Canterbury College
D0349090

ENVIRONMENTAL ISSUES OF TOURISM AND RECREATION

Zbigniew Mieczkowski

University Press of America, Inc.
Lanham • New York • London

4720 Boston Way
Lanham, Maryland 20706

3 Henrietta Street
London, WC2E 8LU England

Printed in the United States of America
British Cataloging in Publication Information Available

Library of Congress Cataloging-in-Publication Data

Mieczkowski, Zbigniew
Environmental issues of tourism and recreation / Zbigniew Mieczkowski.
p. cm.
Includes bibliographical references and index.
1. Tourist trade--Environmental aspects. 2. Outdoor recreation--Environmental aspects. I. Title.
G155.A1M4795 1995 338.4'791--dc20 95- 9062 CIP

ISBN 0-8191-9994-X (cloth: alk: paper)
ISBN 0-8191-9995-8 (ppr: alk: paper)

™ The paper used in this publication meets the minimum requirements of American National Standard for Information Sciences—Permanence of Paper for Printed Library Materials,

Contents

Figures

Preface

This book is the result of many years of research devoted to environmental issues of tourism and recreation. To a large extent it is based on personal experience: I visited most of the countries and individual tourist destinations discussed; I conducted hundreds of on-the-spot interviews with various people, ranging from scientists and government officials to local people. To ensure the reliability of information, I verified it by repeating the same questions in various interviews. Another basic source was the relevant scientific literature based on rigorous data, mainly books and refereed articles in professional journals, representing "hard" science. The book also draws on the so-called "gray" sources— reports, general interest periodicals, journals and newspapers— especially with respect to events which are reported with considerable delay in the scientific literature, if at all. These sources were treated with special caution to ensure their reliability and to minimize anecdotal evidence as much as possible. When the information provided in the book constitutes "common knowledge" repeated by multiple sources, no reference is given, since too many references make reading difficult. The global character of the book required tapping the world literature. Thus, I have benefited from an array of sources in English, French, German, Russian, Polish and Spanish, with English language literature prevailing among my references. I regret not being able to share the photographic results of my field work with the readers.

I hope that this book—the first I know of that gives such a comprehensive treatment of environmental issues related to tourism and recreation—will interest not only scholars but everyone concerned with the out-of-home aspects of leisure, even if not involved professionally. There are four major audiences for this book: first are those in the traditional field of geography—since at least the nineteenth century the pioneers in environmental issues (Hartshorn 1962) and, since the period between the two World Wars, in the study of tourism. The second are those in the rapidly increasing field of tourism who have treated environmental issues as an integral part of the field only since the 1970s; the third are those in the relatively new field of environmental studies that has dealt with the negative and positive impacts of tourism/recreation on ecology cursorily, and will be interested to close the gap. The fourth audience are those in post-secondary and special tourism education courses.

The terminology pertaining to concepts such as "leisure," "recreation," "travel," and "tourism," is based on chapter 2 of my 1990 book, *World Trends in Tourism and Recreation.* The focus of this book is on recreational (pleasure) tourism and recreational excursions, i.e., recreational trips of less than 24 hours duration. The term "tourism" is often used in the text instead of the cumbersome "tourism and recreation." Other introductory information pertains to the mode of most profitable use of the book: I have written the text to be read sequentially; however, individual chapters and sections of the book may also be read for reference, without the need to read the entire text from the beginning to the end. The readers may also find my cross-references useful.

ENVIRONMENTAL ISSUES OF TOURISM AND RECREATION: THE FOCUS OF CHAPTERS 1 - 10

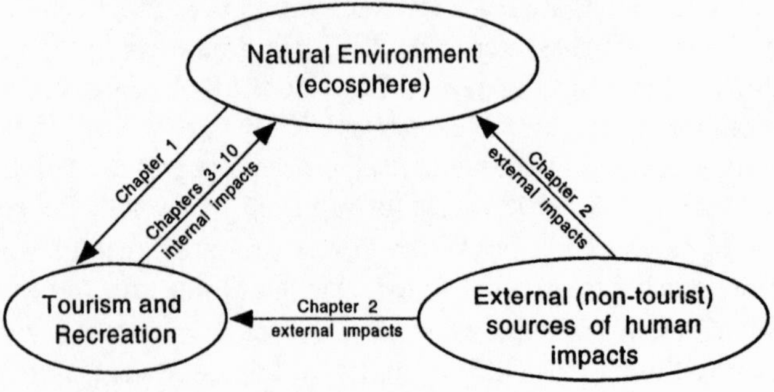

Preface

This interdisciplinary book discusses the environmental aspects of tourism and recreation not in isolation from other factors and phenomena, but in a wide holistic context of the inter-relationships and interactions between other nontourist parameters shaping the ecosystems of our planet. The structure of the book is simple (see figure, p. xii). The book may be divided into three parts. The first is composed of two chapters focusing on tourism and tourists, and natural tourist resources (the tourism-related part of the ecosphere) as objects of impacts. Chapter 1 focuses on the natural or nonhuman impacts on tourism and tourists, and chapter 2 deals with the external or nontourist human effects on natural environment as part of the tourism product. Thus, the impacts indicated by arrows in the figure are exerted on tourists and tourism, as well as on the tourism-related part of the ecosphere. In contrast, the rest of the book (chapters 3 to 10) treats tourism as the subject, i.e., the source of impacts on natural environment. Part 2 (chapters 3 to 6) concentrates on the positive (chapter 3) and negative (chapters 4 to 6) impacts of tourism on the natural environment. The negative effects of tourism are given the most attention and are discussed from the following angles: chapter 4 contains a synoptical analysis of negative impacts, their key parameters, the agents and factors responsible for surpassing the limits of recreational carrying capacity of a tourist destination, and the resulting tourism overdevelopment and overcrowding; chapter 5 examines the negative impacts of tourism on individual environmental elements; chapter 6 focuses on their effects on various types of ecosystems. In part 3 (chapters 7 to 10), I suggest various ways and means to minimize the unfavorable effects of tourism on nature, and measures aimed at making it environmentally sustainable. Specifically, chapter 7 is devoted to the issue of carrying capacity, chapter 8 to the role of agents responsible for the minimization of impacts, chapter 9 to planning and management. While chapters 7 to 9 focus on environmentally sustainable tourism in general, chapter 10, the final chapter, is devoted to a special category—ecotourism.

The index focuses on names of authors. Unfortunately, it was feasible to include only the most relevant geographical names—otherwise the index would be unmanageably long.

The earlier drafts of the book were subjected to the scrutiny of seven specialists in various fields that reflect the interdisciplinary character of tourism. Their criticism was used to improve the text. I would like to take the opportunity to thank my brother, Professor Bogdan Mieczkowski, Department of Economics, Ithaca College, New York; Professor William Pruitt, Department of Zoology, University of Manitoba, Winnipeg; Professor John Selwood, Department of Geography, University of Winnipeg; Professor Ludmila Ilina, Russian Academy of Sciences, Moscow; Ms. Muriel Smith, United Nations Association; Mr. Yanek Mieczkowski, doctoral candidate, Columbia University, New York City; and Mr. Norman Wiebe, McGregor Collegiate, for their time and valuable comments. Nevertheless, I am taking the responsibility for any errors or omissions. Additionally, I would like to thank Ms. M. Halmarson for the preparation of figures.

Introduction

The Nature of Impacts

Although modern tourism started in the middle of the nineteenth century (Mieczkowski, Z. 1990: 59–60), contemporary mass tourism is largely a phenomenon of the more recent decades following the end of the Second World War, and especially the 1950s. Indeed, it is one of the most significant and characteristic socioeconomic phenomena of the present age. Since the Second World War, tourism has grown at an unprecedented pace, faster than most other economic sectors, and has developed into arguably the world's largest industry. At present tourism accounts for over 6 percent of the world Gross National Product and employs over 130 million people, more than 6 percent of the global work force. Domestic and international tourism account for about $3 trillion in revenue. International tourism is approaching the impressive figure of 500 million arrivals and $300 billion in receipts per year. This makes it the second-largest item in international trade, with a share of 5 to 6 percent. Taking into account the annual total figure of over four billion tourist arrivals worldwide (more than 10 percent are international arrivals), one can conclude that practically everyone in the developed world, and a substantial and quickly growing minority in the Less Developed Countries (LDCs), have been tourists at least once in their lives. The share of the Developed Countries (DCs), mainly members of the Organization for Economic Cooperation and Development (OECD), is still between 80 and 90 percent of world tourism (depending on various criteria of classification and subject to inadequacies of world tourism statistics). However, the LDCs, with the exception of Africa and parts of Middle East, have consistently improved their position in terms of arrival and receipts, especially on international tourist markets.

Increasingly, countries and regions turn to tourism as a viable option and mechanism of economic development, and the participation rates (tourists as percentage of the total population) are growing at a proportionately faster rate in comparison with a country's other economic growth sectors. In fact, at present tourism constitutes an inseparable component of modern life for practically all but the poorest in the DCs and for increasingly significant sectors of population in the LDCs, especially in southeast Asia and parts of Latin America. Therefore, tourism has been the focus of growing attention, not only for scholars, but also for politicians and the public at large.

Since about 1973, the exponential growth of tourism, characteristic for the 1950s and 1960s, has subsided. Nevertheless, in the developed world, which has entered the post-industrial era, the relative socioeconomic importance of tourism in the fabric of human life will increase at a faster pace than that of other economic sectors, as humanity progresses to a new predominant culture, the culture of the quality of life. We are moving away from a quantitative, economic lifestyle, to a quality lifestyle. Tourism is increasingly becoming a preferred way to utilize one's discretionary income and leisure time. As a result, the long-range Tourism/Leisure (T/L) ratio, both in terms of time and money spent, is steadily rising (Emery 1981). Moreover, recreational tourism has, since at least the middle of the nineteenth century, constituted the most important part of tourism (Mieczkowski, Z. 1990: 77-91). It is slowly but consistently increasing its share of total tourism, mainly as a result of business travel and visits to friends and relatives.

A superficial look at tourism as a field of research and as a practical economic activity may lead to the incorrect conclusion that it is simple, obvious, almost trivial, self-regulating, and therefore not worth serious research endeavor, planning, or government intervention. Yet, there is enough evidence that such a *laissez-faire* attitude has been costly because it disregards the substantial economic, sociocultural, and environmental impacts. Indeed, the world—faced with adverse consequences of unregulated and unplanned (or inadequately planned) tourism development—is gradually abandoning this negligent attitude. Tourism research and planning are gaining respectability for reasons based on their economic, sociocultural, and environmental usefulness.

There is also a growing appreciation of the intricacy of the subject. Indeed, tourism constitutes a complex of diverse and fragmented components and phenomena that relate, in some way, to practically every visible and invisible aspect of life. No other economic sector involves such a critical interplay of diverse economic, social, political, and environmental factors. These factors interact in widely differing conditions of individual countries and regions. The complex nature of these interactions requires an integrated holistic approach, carefully analyzing the cross-sectoral linkages in a truly interdisciplinary way (Newson, M. 1992: 258). From the point of view of the present book, it is particularly difficult to distinguish tourism-induced environmental impacts from others.

Within the vast field of contemporary tourism research, I am interested in aspects aimed at two objectives. The first objective is the investigation of trends—patterns, regularities, and directions in which the development of tourism is proceeding. The trends should be examined within the dynamics of their interactions, both the internal (i.e., within tourism) and external (i.e., interactions with other economic sectors). The second objective is to inquire into the impacts the environmental, economic and sociocultural consequences of the actions and processes associated with tourism. I attempted to analyze the world trends in tourism and recreation in my previous book (Mieczkowski, Z. 1990). The present book turns to the impacts of tourism on the natural environment (ecosphere).

The Three Categories of Impacts

The diversity of tourism's impacts may be simplified by grouping them into three main categories: economic, sociocultural and environmental. Other impacts are treated in the literature, but they could be conveniently included into these three major groups without committing significant inaccuracies. For example, technical impacts could be regarded as a part of the economic impacts while psychological and political impacts may be viewed as parts of sociocultural impacts.

The threefold categorization of impacts should be regarded as purely pragmatic, useful for analytical purposes. But in the real world things are much more complex than in theory: the economic, sociocultural and environmental systems overlap significantly and the impacts coincide (Fig. 1). Tourism is holistic in nature, combining various components and aspects into an integrated dynamic whole. Thus, the economic issues become more and more intertwined with the environmental and sociocultural ones; one cannot think about effects on the environment in isolation from the other impacts of tourism. The artificiality of such strict segmentation becomes apparent when one considers as an example, the collision of a car driven, by a tourist, with a grizzly bear; the impact of such a coll-ision is not only environmental but also economic and social (Butler 1986: 77). These interactions occur not only on the local and regional scale but also increasingly on the national and global scale, making the analysis much more complex.

The lack of clearly defined limits between the three main impacts of tourism, and even between tourist and nontourist impacts, makes it difficult to present the discussion within tight, textual compartments, and more importantly, to recommend a course of action that takes into account the dynamics of the whole. Researchers are coming to the conclusion that not so much the characteristics of the parts but rather the dynamics of the integrated totality plays the determinant role (Muller, H. 1985: 19). Therefore, while focusing on the details of the three impacts, researchers should never neglect the totality of the issues resulting from their interaction.

Figure 1

THE INTERACTION BETWEEN TOURISM IMPACTS

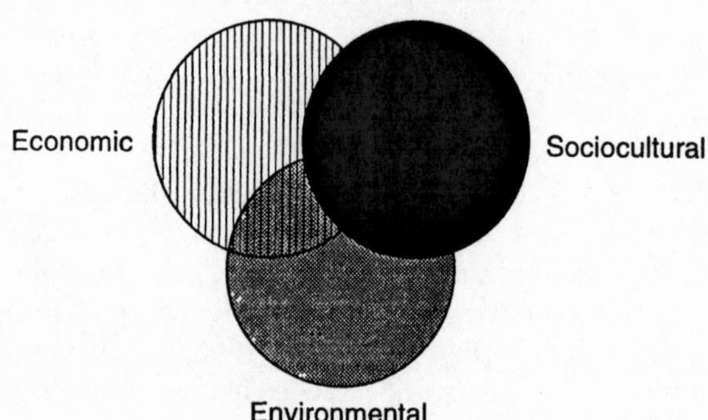

Evaluation of the Environmental Impacts

Among the three impacts, the economic effects of tourism have undoubtedly played the dominant role until the 1960s, not only in the professional literature, but also in the arenas of practical decision-making. With the focus on the economic benefits obtained by the areas of destination, the adverse noneconomic (sociocultural and environmental) impacts of tourism were almost totally ignored. Environmental costs were disregarded because nature was viewed as an inexhaustible renewable resource. However, these views have been largely discarded since the 1960s, as the negative effects of tourism were brought to light in the new era of growing environmental and social consciousness. The startling realization was that the environmental and sociocultural impacts of tourism were frequently negative, and in the long term, the economic effects were by no means always beneficial. Consequently, tourism's reputation has become somewhat tarnished. Thus, a more comprehensive and balanced view has gained acceptance: tourism causes not only positive but some negative impacts as well.

Research into the issues associated with the three impacts influences decision-makers involved in a hotly-debated issue: to develop tourism or not to develop. If the answer is positive, there is a host of often controversial questions pertaining to the details of development. In practical terms, the battles between the advocates of unrestricted tourism development and the forces opposing it, because of its negative noneconomic impacts, are fought in the media and in political arenas. The various views on this matter represent a veritable continuum (see section 8.2).

The debate over the advantages and disadvantages of tourism has raged incessantly and will probably continue for a long time. Some of the reasons why this debate has been so prolonged and so acrimonious lie in the difficulty of a truly objective evaluation. The discussion is often tainted with emotions, subjectivity and vested economic interests. Indeed, the elements in the evaluation of the three impacts are difficult to quantify. The quantitative way to evaluate the impacts of tourism is to express them in terms of monetary value. However, this is feasible only as far as the economic impacts are concerned. The noneconomic impacts (benefits and costs) are, to a large extent, not directly market-related, and are, therefore, difficult to express in terms of money, although there are increasing attempts to do so (see section 8.5). It is also difficult to conduct a quantitative assessment of the advantages of preserving environmental and sociocultural values when facing the pressures of economic development, especially in a world where the quest for jobs and economic gain seems to be a paramount concern.

Are the Impacts Symmetrical or Asymmetrical?

The impacts of tourism are usually treated in the literature asymmetrically, i.e., tourism and tourists affect the destination, but the destination does not affect the tourist. Although the fundamental issue is one of how tourism impacts destinations, one cannot deny that destination impacts tourists and tourism. Indeed, tourism and tourists are not only subjects but objects of natural, economic, and sociocultural impacts at their destination (Fig. 2 illustrates this two-way interaction between "tourism" and "environment"). Tourists are affected in various ways, both positively and negatively, and these effects— given relatively little attention by professional literature—often last for a long time after vacations end. Especially significant are positive and negative impacts on tourists' health or the sociocultural benefits enjoyed by visitors, such as intellectual enrichment, artistic appreciation, and increased understanding of human issues. At the same time, the sociocultural impacts of tourism on the host communities has received mostly negative assessment. However, in this book devoted to the environmental aspects of tourism, these nonenvironmental considerations are deliberately not focused upon.

Figure 2

THE INTERACTION BETWEEN TOURISM INDUSTRY AND TOURISTS WITH THE NATURAL ENVIRONMENT

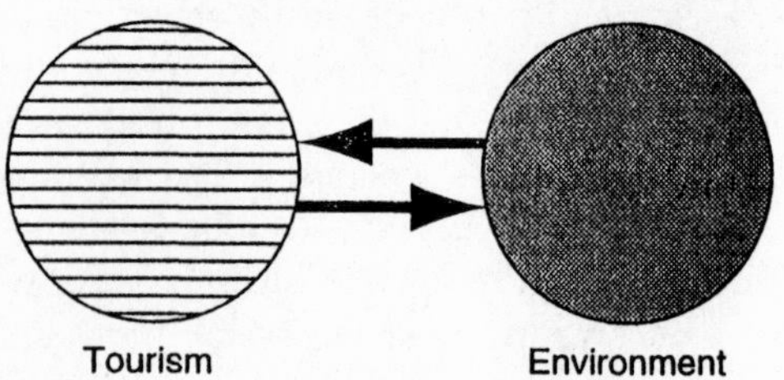

This book attempts to discuss the environmental issues of tourism in a more balanced way than the existing literature, which pays disproportionate attention to the "one-way" impacts of tourism on environment. In reality there exists an intricate system of dynamic interactions between tourism and environment. Therefore, chapter 1 discusses the impacts of environment on tourism and tourists, and chapter 2 is devoted to external (nontourist) human impacts on tourism resources. However, one should not regard the interaction between tourism and environment as completely symmetrical: clearly tourism is, and will be, the dominant factor impacting on destinations. Therefore, in the specific context of this book the focus will be on the impacts of tourism on the natural environment.

Environmental Impacts of Tourism

The notion of "environment" in its broad and comprehensive sense is understood as the totality of all external conditions, both physical and human, in which an organism, a person, a group of people, a society, or humanity as a whole, is living. This notion of "environment" includes not only the ecosphere, i.e., atmosphere, lithosphere, hydrosphere and biosphere, but also human (economic and sociocultural) factors, and is frequently used in the literature. For example, Liu and Sheldon (1987) adhere to this broad concept of "environment." This inclusive view is prevalent in the professional literature on tourism. Anther roughly equivalent all-encompassing term applied in scholarly literature is "geographical environment." However, in scientific literature the notion of "environment" is limited to "natural environment," or nature, and disregards the human element as much as possible. In fact, as will be explained later in this book, many scientists claim that nature would be in much better shape without humans. Some scientists regard the term "environment" as a much misunderstood concept and advocate the use of the term "ecosphere" instead (McLaren 1993: 59).

The environmental impacts of tourism, the focus of this book, should be regarded here as impacts on the ecosphere, i.e., on the natural or physical environment, including components, phenomena, forces, and processes associated with air, water, rocks, soils, plants, and wildlife. "Environment," in this sense, may be defined as the combination of non-living, i.e., abiotic, physical components, with biological resources, or the biosphere, including flora and fauna. The abiotic and biotic elements interact in a series of ecosystems, i.e., communities, composed of various individuals living in a given area and interdependent on one another. In this book, we use the term "natural environment" as it is used in scientific literature, and at variance with most scholarly publications on tourism. Such a narrow understanding of the term "environment" prevails among scientists, including geographers (Dunbar, G. 1991: 50). However, even when talking about the "natural environment" one should realize that it does not exist per se. Since the beginning of the industrial revolution in the mid-eighteenth century, all environments on this planet have been increasingly modified by humans to such a degree that many scientists fear profound, yet largely unknown, consequences for the survival of life on our planet.

Any discussion about the interaction between tourism and the natural environment must acknowledge the human element. Therefore, political, economic, social, and cultural dimensions of tourism's environmental issues receive a wide coverage in this book.

All human activity modifies the environment to some extent, both negatively and positively. Although I agree with Richard Butler (1986) that the division of tourism's impacts into positive (benefits) and negative (costs) is simplistic, I find it, nevertheless, operationally convenient provided that we clarify the variability and complexity of the two sides and emphasize that, they differ between themselves in degree and relative importance. There is no question that from the purely ecological point of view, tourism's negative effects on the environment substantially prevail over the positive ones. Humans must, therefore, minimize the negative and maximize the positive effects to arrive at optimal solutions. Tourism should be not only economically viable and socioculturally acceptable but also environmentally sustainable if it is to be a positive force in the world. In other words, the impacts of tourism on destinations should be, at best, beneficial, or at least neutral and not harmful. They should occur within the limits of social and environmental carrying capacity (see chapter 7) and according to the broad goals of environmental protection and sustainable development. The emphasis of this book is on the environmentally negative effects of tourism, on such undesirable changes as the destruction of rock surfaces, degradation of soil, water resources, vegetation, and wildlife; as well as damage to whole ecosystems. The analysis of these impacts is followed by a discussion of measures designed to cope with these problems and move us closer to our goal of sustainable tourism.

It is in the best interest of the tourism industry to preserve a healthy and clean environment because natural resources, such as the beauty of the landscape, pure air and water, attractive lakes, beaches and forests, are not only essential to the quality of human life, but also an integral part of the tourism product. In this unique situation of tourism, and of no other economic sector, one faces the strange paradox of "tourism destroying tourism" by despoiling the environment (Pearce 1980: 115; Krippendorf 1982: 136). The essence of this negative impact will be investigated in chapters 4–6. What may be said here is that such a scenario is self-defeating and self-destructive. The treatment of the natural environment as inexhaustible and perfectly renewable is suicidal, not only for the non-material but also for the business side of tourism. Indeed, we can supplement the French adage, "*Je detruis ce que j'adore et j'adore ce que j'ai detruit*" (I destroy what I admire and I admire what I have destroyed), and Oscar Wilde's observation that, "each man kills the thing he loves," by a warning that tourism is "killing the goose that lays the golden eggs." As Turner and Ash (1975) put it: international tourism is like King Midas in reverse, "a device for the systematic destruction of everything that is beautiful in the world." Despite the undeniable dramatic hyperbole in these sayings, they serve as warnings to take greater care of the ecosystems, and as an incentive to develop environmentally sustainable tourism.

Chapter 1

Environmental Impacts on Tourism and Tourists

1.1 *The Importance of Natural Environment for Tourism*

Most economic sectors function, to a certain degree, in an undesirable natural environment: manufacturing and agriculture may thrive for a limited time, but not long, in an environment negatively affected by human impacts. However, adverse environmental conditions spell immediate trouble for tourism. The reason for this high degree of sensitivity to natural environment is that tourism is the only economic sector that offers natural environment as a very important part of its product. "The landscape is the real raw material of tourism. It is the reason for the existence of tourism as well as its economic driving force" (Krippendorf 1982: 136). Indeed, the tourism sector of the economy sells the environment to the tourists. Hence, one can expect no high quality tourist product without a high quality environment.

Therefore, tourism is highly dependent on environmental quality, and its ultimate success or failure is closely associated with an attractive, healthy and pleasant natural environment. Of course, the tastes and preferences for specific types of environment differ between various historical periods (Mieczkowski, Z. 1990: 43–57), societies and cultures, and market niches. However, there is no doubt that most people enjoy such diverse natural landscape features and phenomena as mountains, picturesque rock formations, waterfalls, geysers, powerful rivers, beaches, aurora borealis, seas and oceans, coral reefs, wildlife and vegetation, and volcanoes (even erupting volcanoes viewed from a safe distance).

If the landscape is in some way negatively affected, tourists will stay away, even when damage is only perceived and not real. There are many examples of oversensitive tourists who would not visit areas affected by social, political or natural disasters for a long time after all danger or inconvenience ceased to exist. For example, it is a well-known fact that tourists are reluctant to visit places affected by hurricanes even years after the repairs to hotels and basic infrastructure had been completed—they are under the mistaken impression that, the natural environment has been permanently affected.

An interesting survey of tourists' opinions about the importance of high quality environment was conducted in West Germany in 1985 (Hamele 1987: 15–32). According to its findings, 72 percent of the tourists regard high quality natural environment as the primary condition for a successful vacation. In all tourist groups interviewed, well over 50 percent of respondents indicated that an undisturbed natural environment constitutes a condition *sine qua non* for their vacation. Answering the question about the importance of the preservation of natural environment, 94 percent of the tourists responded that it was a very important or an important matter.

The findings of the survey bring Hamele (1987: 28) to the conclusion, that "travel gives the only actual possibility for contact with undisturbed nature". Answering more specific questions the respondents indicated that they are primarily attracted by beautiful landscapes (66 percent), healthy climate (60 percent) and clean air (55 percent). Interesting, too, are the respondents' perceptions of their own country: within the former West Germany the only positive image is enjoyed by Bavaria, whereas, the other *Länder* (regions) of the pre-unification FRG were evaluated as neutral or outright negative. Outside Germany the best environmental images were attributed to Scandinavia, Austria, Switzerland, Greece and South Tyrol, whereas poor environmental images were indicated for the northern parts of France and Spain, for Poland, former Czechoslovakia, the United Kingdom, Belgium, and Italy. Many of the respondents indicated that environmental problems influence their decisions not to travel to the affected area.

Another aspect of sensitivity to environmental issues is the tourists' attraction to particular natural environments, e.g., some individuals prefer mountains while others prefer beaches for their vacations. Christopher Becker (1969: 121–124), in his early study on attractiveness of small islands, shows that insularity constitutes an important attraction for German tourists visiting the islands dotting the coastlines of Europe. He even coined the terms "island feeling," *Inselgefühl,* and "island consciousness," *Inselbewußtsein*. This market preference was later used in the publicity for island vacations all over the world, such as the advertising pamphlets for the Caribbean Islands. It is also a well-known fact that German tourists have changed their tastes during the present century: previously they preferred the mild topographic forms of Mittelgebirge, nowadays they prefer the spectacular splendor of the Alps.

1.2 *Positive Impacts of Natural Environment on Human Well-Being and Health*

The impact of natural environment on tourists reaches well beyond the immediate impact on their senses. It reaches beyond by providing a perfect antidote to our hectic and complex existence. By freeing us from noise and distractions, the processes and rhythms of nature provide valuable insights into our personal transitions. In addition, contacts with nature influence our physical and mental well-being and health. It has long been known that viewing nature, e.g., observing fish in aquariums, lowers blood pressure. There is also evidence of clear benefits not only for tourists' health but also for their education and their aesthetic appreciation of the beauty of landscape.

> Various studies have shown that nature scenes—views of water and vegetation, particularly—elicit positive feelings in people, reduce anxiety in those who are stressed and significantly increase the amplitude of alpha brainwaves. High alpha amplitude is associated with feelings of relaxation. When we experience beauty, then, we seem less likely to have stressful thoughts and physiological arousal (Justice 1988: 100).

Dr. Justice ascribes the benefits of natural beauty to the "release in the brain of opioid substances—endorphins." In a well-publicized study, based on an experiment conducted with two groups of post-operative gallbladder patients, Roger Ulrich, Department of Geography at the University of Delaware, reports that hospital rooms with views of trees and grass outside the windows have a positive effect on the recovery rates of patients, when compared with recovery rates of a similar group of patients given rooms with a view of a brick wall (*Prevention* August 1984: 7).

> Those patients with the tree view spent significantly less time in the hospital after surgery, required substantially less painkilling

medication and had fewer negative ratings from nurses on their recovery (Justice 1988: 100).

The detrimental impact of total isolation on patients in windowless hospital intensive-care units has been recognized for some time. In fact, U.S. federal law requires that all inpatient hospital rooms constructed or remodelled after 1977 include a window or skylight (*Time* 26 March 1990). In 1990, Stanford University Medical Center's cardiac intensive-care unit installed computerized "windows" in three rooms. These $9,000 four-by-five-foot artificial "windows" simulate the progress of daily light changes and the passage of time from sunrise to sunset using a computer-controlled light box behind a blowup of a 35-mm slide that depicts a beautiful landscape. An electronic digital timer produces 650 separate light changes every 24 hours.

There is strong evidence that not only do images of beautiful and serene landscapes, but even a live or recorded voice describing them causes relaxation and reduce stress (Delaney and McVeigh 1991: 117). Many stores in North America and Europe now offer recordings of such pleasant sounds as waves lapping on the shore, babbling brooks, or wind in the trees. A Japanese research project into the labor productivity of keypunch operators confirmed the hypothesis that workers are sensitive to air quality: dramatically fewer errors were made when scents of jasmine, lavender, or lemon were added to their office air. There are also plans to accompany freshening fragrances with the synthesized sounds of ocean waves and babbling brooks (*World Monitor* March 1992).

The impact of natural environment on tourists is generally much more pronounced than on hospitalized or working people. Here the effects extend well beyond the psychological benefits. The direct curative properties of natural resources have been known since antiquity (Mieczkowski, Z. 1990: 47). Indeed, health tourism, which today attracts millions of tourists all over the world, has a long history, the main forms being balneology, hydrotherapy (e.g., Vichy, France), thalassotherapy (e.g., St. Malo, France; Dead Sea, Israel and Jordan), climatotherapy (e.g., the Alps, especially a resort in Davos, Switzerland, where one could go to cure tuberculosis). In the deserts of western China hot "sand bathing" is used to cure rheumatism and arthritic diseases. Health tourists from all over the world stay in the Wieliczka Salt Mine in Poland to cure their respiratory ailments.

These forms of natural cures have thrived from antiquity to the present, particularly in Europe. The perceived importance of health tourism was reflected at the Congress of the International Association of Scientific Experts in Tourism (AIEST) which took place in 1989 in Budapest, Hungary (*Traditional Spa...* 1990). The congress was devoted to European spas and health tourism and focused mainly on balneotherapy (Kaspar 1990). There is a large body of scholarly literature discussing these issues and the significance of associated impacts (e.g., Janot 1988).

These types of health tourism are much less popular in North America than in Europe, where health resorts number well over one thousand. Scientific aspects of health tourism seem to be well researched (Zinnburg 1978: 75-76). However, even in Europe (since the beginning of the century), with the successes of surgery and drug therapy, there is less reliance on the curative properties of mineral springs. As a result, there is a trend to treat patients in the health resorts holistically rather than entirely with natural cures. "Treatment based on the natural resources available in health resorts has been integrated with pharmaceutical and surgical therapy" (*Health and Tourism* 1979: 5).

One of the main organizational forms for health tourism is its combination with social objectives: social tourism (*Health and Tourism* 1979: 6–9; Mieczkowski, Z. 1990: 321). Social tourism is a more accessible form of health tourism. Due partially to government subsidies, health tourism is no longer the exclusive domain of the wealthy, as it was prior to the First World War. However, there is one characteristic feature of vacations in health resorts which remains unchanged: the social interaction between participants (Mieczkowski, Z. 1990: 56) and the psychological benefits associated with this interaction and relaxation in congenial company (Kaspar 1990; *Health and Tourism* 1979: 8) There is also an increasing trend towards multi-functionality, e.g., combining skiing and health holidays in Austria (*Health and Tourism* 1979: 5).

1.3 *Negative Impacts of Natural Environment on Tourists and Tourism Resources*

The natural environment, unfortunately, is not always beneficial to tourists and tourism resources. Tourists, tourist planners and those working in the business should be well informed and keenly aware of negative phenomena, especially if associated with threats to the life and health of tourists and to the potential destruction of facilities. The rest of this chapter will be devoted to these issues.

One could divide the negative impacts of natural environment on tourists and tourism resources into two major categories:
1. Impacts caused by external natural factors completely independent from humans, such as volcano eruptions or hurricanes, and thus unpreventable.

Figure 1.1
CAUSES OF NEGATIVE IMPACTS OF ENVIRONMENT ON TOURISTS: A CONTINUUM

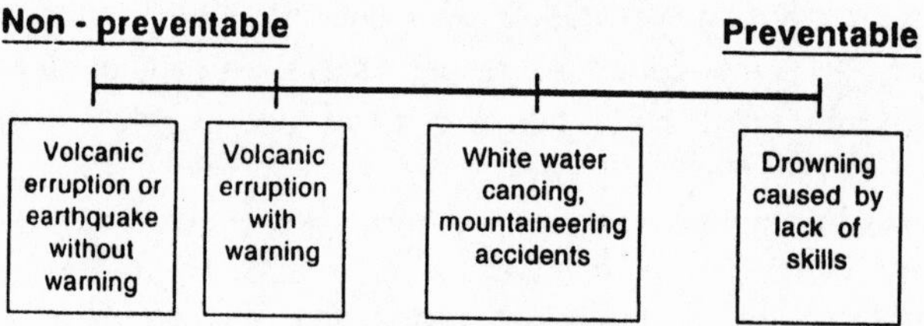

2. Impacts caused by the environment due to lack of caution by tourists, e.g., fatalities from white-water rafting, or canoeing and mountaineering accidents. These effects of nature on tourists are, in various degrees, preventable (Fig. 1.1). Indeed, tourists tend to be offguard during their vacations, which results in a disproportionate number of accidents compared to those at home (Turner and Ash 1975: 230). Tourists frequently ignore the fact that they are at risk from certain elements of the natural environment. For example, while some attacks of grizzly bears on tourists have been completely unprovoked (attacks on sleeping tourists, especially menstruating women), other fatal encounters have been caused by tourists irre-

sponsibly approaching the animals. Charges of bisons on tourists have resulted totally from lack of caution on the part of the tourists. In fact, a continuum exists: from completely tourist-independent factors and phenomena as sources of impacts, through a "gray" transitional area, to totally avoidable impacts caused by lack of caution or judgment of tourists.

The categorization according to the criterion of culprit has undoubtedly significant merits. It helps one to realize the cause of the impacts and wherein lies the blame for any given effect. However, there are too many interfaces between these two categories to clearly distinguish a culprit. As well, although environmental determinism has been discredited for a long time, people often go to the other extreme and do not take natural factors adequately into account. When developing general and tourism infrastructure, they completely disregard potential environmental impacts, e.g., building hotels too close to the ocean beach or in avalanche-prone areas. There is also another circumstance which makes pinpointing the real culprit difficult: government agencies and the tourism industry often engage in the cover-up operations to conceal or minimize any dangers, both environmental and human, at tourist destinations. Thus, tourists are frequently innocent victims rather than culprits.

Because of these categorization problems, I have decided for this book to follow a four-fold classification of natural events and processes that negatively affect tourism resources and tourists:

1. Natural disasters threatening human life and destruction of tourist facilities.
2. Other natural factors and phenomena hazardous to health and life of tourists.
3. Dangerous contacts of tourists with wild animals, plants, insects.
4. Environmental diseases.

1.4 *Natural Disasters*

Natural disasters can be defined as life-threatening and property-damaging, short-term geophysical events of violent nature. People do not have time to adapt to these as they would to long-term changes. Therefore, "disaster management" is the only course of action to follow to minimize dangers and losses. "Disaster management" includes a whole range of activities aimed at timely prevention, adequate preparedness, successful rescue action during emergency, and efficient recovery. Murphy and Bayley (1989) classify human response strategies to disasters in four stages: assessment (identification of potential risks), warning (advice of caution given to relevant parties), impact (implementation of emergency measures during disasters), and finally recovery, subdivided into four periods (emergency, restoration, replacement and reconstruction, and betterment).

One can subdivide the natural disasters affecting tourism into three types according to their cause:

1. Meteorological, such as hurricanes, typhoons, cyclones and tornadoes, floods, snowstorms, and sandstorms.
2. Tectonic and geomorphic (geological), such as earthquakes, volcanic eruptions, tsunami, landslides, rockslides, rock avalanches, snow avalanches, and mudflows.
3. Other natural disasters, such as forest fires, especially in National Parks (e.g., Yellowstone or Yosemite).

1.4.1 *Meteorological and Hydrological Disasters*

The terminology in this area is rich, although some of the terms may designate similar phenomena—thus, meteorologically there is no essential difference between hurricanes, cyclones, typhoons and, to a lesser degree, tornadoes. The difference between hurricanes, cyclones and typhoons is not in substance but in local terminology. All of them are essentially low-pressure systems, from several tens of kilometers (e.g., hurricane Andrew in late August 1992 cut a path of destruction about 60 kilometers wide in the southern Florida tourism area) to several hundred kilometers in diameter, formed over tropical oceans and moving at various speeds. They are characterized by violent winds, as a rule over 120 kilometers per hour, but that sometimes exceed 200 kilometers per hour. In the Atlantic, and east of the International Dateline in the Pacific, they are called hurricanes. In the western Pacific, west of the dateline, they are called typhoons, while in the Indian Ocean they are designated as cyclones. As a rule, these storms are associated not only with high-speed winds and destructive waves, but also with torrential rains. To identify the year and location of storms as they occur in the Atlantic and Pacific basins, meteorologists at the National Hurricane Center in Miami use an alphabetical system of male and female names.

The greatest impact on tourism from hurricane-type storms occurs in the Caribbean, which experiences about six severe hurricanes annually. The hurricane season here lasts from June 1 to the end of November (with the peak period from the end of August to the middle of October). Surprisingly, there have been no reports of fatalities among tourists in the Caribbean, probably because visitation during the hurricane season is low. Although the death toll seems to be limited to the local population, there has been considerable economic damage to tourism, mainly because of destroyed general and tourism infrastructure. This results not only from the sheer force of the wind, but also from destructive storm surges, such as the almost seven-meters-high surge caused by Hurricane Camille in 1969 off the Mississippi coast (Muller and Fielding 1992: 173). In the Caribbean, international aid is not sufficient to cope with the destruction, which in some cases is so considerable that a whole winter tourist season is lost. For example, the entire 1989–90 season was lost in St. Croix following Hurricane Hugo.

Natural tourism resources are also frequently affected, e.g., the vegetation is levelled. This occurred in September 1989, when Hurricane Hugo did considerable damage to the El Yunque U.S. National Forest on Puerto Rico and destroyed the St. George Village Botanical Garden on St. Croix, U.S. Virgin Islands. In the fall of 1991 Hurricane Bob uprooted and defoliated the vegetation of Cape Cod, Massachusetts, dramatically altering the landscape (*New York Times* 15 September 1991). Hurricane Andrew, in late August 1992, did considerable damage to the Everglades National Park. Hurricane Iniki, in September 1992, devegetated parts of Kauai Island, Hawaii, and caused substantial losses of general and tourism infrastructure.

Equally destructive are the typhoons of the western Pacific. For example, in October 1991 Typhoon Ruth killed 36 people, who were crushed by falling trees and buried by landslides, and did considerable infrastructural damage to Baguio, the most important mountain tourist resort in the Philippines. Downed power lines caused blackouts. The number of tourist casualties is not known.

There is an inadequately explored link between the hurricane-type winds and the biggest short-term climatic event on our planet—El Niño, which affects weather patterns in widespread areas and with it billions of people, including tourists (Fig. 1.2). The scientific term for El Niño is ENSO—El Niño Southern Oscillation (Mungall and McLaren 1990: 71-72). ENSO is a quasi-periodic variation of climate that occurs at unequal intervals, ranging from two to seven years and lasts from 12 to 18 months. It starts with the water warm-up in the western Pacific and expands to the eastern Pacific, as the prevailing wind blows warm water east towards Ecuador, nudging the jet streams in the northern hemisphere. This causes significant changes to the weather patterns across wide areas of our planet. ENSO seems to be a purely natural phenomenon, although there are speculations that the contamination of our planet with carbon monoxide, carbon dioxide, methane, and sulphur compounds may account for this.

Figure 1.2

TYPICAL RAINFALL AND TEMPERATURE PATTERNS ASSOCIATED WITH EL-NIÑO/SOUTHERN OSCILLATION (ENSO) CONDITIONS FOR THE NORTHERN HEMISPHERE WINTER SEASON

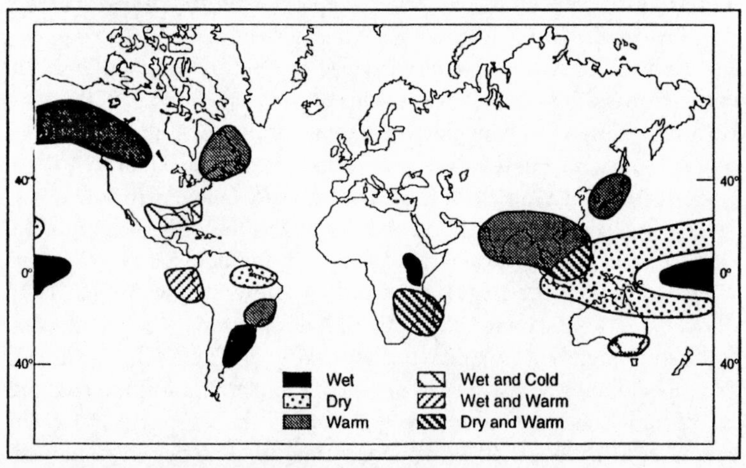

Source: Modified from Ropelewski 1992:476

The local impact of ENSO results in the warming of the equatorial waters of the eastern Pacific. Normally, strong eastern winds in this area push the warm surface waters towards Asia and allow the cool waters from the depths to rise up to the surface. The existence of these relatively cool waters in the tropical Pacific, west of the South American continent, is also reinforced by the cold Humbolt Current which moves northwestward along the western coast of S. America. El Niño disturbs this pattern by replacing the easterly winds with the westerlies and northwesterlies, pushing the warmer tropical waters southeastwards, along the western coast of South America, and deflecting the cool, biologically productive Humbolt Current away from its usual northwesterly direction. The result of these reversed wind and current patterns is an abnormally warm water regime in the eastern tropical part of the Pacific, including the areas along the western coast of South America.

The impacts of these changes are worldwide, and their mechanism is only partially researched. The increased evaporation from the warm water surface of the ocean, associated with strongly convective atmospheric circulation, causes torrential rains and flooding in areas ranging from Chile to the southern and midwestern United States, especially California and Texas. Japan experiences more typhoons than normal because they develop in the eastern Pacific, feeding on energy drawn from warm water, and travel thousands of kilometers westwards to reach the Asian continent. Atlantic and Caribbean hurricanes tend to be milder, however. Other impacts, such as an unseasonably warm winter in North America and droughts in Africa, are not adequately understood.

These changed weather patterns with their torrential rains, violent storms, and floods spell trouble for tourism in the affected areas. There are also other indirect damages and destruction to tourism resources, e.g., coral reefs destroyed by storms and silting from the eroded land. For example, the torrential rains which fell on the Queensland, Australia coast in the summer of 1990–91, flooded the Great Barrier Reef, smothering corals with silt and decreasing the salinity of water to such an extent that large areas of the reef and most of the fish were killed. Nowadays, research focuses on improving techniques of meteorological forecasting of El Niño and its impact on various regions of the world (Ropelewski 1992). Tourism planning will certainly also benefit from improved predicting methods.

The Caribbean is certainly the tourist area most affected by destructive winds. However, they may occur almost anywhere, including the midlatitudes. The most dangerous among them are tornadoes. Tornadoes are essentially spatial miniatures of the low-pressure systems, often developing at the base of a thundercloud. The Unites States experiences more tornadoes than any other country in the world—between 710 and 1,000 annually; most affected are the Great Plains, the Midwest, the Gulf of Mexico, and to a lesser extent the East. Developing over land (in North America between March and September) with distinctive funnel-shaped clouds, tornadoes are, in the northern hemisphere, counter-clockwise whirlwinds that usually affect a small area (between less than a hundred meters to several hundred meters). The wind speeds within tornadoes are normally higher than in oceanic storms such as hurricanes: maximum speeds of tornadoes exceed 400 kilometers per hour. Another difference is that tornadoes are not associated with torrential rainfall. Because of the especially destructive nature of these violent winds, the problem of early forecast, detection, and tracking of tornadoes is crucial. For this purpose, new radar systems have been developed in recent years. Tourists can only partially benefit from the advanced radio warning devices aimed at the local population.

The storm in late January 1990 caused considerable damage to many gardens in Britain, including a major tourist attraction, the famous Royal Botanic Gardens in Kew, England. In other areas of the world, destructive winds occur, although with diminished probability, e.g., the gales that swept across the British Isles in early January 1991. In addition to deaths among local population both on land and sea, there were also victims among tourists. Six Swiss tourists were killed when their van was crushed by a falling tree near Galway in western Ireland, and a couple was swept away by a wave while walking on the beach at Brighton, England (*Winnipeg Free Press* 7 January 1991). In December 1992, the English seaside resort of Blackpool, suffered damages from an Atlantic storm.

The physical damage caused to the tourism infrastructure and resources by such meteorological disasters is not the only problem. Surprisingly, the major problem is psychological: the reluctance of tourists to return after the rebuilding had been completed. Those in affected areas are never sure if tourists will be coming back at the start of the winter season (e.g., December 15 in the Caribbean). Part of the problem is the tourists' terrible knowledge of geography. When they hear that there was a hurricane in the Caribbean, they do not realize that the damage was confined only to a relatively limited path while other areas have not been damaged at all. Florida spent millions of dollars on a worldwide promotional campaign in the aftermath of Hurricane Andrew to convince prospective tourists that the damage was limited to a small area of southern Florida, that elsewhere the general infrastructure and tourist facilities were intact, and that the visitors were welcomed back. Another reason tourists stay away is simple fear. Some stay away for years after a hurricane has hit, and some choose never to return. As a result, the tourism industry is forced to undertake expensive publicity campaigns to embark on a policy of deep discounts on travel costs and hotel accommodation, generous sales in the tourist shops, money-back guarantees, and other concessions to lure reluctant tourists back.

1.4.2 *Tectonic and Geomorphic Disasters*

The negative impacts of tectonic and geomorphic disasters (called less accurately, geological) on tourists and tourism infrastructure may be considerable, especially during and after earthquakes and volcanic eruptions. There is no doubt that the impact of earthquakes on tourism infrastructure and resources is more significant than the danger to the life of tourists. Earthquakes threaten the lives of people almost exclusively by falling buildings and other structures, such as bridges. For example, the April 1991 earthquake in the tropical beach resort and port of Puerto Limon, Costa Rica hit very badly. Although there were no victims among tourists, there was considerable damage to hotels, and tourists jammed the airport waiting for immediate return flights. An earthquake in Yosemite National Park in October 1990 frightened tourists and caused landslides that blocked roads. The 1989 San Francisco Earthquake, significantly damaged the area's tourism infrastructure: among the victims was the coastal resort of Santa Cruz where the loss of many gems of Victorian architecture, built between 1850 and 1910, was a serious blow. The town has recovered remarkably since the disaster.

Earthquakes constitute one of the main threats to the monuments of antiquity in the Mediterranean area, particularly in Italy, Greece and Egypt. More recent buildings of tourist interest, mainly religious structures, have also been affected, as, for example, the St. Francis Basilica in Assisi, Italy. Important tourist areas lie in earthquake zones, such as the St. Andreas fault in California or in the Tokyo area. Seismologists' predictions that these areas were certain to suffer major earthquakes have been borne out. The Los Angeles earthquake of January 1994, and almost precisely a year later, the disastrous earthquake in Kobe, Japan of 1995, both came to pass. Though it is too soon to predict the long-term impact, the immediate impact was severe, with both residents and tourists in fear of the future.

The earthquakes and volcanic eruptions occurring in marine environments, with epicenters at the bottoms of seas and oceans, cause the tsunami, sometimes incorrectly called tidal waves. They have no relationship with the tides. These huge seismic waves travel from earthquake epicenters, underwater volcano eruptions and landslides and reach speeds of up to 800 kilometers per hour. These hit the coasts with walls of water 40 meters high with devastating kinetic energy. *Tsunamis* are especially feared in the Pacific area, where they constitute a potential danger for beach resorts, since they destroy marinas, hotels and other tourist facilities. Examples of destructive impacts of tsunami abound in the Pacific area. For example, on 1 September 1992 an earthquake in the Pacific off the coast of Nicaragua caused a 10-meter-high tsunami that killed scores of people and destroyed property. Hilo, Hawaii was affected several times (Turner, *et al.* 1990: 289). To protect the coastal areas from the devastating impacts of tsunamis, the Japanese built concrete seawalls up to 12 meters high.

As with earthquakes, volcano eruptions endanger the local population more than tourists. However, tourists are deterred by fear, as they were during the 1991 eruptions of Mount Pinatubo, located only about 100 kilometers from the Philippine capital of Manila. The Ring of Fire encircling the Pacific Ocean, where volcano eruptions frequently cause earthquakes, is certainly an important tourist zone. The 1980 eruption of Mount St. Helen's in Washington caused the death of 59 persons. Five scientists and an unknown number of tourists were the victims of the 1993 eruption of the Galeras volcano in Columbia. On the other hand, the oozing type of lava flow of Kilauea, the island of Hawaii, has never threatened tourist lives. Nevertheless, considerable damage has been done to highways and buildings, including tourist facilities such as the Wahaula Visitor Center in the Hawaii Volcanoes National Park, which was completely destroyed in 1989.

Assuming that proper precautions are taken, volcanoes should not constitute a significant danger to tourists' lives. The relatively slow-moving lava flow, if observed from a respectable distance, constitutes a tourist attraction rather than a danger. The glowing natural spectacle fascinates and attracts tourists to such events as the lava flow from Mount Etna, Italy (3,410 meters). The tourist village Zafferana, located on the slopes of Mount Etna, was in danger during the 1992 eruption, but the approaching lava flow was diverted by cement blocks dropped from helicopters and dams of earth constructed with bulldozers. The spectacular fireworks and the rescue action were observed by hundreds of tourists. However, Mount Etna's eruptions occur only sporadically. Whoever wants to view a quasi-permanent spectacle is advised to see the volcano Stromboli in the Tyrrhenian Sea off Sicily, which provides a continuous marvel of nature and draws thousands of tourists. Tourists are not only attracted by spectacular volcanic eruptions but also by areas recovering from the disasters of the past. An example is the increased visitation of Mount St. Helen's in the aftermath of the 1980 eruption (Murphy and Bayley 1989)—indeed, Mount St. Helen's has become an enduring tourist attraction, with visitation increased to half a million annually. The U.S. Forest Service operates a visitors' center with exhibits, a snack bar featuring "Lava Burgers," and a gift shop where tourists can buy volcanic ash for $2.50 a bottle. The more scientifically-minded tourists are drawn to the gradual process of ecological rebirth of the area.

On the Island of Hawaii I had the opportunity to observe a little known aspect of volcanic activity which has a negative impact on tourists' health. The Kilauea volcano emits gases (mainly sulphur dioxide) which are oxidized by air to become sulfates. The result is the so-called *vog,* a haze which is carried by southwestern trade winds toward the Kona coast, a major tourist area on the west of the island. I talked to an asthmatic tourist who had to leave the area. She said that the vog affects not only the health of asthma sufferers, but also people with emphysema and chronic bronchitis.

Volcanic eruptions, although rarely endangering the lives and health of tourists, nevertheless may cause considerable damage to tourism resources. Patagonia, a quickly developing tourist region in southern Argentina, is such an example. The 12 August 1991 eruption devastated much of the attractive landscape of Patagonia, covering large areas with a layer of fine cement-gray ash, composed mostly of silicon, between 10 and 50 centimeters thick. As a result, there have been substantial losses of wildlife (already stressed by over-hunting) and of domesticated sheep. The delicate ecosystem of arid steppe has turned, at least temporarily, to desert. There are now fears that potentially permanent damage has been inflicted on an environment already endangered by human-made decertification associated with overgrazing (Nash 1991).

There is a growing concern about another aspect of volcanic activity that threatens the lives of tourists. Dust clouds composed of volcanic ash have caused a number of dangerous incidents that involved jets flying through dust clouds composed of volcanic ash. The incidents happened in the area of Anchorage, Alaska, which is a major air traffic hub located on the heavily travelled polar routes between Europe, North America and Asia. One of the most serious occurred in December 1989 when all four jet engines of a KLM Boeing 747 stalled at 7,620 meters because of ash from the eruption of Redoubt Volcano, located 177 kilometers southwest of Anchorage. The jet plummeted 3,962 meters before the pilot was able to restart the engines and land safely in Anchorage. The engines had to be replaced. The paint on the jet was destroyed and the windshields so severely damaged that the pilot had to rely partially on instruments to land. Such incidents were not limited to the Alaska area. In 1982 volcanic ash from the eruption of Galunggung Volcano in western Java almost downed two jumbo jets in Indonesia. The volcanic ash problem first came to light after the 1980 eruption of Mount St. Helen's in Washington. Its ash shut down several jet engines, and in one episode the engines caught fire, forcing an emergency landing. The reason for the malfunction: metal components in the volcanic ash melt in the heat of the engine's combustion chamber. This molten, ceramic-like substance hardens in the turbine area behind the chamber and causes the engine to stall by blocking the air flow. Propeller aircraft are not susceptible to such ash damage.

Coping with the volcanic cloud hazards is essential because of the high-density jet traffic in the northern part of the Pacific Basin. Not only are the Alaskan volcanoes a potential threat, but so are the 29 active volcanoes of Russian Kamchatka. However, accident prevention is not easy. Sophisticated satellite monitoring systems have proven to be inadequate because it is difficult to distinguish these clouds from meteorological clouds, especially heavy rain or snow clouds. Also, volcanic clouds cannot be tracked at night. To cope with these difficulties, new satellite sensors are being developed, and laser-based technology, known as "lidar" (light detection and ranging) is being introduced. The problems associated with the early detection of volcanic clouds are gradually being solved, and the Anchorage area got a half-hour's warning on 18 August 1992, before the eruption of Mount Spurr, located 130 kilometers west of the city. The Anchorage International Airport was closed and the population warned well before ash clouds reached the city.

Sometimes the destructive forces of volcano eruptions may be disastrously combined with other devastating processes, such as earthquakes and/or torrential rains. A combination of all three is rare, but did occur in 1991, during one of the greatest volcano eruptions of this century, the eruption of Mount Pinatubo, Philippines. Pinatubo released seven square kilometers of ash and pyroclastic material into the atmosphere, about ten times as much as Mount St. Helen's in 1980. Because after a volcanic eruption the surface is devoid of vegetation, it is prone to erosion, especially during monsoon rains, which wash the volcanic debris down rivers and cause mudflows of volcanic debris called *lahars*. The danger persists for some time, often many years after the eruption: in the case of Pinatubo, the disaster was repeated in late August 1992, as a result of the tropical storm Polly. Although landslides and rockslides, occurring on geologically unstable slopes, are normally caused by earthquakes, they may also be initiated by volcano eruptions. Siebert (1992) reports on research into gravity-driven debris avalanches and mudflows, caused by volcano eruptions. They move even on one degree slopes for long distances. Entering the sea, they cause tsunami. Of course, such disasters may be not entirely natural in origin. Sometimes human factors, such as deforestation and mining, contribute.

Ironically, volcanic eruptions and earthquakes can be dangerous for tourism even if they do not occur. The 1982 volcano alert, issued by the United States Geological Service for the area of Mammoth Lakes, California is an example. As a result of the alert, tourists stayed away for many years, real estate prices plummeted, and the local economy collapsed. The alert proved to be a false alarm. Since that incident the geologists have been much more circumspect in their predictions and are working to perfect their forecasting methods. Indeed, as Siebert (1992) points out, great strides in monitoring techniques have been made in recent years.

Better forecasting methods of earthquakes and volcanic eruptions, based on a network of monitors and satellite-relayed early-warning systems, are not the only measures that can be taken to cope with these natural disasters. Other measures include the implementation of strict building codes, especially for hotels and bridges. The principle of building earthquake-proof structures is to maximize their shock-absorbing capacity. Adoption of more appropriate and "authentic" building styles and techniques might protect against damages. For example, small locally-owned hotels and guest houses in earthquake zones often use lightweight building materials such as bamboo. Not only are such materials less expensive than more solid materials such as concrete blocks, but building tourist facilities with bamboo may also deter the more expensive and environmentally harmful use of tropical wood. This method is being introduced in Costa Rica.

Unfortunately, the damage inflicted on tourism by earthquakes and volcano eruptions is not limited to loss of life and infrastructure—as with areas damaged by hurricanes, tourists are scared to visit such an area for a long time after the disaster. Thus, after the January 1994 earthquake in Los Angeles, millions of dollars were spent for publicity campaigns to ease tourists' concerns and to convince them that it was safe to visit the city.

1.4.3 *Other Natural Disasters*

Snow avalanches, mudflows, rockfalls, landslides and natural vegetation fires are natural disasters on a lesser scale than earthquakes and volcano eruptions, although, as mentioned above, they may be caused by them. The likelihood of their occurrence increases with growing denivelations. They happen mainly in the mountains, especially in those mountains with considerable relief energy. Their impact on tourism is substantial when they occur in tourist areas. Thus, the spectacular development of winter recreation after World War II has greatly increased the danger of snow avalanches in the Alps, the Rockies and the Himalayas. Every winter there are reports about deaths of cross-country skiers traversing remote valleys and the loss of heli-skiers on mountain slopes. However, the danger to downhill skiers using groomed runs appears to be minimal. In order to diminish the loss of life (total elimination of avalanche deaths seems impossible), a number of measures based on scientific research and common sense have been applied. These include such things as triggering artificial avalanches, and strict regulation of tourist movements in endangered areas. Rules of behavior for skiers in avalanche zones are also essential (Wenger 1984: 877-879).

Mountain climbers are at risk not only from snow avalanches but from rockfalls, and their death rate is higher than that of skiers. Another danger is inclement weather, which makes Denali (formerly Mount McKinley) the most perilous peak in North America: 24 climbers (including 22 foreigners) have died on Denali since 1986 (*New York Times* 24 May 1992). This figure pales in comparison with the European data: in July and the first half of August 1992 alone 24 climbers died on the slopes of Mont Blanc. The number of tourists killed in the Tyrolean Alps in 1992 was 113.

Natural fires are an integral part of the environmental process and promote a diversity of ecosystems as habitats for plants and wildlife. Fortunately, fires of the vegetation cover, caused by such factors as lightning, rarely endanger the lives of tourists. However, fires can destroy tourist facilities, such as mountain huts. Chaparral fires in southern California and maquis fires in the Mediterranean region mainly affect primary residences, and to a lesser extent, secondary recreational homes. Fires also damage the "natural" forest landscapes, especially the slow-growing boreal forests. However, not all vegetation fires are natural. Many of them are human-made and should be evaluated negatively, unless they constitute a part of scientific management techniques in national parks.

1.5 *Natural Factors and Phenomena Hazardous to the Health and Life of Tourists*

There are a number of natural factors and phenomena which can be classified as hazards rather than disasters. However, if disregarded or improperly handled, they may unexpectedly endanger the health and lives of tourists. In this section hypoxia and mountain sickness, the impacts of extreme temperatures, and so-called jet lag are discussed.

1.5.1 *Hypoxia and Mountain Sickness*

Participation in adventure tourism requires a certain level of physical fitness on the part of tourists. The challenges of vigorous physical endeavor in various environmental conditions basically contribute to better health and fitness levels. Thus, for example, high elevations increase the production of red blood cells and improve the aerobic capacity of hikers and mountaineers. However, there could be repercussions. In some cases, the high altitudes may lead to the sudden affliction of hypoxia or oxygen insufficiency or the abnormally low level of oxygen in human blood. At high elevations the lungs are unable to supply enough oxygen to the blood, and consequently to the heart. This often happens to trekkers in the Himalayas, to tourists in the Andes or to climbers on Kilimanjaro, Tanzania. Hypoxia leads frequently to the mountain sickness or (high) altitude sickness called *soroche* in the Andes. The symptoms of this sickness are dizziness, headache, nausea, nose-bleeds, insomnia and loss of appetite. In the Alps and in the Rocky Mountains of the United States and Canada it does not seem to constitute a major problem because of lower elevations of these mountains and the fact that the majority of visitors do not venture to the highest peaks.

Mountain sickness may progress to a more severe stage. "The most common form of acute mountain sickness is pulmonary edema, an affliction resulting from the accumulation of fluid in the lungs" (Price 1981: 354). In other words, water from blood collects in the lungs and the body's dehydration reaches extreme levels. Dehydration of the brain leads to hallucinations and loss of consciousness. Death is inevitable unless the sick tourist is brought immediately to a lower elevation. Pulmonary edema is caused by a too-rapid change of elevation to 3,000 meters and over, when combined with vigorous hiking or climbing. Physical fitness may help only to a limited degree, but will not eliminate this affliction. Thus, practically every tourist is at risk, and there is no medicine, no pill which can cure or prevent this affliction. Recently, a specially designed pressure suit, costing thousands of dollars, has been used to save lives, but its application is still minimal. Thus, people are not only suffering—they are dying. There are about 20 deaths from pulmonary and brain edema annually among tourists in the Nepalese mountains (*Der Spiegel* 1991 31: 181).

It is difficult to determine the minimal elevation at which the first symptoms of hypoxia appear, because of the individual variations in the levels of fitness and susceptibility. However, one could generalize that the symptoms start above 2,000 meters for weaker individuals such as the elderly and unfit, and affects many tourists by 2,500 meters. Between 3,000 and 4,000 meters practically all sea-level tourists, even the fittest, will start to experience some altitudinal effects. Price (1981: 353) sets the limit at 4,000 meters. Thus, not only the climbers of Mount Everest (8,848 meters), Mount Kilimanjaro (5,895), Mount Kenya (5,199), Mont Blanc (4,807) should be concerned but also visitors to some important tourist cities such as Lhasa, Tibet (3,658). Less fit tourists should limit their walking, at least for the first several days, in La Paz, Bolivia (3,577—the highest large city in the world), Quito, Ecuador (2,800), Bogota, Columbia (2,644), Addis Ababa, Ethiopia (2,408), or even in Mexico City (2,300), where death by heart attack of the famous British geographer, Sir Dudley Stamp in 1966, may be possibly attributed to the high elevation of the Mexican capital. Another important tourist city located at an elevation of over 2,000 meters is San'a, the capital of Yemen. There are also many mountain resorts all over the world, located well above this altitude. The highest ski resorts are in the Andes (Mieczkowski, Z. 1990: 254), the highest in the world at Chacaltaya, Bolivia, boasting 5,420 meters elevation with a per-day lift ticket price of three dollars (*Economist* 25 December 1993). Staying in high elevation resorts poses not the only danger of altitude sickness for tourists: mere overland travel through high elevations may cause trouble. Therefore, the conductors of the highest passenger railroad in the world, Lima-Huancayo (elevation 4,754 meters), have the equipment to administer oxygen to passengers who need it.

To prevent taking any unnecessary risks, potential tourists who are concerned about their health at high elevations should act before embarking on such a trip. They should find out the elevation of their destination and consult their physician as to any potential danger. Acclimatization seems to be the best method to prevent hypoxia and mountain sickness. Tourists arriving in Cuzco from Lima, are served coca herbal tea and advised to sleep several hours after arrival. According to my experience, that helps only to a limited extent. The problem is not completely solved until the organism acclimatizes, and that may take two or three days. Following several days of acclimatization in Cuzco, Peru (3,399 meters), I felt very good in La Paz, Bolivia (3,577 meters). However, acclimatization is lost in a few weeks if the tourist returns to sea level. Only the local population of the Andes have been found by researchers to acquire a long-term genetic adaptation to life at 3,500 to 5,000 meters above sea level (*Economist* 21 December 1991).

All mountain climbers should adhere to certain parameters if they wish to have a rewarding and trouble-free experience. Starting with the minimal elevation at which the first symptoms of hypoxia and even mountain sickness appear, not only the tourists' health and fitness should be taken into account. Another important variable is the pace of progress up the mountain slope. If the change in elevation is too rapid, even the healthiest, most fit climber will get sick. Acclimatization is essential. I interviewed experienced mountain climbers in Nepal and in Papua-New Guinea (Mount Wilhelm) to find out the best measures against mountain sickness. Minor recommendations were: drink lots of water, eat carbohydrates and take iron supplements. However, the major recommendation was unequivocal: change the elevation gradually. Starting at a level of 2,500–3,000 meters, the climbers should ascend slowly, not more than 500 to 800 meters a day, in order to acclimatize. At about 4,000 meters, the tourists should rest two to three days before proceeding to higher elevations. This is the optimal method to prevent mountain sickness. Nevertheless, one climber mentioned a risky method, feasible only for very healthy and fit climbers with no spare time: attempt a fairly rapid ascent and descend before the onset of the sickness.

However, in reality, tourists seldom enjoy the luxury of time: they are rushed to use their time and money (the climbs are expensive) more efficiently and they, expectedly, get sick. One can argue that the tour operators compress too much climbing in too little time. For example, tourists climbing Mount Kilimanjaro, Tanzania are required to move at an exorbitant pace from 1,840 meters elevation to the peak at 5,895 meters in four days. The majority of climbers experience at least some symptoms of hypoxia. Even one day's rest at 3,780 meters seems to be too short. Another criticism is that the tour organizers, for obvious reasons, do not adequately warn the prospective tourist about the dangers of climbing at high elevations.

With regard to winter sports, high elevation at ski resorts is considered an asset because it contributes to a longer season with more reliable snow cover. But this advantage may be cancelled out by hypoxia suffered by the skiers. In Europe and North America there are no problems with excessive altitudes, because, as a rule, ski resorts are located below 2,000 meters. In contrast, the extremely high elevation of some Andean ski resorts puts much strain on the physical fitness of the skiers (Mieczkowski, Z. 1990: 254). Acclimatization seems to be the only answer. And the added costs to the tourist who must stay longer at the resort before starting to enjoy skiing presumably does not hurt the local tourist industry.

A relatively minor nuisance associated with rapid change of elevation affects passengers of ascending or descending aircraft. The rapidly changing air pressure may cause some discomfort. Swallowing, chewing gum, holding one's nose and blowing are among the many suggestions given to tourists. Jet passengers at high altitudes, may also occasionally be affected by hypoxia, which is aggravated by some human impacts such as cigarette smoking (including "secondary" or "passive smoking"), and alcohol consumption.

1.5.2 *Weather and Climate, Temperature Extremes*

Weather and climate are important environmental factors that affect the degree of comfort experienced by tourists (Mieczkowski, Z. 1985). Of course, "nice weather" influences tourists positively. However, in this section (1.5.2) the emphasis will be on the negative effects of adverse weather patterns. The phenomenon of El Niño and its impact on meteorological disasters has been discussed in section 1.4.1. However, another effect, the temporary changes in global weather patterns caused by El Niño also may impact negatively on tourism business by discouraging tourists from visiting certain areas with adverse weather conditions, lasting for many months. For example, as a result of El Niño, the southern part of the United States and parts of South America suffer from cloudy and rainy weather, with resulting floods. El Niño is also blamed for disastrous droughts in such distant places as southern Africa, northern Australia, and Indonesia. This impact, however, is not necessarily bad for tourism. Long spells of sunny weather in Australia, although harmful for agriculture and communal water supply, attract tourists. El Niño affects Canada and Alaska positively, causing mild winters there. However, skiing may be negatively affected.

Weather and climate in the form of air or water temperature extremes may cause considerable harm to the health of tourists (Dawood 1988: 232–253). Hypothermia and frostbite, heat exhaustion and heat strokes, are examples of such detrimental impacts, as are multiple skin problems, largely caused by climatic extremes (*ibid.* 287–294).

Among the most life-threatening environmental dangers associated with air and water temperature extremes, is the exposure to low temperatures. The danger starts with temperatures of 10° C. to 14° C., to which prolonged exposure may cause much more than mere discomfort: it could result in hypothermia, a potentially lethal drop in body core temperature. On land, outdoor sport participants frequently fall victim to this affliction in winter, and at high elevations, also in summer. The cold air temperature is not the only variable: the windchill factor, humidity, and precipitation also play an important role by accelerating the loss of body heat. Cold water is more dangerous than cold air, since body heat is drained away much more quickly. Thus, swimmers may be afflicted with hypothermia, even if the water is only several degrees colder than the body. The predicted survival time in water of 10° C. is not more than three hours.

Symptoms associated with hypothermia include rapid, deep breathing and shivering, if the body core temperature drops to 35° C. Further temperature drop to under 32° C. is associated with diminished shivering, gradual slowing down of mental and physical processes, clumsiness, lethargy, confusion, inability to communicate, drowsiness, and eventual loss of consciousness (Wenger 1984: 871–872). Death is inevitable unless appropriate measures are taken i.e., rewarming the body by blankets, a hot bath, warm non-alcoholic drinks, and so on. An additional danger frequently associated with low temperatures is frostbite. Severe frostbite may result in the loss of a limb should gangrene set in.

Heat exhaustion is more common among tourists than the hazards of cold because more people travel to tropics and sub-tropics, and in summer to the mid-latitudes, than to polar areas and high elevations. Heat exhaustion may lead to a heat stroke which impairs the heat-regulating mechanism of the body: sweating diminishes and the body temperature rises until death occurs at about 43–44° C. of body temperature (Dawood 1988: 240).

1.5.3 *Jet Lag*

Jet lag, known scientifically as *circadian dyschronism* or *circadian rhythmic disorder,* is a unique, natural phenomenon associated with modern jet transportation, which enables tourists to cross many time zones in hours instead of days or weeks. This rapid transfer into different light and darkness (LD) conditions disturbs the circadian biological rhythm regulated by the human body-clock gene, located in the brain. The result is fatigue, headaches, sleeplessness and other unpleasant physical effects. According to my experience, the negative effects of jet lag are especially pronounced in tourists flying in the easterly direction, e.g., on a transatlantic flight from North America to Europe. The result is confusion of body functions, whereas flying west causes less trouble: it only makes the day uncomfortably longer. There is a plethora of methods to minimize the adverse impacts of jet lag, including special diets (Ehret and Scanlon 1983). I find that special diets are not helpful and recommend exercise, no alcohol, moderate eating, and adjustment to the LD of the destination in the form of timely light exposure. This includes artificial light as well as sunlight, shortly before departure, during the flight, and especially after arrival. These measures help to reset the body's biological clock, as does the use of mild sleeping pills. However, these measures only alleviate but do not solve the problems of jet lag.

It seems, however, that there is a solution on the horizon (Brody 1992). In the not-too-distant-future, jet passengers may be administered a melatonin pill which will reset their body-clocks to the new light-darkness (LD) rhythm. Melatonin, not to be confused with the skin pigment melanin, is a sleep-inducing hormone, stimulated by darkness and inhibited by light. It is normally produced by the pineal gland, located in the center of the brain. Melatonin pills induce sleep quickly without the addictive effects of drugs. Until melatonin is easily available, one has to follow the advice of Mrosovsky and Salmon (1987) who recommend outdoor physical exercise, such as jogging, to accelerate the rate of resynchronization to the new LD cycles. According to their research, jet travelers who have crossed many time zones adjust faster to the LD cycles at the destination by combining exposure to light with physical activity.

1.5.4 *Other Natural Hazards*

There are still a number of the natural hazards that may inconvenience or endanger tourists and impact on tourism facilities. Some of them are sea- and motion sickness, water undercurrents, falling trees, radioactivity, and hypothetical long-term climatic change. The last four will be discussed here briefly. In areas such as the Gulf of Guinea or along the Southeastern coast of Australia, swimmers should be aware of dangerous undercurrents which can threaten their safety. Wenger (1984: 872–876) points out the value of trees in recreation areas; however, he warns against dangers to life and property from falling trees. Weak trees with shallow root systems fall as a result of strong winds, but a tree or a branch may also fall in a situation where the wind is completely still. On a perfectly calm day I was almost killed by a falling branch on a street of Port Moresby, Papua-New Guinea. Wenger sees several factors affecting hazards in trees: species, orientation to prevailing strong winds, rots (mainly affecting hardwoods), hollow trees, snags, and leaning trees. After hazardous trees are identified, there are three response strategies instrumental in coping with potential hazards: removal of the tree, rerouting visitors farther away from possible falling trees, and intensive management measures such as pruning and reinforcement.

Sometimes even benign forces of nature may turn against vacationers. Thus, it is possible that well-intentioned and beneficial natural cures not only fail to achieve the expected results but also bring harm to the tourists. For example, the thermal baths in a German resort of Urach (Swabia) have caused undesirable side effects for users, from too-high natural radioactivity of the water (*Der Spiegel* 1989 36:77–80).

The hypothetical long-term climatic changes, whether natural or human, may also harm tourism. For example, the impact of the greenhouse effect on global warming may threaten tourist beaches and beach resorts all over the world because of the rising sea levels caused by the melting of polar ice. Tourists are not in danger, but tourism facilities may well be profoundly affected. Especially endangered are the low-lying coral islands of the Caribbean and the Pacific (the highest point in Kiribati is only 2 meters above sea level), and coastal barrier islands built of sand. Indeed, the destructive advance of the Atlantic seems to be well on its way at the Eastern seaboard of the United States, where 295 barrier islands are quickly eroding under the onslaught of waves. Rising sea levels may also impact tourism in the coastal areas of countries such as Egypt, Gambia, Senegal, Thailand, and the Maldives. Another hypothetically possible impact of the greenhouse effect on tourism is the duration of the tourist season: while some areas may experience the lengthening of the summer season, skiing at lower elevations could suffer.

1.6 *Contact of Tourists with Fauna and Flora*

In this category, we explore the hazards that stem from tourism coming in contact with the flora and fauna of air, land and sea. On land, the large carnivores (bears, tigers, lions, leopards, hyenas) are not the only threat to the health and life of tourists. There were also many attacks, sometimes deadly, by bisons, buffalos, elephants, and even hippos and wild pigs. I witnessed an unprovoked attack by baboons on tourists near Capetown, South Africa, and successfully recovered my bag of maps from a baboon (although such an action was not entirely safe). Other tourists involved in this attack not only lost their lunches but were scratched by these animals. One of my friends has been divebombed by magpies in Perth, Australia. I had to ward off domestic dogs with stones several times during solitary hikes in various parts of the world. This can happen almost anywhere, even in an affluent suburb of Sydney, Australia. Domestic dogs are, of course, not wild animals.

Even animals that are basically not aggressive and generally avoid humans, such as black bears, can kill. Attacks of black bears on tourists are extremely rare; however, they do happen. According to the Canadian Encyclopedia, between 1900 and 1986 there were only 27 cases of black bears fatally attacking people throughout North America. One of the latest incidents was the death of two tourists in Algonquin Provincial Park, Ontario in October 1991.

The dangerous encounters between tourists and large wild mammals occur mostly in national parks, where the responsibility for managing both tourists and animals lies with the authorities in charge. The optimal approach is to strike a reasonable balance between the interests of tourists and the well-being of animals. Therefore, a number of measures have to be taken to assure a reasonable *modus vivendi* between tourists and animals.

First of all, tourists must modify their behavior. Brochures and campfire programs instruct the visitors, who are advised to be cautious, especially in the darkness of the night. Tourists must learn to keep a safe distance and never appear to threaten the animals, including elks and other ungulates. They should also avoid surprising a female (especially a bear accompanied by its young), getting between a mother and child. Tourists should also not disturb an animal feeding on its prey. Menstruating women are advised not to hike in grizzly country.

The best method for minimizing dangerous confrontations between wilderness campers and wild animals like bears, is to limit access to human food. Feeding is banned and bearproof garbage containers are used. Refuse is disposed of outside the parks. In the wilderness, campers are advised to store their food out of reach of bears by hanging it in counterbalanced sacks on tree branches that are too slender to support the weight of a bear (Edington and Edington 1986: 164–65). Nuisance animals are tranquilized and transported to distant parts of the park. If they return, they are destroyed.

Rabies is another danger associated with dogs and some wild animals, such as skunks, raccoons, foxes, bats, and mongooses. Although there are large areas of the world free of rabies (Dawood 1988: 173), tourists, especially wilderness hikers, are concerned about this deadly disease (although a simple prophylactic injection is now available). Rodents are dangerous not only because of rabies, but because they are frequently carriers of viruses. Venomous snakebites are also deadly. Long trousers, boots, careful movements (especially at night), and cautious collection of firewood are advisable precautions. In areas such as the eastern Mediterranean, venomous scorpions are a danger.

Insects, unless carriers of disease, are rarely more than a considerable nuisance. Some tourists may experience allergic reactions to insect bites, though, particularly wasps and bees. Spiders can be a problem in the tropics and subtropics. The recent invasion of Texas by the African bees, known for their aggressive nature, may impact negatively on tourism business. The problem of insects in recreation areas is associated with the hotly disputed question: to spray or not to spray?

Tourists' contacts with animals at sea seem to be less threatening and the number of victims is much smaller. Sharks are the most feared (Fig. 1.3). "Sharks claim about 50 lives each year out of 100 reported attacks, mostly between latitudes 30° North and 30° South" (Dawood 1988: 170). This grim statistics may underestimate the number of fatalities, which some may be registered as drowning. The most common areas for shark attacks are the Pacific coast of the Americas, the South African coast (especially near Durban) and the southern coasts of Australia. In the United States, there are about fifteen shark attacks annually, mainly on Florida's eastern coast. The increase of tiger shark attacks near Hawaii is attributed to overfishing, which deprives the predators of their normal food. Out of the total of about 250 shark species, fewer than 30 have been involved in attacks on swimmers. Most dangerous are the great white shark, tiger shark, hammerhead shark, mako shark and bull shark (Edington 1986: 139). Tourists are advised not to swim beyond the coral reefs, not to swim alone, and to use guarded beaches. To protect the Durban beaches, anti-shark steel and plastic nets are used.

Because of shark attacks on recreationists, there has been increased killing of millions of these predators—to such an extent that there is concern about the future of the species. The arguments in defense of the sharks range from their role as indispensable parts of the marine ecosystems at the head of the aquatic food chain, to the scientific value of research into the sharks' super-immune system, a potential source for new antibiotics. Therefore, measures are being taken: the U.S. National Marine Fisheries Service has placed a quota of 2,436 metric tons for 1993 and 2,570 metric tons for 1994 on the catch of large sharks by commercial fishermen within the 200 nautical miles of the Atlantic and Gulf coasts. The

Figure 1.3

GEOGRAPHICAL DISTRIBUTION AND SEASONAL INCIDENCE OF REPORTED SHARK ATTACKS

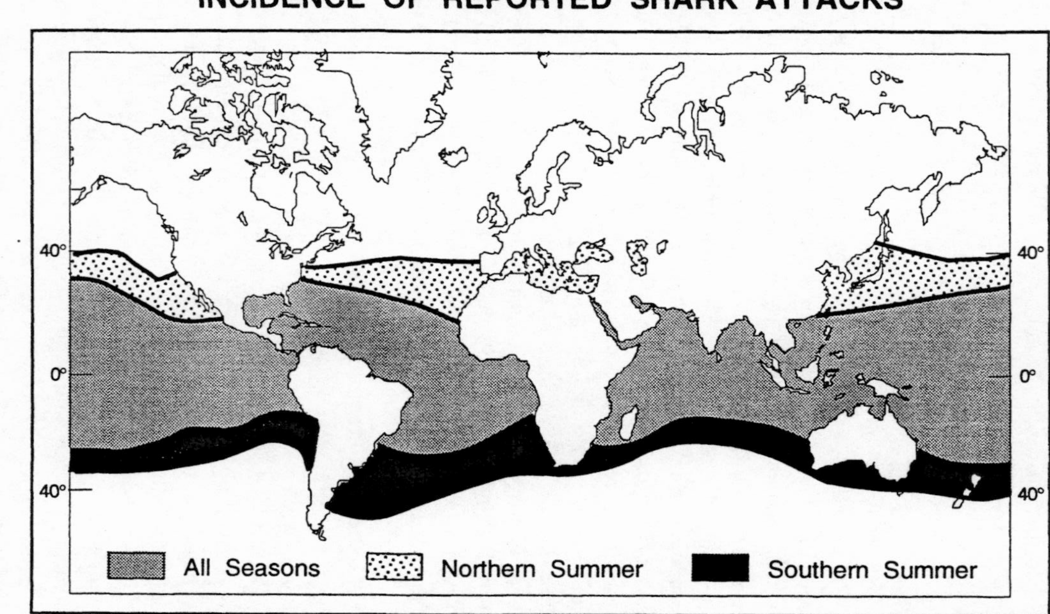

Source: Edington and Edington 1986:138

imposition of these quotas should enable the sharks to rebound to sustainable levels by 1995. Recreational shark fishing will be little affected because the present limit of four sharks a day is considered high.

Other forms of marine life that adversely effect tourists are stings from venomous jellyfish (Medusa) that are found in the warm seas in the Caribbean, northern Australia, Mediterranean, and parts of the U.S. Atlantic seaboard (e.g., Chesapeake Bay). Jellyfish are more frequent in the summer off-season than in the winter season (e.g., in the Caribbean their reproductive period falls between April and June). Their stings are rarely deadly but are very painful and cause considerable discomfort. Jellyfish also plague tourists in the Mediterranean coastal regions each summer. They have increased in number since the middle of the 1970s and there is suspicion that this may be due to higher pollution levels in the Mediterranean (Vadrot 1977).

Tourists should also avoid direct physical contact with poisonous flora, especially with grasses, bushes, and vines such as poison ivy, poison oak, poison sumac, and death angel mushroom. Appropriate clothing and thorough washing of affected skin is advised.

1.7 *Environmental Diseases*

The impacts of various natural environmental systems and components of the environment on human health is investigated through medical geography, an interdisciplinary science that combines geography with medicine and biology (Prokhorov 1979: 58; Meade, *et al.*, 1988). The field of medical geography aims to assist in the optimal use of natural environment, and to improve human well-being through prevention of environmental disease. The commission on medical geography of the International Geographical Union reflects the successful research endeavors of many geographers all over the world, particularly in the United States, Canada and the former Soviet Union. Medical geography acquires practical importance when linked with travel (or tropical) medicine, one of the subspecialities of general internal medicine and infectious disease research (Mayer 1989). Its role is bound to grow with the increasing mobility in international tourism as greater numbers of people travel from the DCs to the LDCs, and the exposure to endemic tropical diseases becomes more frequent.

The former Soviet Union has yielded much research in the medico-geographical field (Raykh 1987; Prokhorov 1979). A team of geographers from the Institute of Geography, USSR (now Russian) Academy of Sciences in Moscow produced a series of medico-geographical maps of the world—these were included in the "Atlas of Natural Environment and Natural Resources of the World." The maps demonstrate the environmental prerequisites for the spatial diffusion of various diseases that affect not only local populations but tourists. In this case, it was impossible to isolate purely natural from socio-economic factors. Therefore, environment in these maps is treated in the wide sense, including socioeconomic aspects.

Despite the problems mentioned above, one can clearly distinguish between environmental diseases, i.e., those caused by natural environment, and diseases brought about by human, i.e., socioeconomic factors. Therefore, the discussion in this section (1.7) will be limited to diseases caused by the natural environmental factors, and excludes diseases generated by human factors, such as lack of hygiene. Such diseases as cholera, or AIDS—diseases caused by social factors, will not be discussed.

1.7.1 *Infectious Environmental Diseases*

Diseases caused by the impact of natural environment, without human interference, may be divided into two groups: infectious and non-infectious. To the infectious category belong the natural plagues propagated by the so-called vectors, such as ticks, mosquitoes, and snails that act as carriers and transmitters of viruses, bacteria, or other compounds causing infectious illnesses. Tourists from midlatitudes lack the partial immunity to local diseases enjoyed by residents of the affected areas. They also lack the experience and knowledge of how to stay healthy. For example, most tourists are not informed that in the tropics, especially in Africa, standing pools of inland water are frequent habitats for the snails that are vectors of *schistosomiasis* (*bilharzia*), or snail fever—a debilitating and sometimes deadly disease that affects 200 million people worldwide.

Tourists should not rely on the promotional literature when looking for ways to stay healthy during their vacations, especially in tropical countries. Travel agents, for obvious reasons, are also reluctant to provide potential tourists with honest information in this respect (Dawood 1989). The best sources of information are scholarly books from practical advisers such as Meade, *et al.* (1988), Pyle (1979), Edington and Edington (1986: 96-134), Dawood (1989), or annual government publications such as *Health Information for International Travel,* published by the U.S. Department of Health and Human Services. These sources not only provide the necessary information about infectious diseases worldwide, but world maps of affected areas. Sick tourists, upon returning home, are increasingly treated by clinics specializing in tropical diseases, rather than by family physicians (*New York Times* 26 May 1991).

There are three major problems associated with these diseases: first, such viruses and parasites are subject to unanticipated mutations which makes successful cures more difficult. Secondly, the viruses are increasingly drug resistant (e.g., chloroquine) because the resistant mutants survive. The vectors of the disease, such as mosquitoes, also develop growing immunity to insecticides. Thirdly, the causes of these diseases may be not entirely "natural." Human factors, such as overpopulation and lack of hygiene, may also contribute to the spread and mutation of viruses. One could also add another concern associated with the possibility of global warming: the spread of vector-insects to highland areas presently free of tropical diseases. In this section the most dangerous of the wide spectrum of these diseases will be discussed.

Among the health threats to tourists travelling in tropical areas, the greatest is malaria, "the most serious tropical disease in practically all affected countries" (World Health Organization 1990: 15). Malaria is spread by the bite of the anopheles mosquito which acts as a vector (transmitter) for the parasite *plasmodium falciparum,* "responsible for most malaria mortality" (WHO: 1990: 13). The main symptom of malaria is high fever. Malaria is not entirely caused by natural environmental factors, however. Human factors are also involved in the spread of this disease: stagnant pools of water, water accumulating in garbage or trash (e.g., discarded old tires), clearing of tropical forests, and increase of irrigation are some of the human factors that affect the mosquito's breeding habits and have considerable impact on the constantly changing intensity and spatial diffusion of malaria.

The primary victims of malaria are not the tourists but the locals: worldwide over two billion people (i.e., more than 40 percent of the world's population) are constantly at risk from malaria. Nine

Figure 1.4

EPIDEMIOLOGICAL ASSESSMENT OF THE STATUS OF MALARIA, 1988

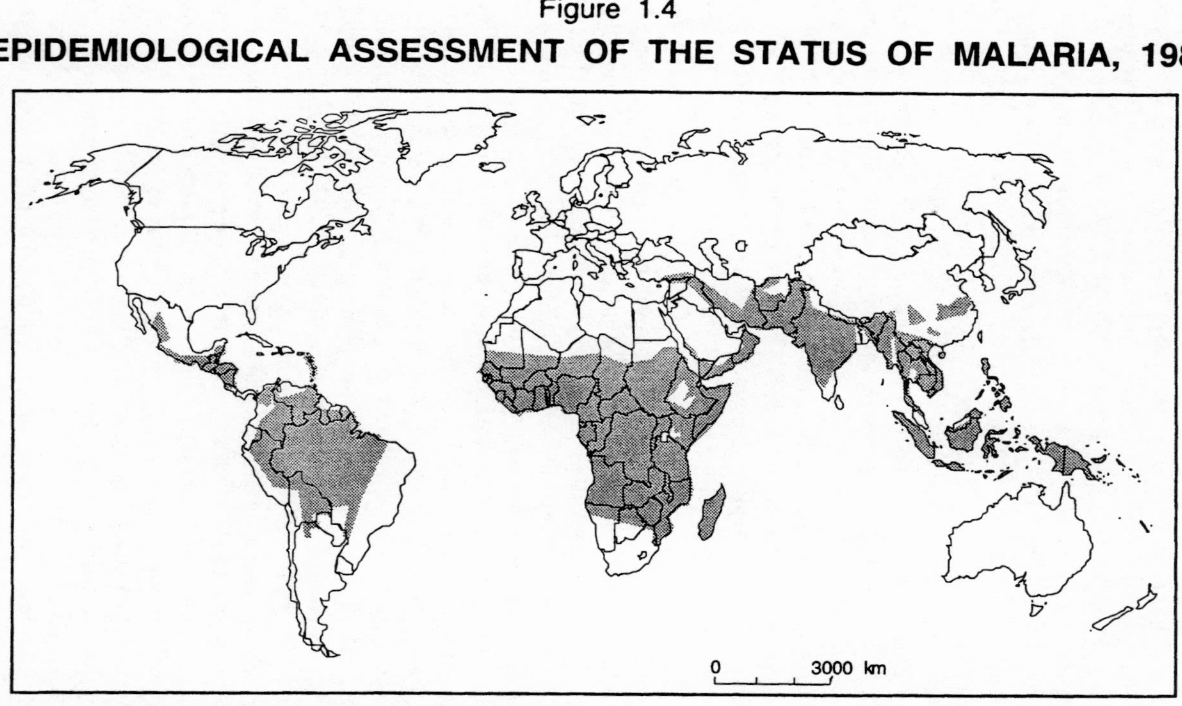

Source: World Health Statistical Annual 1990

percent of the inhabitants of our planet live in areas "where there is intense transmission...and where no antimalarial programs are fully implemented" (WHO 1990: 11). Between 200 and 300 million people in more than 100 countries are infected by the disease each year (WHO, 1993) with more than 100 million acute illnesses a year: 97 million cases in Africa, nine million in Asia, and one million in Latin America (Fig. 1.4). The number of deaths alone in sub-Saharan Africa is estimated at between 1.4 and 2.8 million annually. The statistics on malaria morbidity and mortality are unreliable, mainly because the affected countries habitually under-report them in order to conceal their political and socioeconomic inadequacies. In some instances there is an unwillingness to tarnish the image of a destination in the minds of prospective tourists.

The area affected by malaria does not reach much beyond the tropics (WHO 1990: 1). Tropical Africa, reporting 40 percent of the world's cases, is the region of greatest risk, although there is suspicion that the real percentage is as much as 90 percent. Among African countries, malaria is a major cause of death in Senegal, Zaire, Burundi, Zambia, Botswana, Swaziland, and Madagascar. Recently, there has been a dramatic increase of malaria in Latin America, especially in the quickly developing rain-forest regions of the Amazon Basin of Brazil, such as Rondonia, and in some parts of southern Asia, such as Cambodia. The morbidity in Thailand is stagnant, but the mortality has decreased. However, substantial progress in limiting the disease has been achieved in China (WHO 1990: 12–13).

Understandably, tourists also are at risk. If they do not take the necessary precautions, they frequently fall victim to this debilitating and potentially deadly disease. Unfortunately, the development of a reliable vaccine is not expected before the year 2,000 (*Economist* 10 March 1990), and the present vaccine is only partially protective (New York Times 13 February 1994). Moreover, existing drugs such as Chloroquine and Fancidar, are increasingly ineffective because the mosquitoes responsible for the spread of the disease have developed growing resistance to these drugs and insecticides. This is why malaria, thought to be nearly eliminated by insecticides such as DDT in the 1950s and 1960s, has been on the rise worldwide again since the 1970s. It now constitutes a growing threat to the life and health not only of residents but of tourists. Health workers now focus more on protecting people than on destroying mosquitoes. In addition to taking anti-malarial drugs, tourists are advised to be especially vigilant around dusk, to sleep under cotton or nylon bed-nets which have been dipped in an insecticide solution, to use insect repellents, and to dress in light colors: socks, long pants, long sleeve shirts, proper shoes. Special vigilance is recommended during the seasonal outbreaks of the rainy season. Tourists visiting the tropics should consult the newest WHO data on about 105 countries which are threatened by malaria. They have to do this well before the departure, because the anti-malaria medication should start to be administered about two weeks before the arrival at the destination. According to the World Health Organization regulations, the interiors of airplanes originating in areas affected by malaria are sprayed, to the great annoyance of tourists, to kill any stowaway mosquitoes.

Another potentially deadly disease transmitted by mosquito (*Aedes aegypti*) is dengue fever, which is characterized by fever, headaches, severe joint and muscle pains. Dengue fever strikes millions of people (although considerably less than malaria) and "is now prevalent in the Caribbean, South and Central America and laps at the shores of the United States" (*New York Times* 22 August 1989). Tourists should know that dengue fever is spreading in Mexico and the Caribbean. The same problem has been reported from the Pacific area, especially French Polynesia. Richard Dawood admits the recent dramatic outbreaks in the Americas, but he also emphasizes the dangers of dengue fever in India and southeast Asia (Dawood 1988: 117). As with malaria, there is no immunization against dengue fever.

An entirely different tropical disease of Africa, affecting people and cattle, is sleeping sickness caused by small parasites called *trypanosomas* that are transmitted by their vector, the tse-tse fly. It is mainly confined to uninhabited areas occupied by virgin forests, partially under protection of the national park systems. Ironically, the existence of sleeping sickness in national parks protects these areas against the encroachment of people with their cattle, because wildlife (but not domestic cattle) are immune to this disease. This circumstance creates a unique situation where tourists, participating in wildlife safaris in national parks, are in more danger than the locals and their cattle, who live mainly outside the infested areas. For obvious reasons, tourists will never find any information about the dangers of this sickness in the tourism promotional literature. The picture with respect to drugs and immunization against sleeping sickness is a bleak one (*ibid.* 131).

Tourists in the midlatitudes are not spared from vector-borne diseases. The most common tick-borne disease in the United States is Lyme disease, that affects between five and ten thousand people annually. The principal vector for Lyme Disease is the tiny deer tick (*Ixodes dammini*), which develops on host animals such as deer. The ticks are parasites of the deer, but get infected with the Lyme bacterium by feeding on rodents, which carry the germ. The infection is transmitted from host to host animal by tick, and finally to humans who experience severe flu-like symptoms. The disease is potentially dangerous to life because of severe complications such as meningitis, neurological disorders, and arthritis. Lyme disease may cause death if not attended to. However, recent progress in antibiotic treatment methods practically guarantees the cure in all cases that are diagnosed and cared for within one month. Only a very small percentage of patients have suffered from long-term consequences.

The regions that pose the greatest threat of Lyme disease for tourists are important tourist areas in the United States: New England, Appalachia (especially New York State), Minnesota and Wisconsin. The recent spread of the disease is associated with the increased reforestation in the eastern United States, thus creating the habitat for the deer which serves as a the main host for the vector (tick). The recent spread of recreational settlements and affluent suburbs in the wooded areas ("woodburbs") has increased the exposure of people to the disease. Because the diagnosis of Lyme disease is difficult, doctors frequently use maps to determine if the patient was exposed to contaminated ticks. However, medico-geographical research is impeded by lack of funding from local health budgets, partially because some fashionable vacation spots are unwilling to finance tick surveys that might label them as Lyme disease areas (Rosenthal 1993). Prevention seems to be the best method in battling the Lyme disease: avoiding tick bites by proper dress, insect repellent application, and removing the ticks that are discovered on the body. Special precautions should be taken in June and July. There is no vaccination against Lyme disease, although successful progress in developing one has been reported—according to The Proceedings of the National Academy of Sciences, a vaccine is in the stage of human clinical trials (*New York Times* 16 June 1992).

In the western United States, and more recently in the piedmont region of the southeastern United States, tourists are plagued with Rocky Mountain spotted fever (RMSF) or tick-borne typhus (Meade, *et al.* 1988: 78), spread by wood ticks and dog ticks. Its symptoms include flat red spots on the body, fever, severe headaches, general body pain, coughing, nausea, and vomiting. If left untreated with antibiotics, the disease may lead to the infection of the central nervous system, and finally to shock and death. RMSF is confined to North America; however, a similar affliction is also known in Europe. It is the tick-borne-encephalitis (TBE), and is caused by the animal-hosted European tick. It is found among tourists in Slovenia, Croatia, Styria (Austria), Bavaria, parts of Hungary, and northeastern Poland. There is an immunization against this disease. As in all diseases caused by ticks, tourists are advised to avoid uncut grasses and weeds, habitats preferred by ticks. Other measures include the use of insect repellents containing the chemical Deet, which can be sprayed on skin or clothing, and wearing light- colored clothes to spot the ticks more easily. Long pants are a must and should be tucked into socks or boots. Long-sleeved shirts should be tucked into pants.

1.7.2 *Non-Infectious Environmental Diseases*

The sun's rays have been the source of all life since the beginning of our planet. However, not all that comes from the sun is a blessing: one component of solar radiation, ultraviolet rays (UVs), is potentially deadly to life. Fortunately, our planet has a protective shield, the ozone layer in the stratosphere, about 15 to 30 kilometers above the earth's surface, that acts as the Earth's sunscreen. The ozone layer safeguards plants, animals, and in more recent geological history, humans, from the harmful effects of the UVs. This layer absorbs part of the UVs, limiting the amount reaching earth. The strength of this protection has not been constant during at least the last 600 million years. The ozone layer has fluctuated throughout geological history; living things have constantly adapted to these fluctuations: e.g., UV light damages and stunts marine phytoplankton. Normally, the adaptations of all forms of life, mainly through production of protective pigments and development of sun-blocking compounds, have kept pace with the quantitative UV changes. In addition to the secular changes in the ozone layer, natural annual fluctuations also occur. The reasons for these natural variations of the ozone layer are not yet adequately understood. The evidence is rather fragmentary, e.g., chlorine, sulphur, and dust injected by volcano eruptions, such as the 1991 eruption of Mount Pinatubo, Philippines, trigger ozone thinning reactions over the tropics, and maybe worldwide.

Humans protect themselves from harmful impacts of the UVs by producing UV-absorbing melanin pigments in response to sun-ray exposure. However, some fair-skinned people have limited ability to produce the pigment and are at risk of sunburn. The risk exists for anybody if exposed to too-large doses of UVs. The potentially lethal disease of skin cancer is another risk of overexposure to UV rays, and especially affects fair-skinned people in high elevations and lower latitudes where the UV intensity is at its maximum. Where the angle of the sun's rays is the largest, in the tropical and subtropical regions, the permanent residents have gradually developed, through a slow processes of mutations, an appropriate protective mechanism: dark skin. However, in the modern age, the incidence of skin cancer has increased in the DCs because of a trend to sun-worship outdoor recreation, especially at the beach. The wish to acquire a sporty, suntanned look, associated in the DCs with health, youth, beauty, and success, has proven to be a mixed blessing. Recreational exposure to the sun's rays is today the cause of more skin cancers than is occupational exposure (Dawood 1989; Marks 1989).

Millions of recreationists, many of them tourists still unaware of the odds against them, continue to play the dangerous game of solar roulette. According to the American Cancer Society, these odds are worsening at an alarming rate because this essentially environmental affliction, cancer caused by the sun's ultraviolet rays, has been exacerbated for the last hundred years by depletion of the protective ozone layer, which blocks part of the sun's ultraviolet radiation. This depletion is not caused by natural impacts but by the emissions of chlorofluorocarbons (CFCs) and other chemicals, such as halons contained in fire extinguishers, methyl bromide used as pesticide, carbon tetrachloride, and methyl chloroform. However, the CFCs are regarded as the main culprit. These harmful chemicals are released into the air, where they slowly ascend to the stratosphere. It may take more than 30 years after the emission for the CFCs to reach the ozone layer and react with the ultraviolet rays of the sun, where they turn into the ozone-destroying chlorine monoxide (Cl0). That compound, in turn, breaks down the ozone molecule by depriving it of the third oxygen atom. The offending chemicals remain in the stratosphere for a long time, up to a hundred years, until they decompose. The degree of damage to the ozone layer depends not only on the absolute amount of the CFCs but also on specific atmospheric conditions. Despite this recent adverse contribution of human factors, the impact of the UVs on tourists and recreationists is discussed in this book because "natural" UVs predate the appearance of the CFCs. The human variable (CFCs and other compounds) has only very recently entered the ecological scene, substantially worsening the negative impacts of the UVs and dramatically increasing the incidence of skin cancer.

Crutzen (1992) calls the recent increase in UV radiation "almost a truism." The thinning of the stratospheric ozone layer was discovered by researchers in 1985 in the southern polar region, and labelled "the Antarctic Ozone Hole." Later, scientists found a similar depletion in the northern polar regions and called it "the Arctic Ozone Hole." The latter, more severe than the former, seems to expand farther to lower latitudes than the former. The "holes" (in reality not real holes, only the thinning of the ozone layer) do not last the whole year. They are thinnest in the spring, and are becoming more severe from year to year, consistently spread to the lower latitudes (up to about 45° N. for the Arctic Ozone Hole). There is also some evidence that the annual ozone hole lasts longer, extending from spring until summer, the beach season. Although the ozone depletion is most pronounced in the higher latitudes, all areas of our planet are to a certain extent affected.

The link between the ultraviolet A and B solar radiation and skin cancer in overzealous sunbathers, skiers, mountain hikers and other outdoor recreationists is firmly established. The damage cripples the p53 gene, which normally prevents riotous cell growth. When the p53 gene mutates under the impact of the UVs, it is unable to perform the task of a tumor suppressor, and the cells start to divide unchecked, leading to a full-blown malignancy. Untreated, skin cancer spreads to other parts of the body and can lead to death.

The American Cancer Society reports that the annual number of new skin malignancies in the United States is 600,000 including almost 28,000 cases of malignant melanoma (*Time* 30 July 1990). Most of these cases are caused by excessive exposure to ultraviolet rays from the sun. Malignant melanoma, the deadliest type of malignancy, appeared in about 32,000 U.S. residents and killed 6,500 in 1991. It is increasing by about 7 percent annually in the United States. The other forms, basal-cell and squamous-cell carcinomas, are less lethal but still dangerous if not treated in time. The recent increase in skin malignancies may be attributed to the fact that the effects of the sun exposure are cumulative. It takes as many as 20 to 30 years of exposure before malignancy begins. The results on the population in the DCs are showing up now, especially in Australia. There is evidence that total cessation of exposure, even for a long time, may not help: the recreationist, who abused sunbathing in his or her youth, may get skin cancer at old age. The UV damage to the protective gene p53 may occur more than 50 years before cancer appears.

The danger of carcinomas and melanomas increases with the lightness of the skin of the sunworshipers. Therefore, the incidence of malignancies is the highest among people of northern European origin; they should take special precautions. Another reason for the increase in the incidence of malignancies is geographical location: the lower the latitude the higher the danger. In higher latitudes, solar rays strike the earth at a more oblique angle, taking a longer path through the atmosphere, where the ozone layer absorbs more of the ultraviolet light before it can reach the surface. The intercontinental, international, and national migrations of people from higher, less sunny latitudes to subtropical and tropical areas have significantly increased the rates of skin cancer because of increased exposure to the harmful UVs. The best example of an intercontinental migration from mid to low latitudes is Australia, settled mainly by fair-skinned British and Irish. Australians love the sun—indeed, "sun worship" seems to be part of the Australian national identity. Within their own country, Australians migrate to Queensland, which is known for plenty of sunshine and beautiful beaches. As a result, Australia, and especially Queensland, the Sunshine State, leads the world in skin cancer rates. According to Marks (1989: 8), two out of three Australians will develop some form of skin cancer by the time they are 70. The number of new skin cancer cases reported in 1988 was about 145,000. Deaths in 1987 amounted to 1,027 and are on the increase. The incidence of malignant melanoma in Australia is 12 times higher than in Britain (Marks 1989: 9). The threat of skin cancer in the United States has also increased: Americans have been moving south and southwest to sunnier states known as the Sunbelt, and enjoying the improved outdoor recreation opportunities of these areas.

There are many uncertainties about the ozone layer and skin cancer. Marks warns that a one percent decrease in the ozone layer would lead to a two percent increase in ultraviolet radiation, and a huge increase in skin cancer. These are speculations for the future. What seems reasonable right now is to protect recreationists and tourists from skin cancer. Australia, naturally, is the world leader in anti-skin cancer campaigns. The issue should be given wide publicity because recent surveys revealed a high degree of ignorance about the adverse effects of unreasonable skin exposure to the UVs (*The Guardian* 27 July 1993).

Tourists and recreationists are advised to take certain precautions: stay out of the sun between 10 a.m. and 3 p.m., use UV absorbing sunglasses and sunblocks with a sun protection factor (SPF) of at least 15. Wear wide-brimmed hats and protective clothing. Authorities and the tourist industry should provide more shade in recreation areas. But it does not mean that people should shun the sun. Recreationists and tourists should be knowledgeable but not panicky on issues of skin cancer prevention. In this respect, not only government and schools but also the media may play a useful role in educating the public. There are also some indications that proper nutrition may help in neutralizing free radical reactions generated in skin by UV rays. Therefore, antioxidants such as water- soluble vitamin C, oil-soluble vitamin E and A, and mineral selenium are recommended. Carotin also absorbs UV rays, preventing free radial damage (Erasmus 1990).

To inform the people about local UV radiation, programs have been started to provide data about the current degree of ozone depletion in affected regions of the world. The advisory program introduced by Environment Canada in May 1992 is the most advanced in the world. It follows the Ozone Watch Program launched in March 1992 and provides information about the percentage depletion of the ozone layer in various areas of Canada. The two programs are funded through the federal government's $25 million Green Plan of 1991. The Environment Canada Advisory Program makes provision for the release of a daily index based on a scale of 0 to 10, with the highest number reflecting the typical intensity of UV on a clear summer day in the tropics, where the ozone levels are lower and UV levels higher than in any other latitudes. The scale is divided into four categories: low (0-3.9), moderate (4-6.9), high (7-8.9) and extreme (over 9). The rating of below 4 gives fair-skinned people more than one hour to get a sunburn. Between 4 and 6.9, the time is about 30 minutes, and between 7 and 8.9 it is 20 minutes. The over 9 index is described as extreme, with a sunburn time of 15 minutes.

The indexes released daily by Environment Canada are based on predictions for various areas of Canada made the night before, and take into account the time of the year, the amount of sun radiation, the degree of cloudiness and the amount of ozone present in the stratosphere. In addition to these daily indexes, Environment Canada also indicates how many hours a day the UV values will be above 4, and whether forecasted cloud or rain will lower the potential for UV exposure. In June 1993, the World Meteorological Organization has adopted Canada's ultraviolet index as a universal standard for measuring the amount of radiation to which people are exposed every day.

The medical research field and profession is recently advancing beyond new methods in combatting skin cancer in recognition of the fact that such postfactum or reactive measures play a positive role, but do not solve the problem. Thus, medical research is working on proactive preventive methods of protecting tourists and recreationists from the pernicious impact of UV radiation. These methods could be subdivided into two groups: development of sunblocking lotions, which is already well advanced, and improved means of acquiring a suntan without exposing the skin to sunlight at all. Since about 1990 there has been a new generation of cosmetic self-tanners or sunless tanners (STs) on the market. These lotions and gels contain dihydroxyacetone (DHA) which reacts chemically with the proteins in the upper layer of the skin (epidermis). The effect of a beautiful tan is achieved in just three hours and lasts for several days as skin cells are sloughed away. The intensity of the tan depends on two factors: the concentration of the DHA in the lotion and the quantity applied. The results have been encouraging so far: recreationists tan in the shade without the risks of skin cancer and wrinkles.

Another recent development which promises longer-lasting effects is the skin tan injection, reported by the Journal of the American Medical Association. This process promotes the production of melanin in the skin (the substance responsible for skin color) and acts as a potent sunblocker. This is achieved by injecting a synthetic version of melanocyte-stimulating hormone (MSH). Ten injections over 12 days were enough to cause the darkening of the skin by all research subjects, without side effects. Although the injection needs further research, the promise of safe tanning without the dangerous exposure to the UV radiation and premature skin aging is there (Gutfeld 1992).

On the international level, there are efforts to limit, and ultimately phase out completely, the use of the offending CFCs. In 1987 an international agreement called the Montreal Protocol was signed by 24 DCs, and promised the reduction of CFC emissions by 50 percent by the year 2000. In 1990, it was amended, stipulating a complete ban of CFCs by 2000. The 1992 Copenhagen meeting decided to phase out the CFC emissions in 93 participating countries by the end of 1995, and to set up a fund to help poor countries switch to CFC alternatives. Researchers are working with a sense of urgency on the development of relatively harmless but more expensive CFC substitutes, such as hydrofluorocarbons (HFCs) and on safe methods for the disposal of used chemicals. Even large producers of offending chemicals, such as Du Pont, have joined the ranks. However, there is also a problem of cost to the LDCs and the former Soviet bloc countries in applying the ozone-friendly technology. Because the DCs are mainly responsible for the recent human-made depletion of the ozone layer, ozone- linked foreign aid programs are being developed.

In addition to the effects of the UVs on skin cancer, there are also some other possible negative long-term impacts, such as the increased risk of eye cataracts. Even if the UV light does not cause tumors, it may lead to oxidative processes in the body that weaken the immune system (called *immunosuppression*), which is associated with decreased ability of the body to fight diseases, e.g., AIDS, herpes, tuberculosis, and other nonskin forms of cancer (Legro, *et al.* 1992: 118). The possible impact of increased UV radiation on global weather patterns is also being investigated.

Beyond the health concerns, scientists worry about the ability of ecosystems to adapt to too-rapid UV increases. For instance, photosynthesis, in which carbon dioxide and water are converted into carbohydrates, may be impeded by UVs, damaging the marine phytoplankton that anchors the marine food chain. Subsequently, algae, krill, fish and other components of the marine food chain may suffer. Potential deceleration of protein formation could disrupt food production. However, these possible impacts are still inadequately researched; some of them may prove to be only unsubstantiated hypotheses.

Chapter 2

External (Nontourist) Human Impacts on the Natural Environment as Part of the Tourism Product

In this chapter the impact of the external (i.e., nontourist) human factors will be discussed. These include industry, agriculture, mining, transportation, and human habitation, and their impact on the natural environment, especially on that portion of natural environment that constitutes the part of the tourist product and is regarded as a tourist resource (Fig. 2.1). Tourist impacts on environment are regarded as internal (Fig. 2.2) and treated in chapters 3 to 10 of this book. This chapter, after a historical review (sections 2.1 and 2.2), approaches the external impacts from two angles: the first one focuses on socioeconomic criteria of human impacts on environment. Thus, the external impacts in the First, Second, and Third World are evaluated in sections 2.3–2.5. This analysis is followed by an evaluation of the nontourist impacts on various ecosystems (sections 2.6–2.9). As an additional quasi-ecosystem, the physical environments of large cities are discussed, partly because they are gaining importance as tourist destinations and cannot be ignored.

2.1 *No-Human-Impact Scenario*

The optimal scenario for the natural environment or, in this context, for ecosystems, is one of no human impact at all. Practically, such a scenario assumes absence or virtual human absence: consequently, in this case, the term *ecosystems* is more appropriate because the term *environment* has a meaning only in a situation when there is an interaction between a subject and an object, in this case humanity and the communities of organic and inorganic elements, i.e., ecosystems.

In the absence of humans, for the most part of our planet's history, ecosystems evolved according to their own internal dynamics and under external natural impacts. Thus, in a *no-human-im-*

Figure 2.1

RELATIONSHIP BETWEEN TOURISM PRODUCT AND ENVIRONMENT

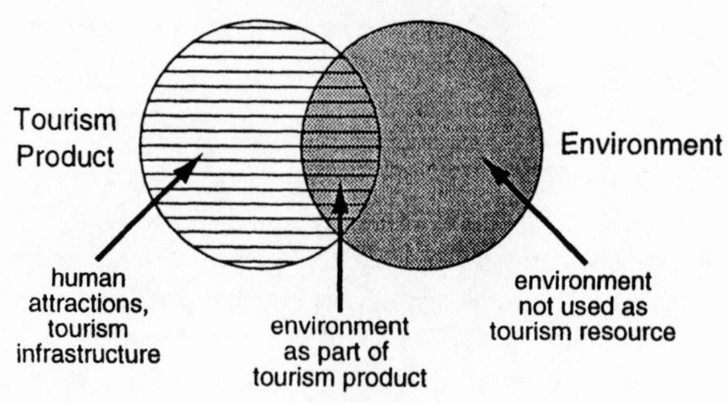

Figure 2.2

INTERNAL AND EXTERNAL IMPACTS ON THE NATURAL ENVIRONMENT

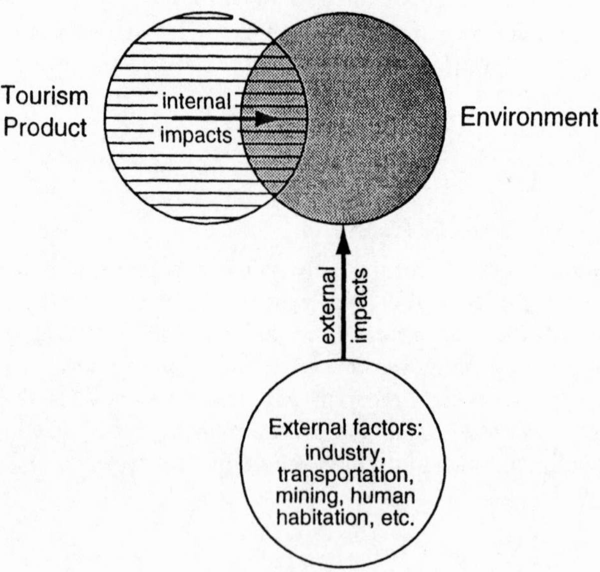

pact scenario natural processes occur completely undisturbed. There may be some occasional disruption of the processes, by such incidents as volcanic eruptions, impact of meteorites, or violent meteorological events. However, after each event nature inevitably returns to some kind of dynamic equilibrium. In addition to short-term disturbances, long-term changes are also taking place: nature or natural ecosystems are not static but dynamic and the processes of evolution are proceeding. As Friedrich Schiller, the German poet put it: "The world is perfect, in all places, where man does not enter with his problems" (*Die Welt ist vollkommen, überall, wo der Mensch nicht hinkommt mit seiner Qual.*) Thus, nature of highest quality is one unimpeded by human presence and by activities connected with that presence. In a sense, any human presence brings about at least some measure of modification of nature—once humans enter the picture, their actions are invariably associated with at least some negative impacts, or as economists call it today, negative externalities.

2.2 *Human-Impact Scenario*

Since hominides, our human-like (anthropoid) ancestors appeared on our planet over four million years ago, the scenario of no-human-impact on the ecosystems has been gradually changing. Most of this period shows so little human (anthropogenic) impact of hunters-gatherers that it can be safely ignored, with some exceptions, such as during the Pleistocene the overkill of the mammoth. However, contrary to some views prevalent in science until recently, there is enough evidence that the Holocene impact on certain areas has been relatively significant: there was an acceleration of human impacts with the inception of agriculture, about ten thousand years ago, when the pace of the adaptation of nature to human needs quickened considerably. These changes, although significant locally or regionally, never acquired global dimensions. These findings contradict the myth that early humans, including those existing prior to recorded history, adhered to the romanticized image of the "noble savage" developed in the eighteenth century by Jean Jacques Rousseau. The "noble savages" were supposed to live in complete harmony with nature without doing any harm to the environment.

> This view holds that neolithic agriculturists feel a reverence for nature, live in harmony with their environment, practice a conser-

> vation ethic, and avoid the short-sighted destructive exploitation rampant in industrial societies" (Diamond 1986: 19).

Indeed, most ancient societies, with a few notable exceptions, neither had the technology nor sufficiently large populations to exert any significant impact on their environments. Nevertheless, the idealistic "noble savage" model is a myth: there is enough scientific evidence (in the form of available written records) that the prehistoric societies frequently destroyed the environment by ecological mismanagement (mainly deforestation and over-hunting) creating, to use the contemporary terminology, "threatened and vulnerable areas" (Eldredge 1991: 212). Indeed, there are instances when ancient people ravaged their ecosystems, and ultimately themselves, into calamity.

The classic example of such ecodisaster is the deforestation of Easter Island between the fifth and sixteenth centuries A.D. Forests were cut to make space for pastures and other agricultural purposes to provide the growing population with food. The consequence of this imprudent action was water erosion that leached out the nutrients from the volcanic soil. Wind erosion completed the destruction. Soil formation processes stopped, fertility decreased, and the land became barren. Despite adequate precipitation, chronic drought set in, resulting in diminished water supply for both domestic use and agriculture. Even fishing was impossible; fish were driven away from the coastal sea that had become contaminated with fresh water mixed with the eroded material. Another consequence of deforestation was lack of timber for the construction of fishing canoes and for fuel to cook food. When the population exceeded the carrying capacity of the island, the people started to starve. Internal struggle for food and other resources led to warfare and cannibalism. The ultimate result of the Easter Island ecocide was the demise of a Polynesian civilization famous for its *moai*—giant statues carved out of the volcanic rock—the main tourist attraction of the island today.

One of the most comprehensive sources dealing with the destructive human impact on the environment of the pre-Columbian America is the work of William Donevan (1992). He describes the devastation of American landscapes by severe erosion and the partial recovery by 1750 due to the depopulation of the continent during the early colonial era. Indeed, North and Middle America provides many examples of adverse environmental impacts of ancient societies: the repeated abandonment of the Mayan sites in Yucatan and today's Guatemala were the consequence of erosion brought about by deforestation (Turner, *et al.* 1990: 37). The collapse of Maya civilization around the year 900 A.D. was caused not only by civil wars but also by over-exploitation of the rain-forest ecosystems. This led to the exceeding of the carrying capacity of the land. Farther north, the aboriginals living in the magnificent structures of Gran Chaco Canyon (now in northwestern New Mexico) between 1000 and 1200 A.D., destroyed the splendid pinyon-juniper woodlands to satisfy their needs for fuel and construction of their dwellings. The subsequent generations could not exist in a landscape increasingly devastated by erosion. With agriculture severely affected, they had to leave (Diamond 1986: 20). There is also enough circumstantial evidence that the Inca and other native people caused a considerable deterioration of the environment well before the arrival of the Spaniards in America. In Europe, the Vikings totally destroyed the forests of Iceland shortly after they settled there (*Poznaj Swiat* 1989: 10).

Less documented is the environmental impact of the Mycenae culture (1600–1000 B.C.) on ancient Peloponnesus (Diamond 1986: 20). Initially, they thrived using terracing and soil conservation. It is possible that the subsequent abandonment of these measures caused the devastation of landscape (slope erosion and valley siltation) and contributed to the end of these civilizations. The Sumerian civilization collapsed, largely due to another environmental sin: salinization and silting of the irrigation systems (Eckholm 1976: 116).

Early civilizations and primitive people not only destroyed whole ecosystems but occasionally eliminated certain plants and animals. The Polynesians introduced exotic species such as rats, pigs, and dogs to Hawaii in the pre-European period (Turner, *et al.* 1990: 357, 359); Eldredge (1991: 206) ascribes the big game extinctions of mastodon and mammoth in the Old World to hunting and correlates the late Pleistocene megafaunal extinctions with the arrival of humans in North America. The Maoris of New Zealand and the Polynesians of Hawaii made some endemic species of plants and birds extinct. The moa bird was completely wiped out by Maoris two hundred years before the arrival of Europeans in New Zealand.

In the early historic time, there are enough written records documenting the devegetation, and especially the deforestation, of coastal regions of the Mediterranean by people and their domesticated animals, particularly goats (Vadrot 1977: 75-81). This process had already started in antiquity. One has to admit that climatic change has played a role, but anthropogenic factors are certainly prevalent. Remnants of these ancient virgin forests may be still observed today in Corsica and Sardinia. In contrast, the devastated landscape of Malta may serve as an example of desertification of Mediterranean forest ecosystems. Another example is the destruction of the Lebanese forests with their magnificent cedars, which started about 3000 B.C. (Eckholm 1976: 27). The destruction was already well-advanced during the Roman period and was completed in the subsequent centuries. The result is today's largely barren landscape of Lebanon.

The pace of human impact on nature has substantially accelerated since the start of the Industrial Revolution in England in the middle of the eighteenth century and later in the nineteenth century in Europe and North America. The rapid expansion of economic activities has brought about a significant degree of anthropogenic degradation, or even devastation, to the ecosystems. The scale has been global and the degree, profound. Practically all human impacts on the natural environment proved to be invasive to the functioning of the ecosystems, and therefore should be evaluated as negative. As Eldredge (1991: 218) puts it:

> We seem to be able to effect more environmental change per unit of time than any other factor ever proposed as a cause for serious bouts of extinction, with the sole exception of the most catastrophic of the bolide impact scenarios.

Two factors were instrumental in this process: a spectacular increase in per capita production and consumption, and rapid population growth. Both of them have substantially increased the use of natural resources. If one adds to these the unrestrained and uncontrolled development of capitalist economies (until recently based on the principle *apres nous le deluge),* the result is the phenomenon recognized as global environmental crisis, which borders on ecocide. Indeed, the negative externalities of human activity have acquired global proportions, prompting Newman (1979: 182) to write about the "worldwide effect" of air pollutants on wildlife, as manifested in "direct mortality, injury and disease, physiological stress and changes in the distribution of certain species." Pollutants found on

Antarctic ice and in anthropogenic dust that contributes to the melting of mountain glaciers, constitutes excellent proof of the global scope of human impacts on the environment.

The acceleration of human impacts on environment since the beginning of the Industrial Revolution has resulted not only in the globalization of the effects but also in significant quantitative and qualitative increases of stress exerted on the ecosystems. Some ecosystems have become so overburdened, that self-regeneration is difficult—in other words, the limits of carrying capacity have been exceeded (see chapter 7). In such conditions, the ecological balance may be disturbed by relatively small additional impacts. These impacts frequently occur in places distant from the affected area, and takes considerable time before the damage becomes apparent. This characteristic feature of negative human effects on ecosystems is called by Wall and Wright (1977: 3) "spatial and temporal discontinuities."

These profound environmental upheavals of the last 200 years have completely reversed the former relationship between humanity and the environment: nowadays people are no longer surrounded by wilderness, but what is left of wilderness is surrounded by people. Today the scenario of absolutely no-human-impact is not valid, even on a local scale. There are no completely undisturbed natural ecosystems on this planet. Therefore, one may speak about the no-human-impact scenario only in relative terms, on a strictly local scale, referring to the comparatively small wilderness areas set aside in national parks and reserves, with limited or no human access.

Ironically, there have been some examples in the current century when war or political trouble created unintentional zones of limited human impact, because hostilities in the area restricted economic activities, such was the case of civil war in Nicaragua, which prevented logging and clearing of land for pasture (*Conservation by Conflict* 1992). In some extreme cases one could speak about *relative no-human impact,* because access to certain areas was denied for everyone, including tourists. The first example of such a situation is the demilitarized zone, 4.5 kilometers wide, between North and South Korea. The Korean zone has existed since 1953 and there are no signs of its liquidation in the foreseeable future. The second example is the border zone that existed between East and West Germany. The East German zone, fortified in 1961 to prevent people from fleeing to the West, was 1,378 kilometers in length and of varied width. It disappeared in 1990 with the unification of Germany. The third example are the Mai Po marshes, which served in the years of the "cold war" as a no-man's land between Hong Kong and the People's Republic of China: it is a wonderful habitat for birds migrating between Siberia and Australia. Nowadays tourists are allowed access to Mai Po on four-hour guided tours.

In these cases, nature was allowed to evolve without any human interference for many years. A major part of the Harz Mountains of Germany, with the highest mountain Brocken (1,122 meters above sea level), was an important tourist area before the Second World War, and was entirely out of bounds for visitors between 1962 and 1990 due to East German policy. There was a joke in East Germany that Brocken was the highest mountain in the world because it was "unreachable": indeed, climbing Mount Everest was easier. After the unification of Germany, environmentalists expressed their concern that these relatively untouched landscapes now become despoiled by tourists invading the former border zone in large numbers. For this reason the Harz National Park (*Nationalpark Hochharz*), centered on Brocken, was established. The idea was to accommodate hikers while leaving ecologically sensitive areas off limits for tourists. The creation of the national park was helpful, although it did not solve all the problems of tourism impact (*Der Spiegel* 1990, 44: 52–61).

2.3 *External Environmental Impacts in the First World*

The devastation of ecosystems worldwide is caused essentially from unrestricted growth of population and economy, which vary quantitatively and qualitatively from continent to continent, and from country to country. To generalize about the quantitative and qualitative aspects of these impacts one has to take into account significant differences in utilization of the environment between countries (societies) according to their political and socioeconomic systems and their stages of economic development. As the prime minister of India P.V. Narasimha Rao pointed out at the United Nations Conference on Environment and Development in Rio de Janeiro in June 1992, "we have one planet and several worlds."

It is fair to assume that the higher the level of economic development of a country, the greater the negative environmental impact. There is ample evidence that quality of the environment has been most affected in the 23 economically developed countries of the so-called First World, all members of the OECD (Organization for Economic Cooperation and Development). These countries with democratic political systems and market economy are also called Developed Countries (DCs). Since at least the early nineteenth century, the societal goal in these countries has been economic growth aimed at improving the prosperity of the people, although initially, state power, business profits and expansion predominated. Left unchecked, this development has led to significant environmental deterioration.

However, since the 1960s, the scenario of unrestrained growth has began to change. People have found that the democratic systems of the First World are the best way to cope with environmental deterioration, due to the relatively well-functioning mechanisms of checks and balances between the legislative, executive, and judiciary powers (see chapters 8 and 9 below). The input of public opinion, inspired by various environmental groups arranged in NGOs (Non-Government Organizations), has gained a significant influence on the decision-making processes. Such groups have exerted pressure on governments at all levels to regulate economic and social development in a symbiotic, sustainable interrelationship, in which a healthy natural environment ultimately coincides with the concerns of all people. As a result of these changes, the environment in the First World has improved in the last 30 to 40 years, not only on the per-capita basis but also, in many instances, even in absolute terms. According to Grossman and Krueger (1991), absolute and per-capita pollution increases in the early stages of industrial development. Subsequently it drops as a result of anti-pollution measures, and as adequate resources become available to tackle these problems. The more recent trend to desindustralize is also helpful. Some of the LDCs (Less Developed Countries), such as Mexico or Brazil, now experiencing the process of intensive industrialization, may be the worst environmental offenders at the present time, but they are just entering the green gate. In contrast, India and East Asia (e.g., China) are now assaulting the ecosphere with little restraint.

In the First World, various environmental NGOs have been using their political clout to influence the governments to take appropriate measures in saving the environment. The degree of success varies according to time and place, depending to a large extent on the resistance of vested economic interests. However, the validity of the environmental cause is being gradually accepted, and government controls are being introduced. Though these are belated and inadequate, the destruction of the environment has been increasingly checked. As a whole, undeniable progress has been achieved during the last 25 to 30 years.

Nevertheless, the political battle between diverse interest groups is being waged on a national and international scale. Not only are the various local ecosystems in jeopardy, but so is the global environment. Indeed, as I. Wallace (1990: 264) put it, "modification of the natural environment in the course of economic growth has reached such a scale that global consequences may flow from relatively localized (i.e., subcontinental) human interventions." This statement may be illustrated by the example of the depletion of the ozone layer discussed in section 1.7.2, and global warming. The First World countries take most of the blame for the damage to the protective ozone layer because they constitute the main users of chlorofluorocarbons (CFCs) that are the source of the problem. Similar is the situation with the emissions of carbon dioxide (CO_2), methane, and other "greenhouse gases" that cause global warming, although the greenhouse effect theory, in contrast to the depletion of the ozone layer, is controversial and much disputed. Some of its critics challenge the theory per se; others disagree on the extent of the danger and on the pace of future global warming. The ozone depletion theory, however, appears to be firmly established.

When looking at specific types of impacts, one has to single out manufacturing and transportation, particularly those that rely on fossil fuels, especially coal, and extractive industries as the worst offender. They are the main contributors to air and water pollution, and toxic waste disposal. The principal environmental impact of transportation is air pollution caused by motors burning fossil fuels, mainly oil. The automobile (including automobile-related impacts, such as salting of highways to control ice) has been blamed as one of the prime culprits of environmental damage. The resulting acid rain affects tourism resources, such as the European and eastern North American forests (e.g., Vermont's and Quebec's maple groves) and lakes, although not all scientists agree that the automobile is the main culprit. Other dangers linked to the increasing movement of explosives, toxins and other hazardous materials on highways and by railroad. The press reports various accidents, mainly collisions and derailments, causing spills of hazardous materials and even explosions. Tourists are sometimes victims of such catastrophes, as they were in the 1978 explosion of a passing truck which killed nearly one hundred campers at Spain's Costa Brava. Because the automobile belongs only partially to external or nontourist impacts on the environment, remarks are limited in this chapter to the external impacts, with tourism as an object of impacts. More attention is devoted to this issue in chapters 5 and 6 where tourism will be discussed as the subject of impacts.

Modern agriculture, with its use of chemicals, is also increasingly criticized. The overuse of herbicides, insecticides and pesticides, and fertilizers by agriculture in the DCs is a source of ground and water pollution and eutrophication (the enrichment of water with dissolved nutrients and algae, which deprives it of oxygen). In parts of the United States and western Canada, the overproduction of subsidized beef is associated with overgrazing and results in erosion, desertification and landscape degradation. Animal husbandry is also polluting the air (criticized by the International Round Table on Swine Odor Control) and water, another recreational resource, by the penetration of animal waste into the underground water and subsequently into rivers and coastal marine ecosystems. For example, this occurs as a result of the rich Amish animal husbandry of Lancaster County, Pennsylvania, which pollutes the Susquehanna River and the Chesapeake Bay, both major recreation areas. The contamination of Swiss lakes with animal waste is discussed in section 2.7 below. In some cases the farm animals may spread diseases, for example, poultry farms have been associated with effluents rich in fecal coliform bacteria. The contribution of agriculture to air pollution, including smog and ground-level ozone, results mainly from the burning of crop residues, such as stubble, and fouls the fall outings of tourists and recreationists.

With respect to logging and the preservation of forests in the DCs, one may generalize that the situation is under control (Turner, *et al.* 1990: 195ff), despite some regional and local problems. The forested areas and the yields are increasing due to forest reversion, as agriculture abandons marginal land, to replanting programs, and to modern silviculture combined with scientific forest management. However, this "industrial forestry" or "tree farming" is criticized by environmentalists for fundamentally changing ecosystems, using pesticides and fertilizers, and for unacceptable harvesting practices, such as clear-cutting. Environmentalists favor substituting the tree-farming with ecoforestry, which would restore the original biodiversity of wooded environments. Nevertheless, it seems there is an abundant supply of secondary forests for logging, and the primary, old-growth forests should be saved. Unfortunately, virgin forests, these unique biodiverse ecosystems providing habitats for endangered wildlife such as the spotted owl, and of particular interest for nature tourism and recreation, are in trouble in the DCs. These primary forests are now the principal battlefields of environmentalists and the loggers.

In North America, there is a growing concern about logging in the old-growth forests of British Columbia, Washington, and Oregon, which threatens the survival of "indicator species" and thus the biodiversity of large ecosystems. Environmentalists criticize not only logging per se, but also the construction of logging access roads regarded "as an important element in the dramatic decline of the old-growth forests" found in the Cascade Mountains of Oregon and Washington (Knickerbrocker 1993). The roads, built by the U.S. Forest Service, cause erosion and sedimentation, fragment the habitats of grizzly bear and other wildlife species, impede wildlife migration, and decrease scenic beauty. They give access not only to loggers, but also to poachers and campers. Logging and logging-road construction of the U.S. Forest Service, while trying to reconcile the incompatible agendas of protecting forests while developing them for harvest, is blamed by environmentalists for yielding too much to the logging interests.

In addition to environmental impacts inflicted by human economic activity and habitation, there are examples of bizarre external interference with the landscape of the DCs which, in my opinion, appeal to the tastes of superficial tourists, but in essence create eyesores and distort natural and cultural landscapes. Moreover, they cause some dangers to onlookers and constitute a considerable waste of money. The examples are the two simultaneous spectacles of the new public art in the United States and Japan, lasting for two weeks in October, 1991: the unfurling of 1,760 giant yellow umbrellas, designed by a landscape architect Christo. The umbrellas, each 6 meters tall and weighing 203 kilograms, were unfurled along an 29-

kilometer expanse of the Tejon Pass in California. At the same time 1,340 blue umbrellas were unfurled in the Sato Valley, 120 kilometers north of Tokyo. The cost of *The Umbrellas: Joint Project for Japan and USA* was US $26 million. Two deaths resulted from this spectacle: a woman tourist was killed in California when strong winds tore an umbrella loose from its foundation and crushed her head against a boulder; in Japan a crane operator was electrocuted while dismantling the umbrellas. Fortunately, after two weeks the spectacle was over, and the landscape returned to its original state.

This was not the first escapade of Christo in "correcting" nature. In 1971 he built an orange curtain across a valley in Rifle Gap, Colorado, and in 1976 he erected the 40-kilometer white fence near Petaluma, California. He certainly did not improve on nature; he merely contributed to the visual pollution of the landscape by introducing his expensive eyesores, reflecting the pattern of overindulgence and overconsumption typical of the DCs (see chapter 8 and 10).

Another eyesore is the seemingly environmentally benign form of wind turbines. Although originally designed as pollution-free alternatives to traditional energy sources, wind turbines clutter the landscape, cause visual degradation of the environment, and kill birds. The towers on which the turbines are located, cover relatively large areas, spoiling views and creating noise pollution in tourist areas such as Snowdonia National Park in England (McLeod 1992). The media have recently reported a controversy surrounding the construction of new wind turbines in Wales (*Economist* 22 January 1994). I tend to agree with the "eyesore" critics, after viewing the wind turbines in the southern part of the Island of Hawaii. As for the noise, new models are allegedly quieter.

The environmental pressures on the DCs, and the resulting deterioration of the quality of life prompts some inhabitants of affected regions to migrate. Thus, many Californians, who for years enjoyed the natural tourism and recreation amenities of the state, now cannot stand the stresses resulting from too rapid population growth and economic development: highway congestion, smog, despoiled landscapes, water shortages, and many other environmental ills. Although there still exists a net immigration to the "Golden State," more people than ever before choose to leave.

2.4 *External Environmental Impacts in the Second World*

The so-called Second World, i.e., the communist bloc, led by the Soviet Union and traditionally hostile to the First World, does not exist at the present time. Nevertheless the model of former communist countries, with their economies in transition to the market system, stands as a distinct group of nations, with specific problems inherited from the communist era, that affects their socioeconomic development (some may say misdevelopment). The remaining communist countries, all outside Europe, belong to the past communist model, with overdeveloped heavy and military industry and underdeveloped consumer industries and services. At the same time, however, these countries display a number of features, which suggest their inclusion into the LDCs (Less Developed Countries) or the Third World.

The countries with centrally planned (command) economies (communist countries), i.e., the former USSR and European members of the former CMEA (Council for Mutual Economic Assistance, named COMECON in the West) called themselves socialist. They were, however, essentially feudal, ruled by the dominating class, the *nomenklatura,* which was interested in the preservation of power and associated privileges and not concerned about the natural environment. "That system, one of the most monstrous in history, destroyed not only people and their souls but nature as well" (Havel 1992). Any opposition was crushed with monumental brutality. The will of the "socialist" states represented by its nomenklatura, was all-pervasive.

The ultimate purpose of this policy was twofold: externally the aim was to defeat capitalism by whatever means and achieve worldwide victory of the system; internally, the communist states pursued the singularly inefficient path of forced industrialization. They focused on producer goods, such as iron, steel and chemicals, with armament production given the highest priority. These were also the most environmentally destructive. This economically and politically distorted growth was forcefully imposed by law, and the basis of the "socialist" elitist leadership. Anything perceived as obstructing the fulfillment of economic plans was ruthlessly destroyed. Bogdan Mieczkowski (1991) provides further economic analysis of dysfunctionalities of the centrally planned and the free market systems. As well, Marxist doctrine, by according no inherent value to resources, contributed to their profligate, and environmentally harmful use (Kotov and Nikitina 1993: 11).

One can easily imagine that, in such conditions, nature was raped at the will of the party and the military-industrial complex. The communist plans were met at the terrible price of environmental despoliation, and nature reserves were used for military purposes, including nuclear facilities (Boreyko and Lystopad 1994). The forces defending the environment were too weak to influence the almighty communist parties and governments steered by them. Environmental legislation was largely ineffective (Hall, D. 1991). Many environmentalists were fired from jobs, persecuted, and even jailed. But the feeble ecological protests of the early 1980s have grown since 1985, in the years of Gorbachev's *glasnost* and *perestroika* (openness and restructuring), into powerful anti-communist political movements which ultimately overthrew the communist power (Feshbach and Friendly 1992).

The communist experiment, the most disastrous socioeconomic experiment of human history, based on limitless exploitation of people and nature, produced some of the worst environmental calamities the world has ever seen. The economic growth and militarization of economy at any price led to critical environmental situations in practically all communist countries. The destruction of ecosystems that included natural and human resources important for tourism, has reached levels unprecedented anywhere else in the world (Komarov 1980; Feshbach and Friendly 1992). Although all of the European members of the Soviet Bloc and the former USSR are not communist anymore, they have to face the awful legacy of "real socialism" (Hughes, 1991). The worst offender today, as was in the communist past, is pollution caused by electrical energy production and domestic heating, based mainly on coal and lignite, particularly the soft, sulphurous sorts used in Silesia (Poland), Saxony (Germany), and Bohemia (Czech Republic), and unsafe atomic power. Profligate energy use increased the damage inflicted on the environment and poisoned peoples' health (Giles *et al.* 1991; Bajsarowicz 1989a, 1989b).

This negligent, even criminal, attitude to the environment, culminated in the 1986 explosion at the atomic station in Chernobyl, Ukraine. This contaminated large areas with radioactivity. The devastating radioactive contamination on the Chukchi Peninsula in the Russian Far East caused by atomic bomb tests, has been criticized by the eminent Soviet scientist D. Lupandin and People's Deputy to the Supreme Soviet Ye. Gayer (Lupandin and Gayer 1989). Other areas of radioactive contamination are Novaya Zemlya, Preduralye, Southern Urals, and the Semipalatinsk area of Kazakhstan (Bulatov 1993). The communist ecological catastrophe afflicted large regions of the former Soviet Union, such as the Baltic and Aral Seas, the Kola Peninsula, the Volga basin, southern and central Urals, Donbass, and Kuzbass. About 15 percent of Russia's territory qualifies as environmental disaster zones (Kotov and Nikitina 1993: 12). Short- and medium-term prospects for improvement are dim, because the country does not have the financial means and organizational structure to cope with environmental problems, and the situation is expected to get worse *(ibid.)* Because the governments of the former Soviet republics have other priorities, it seems at the present time that only local and national NGOs are able to act on behalf of the environment (Williams, M. 1994). These NGOs have excellent ideas and much energy, but few financial resources to pay their expenses, however. Growing international tourism from the First World is a potential source.

The still remaining communist countries are all located outside Europe: China, North Korea, Vietnam and Cuba. They could be best classified as developing countries (LCDs) with a centrally planned economy. All of them are characterized by the same criminal neglect of environment as the former Soviet bloc. However, they also display similar problems, associated with the pressure exerted by exploding populations on limited natural resources and the urgent need for economic expansion to provide the means of survival for their citizens.

The results of such policies are apparent. China's environment, and with it also her tourism resources, is threatened by ecological disaster, caused by reckless economic development strategies that disregard the preservation of nature. Especially disastrous from the environmental point of view is the heavy reliance on coal as fuel for the production of energy, which results in monumental pollution problems; these affect not only China but also its eastern neighbors, Japan and Korea, which are being "invaded" by polluted air masses carried by prevailing western winds. Regional and local tourist resources suffer too: the scenic Guilin area is plagued by air pollution from nearby chemical plants, discoloring the rocks; the rocks of Dafeng Shan area have turned white; and the karst ecological system has been destroyed and the trees poisoned (Smil 1984: 121).

2.5 *External Environmental Impacts in the Third World*

The treatment of the environment by the Less Developed Countries (LDCs) reveals some of the inadequacies of the two previously discussed socioeconomic systems because, although the majority of the LDCs adhere to the free market principles, a number of them have followed, in various degrees, Soviet-inspired policies of socialization. Despite these policies, there are certain features of environmental destruction which are characteristic for most Third World countries. Most scholars agree that the root of their environmental problems is the population explosion (Turner, *et al.* 1990). According to the United Nations Population Fund, the world's population is growing by almost 100 million annually, 97 percent of this in the LDCs. Therefore, without radical change in the reproduction patterns in the Third World, the pressure on the ecosystems, both in the LDCs and beyond will increase, no matter what other measures are taken to improve the environmental situation. Thus, the decrease of birth rates in these countries is the *conditio sine qua non* for the future of the environment, which cannot sustain such rampant population growth. Of course, population control should not be regarded as a panacea for the economic problems of the LDCs: to achieve success, it has to be combined with other development measures.

The growing populations require constant tapping of new and new natural resources, with little improvement in standards of living. The result is growing global environmental deterioration, manifested in devegetation (including deforestation), soil erosion, water pollution and decimation of wildlife, either directly by overhunting or indirectly by habitat destruction. Desperate for new agricultural land and fuel (wood and charcoal), the landless poor all over the developing world, and especially in sub-Saharan Africa and South America, burn or cut down the forests, gradually destroying the fragile ecosystems, with their unique biodiversity and irreplaceable gene pools. Of course, trans-national corporations also play a role in this environmental destruction.

Clearing the tropical rain forests mainly by burning to make space for crops, pasture, and mining, destroys not only the local ecosystems, but endangers the global climate. Such burning constitutes an environmental threat of global proportions because of the release of carbon dioxide which contributes to global warming (see section 2.3 above) and other environmental problems. Also, forest fires in lower latitudes also contribute to the increase of ground-level ozone in the atmosphere due to the intense radiation of the sun. The quest for new agricultural land results in the cultivation and grazing on unsuitable lands such as desert margins and steep mountain slopes. In the African Sahel region, the most striking phenomenon is the gradual shifting of vegetation zones towards the south: "Desert creeps into the steppe, and while steppe loses ground to the desert it creeps into the neighboring savannah which, in turn, creeps into the tropical rain forest" (Eckholm 1976: 61). Most of this desertification, if not all, is caused by people. Indeed, nothing is safe from the constant human onslaught on the environment. Even national parks are threatened by agricultural expansion to increase the food production for local consumption (see section 2.9 below).

There are other reasons for the environmental rape taking place in the Third World: the LDCs argue that the DCs have developed their economies with total disregard for nature for a long time; therefore the LDCs now have a right to pollute until they achieve a comparable level of prosperity. The Third World countries are also, as a rule, burdened with huge external debts to the DCs and urgently need to export as much as possible to pay the interest and principal. They need foreign currency to import manufactured goods, and in many cases food for their exploding populations. Their products have to compete on global markets by keeping the costs of production as low as possible. Taking care of the environment makes their exports more expensive, and thus less competitive.

All these necessities induce the LDCs to accelerate the pace of environmental destruction. The classical example of these policies is the logging of virgin tropical and subtropical forests to export lumber to the DCs, particularly to Japan. Thus primeval forests, most of them tropical rain forests of Brazil, Thailand, Myanmar (formerly Burma), Philippines, Indonesia, Papua-New Guinea, and Malaysia increasingly fall victim to the chainsaw. Excellent prices for tropical timber are an added incentive to clear more land. Among the other export commodities, one has to mention coffee, tea, cocoa. To expand the plantations deforestation is necessary.

This forest destruction in the LDCs causes global climatic change and the risk of mass extinction of plant and animal species. Animals are at danger not only because of the loss of habitats but also because of poaching. The tropical rain forests of Amazonia, Central America, Southeast Asia and Africa containing the gene pools for future food and drug sources are most at risk. These reservoirs of biological diversity are indispensable factors of human survival and important tourism resources, especially for the fast growing sector of scientific tourism.

Wildlife preservation has repercussions for the environment as a whole. In fact, much should be done in this respect: some Asian countries, among them China, South Korea, and Taiwan, are still criticized internationally for the importation of animal parts, valued as medicines or aphrodisiacs. For example, in Taiwan powdered rhino horn is considered a fever reducer, and tiger bones, eyes and penises are prized as aphrodisiacs. Bear gall bladders are used in East Asia as aphrodisiacs. Some Arab countries, such as Yemen, import as rhino horns for use as dagger shafts or, in powdered form, as aphrodisiacs. This demand has reduced the world rhino population from 80,000 in 1972 to about 10,000 in 1992 (2,000 are the black rhinos). There is no medical evidence of any beneficial impacts from these materials; nonetheless, animals are slaughtered for the placebo effect to satisfy the beliefs of gullible people. In response to this outrage, environmental NGOs are increasingly lobbying for trade sanctions against countries that import endangered wild animal parts for medical use; unfortunately, no action was taken until CITES (Convention on International Trade in Endangered Species) joined the NGOs in condemnation (see section 3.6).

Another source of foreign currency is beef that is exported to the DCs, notably to the hamburger-hungry United States. This requires the expansion of grasslands, again at the expense of forests (Turner, *et al.* 1990: 190–197). In the Amazon, the destruction of tropical rain forests for ranching and agriculture has acquired devastating proportions in the last 30 years. The environmental repercussions are not only global, but regional and local because soils render good crops for only a few years, then become infertile. Subsequently, they cannot support agriculture or restore the forest, because torrential rains wash away the unprotected thin topsoil and leach out the scant nutrients. Some countries, such as Zimbabwe, try desperately to increase their exports particular crops, such as tobacco, which leads to the spread of cultivation, again at the expense of the forests. The process of curing (drying) tobacco requires fuel. Because oil, gas, and coal are too expensive for poor countries, wood becomes the obvious choice.

Not only do agriculture, ranching, and logging (for export, construction lumber, and charcoal production) jeopardize the tropical forests. A more recent culprit is mining, especially open-pit mining which scars the environment into a lunar landscape. This primary activity does more than just ruin the landscape by devegetation: it also poisons it. Gold mining, which uses the toxic chemical mercury to amalgamate gold, is particularly hazardous. Clearly, the ensuing contamination of the environment kills fish, wildlife, plants, and ultimately affects people.

The Third World is implementing ambitious plans of accelerated industrialization. To lower the costs of production and thus improve its competitiveness, the manufacturing sector of the LDCs is not eager to incur the costs of minimizing its ecological impacts. Because industrial development in the Third World is taking place almost exclusively in large cities, and because its impact is difficult to distinguish from that of communal uses, I will deal with this issue in section 2.10.

Another environmental scourge in the LDCs is war, including civil war. Internal political disturbances have devastated the ecosystems in places such as Uganda and Assam, India. In Uganda, many years of civil war virtually wiped out the big game in its national parks (there are only few wild animals left outside parks in Africa). Civil wars also devastated the environment of Angola and Mozambique. About half of Mozambique's coastal mangrove forests were cut, and in Angola the UNITA rebels exported huge amounts of valuable teak. Most of Angola's and Mozambique's elephants were destroyed. One of the victims of the Rwanda civil war was Mrithi, the huge male gorilla who appeared in *Gorillas in the Mist.* Mrithi was caught in the crossfire between rebel and government soldiers in May 1992 (*Newsweek* 8 June 1992). The death of the silverback, who had been seen by more people than any other gorilla, has constituted a severe blow to the tourism that has helped finance the efforts to save the gorillas of central Africa from extinction. The 1994 civil war and famine in Rwanda has increased poaching by hungry population but, so far, there have been no reports of harm to the gorillas. In America, the civil war in El Salvador has devastated the country's environment. The war exacerbated deforestation, soil erosion, mud slides, dust storms and silting of water courses already at risk from population pressures (*World Press Review* March 1990: 56).

The news from Asia is also discouraging: the survival of tigers and rhinoceroses in the Manas wildlife park of Assam is threatened by civil war (*New York Times* 12 November 1989). Other environmentally devastating hazards of war are the chemical defoliants (Agent Orange) which destroyed 12 percent of the forests in Vietnam, and consequently wildlife habitats. More than 20 years after the cessation of hostilities, a slow process of ecosystem recovery is taking place. However, the unfortunate legacy of Agent Orange remains in the form of one of its components, the weed killer 2-4D used on our lawns. The U.S. Drug Enforcement Agency (DEA) is using chemical and biological compounds to eradicate the coca crops in Peru's Huallaga Valley (*Der Spiegel* 1990, 27: 138–140). Consequently, the proponents of the legalization of drugs have added environmental concern to their arguments.

Ecological destruction on a much larger scale occurred after the Gulf War in February, 1991. Withdrawing Iraqi troops ignited 752 oil wells in Kuwait. These burned out of control for months and were extinguished only in November, 1991. The result of this eco-terrorism has been disastrous not only the immediate region, but globally. For example, the amount of air pollution from the oil-well fires equalled the annual quantity of poisonous emissions from all the world's automobiles. The oil spills in inland Kuwait created huge oil lakes. It has taken several years to clean them up (Ibrahim 1992).

2.6 *External Human Impacts on Marine-Coastal Ecosystems*

The preceding sections (2.3–2.5) discussed the external impacts on environments in various socioeconomic systems and levels of economic development—the focus was on the causes of the external impacts. However, one may also focus on the objects of impacts, i.e., the ecosystems. Such a treatment of the topic provides different insights, showing how the external impacts affect various natural communities. The following discussion (sections 2.6–2.8) will address three basic groups of ecosystems: marine-coastal, inland (focusing on fresh water resources), and mountain. Conforming to the approach of this chapter, sections 2.6–2.8 will concentrate on the external (nontourist) impacts. The tourist impacts on the same ecosystems will be discussed in chapter 6.

Marine-coastal ecosystems are known for their fragility, and therefore constitute a matter of growing concern because they are especially valuable as tourism resources. Because of the twentieth century trend towards water-oriented recreation, particularly in its maritime form, it is obvious where the vital interests of the tourism industry and the tourists are: in the preservation of the marine environment, especially in coastal areas. Since the 1960s we have realized that the oceanic pollution has reached epidemic proportions, we have realized that the marine and maritime coastal ecosystems are threatened by human impacts such as oil spills and dumping (including deep sea dumping, in depths of 4,000 to 5,000 meters) of toxic and nontoxic industrial waste. Maritime ecosystems also have to absorb agricultural runoff (fertilizers, pesticides, herbicides, insecticides, animal waste), raw sewage, and other habitation waste and chemicals. Maritime waters are deteriorating further because the major part of land-based waste conveyed by rivers, drainage ditches, and by the water table, ultimately will end up in the global garbage dump—in oceans and seas.

There is a widespread assumption that the vast oceans and seas that cover more than 70 percent of the world's surface have an unlimited capacity to neutralize any waste, either by the self-purification process or by the permanent sedimentation in their depths. This statement requires some discussion. Sea water depends on the capacity to absorb offending materials and compounds. The large spaces of open oceans have a substantial carrying capacity—an ability to absorb and dilute contaminants with little harm to the marine life because of their lower concentration in the water. This considerable carrying capacity allows the self-cleaning processes to act to the full extent, especially in warmer waters. Thus, the wide expanses of the open oceans can absorb considerable amounts of toxic and nontoxic materials. However, pollution is a real danger on overtaxed coastal waters, and waters between the land and marine ecosystems, such as river estuaries, where the concentration of pollutants reaches the maximum. In such conditions, waste absorption capacities are overwhelmed. Rampant economic development and urbanization along the U.S. Atlantic and Pacific coasts, the Gulf of Mexico, and along the Mediterranean coasts, especially in France, Italy, and Spain, are examples of polluted coastal waters. At the same time they are major areas of water-oriented recreation and recreational tourism.

Other marine ecosystems with high concentrations of pollutants are the internal seas, such as the Baltic, Black, Caspian and the Mediterranean Seas, and to a lesser extent the North Sea, which is open on one side. Internal seas are more vulnerable to pollution from rivers that empty into them from all directions. The relatively small volumes of water contained in them (as a rule they are more shallow than open oceans) and their limited access to the world oceans impede self-purification and contribute to increased concentrations of pollutants.

The pollution problem of the coastal waters is being aggravated by increased population at the seashores. The reasons for this trend, which has been developing since the 1950s, are mainly economic such as the efficiency of ship transportation. However, in the DCs, people want to live close to the recreational amenities of an attractive seashore, such as the Mediterranean.

A critical situation has developed in the Mediterranean Basin, the world's leading area in beach recreation and recreational tourism. The Mediterranean is the most polluted sea in the world because of dense population, agriculture, industry, and busy oil traffic (Vadrot 1977: 24-56). Hamele (1987: 118) states that the Mediterranean contains 50 percent of the world's oil and tar pollution. Another internal sea, the Black Sea, has been "enriched" by radioactive fallout from the 1986 nuclear plant accident at Chernobyl, Ukraine. Pollution of internal seas is disastrous for tourism: hundreds of beaches on the shores of the Mediterranean, Black, and Baltic Seas have been, at least temporarily, closed to bathers and swimmers. The collapse of sport fishing, proliferation of jellyfish and the threat to food and fresh water supply are additional deterrents. In some places the situation is so grave that one wonders if the wildlife in these areas would actually be rather better off in an artificial environment. For example, one could question where is it better for the beluga whales to live in the deadly polluted estuary of the St. Lawrence River or in the clean tank of an aquarium. Various types of industrial and habitation waste (e.g., raw sewage) are being dumped into coastal waters with devastating results for both commercial and recreational fishing.

Nontoxic sea pollution does not make all marine animals sick. However, it may stunt their growth rates. For example, scientists found that whales off the Newfoundland coast are small for their age. In contrast, toxic pollution represents a much greater threat to marine life. There have been numerous reports of marine life killed by toxic pollution and pollution-aggravated viral diseases, such as the mass deaths (called *die-offs* by biologists) of dolphins in the North Sea in 1988 and in the Western Mediterranean in 1990. The disease spread to the Ionian Sea in 1991 and to the eastern Mediterranean in 1992. Autopsies performed on dead dolphins showed that the cause of death was a disease, caused by the *morbilli* virus. Viral diseases have been known to develop naturally, but toxic pollution, is regarded as an aggravating factor. And indeed, high concentrations of toxic PCBs (polychlorinated biphenyls) were found in the bodies of the dolphins. The impact of these chemicals is not yet well understood.

The concern of scientists toward the welfare of marine life extends to humans. Humans swim in the same polluted waters and eat the same toxic fish that cause viral and bacterial diseases. The disposal of raw sewage into the marine ecosystems is a widespread practice that victimizes tourism. Raw sewage, carrying coliform bacteria and viruses, has been blamed for health-threatening pollution on beaches, from New York and New Jersey to Jurmala, Latvia. As a result, tourists and local recreationists are forbidden to swim in numerous coastal waters. Chris Ryan (1991: 101) describing the sorry state of Sydney's beaches quotes a researcher: "Bacteria lie in wait—capable of causing diarrhea, vomiting, salmonella, enteritis, hepatitis, cystitis, skin rashes, infections of the nose, ear and throat, and for unvaccinated swimmers, even typhoid and polio." Victoria, British Columbia is visited by 3.1 million tourists annually with tourist receipts surpassing three quarters of a billion dollars. The loss of business has been substantial after bad publicity in the summer of 1991. However, raw sewage is not the only substance that threatens the health of tourists and recreationists—various substances dissolved in water are also a menace. Mercury poisonings were reported at the Bay of Cartagena, Columbia, and heavy metal in the Mediterranean (Civili, 1987).

Some of the worst threats to coastal waters are the algae, both toxic (e.g., *Caulerpa taxifolia*) and non-toxic (so-called red and brown tides), that are found off the shores of the Mediterranean, North, and Baltic seas, and on the eastern seaboard of the USA. The algae are fed by air- and water-borne nitrogen compounds emitted by motor vehicles, power plants, manufacturing industries and by nitrogen and phosphorus compounds (usually nitrates and phosphates) in agricultural fertilizers that are flushed down the rivers. Raw sewage also feeds the algae. Overfertilizing the water leads to eutrophication, i.e., enrichment of water with dissolved nutrients, that promotes growth of algae. This deprives the coastal ecosystems of oxygen and suffocates marine life. Algae are most prevalent near the mouths of large rivers and near urban sewage outlets.

The algae problem cripples tourism in many areas. For example, the 1989 tourist season in the Northern Adriatic was ruined because of an especially high degree of contamination, with a loss of $800 million in tourist revenue (*New York Times* 16 August 1989). The number of German tourists, who constitute the major market for the area, dropped by 30 percent from 1988 (*Der Spiegel* 1989, 29: 165–166). The main source of algae-feeding nutrients in the Northern Adriatic is the Po River, the largest river in Italy. The basin of this river supports large concentrations of population and industry, and is located in the most important agricultural region of Italy. The tourism industry is the victim of indiscriminate pollution. The lifeless reddish or brown anoxic water is awful to swim in, and the algae secrete a slimy, gelatinous substance. The unpleasant impression I experienced is of touching a snake. To protect swimmers from algae, desperate resorts put up booms, similar to those containing oil spills. But this does not solve the main problem.

Another nuisance is the nonbiodegradable plastic garbage found in various forms, which poisons marine animals, and ensnares birds, turtles and marine mammals. Here some relatively small part of the blame may be attributed to internal or tourist causes, since tourists and plastic bags tend to travel together (see section 5.6.2 below).

A devastating form of external impacts on marine ecosystems are the oil spills not caused by tourism, but affecting it in a detrimental way. Much of the blame for these ecological catastrophes can be placed on ship owners who want to cut their costs by transporting oil in the largest ships with the thinnest hulls and smallest crews. There is an urgent need to regulate the oil traffic in national and international waters, including the double hull requirement. In recent years, there have been many oil spills which devastated important tourist beaches and other sites visited by tourists. Examples of such spills are the 1978 Amoco Cadiz disaster off the coast of Brittany, France; the 1989 spill off the coast of Washington and British Columbia; and several minor spills in the Caribbean. However, the most publicized was the 1989 Exxon Valdez oil spill off Prince William Sound, Alaska. The oil spills take a longer time to be absorbed and dissipated by northern ecosystems than in warmer environments like the Persian Gulf. There is compelling evidence that the Exxon Valdez oil spill will have long-lasting impacts, and Prince William Sound will take decades to fully recover (Mauer 1993). The break up of the tanker Braer off the Shetland coast in January 1993 was mollified by hurricane-force winds. The impact of the oil spill severely affects wildlife. Thousands of birds perished, severely affecting bird watching, one of the main sources of income of the local tourist industry.

Other oil spills are the result of war. The 1991 ecoterrorism of Sadam Hussein, mentioned in section 2.5, extended also to the sea: his deliberate oil spills into the Persian Gulf destroyed coral reefs off the coast of Kuwait and severely affected the populations of migratory birds, especially waterfowl. This, however, had a negligible impact on tourism, because it took place in an area not popular with international travellers (Ritter 1986) only local recreation has been affected.

There are other sources of oil pollution of the seas. Tank washing, ballast dumping by oil tankers, and other small releases of oil by ships, add up to substantial amounts, especially in waters with high volumes of ship traffic. (In addition, the water dumped by tankers is often contaminated by various viruses and bacteria harmful to marine plants and animals.) Oil is also detrimental to marine life: relatively small amounts of hydrocarbons in water cause the death of zooplankton and phytoplankton, the bases of the marine food chain. According to Vadrot (1977: 64), the existence of even a thin film of oil on the surface of water results in diminished precipitation, because the wind cannot lift the microscopic mineral particles from the top water layer. These particles would play the role of "cloud seeders," causing rain when a certain condensation level has been achieved. Instead, the winds are charged with the lighter, more volatile elements of hydrocarbons, and carry poisoned air to the coast, killing vegetation. Vadrot notes that this happened to the evergreen forests near the Italian beach resort of Viareggio. The surface oil film also decreases the aeration of water and causes the level oxygen level to drop, slowing down the self-purification process of the polluted water. There is an indirect negative impact of oil pollution—the hydrocarbons act as a solvent for other damaging compounds. This accelerates their assimilation by marine organisms, and ultimately by people. Thus oil, itself a poison, multiplies the pernicious effects of other pollutants by facilitating their entry into the food chain. This has been observed in the bay of Muggia, Italy (*ibid.* 64).

Living coral reefs are among the most important tourism resources of the sea, enjoyed by swimmers, snorkelers and scuba-divers. They also shelter millions of marine organisms, and act as protective barriers to coastal erosion. Unfortunately, humanity has not recognized their positive role and for many years has assaulted them with predatory fishing methods; for example, dynamite fishing, the use of cyanide to stun fish, and the use of steel balls tied to lines to scare fish into the nets. Coral reefs have been further destroyed by ships and their anchors, and indirectly by pollution and silt coming from deforested land. In some areas, notably in Sri Lanka, India, Maldives, and east Africa, coral reefs are mined for building materials (Simons 1993).

The most significant coral reef in the world is the Great Barrier Reef, which extends for some 2300 kilometers along the coast of Queensland, Australia. There is growing concern about the future of this "eighth natural wonder of the world." The reef is being destroyed by proliferation of *Acanthaster planci,* a starfish that measures about 20 to 30 centimeters wide and is commonly known as the "crown of thorns." Starfish, which feed on the reef, became a problem in the late 1960s. Their numbers decreased in the middle of the 1970s but by the 1980s, however, the starfish returned with a vengeance. They not only destroy the important fishing and tourism resource, the coral reef, but because of their poisonous spines constitute a danger to anyone touching or stepping on them. The invasion of the Great Barrier Reef by starfish has devastated the tourism industry of Queensland. The world's first floating hotel, known as the Barrier Reef Floating Hotel operated for only a few months at the reef in 1988 before it was towed away, for lack of business, to Ho Chi Minh City (Saigon). I saw it there, empty, in December of the same year.

Scientists are divided about the causes of the unusual proliferation of the starfish and intensive research continues. There is some conjecture that the main culprit is human pollution, and above all, overfishing predators, such as Emperor fish, that eat starfish. Again, the natural balance of the coral reef ecosystems has been disturbed by humans.

The Great Barrier Reef is not the only coral reef affected by external impacts. Similar problems occur in other tropical waters. The reason for the "bleaching" in the Caribbean is a combination of natural factors (sun's ultraviolet radiation) and human impacts. The reefs lose their color and become transparent because the organisms giving them their natural colorations cannot survive stresses such as pollution, busy ship traffic, and rising water levels caused by global warming. The causes of reef deterioration in the Caribbean are various, and include unusually high water temperatures which may cause the corals' death.

The reefs in the vast expanses of the tropical Pacific face another type of anthropogenic environmental threat to tourism resources: modern weapons of mass destruction. Although the USA (Bikini and Eniwetak atolls) and Britain stopped nuclear testing in the early 1960s, the residual radiation still persists, the affected atolls are still not habitable, and tourism potential cannot be realized. There is still nuclear bomb testing in French Polynesia (Moruroa Atoll). More recently, the Pacific has become the garbage dump of the world. The attempt of the Bush administration to use the Johnston Atoll for the destruction of unwanted chemical weapons has met with the resistance of all tiny independent states in the Pacific (*Economist* 27 October 1990).

The military use of the maritime environment is not limited to the free-market economies. On balance, the countries of the former Soviet Bloc have shown more disregard for the health of its citizens, including tourists. For example, the Soviet press reported that in February and March of 1989, the Baltic Fleet of the Soviet Navy exploded a number of smokescreen bombs near the coast of Latvia. As a result, parts of the bombs were washed onto tourist beaches—tourists collecting amber were in danger of picking up amber-like pieces of phosphorus, which explode when exposed to air and the warmth of the human body. There are other external threats endangering tourists: According to a press report, six tourists swimming off the coast of Sardinia were sucked to their deaths down an industrial pipeline (*European* 2 September 1993).

2.7 *Inland Ecosystems*

The inland ecosystems, located on lands with low relief energy, (flatlands), historically constitute the oldest recreational locations, developed when tourists feared the mountains and were not interested in the sea. These ecosystems are generally more resilient to human impacts than the seashore and the mountains. Recreational activities in such areas are largely water-related, and consequently focus on inland waters: rivers, lakes, and wetlands (Mieczkowski, Z. 1990: 256-257). In the broader context, the quantitative and qualitative problems of inland (fresh) waters constitute one of the most difficult environmental problems of the world. This section will deal with them from the point of view of external impacts on tourism.

First of all, I will discuss the quantitative dilemmas of water supply for tourism and other economic sectors. Fresh water is basically a renewable resource; it is, however, also a finite one, i.e., its quantity does not increase to meet rising demand from an exploding population. Thus water is becoming an increasingly scarce resource on the global scale, and not only in specific regions with dry climates, such as southern California, the Middle East, large parts of Africa, and the small islands of the Caribbean and the Bahamas (section 6.2.3.3), where renewable water supplies in cubic meters per person are diminishing at a frightening pace. The situation is deteriorating despite recent technical and scientific advances, including the economic desalinization of sea water, development of crop strains that make irrigation with brackish water possible, and the use of salt water for cooling of industrial operations (Lvovich and White 1990: 238). The demands of a fast-increasing world population on the world's stable fresh water resources are growing. International competition for fresh water results in political friction and even the threat of armed conflicts, especially in the Middle East.

Tourism is, naturally, in competition for water with other economic sectors. In some places, especially on islands, lack of water limits tourism development. The allocation of scarce water for tourism has to be justified on the basis of *opportunity costs.* In most cases, giving priority to rational tourism water use over other competing sectors makes economic sense. However, one cannot ignore social needs that reach beyond the cost-benefit calculations. Unfortunately, despite all these demands, some uses of water all over the world, including the western United States, cannot be regarded as rational. For example, farmers are provided with free or subsidized irrigation water which is often used wastefully. As a result, large amounts of water are removed from rivers which upset the ecosystems and, in particular, damages the delicate fish habitats essential to recreational fishing.

The problem of water quality impacts significantly on environment as a tourism resource. Pollution of fresh water by agriculture (pesticides, insecticides, herbicides, fertilizers, and animal waste) and industry may ruin tourism, or at least affect it negatively, as in Puerto Rico. Most major rivers in the DCs such as the Rhine, Rhône, Mississippi, and the St. Lawrence, have for a long time been unsuitable for swimming. River pollution in the LDCs is a more recent occurrence, and is not as severe as in the DCs. However, the situation is quickly deteriorating in the Third World, whereas there is some improvement in the First World countries. The problem is that while in the DCs anti-pollution measures have been implemented on a large (although still inadequate) scale, the LDCs do little to cope with the deteriorating situation. For instance, open-cast mining not only devastates the landscapes leaving them susceptible to erosion (including river bank erosion), but also affects water runoff patterns, and often poisons the water in rivers with toxins. As mentioned previously, gold mining uses highly toxic mercury to amalgamate gold. The result is the contamination of not only the river water, but also fish, and ultimately the people who eat the fish. However, the main sources of river pollution are industry, agriculture and human habitation. In this connection one has to wonder why the extremely polluted holy Ganges River, although shunned by tourists, seems not to do any apparent harm to the faithful pilgrims (religious tourists) taking ritual baths in it. This phenomenon is under scientific investigation.

Another case of potential harm to tourists is polluted water vapor. Visitors to Villa d'Este, in Tivoli, Italy had an unpleasant surprise in 1990 when they found the magnificent fountains turned off. The Aniene River, the source of the fountains' water, was badly polluted and contained microorganisms that could cause illness in tourists when vaporized and inhaled (*New York Times* 17 February 1991). After clean-up measures were completed, the sparkling fountains were turned on again. As a continuing precaution, however, tourists must now view the pools, and fountains at a distance, from behind a rail (*New York Times* 19 May 1991). In most cases, however, it is impossible to turn off the source of water. The mist spewing from the Niagara Falls contains toxic chemicals, PCBs, chloroform and chlorobenzens (*Winnipeg Free Press* 7 May 1987). These chemicals are known carcinogens, and it is believed that tourists, because of their short stay at the falls, are not in danger. However, some as yet unknown impacts on the tourists' health should not be excluded.

Another environmental problem associated with rivers is the development of hydroenergy. Up to about the 1980s the advantages of hydroenergy development, such as production of cheap and clean electricity, flood control, irrigation, and transportation, were emphasized. Tourism also benefited from the creation of hydro reservoirs ideal for water sports such as swimming, sailing, motorboating, and water-skiing. However, in recent years, environmental concerns have been raised about such issues as loss of agricultural land, wetlands and forests; the necessity of relocation of thousands of people; and the obstruction of wildlife migration routes (caribou). Losses for tourism also could be significant. First of all, the natural beauty of the landscape is frequently destroyed by hydro dams. Many spectacular waterfalls, such as Churchill Falls in Labrador, vanished as a result of hydro construction. The second tourism-related drawback of hydro projects is that the rivers that support activities like white-water kayaking, canoeing, and rafting are altered so severely that these activities cease, and recreational river boating is significantly impeded. The third disadvantage is the impact of hydro development on tourist bioresources: wildlife habitats, including inland wetlands, are often destroyed, and recreational fishing is negatively affected because the fish migration routes, e.g., those of salmon, are blocked (fish ladders do not solve the problem adequately). The travelling times of juvenile migrant fish downstream from the spawning grounds increase. This prolongs their exposure to predators and higher water temperatures in the reservoirs that make them susceptible to disease, and may even kill them. Turbines pose additional danger for the fish if the dams are not provided with appropriate screening devices. Despite this evidence, the impact of hydro projects on fishing is not entirely negative: in some cases, such as the Kara-Kum project in former Soviet Turkmenia, fishing has improved as a result of the dam on the Amu-Daria River.

The fourth disadvantage is the irregular flow of water in the dammed rivers. This is especially frequent in cases where inadequate regional network links provide for energy transfer from alternate sources during the peak periods. Sudden releases of water from the reservoirs occur when the spillway gate is opened, when turbines work at full capacity during periods of peak electricity demand. The result is a sudden upsurge of turbulent water downstream from the station, followed by a trickle during the low demand time. Clearly, these radical oscillations of water flows are not only inconvenient for downstream recreationists, but can be outright dangerous. Boaters, campers, fishermen may be swamped by a sudden wave and endangered by a strong, fast current. Once in the water in such conditions, a swimmer faces a difficult challenge to reach the shore. The sudden water releases from the hydro reservoirs also cause bank erosion and ruin fish-breeding grounds. A side effect of the changing water levels is that the rocks both upstream and downstream from hydro dams become slippery, even when they appear dry. An individual fishing or walking on the shore may slip and fall into the swiftly moving water.

Another specific type of environmental hazard associated with hydro dams is found in projects at high latitudes, particularly in northern Canada. There is preliminary evidence, now being researched, that the water in hydro reservoirs breaks down peat. Peat vegetation covered with water dies and decomposes. Carbon dioxide and methane, the greenhouse gases stored in it, are released into the atmosphere, thus contributing to global warming. If the hypothesis proves to be valid, tourists and recreationists will again join the environmentalists in the call to preserve the peat marshes of the North.

All these arguments against the construction of new hydro dams cause long delays and even cancellation of new projects. Difficult decisions have to be taken. The critics of the huge Yangtze project in China claim that it will ruin the tourist attractiveness of the famous Three Gorges, destroy fishing and destroy a number of historic landmarks. However, these losses must be considered against the alternatives: construction of large thermal-electrical power plants which would produce an equal amount of energy and result in considerable pollution of air and water normally associated with that type of energy generation. Thus, the issue is far from clear. The Chinese authorities insist that the benefits of the Yangtze project will outweigh the costs.

Lakes are an important resource for recreation and tourism, including health tourism (e.g., Dead Sea), and their pollution by industry, agriculture and human habitation constitutes a growing problem. The most obvious seems chemical pollution, toxic runoff and acid rain that destroys the entire food chain in some lakes. However, most people are oblivious to the fact that the lakes (and to a lesser extent also rivers) all over the world are affected by *thermal pollution* (i.e., increasing water temperature) and the introduction of unwanted nutrients into the water. These lead to *eutrophication* and development of various weeds, including algae and hyacinths, that are the enemies of water-related recreation. Hyacinths are especially widespread in tropical and subtropical areas. I observed them on Lake Inle in Myanmar (Burma).

Most people will be surprised to learn that some of the allegedly crystal clear lakes of Switzerland, a major tourist resource, suffer from pollution (*Der Spiegel* 1990, 23: 178-183, *World Press Review* December 1991). Smaller lakes located in agricultural areas are most affected. The damage is mainly by agriculture and animal husbandry where the animal waste (especially from pork production) is used as organic fertilizer. The waste filters to the groundwater, and ultimately contaminates the lakes. The result is the growth of algae that deprives the lake water of oxygen. Concentration of phosphorus in the water reaches 400 milligrams per cubic meter, as compared to the sustainable level of 30 milligrams per cubic meter. Another lake that constitutes a significant tourist resource and is in danger from external human impacts on its environment, is Lake Salton in southern California. The culprits, in this instance, are heavy metals and agricultural runoff. The salinity in the lake is increasing, and now ranges between 3.9 percent to 4.3 percent as compared to 3.5 percent in the ocean. The fish and wildlife in the Salton Lake Recreation Area are in danger.

There have been environmental concerns about the Great Lakes for decades. This prime North American recreation area certainly deserves maximum attention. Toxic chemicals, such as dioxins in Lake Ontario, mercury in Lake Superior, and the threat of algae feeding on phosphorus and nitrogen compounds on Lake Ontario and Erie, have affected both people and wildlife in the form of disease and genetic abnormalities. Since the opening of the St. Lawrence Seaway in 1959, scientists report increasing contamination of the lakes' water with various exotic organisms, such as non-native fish and algae, and more recently zebra mussels, carried in the ballast water of ships that travel to the Seaway from everywhere in the world. The zebra mussel (*Dreissena polymorpha*), a small mollusk from the Caspian Sea, clings to almost any submerged hard surface (Ross 1994), and is proliferating at an alarming rate, thus causing imbalances to the Great Lakes ecosystem. To cope with the environmental problems of the Great Lakes, a bilateral agreement was concluded between Canada and the United States in 1972 and an International Joint Commission was established to monitor this environment. Despite undeniable progress in cleaning up the lakes, their plight seems far from over. Unfortunately, both partners are violating the agreements and there is no improvement in sight. External human factors are mainly responsible for the environmental deterioration of the Dal Lake, the jewel of Kashmir, India. The causes are overfishing and excessive fertilization of the cultivated areas of the region, which results in enormous weed growth. Farther away, the hills and mountains are being constantly deforested and overgrazed, which causes increased runoff, erosion and silting of the lake. Another negative external impact is the growing discharge of raw sewage into the lake, the result of a rapidly increasing local population. Admittedly, not all impacts are external. Tourism is also partially to blame (see section 6.3.2).

Finally, one has to mention a remarkably important tourism resource endangered by external human impacts—wetlands, those valuable ecosystems of land and water. The environmental value of wetlands is beyond question. They provide crucial plant and wildlife habitats, control water quality, maintain soil moisture levels, moderate flood levels and protect shorelines from erosion. Thousands of hectares of wetlands are lost annually to the expansion of industry and agriculture. The quality of wetland environments also suffers. For example, as a result of oil exploration and exploitation, *drilling waste* (i.e., water contaminated with oil and gas) enters the groundwater of the wetlands. Another threat to wetlands is the dropping of the water table, caused by the excessive use of water for industrial and domestic purposes. A good example of such an ecosystem is Florida's Everglades, a valuable wetland which is drying up, endangered by the settlements and industries that are expanding in southern Florida. The water deterioration of the Everglades is a well-documented problem. Water, the source of life of the Everglades, has been drained, diverted, and polluted to such an extent that the wildlife has been decimated and habitats destroyed. Everglades water is being contaminated by agricultural and habitation run-off, especially by phosphorous compounds from fertilizers used in Florida's cane-sugar agriculture, and by detergents promoting the growth of algae and other exotic plants. The impact of tourism and recreational subdivisions on the Everglades will be discussed in section 6.3.3.

2.8 *Mountain Ecosystems*

Mountain environments deserve special attention while discussing the external (i.e., nontourist) environmental impacts, for several reasons. Firstly, as Eckholm (1976: 74–75) points out, "mountain ecosystems have been ignored so long in comparison to other natural areas" by research and governments, and the interest paid to them is relatively recent. The second reason is that mountain environments constitute valuable tourism resources, arguably second in importance to the coastal ecosystems. Third, mountains are among the most fragile environments, extremely sensitive to human impacts. Price (1981: 419–420) discusses the reasons for the fragility of mountain ecosystems:

> Climatic extremes, brevity of the growing season, lack of nutrients, low biological activity, low productivity, youthfulness, island-like character, steepness of slopes, and the basic conserva-

> tism of the dominant life forms, all make the rate of restoration to original conditions after disturbance slow: in some cases, the original conditions may never return... Restoration is hampered by the marginal conditions of exposed, steep slopes with their thin and poorly developed soil.

Satchel and Marren (1976: 72) supplement these characteristic features of mountain ecosystems by slow growth of vegetation, and high percentage of sensitive plants, such as mosses and lichens. Mountain ecosystems are extremely complex webs, made up of closely interacting elements. For example, in the Alps, the Arctic glaciers almost meet the valleys, which are Mediterranean in character. This explains the susceptibility of mountain ecosystems to human interference. In particular, they lack the response mechanisms to human activity. Wenger (1984: 8) provides an example of the slowness of the recovery of the mountain ecosystems from human damage. A military facility in the western United States built at 2,472 meters of altitude in 1747 still bear scars to the landscape now because of the retarded pace of biological processes.

The fragility of the mountain ecosystems is evident from the data on air pollution. Global air pollution, particularly the industrial and automobile emissions of sulphur dioxide, affects the mountain environments especially strongly because airborne pollutants, mostly acid rain, are deposited in the mountains by *acid fog* (ground-hugging clouds) and precipitation coming from pollution-carrying clouds. Acting as a sort of vacuum cleaner of the atmosphere, clouds carry the pollutants for considerable distances, and because of the orographic effect, dump them more in the mountains than in the lowlands. This phenomenon has been observed all over the world, especially in the mountains of the DCs, located at short distance from industrial regions. Thus, such mountains as the Appalachians, the Alps and the German Mittelgebirge, e.g., the Schwarzwald, and other European mountains located to the north of the Alps, suffer most from external sources air pollution. The main victim of these deadly deposits is mountain vegetation, particularly the forests, which are dying and causing soil erosion with associated problems. Thus, the Schwarzwald (Black Forest) is becoming the "Yellow Forest."

The dangers of environmental degradation of the mountain environment are not limited to air pollution. In fact, the human impacts occurring within the mountains are more destructive and their effects increasingly devastating, especially in the Himalayas, the Andes, and the African highlands. There are two reasons for this rapid deterioration. Firstly, the steep mountain slopes cannot sustain the same degree of human use as the lowlands. Secondly, the population explosion in the LDCs is putting a growing strain on mountain ecosystems.

The Himalayas and Himalayan foothills in Nepal are classical examples of ecological degradation caused by local population pressure wiping out the natural resource base. The destruction of the protective forest cover, which is being cut down for fuel, and cleared for the expansion of agriculture (including grazing), causes slope instability. With it come all the dire consequences of soil erosion and landslides, especially during the monsoon period. As the thin mountain soil washes away, the damage is likely to be irreversible. The loss of important tourism resources is the consequence of the destruction of mountain forests. However, frequently the impact is indirect, as in the case of the Lijiang River, which flows through the spectacular mountains of Guilin, the major tourist attraction of southern China. The flow of the river has diminished substantially in recent years, due to the excessive tree felling which was undertaken to expand crop cultivation in the highlands around the river's source. This could make boating for tourists down the river impossible.

Not only does agricultural development constitute a threat to mountain environment, but so does local industrial development. The flat topography required for industrial plants in the mountain valleys means competition with hotels and other tourist facilities. Moreover, industrial enterprises pollute the landscape visually, contaminate water and air, severely damaging both the environment and tourism. Air pollution is especially dangerous; valley topography makes dissipation of polluted air more difficult, particularly in the case of a thermal inversion, discussed in section 2.10 below.

One realizes the environmental importance of mountain ecosystems when one understands that ecological changes taking place the mountains have impacts on the lowlands. The concern about the preservation of mountain ecosystems is limited to their locale, and reaches far beyond their significance as a tourism resource. Pollution of any type affects not only the mountains but also the lowlands: the mountains contain the water sources and reservoirs for most of humanity. Consequently, the pollution of the fresh-water resources in the Alps endangers the water supply for a large part of Europe. Another hazard is erosion and flooding emanating from the mountains. The force of gravity can severely affect the lowlands, as it did in the flooding and silting of Bangladesh, although Ives and Messerli (1989) express some doubts. New research suggests an additional culprit: the destruction of wetlands on the Ganges and Bramaputra flood plains (*Earthwatch* March/April 1992: 4).

The devastation of mountain ecosystems has to be stopped. The present human impacts constitute a threat to tourism, which will suffer or even disappear if the mountains become denuded eyesores unable to attract people at leisure. Tourism is based on the preservation of these scenic refuges of nature.

2.9 *Protected Areas and Wilderness*

The most important repositories of ecosystems, aimed at the conservation of nature in both DCs and LDCs, are national parks and other reserves, such as national forests, wildlife refuges, and provincial parks. In national parks, the preservation function is paramount. Some reserves adhere to the principle of multiple use, and here a delicate balance between preservation and use must be sought. One should also not forget that these areas are important tourism resources, and that in the majority of instances, tourism provides the economic base for their existence. Unfortunately, even these last refuges of unspoiled nature do not escape the detrimental impact of external factors. These operate in various ways in different socio-economic situations, and set the parks of the LDCs apart from those in the DCs.

Many parks in the LDCs provide only a relatively minor measure of protection. The encroachment of agriculture, based on the arguments that people's needs are more important than animals' needs, affects the parks. Logging and mining are widespread, as is oil exploration and exploitation. Sometimes logging is undertaken for reasons other than timber supply and clearing the land for agriculture: the palms of Iguazu National Park in northern Argentina, are being illegally cut for their cores, or "hearts of palm," considered a gourmet treat (*World Press Review* March 1992: 53). An oil spill in a national park in eastern Ecuador is another example (*Der Spiegel* 1991, 26: 160–162).

Poaching in the parks is a permanent problem all over the world (Mieczkowski, Z. 1990: 235–242, 270). Poaching threatens wildlife in all national parks and wildlife reserves, even in North America, but parks located in the LDCs are most affected (Otichillo 1987). Elephants, rhinoceroses, mountain gorillas, and alligators are most endangered. Despite drastic measures used in some countries such as Kenya or Zimbabwe, the problem is extremely persistent. The results are disastrous not only for the tourism business but for the visitors themselves: tourists are sometimes attacked by poachers. Several such incidents were recorded in Kenya in 1990-92.

A different set of problems must be faced in the national parks of the DCs, which, despite stricter law enforcement within their boundaries, are not spared from environmental impacts coming from outside the parks. The national parks in North America, the magnificent "temples of nature" surrounded by the sea of civilization, warrant special concern. The problem is that the parks are parts of larger ecosystems extending beyond their boundaries. Wild animals wandering out of the parks into the adjacent countryside are the victims. This is undergoing rapid development and population increase, often by retirees looking for natural amenities. Thus, in recent times, the pressure of civilization is expanding not only to the buffer areas surrounding the parks, but to the boundaries of the parks themselves. Probably the most externally endangered in North America is Everglades National Park, which protects and is part of the Everglades ecosystem discussed in section 2.7. above.

The diversion of water for human use from national parks may substantially impoverish such resources as scenic rivers, fishing areas, wildlife habitats, and wetlands. Near Yellowstone National Park, for example, the production of geothermal energy or operation of mineral health resorts that tap the water near the parks, may affect the underground aquifers that feed the park's geysers, hot springs, fumaroles, and mud pots. Similarly, oil, gas, mining and mineral exploration in the vicinity of the parks constitute a potential threat to their ecology.

A separate external problem for the parks has been air pollution and acid rain that often reaches the parks from faraway sources. Alarming reports have appeared about this since the mid-1980s. The problem seems worst in the eastern United States, particularly in the Appalachians, because of the proximity of major conurbations. The Great Smokey Mountains National Park in North Carolina and Tennessee, the most visited national park in the world, is often overwhelmed by man-made haze. Sulfate particles and acid rain are steadily degrading the air quality and destroying vegetation in many North American parks. There is evidence that both deciduous and evergreen forests (located at higher elevations) are being damaged. The sources of pollution such as smelters, coal-fired industries and power plants, often situated at considerable distances from the parks, emit sulphur compounds which are deposited over wide areas in the form of acid rain. Another culprit is ground-level ozone, usually with automobile exhaust and vegetation fires from farming and ranching (Simons 1992a).

The list of national parks affected by external air pollution is long and includes such remote locations as Bryce Canyon in Utah and Glacier in Montana (*United States National Park Service* 1988). The smog over Grand Canyon National Park is especially obnoxious in winter. The source of the haze is the sulfur emissions from the coal-fired Navajo Generating Station in Arizona, located about 25 kilometers to the northeast, although the company argued that the causes of smog were to a large extent natural (*New York Times* 15 October 1989, 2 November 1989, 2 February 1991). However, in August, 1991 the Environmental Protection Agency (EPA) ordered the plant to install scrubbers, expensive pollution control devices, to eliminate 90 percent of sulphur emissions. On the basis of the available material one can conclude that the Navajo Generating Station is responsible for most of the winter pollution, and Los Angeles and other urban areas of southern California for summer pollution of the Grand Canyon National Park. A recent air quality study in the Grand Canyon area found traces of methyl chloroform, a chemical used in the Los Angeles based aerospace and electronic industries, in the canyon's atmosphere (*Time* 10 July 1991). The same sources are responsible for fouling the air in Kings Canyon and Sequoia National Parks. However, there may also be some natural causes for the haze over the Grand Canyon. An additional threat to the Grand Canyon is the wildly fluctuating level of the Colorado River, brought about by releases of water from the Glen Canyon reservoir to meet the demands for hydro-electricity. Surges, almost four meters high, erode habitats, endanger Indian archaeological sites, and raise complaints from tourist boaters travelling down-river in the canyon. Appropriate Senate legislation forbidding such practices is now in place.

Besides the national parks of North America where economic activity is banned, are the areas of nature reserves. Along with the preservation function, some of them allow for multiple use, i.e., logging, grazing, mining (including oil drilling), and military combat training, are permitted. Representative of such areas are the wildlife refuges and national forests in the United States and some provincial parks in Canada. These areas are often buffer zones surrounding the parks. Typical in this respect are the national forests surrounding the Yellowstone National Park.

As indicated in section 2.3, some primary forests in North America are under the threat of logging (especially clear-cut logging). This pertains also to the virgin forests in the wilderness areas of the U.S. national forests, and provincial parks in two Canadian provinces. There is increasing evidence that some forest ecosystems, especially old-growth forests, may never fully recover, once logged, mainly due to the loss of valuable species (Dold 1992b). In Canada the logging issue affects Wood Buffalo National Park in Alberta and the Northwest Territories. To advocates, logging jobs are considered more important than habitats for wildlife. These issues are fought in political arenas.

In addition to obvious environmental impacts, such as destruction of wildlife habitat and soil erosion, logging blocks rivers to fish migration, (e.g., to salmon in the west of North America), and fouls riverbeds by decomposing debris. Although such practice is banned, old logjams still cause problems on some rivers. Environmentalists also argue that deficient reforestation programs result in a deterioration of forest quality.

Agriculture, logging, mining and other nontourist activities in the immediate vicinity of parks which do not enjoy a buffer zone, directly threaten the survival of park ecosystems. One of the most extreme examples is Riding Mountain National Park, Manitoba, Canada, where there is a troublesome interface of the park ecosystem with agriculture.

2.10 *Physical Environments of Large Cities*

Cities, especially large cities, are specific, completely human-made environments. They serve not only as sites of permanent residence to millions of people but also contain important tourism resources and facilities: especially important are the cultural and recreational attractions. Urban tourism is on the rise worldwide for several reasons, such as increased interest in culture. This interest results from improved education and possibly a slight shift from beach tourism.

This section discusses some of the external impacts on the physical environment from large urban agglomerations. Of course, these are not the most important problems of contemporary cities, and especially of mega-cities. One has to realize that at the root of the urban plight are socioeconomic problems which will not be discussed here, although there is a link between them and the issues of the urban physical environment.

There are essentially three external (nontourist) sources of environmental disturbance in urban areas: first, human habitation (including heating, air conditioning, cooking), second, transportation (mainly automobiles), and third, industry (including energy production). The relative importance of each of them depends on local conditions. However, generally the main culprit in the DC cities is not industry, as it was in the past. There are several reasons for this: the first is the increasing use of antipollution measures, including high-tech devices, the second is that the worst offenders have been removed from the urban scene to extra-urban areas or even abroad, and the third is deindustrialization that has caused heavy industry to die. Nowadays, the main source of pollution in the DCs is the automobile—two thirds of the smog in Los Angeles is car-related. In the LDCs the situation is more complex. Industrial polluters are still despoiling the environment, but the car, especially because of nonexistent or inadequate emission controls, is becoming the source of major concern, as it is in Mexico City.

The main environmental problem caused by all three sources seems to be the air pollution (WHO/UNEP 1992) by particulate matter, sulphur dioxide, carbon monoxide, carbon dioxide, nitrogen oxides, ground-level ozone (the main cause of smog), and lead compounds. In the LDCs lead from gasoline is a major problem. The most significant worry is the health of permanent residents endangered by longer exposure; tourists staying at the destination merely a short time are less affected. Practically, only tourists with pre-existing health problems are at risk. Tourists who are in good health stay away from polluted cities or limit the duration of their sojourn because they simply do not enjoy such environmental conditions. Indeed, there is no other option but to leave: pollution affects the well-being and health of tourists even in air-conditioned hotel rooms, because air-conditioning removes only some particles from the air but fails to filter out noxious gases. Tourists with respiratory problems like asthma, emphysema, and bronchitis should take necessary medical precautions while visiting the most polluted cities of the world, such as New Delhi, Calcutta, Bangkok, Jakarta, Teheran, Shenyang, Shanghai, Beijing, Seoul, Mexico City, Bogota, Saõ Paulo, Madrid, Milan, Paris, the Ruhr district, Silesia, Los Angeles, New York, Chicago, Detroit, and the cities on the Mexican side of the U.S.-Mexico border which also pollute the adjacent US cities. Smog (see section 5.2), a combination of fog with pollutants, (mainly ground-level ozone) is the hazard of many large urban agglomerations, but is especially prevalent in Los Angeles. Smog killed thousands of people in London, England in 1948, 1952 and 1956. Now, after the implementation of stringent antipollution measures by local authorities, the situation in London and in other heavily polluted cities (especially in Japan) has improved.

Smog is, as a rule, aggravated by two natural factors: elevation and topography. Pollution in cities located at high altitudes is exacerbated by oxygen deficiency in the atmosphere. This causes car engines to burn inefficiently and release unburnt hydrocarbons. These react with the sun, producing, by photo-chemical processes, ground-level ozone which attacks the lining of the lungs, irritates the eyes and nose, and causes asthma attacks. A mountain basin or valley city may also aggravate the impact of air pollution because the air has a tendency to stagnate. Such locations are also at risk of thermal inversions that trap polluted air by a layer of warmer air. Examples are Los Angeles; Denver, Colorado; Mexico City; Athens, Greece; Santiago, or Ulan Bator in Mongolia.

Air pollution in large cities weakens the human immune systems, endangering people with a number of diseases: it is linked to the exposure to viruses and bacteria that cause infectious diseases, such as salmonella and hepatitis. They can be contracted simply by inhaling bacteria and viruses that are suspended in the air in a substance called *fecal dust.* Other short-term health effects await tourists. Such pollutants as ozone and nitrogen dioxide may cause everything from skin reactions and eye irritation to increased susceptibility to heart attack. Bronchitis and other respiratory ailments are also pollution-related.

Urban pollution damages the physical well-being and health of tourists and recreationists. It particularly affects athletes and recreational runners, and other outdoor sport participants because they breathe more deeply than walkers, and often through the mouth, thereby bypassing the nasal passages which help filter out water-soluble compounds such as sulfur dioxide (*Wellness Letter* August 1992: 7). Thus, modern tourists and recreationists are involontarily breathing in such components of car exhaust as sulphur dioxide, ozone, carbon monoxide, nitrogen oxides, lead (in the LDCs), and suspended particulate matter. The smaller the particles, the deeper their penetration into the lungs. Therefore, the health of deeply breathing recreationists is a special concern.

Secondly, urban air pollution degrades recreation and tourism resources of the cities: vegetation in the city parks, historical buildings, architectural monuments, museums and the paintings, sculptures and artifacts they contain are all at risk. Unfortunately, tourism is much too often blamed as the culprit. Readers of the article, "Rome crumbles before the tourist hordes" (*Financial Times* 22 December 1978) will conclude that the title is misleading, because the material contained in the article clearly demonstrates that tourism is not the main source of air pollution in the "eternal city." The real environmentally destructive forces in Rome are not only from human habitation (especially the use of coal and oil for heating), but from the local automobile traffic roaring within meters of the Colosseum, the Arch of Constantine, and other monuments of ancient Rome. The devastation of these monuments of antiquity is caused mainly by sulphur and nitrogen compounds from car exhaust. Sulfuric acid reacts with calcium carbonate in marble; the resulting gypsum ($CaSO4$) just falls off, leaving faceless sculptures and reliefs. Additionally, monuments such as the Colosseum also suffer from traffic vibrations.

It is true that tourism is responsible, to some small extent, for the damages. However, everyone who observed the mad traffic of

Rome can testify that tourist buses and cars are only a tiny part of Rome's motorized traffic, mainly motorists commuting to work, and including lunch trips that contribute to four rush hours a day. The problem lies not in tourism but in allowing heavy traffic in the ancient part of the "eternal city." This relatively small area should be reserved exclusively for pedestrians, as has been done in many other cities. Tourists would benefit from sightseeing in peace, away from fumes or noise, if such a measures were taken in Rome (and in other cities which still allow cars in close proximity to the treasures of the past and the main pedestrian areas). The Italian government has acted belatedly by introducing a number of measures which have improved the situation somewhat: introduction of a "blue zone" (all-pedestrian zone) in a part of the city's historic center and limitation of automobile traffic by odd-even number license-plate on alternate days.

The threat of air pollution to ancient architecture is not limited to Rome. Similar problems occur in Florence or Madrid, where the paintings in the Prado Museum have suffered from urban smog. In Cologne, Germany, the sandstone carvings on the cathedral have been damaged by acid rain. In Segovia, Spain, the granite Roman aqueduct, the main tourist attraction of the city, is in danger of disintegration as a result of air pollution and passing vehicle vibrations.

However, the greatest threat to the monuments of the past is in Athens, Greece. The Athens metropolitan area is surrounded on three sides by mountains. Such topography causes the air to stagnate. Human factors have increased the dangers. Out of the ten million Greeks, four million live in Athens. About 50 percent of Greece's industry in located in the capital and there is also an extreme concentration of automobile traffic. Such unfavorable natural and human factors result in environmental disaster. A brown smog, called locally *nefos,* hangs over the city most of the time, especially during thermal inversions. The air pollutants carbon monoxide, sulphur dioxide, nitrogen dioxide, and lead destroy the ancient buildings. As in Rome, acid rain containing sulphur dioxide reacts with the marble of the Parthenon, turning the surface into extremely fragile gypsum. Not only do architecture and people suffer from Athens' air pollution, so does the city's reputation. Nefos

Figure 2.3

POLLUTION OF MOSCOW: View from space (1993)

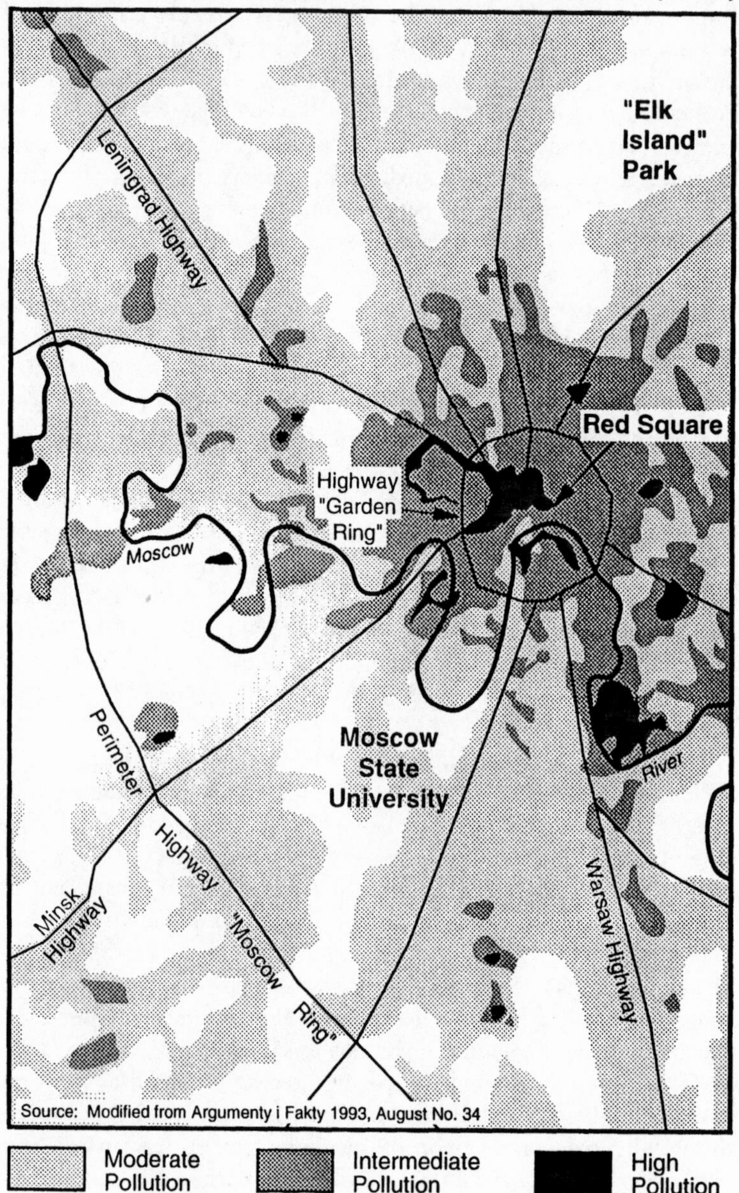

was probably one of the reasons for the failed bid of Athens for the 1996 Olympic Games. It is also responsible for the hazards of take-offs and landings at the Athens' International Airport. For example, the October, 1979 crash of a Western Air Lines jet, which killed 73 passengers, has been attributed to this factor (*Time* 12 November 1979).

To improve the situation a whole set of measures is being undertaken: limits to traffic and industrial development, installation of antipollution devices in plants (including power production), electrification of traffic, liquidation of siesta break (which causes unnecessary traffic), expansion of the subway system, and introduction of pedestrian and green areas. However, the city fathers have stopped short of a complete ban of automobiles from the city center.

While the automobile is the main cause of air pollution in the First World countries of Western Europe, in the former communist countries of the Second World, heavy industries, especially iron, steel, and chemical industries, are responsible for their environmental disaster. Moscow's air is heavily polluted, especially in the city center and in some suburbs known for their "dirty" industries (see Fig. 2.3). Cracow, Poland, located in a poorly-ventilated valley, is in danger of losing its leading tourist attraction, the medieval center of the city. Although this valuable part of Cracow lies in an all-pedestrian zone, it is severely affected by air pollution from sources 8 and 15 kilometers away. The offending industries are the gigantic steel mill *Nowa Huta* and the huge aluminum plant in Skawina. The automobile is a relatively minor factor, although one has to take into account that all gasoline sold in former communist countries is leaded. The main cause of damage are soot and acid rain that eats away the monuments of the past—for instance, the figures of the twelve apostles in front of St. Peter's and Paul's Church have lost their faces to pollution. The capital of the Czech Republic, Prague, and adjacent industrial cities suffer similar hazards. Here low-quality brown coal used by industry and for heating is the source of smog, acid rain, and other forms of atmospheric pollution. This has reached such disastrous levels, that in February 1993 a "natural disaster" state of emergency was declared in three Bohemian cities (*Winnipeg Free Press* 14 February 1993). In addition to air pollution, the exploitation of brown coal in this part of Europe by open pit method scars the landscape.

The characteristic features of air pollution in the cities of the LDCs show certain similarities to those in the former communist countries, i.e., the main culprit is industry. Pollution is very severe in some of the megalopolises: in fact, the most polluted city on earth is not in the First or in the Second World but in Mexico. Mexico City suffers from both industrial and car pollution caused by more than three million cars and 35,000 industrial sites (Turner, *et al.* 1990: 583; *Time* 11 January 1993). A huge agglomeration of people and industry, combined with lax and corrupt enforcement of environmental laws, create a crisis situation of major proportions. Additionally, the topographic features of the city aggravate the situation; Mexico City is surrounded by a semicircle of volcanic mountains, rarely visible because of smog that trap the polluted air. The prevailing winds come from the open north but the topography does not allow the polluted air to escape. Thus, the city is shrouded in chronic brownish smog caused mainly by automobile exhaust (Turner, *et al.* 1990: 583). The peak air pollution season coincides with the winter dry season when the tourist visitation reaches its peak.

There is still another factor contributing to the stagnation of polluted air over Mexico City. Once released into the air, the pollution is pressed down by inversions of hot air. These thermal inversions are typical in winter, and frequent on early mornings in summer. Because of the high elevation of Mexico City (2,225 meters), the amount of oxygen available is reduced by 23 percent. Thus, people have difficulty breathing, and fuel in the motors burns less efficiently and emits more pollution. As mentioned previously, such inefficient burning produces ground-level ozone; surface ozone pollution in Mexico City is regarded as the world's worst. An official ozone index of below 100 deems the ozone level satisfactory, but in Mexico City it frequently climbs to over 300, which is regarded as "very dangerous" (*Economist* 4 April 1992). On days when pollution in Mexico City is at its peak, migrating birds fall poisoned from the trees. Athletes and recreational runners are warned not to run in the city parks practically all the time.

The Mexican authorities have initiated a number of measures to cope with the city's pollution, among them the closure of polluting factories, emission controls for factories and motor vehicles, introduction of non-leaded gasoline, mandatory emission controls on new cars, and various methods of limiting car use, such as prohibiting access to the city during specific days of the week, for certain cars. However, enforcing this is another matter. The government could also pay attention to public transportation.

Much smaller cities in the LDCs have problems associated with valley locations. An example is the increasingly popular tourist destination, the Katmandu Valley in Nepal. The capital city of Katmandu is especially polluted and tourists often prefer to stay beyond the smog of the urban area in one of the mountain lodges located above the rim of the valley. The sources of pollution in Katmandu are brick kilns, cement factories, and, increasingly, the car.

Another large Third World city plagued by environmental problems is Cairo, the capital of Egypt. Like Mexico City, Cairo is also shrouded in a perpetual poisonous haze. Industrial pollution is high, traffic is heavy, and traffic police show high lead and carbon monoxide levels in their blood. Industry, including cement factories, pollutes without restraint. Not only are the historic buildings affected, but so is the resort of Helwan located at a short distance from the capital.

In Latin America, Saõ Paulo, the most industrial megalopolis of Brazil, quality of life is quickly declining as a result of overcrowding, air, and water pollution. Major Chinese cities have similar problems. Here the use of brown coal as an energy source and for heating exacerbates the pollution problem. The maquiladora zone on the Mexican side of the border with the United States is an example of a Third World area that impacts the First World. Thus, e.g., Ciudad Juarez, Mexico, contributes to a source of air pollution in El Paso, Texas. As a result, El Paso substantially exceeds the maximum standards for ozone, carbon monoxide and particulate matter.

In Asia, airborne sulphur dioxide and other pollutants are corroding the marble of the seventeenth century majestic Taj Mahal Mausoleum in Agra, India. The nearby 8,000 industrial plants (including several iron foundries and an oil refinery), and the three million inhabitants of the city of Agra are the culprits in the damage to the white marble of the mausoleum. In 1987 the Indian government decreed that no polluting enterprises could be built within forty kilometers of the Taj Mahal, and in 1991 it ordered the iron foundries to install scrubbers and filters on their smokestacks. In

1993 all 212 factories in and near Agra were ordered by the Supreme Court to install pollution control equipment (*New York Times* 5 September 1993). However, there is no evidence that the quality of air in the area has improved.

Sulphur dioxide and nitrogen dioxide, after reacting with sunlight and moisture in the clouds, may damage architectural monuments by acid rain, even if they are located at considerable distances from the source of pollution. Two good examples are the Buddhist temple at Borobudur, Indonesia and the Mayan ruins in Yucatan, Mexico. Although in both cases the oil wells, oil refineries, and manufacturing plants are located a distance of up to 500 kilometers from the ruins, their pollution still affects them.

A peculiar source of air pollution associated with the poorest of the DCs is the dust kicked up by traffic on unpaved streets, or roads, noticeable in Banjul, Gambia, an important tourist gateway. In Banjul the haze is red because of the color of the soil.

Air pollution is certainly the main environmental problem of contemporary large cities. However, recent trends indicate a significant improvement in most cities of the First World, a stagnant situation in the Second World, and deterioration in the Third World.

Another severe man-made predicament affects the physical environment of some cities in various parts of the world. This phenomenon of "sinking cities" is associated with artificial subsidence caused by ground water, oil, and gas withdrawal, and by the lowering of the water table, due to intensive, and often excessive, use of this resource by humans. The catastrophic "sinking" of Venice, due to the industrial development of the Maestre area on the mainland, has stopped since the artesian wells have been capped. Mexico City and its historic buildings is also sinking as water is pumped out of the underground aquifers faster than it can be replaced. Concrete piles had to be installed to shore up the tilting 400-year-old Metropolitan Cathedral.

Lowering of the water table is also the reason for the increase in the tilt of the twelfth-century Leaning Tower of Pisa in Italy. For hundreds of years the tilt of the top of the tower was increasing by 1 millimeter per year, and reached 4.80 meters off-center in January 1990 when the 55-meter tower was closed to tourists. The economic impact of this closure has been heavy, taking into account that about 800,000 tourists climbed the 294 steps to the top annually, paying over three dollars for this privilege. The authorities are doing their best to save the tower from falling. In 1992 a girdle of 18 steel bands was installed around the base of the tower, which was also reinforced with concrete. In 1993 a total of 600 metric tons of lead ingots was placed in two stages at the base to pull the tower back. The idea was to stabilize the lean by "controlled subsidence," meaning that the ground below the northern flank of the tower would be lowered to provide a more level base. So far the lean has decreased by 4 centimeters. The ultimate aim is to reduce the lean from 10° to 9° (*New York Times* 8 November 1989; *New York Times* 28 October 1993; *World Press Review* April 1994). The city of Ravenna, Italy, famous for its Byzantine frescoes is also at risk from human-induced lowering of the water table.

In Copenhagen the reasons for "sinking" are partially geological: the isostatic uplift of Scandinavia since the end of the last ice age currently proceeds at a rate of 3 millimeters annually. This geological problem is substantially exacerbated by human factors, however, such as deep basements, underground parking lots, and deeper sewers, which have lowered the water table. The paving of much of the city's surface has also prevented the rainfall from effectively seeping underground. The combination of these natural and human factors has caused a drop in the groundwater table that has endangered the most valuable architectural monuments of the city, buildings constructed over 300 years ago on wooden (mostly oak) three-to-eight-meter-long piles, driven into the marshy ground. Deprived of water, the piles dry out and rot, and the buildings start to sink. Among these is one of the royal palaces at Amalienborg. Costly procedures are required to save the endangered buildings.

Not only falling, but rising water tables may cause damage to the environment. The Nile Valley in Egypt, with its many archaeological treasures, is a good example. Here the water table has risen, mainly as a result of the Aswan Dam on the Nile River. Added to this is the seepage of irrigation water, and still worse, seepage of polluted sewage water from leaking urban pipes. The resultant rise of the water table gradually undermines the foundations of buildings and dissolves mineral salts from bedrock and soils. Many ancient buildings are made from soft and porous sandstone which, sponge-lime, suck this salty water from the ground. When the water evaporates, the salts crystallize on the surface, and cause the stone to crumble into dust. This problem afflicts the Great Cheops Pyramid and the Sphinx, which is in great danger of destruction.

There is a long list of remedies to save the physical environment of large cities for tourists and for residents. It includes such measures as the introduction of alternative-day driving rules for cars, based on even and uneven last numbers on the license plate, increasing the parking fees, banning cars from the most valuable downtown areas by creating exclusive pedestrian zones, promotion of public transportation (particularly its underground form), limits to industrial development (especially to polluting industries which should be located or even relocated to extra-urban areas), provision of more open park space, and introduction of strict noise controls (as in Toronto, Canada). An interesting initiative has been undertaken in Copenhagen since the spring of 1992, where both residents and tourists are allowed to borrow solid tire white bicycles free of charge. This initiative has been followed by Zurich, Switzerland. Many megalopolises such as Tokyo, Bangkok, and Mexico City provide daily information in the media on the level of pollution in various parts of the city.

Finally, one has to mention the problem of cityscape—of the physical outlook of the city. Tourists and city residents enjoy a well-planned city with plenty of open green space. Lack of parks and trees, shanty towns (called *favelas* in Brazil and *pueblos hovenes* in Spanish-speaking America), garbage, dirt, stench, chaotic traffic conditions, and other scourges of a badly planned city repulse tourists. In this respect urban cores of some cities of the DCs, are generally in better shape than urban centers in the LDCs. They can afford the reconstruction of city centers and introduce such measures as pedestrian-only shopping malls in the "blue zones," the relocation of offending industries, and strict emission controls for industry and transportation. These policies have led to gentrification of many city-core areas in the DCs and made them attractive to tourists by radically changing their physical appearance. However, most city centers are suffering "urban sprawl," i.e., the post-Second World War development of the suburbs, especially in the United States. The process of suburbanization has been severely criticized by James Kunstler (1993), who regards them as sterile zones compelling their inhabitants to the tyranny of compulsive commuting in an oil-dependent economy.

2.11 *Conclusions*

The purpose of this chapter was to demonstrate that the main culprit for the environmental deterioration, on local, regional, and global scale is not tourism, but rather external factors outside of tourism, such as agriculture, industry, transportation and human habitation, that use natural resources, including land. Even in cases of shared responsibility for ecological damage, tourism is definitely not the main source of negative ecological impacts. Even in Hawaii, a major tourist state, economic development and rapidly growing resident population pressure are the main causes of environmental problems, not tourism.

Chapter 3

The Positive Impacts of Tourism and Recreation on the Natural Environment

The discussion in chapter 1 and 2 focused on tourism and tourists as objects of natural and external (nontourist) human impacts, respectively. Starting with chapter 3 the emphasis shifts to tourism as the source of environmental impacts. In other words, tourism is the subject and natural environment is the object that is modified and transformed by the tourism industry and tourists. Extremists evaluate these impacts as either totally positive or totally negative. This book will contribute to a balanced assessment of both positive and negative aspects of tourism's impact. In chapters 4, 5, and 6 a pessimistic approach prevails: these sections concentrate on the negative environmental impacts of tourism.

Two words of caution: first, one has to realize that in talking about positive and negative impacts of tourism we are only operating with relative notions: All human impacts on nature are actually negative: to paraphrase Theodore Roosevelt, humans cannot improve nature, whatever their actions. Second, while dealing with a complex system of interrelationships and interaction in the real world it is not always easy to distinguish between the tourist and nontourist sources of impacts.

3.1 *External Versus Internal Impacts*

Tourism is frequently and correctly accused of negative impacts on natural environment. However, as discussed previously, one should not forget where the main cause of today's worldwide environmental malaise lies. It is certainly not tourism—the primary reasons fall well outside the tourism industry (Gunn 1987: 234). As pointed out in section 1.1, tourism is a relatively minor culprit because, unlike the other economic sectors, an attractive and healthy environment tis inherent as its product. Consequently, tourism is more vulnerable to environmental deterioration than other economic sectors (Fig. 2. 2). Therefore, a balanced and sustainable natural environment is essential for the survival of tourism: protection of watersheds, conservation of diverse wildlife and plant habitats (with their all-important gene pools) are some of the benefits associated with tourism development. In this unique situation, natural environment (in this book called simply environment), constitutes a tourism resource—and is considered a part of tourism's product (Mieczkowski, Z. 1990: 204). The relationship between tourism (or tourism product) and environment is that of interface. This overlap between tourism and environment constitutes the "environmental part of tourism." Outside this overlap remain human attractions, tourism infrastructure, and that part of the environment which is not used as a tourism resource (Fig. 2.1).

3.2 *Tourism—A Theoretically "Smokeless Industry"*

If we accept the premise that practically all human impacts on nature, including the impacts of tourism, should be evaluated as negative, we have to establish certain parameters to evaluate the role of tourism as a factor influencing the ecosystems. Is it possible to find something positive about the environmental effects of tourism if any tourist activity modifies and transforms the natural environment at least to a certain extent (Williams, P. 1987: 386)? The answer is yes, but only when comparing tourism with other human activities. Thus, for example, one could successfully argue that, as a rule, the quality of the natural environment is superior at tourist destinations to those in nontourist areas. Indeed, tourism has considerable potential for environmental enhancement. For tourism, environment represents not a handicap to be overwhelmed by or cope with, but a resource of central importance and an opportunity for improvement.

High quality natural environment is a part of the tourism product. "High quality environment is essential for tourism...is tourism's *raison d'etre*" (OECD 1980: 21–22). Multiple surveys confirm the hypothesis that the quality of natural environment constitutes "the primary factor that attracted the present-day tourist, even in countries with an outstanding cultural heritage" (WTO 1983: 28). Residents of tourist destinations also demonstrate a high degree of awareness of both positive and negative environmental impacts of tourism (Liu, *et al.* 1987).

In this context, any violations of the ecosphere by tourism are examples of "internal impacts," i.e., impacts of tourism on tourism and tourism resources, veritable tourism-killing-tourism situations, and not compatible with the vital self-interests of the industry and its clients—the tourists. These dangerous aberrations in the pursuit of short-term interests destroy, in the long term, the very essence of tourist supply. Thus, tourism is, at least in theory, a "smokeless industry," an ecology-oriented sector, a logical partisan of environmental conservation. No other economic sector is so vitally and so directly concerned with environmental quality. This concern reaches well beyond natural environment and extends to economic and sociocultural environments. Using the terminology of economics, tourism creates positive environmental externalities. Therefore, the tourism industry, both in theory and practice, should not only act conscientiously to minimize the negative internal impacts on the environment, but also monitor and participate in the struggle against the unfavorable (i.e., nontourist) impacts. At the social and political level the tourism industry should be expected to participate in the environmental movement, lobbying for necessary measures against all destructive human impacts on nature. Why this scenario, remains in the sphere of "wishful thinking" will be discussed in chapters 4 to 6.

According to an OECD study (1980: 51–53), the environmental objectives in tourist areas include the protection of both the health of the local population and tourists. This requires the maintenance of environmental quality standards "at least as high as in the industrial areas" because "tourists are entitled to a better than normal environment recuperate." Another objective is the maintenance of a high quality of environment to satisfy the long-term interests of the tourist industry in safeguarding its profitability. There will be no demand for tourist services in environmentally degraded destinations.

Therefore, tourism frequently contributes to environmental improvements, not necessarily improvements correcting nature, but those that correct ecological outrages inflicted by other sectors of economy, or by impacts of human habitation. Indeed, "in a number of places tourism has helped to improve the environment" (OECD

1980: 8). However, not everybody agrees with this statement—some believe that the impact of tourism is always negative. An interesting argument is provided by an anonymous writer representing the World Tourism Organization (*World Tourism* 1977 137: 24). A critic complained that tourism caused beach pollution in a resort. A resident replied: "You should have seen our beaches *before* tourism came. They didn't even bother to take the sewage as far as the sea. It was tourism that caused the authorities to pull up their socks."

The very existence of tourism is unthinkable without a healthy and pleasant environment, with well-preserved landscapes and harmony between people and nature. Therefore, the most desirable relationship between tourism and nature is, using Budowski's terminology, a symbiotic one, reflecting harmonious cooperation. In such a relationship the adverse impacts of tourism on natural ecosystems are minimized so that tourists are able to enjoy undisturbed nature (Budowski 1976). Budowski points out that the symbiotic relationship between tourism and conservation results in physical, cultural, ethical, and economic benefits. Today we would call such a relationship environmentally-sustainable tourism, discussed in detail in chapters 8 to 10. In this optimal scenario, tourism creates incentives for the preservation of natural and human attractions that might otherwise suffer, not only from lack of appreciation and enjoyment (especially in the LDCs), but also from lack of financing.

Indeed, tourism provides not only appreciation and enjoyment of beauty, but also income. "Natural scenery and historical sites or traditional towns and neighborhoods, untouched by 'progress,' suddenly become economic assets" (Cohen 1978: 218). Thus, many regions and countries embrace tourism as a solution to their economic problems (unless the opportunity costs indicate that alternative development options should be pursued). An example of a solution in favor of tourism is the Hula Valley in northern Israel. In the 1950s, the valley was drained to increase badly needed agricultural production. However, in the 1990s the economic priorities changed, and the government decided that tourism development represented a more profitable option. An additional factor was that dried peat soil at the bottom of the drained marsh had decomposed and released pollutants that were once filtered by the marsh, thus making the land a wasteland unfit for farming. Taking all these considerations into account, the government decided to act, reflooding 600 hectares in the center of the Hula Valley and reintroducing the original flora and fauna over the term of the three-year project. The wetland wildlife park will be a tourist attraction and the raised water table will benefit the adjacent farmland (*New York Times* 15 December 1993; *Christian Science Monitor* 29 April 1994).

Resource utilization by symbiotic tourism also guarantees the sustainability of ecosystems, i.e., their unimpaired preservation for the benefit of future generations. Tourism treats natural resources as renewable by using them mainly (but not exclusively), in a non-consumptive way. This type of use increases the carrying capacity of tourist areas and secures the sustainability of the resource base. Another positive aspect of resource utilization by tourism is its decreased competitiveness for space, combined with relatively low opportunity costs. This is due to the fact that areas of exceptional scenic value are usually less fertile and suitable for alternative economic development. Savannahs are too dry for agriculture, wetlands too waterlogged, mountains have poor soils and the high relief energy makes them difficult for cultivation and industrial construction. All of these ecosystems are good examples of areas potentially valuable for tourism, but of limited interest to other economic sectors. Some national parks of sub-Saharan Africa, e.g., in Malawi, are infested with the tse-tse fly, the vector of sleeping sickness, which renders them unsuitable for human habitation and cattle breeding.

Symbiotic tourism, at least in theory, presents the best development option most of the time and in most places. Environment-friendly symbiotic tourism not only helps to preserve nature, but also prevents large scale expansion of other industries, such as heavy industries and mining, that are especially destructive of the natural environment.

Various other forms of tourism contribute to the environmental cause by preventing the development of ecologically destructive economic activities. The 1992 decision of the Egyptian government to stop issuing new oil exploration licenses for the Red Sea coastal region of Hurghada is an example. The expansion of beach resorts, instead of oil exploration and exploitation, is planned for this region, with the number of beds increasing from 10,000 to 25,000 beds. Tourism seems to present an environmentally superior development option for this rugged Red Sea coast.

Often the mere presence of tourism in an area prompts the authorities to undertake clean-up actions. May suggests that a concern over tourism income was the driving force behind the upgrading of the sewage system in Srinagar, India. This was necessary to stop the water pollution of Lake Dal (May 1991: 115–116). Similar concern about the Mediterranean beaches has contributed to the antipollution measures undertaken by the Mediterranean Action Plan (Vadrot 1977). Taking good care of nature certainly means good tourist business. Thus, a hotel in the Sharm-al-Sheik area, Sinai Peninsula, Egypt, is financing a migratory bird rescue center, which cares for sick or injured storks and releases them. Hotel visitors are thrilled to visit this animal hospital.

Even in areas where the natural environment has been modified and transformed by human activity to a considerable extent, the beauty of the landscape is an asset to tourism marketing. Consider landscape beautification contests between localities (frequently featuring the most attractive flower gardens), and the promotion of various areas as "green destinations."

3.3 *Positive Impacts in the DCs*

Positive impacts of tourism on environment operate in various ways, according to the socioeconomic structure of different geographic areas of our planet. In sections 3.3 and 3.4, these variations will be discussed from the perspective of the First World (DCs) and the Third World (LDCs). There are three features that distinguish the model of positive human impacts on the environment in the DCs from those in the LDCs. The first is that the relationship between humans and environment derives its strength from the philosophical and ecological roots dating back to the eighteenth and nineteenth century philosophy of Enlightenment and Romanticism, and the ideology of conservation developed in the United States in the second half of the nineteenth century (Mieczkowski, Z. 1990: 53-57). These basically noneconomic approaches to conservation have undoubtedly contributed to the widespread understanding of ecological problems and to the environmental consciousness and ethic, i.e., awareness and appreciation of the value of conservation (Gunn 1987: 231, Mathieson and Wall 1982: 97; Marsh, 1986: 217).

The second feature of the positive impacts of tourism in the DCs is that the translation of theory into practice is more feasible in the DCs because they can afford to. No other industry is prepared to pay for conservation, no other industry has so contributed to improvements in the quality of natural environment, either directly or indirectly (through taxation of the tourism industry by governments in order to improve the environment). Therefore, despite the focus on negative impacts of tourism, many authors do not forget to point out the positive ones (Mäder 1988: 94–95; Cohen 1978: 217; Mathieson and Wall 1982: 95ff; Pearce *et al.* 1989: 238– 239).

The third characteristic feature is the democratic political infrastructure of the DCs. This includes the increasingly influential NGOs that advocate conservation through means such as the media, pressure on legislators and governments, and public participation in environmental decision-making. This political system creates favorable prerequisites for the development of environment-friendly attitudes and policies. Chris Ryan (1991: 102) indicates that the tourism industry "can become an ally of environmental conservation groups, as there is a common cause in preserving the quality of the landscape." He gives examples, "where tourist business organizations have appreciated the need to enhance landscapes so as to simultaneously enhance the quality of the tourist experience." According to Ryan, the partnership between tourism and landscape conservation has been most effective when dealing with the urban landscape (cityscape). In many cities, tourism contributes to the process of gentrification (urban renewal) of core areas that have experienced decline. Tourism's financial support encourages habitation of formerly depopulated inner cities, especially historic cores, and also fosters their pedestrianization. The provision of open space in the cities for local recreation and the enjoyment of tourists has also been adequate in the DCs. In some U.S. cities, where the city fathers neglected to set aside sufficient park space, the citizens, for lack of other opportunities, use cemeteries. This causes bitter criticism and social friction. In extra-urban areas, especially in wilderness, tourism and recreation organizations strongly advocate nature preservation, e.g., the Manitoba Recreational Canoeing Association protested against logging in the Nopiming Provincial Park (*Winnipeg Free Press* 29 July 1992). These sorts of contributions of tourism are well known in the post-World War II scenario of the DCs.

Generally, in the DCs there are powerful agents, namely governments and private organizations, concerned about the ecological implications of the negative impacts of human activity, including tourism, on natural environments. These organizations operate on a local, regional and global scale as promoters of the conservation of ecosystems and as defenders of nature against environmentally destructive impacts of tourism. This does not mean that the economic contributions of tourism are ignored. On the contrary, their role is significant, especially on the community level (Murphy 1985).

Examples of the positive role of tourism and recreation in the DCs abound. Let us start with local small-scale improvements. Many urban parks, both prime tourist attractions and a source of enjoyment for local residents, have been fashioned from adverse environmental conditions in human-made quasi-natural environments. The most famous urban parks in the United States, Central Park in New York City and Golden Gate Park in San Francisco, were developed in the nineteenth century, from useless, ugly wastelands or outright garbage dumps (Wagner 1971: 68). The Butchart Gardens, near Victoria, British Columbia, are a former quarry. Sea World in San Diego, California, and the adjacent area of Mission Bay, were garbage dumps until 1950. Teufelsberg Park in Berlin was developed on a pile of rubble collected from the ruins of the Second World War. Even golf courses have been developed in areas destroyed by former economic activities, such as the Quarry Oaks Golf Course near Steinbach, Manitoba, which occupies an abandoned gravel pit. Similar improvements have been made to former open-cast mines used for water-oriented recreation. Such changes in land use should unquestionably be regarded as environmental improvement.

Urban open space and parks were the highest priority among the environmentally enlightened and socially progressive circles during the nineteenth- and early twentieth-century Europe and North America. These endeavors were frustrated and the opportunity missed in many U.S. cities. This lack of care has contributed to the present social problems in urban areas, with little recreational space for not only tourists but more importantly, local recreationists.

However, already in the late nineteenth century, the environmental emphasis in the DCs had begun to shift from urban to extra-urban areas, where tourism and recreation have also contributed to the improvement of ecological conditions. For example, for many years and in many places the beaches have merely been convenient places to dump garbage. Ultimately, this accumulated waste washed out to the polluted sea. However, after the discovery of their recreational value, many beaches around the world have been cleaned up; restored into environmentally sound areas that meet the recreational needs of people. These are examples of rehabilitation of natural environment by tourism development, and goes beyond simple protection and preservation of existing natural ecosystems.

In the DCs, the most significant form of environmental conservation of ecosystems threatened by development are the national parks and equivalent reserves. They focus the attention of conservationists on the most efficient tools of conserving the natural ecosystems (Mieczkowski, Z. 1990: 266–290). To effect the necessary political and economic support for this form of nature conservation, conservationists must provide environmental appreciation and increased public awareness. Protection of scenic and cultural heritage enjoys much more public support if based on the practical tourism experience of millions of people than on the theoretical considerations of a few distinguished thinkers. Not only do the needs of tourists work in favor of conservation (the demand side), but so do the economic interests of the destination areas (the supply side).

In some cases the "setting aside" of nature reserves reaches beyond the mere conservation function: significant environmental improvements and/or restoration often occur. For example, one of the main achievements of the New Zealand's Kapiti Island reserve, established in 1897 off the North Island, was the elimination of exotic species introduced in the past by Maoris and European settlers. Exotic species, such as rats, dogs, sheep, goats, pigs, deer, cattle, and cats, have devastated the ecosystems of New Zealand. The main victims were native birds, and their regeneration has been the focus of Kapiti. Once a bird species has reached safe numbers, breeding pairs are airlifted to other parts of New Zealand. This unique sanctuary enjoys great popularity among the Kiwis (New Zealanders), but only 50 people daily are allowed to visit the reserve. Thus, in this case the economic return is relatively modest.

Despite the undeniable successes of tourism financing nature conservation in the DCs, there is still room for improvement. The survey of all state and provincial travel bureaus in the United States and Canada, conducted by Defenders of Wildlife in 1987-88, shows that the economic benefits associated with nonconsumptive wildlife recreation in North America are not fully realized (Vickerman 1992). There is a lack of understanding of the issues, and the absence of data on wildlife resources and the level of public interest in wildlife viewing hinders the agencies' ability to take appropriate action. Sara Vickerman suggests financing conservation by increasing investment in habitat acquisition and management. The funding sources proposed by the author are: taxpayers' money, "abuser fees," (also called mitigation fees, including real estate development taxes, severance taxes on minerals, sand and gravel, etc.), user fees (including increased fees for the use of vehicles, boats, trailers, and taxes on binoculars, cameras, camping gear, etc.), and a portion of the so-called "sin taxes" on cigarettes and alcohol.

Tourism not only finances conservation but helps it in many other indirect ways: the mere presence of tourists discourages poaching and other environmentally destructive activities. The interest tourists show to the natural environment enhances the pride of locals, both in their natural heritage, and in the economic and noneconomic value of nature conservation.

3.4 *Positive Impacts in the LDCs*

As discussed previously, the concept of symbiotic tourism in the DCs reaches back to its eighteenth- and nineteenth-century philosophical roots. As a result, the proenvironment stance in the First World contains not only economic arguments, but noneconomic ones as well. In contrast, the considerations for nature conservation in the LDCs are based almost exclusively on economics (with some exceptions associated with the Asian religious philosophies—see section 8.3). Ideology has no role because in the desperate economic situation of the Third World, most ecosystems are under constant, intensive pressure for alternative use, especially logging, fuel collection, and agriculture. Thus the wildlife in western Africa was already destroyed before tourism could save it; and mainly the tourism-financed modest revival is a recent occurrence.

In the LDCs, international tourism is acting as rescuer of nature by offering alternative economic options for resource use. If the economic advantages of nature conservation for tourism surpass those of other uses, then the preservation of ecosystems represents the most financially viable option. This is proving to be the case in many instances. To reinforce the economic arguments in favor of nature conservation, proponents of tourism and conservation use noneconomic approaches to stimulate pride of local residents in "their" lions, gorillas, and the attractiveness of their ecosystems. However, these considerations are completely ineffective without the promise of economic rewards.

In the LDCs, as in the DCs, the most appropriate form of nature conservation are the national parks and equivalent reserves. International tourists, mainly from the DCs, play a key role for the survival of the parks. The establishment of new parks improves a country's chances on the international tourist market; for example, the new national park in Dominica "became immediately a strong theme in the promotional literature on the island's attractions" (Stankey 1989: 11). However, Africa offers many poignant examples of the role of national parks in saving endangered ecosystems and individual species. The destruction of ecosystems in Africa during the colonial and postcolonial periods is a well-established fact. Virgin nature is practically gone, and the remnants in eastern and southern Africa are being saved by the tourism industry, which pays for the preservation of ecosystems within national parks and other reserves. The national parks of Kenya, Tanzania, Zambia, Zimbabwe, Botswana, Namibia, and South Africa represent good examples of tourism, not only stimulating conservation of ecosystems (particularly of wildlife), but also economic development, an efficient earner of vital foreign exchange. For example, the famous Serengeti, Amboseli, Tsavo and Kruger national parks owe their survival to fees tourists pay and other expenses they incur. Tourism contributes to local employment, to the general infrastructure, and to a demand for locally-produced handicraft items—all obvious economic advantages. The financing of conservation efforts by tourism allowed the extension of Kenya's national park system to about 7.5 percent of the total area of the country. There are at present 13 national parks and 24 national reserves in Kenya (Davidson, 1989: 128).

In many areas tourism is viewed as the savior of ecosystems in crisis. Such is the situation in Madagascar, which faces an environmental catastrophe. The explosion of a poverty-stricken population, growing at more than 3 percent annually, has already destroyed 85 percent of the country's forests for fuel (mainly charcoal), for the expansion of cultivation (mainly rice), and for pasture, although much of this tree cutting is illegal. The result is rapid erosion of the red soil. Astronauts in space see a red ring around Madagascar—one could figuratively say that the island is bleeding to death. The damage of deforestation to agriculture, forestry, and infrastructure is estimated at between $100 million to $300 million a year (*Economist* 2 April 1994).

Tourism's role in saving the forests of Madagascar is indirect. The industry has capitalized on the tourists' interest in the inhabitants of these forests: the lemurs, a unique endemic order of primitive arboreal primates. The protection of lemurs from extinction is clearly associated with the preservation of their forest habitats against the spread of agriculture—preservation that would be impossible without the cooperation of the Malagasy government. Between 1975 and 1987 they sided with the Soviet bloc and became a "country of socialist orientation." As a result, the island was closed to western tourists, including scientists, and the devastation of the ecosystems became a symbol of "socialist development."

The progressing decay of the USSR in the second half of the 1980s was instrumental in the change of political orientation of the Malagasy government. They now follow the path of a market economy, looking for assistance and guidance from the West. Not only is such assistance well on its way from Western governments, but also from the West-financed international NGOs. The World Wildlife Fund spent $6 million in 1993 alone for conservation and education (*World Press Review* August 1993). In terms of environmental policy, the Malagasy government is determined to cash in on western tourists' interest in lemurs and to create a number of national parks to provide wildlife habitats in the unique ecosystems of Madagascar. These include lemurs (no monkeys), 80 percent of endemic flowering plants, 148 endemic frog species out of 150. So far, four parks have been established. The government is also prepared to conclude "debt-for-nature" swaps with the DCs (see section 9.6.3) and to open the forests to scientific researchers looking for new sources of medicines.

The recent discovery of the dwarf lemur *(Allocebus trichotis),* a subspecies of lemur thought to be extinct, will certainly stimulate "ecological tourism" to Madagascar. The tiny lemur weighs less than 100 grams and is about 12 cm long. In 1985, the golden crown chipaka lemur, also thought to be extinct, was discovered in a forest targeted for logging. The discovery saved not only the lemur from extinction but its habitat from the chainsaw: since May 1991 the habitat of the lemur has been preserved in the Ranomafana National Park, about 350 kilometers south of the capital of Antananarivo (Perlez 1991). In order to compensate local inhabitants for the loss of the forests, a program was developed to train them as tourist guides and hotel and camp employees. The project, which is partly financed by a $3.2 million grant from the U.S. Agency for International Development (AID), also includes plans for improving health, education, and sanitation services in affected villages, and for creating alternative sources of income for the residents (such as vegetable gardening and sustainable forest management). Half of the entrance fees paid by tourists visiting Madagascar's national parks are used for these purposes.

At the present time, preservation of ecosystems in Africa seems to be the main concern in the Third World. However, other continents also contain valuable, and quickly dwindling, nature resources. Here again, tourism is the main financier, be it in the Galapagos Islands with their endemic ecosystems, or India with her tigers. "Debt-for-nature" arrangements, discussed in detail in section 9.6.3, are also becoming increasingly popular. In Latin America, Costa Rica and Brazil are leaders in negotiating such arrangements. In the framework of these agreements, large areas are being set aside as national parks or nature reserves in exchange for repayment of some parts of debts of a LDC by private environmental agencies or governments of the DCs. In such cases the long-term maintenance of the area's reserves depends on tourism patronage, e.g., the bird-watchers that enjoy Costa Rica's national parks, which contain more bird species than Canada and the United States combined. Costa Rica boasts one of the highest percentages of land preserved in parks among the countries of the world (see chapter 10).

Tourism is instrumental not only in the preservation of ecosystems but also of individual species of fauna and flora. Tourism's growing economic contribution to the preservation of endangered species is appreciated, and creates a solid basis for international cooperation. Approximately 600 mountain gorillas live in the remote areas of northern Rwanda, southwestern Uganda, and eastern Zaire. The film, *Gorillas in the Mist*, contributed to their popularity. The most popular reserve has been the Volcanoes National Park (120 square kilometers), located in Rwanda, and home to more than 300 of the world's approximately 600 mountain gorillas. Tourist visitation of the gorillas in the park, conducted by the "Mountain Gorilla Project," started in 1978 and has been a financial success, yielding up to $300 per hectare of the park annually (Kohnen and Braun 1989: 162). The viewing of the gorillas is strictly controlled: no more than six tourists are allowed to join a supervised group to observe the gorillas. The total annual visitation is 5,000 to 8,000 tourists. Children below 15 years of age are not admitted because they are potential carriers of diseases that could endanger the gorillas' health. In recognition of the economic importance of the gorillas, the governments of Rwanda, Uganda, and Zaire developed a plan to coordinate tourism in the shared Virunga Mountains. All three governments recognize the mountain gorillas as valuable tourist attractions and as the best economic option of land use in the area. Despite protection policies, the gorilla habitat is not completely safe from external encroachment by land-hungry local farmers (Mgahinga National Park, Uganda), from government abuses of gorilla tourism, for profit in Zaire (*ibid.*), and civil war in Rwanda. In February 1993 Tutsi guerrillas invaded Volcanoes National Park, ransacked the Karisoke Research Center, established in 1967 by Diane Fossey, and killed Mrithi, the dominant silverback.

For many years the outside world was convinced that lowland gorillas were totally extinct in Nigeria, one of the most environmentally devastated country of the sub-Saharan Africa. However, in the early 1980s about 150 of them were officially "rediscovered" in the eastern part of the country, near the town of Kanyang. At the time of their rediscovery they were hunted for meat by the local population. The Nigerian Conservation Foundation, aiming at the preservation of this westernmost gorilla population in Africa, resorted to economic arguments to persuade the local villagers that the gorillas could be more valuable as a tourist attraction than as meat. A hunting ban on gorillas has been instituted. The federal government was considering the establishment of a national park of 750 square kilometers in the area (*New York Times* 1 August 1988).

Another species being saved by tourism are the little-known forest elephants of the Congo Basin. They are smaller and rarer than their cousins—the savannah elephants of eastern and southern Africa, and their heavier yellowish tusks command more on the lucrative ivory market. Although this market has collapsed since 1989, after CITES (Convention on International Trade in Endangered Species) banned the ivory trade, poaching threatens their survival. Therefore, the three nations of the Congo Basin, Cameroon, Zaire, and the Central African Republic, initiated a project of bringing tourists into the area to finance the protection of animals and employment of local people primarily through the Dzanga-Sangha Forest Reserve in Central African Republic.

Another African example of tourism helping to finance wildlife preservation is the hunting safaris, where the South African method of cashing in on the hunting instincts of tourists are allowed to shoot rhinos with tranquilizer darts. Tourists pay for the privilege, and scientists are relieved from doing this themselves. Not a bad deal at all. The tranquilized animals contribute to objects of research: they are weighed, measured, provided with radio transmitters, and finally released. Thus, the research financed by tourism contributes to the preservation of these animals.

The beneficial impact of tourism on conservation in the LDCs is not limited to saving whole ecosystems and individual wild species from destruction. It extends also some domesticated animals in trouble. In Thailand, the elephants that had been involved in logging operations suddenly became "unemployed." They have become increasingly used by visitors from overseas, not only for short rides, but for "safaris" that last several days. As a result of the growing use of the automobiles, camels in many countries are less needed than before; however, their use for tourists saves them from unemployment, and inevitable death.

The preservation of certain species of flora the national parks are also playing an outstanding role. To the well-known preservation of the sequoias in California one may add the South American redwoods, the ancient alerces (the pride of the Andean Alerce National Park, located south of Puerto Montt in Chile).

The argument presented in this section has been that the noble idea of nature preservation should be based on a sound economic foundation. In other words, the income from tourism and recreation must, especially in the LDCs, surpass the opportunity costs of using the forest for logging or agriculture. Indeed, as C. Tudge (1991: 245) puts it: "Conservation must as far as possible pay its way." In this respect, tourism goes hand in hand with other "soft," nondestructive resource utilization. For example, economic benefits of nature conservation by tourism is the preservation of the gene pools of flora and fauna for the production of drugs and other substances. This may prove instrumental in maintaining the biodiversity, and thus the stability, of the world's ecosystems. While examination of this issue is beyond the scope of this book, one has to emphasize that certain wild species of flora and fauna are especially important for humans. The problem is that scientists don't know which ones. Loss of these species means the loss of unique genetic material that is indispensable to future food supply, for scientific and medical purposes. For instance, the Pacific Yew, *Taxus brevfolia,* the source of a cancer-curing drug Taxol, is close to extinction. The wealth of species in subtropical and tropical forests holds more promise than those in the forests of the mid- latitudes. Thus, according to Balick and Mendelsohn (1991), the value of herbal medicines, combined with other sustainable nontimber forest uses, provides sufficient economic argument for conservation of tropical and subtropical forests. This argument may by strengthened by the potential of gaining other useful substances from the environment without destroying it. An example is the Mpingo tree (African black wood or ebony) of southern Tanzania and northern Mozambique. Its hard wood is used for musical instruments and carvings sold to tourists, but it is now close to extinction as a result of logging and burning to clear land for farming and pastures.

3.5 *Tourism and Wildlife Policy Issues*

The discussion in section 3.4 focused mainly on simple, optimistic scenarios of interaction between symbiotic (sustainable) tourism and environment. However, the situation is often much more complex and things do not fall in place as smoothly as in the cases presented; a number of factors hinder the ability of symbiotic tourism to realize its full potential. To resolve these issues, appropriate policies are essential. This section focuses on wildlife management policies in sub-Saharan Africa, southern Asia, and Russia. One could generalize that this complex interaction between tourism, environment, and the locals is typical for most LDCs and for some areas in the DCs, but these examples are the most poignant. In discussing the role of tourism in wildlife, one has to keep in mind that it could be regarded as proxy for the natural environment.

To put the issues in a proper framework, one needs background information on African economic policy as it pertains not only to the broader economic interests, but also to the well-being of the residents. Sub-Saharan Africa has experienced a number of socio-economic changes during the last 30 to 35 years, after it gained independence from colonial domination. These upheavals had important consequences, not only for the local population, but also for wildlife and tourism. After gaining independence in the early 1960s, the countries of this part of the African continent looked forward to economic development and progress. Instead, despite some initial and rather superficial successes, they have met disappointment and frustration due to the failure of the socialistic and undemocratic governments in Black Africa to develop their economies, and particularly, agriculture. Some of these countries allied themselves with the Soviet Union. Their economic policies were based on nationalization, collectivization (Tanzania), inefficient gigantomania, and suppression of individual initiative. The problems of policy were exacerbated by the unprecedented and economically unsustainable population explosion, characterized by increases of 30 to 40 per 1,000, with Kenya leading the world in this respect. If one adds civil wars, one gets a fatal mix leading to economic deterioration, hunger and famine. Most countries lack the natural resource base for the development of their manufacturing; therefore, agriculture and tourism present practically the only viable alternatives.

Political rulers, mostly pro-Soviet and pro-West dictators, have neglected agriculture and tourism to the benefit of large, conspicuous construction projects such as huge sport stadiums, expensive churches and mosques, giant factories and hydrodams, have proven from the economic point of view, to be "white elephants." Overvaluation of currencies has made exports, including tourism, more expensive, and therefore less competitive, but it has served the political purposes of making food imports cheaper, thus pacifying the urban populations. The political strategy of clinging to power at any price (see Mieczkowski, B. 1991) has harmed national agriculture, which has been unable to compete with cheap imports and to deal with inefficiencies. Agriculture continues largely on a subsistence level. But because of its low productivity, and combined with rapidly increasing agricultural population densities, farming has had to expand territorially to less fertile marginal areas, such as tropical rain forests, mountains, and the savannahs—the last refuges of the decimated African wildlife. Some of these areas have been designated as national parks to secure appropriate habitats for the animals. Thus, the creation has lead to land-use conflicts with residents. National parks and other wildlife reserves have been invaded by the land-hungry local populations, eager to cultivate more land or use it as grazing ground for livestock. Increased poaching is also a problem, and locals do not appreciate the value of animals beyond food or monetary gain from the sale of body parts (Mieczkowski, Z. 1990: 236). The preservation of wildlife has not been linked with economic stimuli for the people living in areas adjacent to the parks; the benefits have been reaped by outsiders. The rewards from poaching, moreover, are considerable. Thus, there are two competitors for the same land: symbiotic tourism and wildlife on one side and the indigenous people with their cattle on the other. The local farmers and cattle breeders, like the Masai of Kenya and Tanzania, complain bitterly that in many instances, such as in the Ngorongoro Crater, Tanzania, and in the Amboseli National Park in Kenya, they had been forced by the creation of national parks, from their ancestral land to make space for animals and tourists. They insist that the needs of the people should be given priority over the needs of animals and foreigners.

The tension between local people on one side and wildlife preservation and tourism on the other is aggravated by the animal depredation of crops in the game dispersal areas, (especially when elephants leave the confines of the reserves and invade the adjacent agricultural lands). This "spillover" of animals into areas outside the parks results partially from the interruption of the natural migration routes of ungulates by park boundaries, and partially from the ban on hunting (causing occasional animal "population explosions" in the national parks). If the carrying capacity of the park, which, for example, is estimated at one elephant per 4 square kilometers, is exceeded, the animals leave their devastated habitats to escape starvation, invade the adjacent areas, and wander the countryside in search of food. Animals such as elephants not only routinely destroy crops, but occasionally kill people. The dilemmas of "people or animals" and "the interests of local inhabitants or the enjoyment of foreign tourists" become exacerbated, and acquire political dimensions.

These issues are complex and contentious, and so are the solutions. My suggestions will be based on firsthand knowledge of the problems, and also on available literature. The first recommendation is political, but has significant socioeconomic consequences: promotion of genuine democracies and a free-market system to replace the former rightist and leftist dictatorships. The disintegration of the USSR has destroyed the *raison d'etre* of these oppressive regimes, and opened the road to democracy and a market system. One does not need to argue that the acquisition of democratic freedoms, including private-property rights, by the people of Africa will release great human potential. It would also result in a successful diversification of economic development, the decrease of government bureaucracy, the improvement of economic efficiency, and secure a role for tourism in the conservation of ecosystems. The prerequisites for the political and economic democratization of Africa have been created with the end of global East-West competition and the disappearance of the Soviet penetration on the continent. This propitious political climate has enabled Black Africa to achieve some successes. A number of civil wars have been brought to peaceful solutions. All these political changes promise a better future for symbiotic tourism, that is environmentally sustainable and supportive to wildlife.

The second broad recommendation relates to the exploding population levels of Africa. East Africa, like most of the continent, is overpopulated in terms of environmental and economic capacity. A long-range solution to its socioeconomic and political problems is impossible without a significant decrease in birth rates. This requires a coherent family planning policy. It appears that modest progress in the field of population control has been recently achieved in some sub-Saharan countries.

The third general recommendation pertains to the need for a radical change in agricultural policies on the part of governments. At present, there is an improvement in the official attitude towards this most important sector of the African economy. This means adopting policies that promote small agricultural initiatives, rather than large prestige projects and poorly planned industrial development, but also create an appropriate political climate for the growth of more competitive and efficient agriculture. This means the abandonment of such abortive socialistic experiments as collectivization and overregulation of agricultural production. Another important measure is the sharp devaluation of national currencies, such as those implemented in early 1994 in the former French colonies of western Africa to make food imports more expensive and local production more economical. This means that exports, including international tourism, are cheaper and consequently more competitive internationally.

The fourth recommendation focuses more narrowly on wildlife and its habitats. First of all, African parks need more financial means for conservation, parks planning, management, and enforcement of law within the parks. The present misery resulted from the steady deterioration of the economy. With the change discussed previously, the chances for better financing have improved considerably. A larger proportion of foreign aid should also be used for environmental protection in general, and for the creation and upkeep of national parks specifically. Such aid will contribute to the future ability to earn foreign exchange from tourism.

The fifth and last recommendation pertains to the needs of local population. One has to balance the interests of residents with the requirements of wildlife conservation and tourism. To achieve this, one has to put an end to the locals' alienation and hostility to wildlife as pests, to alter their perception of national parks as useless playgrounds for rich tourists, and to involve them closely with the conservation and management of wildlife habitats. The historical and cultural roots of this alienation have been explained by Walter Lusigi (1982: 104), who recommends that, "these people must be compensated directly for the use game animals make of their private land and they must benefit directly from the tourist income by being directly involved in the trade at the local level." The local people of the LDCs should benefit from participation in the strictly regulated capture of surplus live animals for zoos, from the restricted grazing of their cattle in the parks on a permit basis, and from controlled hunting (preferably outside the parks and only in times when the number of animals exceeds their carrying capacity). This means the introduction of multiple use into the parks, which is at variance with the practice in the DCs. However, according to Lusigi's concept, this principle would apply to much larger areas than those presently protected. The surrounding lands inhabited by the local population as well as the park itself, would be included in the park's planning and management. This would allow the animals to follow migration patterns currently disrupted by the present park boundaries. Lusigi closes his proposal with a statement that, "to attempt to conserve without the cooperation of the local people is merely to fight a delaying action" (*ibid.* 106). The issue is contentious. Many conservationists express other ideas.

In practice, Lusigi's views conform with the southern African model of wildlife management that advocates sustainable use of wildlife, i.e., a policy of science-based, controlled tourist hunting, and successful control of poaching, as in Zimbabwe, Zambia, Botswana, Namibia, Malawi, and South Africa. The philosophy on which the wildlife management policy of these countries is based could be summarized as follows: wildlife has to be killed in order to be saved. Local residents are not interested in the efforts aimed at sustained conservation of fauna, unless there are economic stimuli to do so. In certain areas of Zimbabwe, substituting cattle with wildlife means more productive and more profitable use of resources. The local population benefits from wildlife-generated tourism revenues from such sources as guide services, accommodation and food in hunting lodges, entrance fees to national parks, hotel taxes, hunting licenses, and souvenirs (including animal products). In such a situation, the local population is more interested in wildlife conservation than in poaching, which is ruthlessly controlled by shooting poachers on sight. An additional initiative to prevent poaching is the dehorning of rhinos, practiced in Zimbabwe. Unfortunately, this measure's effectiveness is limited, because horns grow back quickly and poachers kill even dehorned animals. Another disadvantage is the zero survival rate of calves borne to a dehorned mother, due to her inability to defend her "baby" against predators such as hyenas and lions.

The southern African wildlife management policy has, so far, brought beneficial results. The animal populations remain sustainable within their habitats, which now extend beyond the protected lands of the national parks into the wildlife management areas of the countryside. The local residents are free to switch from raising cattle to wildlife management (the more profitable option) or pursue both. The protection of wildlife and its habitat within the national parks is financed by tourism income. Wildlife depredation on farmers' fields and ranchers' cattle are tolerated because appropriate compensation is paid. Tourism revenues also finance measures aimed at decreasing the depredation, such as fencing and introduction of guard dogs—to deter cheetahs hard-kicking donkeys are recommended (Keller 1993). All these measures help to realize the full economic value of wildlife, be it by consumptive or nonconsumptive use, pursued in southern Africa with various emphasis, from place to place. Some authors even argue that hunting in Africa is economically more valuable and environmentally less destructive than animal viewing (Bonner 1993).

Consistent with such policies, the governments of the southern African countries are advocating the international ivory trade, and also expansion of the strictly regulated trade in meat, skins and other parts of wild animals. Wildlife meat in southern Africa is also used in emergencies: a catastrophic drought forced the authorities to take tough decisions in the middle of 1992. To feed the starving people, 2,000 elephants and many thousands of other wild animals, such as impala antelopes, were killed in Zimbabwe's national parks. The meat was distributed among the local population, and the tusks were added to those stored by the government since 1989 (see below).

The southern African policy allows hunting in national parks, if carrying capacities are surpassed by exploding wildlife populations. Thus, for Zimbabwe the carrying capacity of 45,000 elephants has been established, and the surplus is harvested, partly by tourists. Other animal parts, including skins and ivory, had been marketed before 1989. Since the 1989 ban by CITES of international trade in elephant parts, they have been stored in government magazines with the prospect of future sales, CITES permitting.

Diametrically different from the southern African approach to wildlife is the approach in eastern Africa, notably in Kenya. The only similar element is the struggle against poaching, which, for reasons explained below, has been much less successful in eastern Africa than in southern Africa. The Kenyan authorities frustrated by the catastrophic decrease in the numbers of elephants, which are much less abundant in eastern Africa than in the south of the Black Continent, have been advocating a total ban on hunting and trade in animal parts, including ivory. To cope with occasional animal overpopulations, they suggest contraception programs based on various contraception methods currently being developed (*Economist* 8

August 1993). The east African school of wildlife management fears that once hunting is allowed, the demand for animal parts (especially ivory) will increase, as will prices. The inevitable result will be, according to the east African approach, a return of poaching. Such a stance is supported by the World Wildlife Fund (WWF) and the CITES. In fact, in 1977 Kenya banned "hunting safaris" (an economically lucrative business based on international tourism) and outlawed wildlife trophy sales in 1978. However, since that time, the elephants have been diminished due to poaching, which is practiced by impoverished locals, angered by the absence of economic benefits from conservation. The government lacks resources to control poaching efficiently, and the survival of some wild animal species, such as the elephant, is threatened.

One can see the merits of both wildlife management concepts. In Kenya the wildlife is concentrated in the national parks and can be easily viewed by tourists, while in Zimbabwe the situation is different: wildlife is not confined to national parks but is also scattered beyond their boundaries and outside easy-viewing savannah areas. Thus, in Kenya, strict protection and nonconsumptive tourism may be the best option. In Zimbabwe consumptive tourism, i.e., hunting and consumption of wildlife by locals, could be a better alternative (Adams and McShane 1992).

As mentioned previously, to protect the dwindling herds of east African elephants, the CITES banned the international trade in ivory and other elephant products in 1989. However, the southern African countries, which kill about 2,000 elephants annually, want the CITES to downgrade the status of elephants from endangered to threatened, thus enabling them to sell the stored elephant products, especially ivory, on international markets. The confrontation between the two ended at the March 1992 meeting of CITES in Kyoto, Japan: the decision was to continue the full ban on trade in elephant products. Thus, the eastern African model has prevailed and a total ban on international trade in endangered species (including ivory and other elephant products) is in force. This keeps the controversy alive. The illicit international ivory trade continues to operate but at severely depressed volumes and lower prices. Poaching has decreased somewhat in eastern Africa, but may increase in southern Africa because of reduced funding of anti-poaching programs, financed from the revenues derived from wildlife trade. This clearly illustrates the difference between the situation in eastern and southern Africa and the impossibility of continuing with different policies. A possible solution would be a transfer of surplus elephants from southern to eastern Africa, if such a course of action is economically and scientifically feasible.

The issue of competition between the local population and wildlife habitat is not unique to Africa, and both African management models could be applied to other continents, with modifications. In fact, some overpopulated areas in Asia suffer from problems similar to Africa. The protection of lions and Bengal tigers in India is an example. The apparent success in preserving Asian lions in Sasan Gir National Park must be credited entirely to tourism. Tourism finances the relocation of cattle farms from the area and compensates farmers for losses of farm animals due to predators. Captive breeding programs in zoos have also been initiated to keep the lions' gene pool fresh and to create a reserve of lions for future transfers to other parks, in case of a disease outbreak.

The tiger problem is more difficult because of great demand for tiger skins among wealthy Arabs, and for tiger bones in east Asia where they are used as medicines. As a result the global number of tigers has declined by 95 percent in this century to an estimated 7,000 in 1992 (Browne 1992). However, more recent sources place the figure at not much more than 5,000. About 3,000 tigers (inflated Indian statistics boast 4,300), live in India, and 200 to 300 in the Russian Far East (Chisholm 1994: 36). The remainder inhabit southeast Asia and China. In 1973 the Indian government started Project Tiger, an effort to set aside reserves for the endangered animals. Unfortunately, the expansion of tiger sanctuaries involves the relocation of thousands of villagers (Theft 1989). Another drawback is that tigers kill about 50 people in India annually; there is also a substantial loss of livestock. The economic losses associated with the expansion of wildlife sanctuaries include not only land, but decreased wood supply and grazing grounds for livestock. To cope with these problems a policy of economic trade-offs, financed by revenues from tourism, is being introduced. The locals receive compensation for their losses, special development programs are being initiated in areas adjacent to the tiger sanctuaries, to increase local benefits from the lucrative tourist industry. However, these measures still do not prevent poaching. As long as the people living near the reserves remain poverty-stricken, and demand for tiger parts in China and Taiwan is high, poaching will threaten the survival of the Bengal tiger.

Another country which needs the implementation of an appropriate wildlife utilization policy is the former Soviet Union, especially Russia. In the absence of government intervention, needy residents and greedy local officials exploit wildlife as their private source of income, either by poaching or by allowing foreign hunters to deplete the resource for economic gain. Habitat destruction by logging is also a problem, but is secondary: poaching is the key problem. As a result, the survival of animals, such as the Siberian tiger, is threatened (Chisholm 1994). At present, consumptive and nonconsumptive tourism seems the best option for financing science-based wildlife conservation for Russian NGOs (*ibid.*). For now, the only hope for wildlife conservation falls to the impoverished.

A difficult problem is eliminating the demand for animal parts. In the absence of demand there would be no poaching. CITES condemned Taiwan many times for importing tiger bones and rhino horns—condemnations accompanied by calls for retaliation against offenders in the form of trade bans. And indeed, in April 1994 the United States was the first country to impose an embargo of imports on wildlife products from Taiwan.

Another problem of wildlife management is that of tourist souveniring. (This issue is discussed in more detail in section 5.8.2. 3.) The trouble is that most tourists expect not only experiences, photos and videos from their vacations, but also like to bring home other mementos, such as hunting trophies, butterflies, or shells. Mementos obtained illegally contribute to vandalism or poaching.

However, if consumptive resource use is conducted legally, on a scientific basis, and is essential to resource preservation, it should not only be allowed but promoted. The contribution of hunting, or culling the surplus wildlife populations, to the preservation of natural environments is discussed in section 5.8.2.1. Another tool in coping with problems of illegal consumptive use of wildlife is animal farming (see section 10.5).

Although the emphasis in this section was on the issues of wildlife policy in the LDCs, it does not mean that similar policies are not being applied in the DCs. I will limit this discussion to the example of the Yellowstone National Elk Refuge, which provides the local population with income from hunting and the sale of collected antlers.

3.6 *Zoos and Saving Wildlife*

For centuries zoos have enjoyed a high degree of interest. This interest is associated with *biophilia* (Wilson 1984), the human bond with other species, expressed in the need for contacts with nature, for encounters with living things. However, people have failed miserably to provide proper conditions for captive animals. As a result, zoos have a long and unsavory history (going back to the Roman Circus), of using and abusing captive wild animals for human entertainment. Recently, however, animal advocacy groups, including those in the Animal Rights Movement, have severely criticized aspects of human treatment of animals. This criticism goes beyond tourism and recreation, and extends to the use of animals for scientific experiments. However, tourism and recreation embrace rodeos, circuses, movie-making, and horse- and dog-racing. While agreeing that some may be party to those practices, and that in some of these attractions the animals are mistreated, I take exception to the condemnation of keeping fauna in captivity, i.e., in zoos, aquariums, water tanks and pools for the enjoyment and education of paying tourists and recreationists, and for research. Does this phenomenon demonstrate a negative or a positive impact of tourism and recreation on natural environment? The positive view is taken on this issue.

Since about the 1980s, some environmentalists and animal lovers, including those in the Animal Rights Movement, have questioned the very concept of zoos that deprive animals freedom of movement and their natural habitats. Visitors can observe the results of their confinement: the animals often display odd behavior, such as uncontrollable rocking, nodding, mindless pacing, and head-twisting—signs of their unhappiness caused by living in unnatural conditions. Critics also argue that animals in the zoo are becoming domesticated to such a degree that they would be unable to survive on their own if released into their natural habitats.

Critics of zoos advocate phasing them out. They advise the public to satisfy its appetite for close encounters with wildlife by looking at photos, films, the *National Geographic,* and if they can, with wildlife safaris. The University of Colorado philosopher, Dale Jameson, in his essay "Against Zoos," takes the extreme view that it is preferable to permit species to become extinct rather than to confine them to the artificial environment of the zoos (Birnbaum 1991). It seems such criticism is working to a certain extent, and the visitation rates, at least in some zoos (such as the Winnipeg Zoo in Manitoba and the British zoos) have been decreasing. The first success of the zoophobes was the September 1992 decision to close the venerable London Zoo in the Regent's Park, which had existed since 1828. The Zoo was finally saved by financial reform and the introduction of new attractions, among them the breeding programs for endangered species. The crisis seems to be over, at least for the time being. In the fall of 1993, the decision was taken to close the Vancouver Zoo in Stanley Park. At the same time, however, other important zoos of the world, such as the San Diego Zoo, California, are apparently immune to any trouble, and enjoy high visitation rates. The North American zoos as a whole boast about 200 million visitors annually. Among individual zoos of the world, the leaders are Mexico City with 12 million visitors annually, Beijing with 11 million, Moscow 3.5 million, San Diego 3.3 million (Van Linge 1992: 116).

In principle, one can agree with the critics of zoos. Indeed, wildlife does much better when in its natural ecosystem; the fauna in the splendor of nature is vastly superior to the artificiality of zoos. The criticisms are also valid with respect to caged conditions, notably in the LDCs and in some communist and ex-communist countries. In fact, the cruclest zoos I ever saw were in Tbilisi, former Georgian SSR, and in Teheran, Iran. The conditions were truly appalling, an outrage which should be dealt with promptly. However, the majority of zoos in the DCs have, during the last 30 years, developed a concept of a modern zoo which seeks to approximate the natural habitats of the animals as closely as possible within the framework of economic feasibility and practicality. They are less successful with large land mammals, such as elephants, and with primates and marine mammals, but they certainly do their best, providing as much space as possible, and simulating other conditions of the natural ecosystems. As a rule, the design of modern zoos has changed to reflect the modern attitudes towards nature: water-filled moats separate the animals from the public, and the enclosures' design follows scientific advice; exercise facilities and toys are provided for the animals to play with.

In recent years one of the zoos' problems turned unexpectedly into a positive environmental economic spinoff. The waste products of megafauna in the zoos have been a major nuisance for management, and substantial costs have been incurred to dump manure into landfills. Nowadays, zoos use the services of various compost companies that process and sell the animal waste to eager gardeners. The superior qualities of the exotic compost is twice as rich in nitrogen as cattle or horse manure, but is not as strong as chicken manure. Gardeners also say that the megafauna waste compost keeps away deer and rabbits (*New York Times* 12 May 1992).

The demand of the zoo critics for total elimination of all forms of keeping wild animals in captivity and their immediate transfer to the natural habitats is a superficial one. In the real world the situation is much more complex. My defence of zoos will contain two essential points: first, their educational, public relations, and scientific role, and second, their importance as tools for wildlife conservation.

Keeping a small part of wildlife in artificial surroundings is appropriate because zoos play the role of scientific research labs and of educational forums for the masses. The educational functions of zoos blend with public relations (PR) in promoting the appreciation of wildlife and the environmental cause at large. Of course, the best PR for nature is to create conditions enabling everybody, including those of modest financial means, the aged, the disabled, and the very young, to appreciate the animals in their natural settings. However, this is not feasible because of distance, costs, and travel time. Even if all potential tourists could make such visits, the natural habitats of our planet would not sustain such numbers as not too much wilderness is left on earth—only small areas, real islands in the sea of humanity. The carrying capacity of these ecosystems, left relatively intact, is limited. They are fragile and cannot be subjected to mass visitations without considerable harm. Thus, millions of people who cannot view the animals in the national parks and other reserves can enjoy wildlife in the zoos, and what is also important, can learn about nature. This promotional and educational aspect of viewing wild animals in captivity plays an important role in the campaign to save the fauna, and consequently its habitats (the ecosystems of our planet). Captive wildlife also enables considerably more people appreciate animals by viewing them at a closer range than is possible in the national parks.

My second argument in defense of zoos is that they are now becoming an essential part of modern conservation strategy and a critical instrument in the preservation of biodiversity. The extinction of plant and animal species since the beginning of the Industrial Revolution, and especially in this century, is advancing at an alarming rate. One could speculate that perhaps these extinctions exceed the geological extinction experienced at the end of the Cretaceous period, about 65 million years ago. According to Tudge (1991: 36ff), the main causes of the modern extinction of species are habitat destruction and fragmentation, introduction of exotic species into previously unexposed ecosystems, hunting, and the secondary effects of pollution, greenhouse effect, stratospheric ozone depletion and other global anthropogenic impacts.

Modern human habitation and economic activity disrupt not only various ecosystems but also the ecosphere of the planet as a whole. Evolution has created a complex, interacting structure of life that is being seriously disrupted by humans. Once a chain reaction is set in motion, the negative consequences on the ecosphere are inevitable, e.g., the depletion of the ozone in the stratosphere allows more ultraviolet rays to reach the surface of our planet; the UVs destroy the chlorophyll in plants; in the oceans this diminishes the amount of microplankton; this affects the number of krill feeding on it; less krill means less food for fish, whales, penguins and other birds. The chain reaction affects all life, as the disappearance of one species from an ecosystem may trigger a cascade of extinctions of other species that depend on that species. Some species are also more vulnerable to human impacts and they fall victim to extinction ahead of others.

This catastrophic destruction of valuable gene pools cannot be dealt with by preservation of natural habitats alone. Natural habitats are shrinking in the uneven competition with humans for living space. That there are no habitats left or extremely limited habitats for certain species, and this dooms them to extinction. Another threat is poaching, which is a problem in some areas of the First World, and out of control in most LDCs. It is especially acute in the former Soviet Union, where the desperate economic situation and the disintegration of political power renders law enforcement difficult, and even impossible. To save endangered ecosystems, and thus the future of our planet, humanity has to take a number of measures: a daunting and controversial long-term task is to limit the birth rates in the LDCs and to control the economic growth.

In this context zoos, megazoos (theme parks where animal are kept in semi-natural conditions), and other artificial environments where the fauna are kept captive, are performing an important role, providing a modern Noah's ark in saving animal species from the brink of total extinction. Because of their role as guardians of our wildlife heritage, the impact of zoos on nature should be evaluated positively. One should also not forget that visitors to zoos are recreationists and tourists who contribute financially to their upkeep. As for their roles in the preservation of species, the record of the zoos, with their scientific breeding programs, is outstanding, and the argument supporting zoos and their captive breeding programs convincing (*ibid.*). The rationale for protecting endangered species is to breed them scientifically in secure places, often (as in the case of the California condor), far safer than the wilderness. The ultimate purpose is to return them to their wild habitats, ideally in the form of national parks and similar reserves, where the animals will enjoy full protection from human interference. Thus, the chances for successful breeding in zoos are much higher than in the natural habitats. The breeding of rare animals in zoos saves not only their species, but also their genetic material, by providing carefully arranged mating programs which keep the genes fresh and diverse. In this way the rare species may be nursed through crises in much smaller numbers than in the wild. Such programs are financed by the viewing public, tourists and recreationists. The secondary purpose of the breeding programs is to supply new generations of animals for the zoos. As a result, only about 10 percent of zoo inhabitants come from outside (either orphaned or rescued).

There are countless examples of successful rescue missions performed by scientists in cooperation with zoos and other enclosed wildlife sanctuaries. Arguably the most distinguished record in this respect belongs to the zoos of San Diego, California, and Cincinnati, Ohio. Their breeding programs have saved many species, such as bisons and whooping cranes in North America, and sea eagles in Scotland, from total extinction. The bison will, however, never be able to recover its former habitat, and will be confined to national parks and other reserves. Similar programs have saved the European bison, Przewalski's horse (native to Mongolia), the kit fox (the smallest fox in North America), the Formosan sika deer, the white-throated wallaby, the Sumatra rhino, and many other species. In most cases these captive breeding programs have restored the ecological balance of habitats by re-establishing predators. A breeding program conducted by the Toronto Zoo strives to restore black-footed ferrets, which keep the prairie dog population in check across the Prairies.

Some breeding programs are conducted in zoos despite the fact that the animals can still be found in the wild. Panda bears are at risk because of the shaky environmental conditions in the 13 Chinese panda reserves. It seems the only way to save Siberian tigers from extinction is to breed them in the zoos, and release them into the wilderness when the conditions in Russia change. Sometimes it is too late: the protective environment of the Javan National Park was not enough to save the Javan rhino and the Javan tiger, which became extinct during the 1980s. The smaller the population, the more difficult the rescue missions, because the small numbers become inbred (genetically homogenized). Inbred offspring are susceptible to disease, and the breeding success is in doubt. The sub-Saharan cheetah suffers from such a lack of generic variability despite large wilderness populations of about 50,000. Golden lion tamarins and long-haired monkeys, native to Brazil's eastern coastal rain forests are also at risk. The forests that are their habitat are almost totally destroyed: only 2 percent of them still remain (*ibid.* 150). The remaining small group of tamarins that survived their habitat loss was doomed because of inbreeding, illustrating that too-small populations also become extinct. Zoos came to the rescue providing different genetic materials from captive animals and assuring the flow of genes between the captive and wild populations. Since 1983 a number of captive tamarins have been released into the Poco das Antas Biological Reserve in coastal Brazil, with 5,000 hectares largely devoted to the preservation of these monkeys. The results are encouraging because they prove that the reintroduction of captive animals into the wilderness can succeed if it is conducted gradually and scientifically. However, the golden lion tamarins in Poco das Antas will never again enjoy their original habitat: it is gone. Therefore, their limited numbers again raise the danger of inbreeding.

Another species threatened with extinction due to habitat loss are some parrots, including macaws, which have been hunted and trapped by the millions to be sold as pets. To cope with the problem, captive breeding programs have been initiated in order to supply the market exclusively with parrots raised in captivity. Protection from hunting and habitat destruction is also promoted and local people are taught that the colorful parrots in their natural environment constitute an important tourist attraction. To achieve this change of attitudes, advertising and educational campaigns have been launched.

The white rhinoceros, threatened with extinction in the 1920s, were placed in enclosed sanctuaries and have recovered to numbers of about 4,500. Nowadays the black rhinos are similarly endangered. The situation has reached the point where the best way to rescue them from loss of habitat and from poachers may be to confine them to fenced and well-guarded sanctuaries, including megazoos. After successful breeding programs they could be reintroduced into the African national parks. All five rhino species have been declared endangered by CITES, which has banned the international trade in rhino horns since the 1970s.

The Arabian oryx is a symbol of wildlife for the Arabian Peninsula, similar to the tiger of India. However, in the case of the oryx, there is no lack of habitat: the problem were mindless recreational hunters, using all-terrain vehicles (ATVs), helicopters, and high-powered rifles. The result was the total disappearance of this ungulate in 1972. A few specimens, captured for breeding programs in zoos, survived in captivity. Scientists successfully avoided inbreeding, the animals did well in the zoos, and a program to release them into the wild began in 1978. Since then, there have been several releases in Jordan, Saudi Arabia, and Oman. The rehabilitation program of the oryx can be declared a full success, and there are several hundred living in the Arabian Desert. However, their survival depends on attitudinal change of the local population. To achieve this change, the tribesmen are trained as wildlife rangers and an impressive publicity campaign has been launched.

The story of the California condor has been more tragic. These magnificent birds have been brought close to extinction by hunting, pesticides, and lead bullets lodged in the carrion they ate. A recovery program, led by the San Diego and Los Angeles Zoos, started in the 1980s. It consisted of removing the eggs from the nests to hatch them artificially, and capturing the last birds surviving in the wild. Despite criticism the program was implemented and after successful breeding in captivity, the release of the condors into the wild has started. It will be some time before victory of the program can be declared. But survival of the condor may depend for some time on the zoo because of the inherent dangers that the condor faces in the wild.

As discussed, the leading zoos and megazoos enjoy generally high visitation rates. An excellent example of a megazoo that enables large numbers of tourists to experience wildlife, is the Busch Gardens in Tampa, Florida. This theme park, which accommodates almost 3,500 animals, has breeding programs for many of them, including Asian elephants, Nile crocodiles, reticulated giraffes, and black rhinos. There are also special educational programs for visitors, particularly for the children. Scientific research is conducted in superbly equipped animal hospitals.

The newest, and rather expensive trend in the revolution of zoo design is toward bioclimatic exhibits imitating the vegetation and climate of natural habitats (Mansfield 1991). An example of such an arrangement is the African Tropical Rain Forest at Boston's Franklin Park Zoo. According to Howard Mansfield (*ibid.* 66), the famous San Diego Zoo plans to spend $100 million over the next 15 years to convert the entire zoo into ten bioclimatic zones.

A new facility established in 1992 within the Busch Gardens reflects the trend of establishing mini-replicas of natural ecosystems for keeping and displaying wildlife. It is the Myombe Reserve, also called the Great Ape Domain. The Myombe is a 1.2 hectare habitat designed to simulate the primates' natural environment and to encourage their natural behavior. The area is covered with dense, lush, tropical vegetation and houses six lowland gorillas and nine chimpanzees, both listed as endangered species by the U.S. Fish and Wildlife Service. The viewing of the apes is arranged to minimize the disruptions of their lives, with the help of a 30-meter-long glass panoramic area and boardwalk. There is also a breeding program for the resident gorillas.

Similar facilities that have recently opened are the almost one-hectare Tropical Rain Forest at Seattle's Woodland Park Zoo, the one-hectare Amazonia tropical rain forest at the National Zoo in Washington D.C., and the more than half-hectare Lied Jungle at the Omaha, Nebraska Zoo, which is covered by a naturally-lighted eight-storey-high dome. All of them opened in 1992. Some modern zoos specialize in displaying only certain species, such as the Butterfly World, a tourist attraction and research facility near Fort Lauderdale, Florida; or the Appenheul Zoo in the Netherlands, which displays only primates. The zoo management in these facilities have also enforced various codes of visitor behavior, such as forbidding disturbance and feeding of animals. In some zoos visitors are prohibited to eat (Van Linge 1992: 116).

According to Joost van Linge (*ibid.* 115), only about 650 institutions in the world can be classified as zoos or aquaria, based on international standards of quality, education, and research. As a rule, they rely on captive breeding to replenish their collections with only a small percentage of animals coming from outside zoos. To avoid inbreeding, there are well organized exchange programs between various zoos of the world. Surplus animals are sold to other zoos.

There is one aspect of zoos that causes some misgivings. Not all species enjoy the same level of interest. Some animals enjoy a kind of "good image" glamour among the human population. This phenomenon is called *speciesism,* which means discrimination against small and obscure species, especially invertebrates, such as insects, spiders and worms, in favor of big, attractive, cute, furry, and conspicuous ones, such as large mammals and birds. Certainly, people prefer to see and finance the preservation of panda, the symbol of the World Wildlife Fund, than of toads or beetles. People like to view and photograph showy larger mammals and birds, especially ones that are cute, cuddly and loveable, such as pandas; or humanoid, such as primates; or graceful and smart, such as dolphins; or majestic and intelligent, such as elephants and whales; or glamorous, such as the California condor or the bald eagle. These species capture the public's imagination and support. The high degree of tourist interest in Manitoba's teeming garter snake pits is not typical. Generally, less conspicuous and less attractive species such as bats, lizards, frogs, earthworms, insects, and various aquatic species, lacking fur, feathers and facial expressions, do not attract people—moreover, their image is often negative. In the DCs, not long ago predators were mercilessly eliminated. The same happens today in the LDCs, where some very useful animals, such as bats, are considered harbingers of death, and killed on sight. Some ancient civilizations regarded the serpent as a symbol of evil. In the Bible, Satan assumed the form of a serpent to tempt Eve.

Negative or indifferent public attitudes to a majority of species has lead to the lack of support for their conservation, although they also play an important, often critical, role within healthy and productive natural environments. In fact, many wild animals, such as insects, may be regarded as keystone species that hold the ecosystems together. Or they may be regarded as indicator species, which provide signs of the over-all health of the ecosystems. Indeed, the ecological importance of a species depends on its relationship with other species and not on their looks. In this connection, the present worldwide decline of amphibians, such as frogs, toads, and salamanders, concerns the scientific community, but unfortunately, not the public. Professionals are alarmed because the amphibian's skin absorbs pollutants from both the soil and water. They sit on top of the Detritus Food Chain and by serving as food for carnivores of the Grazing Food Chain, provide the essential link between both food chains. Since amphibians are generally stationary and migrate little, their condition may signal contamination of their habitats. The decline of amphibians seems to be worldwide, which indicates the gravity of the ecological situation. One theory of the reason for their plight is the thinning of the ozone layer in the stratosphere. Therefore, amphibians may be compared to canaries who were sent down into the old coal mines; their demise signalled danger. Thus, amphibians must be considered not only a keystone species but an indicator species. The grizzly bear is an example of an indicator species only because it requires large areas in good conditions—but it is not absolutely essential for the survival of ecosystems, as are amphibians or insects. Another example of an indicator species found in North America's lakes are clams. These decrease in areas of recreational motor-boating, because the turbulence increases turbidity and coats the membranes of their grills, cutting off the oxygen supply.

While admitting that speciesism is a problem, one has to consider the following: giving priority protection to larger species saves smaller species at the same time. Secondly, zoos frequently constitute the last sanctuaries, the last safe havens for the big animals, when their habitats are lost, and the captive breeding programs in zoos may be their last chance to survive. Smaller species are more resilient because their numbers within ecosystems are, as a rule, larger; their ecosystems have a larger carrying capacity for small animals. This prevents inbreeding, and the danger that a few individuals may be wiped out by disease and natural disasters.

3.7 *Display of Aquatic Wildlife*

The display of captive aquatic wildlife in large water tanks, pools and aquariums became fashionable after the Second World War in many DCs, especially in North America. Aquariums all over the world attract millions of people, eager to become environmentally educated and entertained. Among the most notable are aquariums in Boston, Baltimore, Monterey Bay (California), Vancouver, Sydney, and Osaka. Two new aquariums opened in May 1992: the largest fresh water aquarium in the world, the Tennessee Aquarium in Chattanooga, and the Oregon Coast Aquarium. The aquarium in Genoa, Italy, was completed in spring 1993.

There are various arguments in favor of the aquariums. The first is the scientific data gained from research on marine mammals in aquariums. Second, advocates claim that the animals taken from their habitat to the aquariums are never endangered species. For example, with a healthy population of 23,000 belugas in the western part of the Hudson Bay, a few individuals taken for display in aquariums and scientific breeding programs will not hurt the population. Third, there is the undeniable educational value of presentations of trained animals, such as dolphins, seals, killer whales (more correctly called orcas). Children who see these animals are not only entertained, but instructed in conservation, earning respect for marine wildlife, and encouraged to study science. In at least four aquariums in Florida (the largest is Dolphins Plus in Key Largo) the tourists are allowed close contact with the dolphins. For a fee, they can swim with them and touch them. Sometimes a portion of the money is devoted to a good cause, such as the funding of research to save dolphins from dragnet tuna nets. The Hyatt Regency Hotel in Waicoloa on the Island of Hawaii runs an elaborate program, supervised by veterinarians. A similar program is available in Xaret, Mexico. Sometimes wild dolphins, if treated gently, befriend swimmers, e.g., scuba divers and snorkelers at the Club Med village in the Turks and Caicos Islands, Caribbean, enjoy the company of Jo-Jo, a friendly local dolphin. More recently, close contact with marine mammals is spreading to the North. Scuba- diving tourists started to swim with the beluga whales in the frigid waters at the mouth of the Churchill River in Hudson Bay, Manitoba.

However, despite these positive values, criticism of aquariums is growing. Display and presentations of trained animals and the swim-with-the-dolphins sessions have been subject to intensive criticism by environmentalists. It seems that the criticism is more justified than in the case of land wildlife in zoos. Whales, such as orcas, grow as large as 9 meters and weigh more than 8 tons. They travel huge distances through the oceans. In the aquariums these marine mammals are confined to a small concrete space, filled with chlorinated water. The result is that many are dying. Concern has also been expressed about the potential, not clearly proven, of orcas and dolphins contracting diseases from humans. In some documented cases, dolphins developed ulcers from the stress of an artificial environment. In September 1992 two beluga whales died in an aquarium in California after being injected with antibiotics. On the other hand, trainers have been badly hurt and at least one was drowned by orcas. The issue is contentious and there is little agreement among scientists.

The criticism is having an affect: the curator of the Vancouver aquarium announced in 1992 that they will stop capturing new orcas from the ocean but will, instead, continue to show and breed them from the stock in captivity. Whales and dolphins already in the aquarium will not be returned to the ocean. The new policy is the result of public pressure. The natural habitat of marine mammals is generally much better than that of large land mammals. Nevertheless, as indicated in chapter 2, they suffer from pollution in many places, such as the 500 beluga whales living in the polluted waters of the St. Lawrence River.

These are the sickest whales in the world. Researchers detected a marked reduction of fertility and, worse, an extremely high incidence of cancer, caused by known carcinogens, such as mercury, lead, DDT and PCBs found in the water. The long-term solution is to clean up the river. The short-term solution is to capture some of the belugas, and place them temporarily in aquariums, with the prospect of releasing them in the future.

3.8 *Conclusions*

The discussion of the positive impacts of tourism on environment presented in this chapter focused on three aspects. First, the mere presence of tourism in an area leads to ecologically beneficial measures, such as clean water supplies, appropriate sanitation and sewage facilities, and prompt solid waste disposal. Tourism cannot develop in an environmentally-devastated area and this creates pressures for clean-up. The second beneficial impact of tourism is in its financial contribution to the costs of nature conservation. The economic input of tourism is generally more important than the input of government agencies and various NGOs. Without tourism success would be questionable. The third positive function performed by tourism is the educational and PR one: people at leisure learn to respect and appreciate nature and the human role in the context of life on earth. Their attitudes, and hence their actions, become environment-friendly—certainly an advantage to the conservation of the ecosystems.

Chapter 4

The Negative Impacts of Tourism and Recreation on the Natural Environment: Parameters, Agents, and Factors of Overdevelopment

Chapters 4 to 6 are devoted to the negative impacts of tourism on the natural environment. While chapter 5 focuses on the effects of tourism on separate elements of the environment, and chapter 6 on its impacts on integrated ecosystems, chapter 4 is more general and introductory. The discussion in chapter 4 starts with the key parameters determining tourism's impact on environment (sections 4.2 to 4.5). Subsequently, the agents of environmental impacts are reviewed (sections 4.6 and 4.7). Finally, the spatial intensity of tourism's impacts is examined using as examples the overdevelopment in western Europe, North America, and the LDCs (sections 4.8 to 4.10). Section 4.11 is devoted to the impact of tourism on the physical aspects of cultural monuments.

4.1 *Introduction*

The factors that influence the extent of tourism's impacts on the natural environment have been discussed at length in the international literature (e.g., Cohen 1978; Barbier and Billet 1980; Hamele 1987; Coltman 1989; Farrell and Runyan 1991; Wall and Wright 1977; Mathieson and Wall 1982; Williams 1987). Thus, there is a solid base for the development of a model of the effects under discussion. One has to agree with Cohen that to talk about the environmental effects of tourism in general terms has limited usefulness. Instead, one has to explore certain key parameters, as well as the agents and factors that play a decisive role in the complex interaction between tourism and ecosphere.

There is complete agreement in the literature on the complexity of such an analysis due to a number of problems. The first problem is that research on environmental impacts is reactive rather than proactive: it is basically conducted post factum (after the fact) rather than ante factum (before the fact). Therefore, it is difficult to establish a baseline, or a status *quo ante* (the situation prior to the advent of tourism) against which the changes brought about by the impacts could be determined, in terms of scope and extent. Recent research (Ludwig, *et al.* 1993; Hastings and Higgins 1994) expresses doubt if such a baseline really exists because nature's boom-and-bust cycles are largely unpredictable, chaotic, irregular and fluctuating, and because controlled and replicated experiments are impossible to conduct in large-scale systems. This increases the margin of uncertainty.

The second problem is of an etiological nature: it is difficult to distinguish between the impacts of humans and the pure impacts of nature—especially those that occur without human participation and not always "at glacial speed" (Goudie 1990). It is not always easy to single out the effects of tourism from other anthropogenic factors, such as economic activities and human habitation (Goudie 1990; Wall and Wright 1977: 4; Williams, P. 1987: 387). In this book tourism impacts are called internal, whereas the other human impacts are regarded as external.

The third difficulty in measuring impacts is the complexity of the interaction between one environmental component and another. A change in one may cause a cumulative and synergetic chain reaction which is difficult to foresee. Thus, even a mild force may lead to cumulative and synergetic environmental damage. Multi-collinearity, i.e., strong association of causal variables, discussed by Harold Foster (1992: 11–12), may also complicate the issue.

The fourth problem is associated with the nonlinear character of most impacts: some of the effects may build up slowly, imperceptibly, and result in long-term dramatic changes. According to Hammitt and Cole (1987: 244-245), in the majority of cases the effects are asymptotic, i.e., the relationship between the amount of use and the damage is curvilinear or logarithmic (Fig. 7.2). This means that the initial light use causes disproportionately high environmental damage, while later increases in use "have less and less additional effect on the resource." (See section 7.3 and section 9.1, point 15.) One has to note that the inflection point (the point at which even a significant increase in impact will cause less-than-proportional environmental damage) may be located at a very low intensity of impact. This inflection point is directly related to the area's resiliency (see section 4.2 below): fragile areas reach the inflection point much sooner than more resistant areas (Pigram 1983; Hammitt and Cole 1987). This nonlinear character of impacts does not necessarily mean that a reduction of use will substantially decrease the negative effect. Thus, "on already impacted sites all use may have to be curtailed before recovery can occur. In fact, in some situations such as on incised trails where erosion is occurring, even elimination of all use may be ineffective. Active site rehabilitation may be necessary before any recovery occurs" (Hammitt and Cole 1987: 245).

The fifth problem in the determination of the impacts are their spatial and temporal discontinuities (Wall and Wright 1977: 3 and 50), i.e., the situations when the causes and effects of impacts occur at various places and at different times. For example, dumping of raw sewage from a hotel may cause undesirable effects far downstream or down the coast. This uneven spatial distribution of impacts makes research planning and management difficult. The results of the impacts are not always immediate: there may be a considerable time lapse between the impact, such as trampling or destruction of vegetation, and the appearance of erosional damage. Another consideration is the recent acceleration of tourism's impact by modern technology, which makes these impacts more rapid than in the past. For example, modern vehicles of transportation and recreation such as airplanes, helicopters, hovercraft and various types of all-terrain vehicles (including dune buggies and snowmobiles), not only enable tourists and recreationists to penetrate virtually everywhere, even to virgin areas previously untouched by humans and their activity, but also cause increased wear and tear of the landscape.

The sixth difficulty is distinguishing between various dimensions of impacts, such as direct and indirect, trivial and serious, innocent and malicious, transitory and non-transitory, avoidable and non-avoidable (Mercer 1990: 289).

One has to take these caveats into account when searching for optimal approaches to the question. First of all, one has to realize that in the interrelationship between tourism and environment, tourism functions as the subject, causing ecological changes, and the environment constitutes the object of tourism's impacts. Consequently, to establish the key parameters in this interrelationship, one has to identify the features of the environment on the one hand, and of the impacts of tourism on the other–impacts which lead to various degrees of quantitative and qualitative alterations of the ecosphere. Thus, there are two sides of the coin:

1. The characteristics of the environment, i.e., the degree of resiliency of the ecosystems to the impacts, discussed in section 4.2.
2. The characteristics of tourism's impacts, i.e., spatial requirements of tourism, and the intensity and seasonality of its impacts, discussed in sections 4.3–4.5. Additionally, the agents and factors of tourism's impacts, such as developers, the public sector, the tourism industry, and tourists should be taken into account (sections 4.6 and 4.7).

4.2 *Environmental Resiliency of Ecosystems*

Not all ecosystems are equally susceptible to human impacts: they differ in resiliency. Urban, i.e., practically totally human-made environments (especially large metropolitan areas), are most resilient because their original natural ecosystems have been almost completely eliminated, and virtually everything is encased in concrete. As a result, there remains hardly anything to be altered—everything natural has been altered already. In the urban setting, the economic and sociocultural impacts of tourism are of main concern to decision-makers, but these issues are not the focus of this book— natural ecosystems, or their elements at various stages of modification resulting from human impacts. In the case of the urban environment, and with respect to cultural monuments, it is advisable to use the term physical environment instead of natural environment (see section 4.11 below).

The resilience of ecosystems to human impact depends on multiple factors. In general, the degree of resilience is proportional to their maturity. This means that complex, mature, ecological communities are more stable than communities at early seral stages, and therefore able to withstand more human pressure.

> In their progression towards climax communities, ecosystems acquire more cybernetic linkages and this increases their capacity for self-regulating adjustment (Satchell and Marren 1976: 2).

The succession of the ecosystems is often arrested at the early sub-climax seral stages by human disturbance, as in the case of recreational use of dunes. In such instances, according to Satchell and Marren (*ibid.* 2–4), larger management inputs are necessary to maintain these areas because of their greater instability and susceptibility to human impacts (Fig. 4.1).

Figure 4.1

THE RESILIENCY OF ECOSYSTEMS AT SERAL STAGES

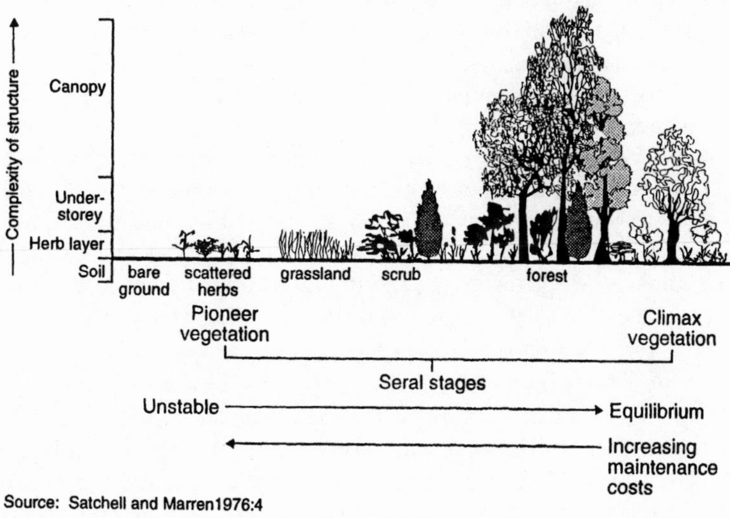

Source: Satchell and Marren1976:4

Secondly, the resilience of the natural environment to direct and indirect human impacts may depend on their geological features. For example, limestones, particularly *karst* landscapes (Sauro and Finlayson 1992: 558) or Alpine *flysch* are susceptible to impacts.

Very coarse-textured soils, such as those based on gravel and sand are prone to erosion (Mieczkowski, Z. 1965; Mieczkowski, Z. 1990: 224- 225). Some soils are susceptible to waterlogging. Thirdly, topography also plays a role: steep slopes are more prone to erosion than flatland. Fourthly, certain climatic features, such as aridity or low temperatures, decrease the resiliency of the ecosystems and their capacity to absorb human impacts. As a result the Arctic, Antarctic and mountain ecosystems regenerate extremely slowly when damaged. Fifth, hydrology factors such as the level of water table and run-off conditions, must be taken into account when evaluating the environmental impacts of tourism. The fragility of coastal ecosystems, such as dunes, is partially associated with their hydrological regime. Wetlands, both coastal and inland, are susceptible to tourist impacts.

Thus, to understand the potential effects of tourism on natural environments one has to take into account all the factors associated with their environmental resiliency. One can then identify certain ecosystems or their elements with low resilience thresholds, such as coral reefs, dunes, mountains with high relief energy, watersheds, wetlands, arid areas and polar regions. Not all of these sensitive types of ecosystems hold the same degree of interest for tourism. Yet in general, ecosystems that attract the attention of tourism tend to belong to the more environmentally vulnerable, such as seashores, mountains, lakes, and coral reefs. As a result, these environments are given a high priority in scientific inquiries for these researchers, trying to establish the degree of resiliency of the ecosystems for the purposes of tourism.

Not only whole ecosystems vary in the degree of their resiliency. Separate components of the ecosystems also differ from each other in their tolerance levels. For instance, particular geological features of various parts of an ecosystem may make these parts more prone to erosion. The same may be said about diverse species of flora and fauna which vary in their resiliency. The investigation of these differences constitutes a considerable challenge for research.

4.3 *Spatial Requirements of Tourism*

Turning from the properties of environment to the characteristic features of impacts of tourism, one encounters a multitude of variables which determine the degree of impacts that affect the environment. In general, the impacts may be subdivided into quantitative and qualitative. Space requirements belong to the first category.

Space consumption by tourism and recreation occurs at the expense of natural or semi-natural (modified) ecosystems. Unfortunately, trends in tourism and recreation indicate that the need for space as a resource is increasing (Mieczkowski, Z. 1990: 211–213). Despite factors moderating the space requirements for tourism (*ibid.* 215–217), the competition for space between tourism and other economic sectors and uses not only creates the problems of computation of opportunity costs (*ibid.* 268, 277) but also exacerbates the controversy between environmentalists and developers. Nadeau (1982: 140) writes that, "leisure has become one of the greatest consumers of space and the data pertaining to the future prospects are alarming."

Not all tourist developments and recreational activities require the same amount of space. There is a continuum in terms of recreational space requirements. Using Marion Clawson's terminology (Clawson and Knetch 1966), one can generalize that user-oriented recreational activities located in urban, suburban, and near-urban areas need less space than the resource-based activities pursued in extra-urban areas. However, the former, as a rule, require space monopoly, i.e., they permanently exclude all other recreational uses from the area they occupy. Tennis courts or swimming pools are good examples of facilities requiring relatively little space, but in urban and resort areas, where land is in short supply, they compete for space with other economic sectors and communal needs. In contrast, resource-based activities, such as mountain hiking, require a large amount of accessory space in a relatively pristine state, (although the activity itself needs hardly any space). However, the ecological envelope (environmental or accessory space), where these activities take place, is considerable. There is still another difference between the two categories of recreational activities: the resource-oriented activities, as a rule, do not require a permanent space monopoly. In some instances, such as with swimming or water-skiing, a temporary space monopoly on a small area may be needed.

Some recreational activities are pursued in any setting, and require almost as much space in urban as in nonurban areas. For example, golf is one of the champions in devouring space: it demands large amounts of valuable, relatively flat land, not to mention severe environmental modification. Golf courses claim not only more space than most other recreational activities, but also water resources, which may be in short supply in many tourist regions (see section 5.6.1 below). Golf is booming all over the world: in Western Europe it is a $10 billion industry, and in the United States twice as much (*Economist* 8 January 1994). The recent increase of golf's popularity in Japan, a country where flat land is in especially in short supply, has contributed to the intensive competition for space with other uses. One can expect that the worldwide expansion of golfing will continue in the foreseeable future, as the post-World War II baby boom generation ages and turns to less physically demanding sport activities.

One of the most important manifestations of tourism contributing to space consumption has been the modern trend in Europe and North America to owning a second home. Country homes and cottages near the city are giving way to homes on the coast or in the mountains, despite the longer commuting time and higher costs. According to Stroud (1983: 308), "recreational subdivisions are placing an immense strain on existing resources in many areas because they require large tracts of land, ample water, soil suitable for septic tanks, and many other basic services associated with a suburban subdivision." Space is devoured not only for individual vacation homes and surrounding lots but also for the infrastructure of a road network facilitating access to these homes, and for utility lines, service businesses, shopping areas, and churches. Roads not only take space but impact negatively on whole ecosystems causing devegetation, erosion, and water pollution (see chapter 6). Another spatial drawback of second homes, frequently built on sea- or lake-shores, is that they bar access to prime recreational resources and scenery for other visitors. Mathieson and Wall (1982: 127) point out the loss of esthetic values of areas with high- density second-home development.

Vacation and recreational home subdivisions use space particularly inefficiently in comparison to other tourist accommodations, such as hotels. They consume much more space per accommodation unit, while their economic impact is relatively low (Krippendorf 1986b: 30). Grenon and Batise (1989: 155) calculated that, for the Mediterranean, space requirements for hotels (including gardens and parking lots), is 40 square meters per bed; for second homes, the figure is 70 square meters. Additional inefficiency is the seasonal and/or weekend use of second homes: they are left uninhabited for most of the year, thus contributing minimally to the local economy. The recent trend to winterize second homes results in increased heating, even during the absence of the owners; this means inefficient use of fuel resources and increased pollution.

Another form of tourist accommodation criticized for devouring space in the most profligate way, is camping (Vadrot 1977: 88- 91). Vadrot cites astonishing figures about the overdevelopment of camping on the French Riviera and evaluates the situation as critical: with 100 square meters per one camping unit, i.e., about 300 persons per hectare, the capacities on the French Riviera in the mid-1970s had been surpassed by up to 60 percent, exerting a devastating environmental impact (see section 4.8). Despite the subjectivity of his capacity measure, Vadrot's arguments have to be taken seriously.

The competition for space between recreational and other uses has been exacerbated since the end of World War II by the permanent human migration trends towards the areas endowed with environmental amenities. Beautiful landscapes, mild climates and beaches are not only desired only by tourists, but by permanent residents. The progress in air conditioning technology has made these north to south population movements easier. Since 1945, millions of people in North America have moved from the northeast and the midwest United States to Florida, Texas and the southwest, especially California and Arizona. In Europe the migrations have taken place from inland to coastal locations, particularly towards the Mediterranean Sea. These permanent southward movements of population have been reinforced by the temporary tourist migrations. In Europe, tourists migrate from the north to the south in summer, in America they do so in winter. Thus, two processes of the modern age have exerted a cumulative pressure on space as a resource: permanent settlement of recreation-oriented migrants and temporary migration, i.e., tourism. Vadrot (*ibid.* 85) calls this phenomenon "overcrowding above overcrowding" (*l'entassement sur l'entassement*).

4.4 *Spatial Intensity of Tourism Impacts*

After the spatial requirements of tourism, its *spatial intensity* must be considered. Tourism development is directly affected by the physical (i.e., spatial) carrying capacity (see chapter 7). This has been surpassed in large tourist regions, such as the Alps or the Mediterranean (see section 4.8). The result has been incredible congestion, a veritable people-pollution of high-density mass tourism—the most criticized environmental issue associated with modern leisure.

Physical carrying capacity is associated with tourism overdevelopment—with high density mass tourism concentrated on limited space. With the movement of almost four billion tourists worldwide annually, the problem of physical oversaturation of limited space becomes an alarming problem: there is no room to accommodate people in the overcrowded tourist facilities, and amenities; and the overloaded infrastructure breaks down. This manifests itself in many ways: gigantic traffic jams on highways and in the sky near the major airports, hours of delays in take-off permits for airplanes from the traffic control tower, planes colliding in the overcrowded airspace, skiers colliding on overcrowded slopes or lingering for hours in ski lift line-ups, long waiting periods for camping permits in many North American national and state parks and other nature reserves, overcrowded campgrounds and beaches—these are only some of the examples of the quantitative growth of tourism. This obsession with growth at any price, this frenetic emphasis on economic success and profit has no end and leads to the degradation of the ecosystems. The situation is most precarious in Western Europe, and less severe in North America. For the time being, the LDCs are least affected, although local pressures are certainly noticeable.

The quantitative impacts of tourism are closely associated with qualitative ones. Quantity tends to impinge on quality, and in many instances it is difficult to distinguish between their impacts. Thus, overdevelopment and high density tourism, large-scale resorts and highway construction, recreational activities, such as swimming, sailing, motorboating, horseback-riding, and the use of ATVs, differ qualitatively in their impact on ecosystems. A comparison between them shows there is a continuum from relatively mild qualitative impacts, introducing hardly any modifications into the landscape, to impacts that cause radical and severe qualitative transformation of ecosystems. Of course, even the most environmentally harmless activities such as hiking or swimming, constitute major environmental problems if overdeveloped, i.e., the quantity then changes the quality.

The question is: What is more damaging, the intensive high-density concentrated development of tourism with the impacts localized on a relatively small territory, (as exemplified by Waikiki on Oahu, Hawaii or Nusa Dua on Bali, Indonesia), or its more even but less intensive spread, like butter on bread, dispersed over larger territories, such as areas of wilderness hiking? These are the spatial problems of local and regional policy and planning which will be discussed in chapter 8. In this chapter (sections 4.8 to 4.10) the issues of spatial intensity will be put into the wider context of tourism overdevelopment in large areas of Europe, North America and the LDCs.

4.5 *Temporal Intensity (Seasonality) of the Impacts*

One should not forget that there is another important quantitative aspect of tourism impacts that could help: the issue of time. The temporal intensity, or seasonality, of impacts should also be considered. There are practically no natural regions on earth where the climatically optimal tourist season would last twelve months a year (Mieczkowski, Z. 1985). In most cases the tourist season does not surpass six months: in the polar regions, as a rule, it is less than two months, and in midlatitudes three to four months. In the tropics, the rainy season is off-season; consequently in the Caribbean the tourist season lasts from 15 December to 15 April, or only four months. Every area has its shoulder period between the high-season and off-season, when the environmental pressures of tourism are somewhat mollified. However, even in the rare cases when the seasonal variations in the weather pattern are relatively small; the seasonality of the tourist flows may be significant because of the holiday-scheduling habits of their strong international markets (e.g., the European tourist market that frequents the Maldives).

Seasonality is evaluated negatively from the economic point of view, because tourist-related investments are amortized over a shorter period. However, environmentally, the off-season gives nature the chance to recover from damages suffered during the high season. Therefore, seasonality of tourism should be regarded as a positive phenomenon as far as the natural environment is concerned.

4.6 *Agents of Impacts: Developers and Governments*

When discussing the agents of environmental impact of tourism on the natural environment, one has to realize that there are four players in this game: developers, the government at all levels, the tourism industry, and finally the tourists themselves. In this section the role of developers and governments is discussed.

The attitudes and actions of the developers of the tourism infrastructure constitute the first variable in the tourism-to-environment relationship. Developers do not act alone but in alliance with the political decision-makers, who are exposed to constant pressure from the powerful construction lobby. However, the contemporary construction industry cannot be regarded as a part of the tourism industry (Krippendorf 1986b: 29). The construction industry develops independently from tourism and is subject to different economic laws and processes. Its interests are frequently at variance with the tourism industry, which concentrates on rendering services and is concerned in the long-range stability and regularity of the economic processes.

Developers have a different time perspective from operators of tourist industry. Their goal is to make profit on an activity that profoundly modifies the natural environment, often treated by them as inexhaustible. Once that is accomplished, they are out of the picture, and any adverse effects of their activity are none of their concern. No long-term self-interest of developers will prevent them from "killing the goose that lays the golden eggs." Unfortunately, "developers are often oblivious to the environmental effects of their activities, or possess only such a limited view of the total situation that they are unable to grasp the implications of their small-scale profit-making operation on the overall environment" (Cohen 1978: 223-224). The conclusion is clear: developers lack long-term perspective, they do not (or do not want to) realize the consequences of the unbridled construction booms. They treat the environment as an inexhaustible gift of nature because our free market system has been, so far, unable to incorporate the cost of natural resources and the value of environmental damage into the prices of tourism products. In other words, environmental costs have not been internalized yet (see section 8.5).

The competition among developers for the choicest properties frequently leads to large-scale construction and often degenerates into overdevelopment. The building frenzy seems never to stop, because single developers, as a result of limited transparency of the market, feel no incentive to do so unless they are sure that their competitors will do the same. In addition, the boom frenzy of high-intensity tourism creates conditions developers are hoping for, namely, an escalation of prices for developed real estate. The result is detrimental to not only the environment, but also to the long-term economic interests of the whole tourist industry. Thus, instead of "short-term pain for long-term gain" the situation is one of "short-term gain for long-term pain." The vital interests and the long-term sustainability of the tourist industry are sacrificed on the altar of short-term profit-making by the developers. The situation is aggravated by speculators who drive up prices in an effort to maximize profits before a possible crash in property prices. A classic example of such a situation occurred among developers in connection with the 1987 America's Cup in Fremantle, Australia (Jones and Selwood 1991).

Single large developers of integrated resorts are more environmentally responsible than multiple "catalytic" developers involved in the construction of a resort (Pearce 1978). Indeed, the first category excels in planning, construction, and management stages, and, because of the limelight of public scrutiny, is more concerned with public approval than the host of relatively small-scale "catalytic" developers. Thus, there are many responsible large developers of "total destination resorts" in North America. The multitude of smaller developers is characteristic for western Europe, where large planned developments of the Languedoc-Rousillon type on the French Mediterranean coast, west of the Rhone Delta, are less numerous.

The expansion of tourism infrastructure is not limited to the development of accommodation, i.e., to the construction of hotels, second homes, condominiums, and campgrounds. It also extends to tourist transportation and associated facilities, such as access roads, drainage ditches, communication lines, parking spaces, electric transmission lines, water supply, and sewage systems. Much of this infrastructure is idle most of the year. Some of the most outrageous environmental abuses are associated with cable cars, ski lifts and other types of recreational transportation in the mountains, especially in the Alps. Jost Krippendorf (1986b: 26–27) criticizes the endless drive on the part of Swiss developers to build more and more of these facilities—all in the name of improving the comfort level of the skiers and shorten the waiting time in lineups. He is also against public subsidization of the construction of this type of recreational transportation.

The development of tourist infrastructure, including transportation (especially access roads, cable cars, ski lifts and similar facilities in the mountains), yields many examples of destructive impacts on the natural environment. These contribute not only to air pollution but also to visual pollution, including such unsightly structures as ski-lift facilities, ski pistes, car-parking areas, and billboards. Examples abound from all over the world: the otherwise impressive ski slopes near Zermatt, Switzerland, are covered with a hideous maze of various types of uphill transportation. In terms of ugly tourist architecture, one could apply the designation "construction garbage," used by Arefyev (1991) to describe some sections of Sochi, a Russian beach resort on the Black Sea. Tej Vir Singh (1989: 166–167) complains about visual pollution in the Manali resort in the Kulu Valley of Himachal Pradesh, India. He criticizes "the makeshift wooden structures, painted slogans and ads on giant rocks in the midcurrent of the Beas River," and advocates the harmonization of hotel architecture with the landscape.

To complete the picture, some developers, as agents of environmental degradation, may refer to their alleged criminal activity. An Italian environmentalist told me that there are rumors in Italy of developers' mafia being involved in suspiciously frequent bush fires, especially in Sardinia. Such fires destroy the tourism infrastructure and create potential profit for the developers from the reconstruction that inevitably follows. Another incentive for criminal activity on the part of developers may be legal loopholes, such as the one in Greece allowing to build on land that has been destroyed by forest fire: once a valuable forest in a protected area is gone, developers are free to act according to their interests. Although not all forest fires in tourist areas are caused by arson, nevertheless, a large percentage of them may be linked with illegal undertakings. The results of this type of criminal activity in Mediterranean Europe are terrifying: about 10,000 forest fires in Italy burned 40,000 hectares in 1993—100 percent more than in 1992; the figures for Greece over the past few years was 6,500 fires and 250,000 hectares devastated (*World Press Review* November 1993: 33).

The second nontourist actor on the scene of tourism overdevelopment is the public sector, consisting of local, regional, and national governments. They have the power to regulate tourism but often do not (see section 8.6). Indeed, lack of environmental concern on the part of developers is frequently reinforced by lack of regulatory action by the decision-makers, individual politicians at all levels, and also by government agencies and communities. Often, they act out of real or perceived concern for jobs, fear of losing tourism revenue, and decline in the property tax base. In some cases, there may be illegal cooperation between government officials and developers. The high costs of environmental impact studies may also act as a deterrent. Stroud (1983) gives examples of communities reluctant to impose regulations limiting tourism development because of these reasons. Local and national governments frequently fail, not only in terms of regulatory proaction, but also, under the pressure of the construction lobby, by actively promoting too-rapid tourism development. This results not only in environmental, but also in economic and social damage. More gradual, planned development is definitely not always in the best interests of the construction industry.

4.7 *The Tourism Industry and Tourists as Agents of Impacts*

The third player in the environmental game, in addition to developers and governments, is the tourism industry. In theory, the tourism industry is more responsible than developers because it operates with a longer view and is concerned with future prospects of the business. However, because of the fragmentation of the industry and lack of transparency of the market, not all units of the tourism sector are able or willing to take a long-term perspective. Therefore, transgressions on the part of single tourist enterprises are frequent. Some entrepreneurs try to decrease their costs by disregarding environmental laws and regulations, such things as garbage disposal or the dumping of raw sewage. Consequently, it is the duty of government agencies to enforce protective environmental laws.

The fourth and last factor of tourism that impacts on environment is the tourists. The attitudes and behavior patterns of individuals or groups of tourists often constitute a significant source of environmental deterioration. There are several factors that have contributed to the increase in the ecological despoliation by tourists and recreationists in the post-World War II period. The most significant is the sheer volume of the market, which today encompasses practically all residents of the DCs. Tourism and out-of-home recreation are no longer enjoyed by a small and educated elite, but are a mass phenomena where practically everyone is a potential participant. This mass participation, while undoubtedly a positive socioeconomic phenomenon, is, environmentally, a negative one.

However, the problem is not only with the quantity but also with the changed quality of tourists. The involvement of everyone in the market, despite its undeniable positive egalitarian aspects, has increased the potential of destructive behavior by individuals with lower educational, and occasionally, even moral levels. Thus, the mass tourism market often includes individuals who lack the eco-conscience that would inhibit them from harming nature. As well, the process of urbanization that began with the Industrial Revolution has diminished human contacts with nature to such an extent that many people do not have a proper understanding of ecosystems, and as a result, cause unintentional harm as tourists. Thus, some modern First World tourists, if they lack the attitudinal prerequisites for such encounters, may prove destructive to the natural environment.

Another aspect of quality are changes in the behavioral patterns of modern tourists. Nowadays many modern vacationers want to escape the everyday drudgery of the city, of social regimentation and codes of behavior, be free to do what they want, and to compensate for the inadequacies of their working existence. They want to have a good time in the relative anonymity of the destination, without the social scrutiny to which they are exposed at home—to forget the usual everyday constraints in a completely changed social environment. As a result, the behavioral patterns of tourists at a tourist destination are quite different than at home. They generally behave in a less responsible way than in everyday life, less responsible not only in the economic and social respect, but also in their interaction with the natural environment. The modification of tourists' behavior is reinforced by the recent trend to shorten the length of stay at one destination and to take more than one vacation a year. This contributes to the lowering of behavioral standards in virtually every respect.

The most extreme type of human behavior, which has not only environmental but also economic and sociocultural implications, is vandalism. Vandalism receives plenty of coverage, not only in the press, but in research (Morrison and Wall 1979). For example, 12 articles contained in *Trends* (1984, vol. 21:1) represent a notable contribution to elucidating the scope, impacts and response strategies with respect to vandalism in recreational setting. In one of them Christensen and Davis (1984: 14) offer an operational definition of vandalism as, "the range of perceptions, attitudes, labels, or interpretations attached to inappropriate (non-normative) behavior in recreation settings.... Vandalism is behavior that depreciates the physical and aesthetic qualities of the environment and recreational experience in recreation settings." Wall and Priddle (1979: 282) define vandalism as an extreme, criminal, and destructive form (subset) of rowdyism. They regard rowdyism as, "a vague term implying rough, quarrelsome, boisterous and disorderly behavior."

There is a long list of reasons for vandal behavior with respect to natural environment. As to the attitudes of young people, constituting the majority of vandals, Wall and Priddle (*ibid.* 283–284) discuss various circumstances, ranging from boredom to the intention to strike back at the establishment. Christensen and Davis (1984: 16) ascribe to vandalism some characteristics of "folk crime," i.e., crime that is so prevalent, and accepted by society to such a degree, that coercive approaches are of limited effect. They emphasize the difficulty of enforcing such laws and, instead of regulatory panaceas, they advocate a "broad-based, diverse approach ranging from user participation to education, official presence, reduced opportunity, and enforcement." In general terms, one may point out that recreationists mirror the behavioral levels of the society at large, and do not constitute an isolated group. In other words, as is the society, so are people during their leisure time.

Examples of environmental vandalism include littering, tree carving, illegal firewood gathering, cutting of trees, defacing rocks, putting garbage into geysers (a typical form of vandalism in Yellowstone National Park), and certain aspects of noise pollution. Vandalism is associated mainly with its economic impact because it involves the destruction of tourist facilities, at the expense of the taxpayers. But it must also be emphasized that vandalism causes considerable damage to the ecosystems. For example, tourists and recreationists have been known to harass wildlife, chasing it in ATVs (especially in snowmobiles). Many animals pay with their lives for this questionable "pleasure." The disturbance of the feeding and breeding patterns of birds by tourists approaching nest sites too closely, or by the noise of their motorboats are well-known examples (Edwards, J. 1987: 79). The reader will find a detailed discussion of these behaviors in section 5.8.

Graffiti, the drawing or carving on rock surfaces, discussed in section 4.10, are the most common form of vandalism. However, some of the graffiti become objects of historical interest if they are relatively ancient. This fact presents the managers with a dilemma: "When does graffiti become historic as opposed to sheer vandalism?" (Gale and Jacobs 1987: 7). Sometimes graffiti enhance the cultural significance of a site and should be included in the interpretative material for that site, as in the case of sixteenth- and seventeenth-century Spanish graffiti in New Mexico.

Another form of vandalism is collecting objects for souvenirs, discussed in section 3.5, with respect to wildlife. Some tourists love to take a little memento home to show to friends and relatives. They cut rare plants, chip geological specimens from unique rock surfaces, pick up artifacts, and even, as Gale and Jacobs (*ibid.* 9–11) complain, cut and blast away rock pieces with Australian aboriginal paintings or engravings. The authors speculate that there was more souveniring in the past, when a lower level of visitation of the sites enabled the vandals to do their work undetected. They also point out that, "much of the most dramatic souveniring was done in the name of science" in order to place the items in museums or private collections, presumably safer places than *in situ.* This course of action was abandoned some time ago. "Only in extreme cases, where items are clearly under threat of destruction, is it acceptable to remove them" (*ibid.* 11). Not only do tourists participate in vandalism and plain robbery of archaeological sites: so do professional robbers. Unfortunately, there has been always a market for ancient artifacts purchased eagerly by unscrupulous collectors, the minority of them being tourists.

There is a form of souveniring which has in recent years acquired frightening proportions: the collection and purchase of fossils by tourists. Fossils have become fashionable. Unscrupulous professional collectors of fossils who sell them to tourists use advanced excavation methods. Not only trilobites and ancient fish, but dinosaur bones or even whole skeletons constitute objects of increasing demand. Collectors deplete the nonrenewable resources of scientific artifacts and destroy important scientific data by unprofessional excavation. As well, valuable specimens are being removed forever as potential objects for museums. Unfortunately, authorities are slow in imposing regulations on these harmful activities.

Littering, arguably the most common offense perpetrated by tourists against the environment, is another form of vandalism. Littered beaches, mountains, forests, and city streets illustrate careless attitudes of people at leisure. A modern example of this is the growing problem of the expedition garbage discarded by mountaineers in the Himalayas and hikers in the Alps (discussed further in section 6.4.7).

4.8 *Spatial Intensity: Tourism Overdevelopment in Western Europe*

The discussion in sections 4.2 to 4.7 focused on the general parameters of the negative impacts of tourism on environment, i.e., on the characteristic features of first, the environment as the object of impacts, and secondly, of the agents and factors of tourism playing the role of the subject impacting on environment. The emphasis was on quantitative aspects of impacts, especially their spatial and temporal intensity. Sections 4.8 to 4.10 will be devoted to concrete examples of environmental impacts that resulted in tourism overdevelopment in various socioeconomic conditions of the DCs (in Western Europe and North America) and the LDCs. Generally, tourism in the Second World, i.e., in the communist and former communist countries, has not been overdeveloped because of its relatively low-priority position among the leadership. Thus, these countries are not discussed in this chapter, although they are not completely blameless in terms of tourism overdevelopment.

The evils of tourism overdevelopment are especially apparent in the 19 affluent countries of Western Europe, most of them members of the European Union. Practically every major tourist region is affected. Even the peripheries are not spared according to Chris Ryan (1991: 99), who complains of overdevelopment in the Lake District, Britain's largest national park. He contends that the levels of congestion and stresses to the road system contribute to the failure of the park to achieve the status of a World Heritage Site. Another peripheral region of Western Europe under threat of tourism overdevelopment is eastern Germany. Tourism during the Communist regime was poorly developed. However, after the reunification, the pressures on some relatively pristine areas, such as Rügen, created an environmental menace which cannot be ignored.

Nevertheless, some regions of Western Europe should be singled out as particularly affected by tourism overdevelopment, namely the Mediterranean, the Alps, and the coasts of the North and the Baltic seas. The Mediterranean Basin is the most touristically overdeveloped region of the world. According to various sources, in the 1970s and early 1980s it comprised between 28 and 33 percent of world's tourist bed supply and a similar proportion of international tourist receipts (Impact of Tourism 1985, Tangi 1977: 336, Vadrot 1977: 82). In the 1950s the physical carrying capacity had been surpassed only in the traditional destinations, such as Nice on the French Riviera, or Torremolinos off the Costa del Sol in Spain, and was limited to relatively small areas. However, more recent overdevelopment, especially since the 1960s, has spread from these focal points to large areas located at the coasts and in the adjacent mountains. According to Grenon and Batise (1989: 238), at present well over 100 million tourists annually visit the coasts of the Mediterranean. This overdevelopment has reached such spatial proportions that at the Mediterranean seashores of western Europe there are hardly any undeveloped coastal sectors left. Overdevelopment, overbuilding, and urbanization of beach resorts has led to excessive tourist densities, resulting in the erosion of the resource base. As Vadrot (1977: 85) points out, in their quest to put as many tourists as possible in direct contact with the sea, the developers have embarked on the construction of high rise accommodations and marinas "with feet in the water" (*pied-dans-l'eau*).

Grenon and Batise (1989: 158–159) present various indicators of tourist pressure on coastal regions of the Mediterranean, and state that the heaviest tourist density is in Malta, five times higher than Spain, which occupies second position, followed by France, Italy, and Yugoslavia. Turkey and Egypt are affected relatively little, and Grenon and Batise (*ibid.* 160–161) suggest a redistribution of Mediterranean tourism to these countries.

Among the Mediterranean coasts the Spanish rivieras suffer most from environmental degradation caused by tourism overdevelopment. In the early 1960s, half of the tourists visited the interior, where they enjoyed museums, churches, cathedrals, Spanish wines, and bullfights. Then the situation changed: in the 1970s the share of coastal tourism grew to 80 percent (Vadrot 1977: 83). The reasons for this change lie in the younger age of the tourists and the increasing trend to beach recreation (including acquisition of the "obligatory" suntan). It also was associated with the chaotic urbanization that proceeded virtually everywhere from the French border to Gibraltar. Various terms are used to describe these processes: *balearization, la saturacion hotelera,* and the pejorative *desarrollismo,* the latter used instead of *desarrollo,* which means "development" in Spanish. The worst affected are the Baleares, which account for about 30 percent of all nights spent by foreign tourists in Spain, and also Costa del Sol and Costa Brava. Morris and Dickinson (1987) criticize the anarchic pattern of tourist growth on Costa Brava, the most beautiful of the Spanish coasts. They report the resistance of commercial interests against the imposition of "any restriction on new development" and express concern that without appropriate rules and regulations the landscape resource will be further eroded. There are also complaints about the state of Spanish beaches, which are described as "extremely dirty," and polluted to such a degree that only three beaches on Costa del Sol were considered clean enough for the Blue Flag status in 1989 (*Sunday Times* 28 May 1989).

The results of environmental deterioration on the coasts of Spain contributed significantly to the slump in tourist receipts in the late 1980s (*Der Spiegel* 1990, 23: 236–237). The situation requires drastic measures against overdevelopment, especially against building without proper permits. It seems, however, that even the enactment of the Coastal Law in 1988 is only a small step in the proper direction. Spanish authorities are reluctant to enforce the law consistently because they are concerned it will jeopardize the flow of tourism development capital from Britain, Germany and the Netherlands (*New York Times* 21 August 1989).

In France the Cote d'Azur (French Riviera) is the most overdeveloped and overcrowded area. Nice, the second busiest airport in France after the Charles de Gaulle airport in Paris, served about five million passengers in the late 1980s and expects ten million in the year 2000 (*Sunday Times* 22 July 1990). Things have deteriorated so much it seems that the most prominent blue in Nice is the blue haze from the traffic jams. The questionable response strategy to overcrowding is, unfortunately, to build more freeways and more facilities, thus creating an unending spiral of overdevelopment. Finally, there is no place left to build on. Land speculation has been so rampant that by the 1970s land prices skyrocketed to unbelievable levels (*Der Spiegel* 1978, 24: 178), giving rise to an ironic suggestion to substitute the name Cote d'Azur with Cote d'Usure (Usury). Discriminating tourists, frustrated with lack of space at the coast, have been moving inland followed, of course, by the developers (Vadrot 1977: 85). According to *Le Monde,* "in the hinterland the struggle goes on for each square meter of land" (quoted in *Der Spiegel* 1978 24:178). This contributes to the degradation of environment, such as the deforestation of hills and mountains of southern France.

The most destructive form of tourism degradation of the environment is the construction of accommodations, including hotels and especially second homes. The latter constitute 80 percent of new capacities built. In fact, hotel capacities in the Alpes-Maritimes of southern France have decreased due to the expansion of alternative forms of accommodation, such as campgrounds and second homes mushrooming everywhere. Their growth is a classic example of the overcrowding and the resulting environmental devastation on the French Riviera. As indicated in section 4.3, the campgrounds in this region went through a period of astonishing development, covering large expanses of valuable recreational land. However, this is only part of the story. The campgrounds are so overcrowded that the land can no longer absorb the pressures for additional accommodation. Vadrot (1977: 87-90) is especially concerned about the state of hygiene, pointing out inadequate sewage treatment capacities, and consequently about the health of the five million campers in this area. As a result of overcrowding during the peak season some tourists resort to illegal practices, such as *le camping sauvage* (wild camping), sleeping anywhere, including urban areas, national parks, and nature reserves. This leads to increased environmental degradation.

The third Mediterranean country that suffers from overdevelopment of coastal tourism is Italy. A good example of an overcrowded destination is the tiny island of Capri in the Bay of Naples, with three million tourists per year and only 12,000 permanent residents. The Italian beaches are also overcrowded: the worst is the coast of the Adriatic Sea, patronized for many years by cheap mass tourism from Germany. Tourists have reacted to the environmental deterioration here by seeking alternative destinations, although, because of the distance, more expensive. However, other Italian coastal areas are not immune from the onslaught of mass tourism either. In the 1960s the Moslem prince Aga Khan, the religious leader of over 20 million Ismaelis, developed the virgin coast of northern Sardinia as an exclusive leisure refuge for the rich, under the name of Costa Smeralda. The environmental impact of this development was rather limited, but the scale of accommodation facilities proved not enough for the prince. In the early 1970s he came forward with a project for mass tourism development of hotels and condos with a total capacity of 50,000 beds. In the early 1980s, after many years of negotiations, the local authorities yielded to the pressure and gave the green light for the project, which was completed several years ago.

As mentioned in section 4.3, there is one particularly threatening aspect of tourism development in Western Europe, where lack of space appears to be an especially acute problem, caused by the desire to own a vacation home (often called a second home or summer cottage), or at least a condo apartment. In fact, second home ownership in western Europe stands at about ten percent of all households, and in Sweden, Norway and France it surpasses 20 percent (WTO/UNEP 1983: 69). The environmental drawbacks of these forms of tourism accommodation were discussed in section 4. 3. Because of the EC arrangements, there are no legal or organizational problems for northern Europeans to buy or construct second homes in the southern part of Europe, including the Alps and the Massif Centrale in France; they are doing this on a mass scale. This building frenzy has caused consumption of natural landscape by cottages, villas, condominiums, shopping malls, restaurants, roads, car parks, and cable cars. Tourism development extends both horizontally and vertically, reaching even the highest Alpine peaks, such as in the Zugspitze in Germany. The environmental impacts are predictable: suburbanization of large areas on this relatively small and overpopulated continent, despoliation of the natural beauty of the landscape, overloading of the infrastructure, erosion and siltation caused by the destruction of the protective vegetation cover, septic tank seepage, eutrophication resulting from lawn fertilizer runoff—these are only some of the problems that plague the area. Another manifestation of the overcrowding caused by the proliferation of the second homes in Western Europe is the phenomenon of "Black Saturdays," when the roads are hopelessly jammed by increased traffic.

It is also no surprise that in the deteriorating environmental conditions of Western Europe, the number of critics of tourism is growing. Groups, environmental organizations, and individuals, such as the cultural historian John Julius Norwich (*The Independent on Sunday* 5 August 1990), want to eliminate at least some parts of tourism. The Orthodox Church of Greece is on record as being hostile to tourism, as shown by its prayer: "Lord Jesus, have mercy on the cities, the islands and the villages of the Orthodox Fatherland...scourged by the worldly touristic wave" (*ibid.*). Indeed, tourism is accused by many religious leaders, writers, philosophers and artists as the universal source of environmental deterioration. Very often the blame is ascribed not only in the sensationalist press but also in scholarly publications. For instance, Van Harsel (1982: 24) writes: "...the biggest environmental casualty has been the Mediterranean Sea, steadily deteriorating, largely as a result of overdevelopment of the coast for tourist purposes."

It is impossible to deny that tourism negatively affects not only the natural but also the sociocultural environment of Western Europe (Grenon and Batise 1989). Having said this, one has to reiterate the thesis of chapter 2 that tourism is not the main culprit: the finger must be pointed at external, i.e., non- tourism-related factors. I am more optimistic with respect to future development: the law of diminishing returns will compel the decision-makers to react when they have failed to proact. Tourists, when deciding on a particular destination, usually act on recommendations of the tourist industry selling the services. Once at the destination, if they find quality below their expectations, they cannot change, especially when the vacation had been prepaid. Because tourist populations change so rapidly, enforcing environmental standards by withdrawal of demand is difficult. However, the tourist market is captive to the travel agents, airlines, and tour operators only in the short run. The economic clout of demand, especially in the modern age of communication, is increasing. Tourists are becoming more sophisticated and informed, and increasingly perceptive to environmental problems at the destination. Thomas Hofels (1991: 13) supports this statement with relevant statistics. International tourists visiting several European countries were asked the following question: "Were you aware of environmental problems during your last vacation in...? The results were as follows:

Yes (%)	*1985*	*1989*
Germany	27%	51%
France	39%	63%
Italy	30%	64%
Switzerland	16%	56%
Spain	32%	65%

As a result of this increasing environmental susceptibility, dissatisfied tourists are withdrawing their demand. This is especially true if their perceived benefit from a vacation falls below their costs, is too crowded, or is marked by environmental degradation. Many destinations with tarnished reputations for overcrowding or other environmental damage are driving tourists away. The Adriatic coast in Italy and the Spanish beaches on the Mediterranean are abandoning sun-seeking European tourists for the more distant beaches of Turkey, Israel, Egypt, Jordan, Seychelles, Mauritius, Maldives, and the Caribbean. Those who cannot afford higher transportation costs turn to domestic destinations.

These trends have been fully confirmed by research, conducted as early as the 1970s (OECD 1980: 56ff). All southern European OECD member countries were investigated in this project, and the research findings established, in a number of concrete case studies, the positive causal correlation between environmental degradation, and declining numbers of tourists (and/or the changing composition of tourists). These early findings were also supported by French research (Vadrot 1977: 84). The results of research conducted in the

1980s fully confirm the investigations of the 1970s. Thomas Hofels (1991: 13) presents statistical data demonstrating that between 1988 and 1990, well before the onset of the economic recession in Europe, the traditional Mediterranean tourism destinations of Italy lost nine percent of tourists and 33 percent of revenues. The corresponding figures for Spain were 14 and 12 percent.

The deterioration of the environment in Western Europe causes not only the numbers of tourists to drop but also affects the quality of the market: affluent tourists drop off first and are replaced by mass tourism looking for bargains, and younger vacationers of modest means. As a result of the change in the composition of the visitors there may be a decline in the receipts, even if the absolute numbers of tourists stay the same or increase, i.e., spending per tourist declines, even if numbers of tourists remain the same. Such a situation exists, according to research findings, in a number of coastal destinations in the Mediterranean, leading to further degradation and urbanization of beach resorts (Smith, R. 1992; Butler 1980).

4.9 *Spatial Intensity: Tourism Overdevelopment in North America*

In comparison with overpopulated Western Europe, the problems of tourism overdevelopment in North America are less acute. High density tourism is intense only in certain relatively small areas, such as parts of Hawaii, California, the Rocky Mountains, the Appalachians, Florida, and some sections of the Atlantic Seaboard as at Hilton Head, South Carolina. With the exception of some problem spots the general situation seems to be satisfactory. A highly developed national park system is owned, planned, and managed by the federal governments of the United States and Canada. The main mandates adhere to the preservation of natural ecosystems. Tourism overdevelopment within the parks is an exception. Examples of such unwelcome intrusions within the Canadian national parks such infamous townsites at Banff or Jasper. These townsites are equipped with modern facilities and amenities, including golf courses. The most publicized example of overdevelopment and overcrowding in U.S. national parks is Yosemite Valley, with 2.6 million annual visitors (MacCannel 1992: 116; Dilsaver 1992).

Overdevelopment of Oahu, the most important island of Hawaii, has been discussed for the last 30 years (Gunn 1987: 230). The density of development in the Waikiki area of Honolulu certainly surpasses that of many metropolitan central business districts (CBDs). Looking out from their skyscraper windows tourists can rarely see picturesque Diamond Head: they end up contemplating another concrete skyscraper. In more recent years the development frenzy has spread to the outer islands, among them to the most fragile and youngest geologically, the Island of Hawaii. Here, tourism development plans run into stiff opposition from the local population. The bone of contention is the continued expansion of hotels at the Koala coast. The perennial question of "how much tourism is too much?" is argued without end. Do the economic benefits justify overdevelopment, high density tourism, congestion and other environmental problems?

Another area threatened by overdevelopment is the Napa Valley, north of San Francisco, California. The valley is a classic example of the precarious symbiosis between agriculture, mainly vineyards, and tourism—25 million visitors spend $160 million annually (*New York Times* 30 May 1988). In recent years there is the increasing concern that tourism is growing out of environmentally desirable proportion. On November 6, 1990 the plan to construct a four-lane highway into the Napa Valley was suspended until the year 2020 due to pressure from citizens concerned with the prospects of an inevitable overdevelopment of the fragile valley.

Not far from the Napa Valley lies Lake Tahoe, shared by California and Nevada, with an area of nearly 500 square kilometers and the maximum depth of 500 meters. Lake Tahoe is considered a natural wonder, a miniature of the jewel of Siberia, Lake Baykal, because of its unique environmental features, such as crystal-clear water. This lake was the battlefield between developers and conservationists for at least 30 years. The shores of the lake have been overdeveloped well beyond its saturation point by second homes, hotels, condominiums, and gambling casinos (on the Nevada side).

The Coachella Valley, part of the Colorado Desert of southern California, was little developed until recently. The wealthy took refuge in the sleepy desert heaven of Palm Springs. This idyllic picture belongs to the past since high-density development has taken over: the valley's population nearly doubled between 1970 and the mid-1980s from 88,000 to 170,000 (*Time* 13 January 1986). Most residents are leisure inhabitants, including retirees. Golfing is their primary recreational pursuit, and the 58 golf courses are voracious consumers of water, contributing, along with the recreational habitation, to a significant drop of the water table.

The Rocky Mountains are in incomparably better shape environmentally than the Alps. The problems of tourism overdevelopment pertain only to certain areas rather than the totality of the mountain environment. Nevertheless, there are local concerns, such as in the famous ski resort of Vail, Colorado. Price (1981: 434) is worried that after 1960, the overdevelopment of Vail has reached the critical stage and complains that:

> Vail, along with its sprawling suburbs in neighboring valleys, is a boom town with an annual growth rate of about 20 percent in skier visits, population, retail sales, vehicle registration, and real-estate values. Unfortunately, the quality of life is not increasing concurrently; Vail's problems have grown in proportion to its population. Crowding, traffic jams, smog, poorly planned developments, visual pollution, strain on county budgets, loss of small-town intimacy, and run-away inflation have taken their toll.

Naturally, some of the developers withdraw after selling the facilities they have built, at exorbitant profits. This explains their lack of environmental concern.

However, in the North American context, there are effective mechanisms in place for coping with problems of tourism overdevelopment: environmentalists, scientists, non-government organizations (NGOs) and, above all, the local people (see section 2.3). These environmental watchdogs have been at work. They have managed to check further development and mollify environmental impacts by introducing such measures as the banning of wood- burning in fireplaces and stoves during the winter. This was to curb toxic pollution (C0, $C0_2$, particulate matter), especially nasty during thermal inversions. Additionally, public pressure thwarted the development of a large ski resort on 1,200 hectares at Beaver Creek near Vail (*ibid.* 435). Similar public resistance was successful in blocking the huge ski development project in the Lake Louise area in the Canadian Rockies as one of the prospective sites for the 1984 Calgary Winter Olympics. More recently, such groups are fighting the increasing number of exemptions from environmental impact assessment granted to new ski developments in the southern part of the Canadian Rockies.

Finally, the point must be made that overdevelopment of Florida, [both external (non-tourist) and internal (tourist)] lies at the root of the environmental problems of that state. The tourist impact on Florida's wetland ecosystems will be discussed in chapter 6. But the sheer quantitative scale of the problem has caused the following cycle: drainage of marshes and swamps; drop in the water table; desiccation; damage to agriculture; to flora and fauna; and finally, harm to tourism.

4.10 *Spatial Intensity: Tourism Overdevelopment in the LDCs*

Environmental deterioration due to growing spatial intensity of expanding tourism is especially dangerous for the LDCs. They are more vulnerable to tourism's impacts than the DCs because of the almost-total absence of environmental pressure groups and/or organizations, and because of the inadequacies of environmental laws and their enforcement. Additionally, the level of eco-conscience in the LDCs is still lower than in the DCs. Therefore, government officials, preoccupied with the economic problems, are less responsive to environmental concerns than those in the DCs. Tourism and recreation in the LDCs is also developing at a more rapid pace than the eco-consciousness of individuals.

All these factors result in tourism overdevelopment and associated environmental problems. Generally speaking, overdevelopment has not attained the same mass proportions as in the DCs, and especially Western Europe. However, there are some destinations in the Third World which resemble the worst examples of the Mediterranean Basin. For the time being the affected areas are rather small and the impacts localized, as in some Caribbean beach resorts and in Pattaya, Thailand; or linearly as in the case of unplanned clutter of ribbon development on Kenya's coast (Dieke 1991: 277) and on some trekking trails in Nepal. Similarly to the Adriatic resorts, Pattaya suffers from shrinking demand as a result of overcrowding and sewage pollution, associated with multiple cases of morbidity and even mortality among tourists. There were reports that "many tourists died" (*Economist* 6 July 1991).

In some places different policies are followed in close proximity and this facilitates the comparison of their effectiveness: the Dutch part of St. Maarten Island in the Caribbean is a classic example of uncontrolled and unplanned development of tourism—it is characterized by all the attendant environmental deterioration. In contrast, St. Martin, the French part of the same tiny island, provides an example of tidy, controlled growth catering mainly to upscale tourism. In this case, neither the local environmentalists nor the NGOs deserve the credit, but rather, the centralized French government does.

4.11 *The Impact of Tourism on the Physical Aspects of Cultural Monuments*

Tourism overdevelopment affects not only the natural but the cultural environment. Because the cultural impact of tourism is beyond the focus of this book, this section will deal exclusively with the physical impact of mass tourism on the cultural treasures of humanity. Vandalism as a form of deliberate destructive behavior was discussed in section 4.7. However, not all actions of tourists are deliberate. In most cases the damage is not intentional and results from simple "wear and tear," caused by mass visitation, accidents resulting from limited space in crowded conditions, and also lack of knowledge and experience (characteristic for children who constitute the most destructive segment among tourists). Carelessness, and most importantly sheer numbers of tourists, inflict considerable physical damage, not only to the natural environment, but also to the cultural monuments of the past.

I will start with the prehistorical cultural monuments, such as the "Quaternary Sistine Chapels." These 17,000-year old paintings of extinct animals were discovered in the Altamira cave in Northern Spain in 1879. More were found in the Lascaux cave in the Dordogne River valley in southern France in 1942. These two sites have been visited by thousands of tourists. However, scientists have found that the perspiration and breath of people in the caves results in a change of their microclimate, particularly in the increase of carbon dioxide, temperature and humidity. Additionally, artificial lights, installed to illuminate the interior of the caves, create favorable conditions for the growth of not only green plants, such as mosses and algae (Edington and Edington 1986: 84), but also of bacteria. As a result, the quality of the paintings deteriorated.

The response strategies were entirely different in each of the two cases. The Altamira is still open, allowing only 15 tourists a day; and the waiting list is full years ahead. The Lascaux cave allows only five scholars daily; they require a special permit and have to go through a disinfection chamber before entering the cave. Their visits are limited to 20 minutes, and they are not allowed to speak while inside. However, the public may enjoy the splendors of the cave by visiting an exact replica called "Lascaux Two," which was constructed over ten years and opened to the public in 1983. "Lascaux Two" admits about 2,000 tourists a day in groups of 35 to 40. Tours are tightly scheduled to achieve its maximum capacity.

Tourists' breathing has also affected the paintings inside the Egyptian pyramids and the murals of the royal tombs in the Valley of the Kings near Luxor in upper (southern) Egypt. Mold, bacteria, algae, and fungi are the result, as they were in Altamira and Lascaux. Similar effects have occurred in the tomb of Tutankhamun. The frescoes have deteriorated to such an extent that the tomb has been closed to the public. The tomb of Nefertari, the wife of Pharaoh Ramses II, located in the nearby Valley of Queens, has remained closed since 1940 for the same reasons, but was reopened after four years of renovations in May 1992 for visits limited to scientists, scholars and dignitaries. In 1990 cracks were found in the interior of the Cheops Pyramid. Scientists attribute them to the accumulation of moisture from the breath of tourists. Even the interior of the seventeenth century Taj Mahal mausoleum suffers from thousands of visitors. In this case, a local flavor has been added by the heavily-scented talcum powders worn by Indian tourists.

Much more turbulent is the story of Stonehenge, the assemblage of monoliths arranged in five concentric circles in about 2,800 B.C. on England's Salisbury Plain, about 120 kilometers west of London. The monument has deteriorated, not only because of the one million annual visitors, who touch the stones and trample the soil, but also because the modern-age Druids hold their summer solstice celebrations each 21 June. The site attracts various groups wanting to hold their rock festivals there. The authorities do their best to keep the intruders away, but still bloody clashes between the police and hippies occurred in June 1985. The impact of tourists on Stonehenge has been so destructive that the monoliths may tumble; there is also evidence of physical damage to the monument inflicted by souvenir hunters chipping off stones. As a result, Stonehenge is now surrounded by barbed wire, and tourists are not allowed to wander inside the circles. For similar reasons, tourists are not allowed to stroll and to climb the mysterious menhirs of Carnac in western France, some of them 50,000 years old.

The cases of Stonehenge and the menhirs indicate that destruction to such monuments may indirectly affect their chances of survival. If located outdoors, the destruction of the surrounding vegetation is likely to cause problems because the feet of the tourists and their vehicles stir up dust. This particulate matter, after becoming airborne, settles on the art objects with predictable results. Such a situation may occur on the Lena River pictographs south of Yakutsk, Siberia. Rarely visited today, this valuable site may be destroyed by an anticipated increase of visitations. Gale and Jacobs (1987: 13) point out that the devegetation of the surroundings of Uluru (formerly Ayer's Rock) in central Australia is a particular problem affecting aboriginal paintings and engravings because of the fragility and slow rates of regeneration of the vegetation cover.

Even the famous cathedrals of Europe are not immune from the physical damage of mass visitation of millions of well-behaved tourists. Indeed, the damage is so considerable that somebody made a suggestion to build a "Notre Dame Cathedral Two" and close the original in order to save it from the ten million annual visitors. In addition to condensation on paintings, sculptures and stained glass windows, there are problems of wear and tear of the marble and granite floors caused by millions of tourists' shoes, and the salt and dirt. For example, St. Paul's Cathedral in London, England has introduced an entrance fee, spending $150,000 to repair its marble floor (*Time* 22 July 1991). Entrance fees to pay for restoration projects are now becoming common. Another strategy to minimize interior damage by visitors is the installment of state-of-the-art climate-control systems, feasible in museums and smaller buildings, like the Sistine Chapel in Rome, but not practical in large cathedrals.

The principal cause of exterior damage to famous churches and other monuments of the past, is industrial, communal, and traffic pollution that has little to do with tourism. However, tourist buses idling in front of such treasures should take part of the blame. To save the monuments of the past, costly renovations are undertaken, such as the present $200 million renovation of Notre Dame Cathedral in Paris.

Physical damage inflicted by thousands of visitors is by no means limited to sacral structures. Relatively small secular buildings of historical value, protected as National Historic Sites (Canada) or within National Historic Parks (USA) also suffer from strain of overuse. For instance, the sheer volume of traffic constitutes a serious physical danger for the former family house of Sir John A. MacDonald in Kingston, Ontario; today it is a historical museum, visited by up to 200,000 people annually. These places were not built for such a volume of visitation.

Physical harm perpetrated on the monuments of the past may sometimes take bizarre forms, such as the damage to the Trevi Fountain in Rome caused by tourists throwing coins into the fountain. The impact of the coins is chipping the marble. Nevertheless, there are no plans to ban the tradition because of the commercial value of repeat tourism: tourists believe that dropping a coin into the fountain ensures a return to Rome.

Another vexing issue is that of graffiti on the monuments of the past. Some tourist attractions are especially vulnerable to this form of vandalism (see section 4.7 above), e.g., the ancient aboriginal paintings and engravings on rocks in Australia. The problem is that these places are easily accessible at any time, because they are located in unsupervised caves or on open rock surfaces. However, one can find graffiti in almost any place, even the least expected. The summit of the Cheops Pyramid in Egypt is not easily accessible, but when I climbed the pyramid in November 1975, I found graffiti covering the entire top flat platform. There was virtually no space for another vandal to place his or her name.

The problem of tourists' graffiti on the monuments of the past has become so drastic in some places that it forced authorities, responsible for these cultural treasures, into action: posters entitled "Behavior Best Avoided" were plastered all over Venice, graffiti artists were threatened with a short jail sentence and a $240 penalty. However, such posters, warnings, prohibition signs, advisory signs are themselves a form of visual pollution, and thus desecrate the sites. The harm of graffiti may be removed by professional intervention; yet, unfortunately, amateur do-gooders often add insult to injury. In March 1992 the press reported the destruction of two 15,000-year-old paintings of bisons in the grotto of Mayrieres, located in the valley of the River Tarn in southwestern France. The culprits were a group of Boy Scouts cleaning the graffiti from the cave walls with steel brushes. This revelation was followed by similar reports from Mexico, where Olmec drawings, 1,000 to 1,500 years old disappeared from the walls of a cave (*New York Times* 21 April 1992).

Physical damage can be inflicted on cultural treasures merely by touching. There is a wide spectrum of destructive touches, by tourists and by tour guides who use their hands or pointers to demonstrate details of interest. Though touching may be purely accidental resulting from overcrowding of the site, it in most instances is deliberate. For instance, tourists touch smooth surfaces of marbles in the museums; the grease on their hands causes the marbles to blacken. In the case of aboriginal rock paintings and engravings in Australia, Gale and Jacobs (1987: 14) suggest that, "visitors feel the need to verify the permanency of the painted image by touching it to test if it will come off. Some visitors even go so far as to pick at the paint. Clearly, touching is an important step in the visitor accepting that the painted image is permanent and therefore of considerable age." The most likely to do the touching are children (*ibid.* 48). The same authors present interesting research results with respect to the likelihood of various items being touched (*ibid.* 48-49).

However, not all touching results from curiosity. Sometimes it may be associated with expression of reverence and appreciation. Gale and Jacobs illustrate this point by quoting a poem expressing deep emotions with respect to the great monuments of the Australian aboriginal rock art. Such fragments of the poem as, "I trace the shape with a pensive finger," "I place my hand on yours," or "Hands touch in greeting" show that even emotional attachment may inadvertently jeopardize the revered items.

There is still another form of touching discussed by Gale and Jacobs (*ibid.* 11–12). Tourist photographers apply a sort of "make-up" of foreign materials to the surfaces to improve the quality of rock art photographs. Gale and Jacobs describe various techniques used to enhance the motifs, and regret that, "many of these applications penetrated the rock surface and have proved very difficult to remove without damaging the art." In some cases the photographers remove the patina from engravings to expose lighter surfaces for more distinct pictures. To do this they scratch the engravings with rocks, thus disfiguring them. Fortunately, these practices have been discontinued; students of art and professional photographers increasingly apply modern techniques, such as stereo photography to enhance images. They also take pictures of engravings when "the site is in early or late light when longer shadows enhance the engraved impression." The remaining threat are the amateurs who, unsupervised, use destructive methods to improve the quality of their pictures.

Chapter 5

The Negative Impacts of Tourism and Recreation on Elements of the Environmental System

5.1 *Introduction*

Following the general discussion of parameters, agents and factors of tourism, and the impact of overdevelopment of mass tourism in chapter 4, chapters 5 and 6 approach the issues of negative ecological effects of tourism from two points of view. The first approach is analytical or disintegrative, i.e., it deals with the impacts on separate elements of the environment, such as air, geology, soils, water, vegetation, and wildlife. The second approach is systemic or integrative, i.e., it examines the impact of tourism on the holistic communities of biotic and abiotic components, i.e., on coastal, inland, mountain, and polar ecosystems (Fig. 5.1). In section 6.1, I argue that the most appropriate is the second approach because it reflects the reality: a multitude of factors inseparably linked within the web of interdependence; and that the impact on one component of the environment acts synenergetically, and often cumulatively on other components. While it appears that one should not treat environmental elements in isolation as disaggregated factors, there are some merits in terms of convenience, in the analytical method. Focusing on disaggregated environmental elements leads to specific insights into the mechanism of the impacts, and solutions to problems. Therefore, for analytical and pragmatic reasons, this chapter is devoted to the examination of tourism impacts on separate elements of the ecosystems. These elements are called *conditionally renewable resources,* and include air, land, water, plants and animals (Ekins, *et al.* 1992: 64).

This chapter may be divided into two parts; the first part focuses on the impact of tourism and recreation on abiotic environmental elements (sections 5.2–5.6); in the second part (sections 5.7 and 5.8) the effects on biotic elements are discussed. The emphasis is on wildlife (section 5.8) because it is considered the most important biotic tourism resource, and because the issues associated with both consumptive and nonconsumptive use of wildlife are more controversial than the other environmental impacts.

Figure 5.1
EXAMINATION OF THE ENVIRONMENTAL IMPACT OF TOURISM

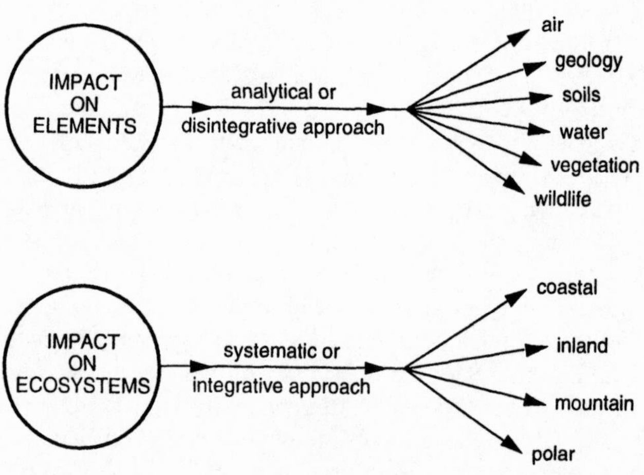

5.2 *Air Quality*

Generally, the hospitality sector, i.e., hotels and restaurants, are not major contributors to air pollution, nor are they profligate in their use of energy resources, at least in comparison with other human economic activities and habitation (see section 2.10). But sometimes tourism-related air pollution may be more critical locally, e.g., in mountain resorts where high-sulphur fossil fuel is used for heating (El Samra 1984: 9), and in isolated tourist resorts, where electricity is generated by diesel-powered plants (notorious as pollution sources). The quantitative and qualitative aspects of tourism's air pollution are determined by the level of government legislation and control, as well as the goodwill of owners and operators, acting in their best self-interest. One could generalize that the negative impacts in this respect are smaller than the impacts of comparative human habitation developments, and especially of urban developments. Secondly, these impacts, as a rule, do not extend beyond the local scale.

The problem of air pollution from tourism acquires different dimensions when one considers tourist transportation, especially the movement of millions of tourists from origins to destinations by private automobile. This is the least efficient and most wasteful mode of transportation in terms of energy utilization, and as a whole, the most polluting agent in the tourist system. Harmful emissions result mainly from inefficient fuel combustion. The automobile industry is gradually introducing more fuel-efficient, less polluting cars. In recent years, special attention has been paid to the phase-out of leaded gasoline which is now almost complete in the DCs, but only in the incipient stage in the LDCs.

It is difficult to determine exactly the extent of tourism and recreation's contribution to air pollution (Mathieson and Wall 1982: 104–105), however, one can assume that it is considerable, because in most DCs the majority of tourists use private automobile as the main means of transportation, e.g., more than 50 percent of international tourist arrivals in Spain, France, and Italy occurs by road. The figure for Yugoslavia was 86 percent (Grenon and Batise 1987: 157). The use of the automobile for tourism and recreation is even more common in North America (Mieczkowski, Z. 1990: 107- 114).

The most threatening form of automobile-caused air pollution is photochemical smog, i.e., elevated levels of photochemical oxidants (including ground-level ozone) in the atmosphere. Smog, mentioned in section 2.10, is mainly formed by reaction of sunlight on two classes of chemicals: volatile organic compounds (VOCs) in gasoline, and nitrogen oxides, which are created when nitrogen and oxygen combine in the intense heat of an engine. Nitrogen oxides and VOCs react in the sunlight to form lung-damaging surface ozone. The most obvious impacts of smog is reduced visibility, eye irritation, and damage to plants. Additionally, automobile engine emissions, some of them toxic, contribute significantly to acid rain, to the thinning of the protective ozone layer in the stratosphere, and, if the theory is valid, to global warming. Air masses poisoned with low-level ozone, acid rain, and other pollutants are not limited by any boundaries; they can move everywhere on the globe. They are the key factors in the "death of forests," or *Waldsterben* (see section 2.8), and affect lakes by acidification. Locally, especially in congested resorts notorious for their traffic jams, polluted air affects vegetation and causes respiratory discomfort to people.

With respect to automobiles, the same rule is valid for both tourist and nontourist movement: the private car is, from the point of view of environmental protection and economics, inferior to public transportation. Research shows that the average emission of pollutants per passenger using private vehicles is ten times higher than that of passengers using public transportation (Turner, *et al.* 1990: 584). However, tourists are reluctant to use public transportation. For instance, Mäder (1988: 100) refers to findings from a Swiss survey on a specific auto route, where 90 percent of tourists used private cars despite the fact that public transportation was readily available. Apparently, like commuters, tourists prefer the flexibility of the private car to the rigidity of public transportation (Mieczkowski, Z. 1990: 107-114); for the relevant developments in former communist countries, see Mieczkowski, B. 1978, 1980 and 1980a).

Compared with the private car, other forms of tourist transportation exert only a relatively minor impact on air quality. Nevertheless, the level of air pollution caused by outboard engines had been underestimated until recently, when research results were published estimating that one powerboat emits 70 times more hydrocarbons than does an average car (*Environment* 1993 35:10, 23). Cruise ships pollute the air only on the local level. Thus, for example, the cruise ships off the coast of the Alaska panhandle "are pumping dense amounts of smoke and obscuring views" (*New York Times* 22 December 1991). The smoke problem is most severe in Juneau, Sitka, and Glacier Bay. The topography of these places, enclosed by coastal mountains, occasionally causes thermal inversions, trapping the polluted air under a layer of warmer air. The incidence of the inversions is highest in summer, during the cruise season. During the summer of 1991, 12 out of 17 cruise ships monitored violated the smoke emission standards that prohibit ship smoke emissions obscuring more than 20 percent of background scenery (*ibid.*). The state authorities, under increasing pressure from local residents, threaten future perpetrators with fines or denial of docking privileges.

Research data is sparse on the polluting effects of air transportation. We know that traffic is steadily growing, but increased capacities of planes and improved standards of fuel efficiency and emission controls have decreased the air pollution per passenger- kilometer flown. The new Boeing 767 is especially efficient in this respect. Nevertheless, more research is needed because air pollution caused by airliners is highly concentrated over North America, Europe, and the North Atlantic route, and also because the jets burn most of their fuel in the turbulence-free lower stratosphere, where pollution may affect the ozone layer. Reduced flight altitudes would increase fuel consumption and costs.

5.3 *Noise Pollution*

There is an aspect of the behavior of tourists which deserves a separate treatment, namely noise pollution. What sets this impact of tourism apart from other effects, is its lack of relative permanency: noise is strictly limited in time, even if its effects on people and the environment are less transient. In fact, most tourists want to escape the high decibels of their workplace and the city, and while recreating, avoid noise as much as possible (rock music lovers being a notable exception). Looking for quiet relaxation may be regarded as simple common sense, but there are negative health effects associated with prolonged exposure to noise, such as sleeplessness, hypertension, cardiovascular diseases, hearing loss, irritability, aggressiveness, and fatigue (El Samra 1984: 10, Legro 1993). Although these are the long-term health impacts of exposure to noise, there is no question that it may be a major stressor to recreationists.

Noise, which may be defined as unacceptable volume (decibel level) and quality (frequency, pattern, purpose, reverberation, and penetration of sound), is as old as humanity. There are negative references to it in ancient Babylonian and Egyptian documents. In about 400 B.C., Hippocrates recognized the harmful effects of noise on the sick. In ancient Rome, traffic limitations were enforced to limit noise. The problem is still with us; not only does noise pollution causes a temporary negative environmental impact, but its effects can also be long-lasting.

The spectrum of noise pollution in recreational settings is wide. It includes such disparate phenomena as screaming in public places; shouting and loud music at campgrounds; air, motorcycle, jet-scooter and motorboat traffic noises, and loud music in restaurants and discos. Construction noises also disturb recreationists. Noise pollution often overlaps with rowdyism, or even vandalism (see section 4.7 above). It is now relatively easy to obtain precise decibel measurements of the exact magnitude of sound by modern instruments (Jones and Barbott 1977). These measures have served as firm guidelines for setting transportation noise standards in nonrecreational settings, e.g., in urban areas or near airports (Nielsen 1989).

However, in the case of extra-urban recreation, the situation is more complex: despite the usefulness of quantitative measurements in decibels, they are valuable only as an auxiliary research tool. Thus, Herbert Kariel (1990: 145) compiled a list of measurements, that indicates the decibel range of noise levels of various sound sources in outdoor recreational environments and at various distances. Nevertheless, a measure of the magnitude of sound, i.e., its loudness, is not necessarily an appropriate predictor of its degree of annoyance. Indeed, noise pollution is linked to more subjective value judgments, with different expectations from tourists than from people at work or in the home.

To resolve this problem, researchers use the Outdoor Recreation Opportunity Spectrum (OROS), a standard similar to the Continuum of Environmental Modification (Mieczkowski, Z. 1990: 258, 263, 265, 281). It is based on participants who have different expectations of what is acceptable (Harrison, Clark, and Stankey 1980). Individual judgments, as to the appropriateness or acceptability of certain sounds, do not deviate much from the standards assumed for the different recreation settings of the OROS. The authors propose such standards of acceptable loudness for mechanical (mainly motors), and nonmechanical (primarily human sound sources) in various recreation settings. Thus, using the OROS model, the noise emanating from a motor vehicle or a chainsaw is considered acceptable at a developed campground but absolutely not acceptable in the wilderness. Thus, what is acceptable and appropriate in one setting may be considered a major annoyance elsewhere along the OROS continuum.

To determine the degree of annoyance for certain groups of recreationists, researchers investigated their perceptions of sound: Kariel (1990) measured the reaction of recreationists to sound by attitude surveys. He found statistically significant differences in the perception of sound between tourists staying at highway-oriented campgrounds and mountaineers at a mountaineering camp. The mountaineers were more susceptible than the campers. In addition to these valid observations, the tourists' perceptions about noise vary according to both time of the day and the duration of the noise: noise bothers them more in the evening (especially during the night) than in the daytime; the longer the noise lasts the higher the degree of annoyance. These observations have been confirmed by tourists who have visited certain Islamic countries, where loudspeakers call the faithful to prayers five times a day—the call shortly before daybreak often wakes tourists up. Sometimes the effects of the same noise may have diametrically different impacts in various situations: Kariel makes the interesting observation that in certain circumstances essentially bothersome noises may become very pleasant sounds indeed, e.g., "the sound of a snowmobile or a helicopter when it signifies that rescue is on the way" (*ibid.* 148).

These arguments support the hypothesis that the physical, quantitative aspects of sound are filtered through subjective social and psychological variables, which classify them as pleasing, annoying, or acceptable (Kariel 1990; Harrison, Clark and Stankey 1990; Driver, Nash and Haas 1987; Legro 1993). Medical research has also discovered that, "women are more sensitive than men to sound–they tend to become irritated by sounds at half the volume than men are" (Legro 1993: 120).

In tourism and recreation there is increasing concern about noise pollution on the part of the governments and the public. Most complaints pertain to air traffic (to a large extent associated with tourism). Therefore, the noise pollution caused by aircraft engines may be classified as an agent of a negative environmental impact of tourism. The primary source is the noise caused by airplanes taking off and landing, especially at large metropolitan airports, such as those in New York City and Los Angeles.

The situation has been gradually improving with the introduction of quieter new planes, such as the Boeing 757, Boeing 767, MD-11, and Airbus A310, the so-called "Stage 3" planes. Noisier planes, classified "Stage 2" planes, such as the Boeings 707 and 727, McDonnell Douglas DC-8 and DC-9, and the early versions of the 737 and 747, are slowly being phased out. Until then, they must be retrofitted with quieter engines or hush kits (*Tourism Intelligence Bulletin*, October 1991).

The International Civil Aviation Organization (ICAO) sets noise standards for airline planes. In 1990 it adopted a resolution urging all countries to phase-out the second generation planes by 1 April, 2002 (Wheatcroft 1991: 120). It appears that the deadline will be met. In the United States and Canada, both federal and local authorities want to accelerate this process in order to solve the problem of noise pollution in airports, by the year 2000. Endeavors to impose and enforce stricter government regulations (such as the Airport Noise and Capacity Act, passed in the U.S. in 1990) encounter some resistance from airlines concerned that their profitability levels may suffer. Some could experience economic hardships if the Stage 2 planes, with many useful years ahead, are withdrawn more quickly as a result of tougher phase-out deadlines. Whatever the final outcome, these new developments are positive, not only because the new engines are quieter, but because they are also more fuel-efficient. This is a powerful incentive for airlines to switch completely to Stage 3 planes. There is an urgent need for agreement on a single international standard for quantifying aircraft noise (Smith, M. 1991).

A second type of noise pollution associated with aircraft is that of sightseeing flights conducted over beauty areas of North America (such as national parks), by fixed-wing airplanes and helicopters. According to the United States National Transportation Safety Board, an estimated two million people took tours in airplanes in 1992, most of them in Hawaii and the
Grand Canyon area (Molotsky 1993). Sightseeing flights are common in many national parks of the United States and Canada. Although their negative effects were long ignored, complaints about their noise mounted during the second part of 1980s. The bad

situation in the Grand Canyon National Park drew vehement complaints, and environmentalists argued that flights over the park should be totally banned. The owners of the aircraft charter companies countered that banning the flights would deprive the handicapped, seniors, and the very young of their only chance to see the Grand Canyon. The environmentalists countered that the air tours do not cater to invalids but to the wealthy elite.

The heated discussion was interrupted by the proverbial straw that broke the camel's back: the collision of two sight-seeing aircraft over the canyon in the summer of 1986. This illustrated the degree of congestion in the airspace over the area. A year later compromise legislation was enacted to limit and regulate the flights: about 50 percent of the park's territory is out of bounds for aircraft flying below 7,000 feet (2,100 m) over the canyon's rim level. The flights are limited to certain corridors; helicopters cannot fly below the canyon's rim; and fixed-wing aircraft cannot fly below 500 feet (150m) over the rim.

Niagara Falls is another area where the problem of sightseeing helicopters has acquired annoying proportions. When I visited the falls in August 1992 I found that in some locations the noise of sightseeing helicopters muffled the mighty thunder of the falls. The disturbance caused by the frequency of the flights (sometimes five helicopters simultaneously hovered over the gorge) was annoying. One month later, on 29 September, two helicopters crashed over Horseshoe Falls, killing four persons. Apparently, lessons had not been learned from the Grand Canyon. In Niagara Falls, the U.S. and Canadian governments are responsible for regulating the air traffic over the gorge; in Hawaii and the Grand Canyon, the U.S. National Transportation Safety Board has regulating power. The board has to draw conclusions from the past: since 1986 it has investigated 11 fixed-wing sightseeing accidents that resulted in 76 fatalities, including 23 in 1992 alone (Molotsky 1993). Hopefully, the inevitable strict safety regulations will hopefully solve the problem of noise pollution over North American scenic areas.

Sightseeing traffic is not the only source of noise pollution over North America's wilderness areas. Military flights bother tourists in many places. Fighter jets and B-52 bombers in training, buzzing at low level, are particularly intrusive. Environmentalists complain that the noise annoys tourists and recreationists who visit the parks for solitude. "You're communing with nature and all of sudden a huge symbol of our military-industrial complex comes screaming low overhead. It's a desecration" (*New York Times* 29 July 1990). Critics also assert that the flights scare wildlife, interfere with migration patterns and have a detrimental impact on the nesting practices of such endangered species as the bald eagle and the peregrine falcon. According to studies conducted by the U.S. Geological Survey at the request of the U.S. National Park Service, low-level flights can damage historic and prehistoric artifacts, crack pictographs and paintings on rock walls, and also cause free-standing walls in ruins to tumble. Some historic adobes, e.g., in Mesa Verde National Park, have been damaged by helicopter vibrations.

However, the issue of military flights is a contentious one; the criticism is not shared by everyone. It is possible that some of the outcry against military aircraft may be prompted more by political anti-militaristic views than by susceptibility to noise. Nevertheless, the prevailing opinion is that the low-level flights should be banned in certain environmentally sensitive areas and the military should conduct their maneuvers elsewhere. So far there are no official regulations, only guidelines suggested by the Federal Aviation Administration that pilots keep to a minimum of 2,000 feet (600m) above ground levels over parks and wilderness areas. However, according to the National Park Service, this advice is "routinely ignored" (*New York Times* 29 July 1990).

Another source of noise pollution associated with the aircraft traffic are planes chartered by advertising companies. On many beaches all over the world, especially on the French Riviera, in California and eastern Australia, a familiar sight are noisy propeller planes flying bulky banners promoting the use of various products, from Coca Cola to condoms. The resulting noise pollution not only bothers the tourists relaxing at the beaches but the local residents as well. Mounting complaints result in proposals to ban this type of noise and visual pollution.

There are plenty of other sources of complaints with respect to noise pollution in recreational settings, such as target shooting, hunting, motorboats on lakes, loud music from cars, motorcycles and trains. People in Germany are annoyed about noise caused by non-mechanized recreational activities, such as the sound of tennis balls hitting the ground (*Der Spiegel* 1984, 15: 179–181).

5.4 *Geology*

The impacts of tourism on geology could be considered rather modest on the global scale, although they may be significant locally. Vandals hunting for souvenirs destroy coral reefs in the Pacific area and in the Caribbean to such a degree that practically nothing is left: while scuba diving off Jamaica I saw reefs that were completely razed. However, it is not only tourists but the tourist industry itself that, if unregulated and uncontrolled, affects the reefs negatively. Polluted water discharged from hotels is often the culprit. Raw sewage has been known to destroy coral reefs in the Caribbean and in the Pacific (such as some sections of the Great Barrier Reef off Queensland, Australia).

Speleologists, (explorers of caves) are considered nature-friendly (see chapter 10). As a rule, they do not damage the caves. However, uneducated mass tourists often strip caves of stalactites and stalagmites and deface the walls with graffiti. As indicated in section 4.11, there is enough evidence of the adverse effects of human breathing on ancient pictographs, paintings and other objects of cultural value in caves. The impacts on the geology of the caves are similar. For example, tourists visiting the Waitomo caves in New Zealand "were warming the cave, increasing air flows, and drying the cave environment" (Hudman 1991:20). Additionally, the increased carbon dioxide eroded the limestone. The solution to these problems was to disperse tourists in smaller groups.

The impact of rock climbers is limited to minor abrasions, and permanent metal bolts, or pitons, drilled into the rocks. In addition, the chalk used by climbers discolors the rock surfaces. However, the vast majority of climbers are nature-loving ecotourists, cautious not to do any harm to the environment. The main tourist impact on mountain geology is exerted not by mountaineers, using alpine climbing techniques, but by mountain hikers, who move on specially designed and designated trails. These trails frequently need significant adjustments on steep rock surfaces to facilitate the movement of people who do not use special alpine equipment. Wall and Wright (1977: 6) indicate that the repeated cutting of footholds can change the character of popular climbs and can "detract from the recreational experiences of other climbers." Additionally, sometimes iron grips and chains are provided to facilitate climbing. Despite their intrusive character, such modifications of geology should be regarded as an unavoidable evil, not only for safety reasons but also because they prevent erosion by stabilizing the rock faces. Trail adjustments for the convenience of people abound in many areas of the world on any steep rocky surfaces, not just in the mountains. Examples of such modifications are the steps carved in the rock on Uluru, in central Australia, or in Taormina on Sicily, and the totally artificial staircases leading to some Buddhist and Hindu temples located in the mountains.

Another negative tourist impact on geology manifests itself in the destructive behavior of some hikers, many of them novices in tourism, who collect minerals, rocks, and fossils that are frequently discarded because of their weight, even before the tourists reach home.

5.5 *Soils*

Soil quality is an important concern for macro- and micro- planning of tourism facilities (Mieczkowski, Z. 1990: 224–225). Recreation activities change the structure, aeration, temperature, moisture and the organic content of soil. As a result, the soil's ability to support plants is reduced. As well, the decreased infiltration rates cause run-off that results in erosion.

The high rates of erosion in the construction phase of tourism facilities is a significant tourism-related impact. Goudie (1990: 148–149) refers to various studies demonstrating the extent of disturbance produced by vehicle movements and excavations. The rates of erosion have been up to 2,000 times higher than those of undisturbed natural areas. After a facility is completed, the roads surfaced, and the revegetation completed, erosion "falls dramatically and may be of the same order as those under natural or pre-agricultural conditions."

Another source of soil disturbance are tourists, frequently contributing to the rapid deterioration of important properties of soils. The main impact is that of soil compaction, caused by such things as trampling by human feet, horses' hoofs, or vehicles. Soil trampling also causes far-reaching effects on the totality of the environment, particularly on vegetation, and consequently on wildlife (Fig. 5.2) In terms of vehicular impact, Off-road Recreational Vehicles (ORVs), also called All-Terrain-Vehicles (ATVs), are especially damaging. The impact of mountain bikes is still disputed, although recent studies show that bicycle tires cause no more erosion or trail damage than the boots of hikers, and obviously much less than horses (Schwartz 1994: 86). Camping and picnicking, because of their concentrated efforts, also contribute to soil compaction.

Figure 5.2
ECOLOGICAL EFFECTS OF TRAMPLING

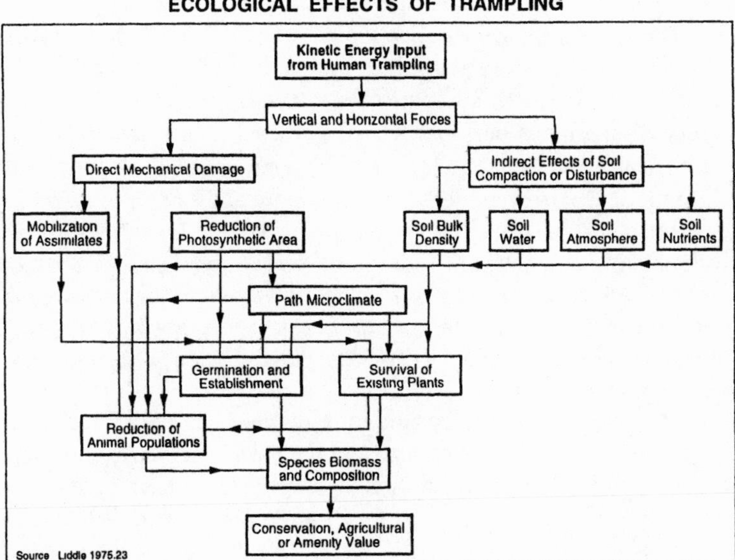

Source Liddle 1975.23

According to Hammitt and Cole (1987: 42–43), the soils most prone to compaction are fine-textured homogeneous soils, such as clay and silt soils, and those of mixed texture, i.e., those with a wide range of particle sizes, such as loams. Soils with scanty litter cover and small humus content are also susceptible to compaction. For coarse-textured soils (such as sandy soils), the compaction may even be beneficial, because by increasing density the soil is allowed to retain more water, and thus promotes plant growth.

However, generally speaking, soil compaction is a negative phenomenon, as it increases the bulk density by packing the soil particles together more tightly and reducing the pore space between them. The soil structure also changes as the aggregates disintegrate and are forced together. The result is a decrease in aeration and water infiltration, leading to an increase of water runoff from precipitation and melting snow. Increased runoff has two major consequences. The first is the reduction of available soil moisture, which may result in the complete absence of vegetation cover. In case of extensive vehicular traffic, it leads to the desiccation of the landscape, as observed in some East African game reserves.

The second consequence of increased runoff is the acceleration of water erosion. As a result, sheet and gully erosion (Mieczkowski, Z. 1965) removes the soil partially or even completely. The latter frequently happens on shallow soils, when bedrock is reached. In such a case, the impact of erosion may be regarded as permanent and practically irreversible—it takes hundreds of years to restore a destroyed soil cover. Gully erosion, once initiated, continues, even if the area affected is later kept out of tourist use. This is especially pronounced on gullied trails, particularly those used by horses or ORVs. They not only compact but loosen it, making it more prone to water and wind erosion. Therefore, gully erosion is more damaging than sheet erosion.

The rate of erosion depends on a number of factors, including the amount and intensity of rain, and the steepness of slope. Campgrounds and picnic sites, although severely compacted, are less prone to erode because of their location on flat terrain. Soil texture is also important: the most susceptible are homogeneous-textured soils, especially those containing fine sand and silt. Also prone to erosion are soils low in surface litter and humus. Surface litter, such as leaves and decaying wood, not only plays a protective role but also provides soil nourishment. Therefore, collecting wood for campfires, especially large pieces, is criticized by some (Hammitt and Cole 1987: 51).

Manning (1979) distinguishes seven steps in the cycle of recreational impact on soils, starting with the removal of surface litter and organic matter from the soil surface, through reduction of macroporosity, water permeability and infiltration, and increase of water runoff, leading to the last step—erosion. These steps summarize the sequence of events discussed above.

Most of the effects of recreational activities on soils do not result from the patterns of the behavior of individuals or group tourists, but from the simple wear and tear of sheer numbers of ORVs, horses, and hikers. The damages frequently require costly repairs, as in the Lake District of northern England where the National Trust recently spent more than $2 million repairing erosion damage on public footpaths (*Time* 22 July 1991). The impact may become so severe in places that Cappock (1982: 273) calls it "tourism gullying," which "is said to be a feature of national parks throughout the world." Examples of such negative impacts are erosion of the surface on high-frequency trails, e.g., on and around Uluru (formerly Ayers Rock) in central Australia, and trampling and compaction of soil in campgrounds. In July 1993 I photographed a 50-centimeter-deep gully in a trail in the Blue Lakes area of Kamchatka, Russia. Though the trail was very rarely used, the gully erosion was well-advanced, due to the extreme steepness of the slope and the use of pack horses. In fact, I was surprised that horses could climb directly uphill without switchbacks on slopes of an almost 40° incline.

Fertile soils are better able to withstand use and maintain vegetation and/or garbage accumulation, whereas shallow soils have little chance to withstand heavy use (Chubb and Ashton 1969: 13). One has also to take the orientation of slopes into account: in some areas of North America, especially in the southeastern United States, slopes facing to the north, northeast and east, are more fertile, and consequently more resilient to camping and picnicking impacts (*ibid.* 15).

The most significant physical damage to soils (compaction and erosion) in fragile environments, such as dry lands and deserts, is the impact of the off-road vehicular traffic. First of all, the Off-road Recreational Vehicles (ORVs) destroy the desert crust, thus exposing the subsurface water to evaporation and causing soil desiccation. Other long-ranging effects of the ORVs on desert landscapes were revealed by the research conducted in the Mojave Desert, California (Iverson, *et al.* 1981). Scientists found that the compaction of the sandy, arid soil increases the bulk density logarithmically, i.e., the largest increase of damage occurs during the first few ORV passes (see section 4.1). These research results could be generalized also for nondesert areas (Hammitt and Cole 1987: 45 and 53). In desert conditions, compaction also significantly reduces the water infiltration capacity (permeability) of the soil and thus promotes the runoff of precipitation. This, in turn, increases the susceptibility of the soil to erosion. The impact of erosion is aggravated by the destruction of the protective vegetation cover, which in desert conditions is thin and patchy, and also by the smoothing of hillsides by the ORVs travelling directly upslope. As a result, the microtopographic irregularities, perpendicular to the movement of the vehicles are subdued. Iverson, *et al.* (1981: 916) came to the conclusion that, "ORV modifications of the desert surface fundamentally change its response to runoff." They also mention accelerated wind erosion after ORV use. The soil of the Mojave Desert would need about a century to restore its bulk density, strength, and infiltration capacity, after being compacted by vehicles. In severely disturbed areas the recovery rate may be hundreds of years.

Management strategies to cope with soil destruction by tourists, such as paving of heavily-used trail sections or construction of boardwalks to fragile dune areas, are advisable; however, they also introduce significant changes to the natural environment. It seems that the best solution is in letting the soil rest. However, this method is not always applicable, especially considering the long recovery rates. Therefore, researchers are doing their best to find other solutions (Liddle 1975: 32–33). More research is required to achieve these goals (Wall and Wright 1977; Liddle 1975).

5.6 *Water*

Water-related impacts of tourism and recreation are a major concern for two reasons. First of all, water constitutes an important resource, a focal attraction, and a medium for a number of recreational activities. At the same time, however, it relates more to human health than to other environmental elements. There are two aspects of tourism's impact on this increasingly important resource: quantitative, i.e., the supply of fresh water, and qualitative, i.e., the problem of water pollution. Each issue will be discussed separately, but one should be aware of their interdependence. Quantitative inadequacies in water supply result in rising concentrations of pollutants, while abundant amounts of water help to dilute and assist in the self-purification process.

5.6.1 *Quantity of Fresh Water*

Tourism is one claimant for the world's scarce water resource (see section 2.7). In general, on a per capita basis the demands of tourism substantially surpass the domestic and municipal demand, which amounts to between 10 and 500 liters daily per person (Lvovich and White 1990: 243). According to Gayray (1981), the tourist per capita consumption of water in Barbados is between six and ten times that of the local population. The same author writes that in a town in southern Portugal, golf course irrigation uses more water than the entire local population. In the Portuguese province of Algarve, the water requirements of golf courses exceed those of the hotels (WTO/UNEP 1983: 10). Grenon and Batise (1989:156) supply data on tourism water consumption in the Mediterranean, revealing higher consumption international tourists than domestic, reaching 600 liters daily per person for luxury hotels; the consumption of campers is relatively small. When one considers that global water withdrawal is 3,600 cubic kilometers per year, and of this, domestic-municipal use is 5.5 percent, then tourism's demand for fresh water seems rather insignificant on the global scale. Nevertheless, because of the limited transportability of water, tourism may locally consume relatively significant amounts of this scarce resource.

Tourism has to compete with alternative uses of water, especially in environments where fresh water is scarce (drylands and deserts). However, for a variety of reasons, lack of water may plague almost any place on earth, at least seasonally, e.g., large metropolitan areas in the LDCs, such as Mexico City or Beijing. Most of this precious resource goes toward irrigation of agricultural crops, which uses almost three-quarters of the world's available fresh water (I computed a figure of 73.8 percent based on Lvovich's data). The problem is exacerbated by the need to provide food for the exploding populations in the LDCs, and by the fact that water for irrigation is used inefficiently. Sandra Postel, vice-president of research at the Worldwatch Institute, stated in a public speech in Winnipeg in February 1993, that worldwide irrigation efficiency averages less than 40 percent and producers could reduce their water use by 10 to 50 percent. This would make a decisive impact on the world's water supply. Tourism also has an important role to play in conservation of water, and each tourism development project in areas of fresh water scarcity should be thoroughly examined with respect to the opportunity costs. In other words, one has to ascertain that the use of water for the project represents the most economically efficient alternative in resource allocation. The issue should be considered in the economic feasibility studies of each tourist project.

Examples of profligate use of water in drylands abound. Lack of water does not seem to limit tourism development in Baja California, Mexico, where an aquifer in a ranch and agricultural valley was tapped to supply water for the resort of Los Cabos. The 338-room hotel called Lost City (part of the resort of Sun City), South Africa, opened in 1992 and uses 10 million liters per day, not only for the personal use of its guests, but also to irrigate its gardens, fill its artificial lakes, and provide a three-storey water slide. It should be noted that such development took place in a drought-stricken part of the country, where the lack of water for local farmers is a major issue.

Mäder (1988: 99) provides the example of the Tunisian oases of Tozeur, Nefta, and Douz, to compare the ample water supply for local hotels (600 liters daily per person) with the scarcity of this resource for irrigation. The powerful pumps of the hotels are lowering the ground-water table to such an extent that the local wells are unable to provide adequate quantities of water to grow dates, fruits, grain, and vegetables. The natural springs dry out and the wells dug by the farmers do not reach deep enough. The result is that the agricultural basis of the oases is shrinking, whereas there are no limits on water for the tourists—including the profligate watering of lawns and decorative flowers maintained for tourists' enjoyment. The daily tourist consumption of 1.2 million liters of water in the Tozeur oasis would irrigate almost 50 hectares of agricultural land, with 12,000 palms (Hamele 1987: 115). Grenon and Batise (1989: 156) complain that the abandonment of cultivated land by the local population leads to a "social wasteland." The local population competes with tourism not only in the desert interior of Tunisia but also in the coastal areas. Thus, according to Tangi (1977: 336) 80 percent of Djerba's population did not have running water in 1974, while 20 percent of the available water was consumed by the hotels.

Another example of a controversial use of water for international tourism is the new Crazy Water desert theme park, opened in 1991 near the Cairo-Alexandria highway in Egypt. The park is an artificial oasis in the desert, and 180 cubic meters of water have to be trucked in every three days from the Nile to keep the water chutes, slides and inner-tube rides operative. Part of the water is used for lawn irrigation and a giant wave pool. The park is operating entirely on free-market principles, and though no government subsidy is involved, there is no charge for the water. Nevertheless, one could question if this is the most efficient use of such a scarce resource in water-starved Egypt.

In the oil-rich Gulf states of the Arabian peninsula, there are few tourists competing for water with the residents, but the local recreation of golfing claims huge amounts of scarce water resources. The users are the local elite: the rich residents and the Western expatriates who enjoy this water-intensive type of recreation. The water that irrigates the golf courses is produced by desalinization plants, which are known for their wasteful use of energy resources. An example of such a golf course, a lush man-made oasis in the Arabian Desert, is the 71-hectare Emirates Golf Club near Abu Dabi. The issue of water use for golf courses in dry areas is a contentious one: some criticize it as the squandering of a valuable resource, some would like the recycled or sewage treatment waste water to be used; some do not regard it as a negative phenomenon at all, as long as the rich recreationists bear the costs.

Certain aspects of water scarcity in the drylands of the western United States, especially in California, Nevada, and Arizona, are associated with the development of tourism. In particular, there are suggestions to increase the use of water for wildlife habitat, and for tourism and recreation operations such as trout fishing and white-water rafting, the latter a $40 million industry. All these increases of water use should be at the expense of heavily-subsidized agricultural irrigation which exerts too much pressure on scarce water resources and does not justify the opportunity costs of such subsidization. The issue is highly controversial because not only tourist resorts, but also manufacturing and housing developments are staking claims on fresh water. Especially tight is the water supply to the fastest growing U.S. city—Las Vegas. Various projects are under discussion, such as the use of unexploited aquifers, buying Colorado River water from Utah and Colorado, and building a desalinization plant on the Pacific for California, in exchange for some of that state's share of the Colorado River (*Economist* 28 September 1991).

Water is scarce, not only in the western U.S. cities but also in the recreational subdivisions, especially in the dry Southwest (Stroud 1983:308-309). Stroud mentions the area of El Paso, Texas, where recreational settlements suffer from an insufficient water supply. According to him, similar situations also prevail, "in many mountainous and plateau regions," such as the Ozarks of northern Arkansas.

The competition for scarce water resources is not the exclusive feature of the drylands. Small islands, mainly located in the tropical and subtropical areas of the Atlantic, Pacific, and Indian Oceans (see section 6.2.3.3) are also suffering. The competition for water between the local population and tourism is most intense during the dry season, which coincides with the tourist season. In fact, in many cases, the capacity of these islands to accommodate tourists is determined by the availability of water. Tourist islands located in the temperate zone, i.e., in the DCs, can afford the construction of expensive desalinization plants. The completion in 1974 of such a plant on the Mediterranean island of Capri, Italy, has solved the problem of water supply for the 12,000 locals and about three million annual visitors, the majority of whom are excursionists. Since the 7,200-ton daily-capacity plant was commissioned, the need to bring fresh water from the mainland by tanker has been eliminated.

Water scarcity also touches some large urban areas in the LDCs, such as Bombay, India, where it constitutes a grave social problem. Tourists living in the luxury hotels in the southern part of the city near the Gate of India enjoy an unlimited supply of water. If they take a walk in the afternoon in the same area, they will witness the residents of nearby slums lined up in huge queues to fill their jars with water, available for just about one hour—from a single communal tap. In 1987, in response to this crisis, the local authorities forbade the construction of new five-star hotels in the area, but would not dare limit the use of water by tourists in the existing hotels. Other examples of cities experiencing a water shortage are Mexico City and Beijing, China, where the water tables are constantly dropping. The supply of water for residents of Goa, India is limited to three hours a day, while tourist hotels use unlimited water. Tropical Africa also experiences water scarcity problems. The inadequacy of the water supply for hotel use in Malindi, Kenya, is notorious. It is exacerbated by the overlap between the dry season and the tourist season. This causes an acrimonious competition for water between tourism and alternative uses. Additionally, there are frequent interruptions in the supply of electricity from hydro stations because of the low water level in rivers at this time of the year.

Competition for water even occurs in some unexpected areas of the world, such as the Indian Himalayas. According to press reports (*New York Times* 3 April 1989), such competition plagues the Darjeeling region, where tourism is of primary economic importance. The tourist boom intensifies the ecological problems of the area by its claim for fresh water. The two water reservoirs, originally built for 20,000 locals, now have to supply 100,000 residents, not counting tourists. The result is that water supplies to the town of Darjeeling are becoming erratic. The communal water tap, located uphill from where most of the locals live, has dried up, and the residents are compelled to go to a downhill location to wash their laundry and draw water from the tap in the public toilet that was built for tourists. They return home from the uphill trek burdened with heavy water jars.

Fresh water shortages may also occur in other areas where basically sufficient precipitation is withdrawn from local aquifers to supply tourist and recreational subdivisions. Such is the case with Florida. In some coastal regions, pumping ground-water for beach resorts may lead not only to the lowering of the ground-water tables and destruction of coastal wetlands (Ranwell, 1972), but also the replacement of fresh water by saltwater in the aquifers (Oglethorpe 1982). The infiltration of seawater into the coastal aquifers occasionally results in soil salinization and ground subsidence. This happens in many beach resorts, such as Djerba in Tunisia, in the Balearic Islands, in places on the Iberian Peninsula, in French Polynesia, and in the Bahamas (Cleverdon and Edwards, 1982).

A careless attitude to water preservation is associated with some tourism areas which obviously enjoy an abundance of the resource. For instance, the managers of Pyeschannaya Bukhta, a beach resort on Lake Baykal in eastern Siberia, seem unconcerned about the occasional overflow in the resort's water tower: the surplus is simply released, gushing for hours, cutting a deep gully in the lake-facing sand slope. As a result, the stability of a section of the slope and the buildings below is jeopardized.

In conclusion, one has to state that the fresh water availability problems could be alleviated by a fundamental change in policy. Water should be treated as a precious, limited resource, that comes with a price tag, not as a free, or subsidized, giveaway paid for by the taxpayers (see section 8.5). This approach would eliminate much of the waste occurring all over the world, especially for the purposes of irrigation. Such a policy would require that tourism also pay the full price for this natural asset, and the present declining block rate system, where rates decrease with increasing consumption, should be discontinued. This should be accompanied with appropriate conservation measures, and where possible, imaginative way of gaining water, e.g., from clouds (coastal fog) as practiced in northern Chile.

5.6.2 *Water Quality*

The second aspect of tourism's impact on water is water quality. This aspect of environment is, as mentioned above, of major concern because it is more directly related to human health than other environmental elements, such as fauna and flora. Tourists and recreationists are vitally interested in preserving the high quality of water for drinking and bathing. Tourism is partially responsible for water pollution but this contribution is often blown out of proportion by sensationalist media and even by sloppy research. One has to stress once more that the main sources of water pollution are external to tourism (see sections 2.6 and 2.7). These include oil spills from tankers and pipelines, viruses, bacteria, insecticides, pesticides, fertilizers and other chemicals dumped into the water systems by agriculture, and the industrial and communal wastes released into the rivers, lakes, and seas.

Recreation, including recreational tourism, is more often the victim than the culprit of water pollution. The pathogens that thrive in polluted waters constitute a threat to the health of participants in recreational activities. Swimming in polluted water can cause ear infections and skin diseases. Consuming contaminated seafood results in potentially deadly infectious diseases, such as hepatitis, dysentery, typhoid and cholera (El Samra 1984). Various toxic elements, such as lead and mercury, seriously affect not only all forms of aquatic life but also the health and well-being of participants in water-based recreation. Hammitt and Cole (1984: 329) emphasize that tourists are exposed to contaminated water in any environment; they advise to remain on guard in extra-urban, and especially in wilderness areas because, "while water is often treated in front country and developed recreation areas, this is seldom the case in back country." Another consequence of deficient water quality is the lack of esthetics resulting from the eyesore of polluted water. Recreationists enjoy clear water and dislike turbidity and suspended solids, even if they do not swim. A severe form of water pollution occurs with the addition of nutrients to the water; this results in eutrophication that promotes the spread of undesirable water vegetation (e.g., hyacinths), which in turn deprives the water of its vital oxygen. Inadequacy of oxygen supply in water impacts on the whole ecosystem and results in the diminished quantity and deteriorating quality of aquatic plants and animals—especially fish, an important resource for sport fishing.

However, blaming external factors for water pollution should not lead to the conclusion that tourism is a completely blameless victim. There is enough evidence to show that unregulated and uncontrolled tourism and recreation cause water pollution on a local scale, thus threatening a resource whose high quality is absolutely essential for the survival of the tourist industry. The most threatening concern is pathogen contamination, caused by improper disposal of human waste. Indeed, in many coastal waters the main sources of water pollution are hotels, resorts and vacation homes that dump raw or inadequately treated sewage. Much of this contains coliform bacteria and other waste materials, some of them toxic. The environmental repercussions of dumping sewage into water bodies are contamination of the food chain by bacteria and viruses, and water anoxia, i.e., oxygen depletion associated with eutrophication (Stevenson 1992: 40).

Among all the water pollutants, pathogens are most dangerous. Pathogens, i.e., disease-causing organisms (mainly bacteria but sometimes viruses), are transmitted to the water by both human and animal feces. The common measures of pathogens in water are total coliforms, fecal coliforms (human) and fecal streptococci (animal). Although coliform bacteria are themselves nonpathogenic, their count is used as an easily measured indicator of the degree of contamination. If the coliform contamination exceeds a certain level, the water is regarded as unfit for swimming and/or drinking. In recreational settings high fecal counts are associated with this lack of or malfunctioning sewage and septic-tank systems in hotels, vacation homes, and campgrounds. In wildland areas recreation-caused impact on water quality is not prevalent, and "does not present a health problem, at least at a large scale" (Hammitt and Cole 1987: 329). The same authors indicate that the dominant source of pathogens in the wilderness is wildlife, and advise recreationists there not to drink unboiled water.

To combat water contamination by pathogens it is essential to provide sewage treatment facilities in tourist areas. Unfortunately, the rates of effective depollution are low, even in the well-established tourist regions of the DCs: e.g., at France's Mediterranean coast it is below 50 percent (Grenon and Batise 1989: 157). The overloaded sewage treatment systems of the French Riviera frequently break down, causing nasty pollution problems. This occurred in 1978 in Saint-Raphael when the local sewage plant could not handle an amount of waste that far exceeded its capacity. As a result, raw sewage was dumped into the sea. At the Spanish Costa Del Sol doctors report skin, eye and vaginal infections by bathers caused by the release of inadequately treated hotel and campground sewage (*Time* 21 August 1978). The scale of tourism-related sea pollution at the Cote d'Azur is well-documented by scientific research and reported in such publications as the French monthly magazine *Science et Vie.* Indeed, tourism is destroying tourism.

In North American recreational subdivisions and single cottages, septic tanks are widely used for sewage disposal. Stroud (1983: 309) indicates that septic tanks may pollute shallow aquifers and "on-site wells." In such situations an environmentally less desirable alternative must be taken—mining the nonrenewable deep aquifers.

The second source of water pollution by tourism and recreation is the massive input of fertilizers, acting as nutrients, and biocides such as pesticides, herbicides, and insecticides, acting as toxins. Contributors to this deterioration of water quality are primarily golf courses and lawns of commercial tourist facilities, but also private recreation grounds, including lawns belonging to second homes. Gardeners often use the special term "to torch" when they mean "to over-fertilize." Water containing chemicals seeps slowly to the groundwater that lies from five to 50 meters under the earth's surface, and led by aquifers it reaches the rivers, lakes, and finally, the sea. Part of the chemicals contaminate the air: as a result, not only nature suffers, but so does the health of recreationists. Unfortunately, golf courses and property owners who refrain from the use of chemicals are still rare.

The third source of water pollution is tourist transportation: cruise ships, motorboats and other recreational vehicles, polluting water not only with oil products (hydrocarbons), but also with human waste and detergents. In practically all DCs, government regulations force boat owners with bathroom facilities to have holding tanks for sewage and to transfer sewage to communal sewage systems. However, to my knowledge, no rules limit engine emissions from powerboats and the introduction of strict emission controls is long overdue considering the extent of the damage. Recent research results contain some unexpected findings: in the United States "recreational power-boating produces 40 times more oil pollution per year than did the Exxon Valdez spill" (Melé 1993: 29). The total annual amount of oil released into water by motorboats in the United States is estimated at between 600,000 and 1.6 million tons (*Economist* 1993 10:32). In fact, pleasure boating produces as much hydrocarbon pollution as all the road vehicles in America (Melé 1993: 34) and the situation is deteriorating: the number of registered motorboats in the U.S. is now 12 million (Melé 1993: 20) and growing. Already about 30 percent of all Americans participate in recreational boating every year (*ibid.* 65). This pollution affects not only the quality of water but also impacts on the air quality (see section 5.2). Especially damaging are toxins contained in discharged fuel, which amounts to about 40 percent of fuel used by outboard motors (Wall and Wright 1977: 33). Some of this discharge may contain highly toxic lead. This chemical contamination of water is most severe in shallow waters sheltered from wind, especially within the area of marinas. Hammitt and Cole (1987: 118–119) provide a detailed list of the impact of chemicals on water. As well, motorboat oil and detergents used by recreationists may also contribute various nutrients to the water, especially phosphorus (in the form of phosphate). Another hazard of tourist transportation that contributes to water pollution is the salt applied in winter on roads leading to skiing areas. This contaminates ground water.

The fourth source of decreasing water quality is individual tourists and their thoughtless behavior, exemplified by littering—throwing garbage, including bottles and cans, into the water bodies. These materials find their way, by gravity, to the bottom of water bodies. As with other forms of environmental vandalism, one cannot expect an improvement without a radical attitudinal change in society at large. As indicated in section 4.7, tourists are simply members of society and cannot be treated as a completely separate element. Therefore, they should not be singled out from their societal context as peculiar environmental villains.

The economic consequences of water pollution are obvious: tourists stop patronizing areas notorious for this problem as they have done with certain resorts. The Mediterranean seas are almost enclosed by polluting continents, and therefore lack the capacity to dilute the pollutants. There is practically no swimming on the southern shores of the Baltic Sea, and on the northern shores of the Mediterranean swimming is an exception rather than a rule. Mäder (1988: 96) expresses his frustration in strong terms, suggesting that the Mediterranean is becoming a toilet. This inland sea occupies only one percent of the world's area but contains 50 percent of world's sea pollution by oil products, and 80 percent of the sewage pumped into it is untreated. The situation has started to improve gradually, after energetic anti-pollution measures were taken. However, things must improve radically before the Mediterranean beaches can clean their tarnished reputation. For the time being, discriminating (and wealthy) tourists are looking toward more distant destinations, such as the Caribbean, West Africa, Kenya, Seychelles, the Mauritius and Maldives. This is not only because of overcrowding, as mentioned in section 4.8, but also because of poor sea-water quality. The less financially endowed stay at home in droves.

Finally, it is important to indicate that scholars are not entirely satisfied with the results of research investigating the impact of tourism on water quality (Wall and Wright 1977: 29–35, Mathieson and Wall 1982: 103–104, Pearce 1989: 239). Indeed, water quality is a complex, multidimensional set of properties which cannot be reduced to a single, common, quantitative, denominator. It changes with variations in space and time, and with the widely-differing quality requirements for various recreational activities (Mieczkowski, Z. 1990: 226). The inadequacies of water quality research are reflected in the substantial variations in water purity standards between countries and regions of the world—standards that differ according to the purpose of use, such as drinking, swimming, or boating. In the United States the drinking water standards are established by the Public Health Service; the standards for recreational uses, however, are subject to local laws and regulations (Wenger 1984: 877). El Samra (1984: 7-9) provides some details of recommendations for water quality standards in tourist areas made by the United Nations Environmental Program.

5.7 *Vegetation*

Vegetation cover is vital for the health of our planet: it impacts on the hydrological cycle; it is instrumental for the preservation of watersheds, global climate, and wildlife. At the same time, it is one of the most important tourism and recreation resources (Mieczkowski, Z. 1990: 233-235). However, recreational use and abuse of this resource threatens the biodiversity of our planet, which is indispensable for the survival of humanity (Wilson and Raven 1992). The positive contribution of tourism to the biodiversity is examined in chapter 3; in this chapter I will focus on the negative impacts of tourism on vegetation.

Although tourism's impact on vegetation, especially forests, is considered negligible (Pawson, *et al.* 1984: 242, 244) in comparison with other uses, tourists and recreationists coming into contact with this resource unavoidably affect it in some way. There are two parameters to consider while discussing the impacts of recreation on the flora. The first is the resilience of the vegetation, the second is the intensity of the impacts.

Regarding the first parameter: plant species vary in their degree of susceptibility to human impact (Kostrowicki 1970; Bowles and Maun 1982: 273-283). With respect to trampling, the impacts on vegetation are strongly correlated with those on soils (see section 5.5). Some of the features that characterize plants resistant to trampling are: low growth, thorns and prickles, flexible stems and leaves, small thick leaves that fold under pressure, flat rosettes of leaves, buds growing on or beneath the soil surface, and rapid growth rate (Hammitt and Cole 1987: 65-66, Satchell and Marren 1976: 50).

Generally resistant to trampling are grasses, sedges and grassland herbs (Satchell and Marren 1976). Grassland vegetation is more resistant than forest vegetation (Edington and Edington 1986: 78) because, "forest-floor plants have large leaves and thin cell walls to allow them to utilize the lower light intensities within the forest, and consequently are particularly vulnerable to direct mechanical damage, by feet, horse hooves, skis and ATVs. By contrast the species which characterize open grassy habitats often have attributes which increase their tolerance to trampling." The bluegrass (*Poa pratensis*) is an example of an impact-tolerant species (Wall and Wright 1987: 21). The most fragile species disappear first, while the most tolerant, sturdy plants can take a lot of abuse, and not only survive but spread. Therefore, the longer the time frame of the impact, the more evident the increase of soil compaction and the decrease in soil moisture. Consequently, there is a change in the composition of the plant cover and a decline in the diversity of species (Fig. 5.3) that precedes biomass losses.

Figure 5.3
IMPACT OF SOIL COMPACTION ON MOISTURE CONDITIONS AND DIVERSITY OF SPECIES

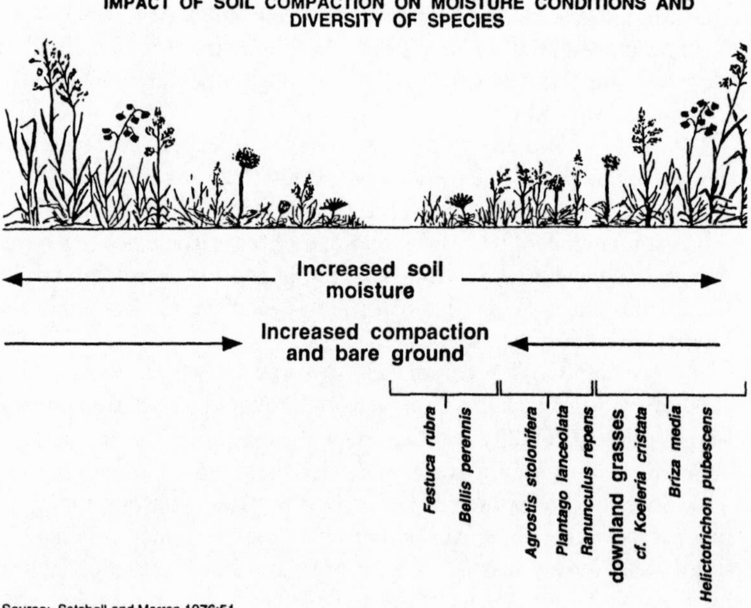

Source: Satchell and Marren 1976:51

The second parameter to consider is the intensity of impact, which is determined from quantitative and qualitative features of the impacts. The quantitative aspect is simple: the more use, the more damage to the environment, with the initial impacts causing the most damage, (see section 5.5 above). This is explained in more detail later in this section. The qualitative characteristics of the impacts are more complex. One could generalize that the degree of the physical damage inflicted by tourism on vegetation varies according to different types of recreational activity: the nonconsumptive, low-technology, low-intensity impacts are generally less consequential than high-technology, motorized mass impacts. Therefore, the optimal scenario is to reduce the impact of all recreational pursuits to a necessary minimum. However, more often than not, such a scenario is untenable, and the reality leaves much to be desired.

The impacts of recreational activities on the vegetation cover may be classified into two categories: direct, such as destruction of plants by their removal or by physical force, and the indirect type. The first type of direct impact is the removal of vegetation, especially forest vegetation, to clear the area for tourist facilities (such as campgrounds and hotels), and for recreational activities (such as boating, skiing and hiking). The major problem associated with clearing is the obvious total loss of vegetation cover with the usual consequences of erosion and siltation. Vladimir Arefyev (1991: 3–4) discusses the tourism-caused deforestation in the resort areas of the Russian Black Sea coast. Torrential rains in 1991 between Sochi and Tuapse devastated the general and tourist infrastructure, and killed 42 people. Arefyev partially attributes the destructive results of this natural calamity to the lack of water-retaining capacity of the deforested mountain slopes.

If forests are cleared to make way for recreational facilities then changes in plant species composition are inevitable because, with the forest canopy removed, the rays of the sun penetrate the ground. However, the impacts of recreational clearing are much more profound than that. The Japanese passion for golf as a vacation activity contributes to the loss of valuable forest areas in southeast Asia, especially in Malaysia and Thailand. I have firsthand knowledge of the destruction of large tracts of virgin forests cleared to make room for golf courses for Japanese tourists in the peninsular part of Malaysia. Hundreds of hectares of virgin rain forests are being cleared, resulting in gully erosion; the large scale devastation of ecosystems includes levelling of natural slopes, building of reservoirs and irrigation systems, changes in ground-water levels, and chemical poisoning of water and vegetation by fertilizers and biocides (pesticides, insecticides, fungicides, and herbicides). The use of chemical compounds on golf courses damages the totality of environment, including the air the golfers breathe. Indeed, golf courses create entirely changed artificial ecosystems, which act as nuclei of environmental deterioration for large adjacent areas. Not only is virgin rain forest lost, but so is valuable agricultural land. The developers use various pressure tactics to force the local peasants to sell their land, including strategic purchases of areas surrounding the proposed site; then they deny access to the residents which compels them to sell.

The second category of direct recreational impacts on vegetation is trampling which, according to Hammitt and Cole (1987: 328), should be singled out as the greatest detrimental direct impact on plants. Trampling leads to significant reductions in vegetation cover and changes in species composition. Trampling is also associated with soil compaction (see section 5.4 above) and the destruction of dead vegetation litter that shelters the soils and provides nutrients to plants. In addition, Hammitt and Cole (1987: 61) express concern about the microclimate of trampled sites: trampling removes vegetation and organic matter, depriving the soil of insulation to temperature changes. This may lead to both heat injury and freezing. The ultimate result of trampling is the decrease of vegetation density, biomass, and species composition. Species more susceptible to trampling disappear, and trampling-resistant species, including exotic species, spread. The result is a decline in the diversity of species (*biodiversity*).

The most destructive trampling results from equestrian and vehicular traffic, such as cars, motorcycles, powered trail bikes, dune buggies, snowmobiles and other types of All-Terrain Vehicles (ATVs). The damage is especially noticeable in fragile environments such as tundra, high mountains, deserts or dunes. Horses destroy not only soil but vegetation to a much greater extent than people, because they exert more pressure per square centimeter and rip the ground open with their horseshoes. Weaver and Dale (1978) conducted a controlled experiment on a sloping mountain grassland in

Montana. They compared the impact of motorcycles, horses and hikers (200 passes of each) on vegetation. Their conclusion was that the motorcycles removed twice as much vegetation as horses, and nine times as much as the hikers.

Even in winter, under the cover of snow, vegetation is not safe from the increasing impact of motorized transportation, such as cars and snowmobiles, and also of skiers and hikers. All cause snow compaction, which destroys the insulating properties of snow cover and results in deeper penetration of frost on compacted areas than on those undisturbed (Hammitt and Cole 1987: 49–50). This makes plants more susceptible to freezing. Similar are the effects of snow compacted by hikers, skiers, and snow-grooming equipment. In such cases the insulating capacity of snow is also destroyed; and the soil freezes about one month earlier and thaws two to three weeks later in the spring (*ibid.*: 50). The resulting damage to the vegetation cover may be critical in high mountains (see section 6.4.6) with their short growing season, frequently limited to one or two months (Wall and Wright 1977: 13).

Trampling by pedestrians inflicts less damage on vegetation than motorized traffic does, but it is nevertheless quite significant. Its impact has been investigated by scientists since the 1930s (Bates 1935, 1938). The direct effects of trampling consist of destruction of plants by physical impact, such as breaking, bruising, and crushing. Tree seedlings are especially sensitive to trampling. Saplings are more resistant, although they frequently break when run over by snowmobiles. Trampling also inflicts mechanical damage to the root system of plants. Westhof (1962) investigated the effects of trampling on the California redwoods and found that their roots are susceptible to trampling around the tree base. As well, compaction increases the mechanical resistance of the soil to root penetration. Consequently, there are fewer roots, and they extend a shorter distance from the plant, making the supply of water and nutrients to the plant more difficult (Hammitt and Cole 1987: 60). The management implications of such findings are obvious.

The pace of damage to the vegetation cover by trampling has become an important management consideration. As it does with soil compaction, the vegetation initially declines rapidly (Merriam and Smith 1974; Wall and Wright 1977). In other words, even light initial trampling leads to disproportionately high damage. Subsequent change is relatively minor. Thus, the relationship between the amount of impact and plant cover damage is curvi-linear, and not proportional (see section 4.1).

For a number of reasons, slopes, especially steep slopes, are the most vulnerable to trampling. As a rule, they suffer from less protection by vegetation than flat areas because the run-off infiltration rates are limited by more than 50 percent (Richling 1971: 453). The trails on slopes are especially damaging for three reasons. First, tourists have a tendency to make shortcuts on curves, and thus contribute to the spatial spread of trails. This occurs less frequently on flatland where trails are straighter. Yet, the lateral spread of the path occurs even on level trails when the vegetation is destroyed, which results in muddy stretches. Hikers respond by detouring to the grassy edges of the trail, thus widening it. Second, on slopes, tourist boots disturb the soil to a greater degree than on flat terrain. "Downhill walkers are potentially more damaging than those going uphill because of their greater impetus" (Wall and Wright 1977: 8). Similarly, Satchell and Marren (1976: 56), referring to data from the Scottish Highlands, indicate that, "the destruction of vegetation by trampling appears to be more rapid as a result of downhill walking on slopes greater than 15 degrees." Weaver and Dale (1978) found that the destruction of the trails was increased when hikers and horses went downhill, and motorcycles uphill. Third, similarly to the impact on soils (section 5.5), the degree of damage inflicted to vegetation by hikers also depends on the type of footwear they use. According to the experience of the park rangers in the U.S. national parks, heavy, lug-soled boots, such as Vibram boots sold in the United States, "have crushed vegetation in high alpine meadows that will take a hundred years to recover" (*New York Times* 18 May 1981). Heavy boots with a thick sole are recommended for rock climbing for safety reasons, because they assure firmer footing. However, on the mountain hiking trails good running shoes are not only less threatening for vegetation but also more comfortable and lightweight.

In addition to the direct impacts of trampling on vegetation, there are also indirect effects. As mentioned in section 5.5., soil compaction leads to the elimination of the pore spaces. This impedes aeration of the soil and infiltration of water into the soil, making the growth and regrowth of the plant cover more difficult.

Compacted soil on the trails lacks moisture; in turn, this inhibits the germination of plants. As a result, new young plants fail to develop and the biomass is reduced (Satchell and Marren 1976: 58). There is also a possibility that other, more resistant plant species may develop. An example of changes in species composition has been supplied by research conducted in California:

> The soil compaction caused by off-road vehicles often killed native plant species and resulted in invasion by different plant species within a few years. The native perennial species required many more years before they showed signs of returning (*ibid.* 58).

The recovery rates of vegetation damaged by trampling differ according to the degree of impact and to the fragility of the given ecosystem. Bowles and Maun (1982), who investigated the variations in recovery rates by plants, generalize that the vegetation after light trampling may take a year to recover. However, the recovery after heavy trampling may take much longer.

The third, most direct impact on vegetation is fire caused by irresponsible tourists. Grenon and Batise (1989: 37) mention the role of tourist congestion in the conflagration of Mediterranean forests. Unintentional causes of forest fires, such as careless smoking and inappropriate handling of campfires, result in conflagration of the plants, and occasionally contribute to the death of animals through asphyxiation due to smoke inhalation. Fatalities among tourists are extremely rare. The intentional causes of forest fires are entirely external because there is no evidence of arson by tourists. The degree of susceptibility to forest and brush fires varies in time and space. Spells of dry weather may occur in most places; this is the signal for increased vigilance. Sometimes the dry area has to be closed to tourists to minimize the danger of fire. On the other hand, areas with year-round dry climatic conditions are under almost constant threat of fire. Nowadays, forest fires are regarded not as an enemy but as part of a natural process. Therefore, in certain conditions, they are considered a tool of wilderness management (Mieczkowski, Z. 1990: 286–287). However, fire policy is the prerogative of the relevant authorities, not of tourists.

The fourth, mostly direct recreational impact on vegetation is the destruction of trees for firewood. This environmental abuse, discussed in detail in section 6.4.5, is most drastic in mountain ecosystems.

The fifth direct impact is the collection of plants (mostly flowers) by tourists. This represents a potential threat to endangered species. I witnessed about 100 Italian tourists eagerly collecting flowers on an Alpine meadow above Cortina d'Ampezzo in northern Italy, although I do not know if this action was illegal. Satchell and Marren (1976: 58) found that picking both flowers and leaves of plants may eventually destroy the population.

The sixth direct impact of recreation activities is on aquatic, mainly freshwater plants. Liddle and Scorgie (1980) report on the effects of wash from motorboats on bank erosion of marginal macrophytes. Of course, the banks of canals and narrow waterways are more susceptible to wash than larger water bodies. Maximum speed limits should be established for various types of boats in specific areas. Aquatic plants differ in their susceptibility to erosion (*ibid.* 187). Boats also damage vegetation by the kinetic energy of direct collision and by pollution from outboard motors.

The impacts of recreational activities on vegetation discussed above, focused mainly on direct aspects. Yet, there are also purely indirect impacts. These include changes in the composition of plant species, which is caused by tourists transferring exotic species from one ecosystem to another. For example, oxygen-eating weeds can be spread by boat or canoe portages from one lake to another. Horse manure may also carry exotic plant seeds to other natural environments. Tourists themselves may bring exotic species from one area to another. The impact of desalination of water for coastal resorts also contributes to this problem, and ultimately changes the marine ecosystems, because they are unable to tolerate the hypersaline and copper-contaminated effluents discharged from these installations (Johannes 1973).

A final example of indirect recreational impact on vegetation is the effect of notorious and ubiquitous littering, which can cause unsightly and undesirable changes to the environment, such as modification of the nutrient status of soil, prevention of soil aeration, and blocking of sunlight. These alterations not only impede plant growth, but can attract wildlife, insects, and ultimately endanger the environment by spread of bacteria and viruses.

Most of the impacts of tourism on vegetation discussed above may be illustrated through the example of camping, an integrated problem that is one of the most environmentally destructive tourist activities. In some campgrounds tourists are blamed for substantial damage to vegetation, including loss of vegetation cover, expansion of bush vegetation into forests, graffiti on trees, littering, poisoning of plants by waste water containing toxins, destruction of vegetation for firewood, peeling of bark to use as kindling, decoration of campsites for grilling purposes, driving nails into tree trunks to support cords for drying laundry, scarring trees by lanterns, and various forms of visual impact on the landscape. Especially vulnerable are seedlings, which are quickly destroyed in campsites. Generally, the overgrowth is less affected than the undergrowth: removal of saplings, seedlings and other undergrowth vegetation for firewood in the vicinity of campgrounds impedes the reproduction of forests when the overstory eventually succumbs to old age (Cole 1989: 144). Hammitt and Cole (1987: 67–68) refer to research in loss of cover and species composition, even in the peripheral zones of campsites and trails.

Boisvenue suggests adopting a number of measures to cope with these, as he puts it, "creeping" problems. Besides the obvious task of educating tourists, he proposes increasing the size of campsites in Quebec's national and provincial parks to 180 square meters and to secure a several-meter-wide wooded buffer strip between campsites. If such a strip is not possible due to lack of space, a clearly-defined boundary between campsites should be created by large rocks or by other means. Rotation of use is also recommended to allow the vegetation to recover from the impact of campers (Boisvenue 1990: 34).

In conclusion, I would like to emphasize the role of research in coping with problems of tourism's impact on vegetation. The first task of research is to supply relevant data on the extent of damage to the quality of the resource, the second one is to suggest appropriate corrective and preventive measures. Barr and Braden (1988: 144) provide important Soviet research data. According to the research conducted in the Russian Federation, the "incidences of diseased trees were 20 to 30 percent greater in areas used heavily by visitors; such areas also had smaller numbers of trees and a smaller amount of tree growth." As a result of these findings one of the Soviet researchers has proposed a four-stage system to measure recreational damage in forests:

• *Stage 1:* Little disruption: trampled areas do not exceed 10 percent of the total, trees distributed evenly, all types of plants normal for that biome are present.

• *Stage 2:* Disturbed: trampled areas represent between 10 and 25 percent of the total forest, sharp drop in rate of tree growth, changes in the composition of the biome. (According to the Russian author, at this stage recreational use should be halted and the forest should be allowed to regenerate.)

• *Stage 3:* Strongly disturbed: trampled areas comprise 25 to 60 percent of the total, few juvenile trees.

• *Stage 4:* Degraded: over 60 percent of the total area is damaged by trampling, young trees are completely absent.

Researchers evaluate the current state of scientific investigations of trampling and other disturbances of the plant cover as inadequate and call for the development of methods, "by which vegetation cover can be maintained or restored on previously damaged sites" (Liddle 1975: 32). Also, research that investigates the hikers' impacts on vegetation, such as the study conducted by T. Foin, *et al.* (1977), should be encouraged.

5.8 *Wildlife*

5.8.1 *Introduction*

For most of history the human approach to wildlife has been purely consumptive; wild animals were simply regarded a source of meat, fur, medicine and other raw materials. Since the eighteenth century there has been a gradual change in the relationship between people and fauna, from consumptive to nonconsumptive uses (Mieczkowski, Z. 1990: 53-67). Today, at least in the DCs, the nonconsumptive recreational use of fauna such as game viewing, bird-watching, and photography prevail. In fact, nonconsumptive uses of wildlife are among the most enjoyed recreational activities in the DCs. According to a 1991 Environment Canada survey, Canadians spent $5.6 billion annually on recreational use of fauna, (about 21.3 percent of it on hunting). According to the survey, more than 90 percent of the Canadian population were involved in some form of wildlife-related activity (Environment Canada 1993: 3). Long-term growth rate in these activities exceeds growth rate of Canada's population. However, the increase is occurring in the area of nonconsumptive use. Participation in hunting is declining: percentages decreased from 9.8 in 1981 to 8.4 in 1987 (Canadian Wildlife Service 1989: 2), and to 7.4 percent in 1991 (Environment Canada 1993: 3). The percentage of United States residents participating in hunting is lower than in Canada: only about 14 million of them hunted in 1991 (*Economist* 12 December 1992)—less than 5.5 percent of the population. These statistics also confirm that hunters spent more per capita than the nonconsumptive users of wildlife.

As far as the impact of these activities is concerned, one could generalize that they affect all aspects of wildlife existence (Fig. 5.4). However, in this illustration no clear distinction is made between consumptive and nonconsumptive uses and their impacts. Although such a distinction is challenged by some writers (Weeden 1979), I will be using it as an pragmatic analytical tool.

Figure 5.4

IMPACTS OF RECREATION ON WILDLIFE

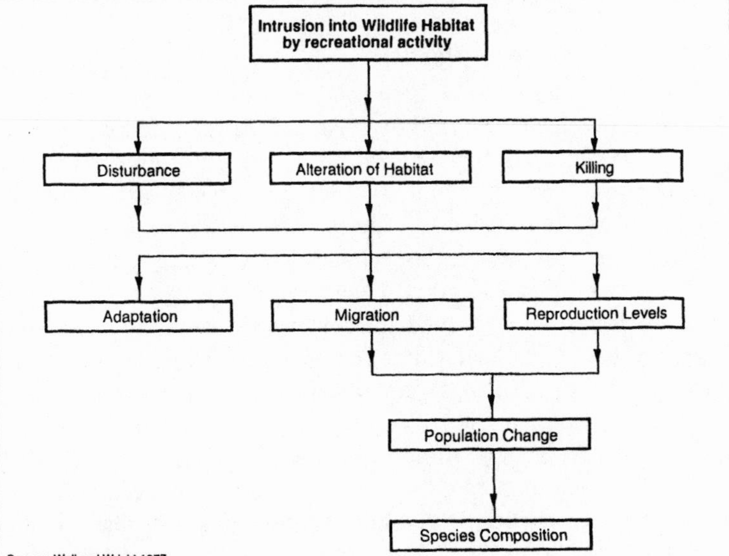

Source: Wall and Wright 1977

5.8.2 *Consumptive Use of Wildlife*

The consumptive use of wildlife, through hunting and fishing, is as old as humanity. Most civilizations have accepted it as a matter of pragmatic expedience, and the Judeo-Christian tradition placed it on philosophical foundations that regard humans as the highest pinnacle of God's creation. Within this tradition other elements of natural environment, including wildlife, are relegated to an inferior position subjected to man's stewardship and to be used as resources for human benefit and pleasure. The purely utilitarian subsistence need has prevailed throughout most of history with some notable exceptions, such as medieval hunting by the nobility. However, since the spread of the Industrial Revolution in nineteenth-century Europe and North America, recreational hunting and fishing in the DCs gradually gained in importance. Today, these activities represent the main type of consumptive use of wildlife, with subsistence and commercial hunting still practiced by some small groups, such as the North American aboriginal population. Commercial fishing still plays a considerable, although decreasing role. The same scenario is spreading gradually to the LDCs.

5.8.2.1 *Recreational Hunting*

The ethics of hunting is a hotly, and frequently emotionally, debated issue between hunters and anti-hunters. In fact, hunting has many enemies who call for its total ban. The anti-hunters insist that recreational hunting is morally unacceptable, and it amounts to speciesism (like sexism or racism). In section 3.6, I referred to speciesism while discussing human preferences for certain animals. In this context, speciesism isolates humanity from the whole animal world—it is an unwarranted anthropocentric attitude that asserts the right of people to deal with other species according to their needs (Singer 1975). Critics of hunting deny humans such rights. They argue that nature should take precedence over human interests, and consequently, people should not interfere into natural processes. Therefore, the term "wildlife management" is an oxymoron.

The hunters counter that killing wild animals instantly by bullet is more humane than death by a predator, when the victim is ripped apart and dies in agony for many minutes. They also claim to be more environment-friendly than their beef-eating critics because animal husbandry causes considerable ecological damage. However, the most important argument of hunters is that nowadays controlled hunting is an indispensable wildlife management tool. Protecting certain species from hunting may result in critical overpopulation associated not only with mass starvation but also with considerable damage to the environment, particularly vegetation. These scenarios happen periodically in some African national parks. In Tsavo National Park in Kenya, for example, the elephants destroy the vegetation of the area, bringing the dynamic ecological balance into disequilibrium, and threatening the biodiversity of wildland areas. One elephant feeds on about 150 kilograms of leaves and branches daily, and needs at least four square kilometers of land. If an area suffers from overpopulation, mass starvation results: in Tsavo National Park in 1970, 5,000 elephants starved to death, and so did other grazing animals (Myers, N. 1994). The elephant situation is particularly difficult in drought years, when food supply is scarce. The overpopulation of fauna, and especially of elephants, devastates not only the environment of the national parks but also inflicts considerable damage to adjacent farmlands and local settlements as animals disperse beyond park boundaries. This occurs because park boundaries are artificial—they do not include wildlife habitats and animal migration routes in their totality.

In such instances, strictly controlled hunting makes sense, not only from the environmental point of view but also economically. Hunters pay dearly for their "enjoyment" in terms of high license fees and other expenses. The necessity for strict control must be emphasized, especially because there is a danger that wildlife overpopulation may change radically to the other extreme, as it did in East Africa in the 1980s. The same animals (such as elephants) may become endangered at a different time. Such boom-and-bust cycles are normal in nature (Hastings and Higgins 1994).

For the most part, the polemics between hunters and those opposed are limited to verbal encounters in public meetings and discussions in the media. However, from time to time, the anti-hunting groups harass hunters by violence. But to my knowledge no country enforces legislation forbidding harassment of legitimate hunters by animal rights groups.

The emotional issue of animal rights reaches far beyond recreational hunting and into scientific research laboratories, abattoirs, pet shops, fur shops, circuses, and rodeos. I addressed some of these issues in section 3.6. Here I limit myself to the statement that certain forms of hunting, such as fox hunting, are cruel and inhumane. Nevertheless, prevailing public opinion all over the world is that sustainable hunting, including recreational hunting, is fully acceptable if it is managed scientifically to avoid ecological decline. Especially important is the prevention of wild animal extinction, the unfortunate legacy of the past. The blame for the extinction of a large number of wildlife species is more properly attributed to external factors, and not to recreational hunting. Nevertheless, since recreational hunting now prevails over subsistence hunting, its impact on fauna must be evaluated critically. For the most part recreational hunting has been an unrestricted and unregulated pursuit because wildlife was regarded as an unlimited resource, there for the taking. The results have been miserable, particularly in North America. Around the beginning of this century, elk and wild turkey were disappearing from eastern Canada; bison had vanished almost completely from western North America. Indiscriminate recreational hunting destroyed some species of wildlife entirely. For example, the passenger pigeon became extinct in North America in 1914. The Edingtons (1986: 51-54) and Peters and Lovejoy (1990: 353-354) cite a number of other wild animal species whose extinction was caused or accelerated by unrestricted and uncontrolled recreational hunting. Myers (1987) sees additional repercussions of such extinctions and population reductions: the more subtle secondary effects on whole ecosystems through "cascades" of species interactions.

As discussed in section 3.6, some species, such as the whooping crane, bison, pronghorn antelope and Arabian Oryx, were brought to the brink of extinction, only to be saved by dedicated conservation efforts. The bald eagle was nearly extinct in the mid-1960s but has recovered to number 6,000 in the contiguous United States (Egan 1992). Hunters had completely eliminated bighorn sheep from the Yosemite Valley in California in the nineteenth century. However, using stock from such sources as zoos with breeding programs (see section 3.6), they have been recently restored to the area. Even primates, such as gorillas and orangutans, have not escaped hunters. The rescue missions by various NGOs and heroic individuals are frequently instrumental for saving the primates. Dian Fossey, who lost her life in her struggle to save the African mountain gorillas, Jane Goodal, famous researcher of chimpanzees, and Birute Galdicas, protectress of the orangutans in Kalimantan (the Indonesian part of Borneo), are among these distinguished individuals.

These rescue actions to save endangered wildlife species would be impossible without enforcement of appropriate hunting legislation and international agreements, most of which have been drafted in the twentieth century. There is general satisfaction with the present hunting laws and their enforcement in the DCs, particularly in cases of endangered species. For example, the U.S. Endangered Species Act of 1973 has effectively enforced total hunting bans and habitat protection. The legal protection accorded many wildlife species has resulted in a rapid recovery of many endangered animals, following both national and international hunting bans. For instance, the recovery of wildlife in the United States has been spectacular. Bison have recovered from about 1,000 in 1900 to the present 30,000; the pronghorn antelope from 12,000 in 1940 to the present one million; the Rocky Mountain elk from 41,000 in 1900 to 772,000 in 1992; the white-tailed deer from half a million in 1900 to 26 million in 1992; and the wild turkey from 650,0000 in 1900 to four million today (*Economist* 12 December 1992). After years of protection, the formerly endangered Florida alligators have recovered so nicely that they are now a growing nuisance in some parts of the state (see section 5.8.3.2). After spectacular recovery, recreational grizzly-bear hunting was resumed in Montana, stirring a controversy between advocates and adversaries who fail to agree if the grizzly is really an endangered species (Egan, 1991a).

On the international scene, the polar bear (*Ursus maritimus*), protected since 1976 by an international agreement, has recovered from the dwindling numbers of the past to at least 20,000 worldwide, and the Russians are now suggesting a resumption of some limited hunting by foreign tourists. The Indian rhinoceros has slowly recovered from near-extinction caused by the nineteenth- century sport hunting. It has been under protection since early this century and now numbers about 2,000. The Indian rhino is also being reintroduced to Nepal from which it had disappeared.

Less spectacular has been the recovery of bird species. Birds have been hunted without restraint for millennia. The era of the shotgun has been especially devastating. Hunting migratory birds in the Mediterranean and in North America has resulted in almost total extinction of some species. Among them were the whooping and sandhill cranes, whose numbers are still far below their levels before the onset of hunting. Nevertheless, the species have been saved by hunting bans and by the provision of appropriate habitats in national refuges and other reserves, such as the Mississippi Sandhill Crane National Wildlife Refuge. Sometimes the costs of the rescue of a single species are high: the price tag for saving the California condor by captive breeding, discussed in section 3.6, was $25 million.

The environmental disruption brought about by unregulated and uncontrolled recreational hunting provides a part of the rationale for government intervention in the form of controlled hunting, managed on a scientifically researched sustained-yield basis. And indeed, such regulated hunting (euphemistically called culling, cropping, harvesting, or population control), despite multiple shortcomings, prevails today in the DCs. Compared with the past, the improvements are undeniable, and support the argument about the feasibility of hunting game-animal populations without their destabilization. It is crucially important to cope with inevitable cycles of population explosion followed by periods of decline caused by natural factors or overhunting that threaten the survival of the same species. The occasional overpopulation of wildlife acquire drastic proportions in Africa; however, they also happen in national parks and other reserves in the DCs (see section 3.5). These discrepancies—between numbers of wildlife and the capacity of the habitat to support them, presents difficult management problems because hunting in national parks is strictly forbidden. Sometimes the animals, under the pressure of deteriorating habitats, venture outside the parks where they are hunted. This happened in 1988 and 1989 when hundreds of bison were killed outside the boundaries of Yellowstone National Park, which had been devastated by catastrophic fires in 1988. There have also been reports of beavers and cougars, sometimes called mountain lions or pumas, invading suburban areas in Canada and the United States.

The advocates of hunting claim that, by eliminating surplus animal populations, recreational hunting performs a role similar to natural predators. However, some scientists, such as William Pruitt, disagree with this evaluation. Pruitt insists that human predation cannot be compared with natural predation because recreational hunting focuses on different sex and age animal groups than does natural predation (personal communication). This valid circumstance could be partially alleviated by appropriate scientific management strategies and by focusing on wildlife survival. Another function of hunting is the scattering of wildlife throughout the ecosystems, preventing animals, such as deer, from congregating in one area where they eat themselves into starvation. Uncontrolled recreational hunting has impacted on wildlife not only quantitatively by eliminating species, but also qualitatively by significantly changing the composition of species in the ecosystems; e.g., by the introduction of exotic species into ecosystems for the purposes of hunting. An example was the introduction of mountain goats by sport hunters in the 1920s into the area which later became the Olympic National Park, Washington. Because hunting in the U.S. national parks is banned, the goats proliferated to such a degree that they now constitute an environmental problem, causing destruction of endemic vegetation and soil erosion. Consequently, they are being shot by park rangers.

Another example of unwelcome change in the composition of species has been the unjustified "control" (elimination) of predators, such as wolves, that suffer from a "bad image" among humans. With the exception of Minnesota, viable wolf populations disappeared from the contiguous United States in the 1920s, killed by bounty hunters and government agents. Nowadays, the wolf population survives in Minnesota, Alaska and in Canada. However, it fluctuates widely in Alberta's and British Columbia's national parks, due to predator control outside the parks (Cabryn 1974). Human-induced distortion of the inter-relationship between predator and prey often leads to the proliferation of ungulates, to the killing of birds and wild boars, and to a plague of snakes.

These problems may necessitate the reintroduction of wolves to reduce the exploding populations of ungulates. Some conservationists have successfully advocated artificial reintroduction of wolves to Yellowstone National Park, arguing that they will have enough ungulates and other animals to feed upon within the park and will not pose a threat to livestock. However, local ranchers and hunters do not agree with this argument and oppose the reintroduction plans, because they perceive not only a danger to livestock but a threat to calf survival rates. This became evident in late 1980s and early 1990s in the Yukon, which led to controversial proposals to allow tourists to hunt wolves in the territory. The decline in elk, caribou and moose populations caused by wolves threatened the more-than-$4-million annual tourist income from hunting. To restore the balance between the two competitors for the game—the tourists and the wolves—the program was implemented in the winter of 1992–93 when 75 wolves were hunted from airplanes and helicopters; thus hoping to increase the numbers of ungulates for hunting. Scientists are divided on the issue of wolf control. Some advocate control because they consider the decrease in the number of ungulates a result of wolf predation, especially predation on the calves. Others insist that the wolf control program was a mistake because wolves killed mainly old or diseased individuals, and that adverse weather conditions, climate and habitat change, and human disturbance were more responsible for the decline of ungulate populations. In Alaska, a plan to kill wolves to save caribou for hunters was postponed in December 1992, following threats of an international tourist boycott.

In Alberta and British Columbia the wolf controversy involves not only tourist trophy hunters of deer and moose, but also ranchers, who demand predator control because of livestock predation. The total wolf population in British Columbia is about 8,000 and growing, expanding to Montana where they had been eliminated long ago. Sport hunters in British Columbia take 400-500 wolves a year, trappers about 50, and about 100 are killed to protect livestock. Environmental organizations threaten a tourist boycott in an effort to force the authorities to stop the wolf control programs.

It is difficult to generalize about the most appropriate management strategies with respect to predators. Everyone seems to agree on one issue: all species in an ecosystem should be preserved because of the importance of key species. This includes predators at the top of the food chain. However, predator control is a matter of controversy. It appears that in some cases it may be unnecessary, in other instances advisable, depending on the species and concrete situations (Edington and Edington 1986: 56–61).

Other environmental problems associated with recreational hunting is the behavior of inexperienced and/or criminally negligent hunters who endanger the lives of local residents and other recreationists. Reports abound of accidental shootings of people. Indeed, some hunters behave in an outright irresponsible way: they shoot at everything that moves; they shoot at signs, insulators and bottles; they shoot from their vehicles, sometimes using headlights to confuse the game; they hunt without license or permission; and they hunt while drunk. Another problem is the inexcusable waste of resources practiced by some hunters. A survey conducted by the Canadian Wildlife Service and the Department of Natural Resources discovered that 46 percent of hunted ducks and 44 percent of geese were "crippled losses,"—this means not retrieved, or retrieved and discarded, sometimes to die a slow lingering death (*Winnipeg Free Press* 24 September 1989). It means that the actual kill might be almost 50 percent less if hunters made a reasonable effort to retrieve the birds. This squandering of a valuable resource, endangered already by external impacts like loss of habitat, drought and disease, and internal impacts like overshooting, is absolutely untenable and is one of the worst examples of the negative impacts of recreational hunting on wildlife. For proper retrieving, each hunter should have a boat or canoe, chest or hip waders, and a dog. The report also criticized hunters who "were not selective and fired at nearly all the waterfowl within killing range." Hunters who are unable to identify various waterfowl species and subspecies, including the restricted ones, are at fault. In fact, hunters frequently shoot at bird species protected by law.

In contrast to hunters' irresponsible behavior, environmentally-sensitive conduct is becoming increasingly common. Conscientious hunters restrain themselves by filling the legal daily bag or using difficult methods of hunting, such as crossbows and bows-and-arrows, or old model rifles. Nevertheless, there are still complaints of local overhunting, even in the U.S. Wildlife Refuges. Yet, calls for temporary total hunting bans or sharp restrictions are not successful for economic reasons (Meier 1992).

Despite incomplete law enforcement in the DCs, generally significant progress has been achieved in these countries, and the situation has been constantly improving under the pressure from various NGOs, environmental groups and agencies (Mieczkowski, Z. 1990: 239). In turn, the hunting lobby keeps a low profile and does its best to improve its image by supporting the preservation of wildlife habitats as primary preconditions for the survival of the fauna. The management of duck hunting in North America is an example. The conservation efforts of powerful private organizations like Ducks Unlimited (with 500,000 members) deserve a measure of praise. Ducks Unlimited not only finances the purchase and efficient management of wetland waterfowl habitats, but also enhances their productivity. This requires heavy investments in water-retaining dikes, and in the creation of artificial islands as homes for waterfowl.

Ducks Unlimited provided the main stimulus for the North American Waterfowl Management Plan negotiated in 1986 between the United States and Canada. This $1.5 billion plan, which ends in the year 2000, is financed by the U.S. and Canadian federal governments, as well as by state and provincial governments of the two countries. Private organizations, such as Ducks Unlimited, are also participants. The plan provides for a $1 billion expenditure in Canada, in recognition that the majority of critical waterfowl habitats are located there. Ducks Unlimited emphasizes that it is not exclusively a hunters' organization: about one-third of its membership are nonhunters. They also support a nonconsumptive use of wildlife. Environmentalists criticize Ducks Unlimited for outdated management techniques, such as predator control (Professor William Pruitt: personal communication).

Recreational hunting in Europe is based on widely-different principles than those of North America. Not only are hunters "managed" but also wildlife habitats The wildlife, especially fowl, such as duck and pheasant, is to a large extent artificially bred. They are then released for hunting, or kept in specially designated areas, such as the moors of Scotland and northern England. The conditions in such commercial estates are artificial: the gamekeepers eliminate all predators, burn the heather to encourage succulent new growth, and prevent the expansion of trees.

Environmental degradation brought about by hunting has decreased significantly because of hunting regulations, bans and quotas (bag limits), but also because such practices as government bans on hunting from motor vehicles and airplanes, using lights at night, and tape-recordings of animal distress calls to lure predators. Another improvement from government intervention took place in Camargue, France in the Rhône River delta. For years hunters had used lead pellets to kill waterfowl. The environmental impact of this practice was disastrous: there was an accumulation of up to two million lead bullets per hectare (*Der Spiegel* 1989, 34: 150–151). This resulted in lead poisoning of practically the whole Camargue ecosystem. The fowl ingested the lead with its feed and became poisoned, because "in the acid and abrasive conditions of the bird's digestive tract, soluble lead salts are formed and produce symptoms of lead-poisoning" (Edington and Edington 1986: 71–72). Lead poisoning exerts a devastating impact on the birds' nervous system, causing muscular paralysis, anemia, and liver and kidney damage (Goudie 1986: 82) The likelihood of death increases with the number of lead pellets ingested. On average, 60 percent of waterfowl was poisoned; the worst affected were ducks. Consequently, the vultures and foxes feeding on the birds were also poisoned.

Despite the fierce resistance of the strong French hunters' lobby (a well-known obstacle to conservation) a new law was introduced in 1991 forbidding the use of lead pellets and mandating their substitution by steel pellets, a more expensive but environmentally safer substitute. Despite the fact that the use of steel pellets may cause accelerated wear to the barrels of some types of guns, it has already been made mandatory in certain national refuges in the United States (*ibid.*: 75). I talked to an American hunter was in favor of substituting lead pellets with copper pellets.

The Edingtons (1986: 71–75) report the incidence of lead-poisoning of waterfowl in various parts of the world: In the United States from 1.6 to 2.4. million ducks died every year after ingesting lead pellets, until they were banned in 1985; in Britain many species are falling victim, even certain nongame species, such as swans. As a result, the famous swan herd on the River Avon at Stratford became almost extinct in 1978. Andrew Goudie (1986: 82) reports that in Britain mallards are the main victim of lead poisoning. As in Camargue, the predators that feed on carrion shot with lead pellets are also affected. This was a contributing factor to the near extinction of the California condor.

Despite these local and regional problems, hunting in the DCs is generally under control. But in the LDCs, the detrimental impact of recreational hunting by foreign tourists increases the pressure already exerted by nontourist factors like subsistence hunting and poaching. Lax enforcement of hunting laws (where they do exist), the lack of funds for wildlife conservation, corrupt government officials, and abusive behavior of foreign hunters (especially from Saudi Arabia, who devastate the wildlife of the Sahara in southern Morocco, southern Algeria, Niger, Mali and Sudan) are all factors that contribute to the problem (*Economist* 27 October 1990). In most instances, the big game trophy hunting has nothing to do with thrill-seeking macho adventure; it amounts to not much more than the execution of animals by high-power rifle, frequently from a car or helicopter.

Poaching is a separate problem external to recreational hunting, outside the focus of this chapter. Nevertheless, it deserves a brief comment. Poachers are not recreational hunters but criminals violating the law. To eliminate their threat to wildlife, efforts are being undertaken to strengthen legislation and law enforcement. Otherwise, poaching gets out of hand. As mentioned previously, poaching is common in the LDCs; it is also a problem, although on a smaller scale in the DCs. In North America, there is an additional problem with unlimited hunting rights for aboriginal people. These allow hunting on government lands all year round; hunting at night with lights is tolerated. These rights, granted in the nineteenth century to provide meat to starving people, are obsolete today and are being abused for commercial purposes. Therefore, they should be reconsidered and adjusted to the present situation.

5.8.2.2 *Harvesting Aquatic Species*

Harvesting aquatic species, or fishing, is another form of consumptive use of wildlife. As with hunting, in certain well-defined, spatially-limited areas, recreational harvesting of aquatic species often exerts considerable negative impacts. However, it is not responsible for global deterioration of aquatic fauna, both in the quantity and quality that became apparent in the early 1990s. The leading culprits are external, nontourist factors, e.g., the commercial overfishing which has been responsible for the devastation of Atlantic cod stocks along the eastern seaboard of Canada, and bluefin tuna stocks in the western Atlantic.

Research into the causes behind the depletion and loss of aquatic species resulted in two important findings: first, that habitats are being steadily degraded by chemical contamination, including accidental spills of toxic materials, deposits of agriculture silt, construction, mines, hydro dams, and river diversions. Second, research revealed that there is usually more than one factor instrumental in the extinction of aquatic species. Therefore, percentage shares of individual impacts amount to well over 100 percent when added up. Thus, overfishing caused mainly by commercial fishing is assigned a causal factor of 15 percent in the extinctions of 40 North American fishes in the last century. This figure may be compared with 73 percent for habitat changes and destruction, 38 percent for genetic mixing, 68 percent for competition from introduced species, and 38 percent for pollution (Brody 1991). In Canada, one occasionally hears complaints, vigorously denied, about overfishing by the aboriginal population, e.g., salmon overfishing in the Fraser River, British Columbia.

It is interesting that the reports from all over the world blame overprotection and the resulting overpopulation of sea lions and seals for the depletion of fishing resources. The sea lions became protected on the U.S. Pacific coast in 1972. The resulting population explosion caused damage to both commercial and recreational fishing, as when sea lions decimated the salmon run at the canal leading from Puget Sound to Lake Washington. They also invaded and damaged tourist facilities, such as the marina in Monterey, and Pier 39 on Fisherman's Wharf in San Francisco. In late 1989 they were a tourist attraction, but when their numbers reached over 600, they became a nuisance because of their noise and smell, and because they block access to recreational boats. Despite these drawbacks, the sea lions of Pier 39 have been accepted as an asset, attracting hundreds of tourists to the restaurants and shops on Fisherman's Wharf.

Similar problems may arise from overprotection of fish-eating birds, such as cormorants. For example, in 1980 Lake Winnipegosis, Manitoba, was described by a leading naturalist as the world's largest nesting ground for cormorants. Since that time their numbers have increased six times to more than 51,000 breeding pairs. Commercial and recreational fishing has been considerably affected by this population explosion; the cormorants consume nearly 7 million kilograms of fish in a season, far more than humans get from the lake. In addition, cormorants are frequent carriers of Newcastle disease, a potentially fatal brain infection which can spread to domestic poultry.

The argument presented above leads to the conclusion that recreational fishing should be evaluated as a relatively minor negative impact on fish stocks on a global and regional scale. However, overfishing by tourists and recreationists may occasionally become the source of local problems, mainly on lakes and rivers. Satchell and Marren (1976: 68) researched the effects of outboard motors on fish, with regard to propeller action, unburnt fuel, nonvolatile oil, volatile oil, lead and phenols (see also data on water pollution by motorboats in section 5.6.2). Although no definite effects were found, there are indications that some tainting of fish flesh may have occurred. Recreational fishing may affect not only the fish resources but other aquatic species. The Edingtons (1986: 74) report that, "injurious lead items included both the split-shot weights which anglers pinch onto their lines and also the larger ledger weights. When these items enter rivers, they constitute a potential cause of death of water fowl: the ingestion of only one lead ledger weight is sufficient to cause the death of a swan by poisoning." The use of angling weights made from nontoxic substances, such as tungsten polymers and steel-based putties, should eliminate the danger of lead poisoning.

The importance of minimizing the negative impact of recreational fishing becomes clear if one takes into account that it is a multi-million dollar industry bringing significant economic benefits to many areas of North America, especially to regions lacking other major resources. Frequently, in lakes and rivers economic benefits of recreational fishing are higher than those of commercial fishing (Mieczkowski, Z. 1990: 238). Over five million Canadians participate in recreational fishing annually; one million foreign tourists, mostly from the United States visit Canada in order to fish.

> "In 1985, anglers accounted for 8.5 percent of the national fish harvest, and some $4.4 billion was spent on goods and services directly related to fishing, supporting an industry that generates over 40,000 Canadian jobs" (*Sustainable Development* 1988, 9:2: 3).

The importance of recreational fishing for the enjoyment of participants and for the long-term health of the tourism industry (especially in remote areas where jobs are scarce) creates the prerequisites for a policy aimed at the sustainability of the resource. Therefore, the governments of the DCs at all levels do their best to develop and enforce sound conservation policies. Indeed, control and regulation should be tightened where and when necessity arises. The primary objective is the protection of aquatic habitats; the second is the protection of aquatic species from over-exploitation. Specific measures are: the reduction of the number of catches by licensing quotas, maximum size limits for oligotrophic lakes, and rotation of areas being exploited. More attention is also being paid to the education of recreationists by promoting fishing methods like catch-and-release programs and the introduction of barbless hooks. The spread of catch-and-release programs in the United States and Canada and in the Sea of Cortez (east of Baja, California) in Mexico proves that an attitudinal change in recreational fishing is well under way.

Finally, one has to refer to a recent trend in the consumptive use of aquatic resources: the expansion of recreational fishing of human-bred fish from artificial ponds, comparable to game farming. The former, in my opinion, should be evaluated positively, especially in regard to the relatively resource-deficient areas such as western Europe, while game farming, as explained in section 10.7., has some significant drawbacks.

5.8.2.3 *Harvesting and Collecting Souvenirs*

A type of hunting that is partially pursued by recreational hunters but mainly by the local population is the so-called "souveniring" (see section 3.5). This is directly related to tourism because it amounts to "harvesting" certain animals to supply shops with souvenirs. These often take the form of animal parts, such as animal skins, furs and turtle-shell jewelry, or whole mounted animals, such as stuffed turtles and mounted butterflies. Trade in live pets is also booming. The Edingtons (1986: 68-69) give several examples of hunting for souvenirs, which has subverted the traditional subsistence hunting. The demand for souvenirs, created by both tourists and nontourists (the latter reached through export) has stimulated the locals to intensify their hunting activities far in excess of their original subsistence requirements. This has upset the delicate balance of sustained yield to such a degree that certain animals, such as huia (*Heteralocha acutirostris*) in New Zealand, became extinct. Mounted specimens of species threatened with extinction, such as two species of pheasant and silka deer (*Cervus nippon*), are being offered, along with other endangered species, for sale to tourists at the Sun Moon Lake resort in the central part of Taiwan.

Insects are increasingly attracting tourist collectors, who either buy them from the locals or collect them themselves. Satchell and Marren (1976: 59) mention specialist collectors who travel as tourists. They collect rare local species of butterflies whose numbers may be reduced or possibly eliminated, especially if "the habitat is limited and specialized." Thus, collection endangers the beautiful butterflies of tropical Borneo, which are caught in nets and sold to tourists in Sabah (see section 3.5). Similarly threatened are the homerus swallowtail butterflies in the mountains of Jamaica, and birdwings in Papua-New Guinea. The protection of butterflies is rather recent. For example, Parks Canada plans to change regulations so it can stop poaching of rare insects from national parks (*Winnipeg Free Press* 8 January 1993). This measure seems to target butterfly collectors especially. Probably the first conviction of tourist insect collectors in the world was in the summer of 1993, when two tourists from European Russia were convicted to pay a fine of an equivalent of $8,000 for the collection of 135 butterflies within the nature preserve of Suntar Khayata in Sakha, formerly Yakutia (*Vostochno-Sibirskaya Gazeta* 5 August 1993).

Turtles, harvested by poor locals in the warm waters of the Atlantic, Pacific, and Indian Oceans, are also at risk from the souvenir trade. The pet trade is also a threat. Turtles perish so their shells can be processed into jewelry, combs, and eyeglass frames. In May 1991, the issue of importing the shells to Japan acquired political dimensions when the United States government threatened trade retaliation against Japanese exports, unless the import of sea-turtle shells to Japan was banned. The Japanese have complied and have promised to gradually phase-out the imports that threaten the survival of the hawksbill turtle.

To provide pets for aquariums, colorful tropical fish are stunned by cyanide that destroys coral reefs off the Philippines; elephants and walruses are still hunted, and frequently poached, for ivory, and are among the casualties of the souvenir trade; live parrots (or their eggs) are taken from their natural environment to supply the pet market. The pet trade focuses on birds, and to a lesser extent, also on primates and monkeys. Some of these animals are used by photographers to tempt tourists to have a picture taken with a chimp or a parrot. The World Wildlife Fund distributes leaflets warning tourists against posing with these animals, and informing them that they were frequently orphaned by killing their mother.

Nonetheless, tourists are only partially to blame for the harm done to wildlife by collection. A large part of the trade and smuggling of live animals and animal parts is conducted within the framework of official and unofficial international trade operations. The OECD statistics demonstrate that Japan was, and probably still is, the biggest importer in the world of wildlife and its products (OECD 1980). Japan imported about 40 percent of the world's ivory, animal parts, and endangered animals as pets, until it complied with the CITES (Convention on International Trade in Endangered Species) restrictions in international trade in endangered animals.

The response strategies to the ecological damages resulting from the trade in animal parts and live animals, are regulation and control advocated for years by various pressure groups. These include the NGOs such as the World Wildlife Fund. Governments have reacted with substantial delays, but since the early 1970s, there has been some action. On the international level, there is the CITES, signed by 130 countries since its founding in 1973. CITES provides a list of endangered (banned) species, and species requiring permits for trade (see section 3.5) that is updated every two years. However, the effectiveness of CITES is limited, especially with respect to the bird trade. Therefore, individual countries may find it necessary to develop their own laws and regulations in this respect. The U.S. congress passed a bill in October 1992, that sharply reduced the number of exotic birds imported to the country, including nearly all of the popular parrot species (*New York Times* 20 October 1992). An example of subnational intervention is Canada's province of Quebec where the Ministry of Leisure, Hunting and Fishing decreed on 6 August 1992 a ban on the importation of a number of exotic animal species (*La Press* 1 August 1992).

5.8.3 *Nonconsumptive Use of Wildlife*

When a mammal or bird is killed by hunters it is gone forever. A live animal may be viewed and photographed hundreds of times. Another additional argument in favor of nonconsumptive use is that it does not harm the animals. This position is considered morally superior; animals are viewed as beings, who like humans, are prone to suffering at the hands of those who abhor the "cruelty" of hunting. The result of these changing social trends is that hunting "is a sport in decline" in most DCs (Backman and Wright, 1990: 356). Therefore, nonconsumptive use is, without doubt, a vastly superior form of wildlife resource utilization, whether it takes the form of a photographic safari of the spectacular megafauna of East Africa, or a whale-watching expedition off the Pacific and Atlantic coasts of North America. The economic considerations of nonconsumptive use of wildlife are, in all cases, superior to noneconomic arguments. In this arena, both the economy and the ecology are clear winners.

A good example of the economic benefits to nature preservation by tourism is bird-watching (birding). Glen Hvenegaard estimates that bird-watching is worth $25 to 30 billion annually in North America. According to him, it is the fastest-growing recreational activity in the United States and Canada. He estimates that there are 30 million bird-watchers on the continent (*The Ottawa Citizen* 4 February 1989). Birding tours to some of the most remote areas of the world are growing in popularity. In North America, the birders congregate in such places as Point Pelee National Park (Ontario), Vancouver Island, southeast Texas, and Chesapeake Bay. Churchill, Manitoba attracts not only North American birders, but also Europeans and Japanese. Birders bring money to the area. Thus, they inject $10 million into the local economy of Point Pelee during the month of May (Canadian Wildlife Service 1989: 3). Sometimes bird-watching may rescue troubled local economies suffering from economic setbacks. Such was the situation of the western Ontario town of Ear Falls, where an iron ore mine closed in 1986. The local authorities are banking on bald eagles to draw tourists to the area.

Wildlife watching on land is being supplemented by wildlife watching on water. Whale-watching is especially popular in the United States and Canada, providing income that, replaces what was formerly brought in by whale hunting. In 1991 the number of whale-watchers in the United States was 3.25 million and revenues totalled nearly $200 million (*Economist* 8 May 1993). The commercial seal-fur business in Canada is finished, but sightseeing tours in the Gulf of St. Lawrence, originating from Prince Edward Island or from Halifax, Nova Scotia, bring in more money than the seal hunt ever did. The tours take place roughly between March 1 and 20, when tourists view the fluffy white harp-seal pups and their mothers.

However, the nonconsumptive use of wildlife cannot be regarded as totally harmless to the natural environment; this approach, although much less invasive than consumptive use may, in certain conditions, cause considerable environmental disruption. Some authors express rather radical criticisms of the nonconsumptive use of fauna: "The very presence of large numbers of tourists disrupts the natural patterns of animal life (far more drastically in fact than did the traditional hunting safari)" (Cleverdon and Edwards 1982: 206). Nonconsumptive tourism may impact negatively on wildlife in two ways: directly by disturbing fauna; or indirectly, by affecting its habitat.

5.8.3.1 *Disturbance*

Disturbance of wildlife by tourists and recreationists may cause two impacts on animals: their behavior may change and they may be displaced from their original habitat (Hammitt and Cole 1989: 329). Recreationists can cause a disturbance of various forms: first is the direct disturbance by their mere presence, i.e., by sight and sound. Tourists approach wildlife at close range, viewing and photographing. It produces excitement and stress in animals which, in turn, may alter wildlife distribution, population structure, and animal behavior. It disrupts their feeding, hunting and breeding patterns, and lowers reproduction levels. Hendee, *et al.* (1990) note a considerable variance between species in terms of susceptibility to disturbance: some species, easily habituate to the presence of humans, while others, such as trumpeter swans, are stress-prone, and abandon their nesting sites indefinitely after just one human disturbance.

The most drastic example of tourist disturbance of wildlife is caused by the concentrations of safari minibuses in Kenya's and Tanzania's national parks. They frequently gather at an extremely close range around a pride of lions, and it is virtually impossible to get a photograph of the animals without including some other minibuses. In fact, the best way to find lions relaxing in the shade is to follow other minibuses. The problem of excessive densities was already noted in East African national parks since the late 1960s (Myers, N. 1972).

Some of these nonconsumptive recreationists will threaten the fauna with much more than their mere presence. The drivers of the photo-safari minibuses are under pressure to provide tourists with the best possible close-up photo opportunities. A successful run, that includes viewing of the "big five": elephant, buffalo, leopard, lion and rhinoceros—normally assures a substantial tip. To achieve this aim, drivers aggressively proceed at reckless speeds and go well beyond the established road network. The easiest animals to see at close distance are lions sleeping in prides. To get better pictures, some tourists throw objects to wake them up. Wildlife are often chased by minibuses, four-wheel-drive vehicles, ATVs, and by airplanes. Tourists want to take photos and clock an animal's speed. This often ends in heat exhaustion and heart failure of the animal, as it did with the adax antelope in Niger's Air Mountains. The effects on wildlife are similar where ungulates are chased by snowmobiles in mid- and high latitudes. Chasing wildlife often results in the separation of newly-born ungulates from their mothers. This destroys the critical bonds between parent and offspring and is tantamount to a death sentence for the newly-born animal.

Mathieson and Wall (1982: 107) cite another example of tourists' disruptive behavior in East Africa: by preventing of cheetah or lion from getting her prey, the animal cubs starve. Cheetahs are not only being disturbed by tourist minibuses during their hunting activities but are interrupted feeding on carcasses. Tudge (1991: 8) reports that the buses attract hyenas and lions which chase cheetahs from carcasses. Tourism pressure forces the cheetahs to hunt during the heat of the midday, instead of in the morning and evening. This causes enormous physiological stress to the animals. The indirect impact of tourists, observed in Amboseli National Park, Kenya, has not only been a change in the cheetahs' hunting hours, but also their departure for less-crowded areas (Perlez, 1991b).

The presence of tourists disrupts the predator/prey relationship not only in the African national parks but also in parks in North America. Ungulates, not as frightened of us as wolves, often graze on or near roadsides. As a result, the supply of potential prey for wolves decreases, kept at bay by the proximity of tourists.

There are other harmful impacts at hand. Even seemingly harmless bird-watchers do damage to the birds. In Churchill, Manitoba, "the bird-watchers' paradise of North America," there is a real danger of nests in the tundra being trampled by tourists. In some cases the birders trample and crush the vegetation surrounding their nests to such an extent that the birds desert them. Young birds starve, and along with any unhatched eggs, become sure victims of predators. There are reports from the Outer Hebrides that bird-watchers trample the fields and beat the crops with sticks to find singing birds. This not only disturbs the birds, but also antagonizes the farmers (*The Guardian* 10 August 1990).

Too much enthusiasm in bird-watching may also cause breeding damage.

> At a resort in Australia, the evening migration of penguins from the sea to the foreshore has proved such a tourist attraction that the introduction of the full range of associated contrived activities—arc lights and watching stands, etc.—has prevented the penguins breeding successfully (WTO/UNEP 1983: 16).

The Edingtons (1986: 39-43) refer to reduced breeding success among colonies of the brown pelican, disturbed by tourists in Mexico, and to crocodile eggs destroyed by predators in Uganda, after the mother abandoned them because of the presence of tourists. Satchell and Marren report about the vulnerability of ducks and geese to disturbances by anglers who flush the birds out of their nests. They also point out that, "breeding failure is often associated with increased predation when the parents are kept from the nest by disturbance" (Satchell and Marren 1976: 67). However, the vast majority of bird-watchers behave responsibly and little harm is done. Thus, the penguin-watchers in the Antarctic keep a respectable distance from rookeries where the birds breed. In Galapagos National Park, Ecuador, tourists do not leave the trails and generally behave with restraint although occasionally abuses do occur. Despite these precautions, certain species react to human presence by simply withdrawing from the habitats visited by tourists and by moving to other places, less suitable for survival and reproduction. Disturbance is usually unintentional, such as when approaching the fauna at too-close range, to watch or to take a photograph. Sometimes tourists may not even see the animal or bird—their mere presence or proximity may disturb the fauna.

Cappock is correct in stating that, "the degree of disturbance is difficult to detect except by careful monitoring." He also suggests that, "disturbance remains a greatly under-researched aspect of tourist impacts" (Cappock 1982: 273). A completely unexplored field of research is the impact of noise on animals. How do they react when buzzed by helicopters or airplanes? The research of human disturbance is not merely inadequate; it is badly needed. We do know that the increased presence of recreationists may have a greater impact than previously believed. Van der Zande and Vos (1984) conducted research on the effect of recreation on bird densities in the Netherlands. They indicate that, "significant negative correlations between recreation intensity and bird densities were found for 8 of 13 species" (Van der Zande and Vos 1984: 1). Another study pertains to recreational disturbance on the common sandpipers in Peak District National Park, England. Yalden (1992) found that the sandpipers, disturbed by anglers and other visitors, take flight about 29 percent more often than they would if undisturbed. They often "are forced to encroach on their neighbors' territories, causing far more fighting" than other riverine birds. They also avoid beaches frequented by anglers. Yalden also studied the distances from approaching humans at which birds take off. Such detailed studies are few.

Rosie Mestel (1993) reports on a study conducted by Dale Lott and Michael McCoy, who investigated the effect of tourism on the behavior of Asian rhinos in Nepal's Chitwan National Park. They concluded that the presence of tourists, viewing the rhinos from the backs of elephants, caused the rhinos stress and behavioral changes at specific distances: they spent less time feeding and more time in an alert position. If tourists exceeded a certain minimal distance, about half of the rhinos left the area altogether, taking shelter in denser vegetation of lower quality for feeding and abandoning the highest quality pasture. The researchers think that this situation may impact on the genetic makeup of the rhinos, by enhancing the reproduction of tame animals and reducing that of timid ones.

Disturbance of wildlife by tourists occurs even in well-controlled situations. Discussing tourists' visits to mountain gorillas in Rwanda (see section 3.4), Chris Ryan (1991: 98) reports the opinion of an expert who recommends screening of prospective visitors for infection. This is because tourists may transmit human ailments, such as colds, flu, pneumonia, and measles to the gorillas.

An example of "death without bullets" is the unintentional killing of animals by means of transportation, much of it associated with tourism, such as by car or motorboat. Roads are virtual "killing fields" for wildlife, especially at night when animals are blinded by the car lights. Millions of animals are killed by vehicular traffic. Some of the collisions between automobiles and wildlife present severe dangers to the motorists as well, especially when large ungulates, such as moose, are involved. The high center of gravity of these animals causes their bodies to smash the windshields of cars; this is often fatal for the driver and passengers. For these reasons the reappearance of moose in upstate New York is criticized by many people, who fear the increase of deadly collisions between car and animal. Such accidents are common, not only in North America but also in northern Europe. Certain species, such as white-tailed deer, are particularly vulnerable to road death because they feed on the grassy margins of roads (Edington and Edington 1986: 169). Scavengers, both birds and mammals, that feed on the carcasses of road casualties, themselves fall victim to traffic. Various prevention methods, such as fluorescent ultraviolet reflectors and ultrasound high-frequency alert devices, warn the animals of approaching vehicles. Some of these have been tested and approved. However, none of them has found a wide application. Even if the animals are not killed by cars, they are at least frightened and stressed by the traffic. Pedevillano and Wright (1987) report that mountain goats in Glacier National Park do not react adversely when being observed by tourists at a mineral lick but respond alarmingly to highway traffic.

Wildlife disturbance is much less significant on tourist trails in wooded areas. The animals seem to get used to them. However, research findings suggest that deer, while unconcerned with people on well-used tracks, flee up to 600 meters when people stray from the paths (Satchell and Marren 1976: 57).

The disturbance of wildlife by recreational traffic occurs not only above ground but subterraneously. Small animals are being crushed underground in their burrows by hikers and especially by ATVs (Edington and Edington 1986: 27–30). Death may also occur indirectly by impact on the snow cover in winter. Julie Jarvinen and William Schmid investigated the effects of snowmobiles on the snow cover. They concluded that snow compaction destroys the subnivean air spaces, reduces the snow depth, and increases density and thermal conductivity of snow. All these changes increase the mortality rates of subnivean mammals in the affected areas, to the point where survival was not possible, and the mortality rates reached 100 percent (Jarvinen and Schmid 1971).

Aquatic animals are not immune to traffic. Noisy motorboats and water scooters scare aquatic wildlife and disrupt feeding and breeding patterns. For example, tourists on water scooters frightened a nesting colony of frigate birds in the Great White Heron Refuge on Florida's Keys to such an extent that this colony, unique in the

United States, fled the refuge in 1988 (Meier 1991). Another menace are motorboat propellers. In Florida they are known to kill or maim manatees. The mortality rates are staggering (Dold 1992a). Manatees (*Trichechus manatus*) are plant-eating mammals, measuring up to 4 meters long and weighing up to 1,500 kilograms. They help control weeds, such as water hyacinths, in fresh water bodies of Florida and Amazonia, thus saving millions of dollars in clearing expenses. They move so slowly that the only way to save them from speedboat propellers is either to ban traffic entirely in known manatee habitats or to introduce speed limits. In this way, mere regulation would decrease the casualties, which are so considerable that the Lowry Park Zoo in Tampa, Florida has embarked on a recovery and release program for manatees wounded by motorboats (*ibid.*). Scientists at the same park also investigate manatees' hearing ability to determine the sound frequencies these mammals are able to hear. The idea is to develop a simple plastic device which can be placed on the hull that vibrates at the right frequency to warn the animals of an approaching boat.

Among the great sea mammals, one should mention the spectacular decline and subsequent recovery of the California gray whale off the Pacific Coast of North America. Numbering 2,000 at the turn of this century, they have since recovered to 21,000 in 1994. As a result, in June 1994 the grey whale was removed from the endangered species list by the U.S. Department of Commerce. The whale is threatened mainly by external impacts, such as offshore drilling and onshore industrial development. High-speed motorboat traffic by recreationists can also endanger the whales. A recent concern is the number of sightseeing boats engaged in a recent upsurge of whale-watching. Whale-watching has become one of the top tourist attractions both on the Atlantic (e.g., Bay of Fundy and the Stellwagen Bank, north of Cape Cod, Massachusetts) and Pacific seaboards of North America (in the Hawaiian waters), and off the coasts of Japan near Okata on Shikoku Island. The operators are doing their best to follow strict guidelines in order not to stress the giant mammals. They do not chase them; they switch off the engines when approaching the whales, move slowly parallel to the course of the animals, or behind them, try not to cross their way, and do not approach them too closely. Airplanes are not allowed to fly closer than 300 meters. Offenders of the guidelines for whale-watching may be fined or even jailed. However, the question of whale disturbance by tourists still remains unresolved and requires more research. Greenpeace is critical of whale-watching. According to that organization, too many boats are taking part, and the distances between boats and whales are too small. The specialists are divided on this issue. Some of them speculate that the noise of the motorboat engines may interfere with the whale sound communication systems, or that the calves may confuse the mother with the tourist boat and become irreversibly separated from the parent (Edington and Edington 1986: 45). All these theories require more research.

Sea turtles are another marine species that is impacted by tourists and recreationists. The propellers of pleasure boats are killing them. They also mistake plastic bags, discarded by careless tourists, for jellyfish, and suffocate trying to swallow them. Beach activities and facilities destroy their nests. Shade provided for the benefit of tourists by vegetation planted on the beach lowers the hatching temperature and upsets the sex balance of hatchlings in favor of males (*ibid.*).

However, disturbed breeding patterns are the greatest danger to turtles. A mother turtle may be scared by tourist noise during her trip to the breeding grounds at the beach. Even if she manages to lay her eggs, they may be destroyed by cars, motorbikes, sandcastle construction, and other recreational activities. When the turtle hatchlings emerge from their shells (usually at night) after a 50-day incubation period, they try to leave the beach for the sea, using the brighter horizons of the water as an indicator of the direction in which to move. In other words, they move towards light reflected off the waves. However, the hotel lights, resort street lights and the headlights of cars frequently induce them to move inland, opposite to the desired direction. They never reach the sea and perish. For example, the leatherback turtle hatchlings wander towards the lights of Tamarindo, a beach resort off the Pacific coast of Costa Rica.

Preventive measures include planting some vegetation to screen the young turtles from the artificial sources of light, or shielding the lights during the nesting season. The latter measure was legislated in Brazil in 1990 (Brooke 1991b). A more radical method is to limit new hotel construction. This was decreed in 1982 at the island of Zakynthos, Greece (Ryan 1991: 96); initially the decree was not enforced because of resistance of the local population, who are eager for tourist dollars (*ibid.*). The situation is still unresolved, but a marine park is under consideration.

In Brazil, environmentalists collect the turtle eggs and incubate them in hatching centers i.e., in artificial hatcheries. After hatching, the young turtles are released into the sea. This measure has been successfully conducted by Project Tamar since 1980, in Praia do Forte, north of Salvador, Brazil. This program, unique in the world, is playing a key role in arresting the worldwide decline of sea turtle populations. The project also includes an education campaign directed to the local population to stop consumption of turtle meat and eggs (Kamm 1986).

Often disturbance of animals results in harm to tourists: large mammals, when disturbed, react violently threatening human lives. Polar bears are not shy about approaching people and their domiciles. Consequently, tourists use electric fences, rubber and plastic bullets and various sprays to protect themselves. The Edingtons (1986: 36–37) cite cases of aggressive behavior in elephants of Uganda. Elephants frequently charge the safari vehicles that approach too closely; usually, however, their behavior is a bluff. However, tourists are well-advised to keep a safe distance from all large land mammals and never separate the young from the mother.

Sometimes animals become habituated to being fed by humans and thus become dependent on them. Habituated wildlife often becomes aggressive while begging for food, and injuries, or even deaths of tourists occur. In North America, animals such as bears or coyotes are especially dangerous. The Edingtons (1986: 36) include mule deer, bighorn sheep and raccoons in the list of animals displaying aggressive behavior when fed artificially. Raccoon bites represent an additional hazard for tourists because raccoons often suffer from rabies. Squirrels and chipmunks are carriers of various infectious diseases. Outside North America some animals attack tourists for food. I witnessed such an attack by a troop of baboons south of Capetown in South Africa: the animals tore the lunch bags from the hands of children, injuring one of them. Even birds, such as the long-tailed macaque in southeast Asia, cause injuries to tourists.

Animals are not only fed directly by tourists: they also help themselves from the garbage dumps located near tourist facilities. Black and grizzly bears are known for this. Polar bears feeding at the garbage dump near Churchill, Manitoba are often watched by tourists in cars. However, other also potentially dangerous animals, such as snakes and disease-carrying insects take part in the human-supplied feast. The Edingtons (1986: 177) report that casual dumping of refuse from tourist sites into the water can attract sharks. Other dangers are associated with scavenging birds, e.g., seagulls in the coastal areas, or Marabou storks in Africa. These may create risks of collisions with light tourist airplanes.

Wildlife used as human food are a potential danger, not only for tourists: it may mean a death sentence for the animal because officials often destroy such individuals when relocation is not an option. Wildlife does not need feeding by humans and can survive quite well if left alone. Hence, the U.S. and Canadian national park management tries to keep bears apart from people as much as possible. Feeding wildlife is discouraged not only by park regulations but also by the education of tourists. Many garbage dumps have been closed and all refuse is disposed in municipal dumps located outside the parks. Campers are instructed to keep their food secured so that the mammals do not associate food with people. In certain cases it is necessary to temporarily bar tourist access to specific areas considered dangerous. This change of policy occurred after several deadly attacks on tourists by grizzlies in the 1960s. Other management strategies include the establishment of permanent no-access areas within national parks. Various designations, such as "strict reserve," are totally closed to tourists; only researchers are allowed to work there.

Another measure is establishing minimum distances at which tourists are allowed to approach wildlife. This may work in some cases, as with whale-watching, but it is almost impossible to enforce in other instances, such as control of minibuses harassing wildlife during photo-safaris in East Africa. It seems the only solution in this case lies in building ditches that prevent the minibuses from leaving the main track. However, such a measure is not always feasible, especially when cost consideration is included.

To limit the number of encounters between tourists and wild animals, authorities sometimes have to establish quotas. This strategy is applied in a number of wilderness areas all over the world. In Glacier Bay, Alaska, not only is a minimal distance of

400 meters between the ships and the whales regulated, but the number of cruisers entering the bay are also limited.

However, all these measures do not mean that tourists are deprived of enjoying wildlife in its natural settings. The tourism industry is doing its best to facilitate viewing and photographing of wild animals, and, at the same time, minimizing disturbance. For this purpose special arrangements are being created and structures built, particularly within national parks. On Kenya's Lake Nakuru, tourists may view animals at very close range from an underground observation chamber, provided by tunnel access. An observation chamber is also provided at the Salt Lick Lodge, where, as in most wildlife viewing places in Africa, maintained waterholes with salt licks in their vicinity, attract fauna and increase the tourists' chances of seeing the animals without disturbing them. At some East African lodges tourists do not need special animal-watching facilities: they view wildlife while eating dinner or from the windows of their rooms. At one of these lodges I observed a leopard eating a goat carcass left by the staff on a tree: the leopard had his dinner at the same time as the tourists. However, it is difficult to condone the arrangement in the Gir National Park in India, where lions are allowed to kill tethered buffaloes as a tourist spectacle (Edington and Edington 1986: 48). In some cases in India, the wildlife observation points are mobile and elevated: tourists ride elephants.

5.8.3.2 *Habitat Degradation and Loss*

The issue of habitat degradation, fragmentation, and loss is the key problem for wildlife preservation (Peters and Lovejoy 1990: 354-355). With no habitat, the animals disappear. The impact of tourism on wildlife habitats is considered relatively minor in comparison with external, i.e., nontourist impact. Thus, logging, not tourism, is responsible for the plight of monarch butterflies in their wintering grounds in the Sierra Madre pine forests of Mexico; it is also the reason for the deterioration of their summer habitats in the United States. Logging in the old-growth conifer forests of the U.S. Pacific Northwest is also decimating the spotted owl (*Strix occidentale*) populations. The loss of forest habitats causes the numerical decline of species. The decline of migratory songbirds that winter in the Caribbean, and Central and South American forests, and migrate to their breeding grounds in the mid-latitudes of the northern hemisphere in summer, can be attributed to this. Both habitats are in danger. However, even habitat loss on one end of the migration route can affect the populations at the other end. The danger to songbird habitats is exacerbated by the suburbanization and the spread of recreational settlements in the United States.

Despite the prevailing negative impacts of external factors, the effects of tourism on wildlife habitat are not negligible; they deserve not only attention but action to minimize their adverse consequences. Undoubtedly, negative qualitative and quantitative changes do occur as a result of tourism development. The qualitative changes consist of habitat degradation when tourists destroy the vegetation by fire and/or trampling, thus depriving the animals of food and places to hide from predators. Littering may upset the ecological balance of the habitat by attracting rodents or certain birds (such as crows and seagulls), which may proliferate and thus change the composition of species in the habitat. Wildlife habitats may be also affected by decreasing water quality, caused by pollution from hotels and tourist boats. I interviewed a Zimbabwean scientist who insisted that elephants are suffering from trunk paralysis as a result of drinking water polluted by tourist boats on Lake Cariba. Tourism-related water-temperature increases may surpass maximal temperatures for spawning and growth of various fish species. Goudie (1990: 200) provides information on these maxima.

Quantitative changes in wildlife habitats are associated with the competition for space between tourism and wildlife. The loser in this competition is obvious, and the consequence is animal habitat loss and fragmentation, resulting from tourism development. Hotels, golf courses, and other tourist facilities, including roads, frequently take space previously inhabited by wildlife.

Examples of habitat destroyed by tourism abound. The expansion of recreational and retirement communities in Florida after 1945 has been associated with encroachment upon and drainage of wetlands. This deprived alligators of a large portion of their habitat. The loss of habitat, combined with widespread hunting, caused the numbers of alligator to dwindle dangerously. The state authorities reacted by banning alligator hunting in 1962 and putting the animals on the endangered list in 1972. The result has been a spectacular comeback of alligators to more than one million (Rother 1991) and their removal from the list in 1987. As the alligators try to reclaim their previous domain, dangerous encounters with humans are becoming more common to the extent that swimming in some of Florida's lakes is dangerous. Although limited killing of alligators is allowed, it does not solve the problem. Alligator attacks on humans average about a dozen annually, and attacks on pets are frequent.

Another North American example is the inadequacy of habitats in North American national parks. As a rule, these habitats transcend the park boundaries. Consequently, wild animals, such as bison, elk, and deer, leave the parks and invade crop and ranching areas.

The habitat problems in African national parks are only partially similar. Animal predation of the adjacent fields is frequent (see section 3.5). To cope with the problem, expensive fences have been built around much of Kruger National Park, South Africa. The northern boundary of Manyara National Park, Tanzania, is equipped with an electric fence that keeps elephants from invading adjoining banana plantations. However, the inadequacies of the habitats within the national park boundaries in Africa are more severe than in North America (Myers 1972). Because of seasonal wildlife migrations the habitats extend far beyond the national park boundaries. Additionally, to cope with the habitat destruction within the park boundaries, there were proposals to temporarily close some parks, such as the Amboseli National Park, Kenya, to allow the habitat to recover, especially the vegetation destroyed by tourist minibuses. However, economically, this proved impossible. Finally, the decision was made to consider banning off-road driving and to distribute visitation more evenly throughout the park (Perlez 1991b). Tourist minibuses are not the only cause of the decline of vegetation in Amboseli: other factors include a surplus of elephants and a rising water table that, due to inadequate drainage, is exhibiting increased soil salinity. The rising water table may be also caused by melting of Mount Kilimanjaro's ice cap as a result of global warming.

In other parts of the world, the development of the Mexican beach resort, Cancun, caused the destruction of two wildlife reserves (Cappock 1982: 274). Another case was the elimination of valuable wetlands by the Languedoc-Rousillon resort development on the Mediterranean coast of France. The plight of koalas in eastern Queensland and New South Wales, Australia, is well-known. The animals depend on a diet consisting almost entirely of leaves and shoots of the eucalyptus tree, locally called the gum tree. Human development for housing and farmland is responsible for the destruction of the eucalyptus forests of Australia. However, tourism, including the construction of resorts and cottages, is also among the causes of destroyed koala habitats. Moreover, the koalas are mainly nocturnal animals, and the fragmentation of their habitat by development inhibits their movements from one place to another. They also frequently fall victim to automobiles. Despite all these adverse developments, koalas in eastern Australia seem to be doing relatively well due to a number of measures. Conservation legislation enacted in 1932 bans export of wild koalas from Australia. Thus, they are not in danger of extinction and can be enjoyed by tourists and recreationists not only in national parks, but in zoos.

A special form of habitat degradation is its fragmentation by roads. According to Mäder (1984), roads disrupt microclimatic areas, expose the animals to predators and constitute broad zones of emissions, disturbance and instability, due to destruction of vegetation and chemical spraying. Roads, including road embankments, dissect the wildlife habitats and act as barriers for the natural daily movements and seasonal migrations of animals. Small mammals are reluctant to cross roads with clearances exceeding 20 meters between the forest margins (Oxley, *et al.* 1974). Roads frequently are formidable obstacles for young animals, who have problems catching up with the adults; therefore they stay behind. Such a separation of young animals from their parents may mean a death sentence. Tortoises, attempting to climb road embankments often fall into ditches; if they become overturned, death is inevitable (Edington and Edington 1986: 168). The implications of roads as barriers to the free spatial diffusion of wildlife genes are obvious. Satchell and Marren (1976: 63) were some of the first scientists investigate the impact of roads as barriers to exchanges between gene pools of neighboring populations: as a result of roads, the animal populations become isolated, the exchange of genetic material impeded, inbreeding inevitable. Mäder (1984: 83) calls it "splitting of gene pools." His research into the changes of species composition in the "biogeographical islands" created by roads, brought him to the conclusion that the species composition within the islands becomes unstable, and therefore of lower value to nature conservation than that in larger areas.

The Edingtons (1986: 171–172) discuss some of the remedial engineering measures which may be taken to mollify the separation impacts of roads on wildlife. Culverts and underpasses, in conjunction with guide fences, are most commonly used. The reindeer walk through special passages under the Alaska pipeline. In the Interlake area of Manitoba, Canada the migrating garter snakes, a major tourist attraction of the area (15,000 visitors in spring), were reluctant to use a tunnel under the highway. Even installing mesh barriers did not prevent the snakes from using the warm highway rather than the cool, dark and damp culvert to cross the road. To cope with extremely high mortality rates, the Manitoba Natural Resources Department staff installed a propane heater in the culvert in 1994. Even more expensive solutions that were considered was the introduction of lights, and putting a grid mesh over the road. Other methods to reduce the road mortality of wildlife include erection of signs warning drivers, and even temporary road closures.

Spatial expansion of recreational communities also fragments animal habitats. For example, the Banff townsite within the Banff National Park, Alberta, hinders the movement of wildlife throughout the rich Bow River Valley.

Chapter 6

The Negative Impact of Tourism and Recreation on Ecosystems

6.1 *Introduction*

Discussing the negative impacts of tourism on separate components of the environment in chapter 5 was useful for analytical purposes. However, in the real world these elements are not as isolated but integrated parts of communities of inorganic and organic components. Nevertheless, dealing with them separately may have indirect implications. Thus, although the 1973 U.S. Endangered Species Act directly protects individual species but not the whole ecosystems to which they belong, the protection of individual species amounts, by proxy, to implicit protection of their habitats—and thus, other species within that habitat. The survival of individual species is unthinkable without the protection of the intricate web of life, interacting within whole ecosystems. Thus, instead of conservation programs degenerating to a popularity contest between the individual species, they must be based on a broader framework of environmental conservation.

Ecosystems are not just the sums of their parts, they are alive in themselves, and interact internally in billions of complex dynamic interrelationships within the totality of inseparable mutual interdependencies. The impact on one environmental component acts synergetically and often cumulatively on other components. Consequently, even small changes within an ecosystem may impact on the whole, frequently in an unexpected way that makes "the course of ecological events intrinsically uncertain" (Satchell and Marren 1976: 16). For example, the existence of wildlife is dependent on vegetation, and wildlife in many ways shapes the vegetation. The loss of one species may injure the entire ecosystem, e.g., clearing vegetation for tourism development disturbs wildlife, reduces habitats, and thus makes animals more vulnerable to hunting pressures. Recreational activities change the composition of species in plant communities, and this, in turn, impacts on wildlife. Erosion triggered by recreational use may contaminate water, causing a chain of impacts on other environmental elements within the same ecosystem.

The components of nature are closely interconnected with each other not only locally and within individual ecosystems, but also globally. In fact, there is only one totally integrated and undivided holistic fabric of life that has taken nature millions of years to develop. Many geographers in the past (especially since the eighteenth century) have promoted the idea of nature as a dynamic, constantly changing whole (Hartshorn 1962). Therefore, the appearance of the Gaia hypothesis in 1979 was not a surprise but only confirmation and an extension of the ideas that life and environment constitute an inseparable whole, an integrated and self-regulating system (Lovelock 1979).

This global system (the ecosphere) may be subdivided into various subsystems (major ecosystems) called *biomes,* which in turn are composed of various subsets or habitats, called *biota.* The ecosystems and their subsets contain elements of intensive interaction between biotic and abiotic elements. However, one should never lose the perspective that in the final analysis all these ecosystems constitute a global whole, i.e., the ecosphere.

The conservation of rich and healthy ecosystems is a guarantee of human survival—hence, the recent interest accorded tourism's role in modifying the ecosystems. Naturally, the emphasis is on the negative effects of tourism, because of the fear that ecosystems may suffer drastic and irreversible changes under the onslaught of relentless tourism development and the masses of recreationists. Indeed, the ecosystems have no immunity against the inexorable degradation syndrome of which tourism is a part.

The apprehension that tourism has the destructive potential to degrade, and even destroy, ecosystems is justified not only by the scale of modern recreation but by the fact that tourism, to a large extent, develops on the basis of delicate ecosystems. Not only are individual plant and wildlife species characterized by various degrees of susceptibility to recreational use, but so are whole ecosystems (see section 4.2). Their rates of recovery from damage also differs. Recovery from recreational use is especially slow in the tundra and in the mountains because of a short growing season and low temperatures (Willard and Marr 1971) or deserts' aridity of climate (Webb and Wilshire 1983). The shallowness and low fertility of soils are a factor in tundra, alpine and desert ecosystems. Such ecosystems are susceptible to erosion; especially endangered in this respect are watersheds and aquifer recharge areas. Some ecosystems, such as biologically simple coastal sand dunes, will not develop any vegetation cover because of inadequate moisture. Recently, tourism has been invading other fragile environments, such as the polar regions and savannahs. Ecologically priceless wetlands are being drained and destroyed to make way for tourism. All these ecosystems, nowadays assaulted by tourism, are sensitive or intolerant to development, and their ecological balance may be easily altered and upset.

However, practically any ecosystem, even the most resilient, will become barren if subjected to the impact of thousands of human feet. The rocky sections of the European Atlantic coast, despite shallow and poor soils, develop an adequate grass cover if left alone, but are utterly destroyed if trampled by too many visitors. Murphy (1985: 47) provides a photograph of Land's End in England, while I photographed a similar situation at Point Raz, the tip of Bretagne, France.

6.2 *Coastal Marine-Land Ecosystems*

6.2.1 *Introduction*

The interface between marine and terrestrial ecosystems are especially vulnerable to recreational impacts for three reasons. First, these are the most desirable places to spend a vacation; tourists enjoy the beach and water-related recreational activities. Thus, 82 percent of both domestic and international tourists in Spain spend their vacations "exclusively at the beach" (*Der Spiegel* 1989, 20: 188). An additional attraction is the *edge effect,* overlapping land and maritime ecosystems (Mieczkowski, Z. 1990: 233 and 243). Therefore, in these areas one can expect the greatest spatial concentrations of tourism, exacerbated by the fact that shorelines are not much more than narrow zones, generally from a few kilometers to several hundred meters in width. The quasi-linear character of this resource use contributes significantly to the concentration of tourist impacts. At the same time, from the physical point of view, shoreline ecosystems are among the most sensitive communities of nature, with a high degree of instability, imbalance, and tendency for change. Generally, beaches may accommodate high-volume tourism, while coastal wetlands are reserved for low-impact activities.

All these circumstances cause a justified concern about the negative impacts of tourism on the coastal and adjacent aquatic ecosystems. This concern is confirmed and documented by multiple scientific research. For example, Edwards (1987) investigated the sensitivity of individual coastal ecosystems in the United Kingdom to various recreational activities. From his research he developed a matrix that evaluates the degree of sensitivity of ten coastal environments to 14 recreational activities. The conclusions of virtually all scholars have been highly critical about the impacts of tourism and recreation on the coasts. This criticism has become increasingly vociferous (Barbier and Billet 1980:15; Hamele 1987: 48; Gunn 1987: 230; Young, G. 1973: 157). In fact, not only are the ecosystems being destroyed by unplanned and unregulated tourism, aimed at short-term profit, but the coastal amenity is lost.

6.2.2 *Marine Ecosystems*

Generally, all oceans and seas can be considered tourism and recreation resources. Practically all water-related recreational activities take place in the coastal waters adjacent to the beaches. Unfortunately, these close-to-shore maritime ecosystems are exposed to extreme pollution from industrial, agricultural and household pollutants, as the sea has become an open sewer for land-based humanity.

Within these external factors, tourism plays a relatively minor, although not negligible, role in this environmental outrage: the marine ecosystems suffer from garbage disposal by hotels and littering by tourists, oil spills and seepage of fuel from cruise ships and motorized boat traffic, and dumping of chemicals, such as kitchen detergents. Organic waste, particularly raw or insufficiently treated sewage dumped into the water by hotels, boats and other tourist facilities, is the source of the growth of algae and other weeds. The Edingtons (1986: 173) refer to research that shows primary and secondary stages of sewage treatment do not suffice to remove nutrients that stimulate plant growth such as algae, from the final effluents. The resulting "blanket weeds," deter swimmers. The weeds also wash up on shore: they smell bad and provide breeding grounds for insects.

Geographically, the marine ecosystems are most affected in areas of top tourist intensity, such as the Caribbean, Florida Bay, the 2,000 kilometer-long Great Barrier Reef of Australia, or the coast of Bali (Hussey 1989). However, water pollution reaches its peak in inland seas, such as the Baltic or the Mediterranean, where the self-cleaning process takes longer than in open oceans, mainly because there is little or no tide to scour them.

The European coastal ecosystems are in the worst shape. In fact, a high percentage of sea and inland beaches in western Europe are unsuitable for swimming. The water quality off some beaches in Britain, Germany, Belgium, and the Netherlands is very low. For example, "a European Community Directive, setting out quality parameters for bathing waters was met in 1987 by only 44 percent of Belgian beaches and 59 percent of U.K. beaches" (*Tourism Management* 1990, March: 88). The parameters used are not known to me, but they are probably close to the limit of 5,000 fecal germs per liter set by the World Health Organization (Haulot 1978: 10). In some places tourism-caused coastal water pollution has become so obnoxious that in the 1960s even the Baltic resort of Travemunde was called *Latrinenmunde* by bitter tourists. This is yet another example of unplanned and unregulated tourism destroying its own roots. The state of coastal waters in the Mediterranean has been a cause for concern since the early 1970s: Tangi (1977) claimed water pollution in the Mediterranean affected the health of swimmers by causing infectious diseases. Even in the Caribbean, which relies, to a large extent, on tourism income, sewage treatment is rare, and tourist boats notoriously dump garbage and sewage into the sea, as they do, for example, in Antigua. In Brazil, the famous beach of Ipanema, Rio de Janeiro is polluted from raw sewage; Acapulco Bay, Mexico is also notorious. Tourism-related coastal water pollution of the Black Sea is also caused by lack of sewage treatment (*Ekonomicheskaya Gazeta* 1989, 20).

The external and tourism-induced coastal water pollution impacts negatively on local economies. So far, it seems that tourist visitation has been most affected on the Italian coast of the Adriatic Sea, on the French Riviera and on the Mediterranean coast of Spain (Costa Brava, Costa Blanca and Costa del Sol). The more polluted western Mediterranean is losing tourists to the eastern part—to the

Turkish and some Greek beach resorts (see section 4.8). Although algae has been a problem in the Mediterranean for some time (Vadrot 1977: 91-92), there has been substantial deterioration recently. The algae effect started on the Adriatic coast of Romagna in 1988, and worsened considerably in 1989 (see section 2.6). The resulting negative publicity, when added to complaints about congestion, caused a significant drop (up to 50 percent) in foreign tourism (Becheri 1991: 230). Despite energetic measures, including those proposed at the 1990 congress in Bologna devoted to marine coastal eutrophication, it seems that most international tourism is lost forever, and the Romagna coast will have to adjust, from up-market German tourism, to short-range, down-market Italian tourism (*ibid.* 234–235).

The North American coastal waters are less affected, but not free of problems caused by polluted water. For example, in the summer of 1992 algae and dead sea grass spread over large areas of Florida Bay, contributing to the "dead zone" off the coast of southern Florida, between the Florida mainland and the Keys (*Newsweek* 2 November 1992). The recreational quality of the whole area has been badly diminished.

However, not only does aquatic recreation suffer from water pollution: so do the coral reefs (see section 2.6). These intricate and highly productive biocommunities of the tropical and subtropical seas shelter thousands of marine species, including fish, crabs and other sea life. In fact, after tropical forests, coral reefs are the second-most species-rich habitat on our planet (Tudge 1991: 31). Apart from their ecological functions for marine life and of protecting the shore from wave erosion, these ecosystems constitute a significant tourist attraction, a source of enjoyment for thousands of snorkelers and scuba-divers, whose numbers are growing significantly.

The research conducted by Woodland and Hooper (1977) fully confirms the finding that external, nontourist human activities are responsible for the destruction of coral reefs, as explained in section 2.6. However, they indicate that, "also walking and collecting can be devastating." They warn that recreational pressure on the reefs is increasingly threatening their very survival. One of the most frequent forms of tourism impact on coral reefs is trampling, investigated by Liddle and Kay (1987). They found that reef species vary in their resistance to "reef walking," and also in the degree of their recovery after being damaged. Generally, the reefs are "highly and equally tolerant to damage in field experiments," but the survival rates of detached fragments were lower. Despite this encouraging finding, there is enough evidence that recreational activities destroy the coral reefs directly by physical contact from scuba divers and by the irresponsible behavior of tourists stripping them for souvenirs (this action is euphemistically called "coral harvesting") and choking them with plastic garbage. As a result, barren coral foundations are all that remain. I saw them while scuba diving in many places in the Caribbean, including some of the former reefs off the Jamaican coast. Residents working for the local souvenir industry are partially responsible for such destruction. Another source of peril are the recreational boats and cruise ships anchoring and running aground on the reef.

Coral reefs all over the world suffer from tourism-induced destruction. For example, in Tonga, coral is used as a construction material for hotels and transportation infrastructure (Brauer 1989: 152). The same happens in the Maldives (Pluss 1989: 142). The reefs off Samoa were mined for the construction of the transportation infrastructure, most of it tourism-related (*Der Spiegel* 1993, 11: 227). The WTO/UNEP workshop (1983: 17) mentions physical removal of reefs to facilitate water-skiing and speedboat activities. The tourist boom on the Israeli and Egyptian coasts of the Red Sea endangers the reefs. The Great Barrier Reef experienced a 40-fold increase of visitation in the post-Second World War period, and attracts 2.7 million visitor-days, with a growth rate of 18 percent per annum (Beeton 1989: 34).

A unique danger for the only living barrier reef in the United States located off the Florida Keys, are the treasure hunters. Treasure hunting began as a recreational activity, and has grown to a professional activity. The hunters attempt to locate and bring to the surface sunken treasures from shipwrecks in the reef area. These activities destroy the reefs. To protect them, the Florida Keys National Marine Sanctuary between Dry Tortugas and Key Largo (an area about 350 kilometers in length) was established in November 1990. A ban on treasure hunting was announced by the National Oceanic and Atmospheric Administration (Rother 1992).

A subject of special concern is the impact of raw sewage from tourist accommodations. Nitrogen and phosphorus contained in the sewage overfertilize the reefs and impede skeletal growth. According to Archer (1985: 48) sewage in the shallow-water zone on the western coast of Barbados causes coral death. Additional damage is inflicted by the deposition of sediment-charged runoff from hotel construction; this smothers the corals physically and decreases light penetration through the water. Johannes (1973) reports the destruction of a large section of the reefs in the Kaneohe Bay, Oahu, caused by excess algae resulting from partially-treated sewage effluents. There are also reports of dying coral reefs off Okinawa, Japan caused by tourism over-development (*Economist* 16 May 1992). The destruction of the reefs also affects land adjacent to the reef zone: beaches are deprived of the natural breakwater, and suffer from wave erosion and loss of property (Hussey 1989: 321). With the reefs gone, one has to build expensive antierosion structures to save the coasts from the onslaught of waves.

Figure 6.1
THE BEACH

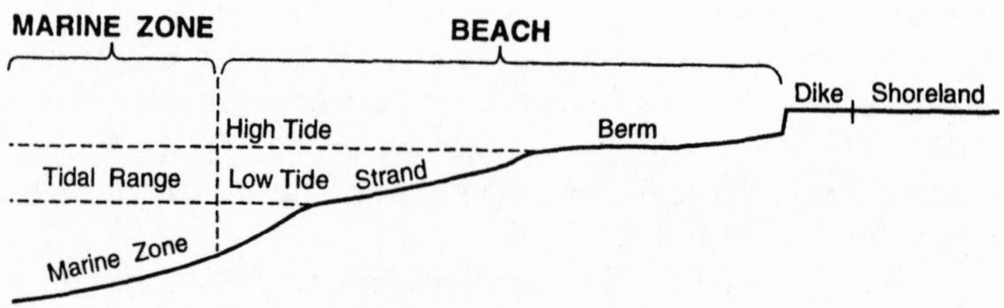

6.2.3 *Coastal-Land Ecosystems*

6.2.3.1 *The Beach and Shoreland*

The beach (Fig. 6.1), whose main components are *strand*, the horizontal intertidal zone, and *berm*, the sandy portion of the beach above the high tide limit (Mieczkowski, Z. 1990: 243–244), is relatively resistant to recreational and other human impact because of its sand (McHarg 1971). However, recent research indicates that the beach is increasingly threatened by interference of human leisure activities that cause regression of the beaches and alteration of the seashore interface. The impact of tourism development and recreational activities is not necessarily confined to the beach proper, but frequently reaches farther inland. It also extends in the opposite direction into the marine zone. In its natural state, most of the sand washed away by waves is replaced by sand from riverbeds carried by rivers and streams to the shore. However, nowadays this source of sand replenishment has significantly diminished because most of the rivers in the DCs are dammed, and coastal development interferes with the natural transportation of sand by sea currents. The waves also erode the part of the beach that is permanently covered with water making it steeper, which increases the force of the waves that destroy the beach. In contrast, gently sloping beaches absorb the energy of the waves.

The construction of tourism facilities in coastal areas affects the beach in various ways. Sand mining for hotel and road construction weakens the beaches and accelerates their erosion by waves. Secondly, the sand may be taken from one place and be deposited in another as a result of the construction of tourism facilities, such as marinas, piers, dikes and hotel complexes. The displacement of sand is always harmful for the "losing" beaches because it endangers adjacent tourism facilities, especially hotels and second homes. The "gaining" beaches may benefit, but not always, especially if marinas are affected by sand blockage. The tourism facilities frequently interfere with natural processes, such as coastal sea currents and *littoral drift,* which is the natural result of waves approaching the beach from an angle and transporting the sand along the shoreline. Piers, jetties, breakwaters, and marinas, which are perpendicular to the coastline, disrupt the currents and littoral drift; this causes the accumulation of sand on the windward (luv) side and loss on the leeward side. This necessitates expensive measures, including trucking of sand to affected places.

In the United States, especially vulnerable are the overdeveloped coastal lands, including fragile barrier islands, on the eastern seaboard from Maine to Texas. The countercurrents to the Gulf Stream carry sand south, renewing beaches with fresh sand, replacing what had been washed away. This natural movement is now disrupted by tourism development of harbors, marinas, piers, hotels, and vacation homes. The decreased sand supply combined with a higher sea level (due to global warming) has resulted in wave action further inland, eliminating beaches and threatening the vacation houses and hotels (Odum, *et al.* 1987: 33). The necessary artificial "beach renourishment" measures—pumping millions of cubic meters of sand to expand and/or create beaches—is not only very expensive, but may not achieve expected results (Nordheimer 1994). The beaches are in trouble on the whole U.S. Atlantic seashore, but especially in southern Florida. The barrier islands on the U.S. eastern seaboard are extremely fragile, composed mainly of protective dunes whose delicate natural balance is being ruined by the wind and wave erosion. This is particularly strong during the winter storm season. This natural process has been aggravated and accelerated by the overdevelopment of recreational infrastructure that further stresses the fragile coastal ecosystems. The western seaboard seems to be less susceptible, although there have been reports of considerable damage from coastal erosion in California (*New York Times* 11 March 1983).

Another type of disturbance at the beach is the presence of thousands of people. One problem is littering by recreationists, which significantly detracts from the aesthetic quality of beaches. Hussey (1989: 321) reports that plastic bags, used by peddlers to package food, fruit, and the like, are discarded by the foreign tourists at the beach in Kuta, Bali. She criticizes "the density of plastic straws" as, "the most startling feature of the beach." Recreationists collect seashells, their cars crush them. There are also changes in the bird species: shy birds go away and the number of bolder seagulls increases, to scavenge for the increased human litter that is their food source.

Figure 6.2
CROSS-SECTION OF COASTAL DUNES

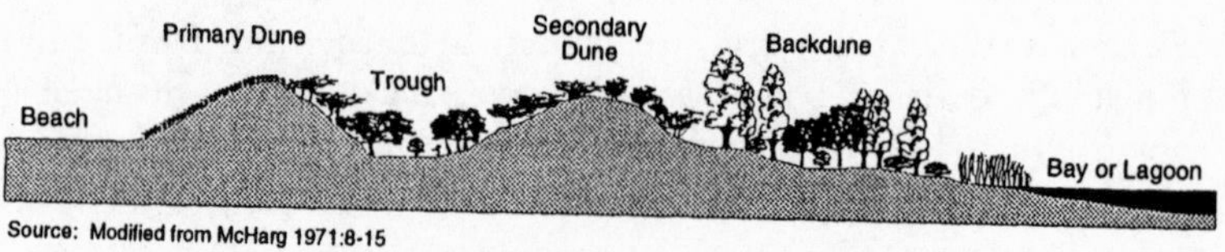

Source: Modified from McHarg 1971:8-15

The shoreland zone extends inland from the beach (Mieczkowski, Z. 1990: 245). The shoreland is frequently protected from wind and waves by environmentally fragile dune ecosystems (Fig. 6.2). The dunes are bound together and thus stabilized by tenuous vegetation of mosses, lichens and grasses. They are extremely vulnerable to human impact; so much so that public access has to be denied. In fact, even a seemingly small amount of trampling will damage the stabilizing vegetation and initiate erosion (Satchell and Marren 1976). Unstable dunes are being displaced inland by wind, an important variable in this process. The fall hurricanes and fall and winter storms on the Atlantic shores of the United States, not only erode the unprotected dunes by the force of wind, but also generate water surges as high as four meters above the normal high-tide level. These storms breach or even wipe out the dunes by force of water (Edington and Edington, 1986: 31). A direct threat to the stability of the dunes is created by irresponsible tourists and recreationists trampling the soil, cutting flowers and branches, and driving all-terrain vehicles (ATVs), which inflict the most damage to the dune ecosystems. The damage is not only direct but indirect. Vehicles operate on the beach, along the inland strandline, where accumulations of seaweeds provide a mulch conducive for colonizing dune vegetation: the motorized vehicles destroy and disperse these useful accumulations of vegetative materials (Godfrey and Godfrey 1980). The best solution is to ban all motorized vehicles, not only from the dunes but also from the beach. If they *are* permitted, their access to the beach should be strictly limited to paved roads, and they should operate below the high-tide strandline. Pedestrian traffic through the dunes should be confined to boardwalks.

Not all parts of the dune ecosystems are equally vulnerable to human impact (McHarg 1971: 8–15). Absolutely intolerant is the youngest *foredune,* or primary. Therefore, any dune traffic on or near it should be banned. The shallow depression (trough) between the primary and secondary (inland) dune is more tolerant, and thus suitable for limited recreation activities. However, to assure survival of the vegetation, under no circumstances should the groundwater level be allowed to fall below the critical point. The secondary dune is, again, more vulnerable, whereas the flatter, more mature backdune, normally the widest component of the dune ecosystem (covered with dense grass, heath, or even forest vegetation) is suitable for development. However, the lack of availability of fresh water may be a limiting factor. A sewage treatment plant is also indispensable. If the dune zone is located on barrier islands, such as on the U.S. Atlantic shore, the next zone inland is the shallow, often marshy, lagoon or bay located between the island and the mainland. This is the most biologically productive area—a wildlife habitat and breeding ground, with aquatic and semi-aquatic vegetation. Lagoons may be used for various recreational activities; however, they should never be sites for hotel or cottage development. Dredging is also not advisable (*ibid.* 14).

Figure 6.3

NATURAL MARINE - COASTAL ECOSYSTEM

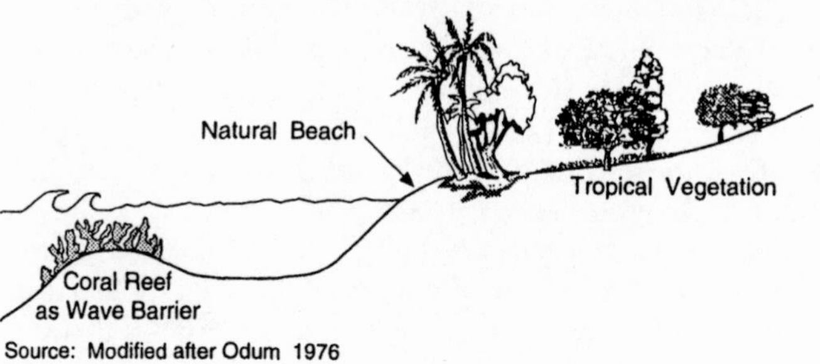

Source: Modified after Odum 1976

Figure 6.4

DESTRUCTION OF MARINE - COASTAL ECOSYSTEM BY TOURISM

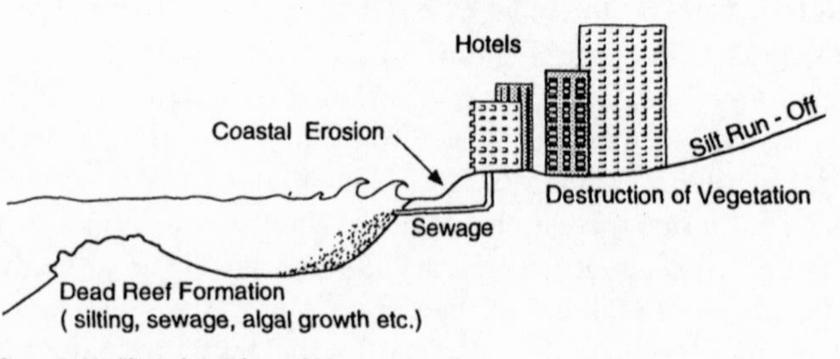

Source: Modified after Odum 1976

The main tourism-related threat to the dunes and the other coastal ecosystems is the tourism infrastructure built in these fragile environments. The result is regression of beaches and alteration of the dynamics between the sea and shore (WTO/UNEP 1993: 17). In fact, hotels, condominiums, and second homes are often built directly in the dune zone, or even on the beach. This ill-advised construction destroys dunes and beaches, and leads to severe environmental consequences (Fig. 6.3 and Fig. 6.4). Thus, many coastal dunes have been dredged and bulldozed into ecological disasters. Additionally, the pumping water from shallow wells may lower the groundwater below a critical level, and cause death to dune-stabilizing vegetation (*ibid.* 11–13). Not only does recreational construction cause these adverse results, there are other, external factors at play—such as the rising sea level, itself the consequence of global warming associated with the greenhouse effect. On the U.S. Atlantic coast the severity of the winter storms is apparent.

The recreational coastal developments in the United States have been influenced by insurance rates. Flood insurance for vacation homes in areas subject to coastal erosion had been unavailable or prohibitively expensive on the private market. In 1968 the U.S. government stepped in with the National Flood Insurance Program to provide imprudently subsidized flood insurance and low-interest disaster loans for the rebuilding of houses destroyed by fall and winter storms. This program was not only environmentally unsound, it was outright ill-conceived because it has fostered destructive and dangerous second-home construction on the nation's shores. As a result of this program thousands of elaborate and expensive second homes and a number of condominiums have been constructed in high-risk zones of the Atlantic coast. Some are built directly on the beach, only to be virtually washed away by fall and winter storms, as they were in late October 1991.

To limit new recreational home construction along the shorelines, the current U.S. government policy is to restrict insurance coverage in recognition that coastal property is threatened not only by occasional severe storms but also by long-term erosion. For this purpose, the 1982 Coastal Barrier Resources Act was passed. The act intends to restrict second-home development in the high-risk Atlantic seaboard areas by prohibiting federal flood insurance and any forms of infrastructural assistance, on lands belonging to the

National Coastal Barrier Resources System. The idea is to identify and map the segments of the shore which are prone to erode, and to limit or prohibit development in such places. The new policy is vigorously opposed by home owners and by the construction industry, who fear a collapse of coastal property values. This would be a direct result of prohibitively high insurance rates or the inability to obtain mortgages for uninsured property. Environmentalists are also dissatisfied and regard the measures as inadequate.

The American case of coastal recreational misdevelopment is perhaps the most drastic in the world. Nevertheless, similar examples, although on a smaller scale, may be found in other areas. The development of Cancún, the largest Mexican beach resort, with more than 1.5 million tourists a year, has obliterated sand dunes, contaminated a large lagoon, and destroyed marine life. The heavy hotel construction too close to shore caused considerable coastal erosion in the Sri Lankan beach resort of Negombo, north of Colombo (WTO 1983). Tourism overdevelopment on the European seashores, especially on the Mediterranean (discussed in section 4.8 above), has wiped out coastal ecosystems on an unprecedented scale (Vadrot 1977: 91–106). Some of the European problems resemble those in the United States: beach erosion, sand mining, water pollution, lack of environmental concern, and littering. Of course, external factors, such as industrial development, intensification of transport, and accelerated urbanization of coastal areas at the expense of inland locations, play a leading role. Among the shorelands of Europe, the most vulnerable to coastal erosion are those located on the North, the Black, and the Azov Seas. As in the United States irresponsible recreational construction too close to the beach and negligent attitudes towards the dangers of erosion created conditions that invited disaster, such as the flooding of the Black Sea coastline of the Krasnodar Kray on 1 August 1991. On 2 January 1992 the Russian government decreed that, while regretting the loss of life, it would take appropriate measures to combat erosion and landslides on the Russian shores of the Black and Azov Seas (*Rossiyskaya Gazeta* 21 January 1992).

6.2.3.2 *Coastal Wetlands*

Wetlands are another coastal-marine ecosystem affected by tourism. All wetlands, both coastal and inland, comprise about six percent of the world's surface (Williams, M. 1990: VII). Since the beginning of history the wetlands have been an engineering challenge for people who tried to drain them in order to destroy malarial mosquitoes and to provide land for agriculture. However, only since the Industrial Revolution have humans acquired the technical and economic capacity to do this on a massive scale. Not only has technology changed, but so has land use: agriculture, industry, urbanization, and tourism and recreation have all contributed to the destruction of wetlands. The realization of negative environmental impacts and economic consequences of such actions have appeared relatively recently.

The biological and economic values of wetlands have been widely discussed (Turner and Jones 1991; Turner, B. *et al.* 1990; Williams, M. 1990; Walker 1990; Mercer 1991). Wetlands stabilize the earth's climate by acting as sinks for carbon, immobilizing it so it does not escape into the atmosphere. As far as the biosphere is concerned, wetlands are biologically among the most productive ecosystems in the world. As excellent plant and wildlife habitats, they provide rich gene pools for fauna and flora and are important as spawning, breeding and nesting grounds. They are also used as resting stations for migratory birds. Wetlands also provide excellent conditions for many leisure activities. However, the benefits reach well beyond the biological and recreational functions: wetlands also act as huge natural sponges as natural flood controls by storing surplus water and gradually recharging the adjacent environments, including the groundwater and underground aquifers. They serve as natural filters that protect water quality; water-treatment facilities that break down toxins and filter polluted water. Their impact on precipitation regimes is beneficial because they provide large spaces for evaporation. Major wetland values, including recreational values, are summarized in Table 6.1.

Table 6.1. MAJOR WETLAND VALUES

Environmental quality values
Water-quality maintenance
Pollution filter
Sediment removal
Oxygen production

Nutrient recycling
Chemical nutrient absorption
Aquatic productivity
Microclimate regulator
World climate (ozone layer)

Fish and wildlife values
Fish and shellfish habitat
Waterfowl and other bird habitat
Furbearer and other wildlife habitat

Socioeconomic values
Flood control
Wave-damage protection
Erosion control
Ground-water recharge and water supply
Timber and other natural products
Energy source (peat)
Livestock grazing
Fishing and shellfishing
Hunting and trapping
Recreation
Aesthetics
Education and scientific research
*Source: Mercer 1991: 274

These beneficial characteristics of all wetlands could be supplemented by the special functions performed by coastal wetlands. Many of them, such as the Mississippi Delta in Louisiana or the Camargue on the Rhône delta in France, are located at the mouths of rivers, and as such, are particularly productive biological communities. By absorbing flood waters, such wetlands help to stabilize the saltiness of coastal lands. They protect human settlements, including recreational subdivisions, by buffeting the effects of water surges resulting from hurricanes and tropical storms.

Scholars realize the values of wetlands. Scientists are teaming up with economists to argue that the opportunity costs of preserving wetlands in their natural state are often lower than the value of wetlands for development (Mercer 1991: 275-276). Attempts have been made also to put monetary values on wetlands (*ibid.* 287-289). At the same time, scholars also understand the dangers: wetlands are not only threatened by development. They are also vulnerable to human impacts, including tourism and recreation, because of their unstable substrata and low elevation. This exposes them to pollution that gravitates down to their drainage basin. Scholars point out that despite some improvements in the DCs, "wetland losses are continuing at alarming rates in many parts of the world" (Turner and Jones 1991: 6). Therefore, the consensus among researchers is unequivocal: they demand conservation and sustained use of wetlands. The following discussion will focus on recreational uses of wetlands, and why drained wetlands, including coastal ones, have become coveted locations for tourism development.

Coastal wetlands include networks of marshes, swamps, and shallow lagoons. The most important categories of coastal wetlands are salt or brackish marshes, freshwater morasses, and mangrove swamps. After a superficial examination of coastal wetlands as potential tourism locations one may conclude that these areas are not conducive to direct tourism development. They do not appear to be appropriate areas for tourism. However, they attract hunters and fishermen, sightseeing tourists, scientific tourists, bird-watchers, and researchers.

Since the 1960s, coastal wetlands have been under direct attack from tourism development. Application of modern technology has allowed drainage of relatively large areas, and dredging and filling of former wetlands for hotel and second-home construction. Indeed, some of the world's most environmentally valuable coastal wetlands have been exposed to the increasing pressure of expanding tourism. This has been especially pronounced on the coasts with their concentrated tourism demand and ensuing congestion. The best example is the Mediterranean coast, where land is at a premium. To gain space for tourism development, the coastal wetlands are drained to make space for beach resorts.

When the French government realized that the carrying capacity of the Riviera had been surpassed, it embarked on an ambitious plan to develop beach tourism in the sparsely populated wetlands to the west of the Rhône delta. For this purpose, in 1963 it set up a public agency, *Mission Interministerielle pour L'Amenagement Touristique de Littoral Languedoc-Roussillon,* which took less than ten years to complete an enormous engineering project that involved draining, dredging, and filling the coastal marshes and saltwater lagoons. The project was completed by construction of a complex of beach resorts, of which La Grande Motte is the most famous. The wetland fauna disappeared completely. The flora "won" thousands of hectares through the forestation of former wetlands. However, this is a totally foreign vegetation cover; the wetland flora has been eliminated.

Florida is another example of coastal wetland ecosystems affected by tourism development: saltwater mangrove swamps and freshwater marshes have been drained for construction of coastal vacation homes and marinas, and diverted to human settlements (Gunn 1987: 230; Odum, *et al.* 1987: 26–31). As a result of accelerated development in Florida since 1945, the supply of fresh water to the coastal zone has decreased and mangrove swamps replaced the freshwater marshes (*ibid.* 29). Today both the salt-water coastal mangrove swamps and the freshwater marshes are threatened by human invasion, especially in the Everglades area (see section 6. 3.3 below).

Coastal mangrove swamps have also suffered from tourism development outside the United States. These ecosystems dominate the coastlines between 25° north and 25° south, with extensions to 32° north and 40° south (Walker 1990: 277). Environmentally they serve as flood control, and also as feeding and breeding grounds as well as a refuge for many species of flora and fauna, including fish. They also supply organic matter to adjacent waters that sustains recreational fishing. The variety of species is astounding (*ibid.* 278). The destruction of mangrove swamps by tourism development may be especially drastic in the LDCs, where the enforcement of environmental legislation is less strict than in the DCs. Such is the case of Igerote, a fishing village 120 kilometers east of Caracas, Venezuela. In order to transform Igerote into a beach resort, the developers destroyed the mangroves, using the notorious defoliant, Agent Orange. Not only were the mangroves destroyed, but so were fish and waterfowl, including the pelican that were meant to be a major tourist attraction of the resort. The bodies of dead fish and birds caused diseases among the local population. The poisoning of the ecosystem necessitated the temporary evacuation of a number of local inhabitants in 1982 (Hamele 1987: 114).

Similar dangers exist in the Caribbean Islands. Bacon (1987: 105–106) reports on the wetland losses due to tourism development in Jamaica. He argues that the threat of tourism expansion to coastal wetlands in the Caribbean may be averted by promoting them as sightseeing tourist attractions. Such a course of action would diversify the tourist supply, "while ensuring the protection of the ecologically and economically important ecosystems" (*ibid.* 105). He has developed a rating system for the evaluation of the attractiveness of individual coastal wetland ecosystems.

6.2.3.3 *Small Islands*

The ecosystems of small islands deserve a separate comment. Particularly interesting are islands located at lower latitudes (e.g., Lesser Antilles, Seychelles, and Maldives) because of specific conditions associated with their dependence on tourism which, together with agriculture, is the basis of their economic sustenance. Narrow resource bases do not allow the local economies to diversify beyond agriculture to become less dependent on tourism. Additionally, they face fierce competition on international trade markets for their fruits and commodities as prices have fallen considerably in recent years. Therefore, the local population increasingly turns to the tourist option to alleviate their economic problems of unemployment and overpopulation. International tourism is especially appropriate since it is a labor-intensive export industry, providing jobs for a large population and hard currency to pay for imports.

However, this tourist connection presents substantial environmental hazards associated with the fragility of tropical and subtropical environments and a shortage of space and water. Shortage of space results not only from the small size of the island but also from the almost exclusive concentration of tourism in the coastal area, where the beaches are the main attraction. Most of the local people also live in the littoral parts of the islands and the competition for space between tourism and local uses (including agriculture) is significant. The outcome of such a situation is congestion and environmental degradation. Another problem, mentioned in section 5.6.1, is the shortage of fresh water on most tropical and subtropical islands, a situation that is more acute than in similar continental areas where water transfers are feasible. Therefore, the competition for water between the local communal and agricultural sector and the rapidly expanding tourism sector is fierce. Freshwater supply is especially stressed during the tourist season because it coincides with the dry season on most tropical and subtropical islands. This creates a barrier to the growth of tourism, for example, in Hawaii and Fiji. Attempts to substitute fresh water with sea water for toilet requirements are criticized, because the salinity inhibits bacterial breakdown of sewage (WTO/UNEP 1983: 21).

The ecological aspects of tourism on small islands differ according to the nature of the island's geology. Low-lying limestone islands of coral-reef origin generally have enough flat land for the development of airports, golf courses, and hotels. However, atolls, i.e., coral islands consisting of a ring-shaped reef that encloses a lagoon, suffer from lack of space. Coral islands also experience severe water shortages due to relatively low precipitation levels (Brauer 1989: 151). This limits any development, including that of agriculture and tourism, and exacerbates competition between them for this precious resource. At the same time the weather patterns associated with little rain satisfy the needs of tourists. The superb white sand beaches, developed on coral sands, and the shallow reef maritime zone, perfect for snorkeling and scuba diving, are additional advantages. The main ecological threats of tourism are its voracious, and frequently wasteful use of water (see section 5.6.1), and the destruction of coral reefs (section 6.2.2).

The environmental constraints and advantages for tourism development on volcanic islands present a different picture. The problem of water shortage is less acute here because the volcanoes "catch" more rain than the low-lying limestone islands. For tourism, a disadvantage is the frequent cloud cover that hangs over such islands and increased precipitation. However, those drawbacks are compensated by spectacular vistas enjoyed by tourists, as, for example, in the majestic mountains of St. Lucia. The beaches of volcanic islands, such as some beaches on the island of Hawaii or on St. Lucia and Monserrat, are frequently poor, rocky, or covered with black volcanic sand, subject to intense daytime heating and, therefore, less desirable to tourists. Some of the volcanic islands, such as Martinique, though, are blessed with white, sandy beaches.

Flora and fauna of small islands are especially vulnerable to recreational impacts because of their small area (Peters and Lovejoy 1990: 356). As a result, environmental degradation occurs more rapidly. The relative ecological isolation of small-island environments resulted in the evolution of endemic species, which are more vulnerable to extinction. Especially dangerous is the introduction of exotic species by tourists, because the endemic species have not developed the necessary defence mechanisms against introduced competitors, predators and diseases. The result of this special vulnerability is the high rate of extinction of island species. Peters and Lovejoy (*ibid.* 356-358) describe the development impacts on a number of important island ecosystems, with an emphasis on Hawaii.

The intensity of tourism's impacts on the ecosystems of small, low-latitude islands ranges along a continuum, from very strong at one extreme to none at the other. Barbados, for example, is under considerable stress particularly from high-density, spatially concentrated tourism. On the highly developed western shore, the main problem is dumping of untreated sewage into the sea from hotels and local settlements. A certain role is also played by discharges from yachts. These destroy protective reefs and result in beach depletion (Archer 1985: 50; *New York Times* 9 December 1990). Sewage and other forms of water pollution threaten marine and coastal ecosystems on a number of other Caribbean islands (Edwards, T. 1988: 65). In the middle of the continuum such islands as St. Lucia and Dominica are less touristically developed; their ecosystems are still more or less unaffected by tourism. At the bottom of the continuum certain Pacific islands are not developed and lack modern amenities, such as electricity. How long can such idyllic environmental and social situations endure before local people to turn to tourism as the source of income?

The Galapagos Islands, Ecuador, should be treated as a special case, because despite the provisions of National Park status for most of their area, the islands suffer from disturbances caused by mass tourism (De Groot 1983: 295-298). There are practically no tourist limits other than on the capacity of tour boats and hotels. Tourists penetrate the islands on small boats run by locals or operating private yachts without proper permits; use illegal trails; leave garbage; and collect shells, rocks and plants. Increasing environmental pressure is exerted by the local population of 14,000, which is continuing to grow at an unacceptable rate of 12 percent per year (Weiner 1991). According to Eric Weiner, the World Wildlife Fund found that during the 1980s about 100 new plant species had been inadvertently introduced to the islands, threatening the fragile indigenous species with extinction. He also reports the case of marine turtles dying after swallowing plastic bags litter that they mistake for jellyfish. The management of the park faces many challenges (see section 9.4.3).

6.3 *The Freshwater Inland Ecosystems*

These are, historically, the oldest areas of recreation, used "when people feared the mountains and did not swim in the sea" (Mieczkowski, Z. 1990: 256). They are mostly lowland rural landscapes with leisure activities focused mostly on water. Therefore, the availability of clean water is essential for the development of tourism in these locations. Unfortunately, inland fresh waters generally show a higher degree of pollution than the seas, first, because of their smaller size and volume, and second, because they are surrounded from all sides by land that is a source of environmental degradation. On the other hand, recreational activities themselves contribute to the degradation of aquatic and coastal ecosystems of rivers, lakes, reservoirs and inland wetlands.

6.3.1 *Rivers*

Rivers are more environmentally resilient than lakes and reservoirs because their waters are less stagnant, continually receiving new inputs. However, these inputs tend to be increasingly polluted. The contribution of leisure activities to this environmental outrage may be substantial. Examples are the riparian and lacustrine ecosystems of the St. Lawrence River basin in Quebec. Nadeau (1982: 141–161) expresses scathing criticism over the situation in the central part of the basin. The degradation of the coastal ecosystems by such external factors such as Montreal's sewage, has been exacerbated by the second homes and their inhabitants, who proved to be outrageously careless in their approach to nature. First of all, property rights extend well into the water, effectively blocking public access to "almost all rivers and many lakes." The devastation of vegetation has caused destruction of wildlife habitats, erosion, the deterioration of esthetic values of the landscape, and unwelcome compositional changes of the ecosystems that result from the rise in water temperature. The erosion has caused silting, which decreases the process of photosynthesis. Another source of harm to the St. Lawrence River basin is the lack or insufficiency of septic facilities in the cottages, which then become an obvious source of water pollution. According to Nadeau, the inefficacy of the septic tanks is associated with the inadequate size of the lots: less than 930 square meters instead of the 3,700 recommended for effective handling of waste. Cottages, recreational facilities, and even roads are built too close to the water's edge, where they thoughtlessly encroach on aquatic ecosystems thoughtlessly placed recreational facilities, and even roads.

6.3.2 *Lakes and Reservoirs*

All types of water bodies are affected by the impact of recreation. However, lakes are most vulnerable because of their relatively small volume and constrained exchange of water. Their self-cleaning process is restricted, mainly because unpolluted inputs are limited and polluted water from surrounding areas is prevalent. Lakes also tend to warm up more than rivers and seas.

Lake ecosystems are especially prone to the process of eutrophication (see section 2.4). This may effectively destroy the life in the lakes, if cottage overdevelopment is allowed. The natural life cycle of a lake progresses from *oligotrophic,* i.e., rich in oxygen, nutrient-deficient, and unproductive to *eutrophic*, i.e., low in oxygen, but nutrient-rich and highly productive, with increased levels of organic matter decay. The waters of such aged lakes become increasingly fertile and shallow. The process of eutrophication may be accelerated by the impact of second homes on lakes, associated with septic fields and the use of lawn fertilizers, detergents, and washing materials that add nutrients, such as phosphorus and ammonia, into the water. The nutrient content of water may be augmented by construction of docks and by recreational activities, such as motorboating, that promote bank erosion. This results in leaching of nutrients out of the soil, especially nitrates and phosphates (both of natural and human origin) contained in the soil at water edges. The nutrient overload in lake water is further exacerbated by wading, swimming, and boating activities that stir up bottom sediments. All these recreational activities make lakes shallower and increase water turbidity, due to suspended solids. Turbidity detracts from the recreation experience of swimmers and boaters by decreasing the light penetration. Furthermore, turbidity reduces photosynthesis and restricts the vision of aquatic animals. These impacts are most severe in shallow water and in narrow channels.

The less advanced the process of eutrophication the more suitable is the lake for water-related recreation and as habitat for aquatic organisms, especially sport fish. Wall and Wright (1977: 29), referring to lakes in the Canadian Shield, state that, "for recreational use, high water quality means low productivity so that lakes are clear, cool and deep." In other words they advocate oligotrophic or mesotrophic (intermediate stage) lakes for recreation rather than eutrophic, where aerobic life forms, such as fish, have limited chances for survival. The authors see the infertility of the soils surrounding the lakes in the Canadian Shield as an asset, slowing down the eutrophication process. Despite the validity of this argument, one has to add an important caveat. The Precambrian Shield of North America is prone to acidification. The rocks are hard and the capacity of the lake water to dissolve decomposing vegetation and animal waste is limited. As a result their ph level is 5.5 or less, which deviates considerably from the neutral optimum level of 7. Recreational activities exacerbate the acidity problems by adding sulphur dioxide (SO_2) and nitrogen oxide (NO_2) to the lake water, and to the atmosphere, in the form of acid rain.

The process of eutrophication leads to oxygen depletion in water. Maintaining a high level of dissolved oxygen in water is especially important because it is necessary for respiration of fish and other aquatic fauna. Oxygen is either absorbed directly from the atmosphere or produced photosynthetically by aquatic organisms under the impact of sunrays. Warm lakes are more susceptible to oxygen depletion than cool lakes because oxygen solubility is inversely correlated with water temperature. Adding nutrients to water leads to excessive plant growth (e.g., algae, weeds) in the *epilimnion* (upper water layers) and decreases the amount of dissolved oxygen. The decomposition of dead organic matter that ultimately falls to the *hypolimnion* (bottom strata) leads to a more significant oxygen depletion in this water layer. This forces the fish to move up to the epilimnion with its higher oxygen levels in order to survive. While there is normally enough dissolved oxygen for their requirements in the upper water layers, the water temperature could be too high for survival of some fish species. The result is the change in species composition: cold-water fish are displaced by warm-water fish and habitat conditions for fish and other aquatic animals generally deteriorate. Plant life may also be affected by oxygen depletion: "some submerged species of aquatic plants are sensitive to low levels of dissolved oxygen and are replaced by more tolerant species" (Hammitt and Cole 1987: 106).

Determining the level of recreational impacts on the sensitive environments of lakes is an important task for research. However, arriving at quantitative data is rarely possible. It is especially difficult to determine to what extent various components of tourism, such as sewage and other wastes contribute to the process of eutrophication, and to what extent agricultural, communal and industrial inputs are to blame (Satchell and Marren 1976: 65). All one knows for certain, as explained above, is that recreational nutrient discharges into lakes lead to their deoxygenization, destruction of plant life, death of fish, and algal bloom. In short, they kill aquatic life.

Much easier to ascertain is the mechanical damage caused by such impacts as direct impact with the shore bank erosion and water turbidity. Bank erosion, resulting from recreational boating (including water-skiing), seems to be proportional to the size and speed of the boat, although speedboats that glide on the water's surface appear to erode less than slower boats. Also, the distance of the boat to the shore has to be taken into account: In the summer of 1990 I measured some erosion damage caused by speeding motorboats in the narrow water courses adjacent to Lake Evoron in the Russian Far East, although there was no damage on the lake shore. Another important variable is the resiliency of soil and supporting vegetation against the mechanical impact of waves generated by the motorboat traffic of local recreational hunters. Generally, it does not seem that bank erosion caused by recreational motorboating exerts a significant environmental impact. However, local effects can be severe, as evident in Manitoba (Professor William Pruitt: personal communication).

Research conducted on water turbidity brought about by propeller action of boats indicates that the effects might be greater in cases where bottom soils are predominantly clay. When the water is shallow and motorboat traffic heavy, the stirring of the bottom mud may result in loss of oxygen in the water, and consequently, in increased fish mortalities (Satchell and Marren 1976: 66). Additionally, the development of the bottom vegetation is highly impeded.

Another recreational impact on lake ecosystems is the presence of boat launching sites and marinas, especially if dredging was conducted prior to construction of the marinas.

Unfortunately, lack of quantitative research data means that information on the impact of leisure activities on lakes and reservoirs is somewhat qualitative and descriptive. Various reports on lake pollution abound: e.g., the once pristine Swiss lakes are today polluted not only by agriculture (see section 2.7) but also by thousands of pleasure motorboats—2,800 on Lake Lugano and 36,000 on Lake Constance (*Der Spiegel* 1990, 23: 180). Similarly the northern, Swiss part of Lago Maggiore is severely polluted by pleasure boats. The "collapse" of the Millstatter Lake in Austria during the early 1970s is largely attributed to unregulated tourist-boat traffic (WTO/ UNEP 1983: 24). However, many quantitative questions should be answered: How much of this environmental damage is due to leisure activities? How much to other (external) sources? How much do the outboard motors pollute? What is the impact of raw sewage release from onboard toilets (see section 5.6. 2)? Noise pollution produced by motorboats is much easier to quantify.

Similar environmental pressures caused by tourism development are being exerted on Lake Shikotsu, located on the least-developed of the larger Japanese islands, Hokkaido. These pressures are aggravated by the recent policy of the Tokyo government to stimulate tourism. Another factor exacerbating these pressures is that Japan is a latecomer to the environmental movement. There are fears that Lake Shikotsu ecosystems, which include such rare birds as swans, may suffer from tourist invasion. The coastal highway has already caused a lot of damage.

Another Asian example, mentioned in section 2.7, is Lake Dal, situated in the center of Srinagar, Kashmir. David Mercer (1991: 272) deplores the extreme tourist pressure that seriously threatens the lake ecosystem. Tourists live in about 1,000 houseboats that routinely discharge raw sewage and other effluents into the shallow lake. The result is eutrophication and the spread of weeds. Because of all the tourist and nontourist impacts on Dal Lake it has shrunk by 50 percent during the last 100 years, and its wildlife is being destroyed. There was a growing concern that the thriving tourism industry may be harmed by these unfavorable developments. The environmentalists' call for a stop of tourism development was unexpectedly successful: political trouble in Kashmir has wiped out tourism in this part of India almost entirely.

One of the most celebrated causes of controversy between developers and environmentalists in North America is over the delicate ecosystem of Lake Tahoe, shared by California and Nevada. The controversy has dragged on for years and the environment of Lake Tahoe continues to deteriorate: just between 1968 and 1985 the transparency of this unique water body declined by one foot a year (*New York Times* 10 March 1985). A typical threat to some Canadian lakes, located supposedly in the wilderness, is illustrated by the situation of Clear Lake in the Riding Mountain National Park. A past policy that allowed townsites and cottages within the national park boundaries means that Clear Lake is in danger because of a sewage lagoon, septic fields, landfill site, gasoline storage units, power boat exhaust emissions, contaminated runoff from cottages, and pesticide run-off from the golf course. All these perils are internal—associated with the impacts of recreational activities in Riding Mountain National Park and its townsite of Wasagaming. Additionally, there are external impacts on the lake, such as agricultural run-off from the surrounding countryside.

However, not all news about the environmental health of lakes is bad. The situation on the Great Lakes has improved: despite proliferations of spirogyra algae in Saginaw Bay, and the plague of zebra mussels mentioned in section 2.7, the cleanup of the lakes is well advanced and tourists are enjoying better environmental conditions, including better fishing, than in the recent past. These positive changes can be partly attributed to the work of the International Joint Commission (Canada-United States). To reduce damage caused by flooding and shore erosion, the commission recommends building up beaches, planting trees to anchor soil, moving vulnerable buildings, building levees and retaining walls, and introducing setback requirements. However, the battles between environmentalists and developers of recreational facilities flare up occasionally, as they did at the Long Point Biosphere Reserve in southern Ontario (*New York Times* 28 March 1993).

6.3.3 *Freshwater Wetlands*

Freshwater inland wetlands occupy much larger spaces than do the coastal wetlands examined in section 6.2.3.2 above. Coastal wetlands are limited mainly to a narrow coastal zone, whereas inland fresh water wetlands take up large areas, constituting significant shares of certain regions. For example, wetlands cover 41 percent of the Canadian province of Manitoba. As a result, their importance cannot be underestimated.

Freshwater wetlands encompass a wide variety of physical and biological environments, such as marsh, swamp, slough, bog, fen, swale, sump, muskeg, moor, mire, heath, carr, pothole and peatland (Bardecki 1984: 3). Some other terms are: bottomlands, bayous, oxbows, billabongs, sinks, kettles. This is probably the reason why there is no consensus regarding a universally acceptable definition of wetland. There is, however, a general agreement among scientists that these wet environments occupy a space on the continuum between totally dry and totally wet environments and that the shallowest ground-water table is at or near the surface for part of the year (*ibid.* 3-4) enabling anaerobic bacterial activity in the soil to take place.

Despite the fact that, environmentally and economically, wetlands have important and beneficial functions, inland wetlands, like coastal wetlands, have long been regarded as "inappropriate" land, which must be "corrected" and "reclaimed." Therefore, swamps and marshes have been drained and dredged for hundreds of years to expand cultivated and forested areas. Free market economies have stimulated the drainage of wetlands by providing tax incentives and subsidies for the conversion of wetlands into other uses, mostly agriculture. The Common Agricultural Policy (CAP) of the European Union has provided high intervention (subsidized) prices for agricultural output, and, in Western Europe, has been the driving force behind the conversion of wetlands to cultivated fields. Agricultural policies in North America are similar. As a result, the losses of wetlands all over the world have been staggering. Thus, in the lower 48 states in the U.S., over half of wetlands have been lost since the 1780s. The reclamation of wetlands covering floodplains has been especially damaging. In this respect, tourism may have played some role. River floodplains should have remained flooded for the benefit of wetland ecosystems that prevent catastrophic inundations, and were used "softly" for recreation and other nondestructive economic activities.

Unfortunately, the real value of wetlands has been recognized only recently, and nowadays, the loss of wetlands to agriculture, forestry, industry, and settlements all over the world is the subject of grave concern among ecologists (see section 6.2.3.2 above). For ages, agriculture has been the most important claimant for space occupied by swamps and marshes, but more recently, a new type of development increasingly demands wetland areas—human leisure time activities. Indeed, many wetlands have been lost, especially since the 1950s, to accommodate such modern human pursuits.

Lacustrine and *riverine* marshes, i.e., marshes located on lakes and rivers, are the primary targets for tourist development. Here land is frequently needed for hotels, marinas, and other tourist facilities. Bardecki (1984: 15) investigated this in a limited area of Ontario and came to the conclusion that recreation development is not a major factor in wetland loss. However, one has to take into account that his project was conducted in Canada, which is blessed with relatively abundant resources and strict environmental laws. In other areas the situation is much more difficult, and tragic destruction is taking place.

This systematic destruction of wetlands is the direct result of the construction of recreational subdivisions and retirement communities in Florida (see section 6.2.3.2). In fact, these developments, combined with the urban sprawl of such cities like Miami, appear to be the main threat to Florida's freshwater wetlands. However, agriculture is still a considerable concern because of the state's intensive citrus-fruit, sugar-cane and vegetable cultivation. Dikes and highways act as dams which destroy aquatic plants and wildlife. "Channels for drainage or boat access and big-wheeled marsh vehicles cut grooves in the peat so water no longer flowed in broad sheets. Water tables were generally lowered more than a meter..." (*ibid.* 30). Odum, *et al.* refer to another consequence of the drainage of wetlands in Florida: Wetlands prevent frost because water releases some heat before it freezes. The loss of wetlands "may have caused frost damage to go further south" (Odum, *et al.* 1987: 26).

Not only have changes in land use contributed to wetland destruction, so has fresh water from wetlands. Thus, a significant part of Florida's freshwater wetlands have disappeared (saltwater wetlands in Florida were discussed in section 6.2.3.2). The expansion of retirement settlements and other recreation-related accommodation is contributing significantly to the plight of Florida's freshwater wetlands. Particularly threatened are large parts of the Everglades in southern Florida (see section 2.7), which are America's largest wetland, and one of the largest wetland systems in the world. The development of tourism and recreation in southern Florida contributes significantly to the loss of this valuable ecosystem (more than half of the original Everglades have been lost) as a result of contamination by chemicals, and desiccation caused by the lowering of the water table. Such dried-up wetlands are susceptible to wind erosion and the invasion of exotic plant species, such as Australian eucalyptus *(Melaleuca quinquinervia)* and Brazilian pepper *(Schinus terelninthinus)*. Eucalyptus drains the land and Brazilian pepper proliferates as a weed, choking all other growth (*Economist* 17 October 1992). The withdrawal of fresh water from the aquifers to supply the Miami region also has qualitative consequences because it permits sea water to seep into them, thus increasing their salinity.

The importance of the preservation of North American freshwater wetland ecosystems has been recognized, and some measures to achieve that goal have been undertaken (see section 5.8.2 above). However, much more needs to be done, and how much will be done depends on the outcome of the political struggle between developers and environmentalists. The environmentalists' position could be summarized as follows: Any development of wetland and the construction of new wells has to be stopped. Where feasible, the old land-use patterns and drainage systems have to be restored, the drainage canals covered, and the protected areas, such as the Everglades National Park, extended (the 1990 extension was too small). It seems that environmentalists have won the battle, and the plan to restore the Everglades marshes has been in progress since 1994. There are similar reports from all over the world (*World Press Review*, November 1994: 39). The battles between environmentalists and developers are fought on all political levels, including local. An example of such controversy involves the approval to develop a golf course in Glen Arbor, Michigan, a resort surrounded by the Sleeping Bear Dunes National Lakeshore, a National Park Service property (Schneider 1992).

Europe has its own "Everglades"-like problems—the Doñana wetlands on the lower Guadalquivir, southwest of Sevilla, Spain. Doñana serves as bird habitat and resting place for birds migrating between Europe and Africa and the Straits of Gibraltar is their route. Together, about one million birds, including the majority of Europe's geese, use Doñana annually. Some of the birds are protected, e.g., 15 pair of Caesar eagles. The mammalian inhabitants include deer, boar and 20 survivors of the very rare lynx. Unfortunately, this remnant of former European wetlands is not safe from the onslaught of tourism development. The Doñana has been invaded by developers eager to build hotels, resorts, golf courses and marinas. Farmers use water from the wetlands to irrigate their rice and strawberry fields. As a result, in the last 15 years the water table has dropped from 2 to 9 meters. Hunters and poachers poison the ecosystem with lead. As with the Everglades, the direct issue is not the relatively small Coto de Doñana National Park (500 square kilometers) established in 1965, but the wetlands that extend far beyond the park boundaries. Tourism development directly threatens these areas and the survival of the wetlands is at stake. In 1990 the European Community's Environmental Agency filed a complaint against the Spanish government for failing to take measures against tourism expansion (in the form of hotels and other tourist infrastructure) that threatened the survival of Doñana. Spanish NGOs also took action and formed the "Save Doñana Movement." The beleaguered Spanish government enacted the "Plan for the Water Management Regeneration of Doñana," envisaging the re-supply of the dried-out areas with water. Land purchases are also planned. The development of ecotourism is suggested as an economic alternative for the area (Simons 1992; *Time* 20 August 1990; *Der Spiegel* 1991, 50).

Regarding the protection of wetlands in the LDCs from tourism development, frequently there has been a lack of political will on the part of government agencies to restrain environmentally destructive tourism development. A good illustration of this is the unchecked tourist invasion of what is arguably the world's largest wetland—Pantanal, 80 percent of which is located in western Brazil, with the rest in Bolivia and Paraguay. Besides the tourist infrastructure, overfishing and overhunting by tourists, poaching has also increased. This is because tourism is a good market for such fashionable items as alligator shoes and venison meals. There are also external forces destroying the Pantanal: gold miners poison it with chemicals while farmers devastate the natural vegetation and poison the environment with fertilizers and pesticides.

North America is the world leader in freshwater wetland preservation. Some controversy surrounds the definition of the term *wetland.* The resolution of this issue is momentous because an agreement on a definition will be instrumental in determining the parameters of preservation by U.S. federal authorities. The definition of wetlands, accepted in 1989, presents the following criteria: First, the availability of certain water-dependent (hydrophytic) plants in the area, and second, the saturation of the soil at or within about 45 centimeters (18 inches) of the surface for at least seven consecutive days during the growing season, or 15 consecutive days of standing water annually. There is scientific evidence that several days of saturation are needed for the soil to lose a sufficient amount of oxygen for the development of hydrophytic plants. According to the definition, about 384,000 square kilometers in the contiguous 48 states qualify as wetlands. This scientific definition is under attack by developers and federal officials who consider it unnecessarily strict, disqualifying development from too many areas. An additional argument against this definition is financial: excessive government funds are needed to acquire the areas, designated as wetlands, from private owners unable to develop them.

Another reason to preserve wetlands is as a habitat for hunting. In this respect the powerful Ducks Unlimited, discussed in section 5.8. 2.1. above, should be praised. Although subject to criticism by environmentalists, Ducks Unlimited throughout its existence (and especially within the framework of the 1986 North American Waterfowl Management Plan) has contributed financially to the preservation of many wetland habitats in Canada and the United States. The wetlands have been preserved not only for waterfowl, but for aquatic plants, for song birds, shore birds, muskrats, beaver, and other species of wildlife. However, as indicated in section 5.8.2.1., Professor William Pruitt (personal communication) regrets that this protection has not been extended to species that might conceivably affect ducks negatively, such as mink, weasel, raccoon, hawk, and owl. Therefore, the wetland ecosystems managed by Ducks Unlimited are ecologically incomplete.

6.4 *Mountain Ecosystems*

6.4.1 *Introduction*

As mentioned in section 2.8, mountains are now the second most popular ecosystem to tourists, after coastal environments, attracting millions each year. As a consequence, these ecosystems also suffer from tourism overdevelopment, aggravated by the fact that they share, with the coastal environments, the same unfortunate characteristics: fragility and sensitivity to human impacts, combined with low ecological carrying capacity (see section 2.8).

Since 1945, mountain ecosystems have been under increasing pressure from human development. Tourism has played a significant role in this. The pattern of tourism impacts on mountain ecosystems vary on a continuum from extremely concentrated to dispersed. Thus, alpine skiers, except heli-skiers, operate in relatively small areas because of their dependence on uphill transportation facilities and groomed ski runs. Cross-country skiers, snowmobilers, winter and summer hikers spread their impact in a more dispersed pattern. In addition, tourists need a means of transportation and access routes to their destinations. They require water, accommodation facilities, food-catering establishments and other resources. All this amounts to considerable stress on the mountain ecosystems, which raises serious concerns about their preservation. The preservation of mountain ecosystems is inseparable from other aspects of conservation. If the unmatched splendor and beauty of the mountains is negatively affected, if they stop providing healthy environments for human recreation and for physical and mental satisfaction and healing, then invariably their other, nontourist-related functions will suffer.

The impacts of tourism on mountain ecosystems vary from continent to continent and from country to country. Best off are the North American mountain ecosystems because they are protected by an excellent network of national parks and reserves. Therefore, the criticism levied below will focus on other areas, especially on the Alps, which seem to be the most affected by the negative impacts of tourism. The following discussion of the effects of tourism/recreation on mountain ecosystems will focus on four impacts: tourism accommodation, road transportation, off-road traffic, and tourists, i.e., hikers, trekkers, and mountaineers (sections 6.4.2–6.4.5). Separate attention will be given to winter recreation (section 6.4.6) and littering (section 6.4.7).

6.4.2 *Development of Tourism Accommodation Infrastructure*

Perhaps the most obvious and significant source of tourism-induced impacts on mountain ecosystems is the spread of tourism and recreation infrastructure. In an environment where flat space is at a premium, the land needed for leisure-time accommodation and for automobile access roads, is often the best available. Secondly, space taken by tourist development is mostly covered with protective vegetation that is lost to a greater detriment than on flatland. Thus, the development of recreational infrastructure is the most damaging type of tourist ecological and visual intrusion into the mountains. This injurious process is nowadays well advanced in the mountain areas of the DCs, to such a degree that one may call it "recreational suburbanization" (or even "urbanization") spreading consistently since the end of the Second World War is mostly due to the construction of second homes, called variously vacation houses, vacation residences, secondary residences or cottages. Developed to a lesser extent, but still substantially, are condominiums and resorts.

In these most spectacular landscapes of Europe the residential deconcentration, most of it recreational, has acquired appalling proportions. West Europeans, enjoying the affluence acquired since the 1950s, display a particular predilection for ownership of leisure retreats, especially individual vacation houses which "consume" much more space than hotels and condominiums. Everyone wants to have a cottage, even a most modest one, preferably in the Alps. This is also the unfortunate prospect for the Carpathian Mountains when free market prosperity spreads to central Europe or when affluent West Europeans develop a taste for that area. The same may eventually happen in former Yugoslavia and Caucasus.

This new trend in recreational land use has found favorable conditions for expansion in the economic and social factors that accelerate this process. Alpine agriculture is in crisis: poor soils, heavy work, and the inability to fully use modern technology has caused the farmers to engage in cattle breeding and dairying, which is associated with lower labor requirements than land cultivation, and with modest incomes per hectare. Initially, the result was not only a drop in land values but also rural out-migration. However, the process of depopulation in the Alps has recently slowed down, and even reversed in some areas, as a result of the penetration of tourism into the alpine environment.

The demand for land, associated with tourism development and the construction of thousands of vacation homes, caused real-estate prices, and consequently taxes, to soar, rendering work in agriculture unprofitable, and employment in tourism and construction relatively attractive. In such a situation the farmers have faced a dilemma: either to sell all their land and migrate to the cities, or to sell at least part of their land, and to switch from agriculture to tourism and tourism-related sources of income. The third solution is to combine employment in tourism with marginal agriculture, which is associated with the German term *Fremdenverkehrbauer*—"tourist farmer" (Stadel 1982: 9). This type of agritourism, based on the principle of multiple use, has proven to be economically viable. Thus, Alpine meadows are used for grazing in summer and for downhill skiing in winter. However, on balance, recreational land use has won the battle with agriculture, and has become the main economic sector in the Alps. In some areas, dominant tourism has completely supplanted agriculture and acquired a position of virtual tourist monoculture (Lichtenberger 1979, Singh and Kaur 1985: 369).

The invasion of the Alps, caused by lowland-generated affluence, propensity to own vacation homes, and the development of other tourist infrastructure, has to a large extent destroyed the beauty of the mountains. The first to go were the choice locations on the south-exposed slopes and at valley bottoms. Subsequently whole landscapes have been covered with cottages, with no space for additional construction. The problem is that in overpopulated Europe, universal ownership of second homes is practically impossible—there is simply not enough space for them, and their cancer-like expansion threatens the very survival of Alpine ecosystems.

Second homes are being constructed in an unplanned and almost unrestricted way, practically anywhere, including traditional resorts (Groetzbach 1985: 149), creating a new and ugly form of suburbanization. The microlocation of the subdivisions does not take into account the physical properties of the terrain, such as the drainage patterns or the degree of susceptibility to erosion (in the so-called *Flysch zones)*, landslides, and avalanches. The construction frequently exceeds the carrying capacity of the basic infrastructure, resulting in a host of problems, such as shortages in water supply, following drying up of wells.

As indicated above, the most vexing impact of mass second-homes development is visual pollution. There would be practically no change in the landscape if old farmhouses were adapted to serve as vacation residences. This should be considered positively as more and more Alpine farmers find mountain agriculture unprofitable and move to the cities, selling their farms. Their houses, together with the adjacent land, are being purchased by the urbanites and converted to second homes. Thus, the rural architecture is preserved. However, the mass development of new suburban-style second homes destroys the mountainscape, especially in areas where their construction is uncontrolled. In such cases, according to Barker (1982: 404), the traditional appearance of the Alpine settlement is lost, and it becomes replaced by a culturally incongruous jumble of quasi-suburban architecture (Lichtenberger 1979, Batzing 1984, Stadel 1982). The vegetation cover disappears as a new automobile access road network to the new subdivisions and to the individual homes invades the lower slopes. Cable ways and ski lifts span the space between the valley bottoms and the mountain peaks. The impact on the whole mountain landscape is so profound that it changes radically in practically every respect. The unique Alpine ecosystems are being destroyed by the exponential growth of a veritable concrete Alpinopolis of leisure exurbia, extending from southern Germany almost to the Po Valley in Italy.

The problem of the environmental impact of tourism is exacerbated by the fact that this impact is distributed, not homogeneously but is concentrated both horizontally and vertically. The horizontal concentration is discussed by Batzing (1984: 61) and Lichtenberger (1979: 424ff). Indeed, tourism hits only selected areas, first of all valley floors and areas considered appropriate or fashionable. Vertically, the impact is differentiated according to the elevation (*ibid.* 431). This differentiation is discussed in sections 6.4.3. and 6.4.6 below. Generally, after the initial destruction of the valley ecosystems, tourism onslaught moves towards the zone of Alpine meadows and rocks.

Barker analyses the impact of tourist infrastructure (mostly second homes), on two models: that of the eastern Alps, covering eastern Switzerland, Bavaria, Austria and northern Italy and the western Alpine model, typical in France. The chronologically older eastern model has developed a symbiosis between tourism and the local pastoral and agricultural communities in the valleys and at lower slopes and terraces. This model reflects the propensity "of German-speaking tourists for participation in local culture, rather than vacationing in enclaves" (Barker 1982: 408). Initially development was mainly confined to the conversion of old farm houses (primarily in valley locations as well as pasture huts situated higher up the slopes), into second homes. However, soon stresses appeared when masses of cottages and trailers surrounded the old villages built in traditional Tyrolean or Swiss style. Then they sprawled all over the lower slopes. Barker complains that this proliferation of vacation residences has been carried to the extreme in parts of northern Italy where planning controls are weak.

The second, more recent western Alpine model, has been developed by large tourism corporations in the French Alps: monofunctional integrated ski resorts, *stations integrées*, i.e., purpose-built "total resorts" have been constructed "ex nihilo" in the unpopulated subalpine and alpine zone above the forest line, bringing the skiers closer to the best and climatically most reliable runs. These resorts are not only economically but visually separated from local communities located in the valleys and on glacial terraces. They are eyesores marring the mountain landscapes, destroying the vegetation cover, causing erosion, and altering the drainage patterns.

The problem of second-home overdevelopment in the North American mountain ecosystems pales in comparison with the Alps. However, some problems are occurring, as for example, in the Adirondacks and the Rockies, particularly in Colorado and Montana (Egan 1991b). Albert Gore (1992: 78) complains about erosion on the hillsides in his native Tennessee caused by new subdivisions depriving the ecosystems of protective vegetation cover.

6.4.3 *Road Transportation Infrastructure*

The intrusion of mass tourism into the mountain ecosystems has been facilitated by the construction of paved roads that have the capacity to bring thousands of tourists, including the very young, seniors, and handicapped, into the heart of the mountains. The recognition of the positive aspects of creating an opportunity for all people to enjoy this superb environment should not obscure the negative impacts associated with the mass intrusion into formerly isolated, and ecologically susceptible areas. The Alps, avoided by people until the nineteenth century (Mieczkowski, Z. 1990: 59), are now visited by over 100 million tourists annually. The consequences for the mountain ecosystems are inevitable: air pollution, noise, traffic jams, dust, destruction of rock surfaces, collection of rocks and minerals, devastation of the vegetation cover resulting in erosion, spread of exotic plant species brought by the motor vehicles, harassment of wildlife, illegal hunting, disruption of traditional daily movement and seasonal migration of animals, and the dangerous habit of feeding carnivores.

Air pollution caused by automobiles (see section 5.2) acquires especially obnoxious proportions in certain mountain tourist regions. Price (1981: 81-83; 433) concludes that the automobile does much more damage in the mountains than in the lowlands. The reason is that the combustion process at high elevations is less efficient because of the low oxygen content of the air. This results in increased emission of carbon monoxide (CO) and particulate matter. The worst situation occurs in the deep mountain valleys. Pollutant dispersal is inhibited, often further aggravated by thermal inversions, common in winter. Lundgren (1987: 52) observed that in winter the polluted air stagnating in the Alpine valleys as a result of *thermal inversions*, causes continuous smog and little sunshine, while the ski areas some 500 meters above are sunny. As a result of this frequent stagnation of air poisoned by automobile and house-heating emmissions, the health of the local population and tourists is threatened. Pollution also increases when traffic stagnates: traffic jams are ubiquitous on the mountain roads. Additionally, the impact of air pollution on mountain vegetation is more harmful than on the lowlands, because of the danger of erosion and the destruction of winter shelter for wildlife. Pollution not only kills the vegetation directly by poisoning but also impedes plant growth because of the reduction of sun penetration. Air pollution is not just limited to valleys, however—forests just below the tree line are especially affected because the toxic substances concentrate slightly below the thermal inversions that usually start at this altitude (*Waldsterben und Luftverschmutzung* 1984).

In consequence, "air pollution under these conditions may actually exceed, on a temporary basis, that found in major industrial areas" (Price 1981: 433). German research, conducted in the Alps, confirms his findings (WTO/UNEP 1993: 13).

El Samra (1984: 9) indicates that, "along certain mountain passes carbon monoxide has been found to reach as much as three times the average urban concentrations." The particulate matter serves as hygroscopic nuclei for condensation of smog, frequent in some mountains, such as the Appalachians. The automobile-caused smog may obscure the most beautiful mountainscapes and cause multiple automobile collisions. To cope with air pollution, the Alpine countries have recently mandated catalytic converters in all cars; there is hope that the situation will improve.

Space is at a premium within the steep mountain topography. Roads with their switchbacks and curves use a lot of it. The automobile roads not only take space but also change the mountain ecosystems profoundly by diverting water courses. Construction of bridges, tunnels, anti-avalanche, anti-rockfall facilities and turnabouts, all change the drainage patterns on the slopes.

6.4.4 *Off-road Traffic*

The mountains, similarly to the coastal and inland ecosystems, also suffer from the invasion of ATVs. The results are predictable: destruction of vegetation, erosion, and harassment of wildlife. However, the mountain ecosystems, with their steep topography, are affected by other forms of off-road traffic, namely the funiculars, cableways, T-bars, chair-lifts and pomas. The landscapes of the Alps are deeply scarred by permanent structures associated with these modern means of vertical transportation that carry tourists from the valley bottoms to the highest peaks. Not only are the slopes physically transformed, but the beauty of the mountainscape is destroyed, especially in the alpine zone above the tree level. One has to see some of the alpine meadows used as ski runs above Zermatt, Switzerland, to realize the extent of the resulting visual pollution. Switzerland alone has over 1,700 such facilities (Krippendorf 1986: 14), and chances are they will multiply still further.

Noise pollution (see section 5.3) in the mountains has some unique features. The topography carries the noise of the off-road traffic to the heart of the mountains, making it louder and more disturbing. Therefore, not only motorized traffic (especially the ATVs), but tourists themselves should be singled out for criticism.

Some of them seem to enjoy yelling inside certain mountain amphitheaters, well-known for their echo effect, such as Königssee in the Bavarian Alps, or several places in the Tatra Mountains (Poland and Slovakia). The idea is to hear the echo of one's voice rebounding from the mountains. This is done with total disregard for other tourists and wildlife. The best response strategy to such behavior is education and regulation: in this respect Switzerland is the world leader.

6.4.5 *Hikers, Trekkers, and Mountaineers*

The fourth agent of tourist impacts on mountain ecosystems are hikers, trekkers, and mountaineers who penetrate deeply into the mountain ecosystems to places inaccessible by mechanical means of transportation. Their main impact is the destruction of mountain vegetation. As a result, herbivores are deprived of their winter grazing areas, and the mountain slopes lose their protective plant cover, especially forests. The result is the loss of plant and wildlife habitat, the destruction of winter storm refuge for the animals, and the disruption of their seasonal migration patterns. Another consequence is the increased danger of accelerated wind and water erosion (tourist's feet turning the trails into water runoff ditches), floods, landslides, mudslides, rock and snow avalanches. Indeed, reports of such disasters have multiplied in recent years (Price 1981, Mäder 1988, Ryan 1991: 96, *Süddeutsche Zeitung* 22 July 1987).

Trampling (see sections 5.5 and 5.7 above) is the most obvious source of direct tourist impacts on mountain vegetation and geology. Human feet trample plants, soil and rocks not only on hiking trails, but also at their edges, especially during wet weather conditions when pools of water accumulate in the middle of the trail and tourists walk at the side of the trail to avoid them. Steep trails and steep "shortcuts" trampled by hasty hikers create favorable conditions for gully erosion, particularly if they are widened to accommodate more tourist traffic.

Bayfield (1979) investigated the rates of recovery from tourist trampling in the Scottish mountains. He found not only very slow rates of recovery but also delayed damage inflicted on some species. One has also to keep in mind that wet uplands suffer more from trampling than dry ones. Especially vulnerable are poorly drained alpine meadows (Price 1981: 429, 430). Shrubs are also more susceptible to damage than grass (Weaver and Dale 1978). Weaver and Dale investigated the damage at various slope inclines. Their conclusion was that the steeper the slope the more damage. Trails on level ground sustained the least damage.

Another study of recovery rates, conducted by Beatrice Willard and John Marr (1971) in the Alpine tundra of Rocky Mountain National Park, found that areas trampled for only one year recover quickly, but the recovery periods increased dramatically with the length of exposure to trampling. This can develop to a point where it may take a thousand years to rebuild a natural climax ecosystem. The authors also note that recovered areas show a change in species composition.

A characteristic feature of mountain ecosystems is that their ability to absorb and assimilate tourism impacts decreases with altitude (Price 1981: 429). This is particularly significant in connection with increased accessibility to pristine high-elevation ecosystems by mountaineers using new sophisticated equipment to climb lofty peaks. Not only does modern technology enable the climbers to penetrate the formerly impenetrable, but their level of skills and knowledge has significantly increased in recent years. This improved accessibility is not without consequences for the precarious high-altitude vegetation, however, and the rock surfaces become scarred by piton holes, rock slides, and suffer other consequences of human intrusion.

Scenic outlooks and observation points of wildlife, because of heavy traffic, are especially vulnerable. In these spots special management techniques seem imperative to prevent still greater destruction. Thus, fencing, paving, boardwalks, and concrete platforms, though artificial, are being constructed as necessary evils. Another method to decrease the damage is to limit the number of tourists allowed into an area.

The generalizations discussed here are found worldwide. However, specific situations of mountain trekking in some LDCs, particularly in the Himalayas (Singh and Kaur 1985) are worthy of mention. 250,000 trekkers, including support staff, in Nepal and Indian Himalayas (Hamele 1987: 115), compete for fuel with the local population by collecting firewood, thus contributing substantially to the destruction of the sensitive high-elevation vegetation. Mäder (1988: 98–100) adds to the discussion about the disastrous contribution of trekking tourism to the deforestation of Nepal, a controversial issue with wide-ranging ecological consequences. One tourist uses about 6.4 kilograms of firewood per day, which equals the daily needs of two Nepalese families. Especially detrimental is the deforestation on higher elevations, precisely the area where the tourists are trekking. The result of this devastation is that the tree line in Nepal was lowered "by several hundred feet" (Boo 1990: 19). The degree of damage in the Himalayas is more pronounced than in the DCs, where mountain hikers enjoy a better and less remote tourist infrastructure, and therefore rely on local resources to a lesser degree. That means that hikers in the DCs are using less wood than the Himalayan trekkers. The second difference is that in the DCs the residents are using sources of energy other than wood, and do not compete with tourists for firewood, as they do in the Himalayas. Third, hiking trips in European and North American mountains are of a shorter duration; most tourists stay overnight either in resort hotels or in well-supplied mountain huts. Fourth, one could generalize that mountain hiking in the Alps and Rocky Mountains takes place mainly at lower elevations than in the Himalayas. Because the vegetation at low altitudes is less sensitive to tourist impact, the hikers inflict much less damage to the ecosystems than near and above the tree line.

To check the devastation of the Himalayan vegetation by trekkers, and to prevent resulting erosion and silting, appropriate measures are imperative. The restrictions or bans on the use of firewood by trekkers have been imposed in Nepal since 1979. Tourists (or rather their local luggage carriers), must haul the necessary fuel, mostly kerosene for portable stoves (Singh and Kaur 1985: 377; Mäder 1988). Other measures include the use of solar energy in lodges. However, those measures, although helpful, are only partial, and do not solve the entirety of environmental problems that result from the impact of tourism in the Himalayas.

The policy of the government of Bhutan should be singled out as exemplary in preventing the tourism-related degradation of mountain ecosystems. This policy upholds the symbiotic relationship between tourism and conservation and follows a "small is beautiful" principle. Unwise tourism development can be worse than no development at all. International tourism in Bhutan is planned and regulated with the conviction that the main concern, besides the preservation of the environment, is the maintenance of the country's cultural heritage. According to the master plan, only 5,000 tourists are admitted to the country annually (Singh 1989: 34). This target figure has been reached gradually; a well-designed phase-in program started with a 2,000 person ceiling. This policy, in contrast to the Nepalese approach, is based on the principle that quality is more important than quantity. Therefore, only relatively few high-spending tourists are allowed into the country to assure a minimal volume of impact associated with maximum economic benefit. Practically all tourists admitted to Bhutan proceed in organized and supervised groups on expensive package tours. Besides, Bhutan's tourism development master plan is holistic in nature by providing intersectoral linkages with other branches of the economy, particularly with agriculture (Singh 1989: 34). It remains to be seen if the privatization of the tourism industry in 1991 will influence this restrictive policy of the Bhutan government *(New York Times* 29 December 1991).

According to the available sources, in terms of its environmental conservation Bhutan ranks first among the noncommunist Himalayan countries. Nepal follows at a considerable distance, although some corrective measures have been undertaken in recent years, especially in the Khumbo and Annapurna regions (Tuting 1989). There is also a trend to increase the fees levied from mountaineering expeditions. Himalayan India, as a whole, has failed to respond to the challenges of mass tourism, which is penetrating the hitherto inaccessible areas by newly built roads. Despite the creation of a number of national parks, India fails to manage them properly (*ibid.* 36). Here Himalayan tourism planning is "ad hoc and impulsive... indifferent to research" (Singh 1989: 181). Nevertheless, in certain regions, such as the Kulu Valley in Himachal Pradesh, the planners deserve some accolades (*ibid.* 167).

6.4.6 *Winter Recreation*

Winter recreation (especially skiing, but also snowmobiling and snowboarding) is a particular source of stress for mountain ecosystems. Its effects on mountain ecosystems may be more significant than those of summer recreation, not only because it is apparently more destructive *per se* but also because the recreational resource use of the mountain ecosystems has, since the 1950s, become associated with "an overwhelming emphasis on winter sports" (Ives

1985: 35). It seems that this prevalence of winter over summer tourism increases with elevation. Downhill (alpine) skiing is now the most popular high-density and high-impact winter recreational activity in the DCs. It grew exponentially between 1950 and 1980, to level off in the 1980s. The number of regular skiers in the Alps today is about 50 million, using more than 14,000 ski lifts (*Economist* 15 February 1992) and more than 40,000 ski runs (Mäder 1988). Such numbers indicate the significance of their impact. Thus, a study by the International Center for Alpine Environments "identified downhill skiing as the most environmentally damaging activity in the Alps" (*Economist* 23 December 1989.

The main damage results from the removal of trees and other vegetation to create ski runs or *pistes*, sometimes expanded to veritable ski freeways (*Ski-Autobahnen).* Frequently the ski runs are associated with the ski lifts into whole integrated systems (*domains skiables* or *ski circuits*). With developments like these, the consumption of space becomes considerable. In the Austrian and Swiss Alps alone ski runs occupy 24,000 hectares of land (Hamele 1987: 114). The loss of vegetation cover deprives the slopes of their major stabilizing and snow-retaining capacity. Ski runs increase runoff: water comes down faster and in larger quantities. Slopes devoid of vegetation become unstable, susceptible to erosion, mudslides, and snow avalanches, which necessitates the construction of costly barriers and other devices that themselves degrade the ecosystem by changing it substantially. "Erosion inhibits the regeneration of the vegetation, especially above 2,200 meters" (Mosimann 1985: 29). In fact, soil profiles on ski slopes may never recover after being deprived of protective vegetation cover (Batzing (1984: 67). The environmental changes associated with ski development also threaten settlements, including those that are part of the tourism infrastructure, located at the valley bottoms: the slopes, denuded for ski runs, are more prone to destruction by flooding, landslides, mudflows and avalanches (Simmons 1988). Water stagnating at the valley bottoms may occasionally lead to the creation of marshes.

The second type of skiing-related damage to mountain ecosystems is slope modification. In the past, the ski runs used to follow the contours of the relief, but today this is not good enough. The ski slopes are being remodeled to render them more "skiable" and to make way for the construction of ski facilities, transportation infrastructure, and parking lots. This modification, called *grading*, is sometimes extensive, especially if bulldozers are used. It changes the slope profiles and upsets their natural balance (Candela 1982). According to Mosimann (1985) this procedure is widespread in the Swiss Alps and its effects are greatest above the timber line where as much as 15 percent of the surface area may have been affected. In places where bulldozers may not be able to do the job, dynamite is used to blast away parts of mountains.

The third damage is snow compaction resulting from ski, snowmobile, and foot trampling on snow. Baiderin (1978), investigating the effects of winter recreation on the slopes in the vicinity of Kazan, Russia, concluded that snow compaction results not only in deeper grass and soil freezing, which prevents good grass development, but also in uneven thawing. It becomes instrumental in initiating the spring erosion process. Satchell and Marren (1976: 56) indicate that compaction "tends to conserve the snow by delaying melting" and increasing runoff. According to Hammitt (1987: 50), compaction of snow by trampling and snowmobiles in the Alps reduces the ground temperature by 11°, as compared to undisturbed snow. "The soil under the compacted snow freezes about one month earlier and thaws in average two to three weeks later in the spring. This shortened growing season is critical to flowering plants" (Hammitt 1987: 50). The skis and the heavy slope-grooming machinery destroy the grass directly, by physical impact, or indirectly by removing the protective snow cover entirely—this leads to a complete loss of vegetation if the slope profile is modified by machines. The problem of vegetation destruction is by far not limited to the ski runs. Down-hill and cross-country skiers frequently destroy tree seedlings invisible under the snow. Satchell and Marren (1976: 56) refer to a Swedish study reporting "severe damage to conifer plantations by snowmobiles with death of pines caused by infection of bruised stems by *Phacidium infestans*."

The fourth type of damage is associated with the efforts of the tourism business to extend the skiing season, which may be becoming shorter as a result of global warming (McBoyle and Wall 1992). Consequently, more and more snow-making machinery is used on the slopes of fashionable European and North American ski resorts. The application of snow-making is limited because it does not work at temperatures above -2° C. Snowmaking is associated with a number of significant environmental impacts, including visual pollution of the slopes. Snowmaking uses water, a resource in short supply in winter. It changes the microclimate and shortens the vegetation growing period, which is already very brief in high mountains. The extension of the winter season by snowmaking may also upset the lifecycle of hibernating animals, such as the marmot. The availability of artificial snow also stimulates skier participation, which results in more recreational impact on the mountain ecosystems.

The fifth category of impacts is *heli-skiing*. The majority of skiers are quite content with the well-groomed ski runs and the standard uphill transportation. There is, however, a sizable group of experts who prefer *heli-skiing*, sometimes called *chopper skiing*. Yet, there is evidence that helicopters are far from environmentally-friendly. Preliminary research results in the Alps and in the Himalayas (Batzing 1984: 65) show that they are a source of severe ecological damage: their vibrations cause snow avalanches; their noise drives hibernating animals from their lairs compelling them to expend valuable energy in digging new ones. As a result, many animals fail to survive the winter. The use of helicopters also improves accessibility to glaciers, especially for summer skiing, contributing to the contamination of water supplies at the source.

All these impacts of winter recreation on mountain ecosystems result in their serious degradation, as illustrated by the quantitative scientific data supplied by soil and vegetation research: nutrient status, humus content, water-holding capacity, and fertilizer retention are much lower on the ski runs than on the undisturbed slopes (Mosimann 1985: 36; Mäder 1988: 100). In the 1980s the development of new research techniques, such as the Geographic Information System (GIS), enabled scientists to obtain more exact quantitative data on the deterioration of the ski runs. Such investigations were conducted within the wider framework of the Man and Biosphere (MAB) project of the United Nations, initiated in connection with the 1992 Winter Olympics. The GIS computers facilitate the combination of data pertaining to various impacts and generalize them on maps scaled 1:5,000 (Hamele 1987: 132–133).

The debate over the environmental impacts of winter sports, and particularly of skiing, has intensified in connection with the large-scale developments associated with the 1992 Winter Olympics in Savoy, France. The environmentalists criticize the losses in vegetation cover resulting from the construction of new ski runs, uphill transportation, and parking lots. They denounce the rerouting of a stretch of the Isère River, the construction of a four-lane freeway from Chambery to Albertville, and the extension of the TGV (*Train de grande vitesse*, high-speed train) to the ski resorts beyond Albertville.

The construction of practically all 1992 Olympic facilities resulted in serious environmental disruptions. All slopes used for competition were modified. The ski-jump in Courcheval involved carting away an entire slope and driving 300 giant piles into the mountainside. Similar methods were used to prepare some of the *pistes*, the high-speed downhill course where the slope had to be adjusted to speeds exceeding 200 kilometers per hour. To construct access roads to the Olympic skiing areas whole mountains were dynamited away in the name of peaceful international competition. Also criticized was the construction of the world's largest bobsled course between La Plagne and La Roche. This two-kilometer-long concrete run, built on geologically unstable ground in an avalanche zone (now devoid of vegetation) has greatly increased the threat to landslides and avalanches threatening the ski resort of La Roche. The cooling system of the course is another environmental hazard: During the February 1992 Olympics, 50 tons of ammonia were used to freeze the ice surface on the course. Ammonia is a volatile chemical that emits toxic fumes, causing respiratory problems. Therefore, local residents living near the runs were issued gas masks. The long-range effects of this chemical pollution are not known.

On balance, one has to point out that there may be some long-range positive aspects from the 1992 Olympic development in store. Additional sewage-treatment facilities have been added to the existing ones, dramatically alleviating the problems of the notorious overflows of raw sewage into the mountain streams. The improvements in the transportation infrastructure may alleviate the notorious traffic jams on Savoy's highways and decrease the associated pollution and accidents on winding mountain roads. The extension of the TGV train service may encourage tourists to use fast and safe public transportation rather than private cars to reach the skiing areas. To fend off avalanches and landslides from roads and ski runs a number of barriers have been constructed. Explosive devices for preventive strikes on accumulated snow have also been installed. Environmental concerns were taken into account in designing the facilities. For example, when building the men's downhill run at Val d'Isère, a special curve was introduced to protect a rare mountain columbine (*World Press Review*, February 1992: 47). Although these benefits may seem weak, they have to be mentioned. On balance, however, the 1992 Winter Olympic site is another example of tourist overdevelopment, detrimental environmentally, and perhaps a white elephant economically.

The unfavorable environmental record of the 1992 Winter Olympics in the French Alps had an interesting impact on the 1994 Winter Olympics in Lillehammer, Norway. The Norwegians intended to break the unsavory pattern and organize the world's first "Green Olympics." The Prime Minister, Gro Harlem Bruntland, former chairperson of the United Nations Commission on Environment and Development, (known for its 1987 report "Our Common Future") played a leading role. Bruntland's government, and specifically the Ministry of the Environment, sponsored Project Environment-Friendly Olympics, an organization mandated to minimize the environmental impact of the 1994 Winter Olympics. The environmentalists, members of the Norwegian Society for the Conservation of Nature, initially fought against Norway's Olympic bid. But once it was clear Norway was designated to host the games, the environmentalists followed the maxim "if you can't lick 'em, join 'em." They made an unprecedented decision to get involved and to work with the Lillehammer Olympic Organizing Committee (LOOC) in developing appropriate environmental guidelines for the planning and construction of sport and tourist facilities associated with the games. Standards included avoiding gigantic monumental structures and slope modelling; the construction of arenas harmonizing with the surrounding topography and cultural landscape; and the use of local materials, such as stone and wood, for building facilities; a focus on energy efficiency and recycling. In particular, the Cavern Hall Hockey Rink was built inside a hollowed-out mountain, and the bob and luge track was sunk into the ground to avoid the ugly support beams of other tracks. Additionally, the Project Environment-Friendly Olympics may boast several victories against harmful location of facilities: the construction of the skating rink initially was planned on protected wetland reserve, was cancelled, and transferred to another location, and the nature reserve was enlarged.

6.4.7 *Littering*

Littering (see section 4.7 above) is rampant in any ecosystem but most damaging, alongside with the polar regions, is its effect on mountain ecosystems. Tourists and mountaineers in the Himalayas, especially the Mount Everest climbers, are notorious in this respect (Pawson, *et al.* 1984: 244). Cullen (1986) indicates that the number of expeditions of climbers and trekkers in the Himalayas is steadily increasing. Their main desire is to achieve success within the allotted time limits, and environmental concerns play almost no role in their behavior patterns. This attitude leads to the abandonment of garbage in their camps, resulting in environmental degradation, water pollution, and health problems. Discarded food, food containers, fuel containers, ropes, tools, batteries, film canisters, broken glass, old clothing, skis, packaging material, medicines, oxygen bottles, cooking equipment, and utensils are left behind at high elevations where natural decomposition and decay proceed very slowly. The impact is exacerbated by the fact that these materials are piling up in relatively few campsites that the trekkers use. To deal with the accumulated garbage, expensive clean-up expeditions have been laboring in the Himalayas.

Responding to the deteriorating environmental situation in the Himalayas, the Nepalese tourism ministry has, since the 1970s, pursued a policy of increasing permit fees for mountaineering expeditions (Tuting 1989). In 1991 it decided to limit the number of climbers and their garbage by raising the fee for a climbing permit on Mount Everest from $1,200 to $10,000 for the first nine members of a party, plus $1,200 for each additional climber (*Time* 7 October 1991). Some additional measures may be advisable, such as payment of refundable environmental protection levies, a requirement that expeditions hire special "garbage" sherpas, enforcement of the regulations by not only liaison officers but also by the headquarters staff, establishment of garbage disposal methods (mainly burning and transport to off-site pits for burning), and scheduling disposal for each site. Self-control must be practiced.

The Alps are also plagued by the problem of littering. Each year, the citizens of Obergurgl, Austria remove about 50 large sacks of empty cans out of the Rettenbach glacier alone. The total amount of litter left by tourists in the Austrian Alps is estimated at about 4,500 tons annually (*Time* 10 September 1984). Indeed, one has to wonder why tourists carry relatively heavy food and drink supplies uphill and fail to carry back downhill the much lighter empty containers, waste, and wrappings. This phenomenon is especially strange in view of the fact that mountain hikers, and particularly backpackers, are the most environmentally sensitive category of tourists. It may indicate that preaching to others is easier than doing it oneself.

6.5 *Polar Ecosystems*

6.5.1 *Introduction*

Polar ecosystems are probably the most fragile of all ecosystems to human impact. On land they function annually only, from just several weeks to not much more than three months. For the rest of the year they lie almost dormant under a cover of snow and ice. Once damaged by humans, the polar permafrost terrain, especially the Arctic tundra, may not recover its original vegetation for a very long time, in fact, up to several hundred years (Satchell and Marren 1976: 56). At the same time polar ecosystems are extremely valuable for the global environment and should be preserved by all means. Polar areas are important because they moderate the impact of the greenhouse effect on earth's climate due to the exceptional ability of the Arctic and the Antarctic Oceans to absorb carbon dioxide more efficiently than warmer waters. This ability is reinforced by the abundance of phytoplankton in the frigid polar waters. Phytoplankton is known to convert carbon dioxide into oxygen.

However, the polar regions are highly attractive for tourism, and unfortunately for their ecology, are enticing increasing numbers of visitors. These fall into two groups. The first category is that of research scientists who normally stay several months and could be classified as business travellers belonging to tourism (Mieczkowski, Z. 1990). The second category, the short-term visitors, participate in adventure and scientific tourism (see chapter 10). Travel to the polar regions, especially to the Antarctic and the high Arctic, is very expensive. Thus, the factor of the distance friction and low accessibility renders mass tourism impossible for a long time to come. In fact, polar tourists are not only better-off financially than most of those travelling to other regions, but also older and better educated (Snepenger and Moore 1989). However, the costs of travel to these polar regions are relentlessly decreasing; responsible organizations and individuals have to plan for the future to ensure safeguards are in place to protect polar ecosystems. But even the relatively small numbers of tourists today visiting the Antarctic and the high-latitude Arctic regions cause considerable concern because of their impact on these delicate ecosystems.

6.5.2 *The Arctic*

Tourism in the Arctic is chronologically older than that in the Antarctic. A significant stimulus for the visitation of the Low Arctic at a reasonable cost has been created by construction of the railroads in the north of the Scandinavian peninsula and in Russia to Murmansk, and in several places in Siberia and the Far East. In North America the most important railroad connection is to Churchill, Manitoba. This destination provides a unique opportunity to see the *aurora borealis* (northern lights), the tundra, polar bears, beluga whales, an incredible variety of migrating birds, and other Arctic wildlife. Tundra buggies are used because of the fragility of the tundra: these special vehicles do not disturb the ground because of their well-distributed weight.

Other methods to reach the Arctic include travel by the Alaska Highway, the Alaska Ferry System, or flights to Anchorage, Alaska. From there one can visit parts of southern Alaska by car. In Canada, there is a 736-kilometer road connection, called the Dempster Highway, that runs off the Alaska Highway between Dawson City and Inuvik. Strict regulations govern the tourist flows on this highway: camping is allowed only in designated campgrounds, the discharge of firearms is prohibited in the 13- to 16- kilometer-wide highway zone (*Land* 1981, 2: 5). Beyond these points travel becomes expensive in the form of commercial air transportation in Alaska, Canada, and Russia.

There is still another outrageously expensive way to see the Arctic: in the second half of the 1980s Salem Lindbad Cruising pioneered annual cruises via the Northwest Passage. Since then, the Northwest Passage cruises on icebreakers and ships with reinforced hulls have become almost annual affairs. A typical route is from

Sondre Strom Fjord, Greenland, to Nome, Alaska. The fare in 1992 ranged from $10,000 to $20,000. The Russians have joined the Arctic cruise business with the 112-passenger icebreaker Kapitan Khlebnikov, which in the summer of 1993 circumnavigated Greenland at a cost of $19,000 to $22,900 per passenger. Another Russian icebreaker, Sovetskiy Soyuz reached the North Pole on August 4, 1991 (*New York Times* 27 October 1991). Cruises are also conducted to the Svalbard (*Spitsbergen*) archipelago by a British company (*Ecodecision*, June 1993) and a Norwegian cruiseline (*New York Times* 7 February 1993). In Canada a 79-meter, 80-passenger Swedish ship Polaris cruises between Churchill, Manitoba, and Halifax, Nova Scotia. The same ship also travels to the shores of Baffin Island, Greenland, Iceland and Svalbard. Ecotourists participating in the Arctic cruises do enjoy the special luxuries usually associated with cruises, and a maximum effort is made to provide them with high quality experience and information. They are transported to the shore by helicopters or by inflated rubber boats called Zodiacs, where they view landscapes and wildlife, and are instructed by scientists-lecturers. There have been no complaints about damages to the Arctic ecosystem.

6.5.3 *The Antarctic*

The environmental importance of the Antarctic region was formally recognized by the 1959 Antarctic Treaty, which banned nuclear and military activity in the area, suspended competing territorial claims by seven Southern Hemisphere nations, and established rules for scientific research. Another historic step in saving the Antarctic ecosystem was undertaken on 4 October 1991, the day of the signing by 26 countries, including the United States and Canada, of the second Antarctic Treaty. It stipulated that Antarctica must remain a non-political continent to be used for the benefit of all nations. The Protocol on Environment Protection, added at the same date, and signed by 40 nations, provides for a 50-year moratorium on any kind of resource exploitation, including mining and oil exploration. It also establishes wildlife protection and waste disposal measures, and puts limits on tourism and marine pollution on both land and water. Tourism is left as the only form of economic exploitation on this continent.

Nevertheless, despite the signing of the second Antarctic Treaty, two principal threats to the Antarctic ecosystems remain: these are the short-term adventure and scientific tourists and the scientists working at the 50 research bases in the region. The Antarctic, the last pristine continent on earth, is becoming an increasingly popular destination for both of these categories of visitors. The number of tourists during the 1993–94 summer was about 8,000, and that of scientists and technicians varies between 8,000 in summer and 1,000 in winter. There is a growing concern about the negative impacts of the quickly growing numbers of these human "invaders." In the 1970s tourism started with nonstop sightseeing flights over the continent conducted by Air New Zealand. However, the flights were discontinued in 1979 after a jet crashed into Mount Erebus, killing all 257 people aboard. Nowadays tourists travel to Antarctica by ship from the cruise bases in Punta Arenas, Chile, and Ushuaia, Argentina (Hall, C. 1992). Those who want to avoid the 1,000-kilometer, 48-hour trip through the stormy waters of Drake Passage use airplanes. The visitors stay only briefly at the Chilean and Argentinean facilities located at the Antarctic Peninsula; they visit some nearby research stations and enjoy "a spectacular helicopter ride to penguin colonies, vigorous walks, and lectures and films on the continent's history and geography" (*Economist* 20 May 1989). Besides these "routine" visitors, there are more adventurous and richer tourists who venture farther. Thus, in January 1988 two groups of tourists, totalling 35 persons, landed in ski-equipped Twin Otter planes at the U.S. Amundsen-Scott Research Station located exactly at the South Pole and stayed there for a few hours. Each tourist paid $35,000 (*Winnipeg Free Press* 26 March 1988). In January of 1989 a group of 11 cross-country skiers reached the South Pole after an arduous cross-continent marathon of 1,060 kilometers in about 40 days. The planned price for this trip was about $70,000 (*Winnipeg Free Press* 22 December 1987).

The 1992–93 Antarctic summer season included new expeditions. The Quark Expeditions organized three trips by the 112-passenger Russian icebreaker Kapitan Khlebnikov. The route of the first trip was from Cape Town, South Africa to Fremantle, Australia via the Antarctic coast, and included a visit to the Russian scientific base Mirny. The fares ranged from $11,975 to $16,475. The second voyage looped from Fremantle via Antarctica, and back to Fremantle. The third started in Fremantle and ended in Bluff, New Zealand. At present there are at least ten ships offering cruises to the Antarctic shores.

The second category of visitors is that of the scientists working in about 50 research stations run by a dozen countries. The relationships between scientists and tourists is an uneasy one (Hall, C. 1992). The scientists complain that the visitors waste their valuable time expecting information and guided tours of the research facilities. Frequently, the scientific experiments are disturbed by intruders. Emergency rescue at tremendous cost and danger to the researchers is taken for granted. In addition, zoologists are not happy that the tourist season coincides with the nesting and breeding season of Antarctic wildlife, and are justifiably concerned that this may disturb the animals. Scientists also criticize the disposal of waste and sewage from the ships, and the danger of oil pollution. The most drastic case of oil pollution occurred in 1989, when an Argentinean ship, Bahia Paradiso, sank in the coastal waters of the Antarctic Peninsula, near the Palmer research station. Although the 316 passengers and crew were rescued, the ship spilled 570 tons of diesel fuel, and the cost of cleanup was $2 million. Other examples of environmentally irresponsible tourist behavior are further noted by C. Michael Hall (*ibid.* 6–7).

The visitors retort with scathing criticism of scientists. They condemn careless littering and disposal of waste (including toxic waste), which seem to be the leading environmental problem in the Antarctic. As well, tourists are horrified by the view of rusty bases which were abandoned and never dismantled. Indeed, scientists apparently inflict more environmental damage than tourists (Riding 1991; Hall, C. 1992). It seems that a compromise between the two groups is possible, and environmental preservation can be achieved by mutual monitoring of each other's behavior.

To enforce the established codes of conduct for tourists, a new organization was formed in 1991, the International Association of Antarctica Tour Operators. The rules of conduct provide for enforcement of strict environmental, and ban tour operators from areas of specific scientific interest or areas requiring special protection. There is a stipulation that at least 75 percent of the staff employed must have prior Antarctic experience. A qualified naturalist must accompany and supervise each group of not-more-than 20 tourists going ashore. While on shore, tourists must remain on trails. They are not allowed to collect or leave anything; they must stay at least six meters away from penguins, nesting birds or seals; they must give animals the right of way; they are forbidden to touch or harass animals. There is no smoking on shore, and garbage must be carried back to the ship. The IAATO supports the environmentalists' call for the designation of Antarctica as a world park. Michael Hall (1992: 8) suggests an international convention to discuss tourism in Antarctica.

Antarctica is certainly not a destination for mass tourism: the cost of visiting it will be a deterrent for a long time to come. Even now, however, the number of tourists should be limited by an international agreement. This should also enforce environmentally responsible behavior on the part of tourists, scientists, and the transportation crews.

6.6 *Deserts*

Deserts generally have a reputation for ecological fragility. According to Noy-Meir (1974), however, they display both resilience and inertia because their indigenous organisms are highly accustomed to variable environmental conditions, characterized by alternations between long stress periods and short favorable interludes. According to him, deserts are flexible, adaptable and tolerant to impacts.

I would like to point out that ATVs (trail bikes, dune buggies and jeeps), disturb the moisture regime of the desert ecosystems by destroying the desert crust and vegetation. This may lead to total destruction of the ecosystem. Recovery from zero level in desert conditions is, indeed, very difficult, more difficult than in other ecosystems. In this sense, the deserts may be considered as environmentally fragile. The Edingtons (1986: 26–27) provide an excellent example of the total destruction of desert vegetation by a single trail-bike race that ran between Barstow and Las Vegas and involved more than 2,500 riders. One result of the vehicles' actions was soil erosion that exposes plant roots. The soil compaction by vehicles also prevents "water penetrating down to the seeds to start the activation process."

Another cause of a complete obliteration of a desert is development, be it for a recreational subdivision or for agricultural development. Some deserts are so remote from centers of commercial expansion that there is no such danger. However, if demand is close by, measures be taken to save these ecosystems. An example is the Lake Wales Ridge in central Florida, a small area, sparsely covered with scrubby vegetation of about 80 square kilometers. The vegetation at the ridge conforms to Noy-Meir's characterization: it is resilient to periodic trials, adaptable, with unusual survival skills, and therefore, the most ancient among the desert vegetation in America (Leary 1991). 40 plant species are purely endemic to that habitat. The proposal has prompted for the first federally designated refuge for endangered plants. To achieve this, the government must acquire about 32 square kilometers of land.

Desert ecosystems in more remote regions, such as central Australia, are attractive not for recreational subdivisions, as in Florida, but for recreational tourism. In these cases infrastructure is not much of a danger to plant degradation and dune erosion, while rock thieving for collection or rock gardens are other menaces. These are typical environmental concerns that affect the Rainbow Valley, about 100 kilometers south of Alice Springs, Australia.

Tourists visiting certain desert areas may be more interested in finding pictographs and enjoying the historical, archaeological, and even religious ambience of the area, such as in the Sahara Desert, Petra, Jordan, or the Mount Sinai area of Egypt. It was leaked that after the Egyptian government planned to build a large resort with a cable car to the top of Mount Sinai, an outcry of protests spread throughout the world, leading to an official denial by the Egyptians (*Time* 9 April 1990). However, it seems that the Sinai desert area already suffers from tourism overdevelopment.

Chapter 7

The Issue of Carrying Capacity

7.1 *Introduction*

This chapter opens the third and final part of the book (chapters 7 to 10). As stated in the preface, this part focuses on planning and management strategies aimed at minimizing the negative impacts of tourism and recreation on the environment, and on methods to render it environmentally sustainable. In this respect, I fully concur with Richard Butler (1993:29) that *sustainable tourism* is an inappropriate term because it may be understood as "tourism which is in a form which can maintain its viability in an area for an indefinite period of time." Therefore, I suggest substituting this with the term *environmentally sustainable tourism.*

The first step in discussing the preventive and corrective measures with respect to tourism's impact on environment, is to discuss the conceptually simple but practically complex issue of *carrying capacity.* Understanding this concept is essential for practical physical planning, management, and decision-making in tourism.

The issue of carrying capacity in tourism and recreation started about the same time as the modern environmental movement in the 1960s. Perhaps one of the stimuli that contributed to the recognition of the problem was the overcrowding of the Yosemite Valley in the Yosemite National Park, California. The concentration of about 50,000 campers during national holidays, and especially on July 4, on the 2 kilometer by 12 kilometer area of the valley floor, was criticized as a veritable camping slum, threatening not only the park ecosystem but also creating social tensions of overcrowding, crime, and drug abuse. Administrators and scholars started to talk about surpassing the limits of recreational carrying capacity, about reaching the saturation point, and about carrying capacity overload.

Researchers went to work on the problem and a substantial body of professional literature, numbering about 2,000 positions (Shelby and Heberlein 1986) was published between the mid-1960s and the end of the 1970s. The majority of the work focused on empirical, and mainly idiographic case studies attempting to establish numerical values of carrying capacities. Among the publications of that period are the studies conducted by the team of researchers associated with the Forest Service, U.S. Department of Agriculture (e.g., Lime and Stankey 1971; Lucas 1974; Wagar 1974; Stankey and Baden 1977; Hendee, *et al.* 1978: 169-188; and Clark and Stankey 1979). In the early 1980s a number of reviews and synthesizing critical publications (e.g., Stankey 1982; Wall 1983; Getz 1983; Shelby and Heberlein 1986) marked the end of this stage of research. Since then, the emphasis has shifted again from general discussion to concrete case studies, probably because a consensus has been reached among researchers and the studies have focused on empirical work, associated with the needs for planning and management.

Another characteristic feature of research has been the shift in emphasis: until the early 1970s, the work concentrated on biological considerations, while since the late 1970s the researchers have focused their attention on socio-psychological factors of carrying capacity (Shelby and Heberlein 1986: 2). This shift is reflected in which the major synthetic work of Shelby and Heberlein is devoted almost entirely to the social carrying capacity.

7.2 *The Concept of Carrying Capacity*

The concept implies that there are limits to any kind of natural resource use. The origin of the concept arises from peoples' concern that the natural environment is likely to sustain damage as a result of overuse and may reach the limits of its sustainability (i.e., a certain critical capacity threshold or the saturation point) called *carrying capacity*. The concern is that if this point is significantly surpassed, an ecosystem will not only loose its sustainability, but will also be damaged and destroyed for a long time, if not forever.

The concept of carrying capacity of the ecosystems under the impact of recreational facility and activity is based on a relatively simple notion of nonhuman carrying capacity (i.e., animal carrying capacity). Historically, probably the earliest calculations are connected with livestock management, such as the number of cows a pasture can sustain, and later with wildlife management. The animal carrying capacity is associated with three categories: minimal, maximal, and optimal (Shelby and Heberlein 1986: 8). The minimal *animal carrying capacity*

Figure 7.1
CATEGORIES OF CARRYING CAPACITY

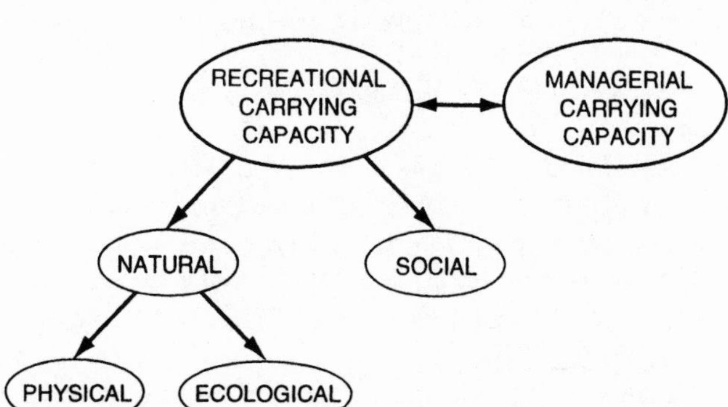

means the number of animals the ecosystems can sustain in stressful times, such as droughts; the *maximal* one indicates the number of animals that may use a given environment without damage; the *optimal carrying capacity* is an intermediate figure and denotes the quality dimension (i.e., the largest and best output for harvesting). Shelby and Heberlein (1986: 10) argue convincingly that the nonhuman carrying capacity is easier to specify than the recreational one because it is associated with the simple equilibrium between animals (i.e., the consumer) and plants (i.e., the food basis for the animals). Such studies use well-established research techniques. The strictly behavioral approach lacks psychological elements normally associated with large individual variations, and is an important argument in favor of greater simplicity of the nonhuman carrying capacity. The *human carrying capacity* is a much more complex category. In a recreational setting there are several categories of carrying capacity (Fig. 7.1). The all-encompassing notion is the *total carrying capacity,* usually called *recreational carrying capacity*, and defined as the maximal volume (level) of recreation use at a given period of time. Recreational carrying capacity:

- does not lower the quality of the natural environment. In other words, the use must not cause an unacceptable degree of deterioration (conceived as a situation in which the environment remains sustainable);

•does not decrease the perceived quality of the recreational experience and the satisfaction of the participants;
•does not harm the broadly defined well-being of the residents (i.e., does not exceed the maximum level of local residents' tolerance to the tourism impacts on the destination).

In connection with this definition, the following remarks seem appropriate:
1. The criterion for the maximum volume of use is preferable to that of the optimal. Any use is associated with some pressure on the environment. Therefore, in theory, the optimal level of use actually means no use at all. Nevertheless, the category of optimal carrying capacity is used for planning purposes as a range of "desirable" sustainable uses (see sections 7.6 and 7.7).
2. The definition of the recreational carrying capacity contains three parts. The first natural carrying capacity, is associated with the natural resource base, an indispensable component of tourism supply (Mieczkowski, Z. 1990: 204) and is, therefore, supply-oriented. The natural carrying capacity contains two elements, physical and ecological:
(a) The *physical carrying capacity,* called facility carrying capacity by the World Tourism Organization (1993: 23) deals with space as a resource (Mieczkowski, Z. 1990: 211-222). It is relatively easy to measure in two dimensions: first, per space unit, expressed in terms of the number of users per hectare of land; second, per facility unit (as for instance, the number of cars in a parking lot, campers in a campground, tennis players on a court, boats in a marina, seats in a theater, or beds in a hotel). According to Yapp and Barrow (1979: 199) the physical carrying capacity relates to the scope of built facilities, including general and tourist infrastructure such as water and electricity supply, transportation system, and tourist accommodation. In most cases the numerical values are easy to determine with a high level of accuracy. However, in some instances, such as finding out the number of golfers who can safely play on a golf course, it may be more difficult.

The physical carrying capacity may be regarded as the most superficial and simple measure of carrying capacity: the number of people that a facility (such as a tennis court, a site, or a theater), for a given activity, can hold at a specific level of facility development. Such a numerical measure may be useful for strictly facility-oriented urban, suburban, and near-urban recreation. In an extra-urban scenario the physical carrying capacity can be determined by the number of people that an area can accommodate, for example, motorboating, especially speed motorboating, water-skiing, and sailing need more space than do swimming or canoeing. Despite its usefulness, however, the importance of the physical carrying capacity in resource-based scenarios is insignificant. Instead, other factors become critical. This shift becomes clear when one considers that a person requires only one linear meter on a wilderness trail to move freely (*Fundaciòn Neotropica* 1992). The physical carrying capacity concept is used, in practice, for managerial purposes, but it is unsuitable for setting the recreational carrying capacity limits. The physical carrying capacity is limited to space only (Kaspar 1982: 98) and as such, is theoretically maximal and practically always too large, because other constraints are much more critical, as they determine the capacity. It may also vary seasonally; for example, it is smaller in the winter because skiing requires the terrain of special quality (*ibid.* 98).

(b) The *ecological carrying capacity* is the second component of the natural carrying capacity. It deals with environment as a resource and is associated with the degree to which the ecosystems are able to tolerate human interference while maintaining the unimpaired sustainable functioning. An alternative term is *natural resource carrying capacity;* however, it is often confused with the term *natural carrying capacity. Land capability* is another frequently used term. *Biological carrying capacity* is narrower in scope because it is limited to the biotic elements (i.e., to flora and fauna), of ecosystems.

The relationship between physical and the ecological carrying capacity depends on the position of the activity on the continuum of recreational opportunity; that is, if the activity is user-oriented and facility-dependent (such as a swimming pool), then the physical limitations of the recreation infrastructure gain more in importance. If the recreational activity is associated with the resource-based extreme of the continuum; that is, it takes place in the wilderness, then physical space is not a problem, but the ecological carrying capacity may be of concern. In this case the limitations lie not in the physical capacity of the infrastructural facilities but in the capacity of the ecosystems. In such instances we can safely substitute the overriding concept of the natural carrying capacity by the more appropriate term of ecological carrying capacity.

3. The second part of the definition of the recreational carrying capacity pertains to the "demand" side in the supply and demand equation (i.e., is demand-oriented). The third part deals with the perceptions of the

local population. Both deal with mostly intangible human perceptions associated with social and psychological elements; and several terms are used to express these concerns (such as social carrying capacity, psychological carrying capacity, perceptual carrying capacity, and socio-psychological carrying capacity). Although socio-psychological carrying capacity is the most accurate term, it is cumbersome to say and therefore, it is not used in this book. Instead, the term *social carrying capacity* is used. Because of the subjective elements, variable in time and space, this type of carrying capacity is still more difficult to determine quantitatively than is ecological carrying capacity.

4. The distinction between ecological and social carrying capacity is clear despite some overlaps (e.g., noise pollution relates to both).

To summarize, physical and ecological carrying capacity deals with resources; social carrying capacity deals with psychological and socio-cultural factors. The relationships between the carrying capacity categories may be expressed by the following equations:

Recreational (total) carrying capacity = natural carrying capacity + social (psychological) carrying capacity

Natural carrying capacity = physical carrying capacity + ecological carrying capacity

7.3 *The Ecological Carrying Capacity*

The basis for ecological carrying capacity is sustained yield, estab-lished for nonrecreational settings (such as forests) for "the achievement and maintenance in perpetuity of a high-level annual or regular periodic output of the various renewable resources of the national forests, without impairment of the productivity of the land" (Chubb and Ashton 1969: 7). In recreation, the equivalent of sustained yield is sustained output of recreational benefits (or a given level of recreational use in a sustained ecosystem.

Research into the ecological carrying capacity has been, primarily, the quantitative measurement of the environmental impact of recreational use on the ecosystems. However, according to Wall and Wright (1972: 3), "environmental impact statements of any kind are extremely difficult to make." They list four reasons which render quantitative recreation impact assessments intricate—and probably not possible at all. I will elaborate on them further.

1. It is extremely difficult to establish a base level for measurement because the primeval environment, before human intervention, is not

known adequately. The present-day "natural environment" has to a large extent, been changed by both recreational and nonrecreational use. Being unable to reconstruct the primeval environment before the presence of humans "means that it will be impossible to fully assess the magnitude of changes brought about by recreation" (*ibid.*).

2. Any use causes some changes. One could ask: how much change is too much? It is difficult to isolate human impacts from natural processes. As discussed in section 4.1, nature is dynamic, not static. It abounds in unpredictable boom and bust cycles (Hastings and Higgins 1994), which make any rigid, permanent, sustainability levels illusory (Ludwig, *et al.* 1993). Therefore, the best advice to researchers and planners is to take into account the most pessimistic scenarios and ride out nature's cycles—"roll with changes in the environment," recognize the uncertainty and risk, and develop flexible approaches to resource utilization and diversified economies based on multiple uses of resources. In practical terms, human impacts on natural processes (such as erosion) may accelerate them. For example, natural shore erosion may be accelerated by the artificial waves created by speeding motorboats. Frequently, nature takes its course unexpectedly and inexplicably because chaos is inherent to dynamic ecosystems (Tilman and Weding 1991); changes occur in the composition of species, such as in explosions of prairie dog or rabbit populations, causing a chain reaction in other elements of the ecosystems, starting with the impact on vegetation. Severe weather conditions, such as ocean storms, also destroy unprotected dunes or second homes built too close to the shore.

3. Spatial and temporal gaps can occur between cause and effect. Erosion in one place, for example, causes siltation in another, frequently distant location; a meltwater runoff following artificial snowmaking in a ski resort may smother an aquatic habitat at considerable distance downstream from the ski area (Jerome 1977). There is often a considerable time lapse between cause and effect (e.g., destruction of a wildlife habitat results in a subsequent decline of animal population, or damage of coral reefs by tourism impact eventually affects the whole marine ecosystem. All these processes may take a long time before the full environmental impact becomes evident. Spatial and temporal discontinuities may necessitate costly studies encompassing large areas, as well as long-range longitudinal research to properly evaluate the extent of the environmental impacts.

4. The complexity of the interactions between various components of the environment make the total impact almost impossible to measure. Chain reactions occur (e.g., changes in soil quality may lead to changes in vegetation) which, in turn, may impact on the water regime and wildlife.

All these problems clearly illustrate the difficulty of arriving at quantitative measures of the environmental impacts of tourism, and, consequently, of establishing firm numerical limits of the ecological carrying capacity. Indeed, the extremely intricate nature of the interactions between various elements of the natural environments render a definitive quantitative analysis impossible. As a result, the numerical values obtained by research should be regarded as guidelines only for decision-makers.

The ecological carrying capacity in recreation varies substantially from one ecosystem to another. As indicated in sections 4.2 and 6.1, some ecosystems are fragile, others are relatively tolerant to recreational impacts. Therefore, the most important task of research is to identify the degree of tolerance of various ecosystems to determine which areas should be protected from recreational impacts and which areas may be used for recreation. The ecological carrying capacity remains relatively stable over time for a particular site or area. It changes only seasonally, and as a result of the variation in weather conditions, especially following unusual weather periods.

Ecological carrying capacity studies belong to every planning process of a major tourism/recreation project. The studies may encompass the totality of ecosystems (i.e., soils, vegetation, topography, and climate) or only some of its components, usually soils and/or vegetation.

Researchers are investigating how susceptible various soils and types of vegetation are to recreational use. For example, sometimes rollers are used to simulate human trampling of vegetation to determine the most resistant grasses in prospective campgrounds (Kostrowicki 1970).

Soils are investigated for their capacity to absorb moisture because that influences their ability to support vegetation. Soils also differ in their capability to withstand trampling (see section 5.5). Trampling is most damaging in a high moisture area, such as a marsh, but may be beneficial on sandy soils that normally retain little moisture. In such an instance, trampling may increase soil compaction, and consequently its water retention capability. However, trampling always damages vegetation (see section 5.7) either by direct destruction of plants or indirectly by soil compaction, which lowers soil permeability and its moisture retention. This affects the plant roots and thus the growth rates of plants. Loss of plant cover results in increased erosion, especially on steeper slopes, thus depriving the ecosystems of soil. In North American conditions, the vegetation is generally most hardy on northwest slopes, especially at lower elevations.

All the elements of the environment interact with one another under recreational use in an infinite number of cumulative and synenergetic impacts, and the subsequent chain reactions may lead to the degradation of the ecosystems. As previously stated, the critical thresholds of ecological carrying capacity vary between particular ecosystems, for instance the process of erosion will start at different stages of damage to the vegetation, or the elimination of plant species will result from various amounts of trampling.

Damage to the ecosystems is easily observed after it has occurred, but difficult to anticipate when it is going to happen and at what level of use. Therefore, it is not advisable to wait until damage occurs: prevention is better than cure. A proactive, not a reactive attitude is recommended.

Another difficulty in establishing quantitative measures of impacts on the ecosystems is that the number of user-units is inadequate as a yardstick. The behavioral patterns of recreationists differ substantially, since some people display environmentally conscious behavior, while others inflict considerable damage to the environment (see sections 4.7–4.9 above).

Despite theoretical achievements, research into the ecological carrying capacity has not achieved its practical goals. Indeed, "little progress appears to have been made towards practical application" (Yapp and Barrow 1979: 192). Regardless of multiple efforts to establish absolute measures for ecological carrying capacity (i.e., fixed quantitative thresholds or saturation points of maximum use), success has been at best limited. There are no scientifically established critical thresholds that could be "interpreted as some objective baseline of science" (Barkham 1973: 221). Barkham remarks that few ecologists *sensu stricto* claim the existence of such thresholds, although, "many ecologists *sensu lato* may propagate this view with the evangelical fervor associated with the environmental crisis. To talk about "unacceptable ecological consequences" is nothing more than a value judgment, valid and meaningful only in the eye of the beholder.

The failure to establish numerical standards of ecological carrying capacity does not mean that research in this field is invalid and futile. In recent times the quest for magic figures of fixed thresholds has disappeared, and the quantitative and qualitative scientific investigations are pursued with different expectations and goals, and from different angles (such as relative comparisons of capacity between various environments and between different environmental impacts). Thus, using various sources, it is possible to establish a relative impact continuum. Some examples are:

- Day hikers, no campfire, no overnight stay. The smaller the number the lesser the impact.
- Hikers staying overnight with campfire.
- Horse parties camping overnight using campstoves.

Figure 7.2
ECOLOGICAL CARRYING CAPACITY

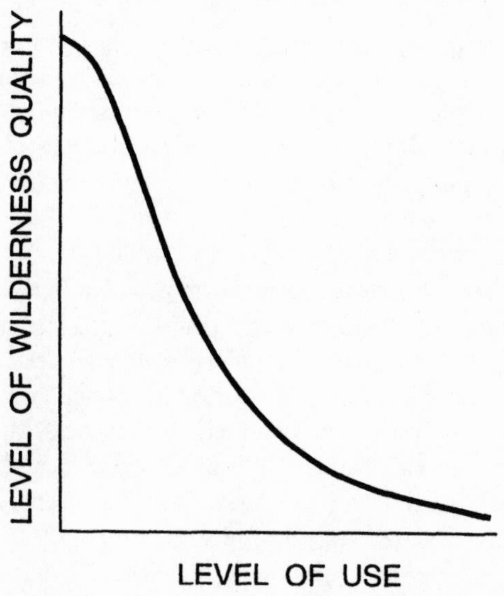

Other research aim to establish correlations between the intensity of recreational impacts and the extent of ecosystem deterioration. An example of such a generalization is provided by Hendee, *et al.* (1978: 180). In the wilderness setting the main damage to the ecosystems does not occur proportionately to use in a linear relationship, but rather curvilinear (see section 4.1, problem 4; and section 9.1, item 15), increasing rapidly in the initial stages of growing recreational pressure on the environment: "The relationship between use and impact is curvilinear, with only slight amounts of initial use producing relatively large changes and additional use producing only small, additional damage" (Wenger 1984: 825). This relationship is represented in Fig. 7.2. For research in carrying capacity, it is especially important to determine the critical inflection point on the curve, at which there is a distinct discontinuity, an abrupt shift, a deceleration, or in certain, rather rare situations a sudden acceleration in the rate of change (Hendee, *et al.* 183). In the latter scenario, this point is a clear indication of the limits of the ecological carrying capacity (Fig. 7.3).

Figure 7.3

ABRUPT SHIFT IN RELATIONSHIP BETWEEN ENVIRONMENT CHANGE AND USE

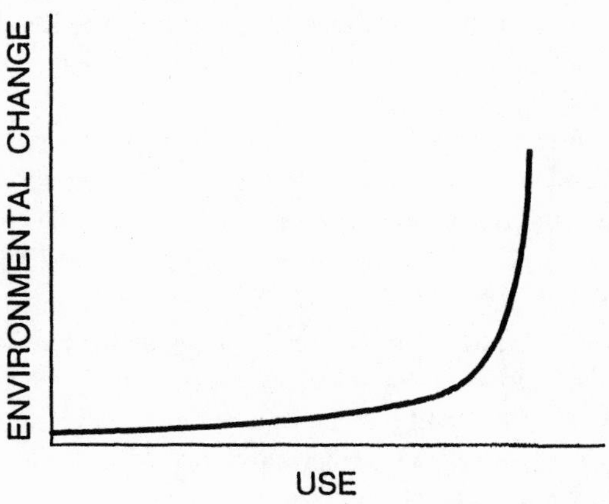

7.4 *The Social Carrying Capacity*

As Getz points out (1983: 231), the early applications of carrying capacity focused on its ecological aspects. However, "later interpretations of the concept have stressed the values and perceptions of users and managers in determining capacity." Thus, a shift in emphasis from purely environmental to socio-psychological aspects has taken place, and the social carrying capacity has become the focus of research.

Social carrying capacity includes a wide range of elements associated with all impacts of tourism: environmental, socioeconomical and cultural. This discussion concentrates on the first element. However, some degree of overlap among the three impacts is unavoidable.

The social carrying capacity is connected with two parameters pertaining to different human groups:

1. participants (users) such as recreationists or tourists visiting a certain destination.
2. the local population living permanently at the destination and encompassing two subgroups: (a) people who derive incomes directly and indirectly from tourism, and (b) residents, such as retirees, not associated with tourism.

In most cases, social carrying capacity constitutes the critical constraint for determining the recreational carrying capacity. At the same time, the social carrying capacity is less tangible than the natural (ecological) carrying capacity, and is more complex to identify because it is associated with subjective human factors that determine the sustained user satisfaction and benefits, as well as the well-being of the residents at the destination.

The main aspect investigated is the socio-psychological (i.e., the perceived number of tourists a destination can absorb before it is evaluated by participants and the local residents as "full" or overcrowded). At a certain point the participants and the local residents will start to feel that the crowds are too large. Researchers are interested in establishing the limits of tolerance to these numbers. Beyond these limits, the destination is perceived by tourists as congested and thus detracting from the quality of their experience, and by residents as threatening their broadly defined well-being. Already, at first glance, such an evaluation lacks objectivity.

Although the concern associated with overcrowding constitutes the most important quantitative aspect of the social carrying capacity, other qualitative components that are not necessarily connected with the number of visitors should also be taken into account. Tourist behavior, such as littering, vandalizing, and making noise, may considerably lower the threshold of social carrying capacity. The behavior of the local population may also impact on the capacity of a destination: if tourists feel welcomed, if the locals render them polite assistance, they may more easily endure some of the inconveniences of overcrowding. If, on the other hand, the attitudes of the locals are negative and they behave in an unfriendly or even hostile manner towards visitors, the thresholds of the social carrying capacity will be lower.

7.4.1 *Carrying Capacity as Perceived by Recreationists*

Figure 7.4

SOCIAL CARRYING CAPACITY FOR USER-ORIENTED RECREATION (high intensity use)

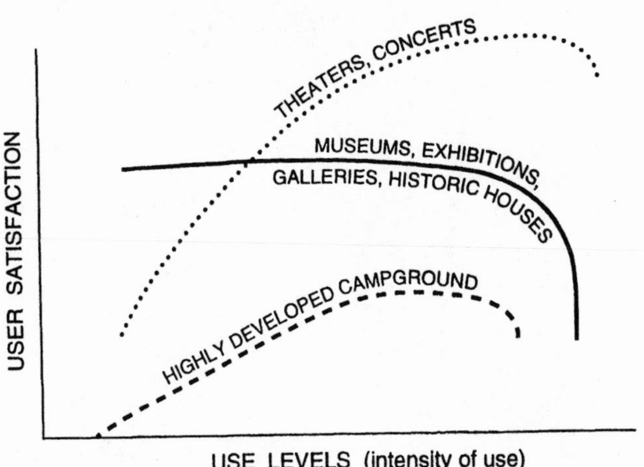

A recreational activity may in itself need little space but could require more or less accessory space or social space—a highly elusive variable because of lack of objective standards (Mieczkowski, Z. 1990: 214). Researchers have been attempting to determine the parameters of this type of carrying capacity by measuring the perception of participants in recreation activities to overcrowding. The purpose has been to establish the thresholds of diminishing satisfaction. Exceeding this point by increasing the number of participants or reducing the available space causes a decline in the quality of the recreational experience, and thus, the satisfaction of users. Sometimes, however, participants may expect, require, and even enjoy considerable congestion to experience a sense of community; for example, rock concerts and some religious gatherings. Occasionally, "undercrowding may be as annoying as overcrowding" (Hall 1974: 392). Thus, people may feel discomfort in an empty theater, concert hall, and campground.

Figure 7.5

SOCIAL CARRYING CAPACITY FOR RESOURCE-BASED RECREATION (low intensity use)

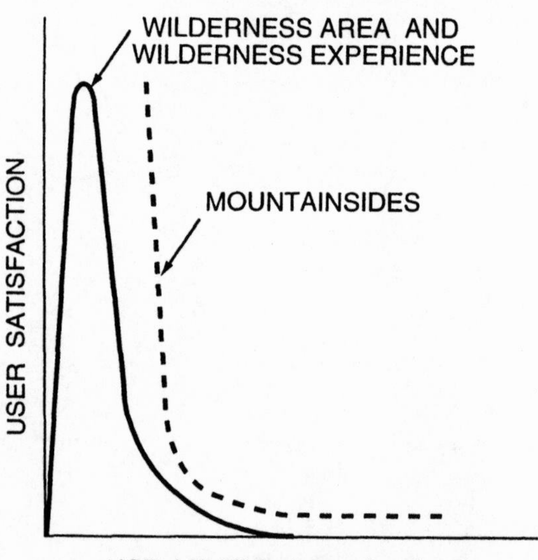

Sources: Modified from Hall 1974:392 and Clawson, Knetch 1966:168

As for ecological carrying capacity, many areas can sustain more use without deteriorating their environment. However, the level of social carrying capacity is, as a rule, lower and differs according to its location in the recreation opportunity spectrum for activities, even for similar activities—such as swimming or bathing (Clark and Stankey 1979), or on the *continuum of environmental modification* for areas (Clawson and Knetch 1966). Consequently, the curves reflecting the relationships between the levels of use and the levels of user satisfaction (i.e., the social carrying capacity), will look entirely different for user-oriented, as compared with resource-based, activities and areas (Figs. 7.4 and 7.5). For resource-based extra-urban areas and activities the social carrying capacity thresholds are relatively low. They increase as one moves along the continuum of recreation opportunity towards user-oriented activities and areas associated with them. Recreationists in an urban park, and especially in an amusement park, tolerate being closer to others than those in an extra-urban park, particularly in a nature reserve.

Figure 7.6

TYPE OF PARTY ENCOUNTERED (1)

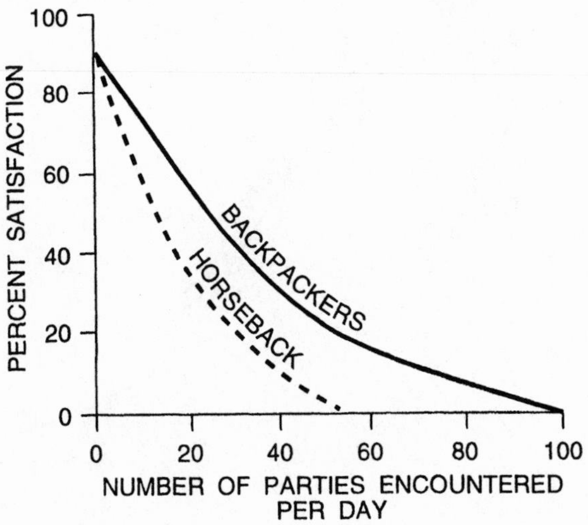

Source: Lucas 1974:8

Thus, the level of social carrying capacity differs according to the specific management goals and objectives for a given area, tailored to a specific recreational experience. As previously indicated, it is not only the activity, but its location that plays a decisive role in establishing the level of social carrying capacity. Therefore, the recreation opportunity spectrum enables the users to match their specific needs with the desired opportunities. Such a solution is preferable to developing recreation areas for a hypothetical "average user." However, within the same spatial setting, the differences between various activities becomes apparent. For example, in the wilderness setting, the levels of social carrying capacity are lower for horseback parties than for backpackers (Fig. 7.6) and for people using motorboats than for those using canoes (Fig. 7.7).

Social carrying capacity's thresholds also differ from one place to another (Dunbar 1991: 134) and in time, both seasonally and longitudinally. They are dynamic concepts characterized by constant change. Their measurements are not valid in the long term. Thus, the social carrying capacity is a subjective category based on human perception.

Figure 7.7

TYPE OF PARTY ENCOUNTERED (2)

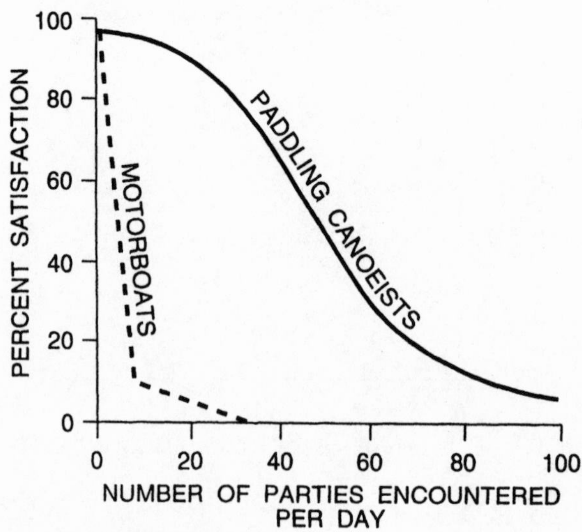

Source: Lucas 1974:9

However, the activity, its location, and time are not the only variables in social carrying capacity. In fact, idiographic variables are so great it is impossible to establish a "magic" quantitative threshold not to be exceeded. The capacity thresholds depend on socioeconomic, cultural, demographic, and psychological characteristics of the recreationists. These characteristics differ with ethnic, social, and age groups, and with the individual. People who are used to living in overcrowded conditions tend to be less susceptible to overcrowding in a recreational setting. Similarly, young people enjoy large gatherings with their peers, but would not have the same kind of fun if large numbers of younger and/or older recreationists were involved. Among ethnic groups, South and East Asians, for example, have higher thresholds than North Americans or Australians. Westerners would not like the Crimean resort of Yalta, Ukraine, where vacationers lie on the beach like sardines, almost touching each other, and seem content.

Psychologically, the widely-accepted division of people into introvert or extrovert has been explored by Plog (1987) for the purposes of tourism (Fig. 7.8). He introduces a lifestyle continuum between two extremes: psychocentric (introvert, passive, not venturesome) and allocentric (extrovert, adventuresome). As a destination becomes more developed, commercialized and overcrowded, it loses its character, authenticity, and specific charm. When this happens, allocentric tourists move on to places that are under less environmental stress. However, psychocentrics continue to patronize the highly developed destinations.

Figure 7.8

PSYCHOLOGICAL CLASSIFICATION OF POTENTIAL TOURISTS

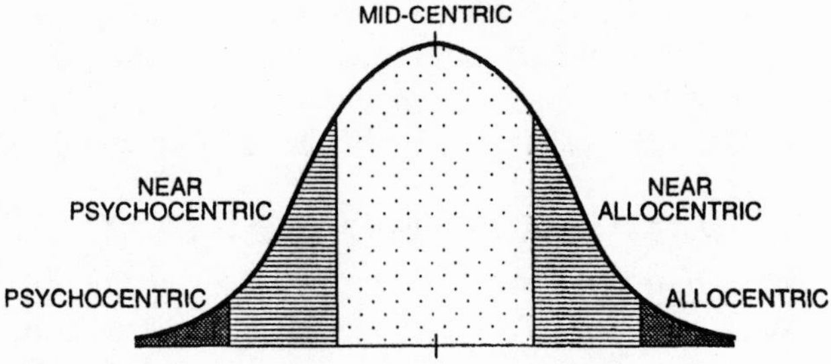

MID-CENTRIC

NEAR PSYCHOCENTRIC

NEAR ALLOCENTRIC

PSYCHOCENTRIC

ALLOCENTRIC

Source: Plog 1967

One aspect of social carrying capacity that is rarely discussed in professional literature, is that recreationists are psychologically flexible and adapt to increased levels of use. Stankey (1982: 67) explains: "...although people may have preferred less contact than they in fact encountered, they might still report high levels of satisfaction by giving priority in their evaluation to other aspects of their experiences...." For example, most recreationists, not just young people, enjoy intra-group social interactions more than interactions with casual strangers.

All arguments demonstrate the weaknesses of the concept of socio-psychological carrying capacity. Without quantitative absolute measures, one can only operate with relative parameters. Still, it is possible to make the following generalizations. Social carrying capacity increases when:

(a) The recreational activity takes place closer to the user-oriented end of the continuum of environmental modification (Mieczkowski, Z. 1990: 258): The more developed and managed, the higher the capacity; the level of psychological and social tolerance is much lower in resource-based areas, even for the same activities, the difference being found in the setting.

(b) The group of participants is more homogeneous demographically and ethnically.

(c) There is a single use.

(d) The participants display a high or equal level of skill in a given activity.

(e) The level of facility development is high, including the closeness of sanitary facilities.

(f) The shape of the recreation site is elongated rather than rectangular.

(g) Dense vegetation offers privacy.

It appears, therefore, that socio-psychological carrying capacity, as perceived by recreationists, depends on a number of intangible variables, such as acculturation, the level of confidence, and the conditions of the facility, and is, consequently, highly variable in space and time.

7.4.2 *Carrying Capacity as Perceived by Residents*

When tourists overcrowd an area, or in any other way impinge on the well-being of an area and its populations, the local residents exert political pressure to put limits on tourism development (Elsasser, *et al.* 1992). This is their only option, short of moving. Residents, however are reluctant to move out.

The list of complaints about tourism's impacts can be many: environmental deterioration; loss of the unique ambience; charm of the area; loss of cultural, social, and moral values; overload of general and social infrastructure; bottlenecks in services and local transportation; lack of parking spaces; too much noise and too many traffic accidents; increases in taxes; and inflation of real estate prices. Such criticisms can be divided into (a) complaints pertaining to environmental damage *sensu largo* (including natural, economic, social, and cultural), and (b) complaints relating to the overload of the general infrastructure, including the economic losses of overuse during the peak season and underutilization in the off-season.

Attitudes of local population towards tourism and tourists were investigated in Barbados and Niagara-on-the-Lake, Ontario. Doxey (1975 and 1976) devised an irritation index, called *an irridex,* to measure the degree of annoyance felt towards tourism development. Doxety found that as the level of development increases, tourist destinations passed successively through five stages: euphoria, apathy, irritation, antagonism, and finally, mutual compromise.

At the euphoria stage, investors and tourists are welcomed. Usually there is little planning or control of tourism development because it seems unnecessary. The apathy stage is associated with the expansion of facilities and an increasing number of visitors. The tourists are taken for granted and their contacts with the locals become more formal. The locals are less enthusiastic, increasingly apathetic, and profit-oriented. Therefore, most planning, if there is any, is concerned with marketing. The irritation stage occurs when the level of development reaches the perceived saturation point, and the residents start to show irritation with overdevelopment. Decision-makers attempt to cope with the situation by expanding the infrastructure, not limiting growth. Antagonism is reached when irritations are overtly expressed, both verbally and physically (e.g., "in Bath, England, in summer 1990, the residents turned their hoses on tour buses in their neighborhoods (*Tourism Intelligence Bulletin,* August 1991). When social friction attains its peak, planners and decision-makers are forced to take remedial action. The final stage, then, is when coping with the mass tourism development. This is usually in the form of a compromise to maintain the *status quo,* acceptable to both the tourists and the residents.

Canestrelli and Costa (1991) suggest that to fine-tune the research so it can be used to accurately study the social carrying capacity, the locals should be divided into two groups and investigated separately: tourism-dependent and tourism-independent residents. Obviously, the locals who depend on tourism for their incomes tolerate negative impacts of tourism more than the residents not associated with tourism. Therefore, Canestrelli regards the latter as critical to the evaluation of the social carrying capacity.

7.5 *Recreational Carrying Capacity*

With objective quantification of the limits of ecological carrying capacity extremely difficult, or nearly impossible, and that of the social carrying capacity definitely impossible, establishing the thresholds for the recreational carrying capacity, seem dim, indeed.

The investigation of recreational carrying capacity (i.e., an integrative approach) is impossible in practice because of the incompatibility of the parameters involved. However, researchers have been attempting to use an indirect path. Usually one of the variables proves to be restrictive, and consequently controlling the recreational carrying capacity. Therefore, it is important to find this critical threshold because it determines only the maximum level of use that should not or cannot be surpassed. Thus, either the ecological carrying capacity, or some of its components, or the social carrying capacity constitutes the overriding critical factor, and researchers have tried to focus their endeavors on one or the other to determine the level of *recreational carrying capacity*.

In most cases, and especially with respect to resource-based recreation, the socio-psychological threshold of use is lower for an individual tourist and a resident, than is the ecological threshold, although in fragile ecosystems, such as wildlife breeding grounds and unstable slopes, the opposite may be true. On the other hand, relatively tolerant and resilient ecosystems may be identified and zoned for more intensive use. If the ecological factors constitute the capacity bottlenecks, then the application of appropriate management techniques such as provision of additional water or paving over an eroded trail, may be feasible. However dealing with socio-psychological factors is much more difficult.

The preceding discussion indicates that in most cases the social carrying capacity constitutes the critical constraining factor for determining the recreational carrying capacity. The social carrying capacity is impossible to quantify. This renders the validity of the recreational carrying capacity questionable. In fact, the "magic numbers" do not exist because the results of research endeavors to arrive at specific quantitative standards of recreational carrying capacity limits or thresholds should be evaluated negatively (Getz 1983; Wall 1983). There is, certainly, a continuum between a strict nature preserve where no use is allowed, and a cityscape where an almost total destruction of ecosystems has taken place. However, the continuum between these extremes is not associated with any specific numerical standards because of the preponderance of subjective elements rendering any objective scientific quantitative evaluation questionable. As a result, the recreational carrying capacity remains an elusive theoretical concept. "It is unlikely that any direct application of the carrying capacity concept will be meaningful or relevant" (Pigram 1980: 563), at least for the time being. Therefore, some investigators have questioned the validity of the recreational carrying capacity concept and suggested discarding it (Wagar 1974; Bury 1976; Burch 1981; Washburn 1982; Becker, *et al.* 1984).

The failure to quantify the recreational carrying capacity and its components should not raise doubts as to the viability or validity of the carrying capacity concept itself. Carrying capacity remains "a fundamental concept in natural resource management" (Hendee, *et al.* 1978: 170). Nevertheless, scientific investigations are continuing with lower expectations and from a different perspective. Experts have realized that the curves illustrating the relationships between use and impacts, both ecological and social, are mainly continuous and rarely provide for abrupt breaking points that would indicate capacity limits. Scientific research cannot identify such capacity limits on the curves, which would indicate that all lower impacts are harmless and consequently acceptable, and all impacts above this critical limit are destructive and, therefore, not admissible.

The second realization is the necessity to develop more qualitative research. Not all values can be reduced to measurable terms, nor are hard quantitative data always obtainable, contrary to the ideas of reductionism (Bosselman 1978: 96). In fact, many variables, associated with carrying capacity are unquantifiable; they are subjects of human value judgments and must be treated as such by research. The intricacy of the interactions within the system of nature-humanity involves "something deeper and more complex than man's analytical techniques can handle" (*ibid.* 98).

7.6 *Managerial Carrying Capacity*

The complex judgmental gap between theoretical models and the real world has to be closed and reconciled by planners. In this connection, the results of scientific research should be regarded not as absolute standards but only as guidelines—as tools or yardsticks for normative planning and management, reflecting the goals and objectives of planners, managers, and decision makers.

When the environment, instead of evolving according to the laws of nature, becomes subject to managerial judgment, planning, and manipulation, the traditional categories of recreational carrying capacity yield to the concept of the managerial carrying capacity which is subject to management manipulation according to the goals and objectives of planning. Managerial carrying capacity is a product of management judgment rather than a precisely defined measure; a decision-making concept, not a scientific concept (Hendee, *et al.* 1978: 172), a means rather than an end (Stankey 1981: 32). Thus, when planners and managers talk about an "acceptable" or "permissible" level of change in natural environment, and about an "appropriate," "optimal," or "desirable" level of development they are suggesting the maximal impacts be limited to levels compatible with capacity parameters, established on the basis of their expert opinions. This implies value judgment or an arbitrary desire on their part to shape the environment according to their strategy, and according to their subjective goals. The objective measure of maximum use, based on natural characteristics of a particular ecosystem when applied as a management tool, is arbitrarily used and temporarily imposed by management and, therefore, subject to change. Indeed, the necessity of the imposition of development limits on tourism/recreation, commensurate with flexible management goals, is, for purely practical reasons, indispensable, and is well documented by the literature, at least since the 1970s (Turner and Ash 1975).

In addition to the judgment of the experts, other parameters must also be taken into account. The researchers working for the *Fundaciòn Neotropica* (1992) admit that management goals and objectives are shaped by personnel, financial, and facility limitations as well. And it is with this knowledge that they computed "effective" carrying capacities for every Costa Rican reserve in their study.

There is another economic consideration. Planners and managers imposing the arbitrary maximal limits to recreational impacts should be aware of the necessity to keep development above certain minimal thresholds for the investment to be profitable. This circumstance illustrates the delicate and frequently controversial balance between environmental conservation and socio-economic considerations. Therefore, in ecologically sensitive areas factors such as profit of the private sector should be supplemented and sometimes even substituted by taxpayers' support in the form of public ownership and resource management. For example, in the case of the North American national parks, participation in decisions and acceptable levels of tourism development are established within the framework of a political process as desirable for the involved parties (i.e., planners, managers, politicians, and taxpayers).

Research into the carrying capacity of sites and areas is an integral part of any physical planning for tourism/recreation, despite the frequently controversial nature of such endeavors. Currently, the concept of managerial carrying capacity uses the physical size of facilities (such as hotels, parking lots, or restrooms) to reflect the volume of visitors that may be accommodated. This is due, in part, to budget constraints (Gunn 1987: 241). Financial realism aside, this concept is being substituted by more sophisticated and refined research techniques, developing more meaningful approaches to this difficult problem. The issue of carrying capacity is also controversial politically, as pressures from the middle-class preservation/ environmental lobby on one side, and the vested interest development lobby on the other. Each has different standards of carrying capacity. No wonder, then, that Getz (1982: 92) concluded that, "the concept of capacity to absorb tourism is fundamentally political in nature."

Space is another limitation of the carrying capacity research. Carrying capacity is essentially a microconcept limited to relatively small areas such as sites, zones, localities, or resorts. Most countries are too large to have the concept of carrying capacity meaningfully applied to them. Although some small countries, such as those in the Caribbean islands, may be evaluated as individual units. But even here, areas under special stress, such as the western coast of Barbados, could be distinguished, and researched as separate territorial units. Lukas (1974: 11-12) demonstrates the uneven distribution of use on wilderness trails: sometimes a relatively small section of a trail attracts practically the entire use. His findings strengthen the argument for a micro-approach to the carrying capacity research, caused by the spatial inequality of recreational use. Therefore, only relatively small spatial units may be properly regarded as uniform enough for carrying capacity research and planning. According to Yapp, "uniform region-wide standards are often impractical" when "applied rigidly (i.e., without adjustments) for local conditions and goals."

If too large an area is assumed to be uniform in terms of the recreational carrying capacity and the use limits are set for the whole area instead for its parts, the threshold of the recreational carrying capacity for the most susceptible parts will soon be surpassed, and vulnerable sites will start to deteriorate long before the other more resilient areas are affected. This, in turn, will lead to problems. Therefore, component parts should be investigated individually because of their different environmental and recreational use characteristics.

The planning process (for details see section 9.3) should start at the national or regional level by establishing regional goals and objectives, and then proceeding down to smaller territorial units such as zones or sites. The results will be variable management goals for each zone or site. In the final analysis, different standards, in terms of limits of use, will be applied for each spatial unit constituting a part of the region. Of course, the larger the spatial unit, the more general and less concrete the planning and management goals, because the "hierarchy of goals" (Yapp and Barrow 1979: 202) progresses from national through regional levels down to increasingly refined objectives for specific zones, localities, and sites. At each level a dynamic equilibrium between various environmental and human variables should be sought. However, the management objectives as to the type of destination to be developed should be the determining factor.

National park planning in North America is an example of such a hierarchy of planning goals and objectives. Planning starts at the national level with the goals for the entire United States or Canadian park system, and ends at the zones and sites with normative standards identifying the limits of use. These standards, established at each level in maximal allowed user-units, such as camper-days, are, on the surface, subjective and arbitrary, but are, in fact, based on solid scientific research and management decisions reflecting the planning goals and objectives.

The time frame during which the changes are taking place should be also taken into account when evaluating carrying capacity for tourism planning. Slow changes in tourism impact give the environmental and societal adaptation mechanisms time to adjust to changes. Therefore, a gradual transformation throughout extended periods of time is healthier than is an accelerated short-term tourism development. As the current societal values of acceptable carrying capacity differ from the future values, so does the perception of carrying capacity. This difference, or potential difference, may create a conflict between short-term and long-term planning of carrying capacity (Barkham 1973: 221).

The units of measurement also constitute a concern. The number of tourists at the destination may be an adequate measure if visitors do not differ among themselves in their impact. However, when more than one recreational activity is involved, and the activities differ in the degree of impact, researchers should focus on volume and level (intensity) of use in various activities.

Decision-makers can cope with the problems of tourism's growth by proper proactive planning and controlled development, rather than using restrictive measures or taking the remedial reactive actions. By anticipating quantitative (dimensional) growth and qualitative (structural) development, planners may also participate in the environmentally-sustainable development of tourism.

7.7 *Measuring Managerial Carrying Capacity*

The failure to establish absolute quantitative limits, or thresholds, of recreational carrying capacity has not prevented planners and managers from adopting some quantitative criteria to express the use in space and time. Thus, for practical purposes of planning and management, a number of quantitative parameters of managerial carrying capacity have been developed. These parameters usually represent ratios between relevant quantities, and are expressed in the form of indexes. For example, the number of facility units is associated mainly with available space—theater seats, campsites, picnic sites, and so on—and use periods or user units—camper-days or boater-days, and are expressed in the form of indexes. Yet, they cannot be identified *per se* with fixed thresholds or standards of recreational carrying capacity. They can only be regarded as statistical tools for comparisons of use between various areas and, more important, as yardsticks for planning and management. As for recreational carrying capacity and its components, they may be only applied as starting points for research and discussion among researchers and planners.

The following open-ended list of indexes or ratios, is based on various sources (Hills and Lundgren 1977; Lozato-Giotart 1992):

- total annual or seasonal number of tourists/local population

- total annual or seasonal number of tourists/area
- tourist beds/local population
- tourist beds/area
- area/tourist beds
- tourists in peak period (month)/local population (the best measure for the irridex)
- tourists in peak period, or per peak month/area
- tourist nights/local population
- tourist nights/area
- tourists present at a given point in time/local population
- tourists simultaneously present at a given point in time/area
- tourist person-years/local person-years
- tourist nights/restaurant capacity
- tourist nights/area of the beach
- area of the beach/tourist nights
- meters of coastline/number of tourists on the beach
- tourist nights/linear kilometers of the beach.

These measuring tools have been used for years in research and planning for various purposes, and result in a number of often conflicting recommendations even for the same area (Lozato-Giotart 1992; Tangi 1977: 340). They are of unequal value, and some may be outright misleading (such as the number of tourists per local population, which does not take into account the length of stay). Using these indexes for comparison, the highest tourist densities are associated with small tropical and subtropical islands, which, as a rule, are located in the LDCs, and contain small local populations and accommodate large numbers of tourists (Cleverdon 1982: 197–204). Yet, even the highest do not always indicate that the saturation level has been reached and that measures should be taken to limit the number of tourists.

A number of other, more complex numerical measures of tourist capacity and density and of hotel density and intensity have been suggested by the OECD (1980:42-43). According to this source, tourist capacity is expressed by a formula relating tourism development to the local population and area, and tourist density by a formula pertaining roughly to the same parameters, and, additionally, taking into account the relationship between the number of tourist nights and the total number of nights spent in the region. Hotel density indicates the hotel potential of a region expressed in terms of beds available per square kilometer; hotel intensity indicates the hotel potential of a region, expressed in terms of beds available per 1,000 permanent residents.

7.8 *Management Strategies & Measures to Modify Carrying Capacity*

With respect to natural environment some general objectives of planners and managers are:

- providing the full spectrum of recreation opportunities which different users can match their recreation needs and objectives
- allowing a certain level of use, which, in the judgment of planners and managers, does not damage the ecosystems
- increasing the critical thresholds of carrying capacity in selected areas or sites by undertaking measures appropriate with their goals
- limiting the use in certain areas below the formerly established threshold levels, if it commensurates with their objectives.

The list of concrete measures used is open-ended. Despite a certain overlap among them, they can be grouped according to categories of carrying capacity: physical, ecological, and/or social. As a result, the theoretical category of the recreational carrying capacity fits the requirements of the managerial carrying capacity in the practical application.

7.8.1 *Modifying the Physical Carrying Capacity*

Physical carrying capacity can be increased simply by expanding existing facilities, such as swimming pools, tennis courts, hotels, campgrounds, and washrooms. The input of capital, labor, and management techniques may significantly increase the capacities, substituting human-made facilities for the natural environment. In extreme cases whole ecosystems may be replaced by artificial environments (Mieczkowski, Z. 1990: 295–296). Examples are artificial beaches, such as at the West Edmonton Mall, or even Ocean Dome at the Seagaia complex in Miyazaki on Kyushu, Japan (*Economist* 18 December 1993). The largest completely artificial skiing facility in the world is the Skidome near Tokyo, with a slope 490 meters long, 100 meters wide, and an 80-meter drop. From an environment perspective, such developments are regrettable; however, they frequently perform a useful role by diverting the demand from fragile natural environments, especially overcrowded national parks, to relatively small, well-developed high-density areas (Mieczkowski, Z. 1990: 152).

Physical functionality of facilities, advocated by Gunn (1987: 232), may also enhance the number of users without imposing an additional load on the environment. Proper designs and structures that efficiently meet the needs of people, including the very young, the aged, and the physically handicapped, increase the flow of tourists and accordingly decrease the pressures on the environment.

Modifying the physical carrying capacity is not confined to developing new or expanding existing facilities, nor by better design of facilities. However, one of the most convenient methods to limit the managerial thresholds of carrying capacity may be achieved simply by intentional lack of facility development, as for example, by provision of strictly limited parking or camping space.

7.8.2 *Modifying the Ecological and Social Carrying Capacity*

As with the physical carrying capacity, the ecological carrying capacity may be increased by input of capital, labor, and management techniques. The application of modern science and technology may also enhance the ecological carrying capacity. In some cases, management techniques, aimed at decreasing the use by tourists and recreationists are regarded as more appropriate. These measures are being undertaken by decision-makers, and their application is frequently subject to intense public debates at political levels. Closely associated, and often overlapping, are measures aimed at improving the social carrying capacity. Some of the measures modifying both categories of carrying capacity are as follows:

- selecting naturally resistant sites, with deep soils of medium texture that can sustain abundant vegetation. Shallow soils, frequently associated with coarse texture and rock outcroppings, are less resistant to use because they do not support vegetation well.
- using artificial soil conditioners and fertilizers
- managing vegetation: seeding, reseeding, or planting vegetation, especially resistant plant species
- irrigation
- taking anti-erosion measures (such as building devices to retard runoff), graveling or paving erodible trails, especially on steeper slopes, or in campgrounds and caves
- rearranging erodible trails by changing their route and/or location
- thinning dense tree cover to let the sun penetrate and to let rain improve soil moisture values; as a result, grass and other lower story vegetation will improve and become more resistant to use;

• walkways, boardwalks, bridges, and other protective devices on building fragile ecosystems, such as marshes
• rotating the use of areas and facilities, such as campgrounds and trails
• using proper landscape design, such as hedges, to protect fragile sites and channel the traffic into more resilient sites
• using various management techniques, such as limiting space for parking, boats, and marinas
• limiting, both quantitatively and qualitatively, facilities (especially overnight facilities), in environmentally fragile and/or protected areas such as national parks
• limiting or discouraging access and use by implementing rationing: permits, queuing, reservations, quotas, lotteries, hunting licenses, restricted length of stay, increasing entrance fees (Beaman, *et al.* 1991), demanding fees for services that may vary from season to season, and applying merit criteria. Stankey and Baden (1977) provide a thorough analysis of the impacts and consequences of various rationing systems
• regulating the size of the visiting parties
• discouraging or forbidding recreational activities such as all-terrain vehicles (ATVs) that damage the environment
• separating areas by use (such as water-skiing and motor-boating from swimming and fishing, and hiking from ATVs)
• providing different spaces between compatible users according to the management objectives for a particular area (e.g., wilderness campers and campgrounds
• zoning the recreation areas for various types and intensities of uses has been successfully applied in various park systems where each zone is assigned a different threshold of carrying capacity
• diverting the demand from fragile resource-based areas to relatively small, user-oriented, high-density areas
• dispersing (redistributing) recreational resources in certain overused areas and opening up new recreation opportunities in underused areas
• encouraging the development of privately owned facilities, especially highly capitalized campgrounds, equipped with "luxury features," located outside the protected areas such as national parks
• time zoning: only allowing a certain limited number of users to a given area at the same time
• dispersing use by staggering the work and leisure periods among the population

•encouraging off-season and weekday participation (and discouraging high season and weekend participation) by setting differential prices and entrance fees
•establishing environmental slogans and guidelines for users, such as "take only pictures, leave only footprints" or "carry out all garbage and waste with you"
•modifying the user behavior either indirectly by education, or directly by regulations
•instructing users in environmental ethics through museum displays, exhibitions, guidebooks, brochures, maps, newspapers, magazines, television, radio, interpretation services, lectures, campfire programs, slide and movie presentations, nature walks, tours, and self-guiding trails and roads;
•combating vandalism and crime: have specially trained rangers and conservation officers enforce the laws and regulations.

7.9 *Establishment and Enforcement of Use Limits*

The decisions about the use limits are the prerogatives of planners, managers, and, most important, of politicians. Since about 1970, a number of decisions have been made by various local, regional, and national governmental bodies with respect to setting limits on recreation in places deemed overcrowded. This restrictive use policy has been spreading with the shortage of resources.

The process of establishing use limits in an area starts at the research level. Hendee, *et al.* (1978: 181ff) suggest that with respect to wilderness this process should start by looking at the ecological carrying capacity from two points of view. First, the character and the rate of change resulting from the recreational impacts should be investigated; second, the effects of human interference on the character of ecosystems, especially the composition of species (including the introduction of exotic and elimination of native species) should be researched. One has to realize that the natural rate of change may be either accelerated or retarded by humans.

This process of arriving at acceptable limits of change is illustrated in Fig. 7.9. The central band labeled *Natural Variation in Rate and Character of Change* represents the natural range of change without human impact. Both adjacent bands indicate the scientifically acceptable margins of change with respect to rate of change and the character of ecosystems, resulting from human impact. Changes beyond these bands are regarded as unacceptable.

Figure 7.9

MODEL OF ACCEPTABLE ECOLOGICAL VARIATION IN WILDERNESS

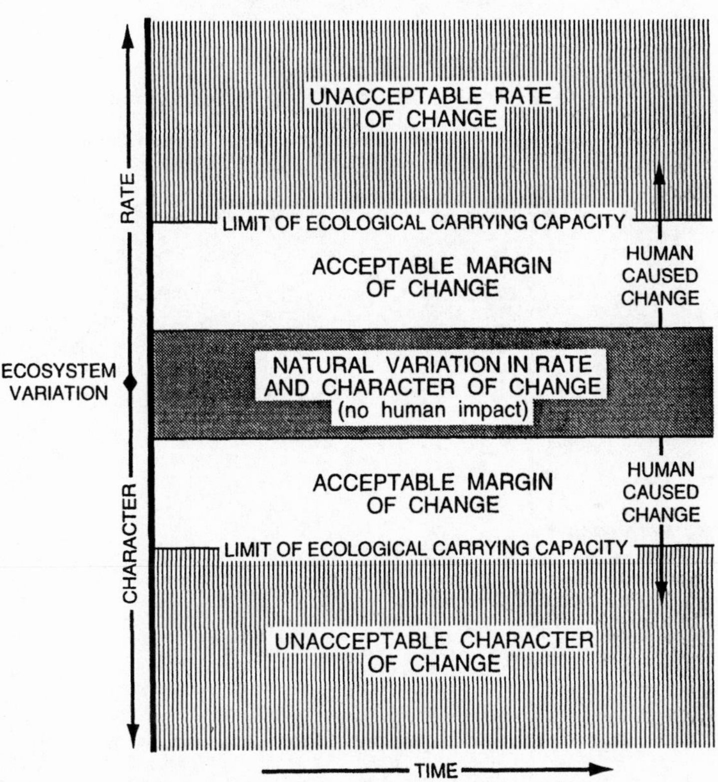

Source: Modified from Hendee et al. 1978:182

The general parameters of change in ecological carrying capacity are arrived at by quantitative and qualitative research investigating each resource element that can be isolated, and by identifying the most sensitive element as the limiting factor. Subsequently, suggestions are formulated, decisions made by planners and managers as to concrete limits or acceptable change.

Public participation in setting the standards of ecological carrying capacity also pertains to social carrying capacity. Here again the research provides the data for planners, managers, and the decision-makers. Hendee *et al.* (1978) discuss whose value judgments should be taken into account—those of the users or those of managers. These two

Figure 7.10

MODEL OF ACCEPTABLE VARIATION IN WILDERNESS EXPERIENCE

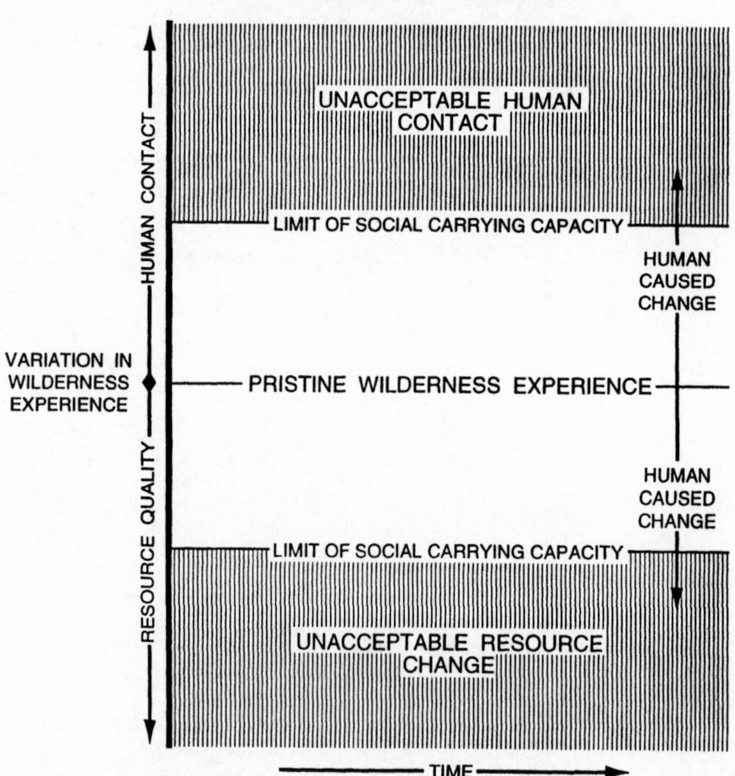

Source: Modified from Hendee et al. 1978:184

groups frequently differ. Moreover, there is usually a wide spectrum of opinion among users. Hendee *et al.* believe that, in the case of wilderness recreation, priority should be assigned to the needs of users with the highest standards of low-use-density recreation in an unmodified natural setting. These standards should be the decisive guidelines for establishing the limits of acceptable change, and consequently the limits of use (Fig. 7.10).

Figure 7.11

USE OF RESEARCH MODELS FOR MANAGEMENT DECISIONS

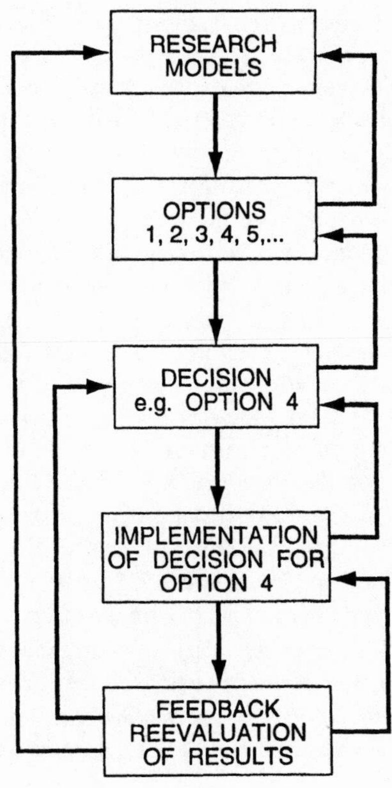

The final stage in this process is the meshing the ecological and social limits of use into a coordinated whole, where all aspects form the basis for the final decision making. Thus, the research models and the options developed by planners and managers form the basis for final decisions. Some time after the standards of use have been put into practice, the reverse process of feedback has to be undertaken. Testing a particular policy in the real world frequently results in appropriate adjustments of the policy (Fig. 7.11).

In discussing the issue of government-imposed use limits on the riverways in the United States, McCool (1978: 5) observes that the implementation of use limits has been easier on rivers in western settings, where access is more difficult or limited. The enforcement of regulations on rivers with easy access at many points is less manageable. The major management problem is the allocation conflict between the outfitting companies and private individual users (*ibid.* 6). The restrictive use policies prompt government agencies towards the identification of other back-country areas outside national parks or designated wilderness, which can provide similar recreational experiences. However, "the availability of alternative areas for back country and primitive recreation experiences appears to be dropping" (*ibid.* 6). The tourist industry may counteract the effects of use limits by substituting some wilderness activities, such as white-water rafting, by other activities belonging to the same "cluster" or "activity aggregate" (Lime and Stankey 1971: 175), or by developing and marketing intermediate types of activities associated with more developed areas.

McCool's research on white-water rafting is a good example of contemporary approaches to establish the thresholds of managerial carrying capacity and, therefore, act for a standard (i.e., fixed determinants of use) for a specific recreational activity. A pioneering study was conducted in the 1970s for the Bureau of Outdoor Recreation, U.S. Department of Interior, and published in 1977 under the title "Guidelines For Understanding and Determining Optimum Recreation Carrying Capacity." This study suggests the ranges of managerial carrying capacity for as many as 55 recreation activities, with the following results:

- The social carrying capacity serves as a the basis for the standards set because it constitutes the main critical factor (bottleneck) in determining the total capacity.
- The survey method applied reveals a wide range of opinions by users. Therefore, it was reasonable to establish relatively wide ranges of

standards reflecting the subjectivity of the issues (for examples see Guidelines 1977: VI-30).

- The range between the minimal and maximal use is called optimum recreation carrying capacity, that is, "the amount of recreation use of a recreation resource which reflects the level of use most appropriate for both the protection of the resource and the satisfaction of the participant." (Guidelines 1977: B-2)
- The ranges of optimum recreation carrying capacities for the surveyed activities were established after surveying users, planners, managers (such as park administrators), and surveyors.
- It is easier to apply the concept of managerial carrying capacity to activities such as picnicking, camping, and tennis, than it is to activities such as mountaineering.

Chapter 8

The Search for Environmentally Sustainable Tourism

8.1 *Introduction*

Chapter 7 was the first of the four last chapters of this book that focused on a wide array of measures to secure symbiotic sustainable tourism and recreation. It concentrated on issues of micropolicy and microplanning, whereas chapters 8 to 10 will focus on macropolicy and macroplanning. These three chapters look towards solutions that address the environmental issues of tourism and recreation from a broad global, national and regional perspective, although local problems are not ignored entirely. More specifically, chapters 8 to 10 discuss measures aimed at prevention and/or mitigation of ecological decline resulting from tourism's impacts, i.e., measures aimed at safeguarding environmentally sustainable tourism in interaction with other global issues. These measures may be discussed from the operational or conceptual point of view.

On the operational level, one can define general parameters, such as human attitudes, education, scientific research, application of green economics, and such factors as the role of government, NGOs, and the business sector, in the development of environment-friendly policies. These parameters are discussed in sections 8.2 to 8.9 of this chapter.

On the conceptual level, one may divide the measures into two categories:

1. *General measures, aimed at environment protection against external (nontourism) impacts.* Although tourism and recreation are not responsible for these impacts, they profit indirectly from the resulting environmental benefits, such as clean air and water, and conservation of fauna and flora. Even though only section 8.10 specifically concentrates on coping with nontourism impacts on nature, chapter 8 puts tourism and recreation in the wider perspective of ecological issues, both nontourist (external) and tourist (internal): Its general orientation is the interaction between external and internal factors from the point

of view of coping with environmental problems;
2. *Specific measures, aimed at environmental protection against tourism's internal impacts.* Chapters 9 and 10 are devoted to this category of measures.

The environmental revolution of the 1960s awakened people to the realization that they share one finite planet with other forms of life and that humanity is only one part of the natural global system—it is not a master of nature but a component, responsible for the sustainable existence of the whole. This revolution has also made us aware that the natural conditions of our planet have deteriorated to such an extent, since the inception of the Industrial Revolution, that further delay of urgent actions to both remedy the present situation, to undertake measures to prevent future environmental degradation, is unacceptable. Ironically, environmental concern has the same roots as environmental destruction. Both are by-products of advanced and prosperous societies, societies in which industrialization, while degrading the environment, at the same time brought about spectacular scientific, technological, economic, and social progress. This is probably one of the reasons why the environmental movement is still relatively weak in the LDCs.

In the DCs, the plight of the natural environment in some regions, such as the Mediterranean, the Alps, parts of northern and eastern Europe and eastern North America, has become especially critical. Consequently, these areas have received priority in the quest for environmental solutions. The DCs—with about 20 percent of the global population and about 80 percent of resource consumption—are recognized as the main culprits responsible for the environmental deterioration of our planet through the global use and abuse of resources. This recognition has led to the rational concentration of endeavors to cope with the threatened ecology in these economically developed regions of the world.

At the same time, the ecological situation is becoming worse in the LDCs. In recent decades the rape of the environment in some parts of the Third World, especially in cities, industrial areas, and industrial/agricultural regions, surpassed the level of the DCs (Klostermaier 1991: 39). Taking appropriate pro-environmental measures in these parts of our planet entails its own, specific set of problems involving the lack of financial means, unwillingness of governments, and population explosion.

Despite these problems, since the 1980s increasing attention has been paid to the ecology of the LDCs. This follows naturally from the realization that environmental issues are global and the health of our planet depends on the preservation of ecosystems all over the world, not only in the DCs. In the LDCs, special attention has been accorded to tropical forests, particularly rain forests, with their immense variety of species and their tremendous impact on world climate. Thus, the LDCs are becoming more decisive players in the international environmental arena. In fact, the future quality of life on earth may be determined by the environmental policies in the LDCs.

Unfortunately, however, the priorities of the Third World lie in the field of economic development and jobs for exploding populations. Dealing with environmental problems is a distant concern; the poor have more urgent needs to satisfy. Indeed, attention to environmental quality is highly income-elastic and the LDCs are holding back on environmental issues. Some of their governments regard the ecological concerns of the DCs as a trick to put a brake on the development of their countries (Keyfitz 1993: 33)

The Earth Summit in Rio de Janeiro in June 1992 indicated that the DCs, facing the reluctance of the Third World to act on environmental issues, must provide a number of concessions in exchange for the protection of nature in the LDCs, including increased transfer of financial resources and improved terms of trade. Technical assistance and transfer of technology also appear to be indispensable; ironically, modern technology that has contributed to the decline of the environment is now capable of restoring and preserving the environment it has historically degraded.

A holistic approach that recognizes the global integrity of eco-systems, from the spatial point of view, must be extended topically or systematically to the factors at play in the environmental game. We must recognize that our planet is one, not only spatially, but also in terms of the agents that impact on the ecosystems. Environmental deterioration in one region affects the whole world, including the favorite vacation areas. However, the detrimental impact of one agent, such as agriculture, industry, or tourism should be evaluated and acted upon, not in isolation but in conjunction with other factors; not only from the local, but from the regional and global points of view. In other words, "think globally and act locally."

In this sense, tourism's impact on environment may be viewed separately from nontourist impacts but only for analytical purposes. In the real world, tourism environmental issues cannot be treated in isolation but must be considered in interaction with external ecological problems—they should be put into the wider regional and global context, together with other human forces that modify the environment. This integrated, holistic approach should prevail, not only with respect to research analysis, but it should underlie planning, decision-making and any concrete management measures aimed at minimizing and mitigating the adverse human impacts on ecosystems, and—especially important in the case of tourism—in maximizing its positive effects. Therefore, it is advisable to integrate all conservation measures, external as well as internal. That is the focus of this chapter.

8.2 *Human Attitudes to Environmental Issues*

The earliest human attitude towards environment was that it was merely a resource. Today that attitude prevails among the profit-oriented development lobby and policy makers concerned with "real bread-and-butter issues" of jobs and profits. These sectors view nature as a commodity to be developed and sold on the free market. In the view of these developers-profiteers (called by Gunn [1972] "developers-exploiters"), business, including the tourism sector, should be completely deregulated and unrestricted in the name of individual freedom and the discipline of the market. These parties believe that the market forces will take care of both the environment and the economy, in the short- and long-term. They believe that tourism should develop without outside intervention, and that decisions about its expansion and the use of resources and facilities should be entirely up to the private business sector. The public at large and the governments at all levels should be kept at arms' length. If environmental problems arise, the proper attitude is to do nothing, in the hope that the market mechanism will solve them. In the political arena, "job protection" is the frequently used slogan to cover up the all-pervading profit protection priority. In terms of land ownership, these extremists would like to see most—or all—public ownership abolished and government-owned land privatized and commercialized, including the North American national parks. Environmental concerns are dismissed by these extremists as irrelevant pathological expressions of fear and despair. Ecologists are called "green

Mafia."

The extremist views of the development lobby represent the vested interest groups who profit financially from tourism, or who are involved in tourism as a tool for job creation. For the latter reason this politically powerful camp is supported by trade unions. The development lobby finds its most ardent advocates among some local groups interested more in short-term economic gain than in keeping their communities environmentally sustainable.

The other extreme on the continuum of human attitudes to environment could be labeled *green fundamentalism* (Loventhal 1990). This historically recent movement of radical zealots and purists represents a societal reaction, an angry backlash to the environmental abuse of Industrial Revolution, that started in the 1960s. It is an attitude that embodies a fear of living, an irrational emotion of "ecological panic," a feeling that any form of human activity harms nature. Internationally, the green fundamentalists oppose a global integrated economy and assume a nationalist, anti-free-market, anti-materialistic, xenophobic, economically self-sufficient and protectionist attitude. Jeremy Seebrook (1991) represents some of these views. Green fundamentalists advocate an anti-development policy halting all economic growth or even curtailing the present level of economic output to protect the environment. They argue against private ownership of land and against human access to natural ecosystems: these have to be protected from any human impact, including tourism. In their view, all of these anti-development actions should be enforced by the heavy hand of the mighty government. What the green fundamentalists struggle for is nothing but an ecofascist totalitarian village state based on a theocratic anticonsumption ideology. Some fundamentalists do not limit their actions to political arenas: they do not shy away from violence (Höfels 1991: 14), and have been known to engage in such tactics as terrorist bombing and assassination, with terrifying implications. Regretfully, this type of ecoterrorism has done considerable damage to the environmental cause.

Green fundamentalism is headed by some writers, poets, sociologists, anthropologists and extremist environmentalists. In countries with a free-market system, these groups belong to the left of the political spectrum. They believe that the impact of tourism should be evaluated negatively; that the undesirable environmental externalities of tourism are inherently repugnant (Mieczkowski, Z. 1990: 347-348) and that tourism should be, if not liquidated, then severely curtailed. This ecological argument is supported by criticism of the sociocultural and economic problems associated with tourism. The negative evaluation of tourism's impacts is also quite common in geographical literature. For instance, De Blij and Muller (1986: 304-305) do not see anything positive in the development of tourism in the LDCs.

Both of these extreme positions are untenable in the real world. There is nothing basically wrong with development. To blame any economic activity, such as tourism in general, for decreasing environmental quality is like blaming literacy for bad writing. Thus, between these two extremes lies a continuum of more-or-less balanced views, that attempt to find symmetric solutions. The immediate challenge is to ensure economic survival in a world where long-range sociocultural and environmental deterioration may ultimately result in economic disaster. A variety of groups of concerned citizens, scholars, government agencies, and NGOs are represented. They attempt to balance out the negative and positive impacts of tourism in specific cases, and help the decision-makers arrive at optimal solutions. They want to see planned, regulated and restricted tourism development based on research and ecologically sustainable management.

Mainstream environmentalists believe that the world needs not just any development, but sustainable development that operates within stringent environmental constraints that maintain and enhance economic prosperity and quality of life without environmental deterioration. In other words, development, including tourist development, is sustainable if it is done in an environmentally sound and esthetic manner that not only leaves the ecosystems unimpeded but also enhances their current recreational value.

The prerequisite for environmentally sustainable development is to remain within the limits of carrying capacity, to minimize the negative and maximize the positive effects of human activity. Therefore, the quest for solutions to environmental problems has to be undertaken in a spirit of balanced compromise, a new equilibrium between humanity and environment with a built-in flexibility. The goal is to achieve economically efficient, sustainable development, and a sustainable natural environment. However, a firm proenvironment attitude that accords basic priority to the ecology is imperative. This attitude requires a fundamental change, a decisive turn in the societal values and attitudes, in both world economic systems and in the production technology and lifestyles. Therefore, where uncertainty exists regarding a specific environmental decision associated with development, it is advisable to give the benefit of the doubt to nature and to side with conservation. As stated in chapter 7, it is preferable to err in favor of environment than in favor of development.

8.3 *Education and Promotion of Environmental Ethics*

At the present historical juncture, there is an obligation to change our societal attitudes toward the environment, as well as to reassess human values and lifestyles with respect to ecology. To accomplish this task, society must promote environmental education. This effort must reach virtually everyone in the society, especially people at leisure. It is these recreationists who, while travelling, are most likely to come in close contact with nature, and thus acquire so-called environmental awareness. Environmental education is an instrument in the struggle against ecological illiteracy, an instrument that promotes a holistic approach to ecological issues, including economic, social, political, and ethical considerations. The purpose of such education is the development of a nature ethic, or environmental consciousness or, to use the newly coined term *biofilia* (Wilson 1984), among the mass population. This is certainly one of the most important preventive and coping measure that can be taken against the negative human impacts on natural ecosystems and in favor of conservation.

Environmental education spreads the simple message that the earth's environment is not an object to be subdued by people, that the resources are not free gifts of nature created for unlimited human use—the earth is a limited place, its resources are finite, our environment is fragile; the past paradigm of human domination over our planet is not valid anymore. In fact, humanity is not the measure of everything, and cannot be separated from natural ecosystems, but it is a part of the biotic and abiotic complex which we call the ecosphere—a part which has to exist with other ecological components in a harmonious symbiosis. If these conditions are not met and the ecosphere's health breaks down, the very survival of humanity may be at risk.

A substitution of the old subjective anthropocentric paradigm by an objective ecocentric one is an essential precondition to successfully coping with the present environmental crisis, of abandoning *laissez-faire* in favor of proactive ethical leadership. Tourism can play an essential role in this educational process by creating environmental awareness among broad masses in the DCs, increasing ecological concerns, which finally lead to the attitudinal change of tourists and their lifestyles. Participation in tourism (especially wilderness tourism), combined with appropriate ecological training contributes to the development of environmental ethics among the masses. This translates into political activism on matters of the environment. Specific issues of the educational role of tourism are discussed by such authors as Jackson (1988), Gunn (1988a and 1988b), and Pigram (1980).

Environmental education should start at the kindergarten level and address people of every age and intellectual level. A recreational setting seems to be an advisable forum for such a process: kids need to learn about nature not in the classroom, but in nature itself—exploring earth, plants, and animals. The supplement to the 29 March 1993 issue of *Newsweek*, entitled "Just for Kids," illustrates the scope of educational effort in environmental ethics, including a substantial list of relevant publications for children. The 200-acre Bicentennial Youth Park in Florida's Volusia County is a good example of a special environmental education program for young children. The park serves as a learning center for thousands of children. It shows the important connection between nature and humanity, and provides the development of environmental consciousness at an early age. To create incentives for school children to engage in environmental activism, large corporations sponsor special award programs for young students who demonstrate outstanding devotion to the environment. Even more important is the development of elementary and high school curricula that integrates general education with ecological knowledge (Ehrlich 1991: 134-135).

In recent decades, environmental educational programs have reached the university level and continued into adult education programs. They perform an important educational role among students and professors whose knowledge of population/resource/environment issues is shockingly low (*ibid.* 133). Therefore, the challenge of becoming more informed acquires important dimensions in the academic world. Various courses in ecology, management, product development, and ethics are being offered primarily by the natural and social sciences departments. Recently, humanities and women's studies have also become involved, the latter advocating ecofeminism. The tasks of the university reach well beyond the expansion of ecological awareness and commitment to the principle and practice of ecologically sustainable development: Scholars in many fields have to satisfy the environmental research needs of the present age (see section 8.4). These combined educational and research mandates in environmental studies found expression in the declaration of the presidents of 33 universities from five continents presented at the Earth Summit in Rio de Janeiro in June 1992 (*University Affairs* May 1992).

Finally, the educational message about ecological issues must be propagated among the out-of-school working population. The media is one means to this end, and so are the popular and scientific publications in the field of ecology and conservation, which are so instrumental in the growing popularity of commercial ecotourism (see chapter 10). To spread the conservation message among the out-of-school population various environmental NGOs, such as the World Wildlife Fund, are developing appropriate educational programs. These are conducted through scientific or adventure field trips and outdoor recreation activities, such as wilderness hikes or scuba diving. Large corporations are increasingly jumping on the environmental bandwagon, propagating ecologically responsible behavior not only among their employees, but also among their clients, the tourists (Ryan 1991: 123).

The number of players in the environmental crusade is growing: In recent years religions have started to play a role in stimulating environmental awareness among the faithful, e.g., the new Roman Catholic catechism treats violation of environment as a sin. In an interview at the Ministry of Tourism in Tunisia, I was told that Islam regards polluting water as a sin.

An interesting source of environmental inspiration, instrumental in dealing with the contemporary ecocrisis, may be found in traditional Asian, and specifically Indian, codes of ethics (Klostermaier 1991). Such elements of the Hindu religion as harmony pervading the whole universe, the integrity of all past, present and future lives, the respect for nature as a living conscious being, and responsibility for the quality of the life cycles go back "to the roots of India's cultural tradition, which indeed has much ecological wisdom to offer and a surprisingly large amount of practical advice to give... At the level of general principle, the Indian lesson is contained in a philosophy of life which encompasses all living beings in a chain of recycling and an intuition of an absolute, tied up closely with nature, together with an ethic that is life-centered and not merely anthropocentric" (*ibid.* 43). Klostermaier sees the educational potential of these ethical attitudes in helping to formulate a number of prerequisites for a universal ecological ethics, which include:

- a code of "ecological duties" parallel to the code of "human rights" of the United Nations;
- recognition of the complexity of nature and a repudiation of the belief that we can scientifically understand and technologically manipulate nature without limit;
- the cultivation of a comprehensive sensibility towards nature which is equally far from a romantic anthropomorphic view as from a utilitarian-rationalistic one;
- restraint in our behavior and restriction of our wants;
- treating nature as a living, conscious being which deserves respect and care;
- a balance between rural and urban settlements;
- a new kind of culture which respects nature in its own right as integral to human civilization;
- an integrated world-view;
- a comprehensive philosophy of life, in which ecological concerns are central;
- co-operation with, and adaptation to, the natural environment rather than conquest and control of nature (*ibid.* 43).

Similar ideas are expressed by other authors. In discussing the ancient Hindu philosophical principles that are so relevant to the relationship of people and nature, Jeremy Seebrook (1991: 175–182) finds it remarkable that they evolved when there was no environmental crisis of present-day dimensions, and that similar basic truths were discovered (or rather rediscovered) in the West only recently.

Other anthropological studies contribute to the growing ecological appreciation of ancient cultures and religions by modern scholars and the public at large. Particular attention is being paid to the nature-centered philosophies and ways of life expressing harmony and balance between humans and their natural environment. In this respect, one could explore the environmental codes of some of the pre-Columbian civilizations in America, such as the Kogi civilization, well preserved in the mountains of northeastern Colombia.

Unfortunately, however, only a minority among the population in the LDCs is educated to behave responsibly toward the natural environment. The least environment-conscious are residents of rural agricultural areas, especially those living in close proximity to national parks. They should also be exposed to nature-friendly ideas, if possible at an early age, because these residents play an important role as stewards of the natural heritage located at their doorsteps. The locals of Africa regard natural vegetation as a source of wood and land reserve for cultivation. Wildlife is considered either a nuisance destroying their crops or a source of meat and commercial gain. These attitudes foster the destruction of virgin forests and the spread of poaching. To counter these disastrous misconceptions and teach the local residents the value of nature conservation, innovative programs are being developed, including guided tours for teenagers and adults into the wilderness, located nearby but rarely visited, and unappreciated by the people. Fitzgerald (1991) describes such an educational program, the Dzanga-Sangha project in the southwestern part of the Central African Republic. Developed by the U.S. Peace Corps volunteers, the project includes guided ecotours into the future conservation zone, and is aimed at educating the local people in ecologically sustainable use of this virgin tropical rainforest area for such activities as licensed hunting, limited logging, tourism and scientific study.

These educational efforts in the LDCs teach the locals about the importance of economic incentives associated with tourism development in conjunction with nature conservation, discussed in section 3.5. Environmental education reinforces the economic considerations by introducing noneconomic values in the form of ecological ethic. In fact, the educational process is enlightening the Third World populations that the issues of ecology are not confined to the North.

In all countries of the world, both poor and rich, tourism plays an outstanding role in environmental education. Especially important are the information/interpretation facilities and centers increasingly provided for the educational benefit of tourists. The Acapulco Document of the World Tourism Organization (WTO) emphasizes the significance of ecological education of tourism-industry employees. Many countries include environmental issues as part of national education at all levels; they also offer a specialized tourism-related curricula (WTO/UNEP 1983: 43). Environmentally responsible tourist behavior can by nurtured by various codes instituted at all levels, starting with the WTO's Tourist Code and Tourism Bill of Rights and ending with local regulations. An example of a national code is the Code of Conduct for Visitors to Britain, published by the English Tourist Board. Some of the 20 points included in the code refer to environmental behavior of tourists, such as respect for nature and refraining from destruction of vegetation, from feeding wildlife, and from littering (*International Herald Tribune* 5 September 1990).

The value of ecoeducation is in making the public aware of the importance of nature conservation. Any concrete action on the environmental front is impossible without the support of the public. This support will be easy to gain, both on individual and political levels, if the masses understand and appreciate the natural environment— hence the significance of environmental education and the development of environmental consciousness. There is enough evidence of meaningful progress in this respect. Public activism on ecological matters is increasing. Environmental ethics has gradually become a part of the mass consciousness in the DCs, and is starting to take hold in the LDCs. However, this optimistic statement should not be understood as a final victory of the pro-environmental attitude among all members of society. Indeed, much work is still to be done, and the educational process will never end.

8.4 *The Role of Research*

Section 8.3 discusses how the basic factors of the ecological revolution are the challenge of education and development of environmental ethics among broad masses of population. However, in order to develop coherent ecological strategies still another factor has to join the equation: the research. Research is becoming increasingly important to environmental policy. Recently, tremendous progress has been achieved in this field. One aspect of research, the use of satellite technology, including remote sensing and high resolution photography, helps students gain a global perspective on the environment. Thus it enables scientists to monitor the dynamics and the rate of ecological changes on our planet and to verify compliance with environmental treaties. Starting in 1972 with the ERTS-1, through five Landsats, and, more recently, the Geographic Information Systems (GIS), scientists have gained powerful tools for detecting, measuring, monitoring, and managing environmental changes (Dunbar, G. 1991: 148–149). Not only are the surface of the earth and its geological structure under scientific scrutiny, but also the total atmosphere. A more recent example is the Mission to Planet Earth program, planned by the National Aeronautics and Space Administration (NASA). The forerunners of this program are already in orbit. The application of these new research methods in the field of tourism and recreation opens unlimited possibilities in modifying their environmental impacts.

Any development, including the ecologically sustainable development of tourism, is inevitably based on the research of its impacts on ecology. Scientific research and the evaluation of consequences of human activities, e.g., in the form of environmental impact assessment

Figure 8.1

SOLVING THE ENVIRONMENTAL ISSUES OF MAJOR DEVELOPMENT PROJECTS

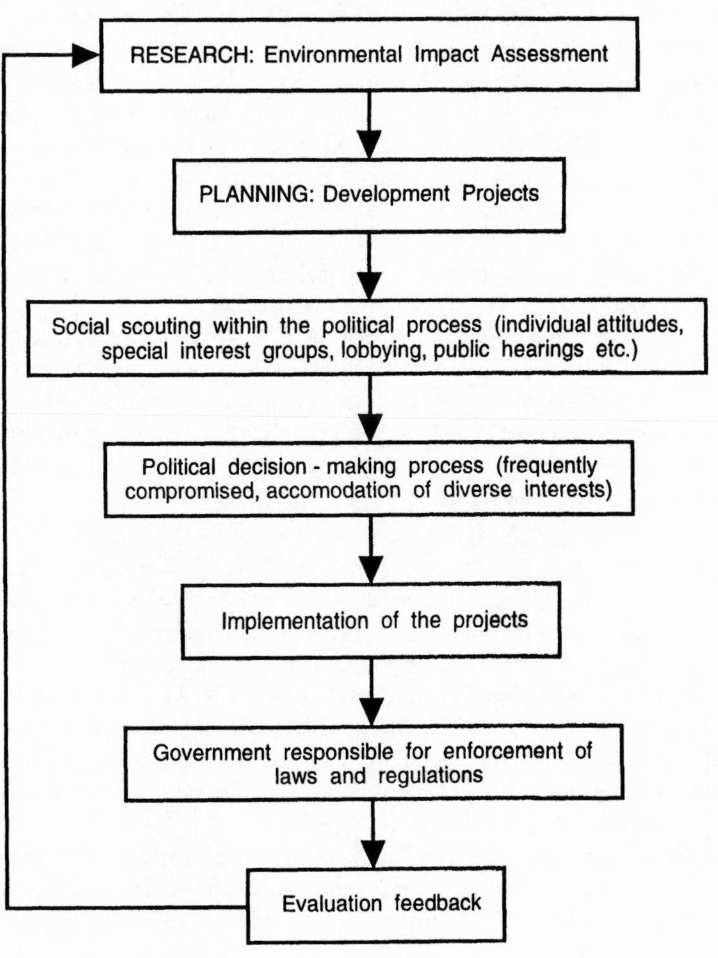

studies, is the essential prerequisite to creating a proper consensus, not only in terms of general policy but also with concrete cases. Such studies form the indispensable basis for the planning process (see chapter 9), political decision-making, implementation and environmentally sustainable management of tourism projects, and for the evaluation feedback (monitoring), which is conducted at every stage of the project and not only after the completion and implementation of a project (as shown in Fig. 8.1). Scientific environmental research is absolutely indispensable before any decision with respect to tourism or nontourism development is to be undertaken. Moreover, ecological research should be not only multidisciplinary (involving a number of natural and social sciences) but, more importantly, interdisciplinary, such as in environmental economics (see section 8.5), and applied economics, such as in biotechnology. Environmental research demands an integrative and practical approach due to the complex interaction of various factors, the cumulative character of environmental impacts, and the spatial and temporal discontinuities (see section 4.1) associated with chain reactions. The increasing practice of risk/benefit analysis is representative of this approach. This concept, examining all sides of an issue, reaches well beyond ecology but takes it into consideration.

Any ecological studies, including those involving tourism, face the difficult task of evaluating the impacts from a long-term perspective. The duty of research is to discern large temporal and spatial patterns, impossible to perceive by individuals whose senses, limited by time and space, are often lulled by apparent sameness, "obscuring dangers that reserve their alertness for sharp contrasts" (Gore 1992: 43).

The researchers studying the environmental issues of tourism have to overcome not only the temporal and spatial limitations which characterize any ecological investigation. They also have to cope with the specific integrative nature of tourism, which interacts with practically all parts of the world system to a much greater extent than do most other economic sectors. Tourism is a fragmented and multi-faceted industry with widespread links to an overwhelming network of interdependencies. This makes scientific analysis and predictions of future patterns extremely difficult. Simple rules of linear cause and effect are, for the most part, useless.

To achieve success, studies of the environmental aspects of tourism should be comparable with each other, in terms of methodologies, scales, and levels used. Comparability should be enhanced by their longitudinal character. One of the most important and difficult fields of research on environmental aspects of tourism is the elaboration of scientific norms of *carrying capacity* (see chapter 7) that safeguard the sustainability of development, and seek to establish the optimal balance between the intensity of land use by tourism and the resiliency of the ecosystems. As indicated in chapter 7, the results of such research have been rather disappointing, though not entirely fruitless.

Thus, despite the fact that knowledge appears to acquire the dimension of a primary "lever" of power in contemporary society (Toffler 1990), the results of scientific research do not always provide ready-made solutions. Indeed, regardless of the scientific roots of most environmental decision-making in the DCs, the solutions are rarely unequivocal, i.e., there is potentially more than one option, more than one alternative to choose from, because as a rule, research is unable to provide the decision-makers with iron-clad results and definite recipes for action. Decision-makers must realize that science cannot remove uncertainty, it can only "narrow the envelope of uncertainty" (Ludwig, *et al.* 1993). Following this logic, we can strive towards sustainability only in relatively temporary terms because of the inherent instability and unpredictable dynamics of nature, with its poorly understood boom-and-bust cycles (Hastings and Higgins 1994). In addition, "the complexity of the underlying biological and physical systems precludes a reductionist approach to management" (Ludwig, *et al.* 1993: 17). The authors postulate that initial overexploitation of ecosystems is "not detectable until it is severe and often irreversible." Therefore, delaying action on environmental issues until "final and completely certain" research results are available is futile and may lead to dangerous consequences. In this connection Nathan Keyfitz gives the following advice: "Where our knowledge is great and the cost is small, we can take big steps: where uncertainties are great and the cost high, the effort will be correspondingly small. In most such matters, delay greatly increases the cost, and where this is so, the steps should be correspondingly large" (Keyfitz 1993: 37).

The choice of one operational alternative from a number of scenarios provided by research is often the result of politics. The final decision on large development projects lies in the hands of government, which is often influenced by various interest groups, each with their own subjective attitude or vested economic interests. Specific conditions of place and time also contribute to the nature of environmental solutions. In other words, conflict resolution between development and preservation of environment varies in space, from country to country, or even from region to region. It also differs in time: the pendulum between environmental concern and economic development, including tourism development, after swinging in favor of ecology in the 1960s and 1970s, in the DCs has, since the 1980s, swung the benefit of jobs and development, to the detriment of the environment. Research has an important role to play in providing the necessary documentation, scholarly argumentation, and updated feedback for decision-makers to enable them to take corrective action.

It is not my task in this book to evaluate the progress of research into the environmental issues of tourism, but, I would agree with the general views of many of the authors quoted that this type of research is inadequate. The complaint of Satchell and Marren (1976: 16), that "the amount of research on the relationship between recreation pressure and changes in soil, fauna and vegetation is negligible in comparison with research on traffic, public health, economic and similar aspects of recreation," is valid to all DCs, and not only in Europe, with which Satchell and Marren were concerned. This observation is confirmed by the WTO/UNEP report (1983: 45) which complains about the research emphasis on tourism's economic impacts to the detriment on the research of the environmental effects of tourism.

8.5 *Environment and Economic Issues: Environmental Economics*

There is no reason to regard *ecology* and *economy* as contrasting antagonistic factors. In fact, they are two parts of a single issue, of a single dynamic. Therefore, they should interact in a harmonious, symbiotic way. Both words are derived form the same Greek word *oikos*, meaning home. In the past, there was no conflict between housekeeping at home and nature's housekeeping. Over the centuries, the two words have acquired different meanings, but their interdependence is evident. Indeed, sound economic policy implies the existence of a sound environmental policy, and *vice versa.* If humanity wants to achieve a sustainable environment, it has to base it on sound economic foundations, because sooner or later, for better or worse, the economic forces will assert their primary role. It is unavoidable that preservation of ecosystems has to be justified in general economic terms. In other words, the long-term economic benefits of conservation should, as a rule, outweigh the costs; failing to incur the costs preventatively will ultimately lead to diminishing economic returns and will compel society to take even more expensive, reactive measures. As a result, the long-term pro-environmental policy is always economically sound because it results in higher natural resource yields and savings on clean-up measures, such as mitigating damage to vegetation and crops, and incurring the medical and social costs of neglect. Such are the basic considerations of a green economy (Pearce, Markandya, and Barbier 1989; Bromley 1991).

The short-term perspective of the cost/benefit calculations looks different. The situation is much more complex and varies from case to case. Energy efficiency, for instance, brings immediate environmental and economic benefits. The preservation of ecosystems in national parks and other reserves often results in instant benefits surpassing costs in the form of tourist payments for the viewing of wildlife, as in the national parks of East Africa. The cost/benefit calculations of nature conservation in national parks indicate both the short- and long-term profitability of such solutions, even if the opportunity costs of the alternative agricultural development are taken into account. The policy of no development at all advocated by ecofundamentalists does not withstand the economic challenge, because of relatively high opportunity costs involved. Their model setting aside huge natural areas, denies tourist access entirely.

Yet, in many instances the short-term economic gain mitigates against the conservation of nature and natural resources. The quest for short-term profits by environmentally destructive tourist development may undermine the long-term regenerative capacity of the ecosystems, and thus contribute to the erosion of living standards and quality of life in the future. Nathan Keyfitz (1991: 5) discusses this issue in a nontourist example of world fisheries: There is no problem as long as the marine ecosystems supply the fish for catch on a sustainable-yield basis. However, overfishing makes the fish scarcer, and according to the law of supply and demand, more expensive. This in turn creates additional incentives to increase catches at a time of diminished capacity of the biological system. What makes sound short-term economic sense contributes to long-term ecological disaster. However, the long-term economic cost/ benefit calculation coincides with environmental considerations. The current plight of world fisheries exemplifies the medium- and long-term issues common to any resource utilization, including the use of natural environment for tourism purposes (For further supporting argumentation see Kolberg 1993). Thus, as Heilbroner put it in his foreword to Ekins, *et al.* (1992), "economics cannot be considered separately from ethical and ecological concerns."

Thus, in the short- and sometimes medium-term, a sound environmental policy may be associated with the loss of current benefits and with increased initial costs that surpass the immediate benefits. The reason for this is that frequently, alongside the economic considerations, noneconomic considerations are also prominent. This is especially significant in tourism development. Such values are impossible to express in monetary terms because the conservation costs are, at least partially, not market-related, and thus difficult to justify from the economic point of view. Because of this aspect of environmental protection, the priority accorded to it by society may mean that costs outweigh benefits and cause a slowdown in economic development. In other words, people have to pay for environmentally sustainable development in the form of higher current prices and taxes. This is the "short-term pain for long-term gain" scenario. The costs of a clean environment may constitute several percentage points of the GNP. Bornet (1979: 46) estimates that amount to two to three percent of Switzerland's GNP.

Another circumstance complicating the environmental cost/ benefits analysis is the fact that the costs of using the environment have been unrealistically low, and in the case of tourism, almost completely free. The resources of nature, including tourism resources, are regarded as a free gift from heaven without any pricetag. The disastrous results of this are evident in former communist countries: natural resources were squandered; pollution abounded. Neither is the West blameless in this respect, e.g., the United States subsidizes the misuse of water resources by underpricing irrigation water for growing surplus crops instead of diverting this precious resource to other uses, including tourism and recreation. Similar misuse of resources result from the U.S. Mining Act of 1872 that allows companies to buy federal land for $5 or less an acre. The European Union's agricultural price subsidization damages the environment by stimulating unreasonably high levels of output that uses too much environmentally harmful fertilizer and expands cultivated areas at the expense of forests, wetlands and marginal lands. These should be left for other uses, including recreation. If these practices of resource misallocation are reduced, tourism and recreation will benefit.

The real costs of resource utilization and environmental protection should not be treated as negative externalities outside the marketplace—as completely uncompensated side effects of economic activities. They have to be internalized and included in economic cost/benefit calculations. Thus, Bosselman (1978: 33) advocates treating the costs of environmental protection, e.g., hotel sewage treatment, as one of the "internal" costs of doing business. In other words, the environmental costs caused by extraction, manufacturing, and use of resources, as well as the costs of protecting the environment, should be added to the costs of production, and consequently to the prices of goods, including the supply of tourist goods and services. Such an enlightened change in the treatment of the economic value of natural resources leads to the development of new ecological accounting (Ekins, *et al.* 1992: 64–67; Repetto, *et al.* 1989: 1-24; Newson 1992: 84ff; Norgaard 1992; Jacobs 1991; Beeton 1989: 34–37). It would internalize the externalities through the inclusion of capital. This includes not only depreciation of human-made capital but the depreciation of natural capital that would be added to the write-offs in the Net Domestic Product (NDP) calculations. The diminished value of that natural capital, including loss of tourism attractions and resources, is largely ignored in conventional economic accounting, even though these important assets contribute to the creation of incomes, jobs, and exports in both tourism and in the nontourism sectors of economy.

The new ecological accounting clearly demonstrates the benefits of nonconsumptive resource use of recreational land (characterized by conserving the natural resource base); it can be compared with consumptive uses like logging or mining. The accounting period should be sufficiently long-term to justify setting aside these lands for conservation and recreation (e.g., as national parks). In light of new ecological accounting a national park, or even a well-managed multiple-use natural recreation area, is not only an ecological asset but an economic one, an asset that preserves the natural capital indefinitely. Presumably, only tangible costs and benefits may be included in ecological accounting. However, there are also intangibles, whose values are difficult to quantify in dollars, such as the health, educational, scientific, esthetic, spiritual, historical, and rehabilitational dimensions of parks. Although these remain outside environmental accounting, they should not be forgotten.

Treating natural resources as "free gifts of nature" and omitting them from economic calculations creates "a dangerous asymmetry" (Repetto, *et al.* 1989: 2). An example of such a narrow approach to costs and benefits is an excerpt from a World Bank document cited by Dennis Goulet (1977: 2): "A tourist project is considered appropriate for Bank financing when the economic rate of return is at least equal to the opportunity cost of capital." This policy does not take into account the environmental costs. As well, disregarding the costs of natural resources in economic accounting results in overstating the value of the Gross Domestic Product (GDP) at the national level, because the costs of natural resource depreciation are not taken into account. To make things worse, the costs of pollution cleanup add to the value of the GDP, but the cost of environmental damage remains outside economic calculations. This dichotomy between economics and ecology provides "false signals to policy-makers" (Repetto *et al.* 1989: 3) to draw heavily on environmental capital, and creates incentives for increased destruction of environment.

The differences between the two methods of economic calculations are substantial, as demonstrated by the examples of Indonesia *ibid.*) and Costa Rica (*ibid.*). The research on Costa Rica used remote sensing, satellite imaging, Geographic Information Systems (GIS) techniques, and detailed field studies to measure natural resource losses. The conclusions were startling. The depreciation in the value of Costa Rica's forests, soils, and fisheries averaged five percent of GDP per year over the 20 years of the study or one-third of gross capital formation. As a result, the economic growth of the country had to be calculated at 25 to 30 percent less and net capital formation at 40 percent less than when done according to the standard conventional calculations. The difference would be still greater if losses of plant and wildlife habitats and tourism attractions were taken into account. This new type of NDP accounting is gradually being adopted by a number of countries; there is even a possibility that the UN might revise its system of national accounts (SNA).

In addition to including the value of natural resources in economic accounting, it is also advisable to accord special treatment to environmental costs of prevention and/or mitigation environmental damage (in other words, investments for the future), by using low discount rates in the economic calculations. The reason for this preferential approach is the existence of some specific features of environmental benefits which put limits to the application of conventional concepts of costs and benefits. First, these benefits are frequently undervalued because of problems associated with putting a market price on them. For instance, it is impossible to put a dollar value on esthetic and recreational values of healthy ecosystems, beautiful landscapes, clean water or the stratospheric ozone layer. Despite undeniable progress achieved in recent years in measuring the value of environment, in people's perceptions calculating the value in tangible monetary terms will be always difficult. Second, "the consequences of some environmental decisions are irreversible. A dirty river may be cleaned up, but a species, once extinct, is gone for good" (*What Price Posterity?* 1991). Third, current environmental decisions may prevent risks that can materialize in the distant future, as, for example, the decisions pertaining to global warming, or to the depletion of the stratospheric ozone layer. Fourth, environmental decisions are frequently associated with a long time gap between incurring the cost and reaping the benefit. In other words, current generations incur the costs and future generations reap the benefits—for example, planting trees today will bring recreational and other benefits in the future.

All these problems with determining the value of the environmental costs and benefits reveal their partially subjective and stochastic characteristics, and the political nature of environmental solutions and decisions. Values include such intangibles as quality of life, quality of human leisure experience, and, in the final analysis, even the very survival of humanity.

Despite these difficulties, the general thinking in scholarly, and increasingly, in political circles, is that the environmental costs should be borne not only by the users of resources but also by the following categories of eco-offenders: 1) polluters, according to the amount of emissions; 2) producers of garbage, according to the amount and type of garbage disposed; 3) the creators of environment ugliness, the so-called eyesores. This means the introduction of fiscal tools in the struggle against environmental degradation. Thus, the environmental taxes should be proportionate to the amount of pollution, garbage, and decay produced, and should take the form of fines for violating the laws, rules and regulations.

Economic incentives and disincentives, used to increase or decrease supply or demand, are the most cost-effective and efficient tools to clean up and prevent environmental deterioration. They work better than the "command" rules, regulations, and controls that have been used mainly so far. Regulation is administratively cumbersome and inefficient from the economic point of view (*America's Parasite Economy* 1992). However, it does not mean that regulation should be declared obsolete—in fact, the "command" measures will be essential for a long time to come. Nevertheless, the recent trend has been the use of fiscal stimuli, such as tax incentives, and various charges, such as *ecotaxation* or *green taxation*— all effective measures to manage demand. This is especially evident in Western Europe, where Scandinavia is the world leader, and to a lesser extent, in North America (Defeyt 1993).

The array of specific fiscal tools to keep the environment clean and green is imposing: charges for automobiles entering the urban centers, traffic congestion tolls, special landing fees for noisy aircraft, returnable deposits on cars to prevent dumping them, gasoline taxation, carbon tax to discourage the use of fossil fuels, air pollution taxes that progressively increase with the amount of harmful emissions, municipal taxation based on the amount of garbage disposed, deposits for returnable bottles. These measures should apply to tourism and recreation enterprises (such as airlines and hotels), and to individual tourists.

From the fiscal point of view, *green taxation* means a shift in the tax base from economically and socially desirable activities, such as hard work and thrift resulting in incomes and profits, to activities that the society wants to discourage, such as harming the environment (Repetto, *et al.* 1992). This fiscal approach stimulates people to work harder, save more, and pollute less. Practically all green taxes are in some ways associated with tourism. However, gasoline and carbon dioxide emission taxes would have the greatest impact on the scope and mode of tourist transportation.

Thus, *green taxation* and other charges and deposits are unquestionably the best methods to get the ecology message across. Creating financial incentives for environmentally responsible behavior (e.g., to save energy through the use of public transportation by tourists and recreationists, or to minimize garbage disposal by hotels and restaurants) is especially effective. Additionally, taxation of polluters and users of natural resources reflects the real costs of goods and services for taxpayers and consumers. On the other hand, environment-friendly producers are being rewarded by tax incentives. Unfortunately, some countries use tax incentives and subsidies which practically stimulate environmental destruction, e.g., Brazil fiscally rewards deforestation of Amazonia (Mahar in Schram and Warford, ed. 1989).

The tax incentives for "green behavior" award economic benefits while the market-based environmental disincentives reflect the ecological, social and economic costs of goods and services, which add to their market prices. Indeed, this is a complete integration of economics with environmental considerations, a real market-based environmentalism—a veritable green economy.

8.6 *The Role of Governments*

Governments play a leading role in environmental conservation. The term *government* must be understood to include the local, regional, national, and international public authorities who bear the ultimate responsibility for environmental protection and facilitate cooperation between various levels. On the national level, agencies responsible for environmental protection are frequently elevated to the cabinet level, as is the case with the U.S. Environmental Protection Agency (EPA). Another trend is to include the environmental rights of people in national constitutions.

Any major human activity pertaining to the natural environment, including tourism, cannot be expected to regulate or police itself. The inadequacy of the *laissez-faire* market mechanism, with respect to the environment, is patently clear. The market, with its law of supply and demand, works at a short, limited extent and at medium-range with respect to goods and services. But the long-term consequences of human impact on environment are categorically ignored. Individuals, groups of individuals, and enterprises focus on short- and medium-term economic results of their activity and lack the direct responsibility for the long-term impacts of these activities on environment. Due to insufficient market transparency, they often act myopically and spontaneously. They are inadequately informed about the totality of the issues, and they rarely anticipate the consequence of their actions—which, for them, appear desegregated from the whole because of the fragmentary nature of most human undertakings. Fragmentation—disassociation of causes from effects—is especially evident in the tourism industry because of its amorphous and highly discrete nature, uneven in size and spatial dimension. Another circumstance is that environment has never been ascribed a market value, and, as indicated in section 8.5, lacks the necessary elements for objective conventional price accounting. Even after the inclusion of natural resources in the accounting system, the value of some environmental impacts and assets is not reliably quantifiable. Nevertheless, unique ecosystems have to be preserved from development, partially for noneconomic reasons.

There are many tourism and nontourism examples that illustrate what happens if natural resource management is left to unrestrained market forces. The results are, as a rule, negative—sometimes even catastrophic—as in the case of the crisis in international ocean fishing, (section 8.5), or the devastation of southeast Asian forests by logging and mining. In the field of tourism, as a result of the Thai government's policy of benign neglect, Elliott (1987) described overdevelopment and environmental destruction. Chapter 4 of this book abounds in examples of such situations from all over the world. Thus, the spontaneity of the market forces quickly leads to ecological deterioration.

These are the reasons that environmental issues should be singled out as a proper subject of government intervention, even in a free-market economy. This does not mean governments take over the tourism industry; it simply means that governments take more responsibility in legislating, regulating, and controlling tourism development and management. These measures include development of voluntary guidelines as well as establishment and enforcement of mandatory environmental standards and monitoring systems. Elliot (1987), Jenkins and Henry (1982), and Cleverdon and Edwards (1982) are of the opinion that active government involvement in tourism is especially essential in the LDCs because of the absence of a developed and innovative private sector.

Emphasizing the role of government in any field seems in conflict with the free-market spirit of our time. The gradual deterioration of the Soviet Union, which culminated with its total collapse on 25 December 1991, has substantially undermined the faith of the Western public in the government's role in the modern state. The conservative idea that, "the government governs best which governs least," and that the role of the public sector should be substantially limited, has been reinforced. Free trade, deregulation, privatization, and scaling down of government subsidies are spreading all over the world. These processes started earlier in the DCs and are now spreading to the LDCs and former communist economies. Even politically communist China has adopted a relatively liberal economic path. All these recent developments in favor of free markets should be evaluated positively. However, they will not lead to the demise of governments and should not lead to passive governments, especially when dealing with environmental issues.

In the present situation, there are not too many proponents of government command economies, in which the government own and manage almost everything (except the frequently flourishing black markets). In fact, market economies have proven to be much more efficient, although far from perfect, in resource allocation and utilization than the "planned" economies. The result has been economic prosperity and improved quality of life for the masses in the DCs. However, government still has a role to play. In reality, the new trends towards increased government activism, including the field of environment, are becoming apparent in the DCs. A typical example is the U.S. administration of president Bill Clinton, in office since January 1993. Although many environmentalists have been disappointed by the executive branch taking into account too much the political realities of the day in their fulfillment of electoral promises on environment, important steps have been taken: the gradual phasing out of low-price logging in a number of national forests, measures aimed at the reduction of carbon dioxide in our air, and the signing of the Convention on Biological Diversity. Tourism and recreation will be among beneficiaries of these pro- environmental measures, as they have been in the past. For example, the U.S. Clean Air Act has contributed to the improved visibility in national parks. However, the new interventionist government policies should be applied intelligently by viewing the market forces, not as an enemy of economic and environmental progress, but as an indispensable ally. The U.S. federal authorities have played a positive role in conservation by their commitment to national parks and other reserves. The withdrawal of these lands from consumptive uses subsidized by the government, such as mining, logging, and grazing, does not mean that they no longer produce revenue. Indeed, these areas produce considerable incomes from tourism, and often surpass the opportunity costs of alternative uses, especially when the new methods of environmental accounting are applied.

Governments at all levels have a very important role to play in the free market economy, including attending to the environmental issues. No other human organization is better able to exercise the appropriate control, to regulate, and to enforce the laws. Governments are charged with taking an integrative, long-term view of the interrelationship between society and the environment to achieve the delicate balance between conservation and sustainable development. Only government has the tools and the power not to cure the symptoms but to go to the roots of the environmental problems. They are empowered not only locally, but regionally and nationally, because ecological concerns encompass large areas. Governments are also able to take into account non-economic (e.g., esthetic) considerations and support them with taxpayers' money. Governments are frequently substantial landowners, and consequently, suppliers of tourism/recreation opportunities. Thus, the United States federal government owns more than two million square kilometers, i.e., over 20 percent of the country's territory (Hammitt and Cole 1987: 4–5). All these attributes enable governments to embark on a proactive course, instead of waiting for the environmental damage to become apparent and sometimes even irreversible. Indeed, anticipation and prevention through proactive measures is not only more advantageous for the environment than *post-factum* reactive measures, but also cheaper. The WTO/UNEP (1983: 32) report cautions that, "taking corrective measures is generally regarded as inferior because it constitutes an ad hoc type of action and often treats symptoms rather than causes."

The government's duty is to represent the interests of the whole of society and not the narrow interests of any particular economic sector, such as the tourism industry, or the interests of the market and its individual boosters, which frequently run counter to the long-term public interests. The government's task is to integrate the environmental policies with other policies, such as economic, social, or cultural, and to place the matters of tourism/recreation in the total context of these issues. An example of such an approach is the Alberta Conservation Strategy Project (Fig. 8.2). To achieve this aim, governments seek support for their actions on environment through mass public opinion, frequently represented by the NGOs. Public hearings on environmental issues are one venue for the expression of voters' feelings. There have been many examples of governments acting successfully as intermediaries between industry and environmental NGOs, and reaching consensus on contentious issues.

One of the basic duties of governments is to establish priorities on the spending of tax money. Decisions about spending priorities are made in the political arena. The recent trends are increasingly favorable to environmental issues, including those related to tourism and ecology.

Take, for instance, military expenses. It has become widely accepted that they are a classic example of the misallocation of public funds. Worldwide military expenditures, according to various estimates, in the early 1990s amounted to between $900 billion and $1 trillion, many times more than the outlays for environmental protection. The output of the defense industry can be regarded as an almost total waste, that stimulates the economy only to a limited extent. The defence dollar sup-

Figure 8.2

ORGANIZATION OF THE ALBERTA CONSERVATION STRATEGY PROJECT

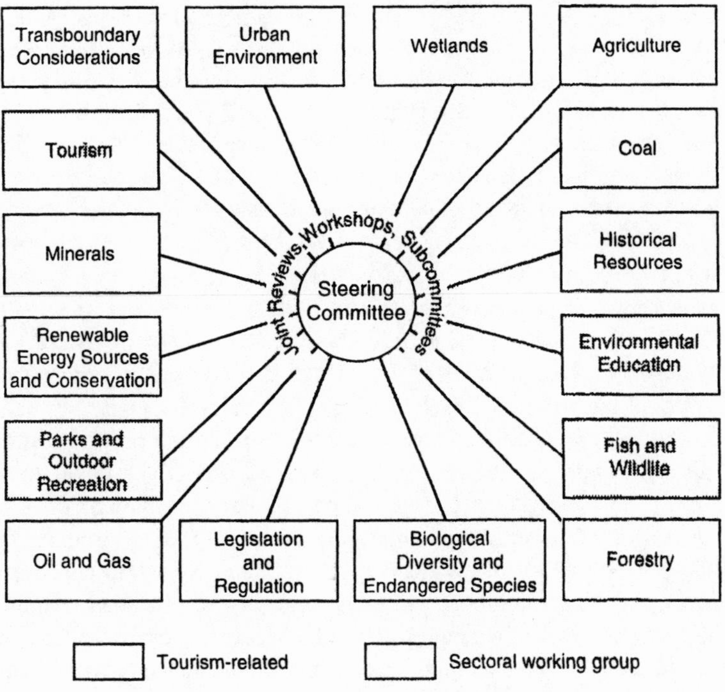

ports fewer jobs than almost any publicly spent dollar. In addition, the military devours a large amount of limited resources and destroys the environment through testing, production, and deployment of conventional, chemical, biological, electronic, and nuclear weapons, by use of artillery and heavy vehicles, and also by fuel spills and irresponsible garbage disposal. This was illustrated most poignantly by the behavior of Soviet and later Russian forces prior to their departure from central Europe and the Baltic republics, from 1990-94. Huge recreational areas and unique ecosystems have been affected by this military "war on environment." For example, one of the most spectacular areas of Kamchatka, Russia that surrounds the three major volcanoes north of Petropavlovsk Kamchatskiy, is "reserved" not as a nature reserve, but as a military "polygon."

However, in the post-Cold-War political situation, the swords are increasingly being converted into environmental plowshares. A novel partnership is being forged between military, or former military, and conservation interests. Lewis (1992) gives a number of examples of such cooperation. The decommissioned patrol boats from the former U.S. naval base in Subic Bay, the Philippines, are used for preventing illegal logging in the Palanan wilderness that represents almost 10 percent of the country's remaining rain forests. A U.S.-based environmental NGO, Conservation International, is responsible for this project. It also uses other surplus military equipment, such as "tents, vehicles, even boots for park people on patrol." Other examples profiled in the Lewis article include green military forces in Vietnam, Brazil, and Venezuela, where the military participates in reforestation programs and in patrolling against illegal hunting, fishing, and logging. In India, retired army men are working in forestation, reforestation, and combating soil erosion in the degraded Himalayas and in the Great Indian Desert. In the former Soviet Union, military equipment is being successfully "converted" to tourist uses. During my trips to remote areas of Asian Russia in 1990 and 1993, I travelled in converted helicopters, jeeps, and ATV minibuses, and used various types of military camping and survival gear now employed for the benefit of tourism. This converted USSR military equipment is one of the few items of quality produced in the former Soviet Union.

Society is concerned about the present and future quality of life, and government policies should conform with this purpose. This requires certain inevitable structural adjustments in the economy. It is likely that environmentally damaging industries facing a lack of public support will go the way of the dinosaurs. Others will accept changes in technological processes and/or introduce new products and services. Governments play a key role in implementing these environment-friendly processes of economic and technological restructuring by pressuring companies to follow the most cost-effective ways to clean-up or to prevent environmental damage. It seems that all the governments of the DCs have jumped on the environmental bandwagon in recent years. A tourism resource base is the direct beneficiary of these actions. Even the economically and politically troubled Russia is taking measures to protect some ecologically endangered areas. An example is a project proposed in the *Law on the Protection of the Lake Baykal,* published by the Russian Press for discussion in the summer of 1993 (*Sovyetskaya Molodezh* 5 August 1993). The protection of the unique, and largely endemic, ecosystem of the Baykal will have an extraordinary positive impact on nature tourism in this area.

The traditional methods of government intervention in protection of the environment consist of promotion of environmental education of children and adults (see section 8.3). With respect to producers and consumers, the main tools, as stated previously, have been legislation, regulation, and control. The list of specific measures that can be undertaken is open-ended. Following is a selection of tourism-related environmental measures that can be undertaken by government:

- limits of access, either locally (e.g., to a specific strict nature reserve) or nationally, by establishment of annual quotas (e.g., Bhutan) or indirectly, by establishing capacity limits (e.g., Bermuda);
- land use; zoning development;
- requiring building permits for any tourism/recreation facilities;
- requiring submission of environmental impact assessments for tourism projects;
- subdivision development control;
- control of public access to water;
- direct acquisition of land with special environmental and recreational attributes;
- purchase of scenic easements (limits or property rights to develop);
- establishment of water-quality standards for sewage disposal;
- regulation of food-quality standards in restaurants;
- emission control standards for automobiles;

•noise abatement requirements for transportation, such as cars and airplane, especially if recreation areas are located in proximity to airports;

•noise standards for hotel-room walls;

•regulation against eyesores.

The degree of government intervention varies from country to country and from area to area, but generally the higher the degree of pressure exerted by tourism/recreation on environment the more essential the appropriate regulation. Thus, in June 1994, the Mexican government drastically curtailed tourism development in the almost 100-kilometer-long coastal zone of the state Quintana Roo between Cancún and Tulum. This relatively pristine area, containing breeding grounds for marine turtles and other rare species, has come under increasing development pressure. The Cancún-Tulum corridor was divided into 45 zones that range from no development at all to low density tourism.

Another typical example of the urgency of government intervention is the overcrowded Netherlands. Authorities strictly control the hospitality industry (hotels and restaurants): restaurants are subject to air pollution regulations, they have to be equipped with special grease catchers, and garbage disposal is regimented to the smallest detail. Hotels, including hotel discos, must be soundproofed to 35 decibels (*Staatsblad van het Koninkrijk der Nederlanden* 1992).

Land-use zoning is especially important for tourism and recreation. Zoning is generally effective, although in recent times the courts, in particular the U.S. Supreme Court (*Economist* 2 July 1994; *Christian Science Monitor* 3 July 1992), have sided with property owners who claim compensation. They argue that nondevelopment clauses for things like wetland protection, enforcement of the Endangered Species Act, or protection from dangers of coastal erosion, hurts their property rights. On the whole, however, zoning seems to be an efficient way to prevent overdevelopment, including tourism overdevelopment. Other government regulation methods include requirements of Environmental Impact Assessments (EIA) of all development projects. This measure is now commonplace in most DCs, and it profoundly affects tourism. In the case of existing enterprises that violate environmental regulations, governments impose fines on polluting enterprises criminal penalties on executives, and ultimately close the recalcitrant polluters.

Another example of government regulation is in dealing with the problem of eyesores. Some of the most notorious eyesores are commercial billboards erected along highways. This creeping ugliness is still ubiquitous in some tourist regions of Europe, for example, in Spanish resorts, and in many LDCs. The greatest progress in eliminating billboards and other eyesores along the highways has been achieved in North America, where legislation restricts their location. The U.S. Highway Beautification Act of 1965, followed by even more radical state laws, may be evaluated as a qualified success. It provides for either removal of highway junkyards and car graveyards, or screening with plantings or fencing of them. Billboards along federal highways, except near commercial establishments, are prohibited. However, the implementation of the bill has not been perfect. Abuses attempting to dilute the original legislation or stall its implementation abound, as in the case of phoney commercial establishments created solely for the purpose of allowing the erection of signs. Another abuse, setting up huge billboards outside the controlled 660-foot zone, has been dealt with by amendments to the law. There are, however, some justified exceptions, such as providing tourists with information about motels or attractions located far off a highway. Yet, even this could be the subject of local controversy and should be resolved on case-by-case basis.

If regulatory measures are insufficient to protect environment from tourism, the government has to resort to the economic instruments discussed in section 8.5. Thus, in recent years governments have added economic carrots to the administrative sticks: they are increasingly using fiscal policies of tax exemption and credit for environment-friendly technology and services, and improving taxation on polluters (Cairncross 1992). A classical example is the carbon tax introduced in some DCs such as Sweden. As a result of the new taxation policy, we are witnessing the introduction of entirely new industries answering to the needs of sound, sustainable environment and promoting prevention rather than band-aid solutions to the past problems.

An important tool in the hands of the government are subsidies. Unfortunately, the record in this respect is not impressive. Frequently these subsidies support a detrimental cause at taxpayers expense. However, there is some improvement on the horizon: environmentally harmful projects and companies are being denied subsidies, and environment-friendly causes are supported. Thus, the United States and Canadian governments subsidize environment-friendly tourist railroad travel, like the Amtrak and Via Rail. The recent introduction of fuel-efficient and non-polluting buses has created the conditions for a revival of this mode of tourist transportation. However, such a revival seems impossible without government subsidies because of the competition of the subsidized railroads.

One of the economic sectors which deserves government support is tourism and out-of-home recreation. Tourism has a unique potential to contribute substantially to the enhancement of the quality of life, and, if properly controlled and regulated by legislation and fiscal policies, it may play an important role in nature conservation and sustainability of environment. Such tourism represents one of the most environment-friendly economic development options to choose from, and is, therefore, likely to expand and increase its share in the world's GNP.

These descriptions of the role of governments are theoretically ideal scenarios, detached in some respects from practical realities. In fact, the inadequacies of government policies and actions in the environmental field are well known. One of the most criticized is the sectorial, disintegrative, and analytical approach of government departments that are frequently at odds with one another (*Our Common Future* 1987). For instance, the development of a cohesive environmental policy on United States public lands is impeded by the division of national lands management among the Department of Agriculture (Forest Service), Department of the Interior (Bureau of Land Management, Fish and Wildlife Service, and National Parks Service), and the Department of Defense. Such an arrangement contributes to the widely criticized economic inefficiencies of government bureaucracies. To develop a comprehensive approach, the administration of all public lands in the U.S. should be placed under a single agency. The realization of these shortcomings does not, however, negate the usefulness of the public sector, which should be viewed as a basis for proactive and remedial measures.

A contentious issue is the competition for power between national governments on the one side and regional and local governments on the other. There are opposing points of view in this respect. The first contends that only local people are in position to exercise appropriate stewardship over the environment, while the other one asserts that only a centralized national government can deal with the environmental issues comprehensively. In general, in the majority of the DCs the central or federal governments have asserted their relative primacy; such a solution has been by and large advantageous to the environment. The role of local input is, nevertheless, considerable, and recent trends indicate that their weight is increasing.

The situation in the LDCs is different, however. In these countries the ineffectiveness of central governments on environmental issues have become apparent (Margolis 1992). The inadequacy of the government apparatus, including dishonest courts and inefficient administrators, opens the way to corruption and sometimes violence. From an environmental perspective, centralized government policies have led to a disregard of nature, to unrestrained overdevelopment, and as a result, to degradation or even destruction of ecosystems (Hassan 1993). The governments' complicity with the private sector in the pillage of natural resources of sub-Saharan Africa and southeast Asia has been most spectacular among the LDCs. Thus, Indonesia leads Asia in the rate of deforestation, followed by Thailand, Malaysia, India, Laos, and the Philippines. There is hope that the present post-Cold-War trend to democratization in the LDCs may contribute to decentralization of decision-making, and consequently to improved management of natural resources. For the sake of environmental conservation, it would be an advantage if the tribal regions within some African countries acquired more local autonomy, or even if these states disintegrated politically and formed economic unions.

The records of various governments on environmental issues vary from benign neglect to extreme activism. The former counsel to the U.S. Senate Committee on Environment, Curtis Moore, argues that in the last 10 to 20 years the world environmental leadership has passed from the United States to Germany and Japan, where government "officials see environmental protection as an opportunity for economic development, not as a barrier to growth" (Moore 1992). Moore supports his contention with comparative statistics ranging from air pollution control to gasoline mileage and energy production. Other supporting material may be found in *Der Spiegel* (1994, 20: 83-95).

Singling out Japan as environmental leader may raise some mixed feelings. As indicated above, internationally Japan has been perceived as an ecological outcast. Internally, the record of the Japanese government is mixed. On one hand, the enforcement of antipollution laws has been exemplary (section 2.10), and Japan is one of the pioneers and leaders in the development of green technology in the field of energy production and manufacturing. Japanese environment-friendly products are sold worldwide. On the other hand, however, the government allowed damming of virtually all rivers, and construction of an inordinate number of golf courses. The record of nature conservation in Japan has been modest.

Recently, the Japanese government, yielding to external pressures of world public opinion, has undertaken a number of measures aimed at refurbishing its tarnished international image. It agreed to curb whaling and to stop importing hawksbill turtle shells. In 1989 it banned ivory imports, and in 1991 it agreed to completely phase out drift-net fishing in the North Pacific by the end of 1992. The issue of curtailing the excessive imports of tropical timber remains unresolved (see section 8.7).

Despite the overriding importance of the industrial giants in global nature protection, small countries are also starting to play an increasingly important regional role. The government of Singapore is outstanding in this respect. The physical environment in this city-state is a delight for tourists: impeccably clean, green, safe, and beautiful. Littering and spitting is punishable by high fines. The Ministry of Environment has even banned chewing gum in Singapore since the beginning of 1992 (*Economist* 1 February 1992). Its industry has been highly regulated and emission controls strictly enforced for a number of years. More recently, Singapore entered the lucrative international market of environmental products and services. In addition to manufacturing green-technology factory equipment, Singapore serves as a consulting center on environment-friendly communal and industrial behavior. The Ministry of Environment set up its own company, Singapore Environmental Management and Engineering, to sell expertise to the countries of East Asia, such as Malaysia, Indonesia, Thailand, and even Hong Kong, Taiwan and south Korea, where it faces stiff Japanese competition. All these countries abused the environment for a long time in favor of rapid economic development. They jumped on the environmental bandwagon only after finding out that to be green is cheaper. For example, the pollution control technology is more energy-efficient.

8.7 *International Cooperation*

In recent years, the importance of government intervention in environmental matters has advanced to the international level. Indeed, protection of the environment is a necessity, not only on the local and national, but the international scale, because environmental concerns reach well beyond national boundaries. As our planet becomes a "global village," the need for international cooperation on environmental issues is imperative; otherwise national policies turn ineffective. In particular, such global environmental issues as the depletion of the stratospheric ozone and global warming should be dealt with on the international arena. Acid rain, on the other hand, is mainly regarded as a regional international issue.

The responsibility for the global environment is entrusted to the United Nations (Wallace 1993). Dealing with these global problems benefits the tourism resource base. In turn, tourism may contribute to the successful solution of these problems. Among the U.N. agencies, an especially important role is played by the United Nations Environmental Program (UNEP).

As a result of the resolution of the U.N. General Assembly, the World Commission on Environment and Development was inaugurated in October 1984 under the chair of Gro Harlem Brundtland of Norway (see section 10.1). The commission submitted its report, entitled *Our Common Future* to the General Assembly in 1987. The report discusses the concept of *sustainable development* manifested by strategies for achieving development goals without the depletion of the natural resource base, and a long-term global approach to environmental issues. In other words, the emphasis is not on development but rather on the *sustainability* of the resource base on which any development (including tourism) depends. The report not only criticizes the present state of the world's ecology but presents a number of recommendations which are important guidelines for the future. Strangely, although the report addresses a plethora of issues in detail, the role of tourism as a factor contributing to environmental degradation and as an instrument of enhancing the sustainability of ecosystems, is conspicuous by its absence. Apparently, the Commission comes to regard the environmental impact of tourism as negligible and its positive input as worthless. I hope that, despite this unfortunate omission, the World Commission regards nature conservation as inseparable from environmentally sustainable tourism.

An agreement of 21 European and North American states, signed in 1991 under U.N. sponsorship, lays out a number of steps aimed at the implementation of the recommendations of the World Commission. The protocol commits the signatories to a 30 percent reduction of their emissions of volatile organic compounds (VOC), mainly from motor vehicles, by 1999. There is no question that this agreement, similar to the Montreal Protocol on the depletion of stratospheric ozone, will be amended in the future to further limit the emissions and also to speed up the deadline.

A more contentious issue is the international coordination of environmental regulation. Controversial questions arise in connection with the endeavors of the General Agreement on Tariffs and Trade (GATT), substituted on 1 January 1995, by the World Trade Organization, to liberalize international trade. Tourism is also affected. The following uncertainties are associated with trade liberalization. Should a trade or tourism embargo be used to enforce environmental laws? Are countries with weak enforcement of environmental laws getting unfair subsidies, and should their exports, including tourism, be treated as unfairly discriminatory against exports from clean and green countries? Should ecolabelling be introduced on a wide range of products to create a competitive advantage? Whatever the answers to these questions, it is clear that international harmonization of environmental laws and regulations, as well as their strict enforcement, should be considered a high priority. The European Union has achieved substantial progress in this respect, and their achievements could play the role of a model for other international efforts to liberalize trade without harming the environment. The existence of these agreements is proof that on the international scale proenvironmental policies are gradually being implemented.

However, Hassan (1993:24) expresses some misgivings about the future of international environmental agreements. He postulates that major revisions to international law are needed to create a new legal framework for cooperation among countries. He thinks that international law is evolving in the right direction by challenging the primacy of the state in view of the transborder and global character of environmental issues. The role of the United Nations is bound to increase in the future (Brzezinski 1993a/b).

A separate issue—the role of international aid in environmental protection, is worthy of discussion because of its tourism connection. The prevailing thinking among donor nations is that the former practice of merely aiding economic growth must give way to ecologically sustainable development. As a result of this attitudinal change, the aid donors are more than willing to support green projects, such as well-planned tourism developments, rather than such environmentally questionable projects as factories, hydrodams, and the use of biocides in agricultural projects. The U.S. Agency of International Development (AID) requires routine Environmental Impact Assessments (EIAs). Among the U.N. agencies, the World Bank has been participating in ecological conservation since 1989 by screening projects based on their environmental effects. The World Bank has been criticized recently by the environmental NGOs for the lack of ecological component in its loan policy. The agency, which distributes more than $20 billion annually to the LDCs (see Dennis Goulot's quotation in section 8.5), invested $1.6 billion in environmental projects in 1992, and presently stipulates that no loan will be given without a comprehensive EIA. In 1993, the Bank used 8.4 percent of its loan capacity for outright environmental projects as compared to only three percent in 1990 (*Economist* 7 January 1994), and cuts programs considered environmentally harmful. Thus, Mexico received a $306 million loan to fight pollution; $80 million was provided for environmental preservation in the region to be flooded by the Yacyreta hydroelectric project on the border of Argentina and Paraguay. Despite continued criticism of the ecological aspects of the Bank's policy, there has been a noticeable improvement, which may in the future polish its tarnished reputation.

The multilateral assistance programs, such as those rendered by international agencies, are supplemented by bilateral eco-aid, e.g., not only the European Union (EU), but the German government specifically, is assisting Brazil in protecting the Amazon rain forest, while the U.S. Export Import Bank (The Exim Bank of Washington) provides credits to sellers of environmental technology and services.

On the regional-international level there is a plethora of international cooperation agreements. For instance, the Council of Europe issued Recommendation No. R (89) 15 in 1989, which pertains to a wide range of environmental issues, including modification of the impacts of tourism and recreation on ecology. The European Commission, the executive body of the Economic Union, has undertaken a number of concrete environmental protection measures, including increased taxes on fuel, which are significant for hotels catering to winter recreation.

Regional international environmental cooperation is especially important in ecologically vulnerable areas, such as the endangered coastal zones, coral reef marine areas, tropical rain forest, or polar regions. There are many examples of cooperation among the E.U. countries in developing policies, guidelines, and management strategies for environmentally sustainable development of coastal zones (*Tourism Management* June 1991: 169). The imposing U.N. Mediterranean Action Plan (Blue Plan), signed in 1976, seems to be working, and the regional ecology is on the way to recovery (Grenon and Batise 1989; Grossman 1981). The international efforts to clean up the Baltic are only in their initial stages. More advanced is the U.S.-Canadian agreement to clean up the Great Lakes (see section 2.7), or the agreement signed in 1983 by 24 Caribbean states and France, Netherlands, and Great Britain. The latter agreement provides for protection of marine ecology, especially coral reefs, against oil spills and other forms of pollution. Various international agreements, such as the Tropical Forests Action Program (TFAP) may also be helpful, if the governments of 70 tropical countries that signed the agreement have the political will to implement it. Japan, the leading importer of tropical timber, is also a reluctant participant. Another example of this type is the Amazon Cooperation Treaty ratified in December 1992 by eight countries: it foresees the harmonization between ecology and economic development, including tourism (*World Press Review*, April 1992).

Other regional international cooperation pertains to the ecologically vulnerable polar areas. Thus, the Arctic Environmental Protection Strategy Agreement was signed in 1991 by United States, Canada, Russia, Finland, Sweden, Norway, Denmark, and Iceland. The agreement encompasses cooperation on oil spill cleanup, nuclear leaks and other environmental emergencies, development of pollution monitoring programs, and holding regular meetings on regional problems. The signatories of the Antarctic Treaty (see section 6.5.3) agreed in 1991 on a 50-year moratorium on mining in the area. However, establishment of a world park in Antarctica for scientific research and limited tourism has not yet materialized.

The arena for international cooperation in tourism is the intergovernmental World Tourism Organization (WTO), a United Nations agency with its head office in Madrid, Spain. The WTO can look back on its 40-year history of commitment to environmental values of tourism, including the period of its predecessor, the NGO (called International Union of Official Travel Organizations—IUOTO). Since 1954 the study of environmental questions has become institutionalized in the activities of the IUOTO and WTO. Not only do they study environmental issues but also the international cooperation in tourism-related protection of nature and the adoption of environment-friendly tourism policy. At present, the World Tourism Organization's Environment Committee, established in 1981, cooperates with the United Nations Environmental Program (UNEP). The 1980 World Tourism Conference in Manila, the Philippines, adopted the "Manila Declaration on World Tourism," an important document that confirms the public sector's responsibility for environmental conservation and advocates the development of worldwide natural heritage policies, established and followed by tourism and for the benefit of tourism.

In 1982, the WTO and UNEP signed a joint declaration, which "interpreted the rationale of the Manila Declaration by underlining the need to achieve a proper balance between tourism and environment" (WTO 1983: 2). According to the joint declaration, "the human right to rest and leisure, proclaimed by the *Universal Declaration of Human Rights,* is interdependent with sound environmental management because polluted and degraded nature is unsuitable for tourist development, and tourism has become a decisive contributor to the quality of life. The improvement of the quality of life is, in turn, regarded as one of the human rights. In fact, environment is a perishable commodity available in limited quantities and difficult to reconstitute when damaged" (*ibid.*). Other achievements of the WTO include the Tourism Bill of Rights and Tourist Code (WTO 1992: 154-159). These documents suggest certain rights and responsibilities of governments and tourists: "The governments' responsibilities for the control of tourist flows and the tourists' responsibilities to behave consistently with the principles of environmental protection" (WTO 1983: 14).

Regional international cooperation on environment among the intergovernmental tourism organizations is also developing. The efforts are directed mainly towards development of sound environmental policies in regional groups of countries such as the E.U. Here the issues addressed frequently go beyond direct tourist concerns, but do serve the cause of conservation of tourist resources.

8.8 *The Role of NGOs*

Neither the national governments nor inter-governmental co-operation can cope successfully with environmental problems and respond to the challenge of sustainable development without the participation and support of broad masses of population. Indeed, concerned citizens increasingly demonstrate their pro-nature stance by organizing themselves into non-profit voluntary associations. These groups, uniting users or consumers of natural resources in favor of environmental protection, are the NGOs (nongovernment organizations). This section focuses on these environmental NGOs, not only tourist, but nontourist NGOs, that impact on tourism and on natural resources used by tourism.

First of all, one has to emphasize a number of advantages associated with the activities of the NGOs as compared with the those of governments. The NGOs are more flexible than cumbersome government bureaucracies (known for procrastinating in decision-making). The NGOs are also more locally involved, they do not deal with grandiose white-elephant programs but rather with small grass-roots projects, such as assistance in the application of green technologies in tourism (WTO/UNEP 1983: 11), provision of funds for the construction of locally owned hotels of modest quality, or for beach improvements. The outlays of financial resources are relatively modest, and the potential environmental harm smaller than in the case of large projects.

Despite their seemingly limited political and economic power, the NGOs have been gaining ground lately. In fact, the considerable political clout wielded by the NGOs, particularly on environmental issues, has become characteristic. At present, they are a powerful social and political force, although their membership and influence is recently in a slight decline (*Economist* 5 March 1994). In the LDCs, they are still weak, but in the DCs they have become powerful forces, pressuring governments and business into action on the environmental front. One could divide the environmental NGOs into five categories according to the level of their activities: local, regional subnational, national, regional-international, and global. On the local level they take various forms, such as Friends of the Lake District in England, and various land trusts in the United States, such as the Jackson Hole Land Trust and Vermont Land Trust (Kunstler 1993: 268-272). These trusts purchase land or receive it in private donations to save natural areas from development and keep them in their natural state. Other examples are benevolent associations, such as Rotary Clubs that sponsor environmental programs (mostly in urban centers) by financing nature trails in parks, various reforestation projects, and recreation programs for children or disadvantaged groups. The local NGOs also encourage their communities to environmental activism on matters of neighborhood concern, such as beach and river bank cleanup or actions against local polluters. They are also frequently involved in protests against environmentally harmful tourist projects, such as the outrageous Puy de Dome project in the Massif Central in France (*Der Spiegel* 1990, 35: 164–166). All these proenvironment activities of the local NGOs counterbalance, to a certain extent, the local development lobby, ecologically insensitive and composed of business people, politicians, and other individuals who fear a decline of revenue resulting from conservation (Butler 1990: 44).

Other NGOs are active in the regional subnational (e.g., state or group of states) and the national arena. Among the national NGOs, those more widely known are the U.S. National Wildlife Federation, National Parks and Conservation Association, Sierra Club, the National Audobon Society, the Wilderness Society, the U.S. Environmental Defence Fund, U.S. National Resources Defence Fund, and Keep America Beautiful. In Europe, well known associations are Italia Nostra, and Keep Britain Tidy, to name a few. The activities of some lesser national "grass-root movements" are discussed by Ekins (1992: 143–157). Some national NGOs are getting increasingly involved in the politics of nature preservation and environmental protection, while others work in restoration ecology projects of national importance. For instance, the Brazilian Funatura is involved in the expansion and administration of nature reserves and debt-for-nature swaps (see section 9.6.3). Funatura received a $582,000 grant from the World Bank to complete and administer a wildlife sanctuary (Brooke, E. 1992). The native NGOs of America, in their struggle to protect their interests—be it in the Amazon or in Nunavut, invariably defend the cause of nature preservation.

It is also interesting to note the existence of prodevelopment and antienvironmental NGOs. One of them is the Alliance for America, based in Seattle. Other NGOs of this category, such as the American Land Rights Association or Wise Use, represent the real estate owners and focus on just compensation for the loss of land value of property—regulated by the governments' environmental legislation. The pejorative label attached to the this camp is "ecorevisionists," while they call themselves "correctionists."

There are national NGOs, which keep out of political activism on environmental issues and concentrate on ecological education and research. An example is the Sustainable Society, associated with the University of Waterloo, Ontario. The Tourism Industry Association of Canada (TIAC) is an NGO that represents tourism business; its environmental initiatives included participation in the formulation of the Code of Ethics for Tourists, Code of Ethics for the Industry, and Guidelines for the Industry (D'Amore 1992).

The fourth category of environmental NGOs consists of regional-international organizations, such as Alp Action, based in Geneva, Switzerland and dedicated to the preservation of the Alps (Covington 1993), or Europa Nostra, a West European NGO that cooperates with the European Travel Commission. However, the best known is the fifth category, the global NGOs, active in the worldwide arena, that includes groups such as Greenpeace, World Wildlife Fund (which covered two-thirds of the cost of creation in 1964 of the Coto Donana Reserve in Spain; Burkart and Medlik 1975: 238), World Conservation Union (formerly International Union for the Conservation of Nature), Conservation International, Nature Conservancy, Earthwatch, Friends of the Earth, and World Resources Institute. These NGOs work on many fronts, ranging from volunteer cleanup programs to scientific research. However, one of their most important tasks is the preservation of ecosystems by promoting appropriate legislation or outright purchase of endangered land. In this respect, the Nature Conservancy should be singled out. It owns an empire of over one million hectares of land sanctuaries, most of them accessible to green tourists and recreationists (*Time* 2 February 1987). Weaver (1991) emphasizes the role of the NGOs in financing environmental protection in Dominica, which has poor beaches but excellent wilderness resources attractive to tourists.

The most controversial aspect of the international NGOs' work is their political activity. Some of them, for example Greenpeace, are occasionally accused of unacceptable methods. There is also evidence of increased political action of NGOs with respect to the North American Free Trade Agreement (NAFTA), which is criticized for its possible negative environmental impacts.

8.9 *The Role of Private Sector and Consumers (Tourists)*

Business, especially big business that consists of giant transnational corporations, has been criticized for a long time as an environmental villain. One of the most virulent critics of business was the eminent scientist, Barry Commoner, the unsuccessful green candidate for the U.S. presidency in 1980. Although his program was rejected by voters and proven incorrect by time, some of his attacks on the environmental policy of big business, especially in the field of energy production, reflected reality. Indeed, when the sole concern of the human economic activity is limited to short-term profit, the environment suffers. In this respect Commoner's arguments sound plausible (Commoner 1990). Maybe his criticism contributed to more environment-friendly attitudes of large corporations in the 1980s and 1990s (see section 9.5.2.3).

One of the unfortunate spinoffs of big business, mentioned by Commoner, is the spread of rampant and prolifigate consumerism in the DCs and among the rich in the LDCs. Consumerism in the DCs has the doubtful distinction of rivaling the population explosion in the LDCs as one of the most significant causes of world ecological decline. Indeed, the modern consumer society threatens to change global climate; to poison air, water, and land; to destroy the vegetation and wildlife; and to exhaust natural resources. Tourism and recreation are also involved in this frenzy of consumerism.

Business is interested in increased production. In order to sell its output it has to stimulate consumption. Already in 1899 Thorsten Verblen observed in his "Theory of the Leisure Classes" that the rich consume in order to display their wealth. He coined the term "conspicuous consumption" (Mieczkowski, Z. 1990: 66). Since, the wave of consumerism has spread from a small elite to most of the population in the DCs. Galbraith (1967) was one of the first economists to draw attention to the persuasive power of advertising which manipulates the consumers to wasteful and environmentally harmful use of resources. Planned obsolescence, big gas-guzzling cars, unrestrained spending, instant rather than deferred gratification, shopping frenzy, insatiable appetite to acquire goods, the mall-centered consumer lifestyle, low savings, the me-generation, infinite wants, quickly changing fashions, measuring success by the level of consumption, keeping up with the Joneses—all these disparate trends and phenomena point in one direction: the degradation of the environment.

We seem to be shifting from a consumer society to a sustainable society (Durning 1992; Ekins 1992). There is evidence that consumer attitudes are changing, albeit slowly, and this affects tourism and recreation. In the early 1970s the perception of ecological damage by recreationists appeared to be "extremely low" (Satchell and Marren 1976:13), but more recent surveys indicate that people appreciate unspoiled nature at their vacation destinations (see section 1.1 above). They are also increasingly better educated on matters of nature conservation, they favor environmentally responsible behavior, and get involved as individuals or as members of NGOs in the decision-making process. They are, therefore, ready for shifts to materially more modest and culturally more diverse lifestyles and consumption patterns. Most recreationists will even make sacrifices for clean and green ecology. Some will donate their privately-owned land or development rights to land trusts in order that natural areas be saved from development.

Consumers are increasingly realizing that the correlation between consumption and happiness is weak, that "more" is not necessarily "better," and that working more to acquire more mitigates against real human fulfillment, against the ultimate aim of life—creative leisure, filled with rewarding sustainable pastimes, leisure that satisfies not so much material, but rather social, psychological, and spiritual needs. Such leisure contributes to the quality of life, and prominently includes tourism and recreation (see "Philosophical Concept of Leisure," Mieczkowski, Z. 1990: 8–11). Therefore, people want more leisure and not necessarily more income, more environmentally sustainable tourism and recreation and less wasteful consumption. The distinction between wants and needs, one of the principles of green economics (Ekins 1992: 31) gradually takes hold, in the public perception. More and more people do not want what they do not need. They are becoming impervious to advertising that attempts to stimulate consumption, to turn their wants into needs. In fact, "green economics is the economics of enough" (Ekins 1992: 31). Studying nonwestern traditions and cultures, such as Buddhism, Confucianism, or Shinto (Mieczkowski, B. 1991: 218- 222) cultures not based on Judeo-Christian attitudes (Klostermaier 1991: 44-46) and participating in the educational process (see section 8.3) may help in changing from consumerism to ecologically sustainable lifestyles.

The attitudes of business are also changing. The corporations increasingly are realizing that the time of *laissez-faire* economics is over. Embracing the environment makes good sense not only from the legal and public relations point of view, but also for the long-term economic benefits; environment-friendly business behavior and production uses less raw materials and is more energy-efficient (see section 8.5). Therefore, major tourist and nontourist companies, and intra--industry and marketing associations contain special departments dealing with environmental issues. The "green" image of large corporations is increasingly important to their customers. For example, the "total destination complexes," i.e., ski resort built by Boise Cascade, have been a success, at least from the environmental point of view. Hudman (1991: 20) cites as an example the Intercontinental Hotels Group, who has published a 300-page manual devoted to what hotels can do toward sustaining the environment. In contrast, small shoestring developers do not care about their reputation, and act accordingly.

For companies embracing the environment means, first of all, self-regulation, self-auditing, self-policing, self-imposed environmental impact assessment, publishing of environmental reports, and striving to be "eco-efficient" (Schmidheiny, *et al.* 1992). Second, business increasingly follows the path of "regulatory negotiation," the so-called "reg-neg," i.e., dialogue, consultation, and cooperation rather than confrontation between industry, environmental organizations and governments (Shabecoff 1984). The leaders of industry are realizing that environmentally sustainable development is not only ethical but also makes good business sense in the long-term, despite short-term costs. They know that sustainable development links together a healthy environment to a healthy economy (see section 8.5). As a result, the leaders of the private sector of economy are prepared to integrate their concern for environment and environmental protection into their business decisions (Buzzelli 1990). In the process of cooperation, under the leadership of the government traditionally hostile interests arrive at compromise solutions. This procedure saves time and money because businesses have found that what the NGOs demand today, the legislators legislate tomorrow, and the governments enforce the day after tomorrow. They are also eager to avoid the costs of litigation with the NGOs. An example of such a negotiated action is the agreement concluded in the spring of 1993 between the United States federal government and Georgia-Pacific, a large logging corporation. The agreement provides habitat protection for red-cockaded woodpeckers on land logged by the company. Third, business becomes interested in providing environmental services, a multibillion dollar industry. California is a good example of this trend (*Economist* 16 November 1991). In Canada alone protecting the environment has become a $10 billion-a-year industry (*Winnipeg Free Press* 3 March 1992). An example of the growing cooperation between business, government, and the environmental NGOs is the President's Council on Sustainable Development established in the summer of 1993. Co-chairman of the council is David Buzzelli, the vice-president of Dow Chemical Company.

The pro-environment effort of industry is especially visible in tourism-related transportation: the automobile industry is experimenting with alternative fuels, the aircraft industry is introducing less noisy planes and limiting gaseous emissions, traffic control agencies try to minimize congestion on the ground and in the air, and all industries strive to decrease waste disposal (Copeland 1992). All these measures are taken not for love of nature but in the self-interest of the companies involved. An example of the partnership between tourist business and conservation is Disney World, Florida, which financed the conservation of Reedy Creek Swamp, an area of about 20 square kilometers adjacent to the famous theme park, and owned by the corporation (Murphy 1986).

8.10 *Measures Against External Impacts*

Sections 8.1 to 8.9 examined measures aimed at coping with human impacts on environment in a wide context of interaction of tourism with nontourist sectors of the economy. Section 8.10 focuses on nontourist issues exclusively. The external (non-tourist) environmental impacts on tourism resources were discussed in chapter 2. I stated that these impacts, and not tourism and recreation, are primarily responsible for the present degradation of the ecosystems. This section summarizes a number of possible solutions focusing on external (nontourist) impacts on environment. These measures aim at achieving a sustainable environment, which is the basic prerequisite for tourism and recreation. The treatment is brief because dealing with external impacts in a comprehensive way is clearly beyond the scope of this book. Nevertheless, the tourism connection is clear.

The DCs have, during the last 20 to 30 years, achieved substantial progress on the environmental front. Their air is cleaner following the implementation of regulatory legislation like the U.S. 1970 and 1990 Clean Air Acts, and many rivers, such as the Thames in England, are again biologically viable and open again to such recreational use as swimming and angling. Nevertheless, problems remain. These problems could be summarized as follows:

1. As the DCs use most of the earth's resources and contribute most to the present environmental predicament, they carry a special responsibility to improve their record in this respect. This is especially true in the field of energy. The development of energy sources and of alternatives to fossil fuels is a necessity. Nevertheless, as the world's dependency on fossil fuels will continue in the next decades, the energy

balance should shift from high pollutants, such as coal, to less polluting natural gas and electricity. A cleanup in the field of energy production will contribute to the decrease of the carbon dioxide emissions, the principal greenhouse gas.

2. The globalization of the world's economy, connected in part with the dismantling of protectionist barriers in trade among nations, necessitates international standardization of environmental laws, rules, and regulations (see section 8.7). Unless this happens, abuses are inevitable. Action should start on the national level. It should be noted that the states in the United States and the provinces in Canada are still far from being uniform in this respect. The second stage in this standardization process is the trade blocs, such as the European Union (E.U.) or NAFTA, while the final level of standardization is the global arena of the World Trade Organization, formerly GATT, which should eliminate contradictions between sustainable green environment standards and freer international trade.

3. Success in coping with overconsumption problems in the DCs, discussed in section 8.9, could bring substantial benefits to the environment in the form of a more moderate use of resources and less pollution. This includes the use of chlorofluorocarbons (CFCs) that destroys the stratospheric ozone layer.

4. The DCs have to work with special intensity at solutions to environmental problems in areas most threatened ecologically. An example of such an area could be the most densely populated country of Europe, the Netherlands. Large concentrations of people, a high level of industrialization, and intensive agriculture have created a fair degree of tension between humanity and environment. Hence, the Dutch support a radical and expensive antipollution program (*Time* 25 March 1991), which profoundly affects tourism (see section 8.6). Another area in ecological dire straits, as discussed in section 2.6, is the Mediterranean, at the same time the most important tourist region in the world.

5. The DCs have to discontinue some environmentally harmful economic practices, such as the subsidization of agriculture, grazing and logging. Especially evident are the results of such policies in the E.U., where farmers, interested as they are in the increase of output clear forests, drain wetlands, and overuse chemical fertilizers.

6. The ecological problems in the former communist countries, the economies in transition from central planning to the market system, are essentially similar to those in the other DCs, but the degree of envi-

ronmental decline is worse (section 2.4). These countries cannot afford any investments in the future, including taking care of grave environmental damage, but have to concentrate their resources on the current political and economic readjustment. Bare survival of their people is at stake there, and the utmost is done to exploit the resources without any future considerations. Thus, for instance, because of the economic benefits of logging for export, such operations encroach on legally protected areas (Rosencranz and Scott 1992: 294). As long as the present dismal state of environment persists in the area, the environment will be damaged, tourism will be harmed, and these countries will remain tourist destinations of low priority. For the time being, the financially strapped governments can do little but rely on the volunteers and the NGOs. Radical change on the environmental front will take place only if the DCs render substantial environmental assistance. Unfortunately, such massive aid is not forthcoming, although there have been some interesting initiatives, such as the 1992 establishment of the Ecofund in Poland. This will administer the debt-for-environment program planned for Baltic Sea cleanup and anti-pollution measures in the southwestern part of the country (Bajsarowicz 1993). Also important are the activities of the U.S. Committee on Poland's environment under the presidency of J. Bajsarowicz.

7. From the point of view of environmental policy, there is a similarity between the Second and the Third World. As indicated in section 8.1, coping with environmental issues is not a priority on the political and economic agendas of the LDCs: their main concern is economic development to take care of their exploding populations. At the same time, population explosion is their environmental problem number one. This crucial condition is intimately tied with the ecological and resource deterioration in the Third World. Without demographic stabilization of the population at replacement levels, no other critical issue of environmental concern is likely to be solved (Ehrlich 1991: 110). "Rapid population growth among the poor helps keep them poor" (Ehrlich 1991: 123). Our global environment cannot sustain the addition of over 90 million people a year, most of them in the LDCs. Failing to break the vicious cycle of poverty and overpopulation, the LDCs contribute to the ecological decline at an accelerated pace. Resources are used inefficiently; natural habitats are destroyed by burning, logging, and fuel wood collection, and by efforts to expand cultivation and pastures.

One cannot blame starving and poorly educated people for their careless attitude to the preservation of forests or wildlife for the benefit of future generations. Such arguments as the necessity for preservation of virgin ecosystems for the health of the planet, for undiscovered drugs and new crops, are not plausible or meaningful to them. They have other priorities and the economics of survival is their most important motive.

The destruction of nature in the LDCs results not only in regional environmental damage but also in the degradation of the global environment. It is true that poor people use much fewer resources per capita than do the rich, but they constitute the growing percentage of the world's population, and aspire to the consumption level of the DCs. To achieve this, they increase the level of their economic activity, and they cannot be blamed for it. They certainly deserve a higher standard of living. But such a standard is associated with increased exploitation of natural resources, and thus with increased environmental pressures. For example, their use of energy resources grows exponentially, and the rising use of charcoal for fuel (e.g., sub-Saharan Africa and Haiti) as well as the burning of coal with high sulphur content, augurs still more environmental damage, as it does in China and India.

As indicated in section 3.5, nature preservation in the LDCs cannot be based on arguments used in the DCs. One has to convince the local people that conservation makes economic sense, that they may use the tropical forests for their subsistence and for the sale of forest products on a sustained yield basis, and at the same time profitably accommodate tourists. If they improve their educational and living standards, they will start to enjoy nature too. Jacques Cousteau already sees an attitudinal change of the population in the LDCs in favor of environmental protection (Wolbarst, ed. 1991: 105). Attitudes also change on the governmental level, as they are doing in Indonesia, the top world exporter of tropical wood, which is now starting to enforce its laws on logging (Erlanger 1989).

However, neither enforcement of environmental laws, nor the creation of economic incentives for local population will save the virgin ecosystems in the LDCs. The Earth Summit in Rio de Janeiro in 1992 made clear the necessity for assistance from the DCs. This assistance can take many forms, such as opening the markets of the First World to industrial and agricultural products of the Third World, transfer of environmental technology, grants and loans for preservation of nature, and debt-for-nature swaps.

Chapter 9

Environmental Planning and Management of Tourism and Recreation

9.1 *Introduction*

Environmental planning and management of tourism is recognized for its great complexity and limitations (Gunn 1988: 17). Indeed, it presents a number of problems and intricate tasks resulting from the unique characteristics of tourism and tourism's impacts. These problems may be summarized as follows:

1. Tourism is a unique industry because practically all the natural non-consumptive—and some consumptive—resources of an area are a part of the tourism product, even if these resources are not owned by the tourism industry: mountains, waterfalls, beaches, forests, lagoons, and so on are free or almost free tourist attractions. They are generally not owned by the tourist enterprises located in the area that benefit from them. The economic value of these tourism resources is difficult or even impossible to establish, and their relationship to the tourism industry is frequently ambiguous.

2. Spatial and organizational fragmentation makes tourism planning more difficult than any other industry, because it is easier to deal with fewer units, relatively concentrated in space and in terms of ownership than with a web of innumerable enterprises, which vary in size from one-person units, such as a taxi-owner-driver or a souvenir hawker, to huge horizontally-integrated hotel chains and airlines and vertical integrations of tour operators with airlines, hotels, and travel agencies. In contrast to tourism, the natural environment is a highly integrated network of inseparable ecosystems. Therefore, planning and management must treat an ecosystem as a whole.

3. Tourism as an economic sector penetrates, like no other, all aspects of human existence: ecological, socioeconomic and cultural. All these aspects interact in such a complex and interconnected way that the

isolation of certain factors, in this case the environmental, is frequently impossible. Therefore, planning and management have to be interdisciplinary in order to integrate all concerns; environmental, economic, social, cultural, and political. While the isolation of environmental factors in this book has focused attention on ecological issues, the other interacting elements have been taken into account as much as possible.

4. Planning should integrate not only the factors mentioned above, but should be a part of an overall integrated plan that includes all sectors of the economy in a harmonious whole. Tourism cannot be isolated from the total economy of an area for which any given plan is prepared. Even in areas specializing in tourism, one should never allow a complete tourism monopoly (tourism monoculture) but plan for diversification to avoid, as much as possible, total dependence on one sector. It is the responsibility of governments to fit tourism into this integrated plan because the public sector is largely responsible for the harmonious allocation of resources to various economic branches, including tourism, and for the general infrastructure of the area of planning within national, regional and local jurisdictions (see section 8.6).

5. Planning tourism is a political process, associated with decision-making about resource allocation between conflicting uses. The choices are, first of all, between tourist and nontourist development options, based on a number of objective and subjective considerations. Tourism is often regarded as the best economic alternative in all cases and situations. Such a blanket assumption is incorrect, and could lead not only to bitter disappointment, but also to substantial economic losses. Hence, tourism planning has to consider the opportunity costs and assess the economic feasibility of tourism development before, and not after, the decision to develop is taken. Sociocultural considerations should be also taken into account.

6. Political choices between various tourism and recreation activities are related to size, location, and resource allocation that may be incompatible in the same place. Planning must zone various activities or make them compatible.

7. Tourism is one of the most ecologically preferable alternatives of economic development because it is relatively benign to nature when compared to heavy industry and a substantial part of agriculture, and because it has a vested interest in the conservation of ecosystems.

Therefore, one could incorrectly assume that it is an industry completely harmless to the ecosystems of our planet, a veritable "smokeless industry" (see section 3.3). This could lead to complacency, to questioning the need for environmental planning at all. But planning is necessary to take appropriate proactive (preventive) and reactive (corrective) measures that anticipate, prevent, and/or mitigate adverse impacts of tourism, even if such impacts do not yet exist. Taking corrective measures is generally regarded as inferior because it constitutes an ad hoc type of action that treats symptoms rather than causes (WTO/UNEP 1983: 32).

8. Planning, including feasibility studies, should reflect not only socioeconomic but also environmental concerns. Following an evaluation of the natural resources of the area in question from the point of view of their attractiveness for tourists, planners should arrive at appropriate conclusions. Negative conclusions as to the suitability of tourism could range from inadequacy of the resource base for development to the determination that a particular fragile or unique environment should be protected from any development at all, including tourism.

9. Environmental planning should not attempt to prevent any change, but only undesirable change (Hammitt and Cole 1987: 195-196). If the change is considered acceptable or desirable, then it may be included in the plan.

10. Environmental planning for tourism should be long-term because of the cumulative nature of impacts, which are discontinuous both in time and space, and as such are not readily identifiable (in contrast to other impacts, such as economic or cultural). This circumstance makes environmental planning difficult because short-term economic interests generally seem to have more political support than long-term considerations. In the LDCs, as a result of the absence of formal property rights or land, planning horizons are shorter, and incentives to protect the environment are weaker than in the DCs (De Soto 1993). In the DCs, where formal property rights on land are strong, public land ownership (which in western North America exceeds 50 percent) is considered an asset for planning and management of tourist resources (e.g., Nevada, Alaska, Utah, Idaho, and California).

11. Planning should not only prevent undesirable environmental impacts but also optimize the positive and desirable impacts of tourism development to ensure its long-term viability. The degree of desirability varies spatially. For example, practically all tourist impacts in the wilderness are undesirable, while in more user-oriented areas some of

the environmental impacts may prove to be beneficial, or at least acceptable.

12. One of the most important tasks of planning is setting goals (*limits of acceptable change*—LAC and objectives and their priorization. Planning development means not only matching its goals and objectives with the resource capabilities but also with the conservation requirements.

13. Tourism development has a tendency to expand spatially. This tendency may be observed at any level and scale. Thus, resorts tend to grow beyond their limits, sites enlarge into the adjacent area. The difficult task of planning and management is to recognize this tendency and take appropriate measures to limit spatial expansion.

14. Tourism planning essentially amounts to prediction of future developments. Its main task is to be proactive—to avoid miscalculations. In environmental planning there is an expectation that the undesirable ecological impacts of tourism are being avoided and the beneficial ones enhanced. However, there is a considerable element of uncertainty in environmental planning for tourism (Newson, M. 1992: 259). It results from the lack of controls possible in laboratory experiments. This "decision-making under uncertainty" requires the continuous monitoring at all stages of planning and development and with ongoing managerial corrective measures—a difficult and expensive process. In this sense, Gunn (1988a: 17) compares planning to an assembly line operation that is continuous.

15. The difficulty with anticipating the amount of impact that results from a given amount of use is compounded by another circumstance. As mentioned in section 7.3, the relationship between use and impact is not linear but rather curvilinear and asymptotic (Hammitt and Cole 1987; Wenger 1984). This means that successive increments in use correlate logarithmically with decreasing increments in environmental deterioration. In other words, the initial impact on ecosystems does the most damage. The inflection point, at which even significant increment in use may cause relatively small damage, depends on the resilience of the ecosystem. In fragile ecosystems, such as dunes, the point of inflection may be reached at relatively low intensity of use. "Since low levels of use can cause significant impact, it is particularly important to control the areal extent of use and impact" (Hammitt and Cole 1987: 197). This is an argument in favor of the concentration of tourism, which is discussed below (section 9.4.2).

16. A severe problem is associated with the implementation of plans. The World Tourism Organization (1983: 18) complains that, "the vast majority of plans had not been implemented." The main reasons for this adverse state of affairs are the length of time associated with the planning and implementation process, and the rapid evolution of world economic situation which renders the plans invalid. Another reason has been the low priority assigned to tourism both in the DCs and LDCs, and the resulting frequent changes in policy. The fourth cause has been the priority assigned to private sector medium-term projects because of their economic advantages. The consequence has been a loss of long-range planning perspective. Another consideration, in the WTO's view, has been the slow pace of integration of environmental protection into the general tourism development plans. All these circumstances contributed to what the WTO euphemistically calls a "high degree of discontinuity in implementation" (*ibid.* 18).

9.2 *Planning Levels*

Planning, including tourism planning, essentially takes place at the macro- (or national and regional sub-national) and micro- (or local) levels. Because tourism is not an isolated sector of the economy, planning should be integrated with general development planning that includes all aspects of human activity. In other words, tourism planning should take place within the framework of comprehensive national, regional and local planning that deals with cross-sectoral linkages, and is aimed at balancing socioeconomic and environmental concerns. This interdependence of all planning components is emphasized by Murphy (1983: 189–193) who recommends the application of system analysis in the planning process. Thus, the integrative approach to planning is an indispensable condition focusing on tourism.

The historically earliest form of planning is its local form, so-called *physical planning,* which has been limited in scope to architectural design, landscaping, and land use. However, the inadequacy of such a narrow approach has been recognized. Thus, Gunn (1988a: 24), a pioneer in the field of tourist planning, argues that the traditional focus of tourism planning on site scale (hotels, restaurants, historic sites, beaches, mountains) underestimates the spatial interdependence "of all the separate entities and fragments that make up the whole." Therefore, in the United States, he advocates larger-scale regional (subnational) planning. In practical terms, such a scale does not reach beyond the borders of a single state. Jost Krippendorf (1967 and 1975), who has focused his research on European issues, thinks that national and regional (subnational) planning is indispensable in the modern age because today we are at the point when regional-international planning has become increasingly essential. The Alps are an example of an environmental challenge that needs such international cooperation, if it is to be saved from the threat of serious resource deterioration resulting from tourism overdevelopment (see section 4.8). Similar regional international planning is taking place in the Mediterranean Basin. However, this type of international planning lacks the jurisdictional power of enforcement, and may be regarded as mere cooperation.

There is some disagreement among scholars about the emphasis and importance of various levels of planning. Krippendorf (1975) emphasizes national and regional planning, while Murphy (1983 and 1985) argues convincingly about the merits of a community approach that safeguards the public participation of tourists and local residents in the planning process. Maybe some of the reasons for this disagreement is that they are dealing with different areas.

It is essential that all levels of planning are coordinated to harmonize the concerns and interests of urban and nonurban areas, and that discrepancies and contradictions are avoided (Gunn 1988a: 271–275). The degrees of co-ordination and development at various levels differ from country to country (*ibid.*: 1988a: 29-56). In some countries certain levels may be underdeveloped, or even nonexistent. This occurs in federal government systems, such as the United States, where national macro-approaches to tourism planning are limited and conducted more on the local and state level. Among countries with centralized political systems the classic example is France. Its system of centralized planning and management, which has inhibited local inputs, is now in the process of gradual decentralization. The centrally planned economies, or command economies, have expanded their national planning at the expense of regional and local planning. All the major, and even most minor, decisions were made at the top.

The liberal democratic systems that prevail in the DCs, are variously called *indicative planning, industrial policy or sectoral planning.* Krippendorf (1982) sees, in these countries, a healthy decentralizing trend in tourist planning aimed at giving more decision-making powers to local people. Examples of such locally influenced policy and planning incentives are limitations on external developers and on purchases of land by foreigners. Hawkins (1980: 257) formulates his views in the following way: "Plans and policies must not be imposed from above; they must evolve at the level at which they are implemented—and, as a general rule, the lower the better." Though recognizing the environmental and socioeconomic benefits of this planning trend one has to re-emphasize the above- mentioned caveats of an often strong prodevelopment local lobby. Krippendorf (1967) warns against egoistic localism (*Partikularismus*). Even in western Australia, where both tourists and local residents support the symbiotic relationship between tourism and environment, "residents place more emphasis on tourism development while tourists give greater weight to environmental protection" (Dowling 1993).

9.3 *The Planning Process (Stages)*

In tourism planning, one has to follow a few general rules, valid at any level. First of all, the principle of sustainability has to be a guiding philosophy adopted as the main goal of planning. In certain cases, preplanning, usually at the political level, may take place, involving general formulation of policy, goals, and objectives. Once these general guidelines are established, the actual planning process is undertaken, involving several stages (see Fig. 9.1, which approaches the same issues as Fig. 8.1 but from another angle). It starts with an inventory, usually accompanied by evaluation (analysis) of resources. Wenger (1984: 810–825) discusses various methodologies and techniques applied by resource inventorying. A good example is the Canada Land Inventory, which assesses the capability of land for diverse uses, including the capability to support recreation activities.

Figure 9.1
THE PLANNING PROCESS

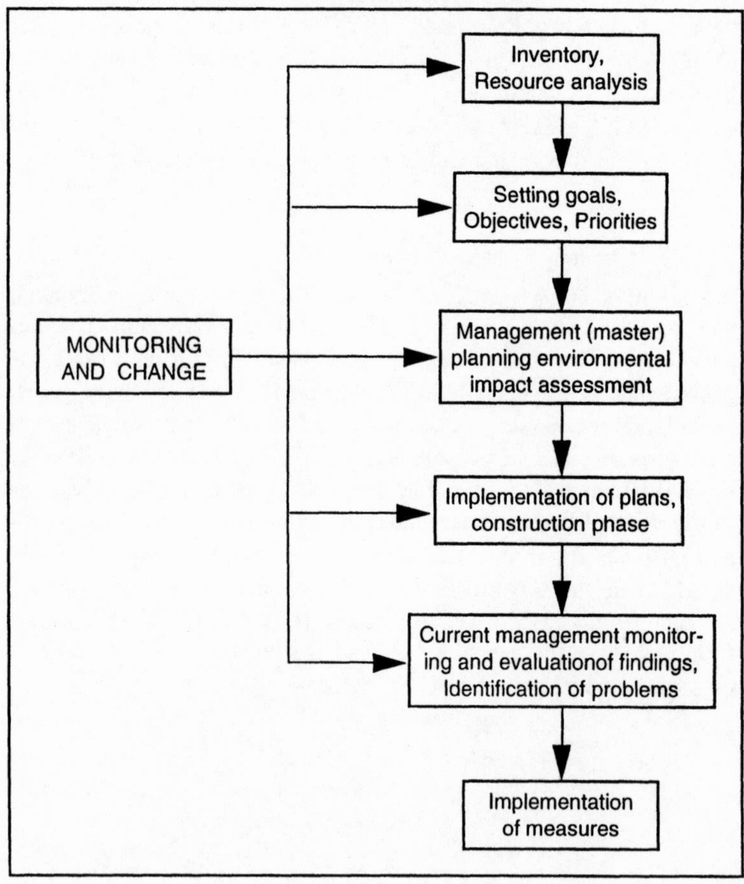

The second stage involves the consideration of various development options and the decisions on setting goals, objectives and priorities. The third stage is the difficult task of the management (master) planning. At this crucial stage the zoning system is elaborated, including specific objectives, and priorities for each zone. Especially essential is the identification of unique and/or ecologically fragile zones where tourism development will be banned or limited. When planning zones for recreational activities, incompatible uses and areas of various tourism intensity should be separated in different zones. To determine the ecological sustainability of the project, planners conduct an environmental assessment of the impacts anticipated in each zone. To secure the quality of the plan, various methods are applied, such as simulation models predicting change in diverse impact scenarios (Gunn 1987: 237). The fourth stage encompasses the practical implementation of the plan, i.e., the development phase, including the construction.

After the plan has been put into effect, the fifth and final operational stage starts. This is when planners discover there is a judgmental gap between the plan and the real world, and not everything is working out as expected. Therefore, monitoring (review), which is recommended at all stages, acquires special importance after the implementation of the plan is begun and the project commissioned. The monitoring stage involves the comparison between the environmental impact levels established by the plan and the actual levels observed. If the latter surpass the former, then management measures, such as Visitor Impact Management (VIM) are implemented to mollify the adverse impacts. Thus, as Hammitt and Cole (1987: 204) put it: "Inventorying is the first phase of a long-term monitoring program. Monitoring is merely periodically repeating the inventory and comparing current conditions both to objectives and previous inventory data." If monitoring detects undesirable changes of the tourism resource base, this provides a warning that some measures have to be taken. On the other hand, monitoring may indicate that planning was correct.

Generally, the purpose of monitoring is to scrutinize how the plan is working in practice to provide the necessary feedback for modifications of the original plan. In our case, such managerial measures aimed at correcting the situation are preventing environmental degradation by tourism. Such a procedure leads to the refinement of the planning principles and strategies. Of course, one has to allow a rather generous time-frame for all planning stages, because only a controlled and moderate growth rate can guarantee the orderly and efficient planning and monitoring process. The course of action that the management chooses is also subject to scrutiny with regard to budget constraints and the effectiveness of the recommended measures.

In recent years, planners have been using the term "strategic planning." This focuses on integrative aspects of planning, on long-term strategies, gradualism in solving problems, and a continuity of the planning process, all aimed at successful coping with change. Strategic planning does not deal with all details normally involved in the standard planning procedures, but concentrates on key issues, challenges, and initiatives. Such an approach is a good one from the environmental point of view because it harmonizes with the features and character of ecological impacts.

9.4 *National and Regional Planning*

9.4.1 *Introduction*

An important part of management planning at the national and regional level is in the division of the territory into tourism regions or zones. Zoning involves setting goals and objectives for each zone—some of the zones are selected for priority tourism development because of their potential, while others may be reserved primarily for nontourism economic activities, or remain undeveloped. Development in various zones is subject to a diverse range of limitations, which are especially stringent in ecologically valuable areas. This includes the total exclusion of tourism in certain unique ecosystems. The objective of planning is setting the tourist capacities and impact parameters for each zone. In this regard, the elaboration of relevant land use plans is essential. The investment in the general and tourism infrastructure, especially in accommodation facilities, is normally concentrated in the zones planned for intensive tourism development, mainly resorts or clusters of resorts. Naturally, these areas also receive most visitation, meaning that these are the high-impact zones.

The most important task of regional planning is to establish the managerial carrying capacities for each zone. As discussed in section 7.6, the managerial carrying capacity represents the desired maximal use level planned for each zone. This prevents overcrowding and limits tourism impacts to a maximum planned level in order to prevent environmental deterioration. Not only is the total visitation important; so are the different types of recreational activities, because of various levels of impacts associated with them. If more than one incompatible activity is planned in the region, then the activities should be zoned to prevent use conflicts.

The simplest tool to control the level of visitation consists of measures to limit the numbers of tourists. In certain cases it may be a proactive measure, sometimes unconnected with environmental protection—such as the policy of discouraging tourism in the past by Albania, Burma, and China. However, in most situations this method is a reactive managerial tool used when the recreational carrying capacities, as perceived by the authorities, have already been surpassed. As detailed in section 6.4, the classic example of limiting access to a country by a quota (5,000 tourists annually) is Bhutan. Bermuda applies the brakes on tourism by putting limits on accommodation capacity, such as on new hotel construction.

On a subnational scale, the imposition of numerical barriers in historic cities, resorts, resort clusters or regions is controversial, resisted by tourist businesses, and advocated by environmentalists. The results vary from case to case, and the quotas are frequently compromised, but the tendency to limit access aimed at preventing overcrowding is discernible all over the world. Among historic cities, the most prominent is Venice where in the spring of 1987 authorities started to ration the numbers of tourists. The "Operation Venice Reserved" provided for a limit of 200 tourist buses and 50,000 visitors a day. However, the operation has run into trouble because nobody could agree on the desirable ceilings. Tourist business regards the 50,000 limit as too restrictive.

When planning zones for various degrees of extensive use, the visitation, and thus the impacts, may be dispersed over the remaining countryside of the region. However, the wide spatial dispersal of tourism and recreation facilities, such as second homes is an environmentally undesirable scenario that has to be avoided. As discussed in sections 4.3 and 4.4, private cottages represent an inefficient use of space because they take a lot of area and are inhabited only during a relatively short time. Therefore, planning has to promote more efficient forms, such small hotels, co-operative condominiums, cottages rentals, and time-sharing arrangements. To achieve this objective, Krippendorf (1975: 120–125) suggests a number of measures, including taxation, regulation, prohibition and others. Most appear to be excellent solutions for crowded European landscapes.

Another caveat for planners is to deter tourism monoculture in the region (see section 9.1, point 4). If possible, tourism should blend harmoniously with other human activities, such as ecologically sustainable agriculture, fishing, and forestry but not mining, heavy manufacturing and energy production. Such an approach is not only economically sound, but also environmentally, because it saves the landscape not only from undesirable nontourist impacts but also from the unmitigated spread of tourist facilities.

An indispensable part of regional planning is to preserve and protect nature from undesirable impacts and possible despoliation of ecosystems. Thus, not only should the protection of separate landscape elements, such as air, water, fauna and flora be safeguarded, but so should whole ecosystems. Only this can guarantee the survival of sound attractive landscapes and the survival of tourism.

9.4.2 *Concentration or Dispersal?*

The issue of concentration (clustering of high-intensity tourism in limited space and deconcentration (such as dispersal of low-intensity tourism throughout relatively large areas) has been a subject of considerable debate in the literature (Bornet 1979, Gunn 1987, Gunn 1988a, Farrell and Runyan 1991, Bosselman 1978, Coltman 1989, Hamele 1987, OECD 1980). The discussion has focused on the advantages and disadvantages associated with both of them, and could be summarized as follows:

1. *Advantages of dispersion.* Dispersion has been used to prevent high density tourism and the destructive impacts associated with it. Spreading tourism over large areas exerts low-intensity impact per unit of space, and therefore less possibility that the saturation point may be reached and exceeded—with the result that the environment may deteriorate. Additionally, the dispersion of tourism makes most "engineering of the landscape" (such as ski lifts) unprofitable, saving us from visual pollution by eyesores. Bornet (1979: 64–65) sees certain emotional aspects in some people's preference of dispersed tourism, such as the ownership of a cottage, sentimental links with the past, a predilection towards primitivism. Thus, while from the purely economic point of view deconcentration means waste of resources, the environmental advantages are limited to all forms of alternative tourism, such as rural tourism and nature tourism (see chapter 10).

2. *Disadvantages of dispersion.* Too-large areas of the countryside are impacted by the uncontrolled sprawl of tourism, especially by the construction of second homes. Bosselman (1978: 145) uses the term "peripheral clutter" in this connection, and Krippendorf (1975) calls it "devouring the landscape." Small developers usually have less trouble with building permits than do developers of larger projects, and as a rule do not need to submit Environmental Impact Statements. The public and the government are not too concerned, because of the perception that small innocuous projects are environmentally harmless. However, while small tourist developments, taken separately, may not threaten the environment, their cumulative effects on the landscape and its ecological health could reach devastating proportions. Thus, one septic tank is harmless, but thousands of them can pollute the ground water and contribute to eutrophication of lakes. Indeed, not everything that is "small is beautiful." The sprawl of tourism over large rural areas may also prevent the conservation of nature in wildlands. The sum of environmental deterioration will be more substantial, because, as stated in section 7.3 and section 9.1 point 15, the initial impact causes considerable damage and the subsequent increase of impacts usually results in less-than-proportional incremental effects.

3. *Disadvantages of concentration.* High-intensity impacts threaten the ecosystems. The carrying capacity of the area is likely to be surpassed, resulting in considerable environmental deterioration, possibly destruction. The social disadvantage is that tourists staying in urbanized environments of cities and resorts are living in the much-criticized "tourist ghettoes" (Hamele 1987). They are deprived of contacts with nature and the local population, and are more or less left to interact among themselves. This is the situation that prevails even in such relatively small resorts as Club Med "villages," that as a rule, do not exceed 1,000 guests at a time.

4. *The advantages of concentration.* The sociocultural disadvantage of concentrated tourism, it could be argued, actually benefits the host societies, because segregation of tourists from the host population protects local cultures through minimizing the negative effects of western behavioral patterns on local population. Another noneconomic "advantage" (we in the West regard it as a significant drawback) had been the "ghettoization" of foreign tourists in the former communist countries, that had taken place for political considerations and had been imposed by the ruling elites. From the economic point of view, the

concentration of tourism in relatively limited space in most countries of the world is connected with a number of internal and external economies which may be mentioned briefly. First of all, there are considerable savings in the form of economies of scale and economies of scope, including better distribution of fixed costs of tourist infrastructure facilities (such as ski lifts or swimming pools), as well as general infrastructure. For example, Bornet (1979: 62–70) reports the results of French and Swiss research into the costs of general infrastructure in tourist areas. The per capita costs of central heating systems, sewage, and water purification facilities is negatively correlated with the size of the locality. At disadvantage especially are settlements with less than 5,000 people, which seems to indicate the optimal size of a resort. The greater economic efficiency of larger resorts is combined with environmental efficiency, because larger facilities have higher engineering standards and pollute less. Another environmental argument in favor of concentration is the superiority of large projects (Bosselman 1978: 146). Indeed, only larger projects have sufficient resources to provide Environmental Impact Assessments (EIAs), or more exactly, Environmental Impact Statements (EISs) which are the products of the EIAs. Because of the conspicuous nature of large projects, they receive better scrutiny by the concerned public, NGOs, and government agencies. In terms of environmental control and management, individual large projects are easier to handle than a multitude of small scattered proposals. More importantly from the environmental point of view, tourism concentration relieves pressure from the areas of dispersed, resource-based recreational areas, and prevents sprawl of facilities "devouring the landscape." This function of diverting demand from fragile, ecologically valuable land is especially significant in coastal, mountain, and small-island ecosystems.

The decision whether to concentrate or disperse is a matter of tourism policy, and may differ from case to case. The choice is between exposing relatively small areas to severe ecological damage, (which requires engineering measures to increase their carrying capacities), or allowing larger areas to be affected by milder impacts. It is a matter of value judgment, as a rule subjective judgment, and should be carefully considered. In this connection, I would like to make following recommendations:

1. On an international scale, one should strive for greater dispersion of tourism. Creating new destinations in the LDCs is especially important.

The benefits of such a solution are obvious: scatterings of impacts over larger areas will decrease the impacts in overcrowded and environmentally deteriorating areas, mostly located in the DCs. This will also contribute to a more even distribution of economic benefits of tourism to the advantage of the poor. The recent improvements in air transportation and its lower costs are playing a welcome role in this arguable transfer of wealth from the DCs to the LDCs.

2. On the national and regional subnational level, an intermediate approach is recommended, combining concentration with deconcentration and using their advantages while minimizing their disadvantages. In other words, the principle of *decentralized concentration* should be implemented (Fig. 9.2). In this pattern, tourists are concentrated in resorts but not confined to them; resorts serve as nodal points for day trips to nature reserves, national parks, single attractions, or clusters of attractions. Zoning should be used as a tool to achieve the strategic purpose of concentrating tourism (and thus its impacts) in terms of location, intensity and duration, in certain zones; within the zones, in tourist centers (such as resorts), and disperse or limit development in other areas. One could suggest a general rule: concentrate in areas of user-oriented recreation located close to urban centers, and disperse in resource-oriented areas located at a distance from cities.

This compromise approach creates optimal opportunities for everybody in the segmented tourist market. Gregarious tourists, who prefer to mix with crowds and to socialize with their peers and enjoy high-quality services, will patronize the large resorts and other areas of concentrated high-impact tourism. The dispersed low-impact tourism will be enjoyed by tourists seeking simplicity, solitude, and the communion and interaction with nature in small resorts, rural areas, and wilderness. Both categories can count on high quality products from their different points of view. In this way the decentralized concentration, by providing a better mix of tourist products, contributes to the diversification of supply for a diversified market.

Figure 9.2

DECENTRALIZED CONCENTRATION IN A TOURIST REGION

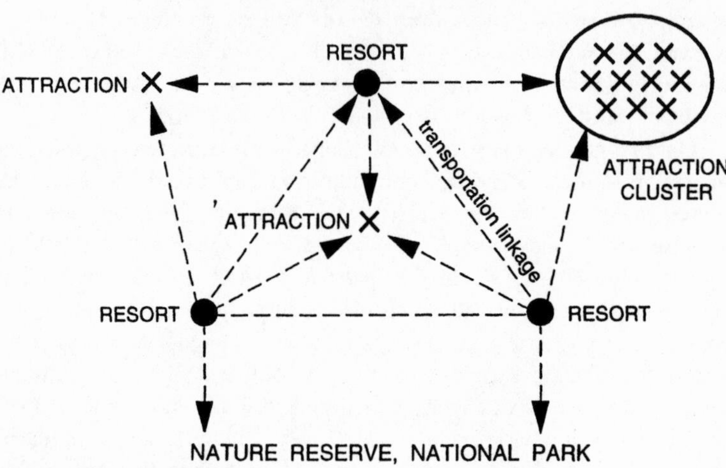

9.4.3 *Small Islands*

As mentioned, the most important task of national and regional planning is the protection of fragile areas from undesirable levels of tourism impacts. The susceptibility of some ecosystems to human interference has been discussed in chapter 6. A small island is a good example of a fragile ecosystem, and its problems have been already examined (see section 6.2.3.3). The planning issues of a small island will be treated in this section because, with the exclusion of islands in the polar regions, they are high-preference tourist destinations and as such are subject to increased environmental stress, especially in their coastal areas. Some of the small islands belong to the microstates, and because they have recently acquired independence, their planning may be regarded as national. Unfortunately, efforts to restrict tourism on many small islands and island archipelagos have met with limited success. Some island governments curb tourism in various ways without initiating any comprehensive development planning. In such cases, the local authorities simply issue orders containing certain measures aimed at decreasing tourist impacts. Thus, the Azores put a ceiling of 5,000 beds on their hotel development to preserve the environment, and imposed a ban on high-rise hotels. The conversion of old inns and villas into small hotels is being promoted. Some islands, such as Bermuda *(World*

Press Review February 1990) and Malta *(Tourism Management* December 1990) while limiting the overall numbers of tourists, want to preserve their status as upmarket destinations. Malta plans to limit tourist arrivals to one million starting in 1994 and has been promoting off-season tourism for many years.

A major environmental problem for tourism planners on small islands is the automobile transportation bottleneck that causes air pollution, erosion, traffic jams, and increasing accident rates. Limited space and topography frequently rule out expansion of the road network or widening of highways. To cope with the situation, various forms of regulation have been initiated. Thus, the Lipari Islands, the islands of Capri, Ischia, and Procida near Naples banned non-resident cars since spring 1989 *(New York Times* 9 July 1989). In Bermuda the density of 220 resident-owned vehicles per kilometer of road belongs to the highest in the world (Teye 1992: 399). On top of this come thousands of international tourists and cruise excursionists, all of them potential car renters. The response strategy on the part of the authorities has been the non-recognition of foreign driver's licenses which makes car rentals impossible. In this way, Bermuda practically bans car rentals and compels tourists to rent scooters that do not exceed 50 cubic centimeters. I rented a bicycle, an environmentally friendlier means of transportation, during my stay on the island. This was a practical option, considering the 37-kilometer lengths and two-kilometer widths of Bermuda. However, Teye (1992) does not mention this environment-friendly means of transportation. Other measures to decrease overcrowding in Bermuda in 1988 are: establishment of a ceiling of 120,000 cruise visitors during the peak season between May and October, limiting the number of cruise ships docked any one time to four, and the elimination of weekend cruise docking (*ibid.* 403).

Limiting tourist arrivals is only a partial solution to the environmental problems of small islands. Therefore, some of them embarked on comprehensive integrated tourism planning. Of note is the Coastal Zone Management (CZM) plans being developed in the Caribbean (Williams, M.C. 1988). These plans contain a number of important initiatives to improve and enhance the environments of these winter tourism destinations of North Americans and, increasingly, of Western Europeans. Since the 1960s, the Channel Islands, part of the United Kingdom, are guided by comprehensive development plans with a significant environmental component aimed at preserving the quality of life (Romeril 1985). These plans provide not only for maximum bed capacities for each of the islands but also for zoning, including *green zones*—passive recreation zones, and areas zoned for nature conservation. The plans are being updated and amended continuously. In some cases the original plans have been substituted by entirely new ones.

The absence of planning on many other islands of the world has been instrumental in severe overdevelopment, as, for example, in the Balearic archipelago. The environmental problems in this area are the main cause of the decrease in arrivals, especially to Mallorca. Tourism on Mallorca creates 70 percent of employment, which is now being threatened. In a belated response to market forces, the regional government of the Balearic Islands introduced the first integrated tourism development plan, which included a number of new environmental standards such as the minimum of 30 square meters of green space per one hotel bed. Additionally, 13 nature conservation zones have been established (Hamele 1987: 52–53). However, already in 1990, a number of management measures had to be undertaken to amend the plan. Among them was upgrading of the infrastructure, including sewer systems and transportation, halt new hotel construction (except four- or five-star accommodations), establishment of a minimum of 60 square meters of green space per one hotel bed, instead of the former 30 square meters; an order to hotels over five years old to renovate; the conversion of cheap mass accommodation "silos" to other nontourist purposes, such as apartments or homes for the aged; and the removal of eyesores, such as french-fry shacks (*Der Spiegel* 1990: 23: 236–237). This course of action indicates the urgent need for improvements of the environmental parameters on the island, aimed at decreased density, promotion of upmarket visitation, and suppression of cheap mass tourism. Considering past experience, one has to be rather skeptical about the feasibility of these measures. To decrease the pressure of beach tourism, the desperate Spanish government tries to market the inland tourist attractions of the Iberian peninsula.

The results of planning on Hawaii, another archipelago and also a "victim" of tourism's invasion, are mixed. Hawaii has a history of regional planning, including zoning, comprehensive outdoor recreation and infrastructure development. However, the enforcement of the 1974 plan that limits the growth of tourism infrastructure has been unsuccessful and it failed to curb overdevelopment in some parts of the archipelago. Nevertheless, there have been some achievements, among them the creation of conservation districts (Myers, P. 1976: 61-69). These districts, composed of publicly owned land and water reserves, encompass a considerable part of Hawaii: 40 percent of Oahu, 55 percent of Kauai, 41 percent of Maui, and 53 percent of the Big Island of Hawaii. The conservation districts are zoned, starting from restricted watershed zones to general use zones allowing "for a long and sometimes questionable list of activities" (*ibid.* 64). However, the districts are threatened by increased development pressures aimed at rezoning some of their most precious parts, the coastal setback. Myers (1976) describes the controversy associated with these issues.

The Balearic and Hawaiian island archipelagos represent examples of island ecosystems under environmental stress of mass tourism. Another type of stress is experienced by the unique and fragile natural environment of the Galapagos Islands, which are planned almost entirely as a nature conservation zone with limited and controlled visitation. In fact, 88 percent of the archipelago is occupied by the Galapagos National Park. There are several hotels in the settlement of Santa Cruz, located outside the park, but there are no tourist accommodations in the park; tourists stay aboard their cruise ships which accommodate about 100 tourists on tours which are on average of six-days' duration. According to the park plans and regulations, the impacts of tourism are strictly controlled (De Groot 1983; Marsh ed. 1986). The archipelago is divided into five zones, two of which admit tourists. There are about 40 visitor sites within the park. The Intensive Visitor Zones admit up to 90 people at a time, the Extensive Visitor Zones only 12. No individual visits are allowed. Tourist groups are accompanied by a licensed guide (one guide per 30 visitors) and stay on trails approximately 1.5 meters wide. Feeding and touching the animals, taking anything, such as rocks or shells, and leaving anything behind is prohibited. In May 1994 the Ecuadorian government barred large cruise ships from visiting the islands.

Unfortunately, these strict regulations are frequently violated (see section 6.2.3.3) and the management has to step in to minimize the adverse environmental impacts. De Groot (1983) advocates better enforcement of the rule of no more than 90 visitors on shore at any one time on any Intensive Visitor Site. He also suggests better control of the violations of park rules by passengers and crews of small ships. For this purpose, fixed scheduling of all boats, large and small, should be enforced. The solution of the private yacht problem lies in allowing the owners to hire licensed guides in Puerto Ayora to accompany them on an itinerary confirmed by the National Park Service.

Another problem on Galapagos is the enforcement of the government-stipulated 25,000 annual limit (although the Management Plan for the Galapagos National Park calls for a maximum of 12,000 tourists a year). However, even this relaxed rule is never enforced. It seems that, in this respect, the short-term economic interests prevailed over long-term environmental conservation, and the number of tourists was about 50,000 in 1992 (Kostyal 1992: 33-34).

Thus, the task of the park planners and managers is complex. It has to focus on strict enforcement of park regulations, including a limitation on the number of visitors, and capping the number of permanent inhabitants is also imperative to prevent the destruction of this unique island ecosystem.

The creation of the Maunga Terevaka National Park on Easter Island set up to protect the ancient stone figures and some natural features, is more recent and will require some time until a definite judgment may be passed as to the success of its conservation measures. The preliminary assessment is rather skeptical (Marsh 1986). Nevertheless, the plan provides for the zoning of the park area into a highly restricted zone (almost 50 percent), a general visitor zone (almost 50 percent), and a small intensive use area (*ibid.* 1986: 228).

On some islands large-scale, high-rise tourism development has been implemented. An example of such an approach is the previously mentioned beach resort of Nusa Dua on Bali. This resort, composed of huge hotels and ancillary facilities, is located on the southern tip of the island, spatially separated from the Bali's cultural and environmental attractions. In 1986, well after Nusa Dua was commissioned, the provincial government issued a decree prohibiting the construction of hotels higher than the palm trees. Another resort, Kuta—located slightly north of Nusa Dua, may be considered a transition zone because it has many small, locally-owned hotels. The international airport of Depensar is located in the same southern corner of Bali. The rest of the island is planned as a nondevelopment zone for tourism: tourists visit this area, travelling mainly by buses. Thus, tourism on Bali is highly concentrated in a relatively small area of intensive development, rather than dispersed over the whole island, which would be environmentally and culturally more damaging. However, there have been various press reports indicating violations of tourist zoning in Bali. Also the order to halt hotel construction in Bali is poorly implemented (*New York Times* 28 1991). I did not observe any of these shortcomings during my stay in Bali in 1983, and I was positively impressed by the concentration of tourism in the relatively small southern area of the island.

9.5 *Planning on the Local Level*

9.5.1 *Introduction*

Tourism development planning on the local or micro level pertains to individual projects or groups of spatially interrelated projects, usually located in close proximity. In terms of land use and other general parameters, planning is based on broad political considerations, many of them already decided on the regional or national level prior to the start of the planning process. Therefore, the elaboration of national and regional plans should precede planning on a local level (Inskeep 1987: 125). As a result of such an optimal scenario, it would seem that tourism policy may play, at least in some cases, a less prominent role in local than in regional planning. The microlevel plans appear dominated by more technical and managerial aspects of planning, including physical planning focused on visual appearance, architectural design and land-use control aimed at minimization of adverse impacts and enhancement of environmental conservation, combined with the promotion of aesthetic values. This may be true in some cases. Nevertheless, it does not mean that political considerations completely disappear from the picture at this level. There is a distinct trend to increasing involvement of the local population in the decision-making process, especially if the residents of an area to be developed are directly or indirectly affected by tourism. As mentioned in section 9.2, local political power is increasing (at least in the DCs) because of the trend to decentralize decision-making (Naisbitt 1984: 100, 103–141, 212, 281), with local residents gaining more say in their own affairs, especially in matters relating to quality of life and to conservation of resources (Murphy 1983 and 1985).

Tourism development at the local level occurs in two ways. The first one is the nodal growth of tourism, which occurs in certain clusters or concentrations, be they urban centers, resorts, or groups of resorts, where attractions and facilities are concentrated in a relatively small space. The second is when tourism is dispersed over large extra-urban areas, frequently in wildlands or in protected wilderness, and the siting and the characteristics of facilities and transportation routes have to be planned to minimize environmental damage. In both scenarios planning should include the environmental impact assessment (EIA) and land-use studies, prior to undertaking any development. As indicated previously, the planning process should continue beyond the development stage into the operational stage, in the form of monitoring and evaluation, in order to ensure that its the goals and objectives are met. If unacceptable impacts do occur, corrective measures should be undertaken.

9.5.2 *Nodal Development*

9.5.2.1 *Introduction*

The nodal (cluster) development pattern of tourism in cities and resorts (including linear concentrations such as coastal zones) represents the environmentally optimal scenario (see section 9.4.2). Tourists either remain confined within the limits of a self-contained cluster, or venture outside on day tours to see attractions dispersed in the countryside. This solution allows for the development of a relatively environment-friendly infrastructure by mitigating ecological deterioration. Such a concentrated general and tourism infrastructure is also used in the most appropriate way, minimizing the negative environmental impacts of mass tourism. Another advantage of concentration is better control of large-scale tourism within limited spatial confines, and the reduction of its impacts on sensitive resources, especially on wildlands. Social contacts with the local population decrease, however, which could be regarded as a disadvantage. The majority of modern tourists prefer socialization with their fellow tourists and/or the participation in intensive recreational activities requiring their full attention, and—fortunately or unfortunately—(this depends on one's point of view) are not interested in contact with local population.

9.5.2.2 *Cities*

The unappealing environmental aspects of American cities have recently been subjected to severe criticism (Kunstler 1993; Borman, *et al.* 1993). Indeed, it is desirable that cities become more attractive to tourists, but these issues are only tangentially linked to the environmental impact of tourism. Cities, including historic cities (Ashworth and Tunbridge 1990), developed in pretourism times, and their natural environment has been almost totally substituted by artificial human elements. This new physical and sociocultural environment, especially in large cities, seems to be resilient to tourism impact. Mathieson and Wall (1982: 124) conclude that "large cities, because of their size, can absorb large numbers of tourists without obvious repercussions." But the carrying capacity of cities is not unlimited, and the task of integrated city planning is to blend tourism harmoniously into the existing fabric of general infrastructure and attractions in order to prevent overcrowding, pollution, and deterioration of the quality of life.

A paramount concern for city planners is the provision of open green space which makes the city not only attractive for recreationists and tourists but also absorbs air pollution, improves water quality, lessens the danger of flooding, abates noise, and renders urban areas more energy-efficient by cooling them in summer and reduces heating costs in winter. Some of these benefits contribute indirectly to the conservation of nature in nonurban areas by decreasing resource use.

A classical example of such an approach to city planning is the city-state of Singapore, where the concentration of over three million people on 639 square kilometers of space presents a seemingly insoluble problem. Nevertheless, due to excellent planning and strict management control, Singapore is one of the most attractive tourist cities in the world. Especially significant is the method of high-tech automobile traffic monitoring that uses fees and fines to limit access to congested areas. Other assets are abundant green space, rigorous cleanness control, and enforcement of stringent building codes, all of which contribute to the city's aesthetics.

The relatively high thresholds of carrying capacity in cities may allow high concentrations of tourism without any significant environmental degradation, and at the same time, may divert some of the demand from fragile extra-urban areas. Such a future scenario of urban tourism increasing its share at the expense of extra-urban tourism may be environmentally desirable, but it depends on unpredictable market forces. Some researchers believe that the opposite will happen because of the degradation of urban concentrations (Farrell and Runyan 1991: 30). This development is by no means certain, in view of the recent gentrification of many city cores (called also inner cities) and the restoration of historic cities (Ashworth and Tunbridge 1990).

Historic cities deserve the special attention of planners because their carrying capacities are much lower than those of large metropolitan conurbations. Certainly, New York City may endure more pressure than large historic cities, such as Rome, Naples or Florence, not to mention smaller historic cities, such as Savannah, Georgia or Charleston, South Carolina. Therefore, not only is careful design essential, but so are stricter regulations and development limits (*ibid.*). This pertains especially to the most valuable core areas, which, as a rule, should be all-pedestrian zones.

As far as the architectural requirements for city hotels are concerned, these may be less stringent than in the extra-urban areas, with the obvious exception of historic cities. In fact, almost any type of accommodations may be represented, starting from private bed-and-breakfast rooms to gigantic hotels that use the economies of scale. Unfortunately, there has been only a limited success worldwide in adjusting the external and internal architecture of hotels to local styles and cultural patterns. Also the development of city parks leaves much to be desired, especially in some U.S. cities and in other cities in the LDCs.

9.5.2.3 *Resorts*

Resorts represent another type of spatial concentration in tourism. The local economy is highly specialized to serve the visitors, sometimes to the exclusion of other economic activities, as well as to the exclusion of local population not directly employed by the tourism sector. Such a situation puts integrated tourism planning in a prominent position aimed at minimizing the environmental, social, and cultural damage.

Resorts are service and facility clusters, which may develop into groups of nodes connected with access-corridors, that are used by tourists to travel between them. Principal facilities and services are located at each node, while others, together with local attractions, are located along the corridors (Beeton 1989: 44–46).

Resorts may develop from a pre-existing community which has embarked on the road of tourist specialization. Or, they may be self-contained resorts constructed from scratch on sites previously devoid of local population (for example, Cancún in Mexico or certain ski resorts in the French Alps). Such "instant" tourist complexes are being designed and planned either by one large corporation or in a coordinated effort by a number of smaller firms. However, the majority of European resorts have grown in symbiosis with existing settlements, such as fishing or agricultural villages. This solution seems to be environmentally preferable, at least for relatively small resorts in the DCs, although not always feasible. If a resort grafted onto a small community develops into a giant, the original local town or village will be completely wiped out: this was the situation with Benidorm, Spain, which grew from a town of 6,000 to a resort city of about 250,000 tourist beds.

The first major task of resort planning is to determine its spatial limits and its size. Resorts should be spatially well defined to prevent their spread (resort sprawl) and to leave the landscape free of construction as much as possible. Their size may vary from an economic minimum to an environmental maximum. Russel Smith's (1992: 306–308) eight-phase beach resort model evolves from a tiny coastal settlement to a multifunctional city, with a separate recreation business district RBD (Stansfield and Ricket 1970) and commercial business district (CBD). This reflects the reality of not only beach resort transformation, but is *mutatis mutandis* applicable to any resort (Butler 1980).

As to the size of the resort and elevation of the buildings, one could follow two diametrically different solutions. The first one adheres to the principle that "small is beautiful" (Schumacher 1975), advised by Clare Gunn (1988a). According to this concept, a resort should be of modest size with low-rise architecture and no gigantic structures. Gunn advocates strict enforcement of growth limits and is opposed to economies of scale in design, planning, and management. These strategies are aimed at preventing the urbanization of resorts, i.e., their transformation into cities, in which the elements of recreation, rest, human dimension, and coziness may be lost.

The second solution, severely criticized by environmentalists, such as Jost Krippendorf (1975), are large resorts, veritable resort cities, such as Torremolinos, Spain, or the Gold Coast resorts in Australia's Queensland, consisting of a number of high-rise hotels and condominiums. Despite the criticism, I do not consider the construction of large resorts or the transformation of resorts into resort cities as an entirely negative phenomenon. Nice has grown to a metropolitan area with the second-busiest airport in France and still attracts thousands of beach tourists who enjoy its specific ambience. Simply, there is a market for such a type of resort. Benidorm, Spain, is a huge resort city, a veritable Waikiki of Europe, with an annual visitation of more than four million. Tourists are housed in skyscrapers and the atmosphere is urban. Despite these drawbacks, however, the resort is spotlessly clean and carefully landscaped, with lots of green space; strict noise controls are also enforced. In a well-designed large resort everything is within walking distance and the environmental damage is limited to a relatively small area of concentrated high-impact tourism.

I think that planners should not strive towards the elusive goal of setting the optimal size for an abstract resort, but should act according to needs and merits of a specific situation. Nevertheless, the capacity limits, usually expressed in the number of beds, should be established, enforced, and harmonized within a resort. To achieve this goal, Gee (1981: 38) recommends either a general plan with broad community support, or self-regulation by the resort industry. He emphasizes that both methods have worked well in the United States because of the realization "that the success of resort operations will ultimately depend on maintaining a pleasant human environment" (*ibid.* 1981: 39). Control of the rate of development may be exercised not only on the general resort level, but also on the specific hotel level by matching hotel capacities with adequate parking, seats in the restaurants, and capacities of sport facilities. Coordination within a cluster of sport facilities is also necessary, as, for example, between the capacities of ski lifts and those of ski runs.

However, there are many cases when resort planning and self-regulation may not lead to desired outcomes, and the authorities, such as government agencies or courts, have to step in to limit resort development. Examples of such actions have multiplied since the 1960s. A pioneer in curbing development has been the most affected area, the French Riviera, where in the early 1970s, court decisions stopped several partially-completed resort developments and withdrew some building permits. The first demolition of a completed hotel was ordered in Italy in 1979 (*Der Spiegel* 1979: 110–111). The order to demolish the 300-bed Hotel Fuenti in Vietri sul Mare near Amalfi was given by the regional government of Campagna under the pressure of the powerful and vocal environmental NGO, Italia Nostra. Hotel builders were accused of obtaining the building permit under false pretenses by providing spurious environmental data. The construction involved rock dynamiting and the destruction of unique vegetation. I do not have a confirmation that the demolition order was actually executed—it is rather unlikely that it took place because a hole in the rock would be equally as unacceptable as an architectural monster (locally called *il monstro.* I suspect that the matter ended with a fine, in the best Italian tradition of reconciliation of differences.

An American example of resort development limitations based on environmental considerations is the removal of unfinished condominiums in the Gateway National Recreation Area on the outskirts of New York City. This was done to clear land for a park (*National Geographic* 1979: 96–97). Another U.S. controversy surrounds the barriers to resort and other construction in ecologically sensitive zones, such as wetlands, coastal stretches, and mangrove swamps (in Florida owners cannot build if mangroves are destroyed by construction). Owners oppose these measures on the basis that they limit private property rights.

After limiting the resort capacity, the second task of resort planning concerns both general and tourist infrastructure. General infrastructure, such as supply of fresh water, electricity, garbage disposal, recycling, and waste management, should be designed according to the highest possible standards. To serve hotels, a sewage treatment plant is indispensable. For the waste discharge from yachts, Jackson (1988: 54) advises the provision of waste discharge terminals and on-shore toilets for boaters.

FIGURE 9.3
EUROPEAN SHORELAND DEVELOPMENT

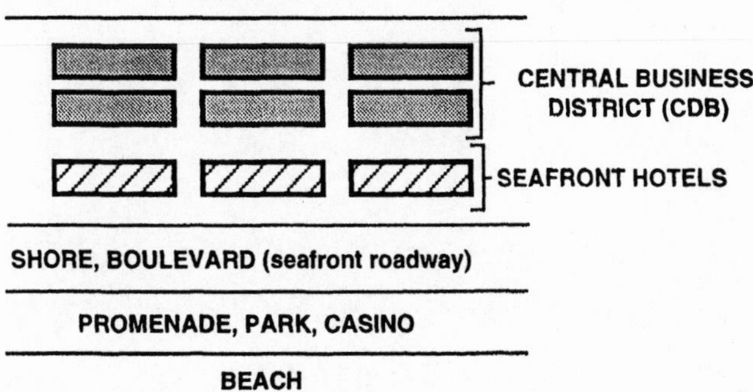

Essentially, part of the general infrastructure is transportation, which deserves special attention. Problems of traffic congestion and visual pollution are especially acute in traditional beach resorts (Stansfield 1969, Stansfield and Ricket 1970; Gunn 1988b: 88–89;

Mieczkowski, Z. 1990: 327–331). Both the European and the United States Atlantic coast morphology of resorts, designed in the nineteenth and the first part of the twentieth century, allows traffic too close to the beach. The traffic flows concentrate parallel to the shore, either in front or closely behind the high-rise wall of beachfront hotels, thus hindering access and obscuring views (Fig. 9.3). Such arrangements were acceptable for creating easy access for horse-drawn carriages. The line of hotels blocking the view and impeding air circulation from the hinterland was not a major problem because of the lack of development inland from the beach hotels. However, the expansion of built-up spaces farther inland and the mass invasion of automobiles into the resort areas have brought a number of severe environmental and safety problems, such as traffic congestion, air, noise and visual pollution, as well as traffic accidents, including collisions between pedestrians and automobiles.

FIGURE 9.4
DESIRABLE COASTAL ACCESS PATTERN

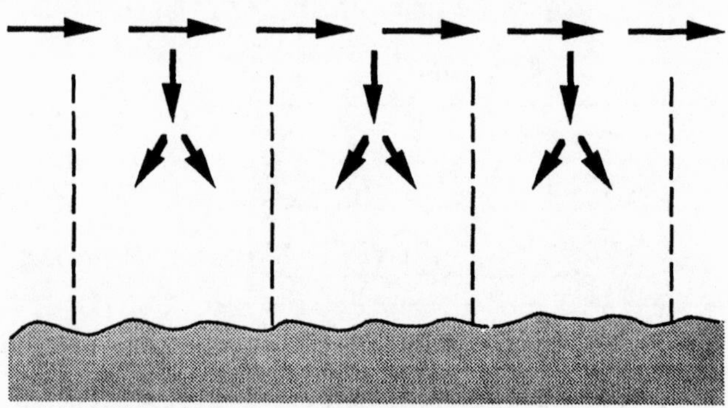

Source: adapted from C. Gunn 1988-89

To solve these problems, new resort designs decisively break with the past. The main high-volume traffic arteries run parallel to the shore, but at a distance. They are connected with the resorts or with sections of the resorts by special access roads, perpendicular to the beach (Fig. 9.4). These roads allow undisturbed traffic flow and terminate at parking facilities with adequate capacity, preferably located at the resort outskirts. The transportation network within the resort must be distinct from external access roads. Gunn (1988: 88–89) advocates such segmentation of traffic but he goes a step further by suggesting "concentrated dispersal" of hotels, i.e., "clusters of buildings or high-rise envelopes along coastal zones" (Fig. 9.5). Recently, an interesting trend in the positioning of buildings in beach resorts is discernible: instead of placing the buildings parallel to the shore, new developments tend to locate them perpendicularly or diagonally. According to the WTO/UNEP report (1983), such approaches are being developed in Denmark.

FIGURE 9.5
COASTAL CLUSTER DEVELOPMENT

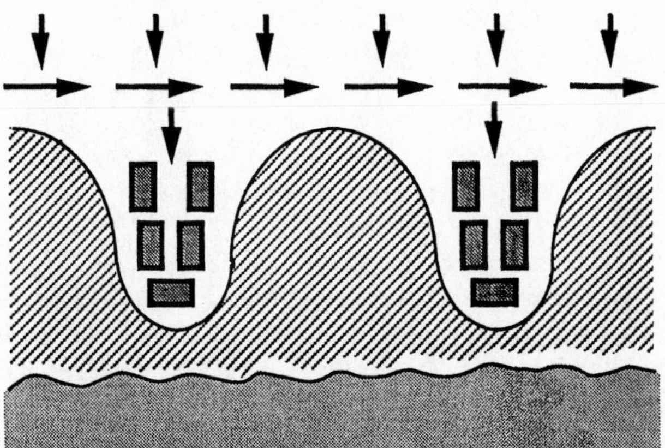

Source: adapted from C. Gunn 1988-89

To minimize the environmental impact of transportation, and to avoid traffic congestion within the resorts (the most frequently cited environmental issue), public transportation, rather than private forms, must be encouraged. Additional measures to decrease vehicular traffic in resorts include promotion of walking and of using bicycles. Motorized transportation has to be banned in resorts located in resource-based areas. In some resorts, the design of the whole resort, or its core, as a pedestrian zone is recommended. The implementation of these objectives is easier in cases of entirely new developments, but one finds such solutions to traffic congestion in old historic cities with narrow streets, such as in Lindos, on the island of Rhodes in Greece.

The third task of resort planning is the design of tourist infrastructure. Planning should establish the proper spatial distribution and design of tourist facilities, especially hotels. Resorts adhere to a wide range of environmental objectives, including a relatively modest, gradual, and cautious pace of development aimed at avoiding the anarchy of a boom, and adhering to strict building codes and architectural design that blends with the landscape.

Environmental considerations in resort design also include protection against erosion and pollution of all kinds, provision of adequate green space, landscaping, preservation, and enhancement of esthetic values. For these purposes, planners set out a number of parameters, such as density of beds per hectare, green space per tourist, beach length per tourist (see section 7.7). To protect tourists from noise, soundproofing standards for hotel walls should be enforced. Things like placing discos at a reasonable distance from accommodation facilities should also be addressed. In many resorts the heights of hotels must not exceed the height of the tops of the trees.

The architecture and landscaping of a resort must be in harmony with the environment, not only in terms of style and motifs of the whole building, but also by the use of indigenous and natural building materials. All the separate elements should be in accord with each other and should blend with the natural environment, complementing the natural beauty and exceptional landscape features. Many recent resort developments have been using local building materials and applying indigenous architectural styles, as with some of the resorts on Djerba, Tunisia. Application of alternative energy sources is also environmentally desirable; the use of solar energy to heat pool water is especially recommended.

In specific cases, such as beach resorts, planning should ensure that facilities are sufficiently set back from the beach to protect them from shore erosion, and for the esthetic reason of maintaining natural vistas of the shore that are unimpeded by high-rise buildings. To regulate construction on shoreland, a number of countries legislate so-called *coastal exclusion* or *restriction setbacks,* laws prohibiting or limiting construction. Generally, the distances are set in meters from the high tide mark, but in certain cases a less precise limit of the permanent vegetation line is preferred (Sorensen, *et al.* 1984: 58).

To protect the beach from erosion and to cope with the dredging and sand-mining problems (Edwards, ed. 1988: 104–109), a number of engineering measures are being taken locally. The solution is twofold: construction of beach protection structures and sand restoration. Thus, beaches are protected by various types of devices, such as piers and walls built from rocks, plastic, grass mats, and so on, with sand being trucked or pumped to the losing areas. Jackson (1988: 53) advises using nonbeach deposits for sand extraction. That was a solution on St. Lucia, where the building boom in the southern part of the island created a strong demand for sand. A quarry located a short distance inland from the Club Med village, but not directly visible from it, satisfies this demand. This is an optimal solution, considering that St. Lucia is known for limited beach sand resources.

Some resorts may require unique engineering solutions, such as hotel construction in areas prone to various natural hazards, like landslides, flooding, high winds (including hurricanes), or earthquakes. Earthquake-proof buildings require more concrete in the foundations and are sometimes built on piles driven deeply into the earth. In site selection, loosely consolidated material, such as sand, should be avoided, and solid rock sought out. Such special measures increase the construction costs—hence the reluctance on the part of developers to apply them. In this respect, the present situation leaves much to be desired: not only are resorts in the LDCs (such as Agadir, Morocco), lacking paraseismic hotels, but so are some resorts in the DCs (such as Nice, with less than 10 percent of earthquake-proof buildings). The November 1968 earthquake in Montenegro, which damaged a number of resorts, was kept secret for fear that bad publicity may harm tourism. However, the more severe quake in April 1979 was widely publicized because of the destruction of two-thirds of the area between Kotor and Ulcinj, which includes such resorts as Bar, Budva, Herceg Novi, and

Petrovac *(Der Spiegel* 1979, 17:136–138). Another example of special needs are tourist facilities in the polar regions. Because of climatic considerations, their design should follow the principle of concentration under one roof. (Mieczkowski, Z. 1974, 1975).

Another technological challenge presents itself in the construction phase of a resort. This is, environmentally, a high-priority stage, because of the particular vulnerability to erosion. Therefore, this stage of resort development should be kept as short as possible. A comprehensive approach at this critical time includes the use of proper methods to minimize erosion, such as excavation of settling ponds, seeding and mulching of bare surfaces, and the erection of rock dams and straw bales (Goudie 1990: 148–149).

Reviewing the environmental records of resorts, one may generalize that if the responsibility for a total resort development (integrated in the sense of self-containment) is concentrated in the hands of one large corporation, then the planning and design process proceeds more smoothly and efficiently from an environmental point of view. Additionally, large corporations, concerned about their public relations image will less likely limit themselves to the traditional costs and benefits analysis, and reach beyond it to analyze the environmental impacts of their projects. Indeed, the environmental impact assessment has become an integral and indispensable component of planning within large companies, even if it is not legally required. This assessment creates the necessary framework for planning and design of a resort (Williams, P. 1987; Edwards, ed. 1988).

There are a number of case studies describing successful design, planning and management strategies. As mentioned, large companies, concerned about their corporate image, receive high marks in this respect. As a pioneer among them, the Walt Disney Corporation, should be given credit for good ecological public relations. A theme park like Disney World, Florida occupies a relatively small space, while, as indicated in section 8.9 above, it saves 20 square kilometers of wetlands. An example of a total resort development whose developers deserve praise for environmental responsibility is the Big Sky ski resort near Bozeman, Montana, built by Boise Cascade (Price 1981: 435). The design of the Club Med villages also deserves high marks: their buildings blend harmoniously into the landscape, and there is no necessity for internal traffic because almost all facilities are within walking distance. Tourists rarely venture outside the village. As a result, environmental impact is contained and successfully minimized. Caneel Bay resort on the island of St. John in the U.S. Virgin Islands provides another example of ecological sensitivity in design. The resort occupies only 160 hectares, and tourists are housed in widely spaced luxurious cottages. The owner of the resort, a Rockefeller company, bought most of the island and donated it to the U.S. government. The land and the adjacent sea are a part of Virgin Islands National Park (Rostenov and Pulsipher 1979: 169).

Among smaller developments deserving environmental praise is the Lobo Wildlife Lodge in Tanzania, designed in local architectural style and harmoniously hewed into a rock out-cropping. The lodge is constructed on piles with a waterhole under the building. This provides fresh water for wildlife that can be observed by the guests at close range. Similarly pleasing to the eye is the Mara Serena Lodge in Kenya. Both harmonize with the surrounding landscapes and create comfortable accommodation for the African safari tourists.

However, not all integrated tourist developments deserve such unequivocal acclaim: there have been a few which raised quite a controversy. Among them are the integrated resorts, so-called "total" ski developments typical of the western Alps, especially the French Alps (see section 6.4.6). The reason for the criticism is the destruction of fragile alpine ecosystems, well above the tree line. Such ski resorts are also under criticism in North America. Indeed, opposition to some projects may cause their demise, as it did with the controversial Mineral King proposal thwarted by the Sierra Club (Sax 1980: 67ff).

A prominent European example of a planned beach resort zone (see section 6.2.3.2) is the huge new French Riviera extending about 180 kilometers between the Rhone River delta and the Spanish border—the Languedoc-Rousillion with 1.3 million beds, and visitation by over five million tourists in 1992 (Klemm 1992). Environmentalists have been highly critical about the project because a valuable wetland ecosystem has been lost as a result. For this reason the French term *valorisation* of environment (meaning improving the environmental qualities of the area) used by the defenders of the project, seems invalid (Bosselman 1978: 62). Nevertheless, one has to take into account compelling socioeconomic considerations, such as the overdevelopment of the Cote d'Azur and underdevelopment of the Languedoc coast, which apparently convinced the French government to develop the latter for tourism (Klemm 1992). While the planning of a single resort such as La Motte seems highly functional, with easy vehicular access routes and a pedestrian zone, not everyone is pleased with the high-rise architecture resembling Mayan or Aztec pyramids that creates an urban landscape (Krippendorf 1975: 93). Klemm (1992: 171) does not agree with such a critical evaluation, and thinks positively about the white condo pyramids that provide views and sunshine for the inhabitants. After visiting La Motte, I concur with Klemm.

Despite the controversy surrounding this project, one has to agree that the architectural design and landscaping of the Languedoc-Roussillon resorts deserve high praise for providing wide boulevards, ample green space, and an ideal solution to traffic problems by keeping long-distance traffic well off the coast, with perpendicular access roads that end several hundred meters from the beach. These are separated from hotels and parking by a wide pedestrian zone. Each of the resorts was built by different architects in a different style. Some of them blend with existing localities, and some, such as La Motte, have been developed as total resorts in an uninhabited area. To avoid overcrowding, a maximum of 800 tourists per hectare of beach was planned (*ibid.* 173). Compared to the chaotic unplanned development of the adjacent Spanish resorts of Costa Brava, the Languedoc-Roussillon stands out as a praiseworthy example of a planned beach resort zone, providing environmentally sustainable tourism for the mass market. Nevertheless, one has to admit that some controversial trade-offs between nature conservation and economic development have taken place. Therefore, Klemm (*ibid.* 180) is only "cautiously positive" about the project.

The design of the resorts on the coast of Aquitaine adhered to a different philosophy than that of the Languedoc, and therefore receive more acclaim from Bosselman (1978: 66–67). The resorts in this area, designed and developed in the late 1960s and the early 1970s (only a few years later than those of the Languedoc), have not destroyed the fragile dune ecosystems. They are small-scale, dispersed and located behind the dunes.

Comprehensive coastal resort development plans sponsored by governments, seem to be on the increase. One of the most recent is noteworthy because of its location between the two largest urban agglomerations of South America, with a total population of 27 million, and huge dimensions—the Turis project in southern Brazil. This project of coastal development between Rio de Janeiro and Santos took 20 years (1975-95). Because the plan is almost complete, one could expect an environmental impact assessment at the monitoring stage. Nicolls (1982) supplies the main technical and economic parameters of the plan, but does not discuss the environmental issues, except for a remark that, "attention was given to beach sand, vegetation and aesthetics," and that there has been "a correlation between physical evaluation and socioeconomic classification" (*ibid.* 197). According to the plan, the 500 kilometer coast has been divided into 19 Homogeneous Tourist Zones plus five island zones. The total amount of beds in accommodations projected for construction in the 19 zones was a staggering 700,000. The plan also envisaged the provision of one million new beds in Rio and Santos.

9.5.2.4 *Historic Sites*

An important local task is the planning and management of historic sites. First of all, planners should do their best to protect historic sites from external impact, such as pollution from industrial plants. This issue is of specific concern to the Taj Mahal mausoleum in India (see section 2.10). Another task is to create pleasant surroundings of the monuments of the past. Although the Taj Mahal is known for its beauty, it is surrounded by obnoxious views in its immediate vicinity. In response to this problem, India signed an agreement with the U.S. National Park Service in 1988 to landscape a park across the river Jamuna from the Taj Mahal.

Another issue is the management of tourists on historic sites, which draw thousands of visitors to a relatively small area. Such numbers can cause a serious environmental menace to the place, threatening the very survival of the attraction. The problem of preventing damage, including unintentional damage, is being solved by limiting access to them. Such a solution has been applied in Stonehenge, England where, until recently, tourists were allowed to wander freely among the stones. At present, they are not permitted to cross the outer perimeter of the monument, (Bender, B. and Mark Edmonds [1992]), while agreeing that this most important prehistorical monument in Britain is vulnerable and in need of protection, suggest more flexible management, allowing more access for alternative visitors, such as Druids, who have a spiritual connection to the site. According to Bender and Edmonds, these groups could be permitted to enter the site at times when there are few tourists.

Similar to Stonehenge, tourists are allowed to view the Parthenon, Athens only from the outside. Other methods which could be applied to cultural as well as natural attractions is making visitation more arduous or difficult. This could be effected by limiting parking space, locating parking farther away from attractions, and increasing entrance fees. Construction of museums and visitor centers may only decrease the pressure to a certain extent.

9.5.3 *Planning for Dispersed Tourism*

The second scenario of local planning and management involves extra-urban tourist locations dispersed in the countryside. The application of the dispersion principle does not mean that tourism is equally distributed throughout the landscape like butter on bread. In the real world there is also a lot of concentration in this scenario, but development is, as a rule, on a small scale. Tourism and recreation facilities are being developed along highways, in designated zones or at individual small, but high-impact sites dispersed in nonurban areas. Even in wildlands the campsites and trails are high-impact isolated places, covering relatively little space—as a rule less than one percent of the total territory (Hammitt and Cole 1987: 330). In fact, this is the decentralized concentration scenario (see section 9.4.2).

Management may decide to take measures to either concentrate or disperse impacts. Normally, both methods are applied in a creative combination of concentrated dispersal in which concentration of use occurs in certain points, such as in campgrounds or linearly along trails. Dispersal takes place if individual campsites are scattered throughout a large wilderness area. Each of the two approaches has its merits, and is associated with some trade-offs. Hammitt and Cole (*ibid.* 253–267) discuss the problem of whether "to concentrate or to disperse" in some detail, and come to the conclusion that, on balance, at least in wildland areas, concentration of use has more merit in terms of minimizing impact. In such cases it is preferable to concentrate the use on the existing impacted sites, and not to attempt to disperse the recreationists. Such a "concentration of use means that pronounced resource impacts, while locally severe, occur only in certain zones and affect a small proportion of any wildland recreation area" (*ibid.* 330).

In this scenario, tourism development and impacts take place in limited space and are characterized by more capital-intensive user-oriented forms, such as commercial and residential developments and recreational facilities, tennis courts, swimming pools and golf courses. At the same time, tourism in extra-urban areas is resource-based and dispersed, frequently taking place in wildlands. Recreational activities are low-impact, such as hiking and mountaineering. Therefore, the most important task of planning is the identification of both zones most suited for intensive development and zones of nature conservation, where tourism is either entirely banned, as in strict nature reserves, or limited to carefully selected sites and trails and to low-intensity activities like hiking and wilderness camping. These zones of limited access are frequently buffer zones that surround wilderness areas designated for conservation, where access may be entirely prohibited. Intermediate areas provide for transitional forms of tourism intensity. Occasionally, whole small countries, such as the Grenadines in the Caribbean, are zoned for low-intensity tourism with limited hotel space and reliance on excursionists, from the neighboring St. Lucia. Generally, management planning in wilderness areas faces the challenges of balancing use with preservation.

Zoning and siting of tourist facilities and recreation areas are the most effective ways of minimizing adverse environmental impacts of tourism in these scenarios. Zoning may occur both at regional and local levels. Regional zoning is developed only occasionally for larger tourist regions, to fit into a framework of regional planning. Thus, the Bavarian Alps have been divided into three zones: zone A has the full transportation infrastructure; in zone B development is permitted only if it does not contradict the planning purposes; zone C is a nondevelopment zone (Groetzbach 1985: 152).

The zoning principle is used much more on a local level than on a regional level in nature reserves, national parks, and recreation areas (see section 9.6). Some zoning may be seasonal, for instance, excluding visitation during the wildlife breeding season. A major challenge of zoning and siting of tourism and recreation facilities arises over the issue of land ownership. There are no limitations in designating areas for protection or limiting development if the land is in public ownership. However, private property requires special measures to protect nature from development. The simplest solution is for government to purchase land from private owners in *freehold ownership (fee simple)*, i.e., acquiring all the property rights within the legal boundaries. However, this method may be too expensive. Another cheaper technique could be applied to preserve scenic areas: the purchase of *scenic easements* (development rights). This arrangement provides for the retention of private ownership rights, but limits development which would detract from the scenic beauty of the area. In some places the government has to legislate or negotiate appropriate easements to allow for recreation uses, such as hiking and horseback riding (Jackson 1988: 52).

In selecting a site for dispersed tourism development, various physical parameters should be evaluated, such as geology, landforms, aspect, exposure, elevation, proximity of water, and drainage. Appropriate places for development should be moderately well drained, not subject to flooding, and resilient (tolerant to human impacts and able to recover from damage). In other words, the land where the tourism impacts are going to take place should have a high ecological carrying capacity (see section 7.3). Also, it is desirable that it be less valuable from an ecological point of view. Valuable and vulnerable areas, such as dunes, highly avalanche-prone unstable slopes, and alpine meadows; or areas of exceptional scenic beauty; and areas with unique resources and/or ecological value, such as wetlands, should be left free of tourism development. Such areas should only be visited on a limited basis in the framework of a plan scientifically designed to prevent environmental damage. Ryan (1991: 124) thinks that provision of self-guided trails may keep tourists away from fragile areas. As far as the vegetation cover is concerned, it should be composed of resilient species. According to Wenger (1984: 834) "durability of vegetation generally increases from lichens, through mosses, herbs, tree seedlings, and shrubs, to grasses and sedges." The undergrowth of older high-density climax forests is inadequate and vulnerable to use.

Zones and sites designated for tourism development should be properly designed in form and content. They should not only be aesthetically pleasing, blending harmoniously with the landscape, but also functional, performing their task most efficiently. This means providing the best service and most satisfying recreational experiences to all visitors, including the aged, the disabled and the very young, with minimal environmental damage.

Landscape design should enhance the aesthetics, the natural beauty and impressive vistas. It should harmonize the linear outline of structures with the contours of land, enhance unattractive areas, and use natural or natural-appearing construction materials. One of the most important problems of landscape esthetics are visual disturbances, the so-called eyesores such as junkyards, car graveyards, factories, power stations and opencast mines that detract from the visual enjoyment of nature. Even some tourist facilities, such as parking lots and trailer parks, could be regarded as eyesores. The best solution to this problem is to eliminate the visual disturbances entirely from the landscape, but this is not always possible. In such cases they should be screened by vegetation.

The design of facilities should adhere to the managerial capacities accepted for the site and to the access routes designated by the planning authorities. An important aspect of design is the enhancement of scenic beauty by the introduction of well-selected vegetation, appropriately laid out throughout the site.

The most vulnerable ecologically are picnic areas and campsites, because of their heavy use. Therefore, their design represents a considerable challenge to planners. The resilience of the site to human impacts and adequate drainage are of primary concern, but proper layout of facilities, washrooms, picnic tables, and tent pads may significantly mollify the impact. In this respect it is important to identify areas of heaviest use and to harden them. Hardening will contribute to still greater concentration of use, and therefore, it is not advisable in wilderness. In such situations woodchips are more appropriate. The pedestrian routes within the site should be functional and as short as possible. Hammitt and Cole (1987: 297) recommend a linear layout for campsites in densely forested back country locations in the northeastern United States. Dense vegetation, rock outcroppings, boulders and rough terrain can also be used to confine vehicular and pedestrian traffic. The selection of trees is also important with respect to their species and age, because tree regeneration on campsites is negatively affected by site use. Therefore, it is advisable to locate campsites in stands of relatively young, long-lived and disease- and insect-resistant trees. For this purpose Hammitt and Cole (1987: 287) provide a list of 27 southern Appalachian trees ranked according to their ability to withstand recreational impacts.

To assist planners in selecting appropriate locations for campgrounds, Mazur (1975) developed an index system of tree species most appropriate for campground location in the Canadian Shield portion of Manitoba: the idea was to avoid locating campgrounds on poorly drained soils. To achieve this, he used various tree species as indicators of soil moisture conditions. The color of soil helps to determine the moisture conditions: lighter colors indicate adequate aeration, and consequently good drainage, whereas darker colors are normally associated with poor drainage. To minimize erosion, campsites should be built on deep, moderately drained loams (Mieczkowski, Z. 1965). Fine-textured soils, such as clay and primary organic soils, should be avoided, because they drain poorly and tend to compact. Sandy soils drain well but are erodible (*ibid.* 1965). Nevertheless, they are frequently used for campsites where erosion can be avoided. As far as the organic soil components in the campsite area are concerned, care should be taken not to deprive the soil of decaying organic matter. For this reason, firewood should be provided to discourage collection in the adjacent terrain. Firewood collection is acceptable only in remote wildlands. Fireplaces must also be provided, not only to prevent fires, but to concentrate the fire impacts.

To avoid ecological deterioration caused by hiking trails, their design should follow certain simple rules. First of all trails should avoid environmentally vulnerable sites, such as those with seedlings and saplings. Also they have to leave unique or susceptible vegetation alone. If their use is heavy, various forms of surfacing may be considered. They range from gravel and wood chips to soil cement and paving. Trail layout should be designed to avert damage to vegetation and erosion, and to secure adequate drainage. Trails should be well defined with adequate width and a comfortable surface to ensure that the walkers are not tempted to stray off the trail. To further confine the hikers to the trail, rough terrain, boulders, rock outcroppings, dense vegetation, or fallen trees may be used. On slopes, trail design must avoid direct upslope routing: the change of elevation should be made as gradual as possible by the design of switchbacks. However, their number should be kept to a necessary minimum, and they should have wide turns that discourage hikers from cutting. Such barriers that compel hikers to stay on the trail can be erected to achieve this. Barriers can be natural, in the form of rough terrain, rock outcrops, boulders, cliffs, and/or dense, thorny bushes (like cacti in dry areas). The trail designers may choose to reinforce nature by piling rocks and encouraging the growth of appropriate vegetation.

Adequate drainage also encourages the hikers to stay on the trail, because to avoid muddy stretches, they invariably widen the trail. Therefore, a trail always should have at least a gentle slope between one and seven percent (Hammitt and Cole 1987: 291). On trails that traverse slopes the outer edge of the trail should be lower than the inner edge, creating a slight downhill gradient (outsloping) to allow proper drainage of the trail surface. To prevent accumulation of drainage on the trail and stop any ensuing erosion, wooden or rock bars to interrupt the flow and divert water are built across the trail at an angle not exceeding 40°. The angle should be fine-tuned to local conditions, decreased if erosion damages the trail, and increased to prevent sedimentation. The bars are to be placed at appropriate distances to stop water from gaining momentum. If the diverted water erodes the slope, ditches or rocks that dissipate the water energy are recommended. Some of the ditches may run parallel along the trail. To divert water off the trail in muddy places, one has to elevate it over the surrounding terrain (turnpiking) and secure these sections of the trail with rocks or logs. If necessary, culverts under the trail are advisable, although this is more expensive. For crossing small creeks, bridges constitute a more expensive but efficient option, especially if the banks are steep or erodible. However, to avoid bridging, a crossing may be arranged with stepping stones placed at an angle slightly downstream to minimize erosion.

Planners and managers are supposed to monitor use on extra-urban recreation sites. If the impacts turn out to be unacceptable, at variance with the goals and objectives of the management plan, then appropriate action should be taken. This means managerial reaction instead of the proaction envisaged by the plan. Thus the management strategies should correct environmental damage if things have gone wrong. The measures that can be taken are twofold: manipulating the visitors and/or the site. Both overlap to a certain extent, but generally in resource-based areas, such as wilderness, it is more desirable to manipulate the visitors than to manipulate the sites. The reverse can be said if one moves along the continuum of environmental modification towards user-oriented areas.

Visitor manipulation is the most effective method to minimize impact. It involves, first of all, education, information and regulation, especially important in view of increasing vandalism (see section 4.7). Provision of information (Ryan 1991: 125) and persuasion (Hammitt and Cole 1987: 209–210) at the site also contributes to behavior modification. A second management tool is entry restriction by means of regulation, either banning entry entirely or limiting it by quotas, licensing, permits, and entrance and user fees. To prevent environmental deterioration the management bans certain types of transportation, such as automobiles, or certain types of activities, such as riding ATVs, horseback riding, power boating or golf. The reduction of use, and thus the decrease of environmental damage, may be achieved by following management techniques: limitation of visitation by putting a ceiling on available parking spaces, permits and reservation systems, limitations to lengths of stay, directing the visitors to other, less vulnerable areas, allowing guided tours or other time-structured outings, prohibiting fires or requiring visitors to carry portable stoves, establishing appropriate entrance fees. Referring to fees, Satchell and Marren (1976: 74) examine "the demand curve for the whole recreation experience" regulating the demand. Some of these measures may also decrease vandalism (Wenger 1984: 830–832).

Management techniques are aimed at maintaining the site in the desired condition as established by planning. There is a wide range of maintenance methods, including engineering, applicable more to user-oriented than to resource-based areas. If the undergrowth vegetation is deteriorating as a result of use, or if the formation of a dense canopy of overgrowth impedes the penetration of sun rays, measures should be taken to thin the tree stands to allow the resilient grasses to grow (Edington and Edington 1986: 94-95). Frequently the application of "gardening" methods—silvicultural and horticultural treatments—may be advisable. The most appropriate measures consist of seeding, watering and soil scarification, especially in compacted areas and on gentle but not-too-steep slopes. Inorganic fertilization, although widely recommended in the literature, should be used sparingly. In my opinion, the introduction of chemicals into ecosystems should be avoided as much as possible. Nevertheless, research presents convincing results that the restoration of vegetation cover combining seeding, watering and fertilization brings about the best results (Hammitt and Cole 1987: 310–312).

"Gardening" is criticized by environmentalists for another reason: it runs counter to the process of natural plant succession (Satchell and Marren 1976: 15). However, allowing the plant succession to proceed in some recreation settings may be contrary to the planning goals for that area. Edington and Edington (1986: 86–93) argue that it may reduce the recreational value of land. Thus, they favor the management of moist grassy parklands, heather moorlands, and flower-rich meadows by allowing grazing ungulates, such as deer, or even domestic stock, to prevent succession to continue toward climax communities. Naturally, maintaining the vegetation at a desired successional stage requires strict monitoring of grazing levels. One has to remember that in other areas where regeneration of tree stands is desirable, domestic stock is a serious environmental problem, destroying tree saplings and seedlings.

Another method of checking plant succession is controlled burning (Satchell and Marren 1976: 80ff).

Another method of preventing the deterioration of vegetation cover involves changing the position of picnic tables. If the area is heavily affected by use and erosion, seeding or replanting with resilient grasses and other plants may be advisable. Some grasses, such as vetiver, undemanding in terms of soil and moisture conditions, provide excellent erosion protection. Bayfield (1974) reports positive results on antierosion measures undertaken in the Cairngorm skiing area, U.K.: reseeding of damaged ground, provision of drains and grading of dirt roads led to recovery unless the depths of debris that bury the vegetation exceeded 7 centimeters.

However, if all recovery measures fail in high-density sites or trails, and the deterioration of vegetation continues, one is compelled to resort to a rest-rotation method, by fencing the site, such as a campground, or closing a trail, and excluding use for several years to allow the site to recover. Paving is another alternative. This could provide another beneficial environmental spinoff: recreationists, such as joggers, like to use paved areas, and may consequently decrease their use of grassed parts of the site.

Monitoring constitutes an indispensable part of both regional and site management. It provides the necessary feedback for taking corrective measures. The literature, such as Wenger (1984: 836–838) Hammitt and Cole (1987: 213–241), and Satchell and Marren (1976: 128–129) provides excellent reviews of monitoring methodology and techniques. In my opinion, the GIS (Geographical Information System) is also a superb computer-based tool to detect any undesirable changes of sites resulting from tourist impacts.

9.6 *Planning and Management of Protected Areas*

Dispersed tourism takes place mainly in protected areas of our globe. This amounts to about three million square kilometers in 120 countries (WTO/ UNEP 1983: 23). These areas enjoy legal protected status, meaning that their ecosystems are safeguarded by legislation, control, regulation, and are subject to land-use policy. Thus, they are mainly under government responsibility. The degree and form of protection vary, but the most important stipulation is that such commercial extractive resource activities as agriculture, hydro-electric power generation, forestry and mining are excluded as much as possible. Tourism and recreation, however, are welcomed in most of these areas. The forms of nature protection include strict nature (ecological) reserves, wilderness areas, wildlife reserves, and most significantly, national parks and equivalent reserves. The sources of funding are ultimately the governments, i.e., the taxpayers, but, on balance, tourism already provides a more significant economic base for nature protection, a trend which will expand as financially strapped governments become increasingly reluctant to invest in the future, particularly when they face the more pressing needs of unemployment and poverty. Tourism and recreation in the protected areas are instrumental in mobilizing political support for nature conservation, as people learn to appreciate the significance of the ecosystems for the survival of life on our planet, and change their values towards quality of life.

National parks are the most important form of nature protection. There are now about 1,500 national parks among 7,000 nationally protected areas in 125 nations, covering about five percent of land on our globe. Most countries, including Canada which protects only 3.4 percent of her land, have to step up their efforts to increase their percentage of protected areas; on the other hand, such countries as Norway, Tanzania and Zimbabwe have more than 10 percent of their land under protected-area status (Canadian Environmental Advisory Council 1991). Costa Rica, with about 25 percent, boasts the highest proportion of protected land in the world. Its growing national park system alone, composed of national parks and seven biological reserves, encompasses 12 percent of the country. Each major ecosystem of Costa Rica is represented.

9.6.1 *International Level*

It is difficult to talk about planning and management at this level, because international organizations, including both intergovernmental and the NGOs, lack authority to enforce decisions. Certain goals recommended by international bodies may be instrumental in nature conservation. For example, the Brundtland Commission (World Commission 1987) recommended that, as one of the prerequisites to sustainable development, jurisdictions protect 12 percent of their land to maintain ecological diversity and preserve gene pools. As a result of this recommendation, many countries, such as Canada, have adopted it as a goal. Besides, inclusion on various international lists provide additional moral boosts and increased commitment to the cause of nature conservation in national parks and reserves. In 1967, the UN published the United Nations List of National Parks and Equivalent Reserves, and in 1972 UNESCO adopted the World Heritage Convention, concerned with the protection of the world's natural and cultural heritage. The criteria for inclusion of an area or site in the World Heritage List demand extremely high standards of outstanding universal values. Therefore, it is a great honor for a country to have its natural or cultural treasures adopted and kept on the list. The threat of loss of the prestigious status may be an important incentive to take appropriate action. For example, the overdevelopment of the resort of Banff (a town of 7,000 residents located within the boundaries of Banff National Park) and the proposed twinning of the Trans-Canada Highway within the park are black marks. Environmentalists argue that such conditions should disqualify the park from the list.

Despite the lack of authority, and because of the resulting inability to enforce international decisions, there are several examples of international cooperation in parks planning and management in contiguous park areas that are separated by international boundaries. The earliest example of such cooperation is the creation of the Pieniny-Tatra International Park on the boundary between Poland and Czechoslovakia (at present Slovakia), established in 1924 (Mieczkowski, Z. 1990: 268). In 1932 the Waterton Lakes-Glacier International Peace Park was established by Canada and the United States. Another form of cooperation is "park twinning," as between Canada's Ellesmere Island National Park and the Northern Greenland National Park (*ibid.* 268).

9.6.2 *North America*

National park systems in the United States and Canada are the best examples in the world of the symbiotic relationship between tourism and nature conservation. However, they are not without problems. Certainly many of them are the victims of their own success, and are affected by the onslaught of millions of visitors. Around 275 million tourists visited U.S. national parks in 1993, and the number is growing by about three percent annually. Since at least the 1960s, if not earlier, there is a widely accepted understanding that it is not enough to admonish the tourists to take nothing but photographs and leave nothing but footprints. Practically everybody comprehends that a *laissez-faire* policy in the parks is untenable, and planning, management, regulation and enforcement has acquired significant dimensions.

The experience of the last 30 years has led to the establishment of new philosophies and approaches to park planning and management, which may be summarized in the following set of recommendations. These are applicable not only to North America but to any country that has sufficient land resources to be designated as protected areas. Unfortunately, there are countries (such as in most of Europe) where it is too late to undertake preservation of large tracts of wilderness; they are limited to modest management of the remaining remnants of natural landscapes. Therefore, these recommendations are not applicable to the majority of protected areas in Europe (*ibid.* 269).

1. The preservation of ecosystem integrity is the paramount principle of parks planning (Woodley 1993). This means that science-based management should wield sufficient power to limit the scale and scope of tourism for the benefit of nature. As Woodley puts it: "Sustainable tourism must be seen in terms of sustainable ecosystems" (*ibid.* 92).

2. Parks should contain significant examples of the complete range of the nation's representative ecosystems, reflecting the diversity of all landscapes (national parks) and seascapes (marine parks). Canada, for instance, follows an ambitious plan for a protected system of representative and unique landscapes. Canada's natural regionalization, developed by the Canadian Environmental Advisory Council (CEAC), encompasses a hierarchy of terrestrial units, composed of 15 ecozones, 40 ecoprovinces, 177 ecoregions, and 5,400 ecodistricts. Parks Canada aims at establishing parks in all of its 39 natural terrestrial regions, which are almost identical with the 40 CEAC ecoprovinces, no later than the year 2000. The total number of new park designations will be 18 in the last decade of the twentieth century. New marine parks will also be designated to assure representation in all 29 natural marine regions until the year 2010. I see severe problems in the fulfillment of these ambitious plans. Canada is facing a prolonged period of budget restraints, and it will be difficult to find the amount of money needed to purchase and manage the huge areas necessary to supplement its existing park systems.

3. It is important to realize that ecosystems transcend the boundaries of the established parks. To support viable biocommunities they should be large enough: Canada considers only areas of 4,000 square kilometers or more as wilderness units. Therefore, as a priority, large units should be set aside to protect whole ecosystems. Smaller protected areas, such as ecological reserves or nature parks, play a supplementary role, "and

complement the major conservation reserves by protecting additional habitat types, or by covering regional variants of habitat" (Canadian Environmental Advisory Council 1991: 25). Landmarks and some national monuments protect specific natural features confined to smaller sites.

4. Because the park ecosystems are not self-contained areas isolated from surrounding lands, they interact with the adjacent ecosystems. Such interactions could perhaps be facilitated by creating bioregions, where the contact between different parks is made possible by protected corridors that allow wildlife and even flora to migrate and thus renew their gene pools and support viable populations. Every park is only a fragment of a larger ecosystem and this is why outward expansion of park boundaries, if feasible, is recommended. If such an expansion is not possible, the areas adjacent to the park should be included in some way into park planning because of the inevitable spatial interaction. In Costa Rica these buffer zones of private lands are designated as "zones of influence" and have local advisory committees cooperating with the parks service. The expansion of the national park boundaries should be accompanied by the designation of new parks, representing new natural regions or ecosystems. This should be vigorously pursued before it is too late.

5. Planning and management should be carried on not for isolated park units, but for whole park systems, even in such a large country as the United States. This approach facilitates matching the segmented tourism market with various parks, not only to the satisfaction of tourists and recreationists, but also to the benefit of nature conservation. For this purpose, parks should be classified into various categories, distributed along the Environmental Modification Continuum, ranging from relatively undisturbed and undeveloped wilderness ecosystems, called by Clawson and Knetch (1966: 36) resource-based areas, to completely changed user-oriented urban environments (Mieczkowski, Z. 1990: 258). In resource-based areas, the protection function is paramount, and the user-oriented areas are devoted to recreation. Naturally, there is a whole diapason of intermediate areas between these two ends of the continuum. Within this spectrum one may accommodate areas with such diverse degrees of protection as strict protection areas (called nature or ecological reserves in Canada); national parks and equivalent reserves; national monuments; managed wildlife reserves such as wetlands, refuges, sanctuaries; protected landscapes such as scenic rivers, trails,

recreation areas (many European national parks would fit in this category); biosphere reserves; and so on. In the North American context, wilderness and most national parks could be placed on the resource-based point of the continuum, while areas where multiple use is permitted, such as the United States national forests and some Canadian provincial parks, in the middle of the parks continuum. In such cases the preservation function is combined with use, including more intensive forms of tourism. Urban parks are located at the other, user- or facility-oriented extreme of the Environmental Modification Continuum. A similar classification, called Recreation Opportunity Spectrum (ROS) is used as a planning and management system by the U.S. Forest Service and the Bureau of Land Management (Wenger 1984: 806-810; Hammitt and Cole 1987: 188–201). This system matches various recreational activities with six desired settings: primitive, semi-primitive non-motorized, semi-primitive motorized, roaded natural, rural, urban. The North American national parks provide low-impact recreational opportunities in the first three settings, and their mandate does not lie in the sphere of the last three ones. This prompts me to suggest that national parks services of both U.S. and Canada should focus their expertise and funding entirely on the resource-based areas, emphasizing wilderness protection, and leave the restoration and management of old textile mills, houses, canals, battlefields and other historic sites to a different, independent agency (Mieczkowski, Z. 1979). Such a focus would facilitate not only better planning and management, but also benefit the cause of environmental conservation by promoting the creation of new parks and the expansion of existing parks. Purchases of land from private owners in areas adjacent to the parks to "round out" the parks and create more complete ecosystems would effect this.

6. As more people travel to the parks, there is a tendency to increase substantially the visitation of parks located at short distances from the metropolitan centers, whereas the remote parks do not register any growth in tourism (Baker 1986b). Baker points out that 90 percent of visitation is concentrated in one-third of the U.S. parks, mainly because of better accessibility and more developed tourist infrastructure. The response strategy to this trend is not necessarily to disperse visitation to the peripheral parks, but rather to create new parks and recreation areas with a certain measure of nature protection near urban centers. A good example is the Gateway National Recreation Area near New York City, where not only are there ample recreation opportunities for the urban

population, but also a surprising amount of wildlife and plant conservation takes place. The expansion of near-urban parks by acquisition of land should proceed at the expense of unused and abandoned areas. The United States Greenway Movement near the metropolitan areas may be of some help in this respect (Peterson 1992). Another strategy is dispersion of demand, i.e., directing people from most popular, and thus overcrowded units in the National Park System, such as the Great Smokey National Park or Yosemite, to less known and underused national parks and forests with good facilities. An analysis of the recent promotional campaigns in the media of the U.S. National Park Service reveals that some lesser known and remote historic parks and sites, such as the Sitka National Historic Park in Alaska, and Adams National Historic Site in Massachusetts, are being promoted. The U.S. National Park Service is also inviting tourists to diverse parks, less popular and remote from major tourist markets. These include Hawaii Volcanoes; Wrangel-St. Elias, Alaska; the Wind Cave, South Dakota; Isle Royal on Lake Superior; Canyonlands, Utah; Dry Tortugas at the western end of the Florida Keys; Petrified Forest, Arizona; and to national monuments, such as Montezuma Castle, Arizona, and Scotts Bluff, Nebraska.

7. An appropriate strategy to decrease tourism pressure on national parks is to provide acceptable substitutions outside the park boundaries by promoting user-intensive facilities, such as golf courses and swimming pools, and also by securing plenty of accommodation in the vicinity of the parks. The location of some attractions, such as wraparound movie screens showing nature films related to the parks should be welcomed in park-adjacent areas. A similar project to that was built by World Odyssey of Los Altos, California in Tusayan, Arizona, near the Grand Canyon National Park. All these near-park developments may divert a part of the demand for the parks. Facility-oriented tourists, who want to have high quality accommodation, good restaurants and lots of fun, are quite content with vicarious "nature" experiences and scenery as a pleasant backdrop for their vacation. Such a suggestion may sound

cynical, but it makes sense from the perspective of environmental protection.

8. Part of the demand for national park experiences may be diverted to lands assigned to the indigenous people for their subsistence, as multiple-use areas, where a measure of nature protection is combined with sustainable use of resources. In some LDCs such areas are called biosphere reserves.

Figure 9.6

THE RELATIONSHIP BETWEEN PRESERVATION AND USE IN CANADIAN NATIONAL PARKS

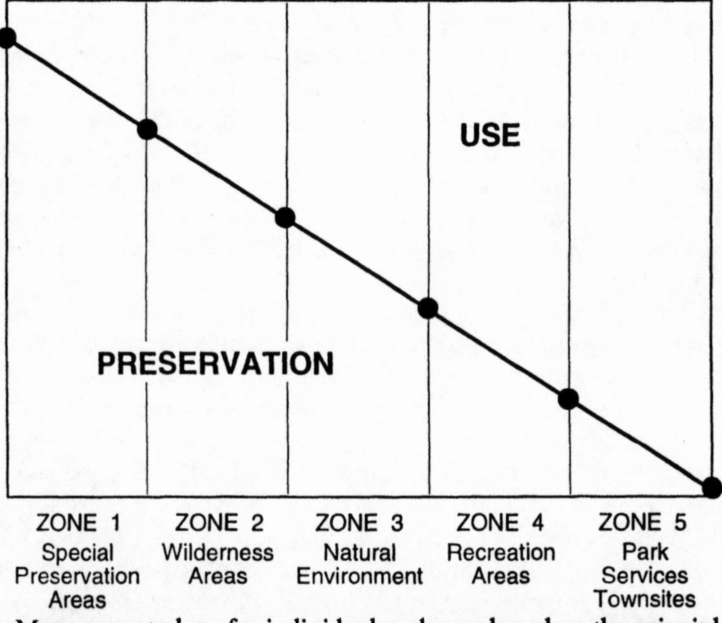

9. Management plans for individual parks are based on the principle of zoning, which follows the philosophy of Environmental Modification Continuum or the Recreation Opportunity Spectrum. The Canadian National Park Service applies five-zone classification for its land use planning (Fig. 9.6): Special Preservation Areas, with strict protection of unique, rare or endangered species; Wilderness Zone, with limited access and widely dispersed use; Natural Environment, with motorized access permitted at the periphery of the

zone and entry only at certain points; Recreation Zone, with a high degree of facility development and easy motorized access; and Park Services Zone, including townsites. Such an arrangement is aimed at separating various uses and associated impacts. Each zone requires different management techniques: the zones close to the preservation end of the spectrum protect especially valuable and fragile ecosystems (such as habitats of endemic animal and plant species), and need more regulation of low-impact tourism and less capital investment and site management. The zones at the opposite end contain ecologically less important and/or more resistant land, capable of withstanding high-impact activities; these should be as small as possible. Landals (1986: 95) recommends lodgepole pine stands for sites of intensive use in the Canadian Rockies. High-impact areas demand investments in visitor centers, campgrounds with full service, boat ramps, site hardening, vegetation management, provision of boardwalks, viewing platforms, handrails, and paved or wood-chip-covered trails. Sometimes even underground parking may be appropriate. The major aim of park zoning is first, to create the appropriate conditions for spatial conflict resolution by separating incompatible activities, and second, to establish the symbiotic relationship between tourism and recreation (not a relationship of conflict or even coexistence [Budowski 1976]).

10. Park management within park boundaries has to take care of management of the ecosystems. The management of the park eco-systems deals with such phenomena as fires. In this respect, the former fire suppression policy has been substituted by the let-it-burn policy. This prevents the accumulation of inflammable dead material and beetle infestation and allows the ecosystems of the parks to regenerate. This happened with Yellowstone National Park after its fire in 1988. A contentious issue is wildlife management. The question is how to cope with the inevitable population crashes resulting from total protection of some species, such as elk or bison. Excessive pressure of some species on their environment destroys the vegetation that supports other species. For example, overbrowsing of aspen and willow trees by elk eliminates the beaver populations in the riparian habitats. Thus the question arises: is the hands-off policy of minimal interference, in place since the 1960s, compatible with the mandate of the parks? Another set of problems arises in connection with the protection of endangered species. In this case, the controversial policy of captive breeding and gene-flow policy may be the only alternative to extinction. There is also a growing reali-

zation that the management strategy should focus not so much on the protection of individual species, but rather on ecosystem conservation. In this connection a difficult question arises: what is the optimal size of a park or reserve if species vary widely in their areal needs (Eldredge 1991: 216)? These are some of the problems the park wildlife managers have to deal with.

11. In terms of facility management, it is recommended to remove all non-essential recreational activities from the parks, as well as unnecessary facilities and services incompatible with the park mandate of conservation. The unfortunate legacy of the past left hotels, shopping centers, restaurants, bars, beauty shops, video-rental stores, automatic-teller machines, swimming pools, downhill skiing facilities, and golf courses within the boundaries of the parks. Unfortunately, the total removal of incompatible facilities is not feasible, but limiting their expansion is recommended. This pertains especially to townsites within the Canadian national parks, such as Banff, Jasper and Wasagaming.

To cope with these development pressures, a more restrictive policy regarding the concessionaires in North American national parks is recommended. In the present situation, they have too much power and, once the contract is signed, virtual 30-year monopolies on doing business in the U.S. parks. Companies managing concessions in the U.S. national parks pay only 2.5 percent of their receipts to the government; this amounts to unfair subsidization by taxpayers. When their contracts expire, every case must be reviewed on its merits. The general policy should be to raise the franchise fees and to shorten the contract periods, say to five years. All the catering buildings should belong to the U.S. National Park Service or Parks Canada.

12. Visitor management is another method to decrease tourist pressure on park ecosystems. The most obvious method of coping with overcrowding is to regulate the numbers of tourists by such measures as limiting access, limiting motorized traffic and providing public transportation. Such management tools as limiting parking space, camping reservations, and visitation quotas have been discussed in chapter 7. They are also subject to criticism, from the right by business, and from the left by opponents claiming that the restrictions "constrain working-class users" (Donnelly 1987). Bella (1987) would also like to see more tourist access to the Canadian parks for social and economic reasons, not to create profits but rather jobs, and to stimulate economic development.

13. Another approach to regulate the number of tourists is to levy entrance fees to public lands, including national parks. In the LDCs these fees, if paid by foreign tourists, should fully cover the costs, including environmental costs. There is no reason for poor countries to subsidize tourists from the DCs, as does Nepal, whose entrance fee policy was criticized by Michael Wells (1993). Wells writes that the park fees paid by foreign tourists cover only about 20 percent of the costs of running Nepal's national parks; only small amounts of that go to pay for nature conservation. The locals benefit little financially, while losing resources such as water and fuel to tourists. Therefore, Wells argues for raising entrance fees to Nepal's national parks and for more benefits to residents living in the vicinity of the parks. He also advocates more investment in nature conservation and management. In his article, Wells contrasts the negligent liberal Nepalese policy with that of Bhutan, whose government requires tourists from the DCs to spend a minimum of $200 a day, as opposed to the $32 voluntarily spent by foreigners in Nepal. Such an attitude seems reasonable considering the fact that foreign tourists visiting Nepal, spend considerable money for long-distance travel. They should also bear the full costs of ecological damage in the parks, pay for nature conservation, and compensate the locals.

The issue of national park entrance fees looks different in the DCs, and specifically in North America where there is no need for fees to fully reflect operating costs (including environmental costs). Here, most of the visitors to national parks are domestic tourists and local recreationists, i.e., national taxpayers. The benefits are spread widely among the whole nation, to both users and non-users of parks. Parks provide not only recreation and education for visitors, but also perform national and global environmental functions, such as conservation of biodiversity, purification of air and water, production of oxygen, and provision of opportunities for scientific research. Reasonable park fees create opportunities for modest-income visitors from nearby urban centers to enjoy nature. It is true that foreign tourists are subsidized by low park entrance fees, but they pay this subsidy back in taxes associated with their other expenses while visiting the country. North American national parks are also one of the main attractions for foreign tourism. If the federal governments complain about lack of funds to run the parks and want to increase park entrance fees, they should be advised to take a hard look at mining, logging, and grazing subsidies they grant to those who take huge profits from public lands but pay for natural resources far below market prices (see section 8.5).

Where tourism and recreational uses are a part of multiple use systems, as in the U.S. National Forests and other public lands, the user fees, according to Repetto, *et al.* (1992: 77–78), should reflect the consumer demand and the incremental costs of providing services. Due to present laws, the authority to change recreation fees, except for accommodation facility use, is severely limited. Therefore, the authors suggest charging differentiated but modest user fees. The National Forest Service estimates that collecting such fees would provide $5 billion revenue annually as compared to timber sales of $800 million in 1991. Thus, the introduction of fair user fees would radically reverse the present situation when timber sales substantially surpass the income from recreation. As a result, this would create incentives for the National Forest Service "to accord higher priority to recreational and environmental considerations in forest management" (*ibid.* 78) at the expense of the ecologically disruptive logging activity.

14. Dispersal of visitors over time decreases the impacts by diverting peak visitation from weekends and the summer season to weekdays, shoulder periods, and the off-season. Various methods may be used: fee differences, ads, allowing motorized traffic during the low-frequency periods and prohibiting it during peak times, and organizing special events. In contrast, one may limit or restrict the visitation during fragile periods, such as spring wetness of the soil.

15. In the United States, it may be advisable to upgrade some carefully selected national monuments and other lower-rank designations to the status of national parks. Such an action would improve the degree of environmental protection accorded to these units because the Bureau of Land Management which is responsible for national monuments, allows multiple use, and the National Parks Service which would take over, bars most consumptive activities within the national park boundaries. An important step in this direction was undertaken in 1994 when the House of Representatives passed the California Desert Protection Act, which prompted the expanded Death Valley and Joshua Tree National Monuments to national parks. The act also creates the East Mojave National Park (6,000 square kilometers).

9.6.3 *The LDCs*

Planning authorities in the LDCs face different problems than those in the DCs, and therefore, the issues have to be discussed separately. There are two areas of concern: designation and funding of new parks and the management of existing parks.

The goal of designation of new parks amounts essentially to setting aside lands for planned and regulated conservation of natural resources. This task is especially difficult in countries where the population explosion exerts continued pressure on the resource base. Additional obstacles are the indifferent, and sometimes even hostile, attitudes towards conservation on the part of disinterested governments and people, who are focused on immediate economic concerns. To overcome these problems, it is imperative that the DCs step in with their resources, not only to pay for putting the conservation measures into effect, but also to compensate the LDCs for the opportunity costs, that is, for the loss of income from logging, agriculture, cattle ranching, mining and other extractive activities. For this purpose a number of wide-ranging initiatives have to be taken.

One of the most important reasons for the inability of the LDCs to designate lands for conservation is their precarious financial situation: most of the LDCs and the former communist countries have accumulated billions of dollars in debt to the DC governments and banks. In order to pay these debts back, the debtor countries encourage environmentally destructive policies of short-term gain. However, it seems that the substantial part of the debts will never be paid back by the financially strapped LDCs. Consequently, there have been an number of proposals to reduce the debt. Defert and Pichot (1988) suggested paying for tourist services in the LDCs by special vouchers, credited to the host country's debt.

However, among all the methods to deal with environmental degradation and the debt problem in the LDCs, one has to single out as most successful and efficient the debt-for-nature swaps. This involves purchases of LDCs' debts in exchange for ecosystem conservation. These swaps create conditions not only for nature conservation, but are also a promise of future economic rewards, including income from ecotourism (see chapter 10). This represents an environmentally friendlier alternative to other economic development options, such as logging, mining, ranching, and agriculture. Only part of the areas involved are designated as zones of strict conservation; the rest is devoted to ecologically sustainable economic development. Permitted in forested areas are: hunting and gathering (including rubber tapping and wildlife farming), and controlled logging. In nonforested areas some sustainable ranching and agriculture is allowed (see section 3.5).

One of the early (1984) proponents of financing environmental projects in the debtor LDCs in exchange for their debts was Thomas Lovejoy of the Smithsonian Institute in Washington, D.C. Following his ideas, in 1987 a number of environmental NGOs, such as the Worldwide Fund for Nature (formerly World Wildlife Fund), Conservation International, and the Nature Conservancy, started buying out these debts from the creditors at a discount and swapping them with the debtor LDCs in exchange for setting aside nature reserves within their boundaries. A remarkable variant of the debt-for-nature swaps has been tried by Conservation International and the Worldwide Fund for Nature in Madagascar. The 1990 agreement was notable as the first to include not only bank debts but trade debts.

Probably the first debt-for-nature swap took place in 1987 in Ecuador. The Worldwide Fund for Nature purchased $1 million of Ecuador's foreign debt at a 65 percent discount. The dollars were changed into the local currency and used to acquire land for national parks. Almost simultaneously, Conservation International purchased part of the Bolivian debt for ecosystem conservation on almost 14,800 square kilometers in the Amazonian lowlands of the Beni River. The price has been deeply discounted: the agency paid only $100,000 for $650,000 of debt. The plan provided for appropriate zoning (protected core zone, forest zone for native hunting and gathering, and watershed forests for sustainable forestry and agriculture) and management of the area. An additional $1.5 million in debt was purchased by the Worldwide Fund for Nature from Zambia, Madagascar, Costa Rica and the Philippines to finance education, training and community projects.

A noteworthy example of debt-for-nature swaps is the case of Guanacaste National Park in northwestern Costa Rica. The natural ecosystem of dry tropical forest has been virtually destroyed, and scientists are attempting to restore it in an unprecedented ecological experiment. The ecosystems will regenerate for the most part naturally, but some seeding and seedling planting is conducted. However, the work is proceeding in a piecemeal fashion because only part of land is available: the rest, 395 square kilometers has to be bought from ranchers and farmers. The Nature Conservancy is attempting to raise $11.8 million for this purpose. The public is being asked to contribute through ads in the press.

The NGOs also used local currency for other purposes that benefit the debtor country: provision of infrastructure, environmental research and education, training of local farmers in environmentally harmless agricultural techniques, and training and hiring of local people as park rangers and tourist guides. An important task is to educate the local people to change their attitudes to nature and to teach them how sustainable development and conservation benefits them economically, in contrast to short-sighted predatory exploitation. There have even been suggestions to present conservation as an additional form of taboo for the Pacific island population (Marsh 1986).

The debt-for-nature swaps have been especially successful in such Latin American countries as Costa Rica, Mexico, and Ecuador, although many other countries, for example, Madagascar, Zambia, the Philippines, and the Dominican Republic have been also involved. As mentioned, even a former communist country, Poland, has joined the trend (Bajsarowicz 1993). It would be highly desirable to include Russia in the debt-for-nature swaps. This is desirable because of the importance of the huge evergreen taiga forests for their benefits to both the world climate and as a future economic resource, including tourism (Ilina and Mieczkowski, 1992). Unfortunately, Russian taiga, especially in Siberia and the Far East, is now suffering from the increasing assault of loggers, including South Korean companies licensed by the Russian government.

Regrettably, the governments of the DCs have not followed these private initiatives of the NGOs with similar actions in channelling a part of their credit assets in the LDCs, and even a part of their foreign aid programs, into the swaps. The first timid steps in this direction were undertaken by the Bush administration in 1991 (Passell 1991). However, there is one caveat that should be monitored: the governments may present these deals as packages which also contain provisions to open up the country to foreign investments. These could include environmentally inappropriate extraction of natural resources in some other part of the debtor country. As for intergovernmental aid agencies, such as the World Bank, there is the hope they will become involved in these deals, particularly as some of them have been criticized for financing environmentally unsound projects.

Another form of foreign aid for conservation is the direct provision of funds for setting aside sufficiently large areas for wilderness preservation. In some cases, like the Mbaracayu reserve in eastern Paraguay, such a course of action may be the solution if a government rejects the debt-for-nature swap for "sovereignty reasons." As a result of such a refusal, a coalition of various NGOs, headed by the Nature Conservancy, has purchased land for the reserve. Another example of such an initiative is the $12.4 million program funded by the World Bank in Mauritius (*World Press Review,* August 1991). In 1988 the government of Niger established the Air and Tenere National Nature Reserve, whose budget is 90 percent financed by the Swiss government, eight percent by Worldwide Fund for Nature, and two percent by a private group, Band Aid. The reserve not only secures the habitat of the addax, an endangered antelope, but also helps the local Tuaregs increase their incomes from tourists eager to see the wildlife, the almost 2,000-meter-high Air mountains, and 40,000-year-old rock pictographs (Brooke 1988).

Unfortunately, there are examples of DCs providing financial assistance to preserve ecosystems in the LDCs which should be evaluated as insincere publicity gimmicks (Jones, C. 1990). In November 1990, Japan paid Malaysia, the world's largest exporter of logs, a paltry $6 million for setting aside two large tracts of land for tribal use in Sarawak on Borneo, and for a vague promise, with no target date, to reduce logging by 30 percent. The plan looks like a tactical ploy to stop criticism for buying about 40 percent of Malaysia's timber exports and thus contributing to the devastation of tropical rain forests in that country. There also have been mixed reactions to the carbon-offset projects proposed by Maurice Strong, chairman of Ontario Hydro. On one hand, nature conservation and nature tourism would be enhanced if Ontario Hydro buys 12,500 hectares of tropical rain forest in Costa Rica for $10 million, to offset its carbon dioxide emissions (similar projects were proposed for Paraguay and Malaysia). On the other hand, the carbon-offset projects are only stop-gap measures. A better course of action would be to discontinue logging of old-growth forests and to cut out the carbon emissions at the roots by such measures as stopping subsidies for fuel industries, increasing the price of fossil fuels, and improving energy efficiency.

Providing free expertise on conservation and related tourism development is perhaps the most popular form of foreign assistance—it is certainly the cheapest among the wide range of options. Examples abound: the trip of a group of U.S. national park experts to Morocco (Baker 1986), the work of Parks Canada specialists and Canadian tourism development experts in the Caribbean, Botswana, western China, and so on, financed by the Canadian International Development Agency (CIDA).

One of the best methods to promote conservation in the LDCs is to interest the local population financially. As discussed in section 3.5, the creation and existence of national parks in the LDCs is often considered to develop with a total disregard of the poverty-stricken neighboring people. Locals are, as a rule, the losers when parks are created: they are displaced from the park area, and the economic benefits from tourism miss them almost entirely. This situation causes local indifference to the idea of nature conservation and can to develop into hostility. This is manifested by poaching, and other illegal use of parks resources, such as firewood collection, livestock grazing and clearing land for crops. Local dissatisfaction can culminates in attacks on tourists. Armed conflicts with park rangers and bloodshed seem inevitable.

Initiatives to create material incentives among the indigenous people and to modify their attitudes towards parks may take various forms, such as the direct infusion of cash for loss of land, annual payments, and salaries for such jobs as tourist guides, park rangers, porters, drivers, road builders, and hotel employees. Financing is also necessary for agricultural improvements, low-interest loans, schools and hospitals. The financial sources for these initiatives should be foreign aid and the income from international tourism. The benefits accrued from tourism create a partnership between parks and the indigenous people, and contribute to their cooperation in the efforts to protect the natural resources of the parks.

A concrete example of the locals benefiting from tourism income is the annual compensation received by the Masai from the Amboseli National Park, Kenya. An additional sum is paid to them for allowing wildlife to use their agricultural areas as migration routes. The most frequent form of financial compensation for the residents are payments for damages resulting from animal depredation on local crops, if the option of park fencing is financially impossible. A more recent form of reconciling use with conservation is by allowing the locals to extract some resources from the parks, such as grass, timber, and plants, as in the Royal Chitwan National Park, Nepal. Fuel collection, beekeeping and rubber tapping may also be allowed in the parks; in some cases limited and strictly regulated hunting on a sustainable basis is permitted (Machliss and Tichnell 1985), although the issue of hunting in national parks, discussed in section 3.5, is much more controversial. This moderate exploitation of the parks' natural environment could take place in the peripheries of the national parks or in their buffer zones. The core areas would be zoned as wilderness for strict conservation, according to the concept of "biosphere reserve." Naturally, more destructive activities, such as farming, cattle ranching, and logging should be completely banned, both in the parks, and their buffer areas. However, the Tropical Science Center in San José, Costa Rica, suggests that logging in tropical rain forests is harmless when conducted in narrow, elongated gaps of a few-meters width. This idea has yet to be tested.

It is advisable that some parks and nature reserves be created in cooperation with and/or for the benefit of indigenous tribes, such as the Yanomami, a tribe virtually untouched by modern civilization, who live in the Brazilian and Venezuelan tropical rain forests of the Amazon and Orinoco. They live off the tropical rain forests as hunters and gatherers in a manner compatible with the conservation of ecosystems. Therefore, the continued existence of the tribes makes sense not only from human-rights and cultural points of view, but also from the environmental one. In the early 1990s, after many years of abuse by governments and gold miners, a large area has been set aside for nature conservation and as a home for the Yanomami by both countries. Venezuela acted first in the middle of 1991 by establishing the Upper Orinoco-Casiquiare Biosphere Reserve, about 80,000 square kilometers in size (Brooke, J. 1991a). Not only are miners banned from this homeland for 14,000 Venezuelian Yanomami, so are missionaries. The Yanomami Park of over 90,000 square kilometers on the Brazilian side of the border in the states of Roraima and Amazonas, was established in late 1991, but it was not until March 1992 that the miners were forcibly expelled by the government. It is not clear if tourists will be allowed into these reservations. That matter is controversial, but tourist access could perhaps be allowed on a temporary basis. This would provide the Indians with income to pay for the opportunity costs of alternative uses and to prevent the Yanomami from selling the mining and logging rights of the area in the future.

In some instances setting aside land for conservation does not require aid from the DCs because the current income from tourism economically justifies such initiatives. An example is Guatemala, which in 1990 established a 10,000-square-kilometer Maya Biosphere Reserve in the northern part of the country. The reserve has been set aside to protect natural and archaeological resources and thus create additional incentives for tourists to visit the Tical National Park and other archaeological sites. Maya ruins are the main attraction for tourists, but these historical places were difficult to protect without conserving the surrounding tropical forests, including the largest freshwater wetlands in Central America. The preservation of Mayan ruins and the enclosing wilderness is the purpose of the Mundo Maya project, which includes not only the Guatemalan reserve, but also relevant parts of Mexico, Belize, Honduras, and El Salvador (D'Amore 1992: 260).

Similar international conservation initiatives, with significant tourist links, were undertaken by Costa Rica and Nicaragua in 1987. Both countries decided to create an international "peace park" in the tropical rain forest along the San Juan River. Much the same arrangement was made almost simultaneously between Costa Rica and Panama. Both biosphere reserves are composed of totally protected core area and surrounded by buffer zones of ecologically sustainable development, ranging from forestry to subsistence agriculture and environmentally friendly ranching. No international aid funding was involved in these projects because the respective governments understand that a sound environmental policy makes economic sense for all sectors, and especially for tourism. The authorities in the Caribbean act similarly: tourism helps finance the management of national parks, as in Guadeloupe and Dominica.

In terms of park management, the most severe problem in the national parks of the LDCs is the preservation of their natural resource base from devastation by loggers, farmers, poachers, and tourism overuse. There are innumerable tourism violations of park environments, such as the development of golf courses in the parks and nature reserves of Thailand. However, the major internal- planning problem of LDCs' national parks, is the ability to remain within the limits of their carrying capacity. Williams (1977) presents some relevant calculations for Zambia. The availability of 40 kilometers of game-viewing roads in the Luangwa National Park does not allow the accommodation capacity to surpass 200 beds, assuming a 60 percent occupancy rate, a maximum of six passengers per vehicle, an average speed of 20 kilometers per hour, and game runs of two hours. Thus, the density of tourist traffic is the independent variable that determines the capacity. Only such a capacity limit will guarantee that the interval between the vehicles is not less than two kms, and, as a result, there is no intervisibility. Williams also calculated the present maximum acceptable capacity of 7,800 tourists daily at the Zambian side of the Victoria Falls, given the present trail network.

Chapter 10

Ecotourism as a Form of Alternative Tourism

10.1 *Alternative Tourism*

There is no question that tourism/recreation represents one of the most environmentally-friendly alternatives for economic use of space: compare an oil refinery to a beach resort, a beef lot to a golf course, (even though a beach resort pollutes water and a golf course uses biocides and fertilizers). But these negative environmental impacts of *homo ludens,* as compared with those of *homo faber,* had been hidden during the "tourism—the smokeless industry" euphoria (see section 3.2), which ended in the 1970s, when the increasing criticism of conventional mass tourism (CMT) focused on its adverse ecological and sociocultural effects. The criticism has been not only about the qualitative character of the impacts but, primarily on the quantitative, specifically the huge numbers of tourists who descend on an area and degrade its ecosystems. These new realizations have developed in concert with the larger environmental movement—a movement that culminated in the 1987 report of the Brundtland Commission (see section 8.7). This report introduced the concept of sustainable development, defined as, "development that meets the needs of the present without compromising the ability of future generations to meet their own needs" (World Commission 1987: 43). As Arthur Hanson, the past president of the Winnipeg-based International Institute for Sustainable Development, puts it, sustainable development is based on the principle of "intergenerational equity," a principle of *not* mortgaging the long-term future for short-term gain. The caveat contained in section 8.4—that we are talking in terms of relative and temporary sustainability—(Ludwig, *et al.* 1993) bears repeating.

The Brundtland report has received an excellent response from around the world. It has been adapted to various economic sectors, including tourism. A definition for environmentally sustainable tourism could be formulated by paraphrasing the United States definition of national parks, as: management of the ecosystems to maintain their ecological integrity unimpaired for the enjoyment of future generations. Another definition of environmentally sustainable tourism identifies it as, a "form of tourism that supports the ecological balance..." (Edwards and Barks 1990: 266). Richard Butler (1993: 29) suggests "a working definition of *sustainable development in the context of tourism*...as: tourism which is developed and maintained in an area (community, environment) in such a manner and at such a scale that it remains viable over an indefinite period and does not degrade or alter the environment...." In other words, these definitions coincide with the model of the *symbiotic tourism* (Budowski 1976), which makes the conservation of ecosystems compatible with the development of tourism.

As a consequence of the realization that tourism is also an environmental culprit, social scientists have started to talk about different options to CMT, which for reasons of economy and convenience, has consistently increased its scale by the considerable expansion of package tours at the expense of traditional individual and family vacations. A welter of new terms has appeared to designate the "new" and "desirable" types of tourism, such as *alternative, appropriate, green, nature, discreet, simple, low-impact, low-density, small-scale, slow-growth, mollifying, soft, environmentally sound, nature-oriented, nature-based, environment-conscious, responsible, concerned, sustainable, special interest, educational, scientific, adventure, rural, farm, ranch, agri-tourism, wilderness tourism, sensitized tourism, and tourism with insight* (in German, *Tourismus mit Einsicht*) . The list is open-ended. Recently, the term ecotourism has become especially popular.

All these terms do not necessarily mean the same thing. In fact, there are significant differences between some of them, although there are many that are similar, for example, rural tourism, farm and ranch tourism. The common feature of such terms is that they are designed to suggest an attitude diametrically opposed to the "hard" and therefore "undesirable" *conventional mass tourism* (CMT). They attempt to minimize the negative environmental and sociocultural impacts of people at leisure by promoting radically different approaches to tourism. All of them have been put under the ambiguous umbrella of alternative tourism (AT) and are presented as the antithesis to CMT (Jones, A. 1992: 102). However, this term is interpreted in widely differing, and sometimes contradictory ways, by various authors. For example, Richard Butler (1990) understands alternative tourism (AT) as up-market package tours of rich people to exotic destinations, mostly wilderness areas, whereas Christoph Becker (1988) defines it as rucksack wandering by young people with limited financial means who stay with locals and (to a large extent) live off the land. In fact, as I argue below, both authors are correct despite the apparent contradiction.

Figure 10.1
THE ALTERNATIVE TOURISM

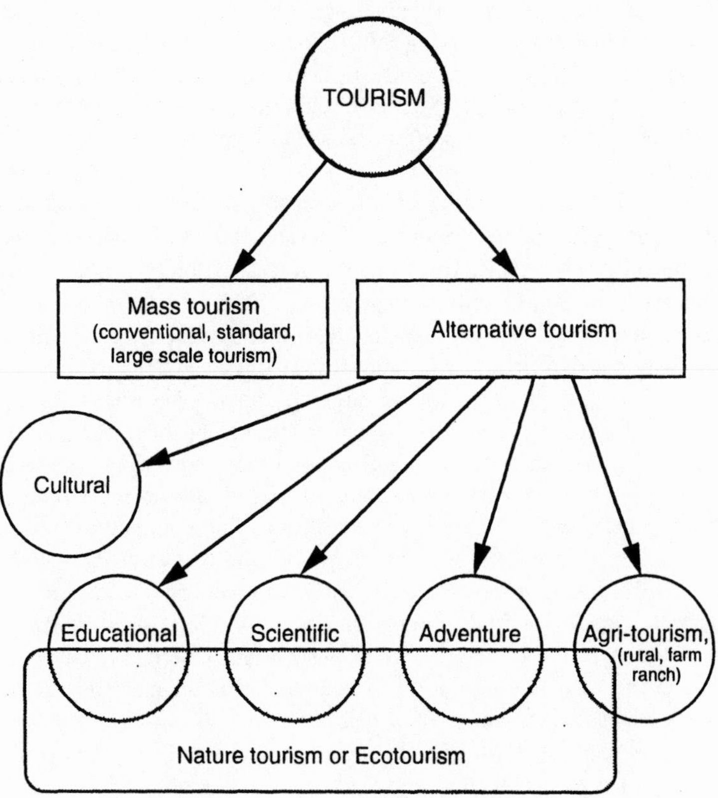

My solution to solve these terminological controversies is presented in Fig. 10.1. Tourism may be divided into two broad categories. The first is CMT, which has prevailed on the market for some time, and there is no indication that this situation may change in the foreseeable future. The second broad category is the alternative tourism (AT), a flexible generic category that contains a multiplicity of various forms that have one feature in common: they are alternatives to CMT. In other words, they are not associated with mass large-scale tourism; they are essentially small-scale, low-density, dispersed in nonurban areas, and they cater to special interest groups of people with mainly above-average education and with good incomes, although this category also includes the "explorers" and "drifters" (Cohen 1978) hiking on low budget through the land, or people spending their vacation on a farm. The participants in AT belong largely to the allocentric type of tourists (Plog 1987). They are generally well-informed, independent-minded, selective, looking for new experience and self-realization. Evaluating the differences between AT and CMT, one could arguably label AT socially elitist.

As to the specific forms of AT, I suggest to distinguish such forms as cultural, educational, scientific, adventure, and agritourism with rural, farm, and ranch subsets. There is some overlap with CMT (e.g., cultural tourism—see Smith and Eadington ed. 1992), but the criteria of distinction is the scale and the character (mainly scope) of the impacts. Another overlap occurs between various types of AT, for example, cultural tourism is to a large extent educational. The form of special interest for us is ecotourism, also called nature or green tourism. Ecotourism is nature-oriented and nature-based, but is not necessarily always practiced in wilderness setting. It is difficult to place ecotourism in the context of AT because, while not coinciding with cultural tourism (as explained in this book) it overlaps with the educational, scientific, adventure, and agritourism forms. Thus, one could say that a significant part of scientific and educational tourism (excluding, some forms like archaeology, and a smaller part of agritourism belong to ecotourism. The extent that adventure tourism be included is a contentious matter, and is discussed in section 10.2 below.

In connection with this classification, one has to emphasize that, although the AT has much better chances to be environmentally sustainable than the CMT, it does not have a monopoly on environmental sustainability. In fact, all tourism should strive to be environmentally sustainable, responsible, concerned, appropriate, and so on—an idea shared by most writers, including the authors of articles in Nelson, *et al.* (1993). In practical terms, this means that *all* forms of tourism, not only AT, should be planned, regulated, and controlled. This is the tourism imperative of our times.

Terminology aside, one has to realize that the forms of AT are not really new. (The Wandervogel movement, before and after the First World War in the German-speaking countries of Europe, is an example of nature-oriented tourism that developed parallel to mass tourism.) Alterative tourism is not a recent phenomenon. It has existed since the beginning of the modern tourism in the middle of the nineteenth century and probably even earlier—since at least the romantic period (Mieczkowski, Z. 1990: 53-57; Jones A. 1992: 102). Therefore, it is incorrect to claim that AT was born by the environmental movement. Rather, AT has been "reinvented" by environmentalists in the wake of growing nature awareness in our society. What is often suggested is to substitute the allegedly "perfect" AT for the allegedly "destructive" and "irresponsible" conventional mass form. I side with authors like Richard Butler (1990), who reject substitution as unrealistic. Mass tourism will stay with us probably indefinitely; Wheeler (1992: 104) predicts even megamass tourism in the future. The reasons are mainly economic: it is cheaper for the participants and it brings economies of scale and scope, profits for business, and, hopefully, also incomes for the local communities (Murphy 1985; Wilkinson 1989; Rostenow and Pulsipher 1979: 40-41), although the latter is frequently far from true. Thus, the problem is not in the substitution of one type of tourism for another one, but rather in mollifying, as much as possible, the negative effects of mass tourism (that is, making all tourism environmentally sustainable).

Two questions arise. Is it fair to place the blame exclusively on mass tourism? Is AT really as harmless to the environment as people think? On the surface, AT appears to be and probably is, more environment-friendly than CMT because it involves less facility development and the participants are more likely to stay in small, mainly locally-owned hotels and budget accommodations, such as campgrounds, or rent rooms from the locals, including bed-and-breakfasts. They use more low-impact, non-motorized and/or public means of transportation, such as the autobus and the railroad. They are also more likely to walk, use bicycles, cross-country skis, canoes, and boats as means of transportation. However, in exotic areas with difficult access, alternative tourists may use high-tech and expensive means of transportation, such as helicopters, while remaining environmentally conscious of their surroundings.

Despite the nature-friendly features of AT, there is no guarantee its impact on the environment will be minimal. In scholarly literature, the misgivings about the alleged benefits of AT as compared with mass tourism are growing. For example, Richard Butler (1990) presents a critical view of some economic, sociocultural, and environmental impacts of AT. Indeed, AT cannot be regarded as harmless to the ecosystems. As indicated in section 9.4.2, the negative impact of dispersed tourism that spreads to new environmentally and socio-culturally fragile areas, may be greater—especially in the long term—than the effects of spatially concentrated and isolated, but frequently well-planned CMT enclaves, pejoratively called tourist ghettos. There is also a danger that some local AT forms may change in time into mass tourism if the demand for previously undeveloped destinations gets out of hand. (In this connection Butler [1990] indicates that to reverse this process, that is, to convert CMT into the alternative forms, is unlikely). Unfortunately, there are many reports about alternative tourism getting out of hand. (*Der Spiegel* 1991 24: 218–226). Therefore, ascribing all the virtues to these alternative options and condemning the CMT as undesirable is a dangerous simplification. As stated previously, the problem is to make all tourism sustainable and environmentally conscious, not to substitute one of its forms for another. Moreover, despite the recent significant expansion of AT, it does not seem that this sector will ever play a commanding role on the market. Jarviluoma (1992: 120) says: "Alternative tourism will always be a fairly minor aspect of international tourism and can never replace conventional mass tourism."

Interestingly, in recent years many LDC actively discourage participants in some forms of AT, such as low-budget rucksack wanderers. They increasingly aim at upmarket clientele to maximize their tourist incomes and minimize the adverse environmental and sociocultural effects. A good example is Bhutan, which allows only expensive package tours into the country (Weiner 1991). Butler (1990: 42) calls such policy "a disguised class prejudice." From the social point of view this approach is elitist; however, from an economics point of view, it is an example of rationing by the purse, and is generally acceptable.

In conclusion, there are two important points to consider:

1. All forms of tourism will exist side by side; each plays an important, albeit different, role in the total tourist spectrum, and each has to find its niche in the segmented markets, as well as in the plethora of destinations through the process of supply and demand being matched along the Continuum of Environmental Modification or Recreation Opportunity Spectrum (Mieczkowski, Z. 1990: 145–201; Jarviluoma 1992). Both CMT and AT are situated at the extremes of these spectra, and should remain there. Indeed, there is a trend to specialize. Policy decisions to change the rate and scope of tourism development should be taken on the merits of a specific case, while the decision-makers and planners should focus their attention on the proper spatial and functional relationship between various forms of tourism at the national, regional, sub-national, and local levels. In certain places, such as in Dominica, AT may be the only choice for tourism development because of the lack of resources for CMT (David Weaver calls this "circumstantial AT"). In other cases the decision to limit tourism to its alternative form may be the result of deliberate policy. For example, Weaver (1991; 1993) argues that following the stage of the "circumstantial AT," the Dominican authorities at present pursue a policy of the "deliberate AT."

In light of this argument, the attempts to convert CMT into AT are not desirable from all points of view. We cannot expect everyone to become an alternative tourist—this would have disastrous social and ecological effects. Therefore, there is no reason to increase the marketing efforts for AT to the detriment of CMT. In fact, the development of AT should be monitored, and deliberately limited, if a threat exists that it may evolve into CMT. However, everyone can move along the Recreational Opportunity Spectrum, not only at various periods of their lives, but even during the same trip (see "add-on" tours in section 10.2). In other words, the same person may engage in both CMT and AT at different times. Thus, instead of hoping that the "new" AT can substitute for the "old" CMT, one should hope for long-range educational influence of AT on CMT. This is the subject of point two.

2. It is important to maximize the educational impact of AT on mass tourism (section 8.3). Such a scenario is entirely feasible, and is discussed with respect to ecotourism, which is a form of AT. But without a decisive change of attitudes and values in society as a whole, without respect, appreciation, and care towards nature, AT's influence on CMT will be minimal. Each small step spreading the sustainable tourism

gospel is a success (such as the establishment of special programs in "ecological tourism" at the University of Costa Rica [Farrell and Runyan 1991: 33]). Still, in observing case studies, one has no problem concluding there is a lot to do (Becker 1988) in this respect.

10.2 *Ecotourism*

According to Elizabeth Boo (1991) the concept of ecotourism emerged from the conversion of two modern trends. The first, on the supply side of tourism, is a trend towards integrating conservation with economic development (that is, promoting the economic viability of parks and nature reserves, especially in financially depressed LDCs). The second trend is associated with the qualitative changes in demand. People are becoming less interested in passive vacations, and want to be active travellers to new destinations, including remote exotic places. In comparison with preceding generations they are more interested in nature and its conservation, and they are likely to be informed and educated. This explains the high rates of growth of green tourism all over the world, and especially in certain most attractive areas. As a result of the merger of the two trends, ecotourism has become a powerful financing tool for nature conservation. The popularity of this term has grown to such an extent that it is used as a buzzword even in politics. For example, the Liberal Party of Canada, in its Red Book (the blueprint of its 1993 election campaign), pledged to develop and promote ecotourism, without spelling out any details.

Ecotourism is a nature-based and nature-oriented form of AT. Other equivalent terms are "nature tourism" or "green tourism." It mainly involves such "environmentally soft" activities as hiking, trekking, nature observation, and nature photography. However, there are some disagreements as to its scope: some researchers include not only nature but also human-made cultural elements, such as archaeological, historical, and anthropological resources. The following two definitions illustrate this approach:

> "Ecotourism" is used to mean tourism based principally upon natural and archaeological/historical resources such as birds and other wildlife, scenic areas, reefs, caves, fossil sites, archaeological sites, wetlands, and areas of rare or endangered species. It differs from mass tourism based upon man-created attractions such as night clubs, restaurants, shops, amusement parks, tennis, clubs, etc. or partially

man-created such as beach front hotels and associated manicured beaches (Kusler 1991: xii).

"We define ecotourism as that segment of tourism that involves travelling to relatively undisturbed and uncontaminated natural areas with the specific object of admiring, studying, and enjoying the scenery and its wild plants and animals, as well as any existing cultural features (both past and present) found in these areas" (Kusler 1991: xii).

There is disagreement among the writers regarding the exclusion of sociocultural elements in ecotourism. For example, Gauthier (1993: 104–105) favors such an approach, while Scace (1993: 63), writing in the same volume (Nelson, *et al.* ed. 1993), regards "cultural heritage experiences" as belonging to ecotourism. The World Tourism Organization (WTO 1993: 21) advocates the inclusion of cultural heritage attractions in remote areas. This implies visiting the anthropological attractions as part of ecotourism. I do not accept the inclusion of human-made elements in ecotourism. Consistent with the approach of this book as to the term "environment" is its meaning of only natural environment, excluding sociocultural and economic elements. Ecotourism should be exclusively reserved for nature tourism. Certainly, there may be an occasional overlap between ecotourism and cultural tourism, for example, historical/ archaeological sites in remote areas in Guatemala or Honduras, where some exposure to nature experiences is involved. Too wide an interpretation of green tourism, however, creates a huge grey area that may be disputed. For instance, is a day excursion from Cancún to the Maya ruins in Chichen-Itza considered to ecotourism? In my view, it is not, but according to the above definition, it is.

Ecotourism overlaps with several types of tourism, such as educational, scientific, adventure, and agritourism. The principal criterion classifying a tourist activity as ecotourism is that it takes place in a natural environment. Given this, not all types listed above should be classified as ecotourism, exclusively. Among them, probably only scientific tourism belongs almost completely to ecotourism, and therefore, deserves special attention. Scientific tourism is a form of ecotourism that helps to preserve the environment relatively undisturbed. The worldwide interest of individuals or groups visiting various ecosystems under the leadership of highly qualified scientists has been increasing for some time (Ilina and Mieczkowski, Z. 1992; Arefyev and Mieczkowski, Z. 1991). Environmentally, this is tourism at its best, because the participants belong to an ecoconscious category of tourists. The benefits of scientific tourism are not limited to saving ecosystems from degradation, however. Tourists gain: by being in touch with nature, they learn to appreciate nature and the importance of conservation. With the improving educational levels of tourists and growing sophistication of contemporary tourism, scientific tourism is increasingly becoming a way for people to spend their leisure time. And in the process, they are becoming conservationists. An interesting example of tourism's alliance with environmentalists was the dispute between the Israeli army and conservationists, supported by tourists, for nature conservation in a canyon in the Negev desert popular with hikers (*New York Times* 23 November 1989).

Another problem determining the scope of ecotourism is associated with adventure tourism. Some types, for example, the bungee jumping from bridges or rap jumping from overhanging cliffs, sport mountaineering, orienteering, hand gliding, horseback riding, white-water rafting, and kayaking, remain outside the scope of ecotourism because they are not authentic, intimate, and meaningful quality-encounters with nature based on scientific, educational, esthetic, and philosophical considerations. They also lack the nature conservation element that is an integral part of ecotourism. These activities are challenging sports within the framework of adventure tourism, but not ecotourism experiences. One could argue about the difference between adventure tourism and ecological tourism. Adventure tourism is in the grey transitional area, where the decision of whether or not to include or exclude a particular activity remains a rather subjective matter. Some scuba diving and most windsurfing in exotic settings could be evaluated as only adventure sport activities, but not as ecotourism, because they are based on the technical aspects of sport skills and lack the elements listed above. I suggest that adventure tourism is inward-looking, self-centered, and a personal challenge to a participant to conquer nature; it is, to a large extent a hurried experience oblivious of the surrounding nature. These features set adventure tourism apart from ecotourism, which is an outward-looking, nature-oriented, contemplative experience that the participant seeks to preserve, not for the benefit of oneself or the ecosystem visited and possibly for the advantage of the whole world.

Without a precise definition of the term ecotourism, however, a meaningful statistical analysis of this type of AT is difficult. In practice, though, the situation is simple: any tourism in a natural setting is classified statistically as ecotourism, even if it is associated with large-scale mass operations and harmful environmental impacts. This is the reality of which I am critical. I regard such an approach as an abuse of a trendy catch term, aimed at increasing profits of the tourism industry that is so eager to benefit from the market trend seeking new vacation experiences. The tour operators want to capitalize on the boom in "eco-tourism," which is growing at about 10 to 15 percent annually, in contrast to a more modest figure of 4 percent for mass tourism (Lindberg 1991: 20). Ecotourism transfers $25 billion from the DCs to the LDCs (Whelan 1988). Thus, to maximize profits, the term "ecotourism" is widely used and abused in promotional campaigns, advertising tours, and activities that actually do not belong to this type of tourism.

The organizational framework of ecotourism relies either on profit-oriented private ecotour operators or nonprofit NGOs. Responsible private sector participation should not be discouraged, but there is a trend among environmental NGOs and nonprofit educational institutions to increase scientific and educational tours to the LDCs. In addition, foreign NGOs in the LDCs have recently shown a tendency to substitute for the financially strapped public sector in a number of initiatives in protected areas (Boo 1990). In fact, many nature reserves in the developing world exist only on paper because of the weakness of national and local government agencies that are supposed to take care of them (Wallace 1993). Therefore, the NGOs tend to substitute for them. This is an development that results from the financial exigencies of these countries, but one should never forget that only the government agencies can provide long-term planning and management as well as legal and police protection of nature reserves for the benefit of future generations. The NGOs lack the power of enforcement, and this is especially important in the LDCs that face growing demands for land for their exploding populations. Therefore, financial means for such agencies as national park services have to be found, and the obvious source is the income from ecotourism. In certain cases foreign aid money could also be used temporarily.

The forms of ecotourism are either individual, "do-it-yourself" (popular in the DCs), or group, including package tours (prevalent especially in the LDCs). As ecotourism is a part of alternative tourism, its operational framework is the same (see section 10.1), that is, it includes, as a rule, small-scale facilities which differ among each other in terms of intfnsity and impact. The low-impact ecotourism is based on minimal general and tourist infrastructure and relies mainly on local resources thus creating higher economic multipliers and fewer leakages than in the CMT. This type of nature tourism is normally associated with more benefits to the local community than those provided by CMT, a circumstance especially important for the LDCs. Accommodations are for the most part modest, food is simple, and transportation is largely limited to nonmotorized means; motorized transportation is restricted as much as possible. The energy sources are often environment-friendly, such as solar or wind power, more by necessity than by design.

Most ecotourists do not mind a degree of hardship to enjoy the extraordinary nature experience: physical rigors are not a deterrent factor. This circumstance is linked with the disputed issue of the level of expenditures. In this respect, ecotourists represent a continuum from Cohen's "drifter," who spends little money, to travellers in remote areas whose expenditures are high although the services received may be modest. What they all have in common is a commitment to spend more if need be to achieve their goal: communion with nature with minimum impact.

The low-impact emphasis in ecotourism is typical for domestic destinations in the DCs, but it is also increasingly practiced in the LDCs. However, the low-impact solutions may not entirely suffice in certain remote locations in the Third World. Here some degree of comfort, such as air conditioning, and more sophisticated means of transportation, such as helicopters, may be essential to cover large distances devoid of infrastructure. These necessities may be supplemented by nonessential luxuries, such as swimming pools and other facilities that may be considered as high-impact despite their small size. Butler's (1990) critical attitude of luxury ecotourism is completely justified.

Most people involved in the tourist market in the DCs are not receptive to the rather modest travelling conditions used by ecotourists. Therefore, to tap potential demand as efficiently as possible, even among the mass "beach tourists," the tourism industry often resorts to offering the "add-on" feature of several days of nature tourism in addition to the standard beach vacation, (Boo 1991: 10-11). Sometimes the package is composed of two parts of about equal duration: for example, one week of shopping, visiting night clubs, and enjoying an elegant hotel and a beach. The other week is spent in the wilderness.

The "add-on" variant has been practiced in places such as Kenya, Costa Rica, and the Yucatan Peninsula in Mexico.

Ecotourists engage in nature study such as bird-watching (the champion among ecotourism activities), nature study, wildlife photography, and the study of marine ecosystems while snorkeling or scuba diving. Ecotourists may be found practically anywhere in the world: from excursions starting with trips to view white seal pups at Iles de la Madeleine, Canada in March, and "wolf tours" in various parts of Canada, to boating and hiking in tropical rain forests in Amazonas. However, the wilderness is the preferred arena for this type of AT. (Section 10.8 is devoted to the world distribution of ecotourism).

10.3 *The Positive Record of Ecotourism*

From an ecological point of view, ecotourism deserves accolades. Its environmental record is sound, not only in theory, but also in practice. Ecotourism is a form of tourism that is associated with empathy between tourism and environment, a real symbiotic relationship with minimal negative impacts. Thus, the World Wildlife Fund investigation reported only minimal environmental problems at all park study sites (Boo 1990).

As indicated, ecotourism is basically a low-impact form of tourism because of its small scale and the activities involved. The participants are motivated by the trends in environmental awareness, health consciousness, and mental and physical challenges of the close-to-nature vacations. They are also, as a rule, better educated than the average population. This is especially true with respect to the scientific tourists who want not only to learn, but also to research nature, understand its functioning, and consequently treat it with respect. All these features lead to the conclusion that they adhere to the principles of environmental ethics because they understand nature and are concerned with the fragility of the ecosystems.

The environmental awareness of ecotourists contributes to nature conservation in other ways, too. Some may act as "informal rangers" who, according to Boo (1990: 22), prevent poachers from killing the animals and provide "information to park managers concerning encroachment into the park, poaching of wildlife or collection of flora, deforestation, or changing ecological conditions, such as fires." Others organize special groups of paying participants to work on various projects such as land reclamation, as in the case of the restoration of derelict land left by open-pit coal mining at Maritsa-Iztok in Bulgaria, which was supported by the Earthwatch (*New York Times* 28 June 1992), or cleanup operations in Japan and Nepal. Some dedicated ecotourists remove litter from protected areas; the most publicized in this respect being the Mount Everest cleaning expeditions, mentioned in section 6.4.7. German ecotourist scuba divers remove garbage from the coral reefs off the Maldives and fly it to Germany for proper disposal (*Die Zeit* 24 October 1994). Assisting scientists in their research, provided by Earthwatch, is yet another form of ecotourism's contribution. Additionally, some ecotours, such as the sightseeing of the area of the oil spill in Alaska's Prince William Sound or tours to the nuclear wasteland of Chernobyl, could be called deterrent trips.

Some ecotourists join protests and lobbying movements organized by conservationists, against wetland destruction and elimination of wildlife, or against logging, mining, or dam construction in unique ecosystems. For instance, Farrell and Runyan (1991: 34) mention the cooperation between conservationists and ecotourist organizations to prevent the clear-cutting of Douglas Fir in British Columbia. Ecotourists also cooperate with environmentalists to prevent the encroachment of destructive activities on valuable ecosystems and support the environmental NGOs in promoting the creation of new parks and nature reserves.

The quality of ecotourism is enhanced by the increasing participation of the NGOs, such as Earthwatch, National Audubon Society, Nature Conservancy, World Wildlife Fund, Sierra Club, Smithsonian Institute, and various wildlife societies, as well as universities, museums, and research centers. These institutions are getting involved directly in the organization and the conduct of ecotourism programs, ecotours, and field courses. In all these ventures, the cause of nature preservation instead of profit is paramount: in fact, many of the ecotours are nonprofit. However, in recent years, as the government grants for research become more scarce in the DCs, the financially strapped scientific institutions have been viewing ecotourism as a source of research funds. Nevertheless, the function of nature preservation is not compromised.

As for the hundreds of private tour operators who specialize in ecotourism (see section 10.7), they have always been profit-oriented, but overall their environmental record does not look bad, especially compared with the CMT enterprises. Most ecotourism operations are small and not volume-oriented, since by their very nature they deal with small groups of tourists and generally observe environmental ethics, both in terms of minimizing the environmental impacts and in employing qualified scientists as guides.

Ecotourism has an outstanding record financing environmental conservation. The ecotour operators make donations to conservation organizations such as the World Wildlife Fund, or contribute financially to the preservation of unique ecosystems. For example, one ecotour company acquired 48 hectares of land (less than half a square kilometer) to enlarge Costa Rica's Monteverde Cloud Forest Reserve (Young 1986). Still, the direct financial contribution of ecotourism companies to the conservation projects (Weiner 1991), including the purchase of land for conservation, seems to be modest in comparison to multimillion dollar debt-for-nature swaps, or gifts from private foundations, such as the $1 million gift from the Chicago-based Arthur Foundation to purchase land for expanding Costa Rica's Braulio Carillo National Park by 204 square kilometers (Young 1986: 362). Nevertheless, even these small purchases should be appreciated as important contributions.

Some publicly owned ecological reserves are underfinanced to such an extent that, paradoxically, they are impeded in performing the important function of nature conservation. Such a problem is encountered even in Costa Rica (Boo 1990) where ecotour operators, such as Horizontes, help to pay salaries of national park rangers because the government has no means to do so and the parks are understaffed. Ecotourism may also render financial assistance by gaining converts to the environmental cause among the tour participants, some of whom may contribute money to green projects either during or after the tour. An additional incentive may be the tax deduction, frequently associated with donations to environmental causes.

Another way ecotourism finances conservation is through the payment of user fees. Kostyal (1992) gives an example of a tour operator who offered a fee to the owner of a forest in Indonesia in exchange for the right to bring expeditions to view a species of the bird-of-paradise threatened with extinction. The owner accepted the offer although he had a tender from a logging company on the table. The resource was saved in the name of the long-term ecological benefit. Ecotourism often serves as an antidote to poaching when poachers are hired as anti-poaching guards, park rangers, park naturalists, tourist guides, cooks, and porters. Becoming concerned about the economic value of wildlife, the locals learn that live animals are much more valuable than dead ones. Western (1982) estimates that, on an annual basis each lion in the Amboseli National Park in Kenya accounts for an income of $27,000. Philip Thresher (1981) computed that a male lion could attract $514,000 in income from foreign visitors during his lifetime as a ecotourist attraction compared to $8,500 as a trophy, and that an elephant herd represents $610,000 annually in tourist revenue. Western contrasted Amboseli's estimated net value for wildlife viewing it as $40 per hectare, with the potential agricultural output estimated optimistically at only $0.80 per hectare. Boo (1990: 16) quotes the results of other research comparing the annual income from park wildlife with the income from potential beef production from the same area. The count was 18 to 1 in favor of conservation. Ceballos-Lascurian (1991: 27) cites the case of the Virgin Islands National Park, United States "which earned an estimated tenfold annual return in benefits over investments." Tobias (1991) computed the recreational value (visitation by ecotourists) of one hectare in the Monte Verde Cloud Forest Reserve at $1,250, while the price the reserve is currently paying to acquire new land is between $30 and $100 per hectare. Tobias suggests that the expansion of the area protected by the reserve is "a well-justified investment." He emphasizes that the recreational value of standing forest is but one of its potential benefits. The total value of conservation reaches beyond the revenues from ecotourism—according to Tobias, it includes "benefits from renewable harvests of many commodities, biological diversity, ecological services, and sites for scientific research." These values are difficult to quantify but they contribute significantly to the benefits of ecotourism. Indeed, the value of live animals is not only higher than that of the dead ones, but protecting whole ecosystems for ecotourism constitutes, in most cases, an economically superior form of land use.

To fully realize the positive aspects of ecotourism, economic cost and benefit studies have to be conducted comparing it to other development options. Johnson (1986) presents a calculation comparing the local economic benefits of ecotourism in the South Moresby National Park, British Columbia, with the benefits of logging. Ecotourism is the clear winner. Laarman and Perdue (1989) analyze the economic impact of low-spending but long-staying eco-researchers associated with the Organization for Tropical Studies (OTS) in field stations in Costa Rica.

The revenues for the local economy are considerable (two to three percent of national tourist receipts), and they constitute an efficient alternative to other resource use. Furthermore, the OTS indirectly generates additional tourism income "by laying a technical-scientific base for management of Costa Rica's national parks and other wildlands" (Laarman and Perdue 1989: 29).

Similar examples of ecotourism paying for nature conservation abound. In many places of the world the turtles, once slaughtered by the locals, are now doing well and draw paying green visitors, as in Costa Rica. In Belize the once-hunted howler monkeys today are housed in the Bermudean Landing Sanctuary and are visited by tourists. The survival of lemurs on Madagascar would be unthinkable without ecotourism saving their ecosystems threatened by logging. In certain carefully selected cases, especially in sub-Saharan Africa, one has to compromise and agree to a measure of sustainable multiple use within the national park boundaries, combining consumptive uses, such as controlled hunting, firewood collection, and grazing, with ecotourism.

The protection of nature in conjunction with ecotourism also involves important external economies that are rarely taken into account. For example, the Parc National des Volcans, Rwanda, has not only provided an income of about $1 million a year in entrance fees and $9 million indirectly for the local economy (Lindberg 1991) and saved the mountain gorillas from extinction, but also protected the watershed from agricultural encroachment. Additionally, for the debt-ridden national economy of most LDCs the income from ecotourism means injection of hard currency, economic diversification, and jobs in the poorest peripheral regions of the country, where most protected areas are located.

10.4 *The Potential to Increase the Benefits*

Researchers unanimously agree that the potential economic and environmental benefits of nature tourism for the local communities in the LDCs are inadequately realized. Many LDCs underestimate the capability of ecotourism and still rely too much on traditional forms of tourism. This situation is changing slowly, and projects that encourage nature tourism are beginning to be promoted. Even if these countries embark on new policies, things do not necessarily work out as they should because of the slow reaction of government bureaucracy. This is not unexpected considering the relatively vigorous expansion of ecotourism in some LDCs, which are overwhelmed and cannot create appropriate organizational frameworks, especially in terms of channelling the benefits to the local communities.

Despite these positive contributions of ecotourism to environmental conservation, there is room for even greater potential. Indeed, the contribution of ecotourism to nature conservation could be more effective if the financial arrangements were more direct. Unfortunately, according to Lindberg (1991), this is not always the case. "Most protected areas around the world are maintained with allotments from national government budgets; related entrance fees, concessions, and taxes go into the general government treasury" (*ibid.* 5). Thus, in some cases the fate of the ecosystems depends more on the goodwill of the public sector than on the income from ecotourism. If the government has other priorities, the environment will suffer. Therefore, Lindberg advocates earmarking the income derived from ecotourism to pay directly for not only the management costs of national parks, but also to compensate local residents for possible losses of other income and for losses resulting from wildlife predation. This arrangement keeps the revenue within the park and in the local community system and avoids its transfer to uses unconnected with the park. Increasingly, such solutions are being implemented in many countries.

Lindberg also advocates price mechanisms and quotas to limit the number of tourists and maximize revenues. A substantial part of ecotourism destinations are endowed with brand rather than generic appeal, characteristic for most of CMT, and therefore pricing is efficient not only in controlling demand but also in increasing park incomes. In practical terms, it would mean increasing entrance fees for foreign park visitors, which are now, as a rule, too low (the Tortuguero National Park, Costa Rica, charged about one dollar in February 1994) or nonexistent (there is, by law, no entrance fee to New Zealand's national parks). In contrast, domestic visitors in the LDCs should pay modest fees, thereby making the parks more accessible to local populations, and giving them the opportunity to appreciate nature. In fact, it seems that the single-fee structure commonly used should be substituted by a two-tier or even a multi-tier system. Such a system would allocate the use of parks not only more equitably, but also allows for maximizing badly needed revenues, by taking advantage of the monopolistic "scarcity rent" of unique resources of such parks as Galapagos, Ecuador. Since late 1994, foreign tourists already pay much higher entrance fees than domestic visitors. In some cases the entrance fees are substantial: the

Parc National de Volcans, Rwanda, charges visitors a day entrance fee of $170 for the privilege to view the mountain gorillas (Weiner 1991). Part of this fee pays for anti-poaching patrols. Some may regard such costs to the tourists as elitist, discriminating against potential visitors with modest finances, but there is no question as to its practical benefits for the environment and for the people of Rwanda. Other potential revenues include a special conservation tax levied by hotels, guide services, and a souvenir trade at the parks.

The practical benefits of ecotourism vary around the world. They are generally positive in Rwanda and Dominica (Boo 1990: 9, 38). On the other hand, often the potential benefits are not being tapped; for example, when direct cash flow to the host community is inadequate (Place 1991; Boo 1990). There are several reasons for this. First, there are few places where tourists can spend money in national parks. Visitor centers, gift shops, snack bars, and lodges are often simply not available. Second, rich national and international entrepreneurs often reap the profits, leaving few jobs for the locals. Place (1991) investigated the Tortuguero National Park, established in 1975 in northeastern Costa Rica. She came to the conclusion that the inhabitants of Tortuguero village, situated on the outskirts of the park, have been inadequately compensated for the ban on the use of the park's natural resources. She concluded that beneficiaries from ecotourism are limited to only a few persons. My visit to Tortuguero in February 1994 convinced me that the situation has improved in terms of job creation as compensation to the locals for the loss of resources following the establishment of the national park. Boo (1990: 37) gives several examples of parks unable to stop encroachment of destructive nontourist land uses, such as mining, agriculture, and firewood collection, on their territory because they cannot offer alternative sources of income. Another criticism is poor management of the parks, caused mainly by their underfunding. The results are an underpaid personnel, low morale among rangers, lack of trained guides, poor maintenance of the trails, and lax law enforcement.

To make ecotourism a viable economic alternative for the local population (following the logic argued in section 3.5) the cooperation of residents is needed, especially in the long range. Enforcing laws is a questionable matter if the locals are hostile because they have been excluded from the benefits of setting aside land as national parks or nature reserves. Therefore, to gain their support, creating adequate economic incentives for them is imperative. One cannot escape the opportunity cost calculation of the conservation efforts. This calculation is more likely to support the conservation argument if ecotourism is drawn into the equation. The locals will not only participate in, but actively defend, the conservation cause if they are convinced of its economic advantages over resource utilization. Such an argument is easier to win when market conditions of price instability and worsening terms of trade for exporting commodities, such as cocoa and coffee, and mining products, such as copper are low, compared to the skyrocketing costs of imports of technology and manufactured goods.

Local populations should be regarded as allies of ecotourism in their conservation efforts. Other potential uses of pristine ecosystems may contribute to preservation as a superior economic alternative to their destruction by logging, mining, and agriculture. As mentioned earlier, nature is the source of medicine and other valuable substances that may be removed from the wilderness without any damage to the integrity of the ecosystems. An example of such an action is the Collaboration Agreement between the Instituto Nacional de Biodiversitad (INBio) in Costa Rica and the United States pharmaceutical corporation Merck & Co. Inc., based in New Jersey. In the preamble to the agreement the partners state that, "INBio is interested in collaborating with private industry to create mechanisms to help preserve Costa Rican conservation areas by making them economically viable." The agreement took effect on 1 October 1991 and had by 1994 provided close to $2 million for nature conservation (the Costa Rican Ministry of Natural Resources and the National Park System are the beneficiaries), staff training, research (University of Costa Rica), and royalties, which are being reinvested by INBio in biodiversity research. INBio is responsible for "the collection and processing of plant, insect, and environmental samples for evaluation for pharmaceutical and agricultural applications" (INBio-Merck & Co. Inc. Agreement 1991, San Jose, Costa Rica). A similar arrangement is the 24-square-kilometer Terra Nova Forest reserve created in cooperation between the government of Belize and a group of traditional healers. The reserve is intended to protect plants used in traditional Indian medicine.

10.5 *The Negative Aspects of Ecotourism*

Despite the praise for ecotourism and its potential, there is no lack of criticism of its environmental practices, nor a guarantee that the standards of environmental ethics will be followed. Ecotourism may eventually mutate to ego-tourism, and "sustainability" may refer to sustaining the business and not the environment (Wheeler 1993: 127). "Sustainable tourism" could evolve into tourism, "which lasts for a long time" (Butler 1993: 138). As mentioned in section 10.2, ecotourism and adventure tourism are often used by unscrupulous promoters as trendy catch words, as a green cover, to denote any place set in an attractive natural setting. Some of the advertising methods are reminiscent of flyers for clearance sales in department stores: "Hurry! Visit a pristine area before the paradise is gone. Come today or you will be too late." This approach is happening more and more frequently (Garcia 1989: 185). In these instances, unsuspecting tourists may believe they are contributing to the benefit of ecosystems, when, in reality they are being drawn into CMT to a far-off and little visited destinations, where there is total disregard for nature. The term "ecotourism" often serves as an alibi for the intensification of pernicious social and ecological impacts. Ecotourism, when used in this way, may be more harmful for the environment than CMT, especially if it is allowed to operate outside the constraints of controls and regulations imposed on other forms of tourism.

The negative impacts of ecotourism may manifest themselves in two forms: (1) the quantitative aspect of overcrowding and (2) the qualitative aspect of ecological degradation. Although the vast majority of ecotourists are environmentally educated, nevertheless some do abuse their environment. But even well-behaved ecotourists constitute a threat to nature by their sheer numbers. An example is the Galapagos Islands (discussed in section 6.2.3.3 and 9.4.3), where in recent years the number of cruise ship visitors has exceeded by about 100 percent the government limit, recently increased from 20,000 to 25,000. According to Elizabeth Boo (1990), the official visitor count figure of 32,000 is incorrect.

Another example of ecotourism "gone awry" is the behavior of tourist guides on Caño Island Biological Reserve off the Pacific coast of Costa Rica. To provide tourists with "milk" from the Vaca (Cow) trees, the guides make a deep cut into the tree. The damage makes the tree susceptible to disease. When confronted, a guide told me, "I can usually get away with this." Indeed, law enforcement by the Costa Rican national park system is weak: Off-shore the island, the fishing trawlers do not respect the three-kilometer fishing ban and fish just few hundred meters from the coast. Ecotourism is environmentally unsustainable and should be put under control.

Still, criticisms of ecotourism are exaggerated, if not entirely false. As such, Buchwald and Dilger (1989) regard scientific tourism as a cover for western imperialism in the LDCs, surely a judgment that has strong "politically correct," but weak factual, underpinnings. Buchwald and Dilger condemn past and present scientific researchers in the developing world as agents working for the DCs. The authors resent the preponderance of European languages, and especially of English, in scientific publications, and the monopoly on exploitative collection of data and other materials, including artifacts, displayed in DC museums. Even debt-for-nature swaps do not find their approval because western scientists who work for western NGOs (which, in turn, depend on DCs' political and corporate donors)—decide which land is to be protected. This, in their view, compromises the whole undertaking as a method to increase the capitalistic exploitation of the LDCs. As well, the authors believe that attaching economic value to protected ecosystems makes it easier for DCs to penetrate the developing world's environment (*ibid.* 50).

Interestingly, nature tourism is associated with quickly growing costs to the taxpayers. In interviews, various officials, including national park rangers, expressed their concern with the ever-increasing costs of irresponsible and/or inexperienced tourists looking for challenges in the wilderness, mountains, or on water. The costs to taxpayers can be in the millions of dollars. For example, in the Yosemite National Park the cost of search and rescue operations was $1,284,000 in 1991 and $1,135,000 in 1992 (*Time* 14 June 1993). Diverting park resources, such as rangers and helicopters, from other services and uses (such as enforcement of regulations) to search-and-rescue operations can add to the cost. To reduce the costs to the taxpayers, various methods aimed at making the tourists responsible for potential search-and-rescue operations are being considered or enforced. Among them are obligatory insurance, posting bonds, and license fees. Costs can also be lowered if tourists observe safety regulations and officials enforce the rules.

10.6 *Measures to Minimize the Adverse Effects of Ecotourism*

Measures to minimize the adverse effects of ecotourism should include some kind of licensing, or at least an official "green rating" by the World Tourism Organization or some highly respectable NGO. Perhaps the Virginia-based Ecotourism Society with membership that includes ecotour operators, conservation professionals, academics, and the tourism boards of several countries, will develop such a listing. Before that can be done, however, standardized criteria need to be established. Some have already been published. An eight-page list of lodgings, ranked on the basis of guidelines for sustainable tourism, was compiled by the Department of Responsible Tourism (part of the Institute of Central American Studies, a private NGO based in San Jose, Costa Rica). Also, there is a book by Evelyn Kaye (1991) that includes listings of hundreds of United States organizations selling ecovacations all over the world, selected according to the following criteria: strong commitment to environmental ethics; a history of concern for the environment; offering programs that abide by environmental rules, and whose leaders are qualified naturalists, environmentalists, scientists, or professionals in their field. The ecotour operators mentioned in the book must also have several years of successful operation documented by letters of recommendation from former participants, and provision of adequate information about the tours. A European example of a critical review of German ecotour operators is provided by Yorn Kreib (1989). He approvingly cites a cancellation of mountain gorilla trips to Zaire by a German tour company because of inadequate local environmental arrangements by the operators associated with the corrupt Mobutu regime.

Another way to curb the abuses of green tourism is to develop guidelines. Although most tour participants are well behaved, tour operators should recommend books and other relevant handouts, including the National Audubon Society's "Traveller's Code of Ethics" (Ingram and Durst 1989; Kostyal 1992), environmental guidelines issued by the American Society of Travel Agents (ASTA's Ten Commandments on Ecotourism—WTO 1993: 142), and any other specific instructions. Usually, these materials are provided free of charge prior to the beginning of the tour. In some especially fragile regions, particularly strict regulations of behavior for both tour operators and participants have been adopted. An example are the guidelines of the International Association of Antarctic Tour Operators (*Tourism Intelligence Bulletin,* October 1991). Special free courses are offered as workshops for scuba divers in Bonaire to teach them how to avoid physical contact with coral reefs by proper buoyancy control, and advice for boaters how to avoid damaging the reefs by using permanent moorings (*New York*

Times 27 October 1991). Ecotourists are also actively involved in information campaigns, urging other tourists to observe, for example, the ban on spearfishing and on collection of corals. The ecotour operators in the Lechuguilla cave in New Mexico insist tourists wear special sneakers into the cave so the delicate rock formations are not destroyed.

Blangy and Nielsen (1993) conducted a survey of 60 ecoguideline sets developed by various groups and for different areas. They found the following:
1. There are substantial differences in the emphasis of the guidelines according to the criterion of who issued them (guidelines' originator). In this respect the authors distinguish between five types of organizations: environmental NGOs, tour operators, public land managers, churches or religious communities, and outdoor equipment stores.
2. The guidelines differ according to the specificity of the area concerned.
3. There are two types of guidelines: (1) do's and don'ts for the public and, (2) codes of conduct for the organization.
4. Guidelines that are also law can be enforced.
5. Most guidelines are friendly recommendations and advice.

The authors then suggest eight strategies to improve the effectiveness of guidelines.

10.7 *Ecoenterprises*

An interesting and controversial spinoff associated with ecotourism is the eco-enterprise, aimed at profiting from the growing biofilia, from the appreciation of the environment, and from the interest in the beauty of nature. In fact, while preserving the ecosystems from mining, logging, agriculture, and ranching, many ecoenterprises create a direct cash flow to the local community. Their products are mainly local or exotic plants and animals catering to internal demand or to foreign markets. However, some of the eco-enterprises do not sell anything; they cater to visitors. Some do both.

The first category of ecoenterprises follows the contentious practice of selling animal and plant products to places that are only minimally extent tourism-related. Environmentally they have certain merits because in some cases they preserve specific ecosystems that otherwise would be free for agriculture or other uses. Ecoenterprises may also contribute to the gene pools for some endangered or threatened species. However, as I argue below, the record of this type of ecoenterprises is not entirely positive from the ecological point of view.

The most important subset in this category of ecoenterprises is animal farming, which has experienced a spectacular expansion all over the world. The list of animals raised on these farms is almost open-ended—bisons, elks, elands, pheasants, and fur animals, to name a few. In North America, game farming and ranching have spread in the western part of the continent. For example, Colorado has game ranches that derive their income not only from hunting, but from selling venison and velvet antlers for the Asian drug market (*Economist* 31 August 1993). Buffalo (bison) ranching is also popular because the meat tastes good and contains more protein, fewer calories, less cholesterol, and less fat than beef or chicken. At present, there are about 150,000 bison in the United States raised on almost 1,000 ranches, in reserves, and on Indian lands (*Economist* 30 April 1994). There is also a potential for future buffalo hunting. Ranching iguanas, practiced in Costa Rica and Panama, provides more meat per hectare than cattle. Iguana meat is regarded as a delicacy and, unlike cattle raising, iguanas do not destroy tropical forests. Turtle breeding is well established in some areas, such as the Dalyan Delta nature reserve in southwest Anatolia, where this development option has been decided upon instead of the construction of a hotel *(Der Spiegel* 1988, 32: 78–79). Michael Robinson (Wolbarst 1991: 150–152) suggests a number of other forest animals for farming, such as the ostrich farms I visited in Zimbabwe and South Africa.

Part of the income of animal farming comes from visitors (entrance fees, souvenir shops, and so on). Additionally, some game ranches are open to hunters of big game, and, increasingly, fowl such as ducks and pheasants.

Animal farming in recent years has been subjected to severe criticism by environmentalists. The primary concern is that animals are taken from their natural environment to replenish stock at the ranches. Animals that escape are another concern—imported sick animals may spread disease among wild species. Exotic animals from faraway places may result in hybridization or displacement of indigenous animals. Clearly, developing a policy regarding game ranching will be controversial, but the demand is growing. In the United States, state governments already have started regulating the game ranching. Internationally, the CITES rejected at its March 1992 meeting in Kyoto the Chinese attempt to register a tiger farm (*Economist* 14 March 1992).

Interestingly, wildlife farming includes not only mammals, but also butterflies which are arguably the only insects loved by people, and reptiles—which are feared alive but loved as raw material for shoes and handbags. Butterfly farms are popular in tropical and subtropical areas, such as Papua-New Guinea, South and Central America (the leader is Costa Rica), Thailand, and Florida. There is no manipulation of the tropical forest ecosystems. The ecosystems are saved from destruction by other resource uses, although special small "gardens," often protected by a net enclosure with "appropriate" plants, are being established directly in the villages or in the core area of the farm to decrease mortality and to encourage breeding of certain prized species of butterflies.

Young (1986) reports that in Papua-New Guinea (PNG), "farming" tropical butterflies with large brilliant wings (a wingspan of up to 30 centimeters) and giant beetles, is bringing income to about 500 small villages. (A pair of butterflies with a 30 centimeters wingspan may be sold for $850. Some villagers are earning $1,200 annually, a significant boost compared to the former average of $50 annually.) As a rule, government agencies are responsible for instructing villagers in insect ecology, and providing equipment and other information. The Insect Farming and Trading Agency, a PNG government enterprise, purchases the insects from the villages, and exports them to collectors, museums, schools, universities, and manufacturers of jewelry, wall ornaments, and inlaid coffee trays and tabletops in various DCs, mainly in Japan and Taiwan.

Butterfly cooperatives are common in the poorer, less-developed countries such as PNG, while in more advanced LDCs, like Costa Rica, the butterfly farms are run by privately-owned companies. A good example is the La Guacima farm on the Central Plateau, Costa Rica, which receives about $6,000 weekly from exporting butterfly pupas. Additional revenue comes from ecotours of the farm. Between 20 and 25 people work as guides and restaurant and gift shop staff (February 1994). La Guacima by cooperating with ecotourism contributes to the local economy and saves the tropical forest from other uses, such as logging and farming.

Butterfly farms do not modify the ecosystems. Even if they did, the International Union for the Conservation of Nature and Natural Resources (IUCN), a United Nations affiliate, does not condemn slight modifications of wild habitats to increase their output, making the conservation more economically feasible. According to Tudge (1991: 7), "it supports schemes in Papua-New Guinea to plant extra food trees in the forest, to increase the population of large, colorful butterflies of the kind favored by tourists."

Crocodile farms are especially lucrative economically. The animals are housed in pens located in park settings. Thousands of tourists visit these farms (in South Africa and Zimbabwe, in Florida, Cuba, and Thailand). Their impact on the survival of the species in the wild may be negative because poachers of wild crocodiles may misrepresent their trophies to prospective buyers as provided by the farms.

Plant farming is another subset of tourism-related ecoenterprises. Costa Flores, the "world's largest tropical flower farm," Costa Flores, located on the Caribbean coastal plain in Costa Rica, on 117 hectares of a park-like setting, employs 150 workers and exports $30,000 worth of flowers daily by air to North American and European markets.

Some ecoenterprises do not sell products—they sell tours and other services. Most of the protected areas used by ecotourism are owned and operated by public agencies. However, Boo (1990:42) draws attention to private protected areas in the LDCs that cater to nature tourists. Her evaluation of these places is positive, citing high-level environmental consciousness, and small-scale, yet reasonable user fees (in contrast to the chronically low or nonexistent fees at public areas). She also gives them credit for local job creation, good management, and minimal leakage. "In all examples observed during the study, local participation in these types of tourism development was greater than in many public protected areas" (*ibid.* 42).

Private nature reserves operate on a strict commercial basis, combining environmental preservation with economic gain. In some cases, the profits earned by the reserves have benefited not only the local communities but also have been used to purchase additional land for the existing reserves, or to establish new reserves (Alderman 1990: 33). In fact, the number of privately-owned nature reserves is rapidly increasing, especially in Latin America. This is a positive development, since many government-owned national parks and other reserves have inflexible policies regarding development. Wright (1993: 5, Fig. 1) gives low marks to profit-oriented ecoenterprises for their high impact and low-local involvement. Many ecoenterprises, however, and especially private reserves, are environmentally responsible.

Private reserves play an important role in ecotourism:

1. They supply tourist infrastructure, especially accommodation and food facilities, outside the publicly owned parks.
2. They provide expertise in scientific interpretation and guiding services, as well as in marketing ecodestinations because of their often substantial marketing budgets (Alderman 1990: 15).
3. They increase the areas "set aside" for nature preservation, and supplement the governments' conservation efforts.
4. Because they are frequently located at the fringes of national parks, they are effective buffers for the ecosystems in the national parks, against external impacts, such as logging, poaching, and expansion of agriculture.
5. Their location adjacent to national parks increases the protected area of park and, consequently, contributes to the biodiversity and improves the effectiveness of species preservation.
6. Most owners are more interested than government agencies in maintaining the ecological integrity of their enterprises—to safeguard the quality of tourist experience and ensure the continued success of their venture. Still, government regulation is essential because some have a short-sighted quick-profit perspective.
7. They create jobs. According to data collected by Alderman (1990: 64) for reserves located in Latin America and sub-Saharan Africa, each thousand visitor nights generated between 32 and 40 employee months. More local jobs are created by private reserves than by the government-managed national parks because they are more interested in providing fuller and better services than the government. This circumstance, in turn, improves the economic viability of the conservation option because the local population is adequately compensated for the loss of other economic opportunities (opportunity costs). In fact, 84 percent of the permanent employees of the private reserves surveyed by Alderman (*ibid.* 16, 64) were from the local community. In some cases economic viability is the condition for the very survival of the reserves, especially in the case of Africa, where the land scarcity puts pressure on governments to use the reserves for agriculture instead of for nature conservation (*ibid.* 48). In cases when an ecologically valuable private reserve is in financial trouble the conservation NGOs should provide aid.
8. They provide recreation and education (*ibid.* 42).

Private ecoreserves can be divided into various categories according to three criteria. The first is ownership and management. Ownership can be by individuals (or groups of individuals) or by NGOs. Individual ownerships are managed as normal businesses, that is, for profit. The second group is more complex because NGOs are nonprofit (their first reserves were supported by membership fees and donations). However, recently there has been a trend toward financial self-sufficiency because of the demand for accountability.

The second criterion is the type of activities in which the reserve is engaged. Some are devoted entirely to ecotourism (including education); some combine research with educational ecotourism, and some blend ecotourism with economic activities similar to those practiced by animal farming (that is, selling products).

The third criterion is the size of the reserves. In this respect, Alderman's materials *(ibid.)* are convincing. The African reserves are larger than their Latin American counterparts. In fact, some of the Latin American reserves are very small (the Bosque Lluvioso bordering from the northeast the Braulio Carillo National Park in Costa Rica, is 170 hectares). Despite its small size, I was positively impressed by the scientific tourism experience the reserves offers— excellently preserved virgin tropical rain forest, carefully designed trails, and a high-quality guided tour. Part of the operation consists of a former grazing range, which is presently undergoing restoration. First-rate restaurant and tourist accommodations take care of the visitors, and their dollars provide jobs for the locals. The farm is open for scientific research. Thus, following this logic, the scientific researchers are ecotourists.

10.8 *Regional Distribution*

Ecotourism is unevenly distributed throughout the world. There are several reasons for this. First, an area must have abundant and/or unique resources. Political stability is another condition. In addition, a location close to markets and with a cooperating government is instrumental. Most of the DCs, and particularly those in North America, fulfil these requirements. Australia and New Zealand, however, are far from the world tourism markets (with the exception of Japan). Their remoteness may turn out to be an asset, preventing ecotourism in the two countries from evolving into CMT.

Figure 10.2

KEY ECOTOURISM AREAS IN DEVELOPING COUNTRIES

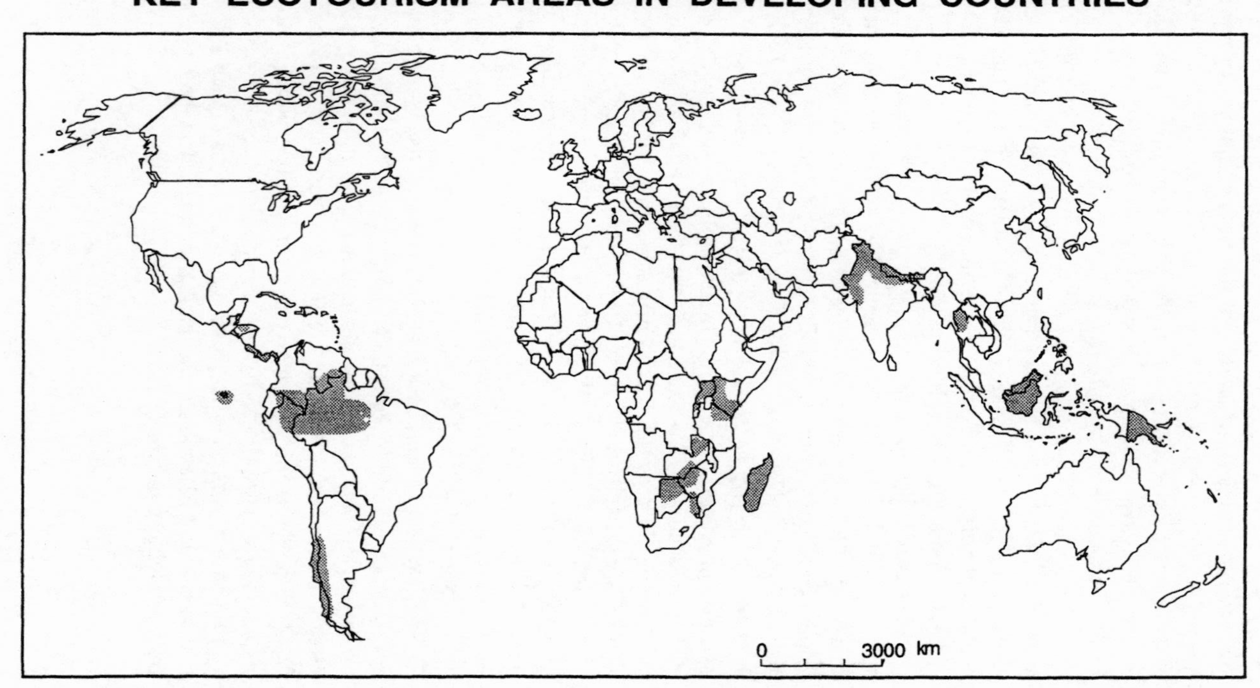

In North America, the outstanding national park systems of the United States and Canada, and other government-owned lands offer impressive opportunities for ecotourism that are adequately used. There are also several nongovernment initiatives. The Nature Conservancy is attempting to finance a 146-square-kilometers tract of tall grass prairie near Pawhuska, Oklahoma. Here, ecotourists can see the restored American landscape. (*New York Times* 19 October 1993).

Recently, however, much more attention is being paid to increased nature tourism in the LDCs (Fig. 10.2.) There is recognition of the extraordinary biodiversity of the LDCs ecosystems, the economic importance of their resources, and the significance of tropical rain forests for the health of our planet. The development of ecotourism is the optimal path to safeguard these values by minimizing negative environmental and cultural impacts. Ecotourism represents the best development alternative for many LDCs because of their environmental fragility, and in view of the past negative experience with CMT. And, from a purely economic point of view, ecotourism, agriculture, logging, and mining may offer the best development option for wilderness areas (see section 3.5).

In the Americas, Belize boasts large rain forest areas and the longest barrier reef in the Western Hemisphere (almost 300 kilometers in length and is an important eco-destination. Nature and marine reserves have already been established by the government. The Bay Islands of Honduras are also developing ecotourism. However, the ecotourist champion in Central America is the politically stable and resource-rich Costa Rica. Its national parks, wildlife refuges, and nature reserves bring more than $300 million per year in foreign exchange from ecotourism. In fact, Costa Rica has become a mecca for ecotourism—so much so that it is becoming overcrowded. More regulation seems imperative. A balance has to be found; more than 50 percent of the country's natural ecosystems have been destroyed by human settlements, logging, agriculture, and ranching. Ecotourism will play an important role in saving what is left. The meager financial resources of Costa Rica's National Park System are supplemented by the private Costa Rica National Park Foundation, funded by various conservation NGOs, mostly United States-based (Young, 1986: 362; Barborak and Green 1987: 144–145). The national park system attracts not only educational and scientific tourists but also permanent research stations, maintained with foreign funds. It protects most of the fresh water supply for the country, and coastal wetlands for fishing.

Ecotourism is facing problems in Costa Rica: overdevelopment on the Nicoya peninsula and the recent drop in national park budget has resulted in the December 1993 downgrading of Tamarindo National Park to National Refuge, which may give a green light for undesirable tourist development in this ecologically sensitive area (leatherback turtle nesting grounds). Costa Rican authorities hope a foreign NGO will buy the land to save the turtles.

Another region where ecotourism is flourishing is the Amazon River Basin, especially in Brazil, Ecuador, and Peru. The boom in Manaos, Brazil, and Iquitos, Peru, is tremendous—even Club Med is considering building an "ecological village." No wonder there are fears that the environmental and economic benefits of green tourism may become eroded if the carrying capacity of the area is exceeded (Brooke, 1991c). For example, in Pantanal, Brazil, the largest wetland in the world (about 200,000 square kilometers) is polluted by agricultural chemicals and mercury from mining, encroached by ranchers, abused by poachers, and invaded annually by over 100,000 uncontrolled "eco-tourists" who litter the landscape with hundreds of tons of garbage, and overfish. This is in sharp contrast to Doris Ruschmann's (1992) rather optimistic picture of the rigorous controls of tourism, allegedly enforced by the Brazilian authorities. This includes the EMBATUR's (Brazilian Government Tourist Enterprise) ecological tourism program, established in 1988, "to control the tourist flow to areas of ecological interest, by using only specialized guides in previously selected areas" (*ibid.* 127). This picture is at variance with my observations in Amazonia, where I was an inadvertent witness to poaching, perpetrated by my "ecotourism guides" in a national park near Manos.

Brazil has a huge national park system of about 300,000 square kilometers. Unfortunately, most of the parks exist on paper only. Well-organized and regulated ecotourism would save unique ecosystems and give the country a chance to end. The present decline in tourism is caused, in part, by images of unsafe areas, widespread poverty, inflation, and the plight of the native population, especially the Yanomamis.

Chile is another South American country where well-organized and regulated ecotourism would have a positive impact. Chile is home to the largest temperate rain forests in the southern hemisphere (about 60,000 square kilometers). These forests are threatened by logging, and ecotourism, in conjunction with other nondestructive uses of resources, may save this ecosystem.

In Asia, the prime ecotourism areas are in India, Nepal and Indonesia. Recently Bhutan began offering ecotourists a two-week tour for $3,075, a three-week tour for $3,950, and a 19-day tour focusing on flora and fauna for $6,200 including air fare from New York (*New York Times* 29 August 1993).

In Africa, in addition to the traditional ecodestinations of Kenya, Tanzania, and South Africa, Botswana offers low-volume, high-price ecotourism to the Okavango Delta—$600-a-day safaris on elephant-back (*Economist* 27 November 1993).

There is a real danger that expanding ecotourism in areas that already support it (including some of those mentioned above) will transform it into CMT. With its increasing popularity, those involved in ecotourism should look elsewhere. Russia, for example, has significant, untapped resources and tremendous capacity to accept the demand "surplus" (Arefyev and Mieczkowski, Z. 1991; Ilina and Mieczkowski, Z. 1992).

Conclusions

The global dimensions of the ecological crisis have alarmed the world since the 1960s. The human onslaught on the natural environment has to stop because it threatens both the quality of life and the very survival of the human species. Coping with environmental problems, however, requires the implementation of a number of reactive and proactive measures on global, regional, national, and local scale. For these problems to be successful, a host of political, social, economic, moral, and attitudinal issues must be tackled. In fact, the earth's natural environment is intimately interconnected with other aspects of life, and cannot be treated in isolation. Humanity, on the eve of the twenty-first century, is facing the challenge of a complex web of correlated issues: stratospheric ozone depletion, climate change, air and water pollution, soil erosion, socioeconomic inequality on a global and national scale, conspicuous overconsumption, self-indulgence and resource waste in the DCs, poverty combined with population explosion and political failure in the LDCs, and social and political tension on all levels, including the threat of a looming North—South confrontation. The list of these interacting issues is open-ended.

This book has dealt with the role played by tourism and recreation in the context of the global ecological drama. Indeed, the environmental issues of tourism cannot be treated in isolation from the complex interaction between humanity and nature because they are an integral part of the ecosphere. Practically any human activity exerts a negative impact on nature, and tourism is no exception. The rapidly expanding scale of tourism threatens the environment by mere quantity of impacts. The pressures on our planet's ecosystems, caused by demands for tourism and recreation are bound to increase more than proportionately to population growth because of improving standards of living, not only in the DCs, but in East and South Asia and Latin America. As the population in these LDCs gradually achieves a certain degree of affluence, the demand for tourism/ recreation will invariably escalate, and this will augment the environmental stress on already limited natural resources.

Tourism belongs to the most ecologically benign economic sectors. In practice, tourism is more often the victim of the assault by other economic sectors than a perpetrator of ecological outrage. Additionally, tourism is an industry that requires high-quality natural environment—it must be clean, attractive and scenic. In this sense, tourism is an ally of the environment to a greater degree than other economic sectors because this desire to preserve the beauty and harmony of nature lies at the very foundation of human leisure activities. As a result, tourism is much more vulnerable to environmental degradation.

This unique feature of tourism elevates the recreational use of land to an prominent position as one of the ecologically most beneficial uses of space. For example, compare the use of an area for an oil refinery with its use as a well-designed and managed beach resort. In addition, tourism is incompatible with ecologically destructive economic activities, such as oil exploration and exploitation, mining, or the chemical industry. The economically negative externalities associated with these activities affect tourism directly. Therefore, environmentally undesirable enterprises have no place on land zoned for tourism development. Thus, tourism/recreation saves the environment from damage and possible destruction by other economic sectors by providing the economic rationale based on the computation of the opportunity costs of tourism development.

Recreational use of land has to compete with other economic sectors, and as such may be often difficult to justify in economic terms. However, there is an important aspect that mollifies the competition that tourism and recreation often use land that would otherwise not be developed. Preferred nonurban tourism locations are mainly on the periphery and on topographically rugged terrain that, because of transportation costs and construction requirements, impede industrial or agricultural development. The competition between tourism and agriculture for land is also diminished by the fact that tourism may locate on land with inferior soil quality. Environmentally, tourist areas are more likely to be included into the systems of protected lands (such as national parks and other nature reserves), and, as such, are protected from ecologically damaging uses. This association demonstrates its beneficial ecological potential. At the same time, peripheral areas may find tourism useful as a tool of economic survival in order to overcome their disadvantaged position, as compared with the industrially and agriculturally developed central regions. Tourism, at least in theory, therefore, should stand in the forefront in the struggle for the conservation of nature.

Unfortunately, tourism does not always manage to fulfill its ecological mandate: unplanned, uncontrolled, chaotic and spontaneous tourism—instead of acting as an ally of nature, sometimes contributes to environmental deterioration, especially in fragile ecosystems such as coastal areas, mountains, and, more recently, deserts and polar regions. Although this aberration of "tourism killing tourism" does not typically extend over large territories and, with some notable exceptions, acquires only local dimensions, the negative ecological effects of recreational activities are particularly annoying because tourism is an activity that should enhance the quality of life.

Still, despite the undeniable negative impacts of tourism (which have received wide coverage in this book), it is impractical to eliminate tourism, or even curtail it severely. The challenge is to cope with its problems. Tourism, if properly conceived and conducted, may play a positive role in the economic, sociocultural, and environmental challenges of the twenty-first century. The importance of science-based, well-planned and regulated tourism as one of the beneficial elements in solving the environmental problems of our planet, is closely associated with the unique feature of the tourism sector, which, unlike other sectors, is directly and intimately linked to the quality of human life.

For a number of years, scholars, environmental activists, business people, politicians, and residents of communities affected by tourism have realized that "those who do not learn from their mistakes are doomed to repeat them." They have analyzed the environmental degradation it can cause. They have also worked on ways to make tourism environmentally sustainable, appropriate, and symbiotic with ecological conservation. This book has suggested a number of measures to prevent, minimize, and mitigate the negative impacts of tourism on the natural environment and how to optimize its positive effects. The most important among them may be summarized as follows:

1. Fundamental changes in societal system of values resulting in lower material expectations and changing lifestyles, from extravagant overconsumption to more circumspect and modest attitudes in the DCs. These changes should affect *homo turisticus* and in the broader sense, *homo ludens* (human at leisure). Such a re-evaluation is impossible without a revival of social, psychological, moral, and spiritual values of our civilization. A significant part of this attitudinal change is the accept-

ance that the natural resources of our planet are finite, therefore, environmental ethics are important. In practical terms, the turn towards nonmaterialistic philosophical standards will promote alternative forms of consumption, more benign to nature. The implications for symbiotic (environment-friendly tourism) are obvious. Tourism, synonymous with environmental protection, may play an important role in the re-evaluation of societal values and in improving the quality of life, not by endlessly increasing consumption of goods and services, but by enriching our lives in experiences, including the enjoyment of unspoiled nature.

2. All tourism, and not only alternative or ecotourism, should be environmentally sustainable. In this connection, growth and development are not interchangeable terms. Thus, the growth of tourism, understood as an increase of scale, should be restrained in most extra-urban areas, especially in fragile and protected ones, where the priorities are those advocated in point 1. Restricted or zero-growth policy has to be promoted as a preferred option in most extra-urban areas, even those without an officially protected status. As a rule, the type of operation should be kept as small as possible to minimize the erosion of ecological quality. Large scale facility-oriented conventional mass tourism (CMT) and recreation should be concentrated in cities and their immediate vicinity, and in some large extra-urban resorts with the proviso of rigorous planning and control. Additionally, this concentration and expansion of tourist and recreational opportunities plays another important role: it diverts the demand from ecologically fragile extra-urban and protected areas, decreasing pressure on them. On the other hand, the provision of nearby opportunities for contact with nature for populations of large metropolitan centers located near nature areas is particularly significant from a social, educational, and ecological perspective. For example, the Gateway National Recreational Area on the outskirts of New York City gives city-dwelling recreationists a place to go without having to travel far distances, thus saving resources and diminishing pollution.

3. Rapid tourism development should be avoided as much as possible because it is difficult to absorb by the ecosystems and the people involved. It is important that development takes place at gradual rates. This assures that appropriate adjustments—in the form of prevention, mitigation and correction may be undertaken.

4. Damage to ecological assets should be prevented and negative environmental impacts minimized, while authentic, intimate, and meaningful educational encounters of people with nature in extra-urban settings (especially in the protected areas), such as national parks, should be encouraged. This ideal should be pursued by all forms of tourism, but especially by nature tourism (ecotourism). The aim is to bring people closer for nature.
5. Make tourism more energy and resource efficient. Especially important in this respect is the increased use of green products and green technology by the tourism industry. The use of low-impact technology is especially significant in transportation. If distance is a problem, public and non-motorized transportation should be used at the expense of private automobiles. Tourism enterprises should refrain from using chemicals polluting ground water. For instance, biocontrol methods should be used instead of biocides.
6. To avoid boom and bust cycles, tourism should be developed at destinations at a well-planned, controlled, slow, and gradual pace rather than in a revolutionary manner.
7. Integrate tourism with other environment-friendly economic sectors, rather than as a substitute for them as a sort of tourism monoculture—a monopoly condition which is economically undesirable because, it is labor-intensive, while at the same time provides only seasonal employment. The souvenir and sport equipment producing industry, environmentally sustainable agriculture, or other ecologically benign economic sectors are recommended. A diversified economy is not only economically rational but also environmentally sustainable.
8. Expanding and improving research into conflicting interactions between tourism and environment will help anticipate and prevent future ecological damage. Especially significant in this respect are investigations of the recreational carrying capacity. The application of the Geographical Information System (GIS) and the Internet communication system may offer yet unexplored potential for environmental research in tourism.
9. An indispensable element in tourism development is planning combined with environmental assessment, zoning, management, control, and monitoring. After priorizing goals and objectives, and evaluating various strategies, the selection of the most appropriate path to be undertaken deserves consultation. In most cases, government is responsible for these activities. It represents the long-term broad interests of

the whole society and not of the short-sighted vested interest groups. The government is better equipped in terms of scientific research and law enforcement capabilities. Nevertheless, in recent years the tourism industry is becoming increasingly involved in the planning process, its self-interest being the main factor in this trend. Planning, together with monitoring, as opposed to voluntary *ad hoc* decisions, should be a continuous process to ensure proper ecological safeguards. Functional differentiation of the planned area is achieved by zoning.

10. Planning is often associated with putting limits on development of facilities and/or the number of visitors. If properly controlled, tourism may thrive even in ecologically sensitive areas without compromising the ecological integrity. The resident populations of destination communities should be drawn into the planning and monitoring process mainly through public hearings. Often, if the locals are relatively young and unemployed, they will advocate development and job creation over environmental protection, while retirees tend to resist tourist expansion. On the international scale, the LDCs are more inclined to overdevelop tourism than are the DCs.

11. Environmental laws and regulations should be toughened and enforced.

References

"A Conservation Strategy for Prince Edward Island." 1992. Charlottetown: Island Information Service.

Adams, Jonathan and McShane, Thomas. 1992. *The Myth of Wild Africa*. New York: W. W. Norton & Co.

Adams, W. M. 1990. *Green Development: Environment and Sustainability in the Third World*. London: Routledge.

Ahmed, S. A. 1984. "Perception of Socio-Economic and Cultural Impact of Tourism in Sri Lanka." Faculty of Administration, University of Ottawa, Working Paper 84-18. Ottawa: University of Ottawa.

Alderman, Claudia. 1990. *A Study of the Role of Privately Owned Lands Used for Nature Tourism, Education and Conservation*. Washington: Conservation International.

Anad, P. A. 1987. "Progress in the Conservation of Nigeria's Wildlife." *Biological Conservation*. 41: 237-251.

———. "World Tourism Organization and Development." 1977. *World Travel*. 137: 23-27.

Archer, D. 1980. *Effects of Tourist Industry in Barbados, West Indies*. Austin: University of Texas.

Archer, E. 1985. "Emerging Environmental Problems in a Tourist Zone: The Case of Barbados." *Caribbean Geography*. 2, 1: 45-55.

Arefyev, V. 1991. "Turism i Problemy Okhrany Prirody." Unpublished conference paper.

Arefyev, V. and Mieczkowski, Z. 1991. "International Tourism in the Soviet Union in the Era of Glasnost and Perestroyka." *Journal of Travel Research*. 29, 4: 2-7.

Ashworth, G. and Tunbridge, J. 1990. *The Touristic-Historic City*. London: Belheaven Press.

Aulitzky, H. 1974. *Endangered Alpine Regions and Disaster Prevention Measures*. Strasbourg: Council of Europe, Nature and Environment Series. 6: 106.

Axtell, Roger, ed. 1985. *Do's and Taboos Around the World*. New York: John Wiley.

Backman, S. and Wright, B. 1990. "Identifying Perceived Constraints to Hunting." *Sixth Canadian Congress of Leisure Research Proceedings*. Waterloo: University of Waterloo, Dept. of Recreation and Leisure Studies: 356-360.

Bacon, P. 1987. "Use of Wetlands for Tourism in the Insular Caribbean." *Annals of Tourism Research.* 14: 104-117.

Baiderin, V. 1978. "Effect of Winter Recreation on the Soil and Vegetation of Slopes in the Vicinity of Kauzau." *Soviet Journal of Ecology.* 9, 1: 76-80.

Baines, G. 1987. "Manipulation of Islands and Men: Sand-Cay Tourism in the South Pacific." In Britton and Clarke, eds. 1987. *Ambiguous Alternative: Tourism in Small Developing Countries.* Suva: University Press of South Pacific. 16-24.

Bajsarowicz, J. 1989a. "Pollution Problems Plague Poland." *Water Environment and Technology.* September: 45-48.

———. 1989b. "Pollution and Solutions in Poland." *Studium Papers.* October: 194-196.

———. 1993. "Environmental Reform: The Polish Model." *Wall Street Journal.* 1 June.

Baker, P. 1986a. "Area Destinations: The Moroccan Experience." *Tourism Management.* 7, 2: 129-131.

———. 1986b. "Tourism and the National Parks." *Parks & Recreation.* 21, 10: 50-73.

Balick, M. and Mendelsohn, R. 1991. "Assessing the Economic Value of Traditional Medicines from Tropical Rain Forests." *Conservation Biology.* 6, 1: 128-131.

Barbier, B. and Billet, J. 1980. "Development Touristique et Espace Naturel." *Limits to Tourism Development.* Berne: Editions AIEST.

Barborak, James R. and Green, Gina C. 1987. "Implementing the World Conservation Strategy: Sixteen Stories from Central America and Colombia." In Southgate, D. and Disinger, J. eds. *Sustainable Resource Development in the Third World.* Boulder. 139-149.

Bardecki, M. J. 1984. *Wetland Conservation Policies in Southern Ontario.* York University Geographical Monograph No. 15.

———. 1985. *Wetland Conservation Policies in Western Ontario: A Delply Approach.* York University Geographical Monograph No. 16.

Barker, M. L. 1982. "Traditional Landscape and Mass Tourism in the Alps." *Geographical Review.* 72, 4: 395-415.

Barkham, J. P. 1973. "Recreational Carrying Capacity: A Problem of

Perception." *Area.* 5: 218-222.

Barr, B. and Braden, K. 1988. *The Disappearing Russian Forest: A Dilemma in Soviet Resource Management.* London: Hutchinson.

Bates, G. H. 1935. "The Vegetation of Footpaths, Sidewalks, Cart-Tracks and Gateways." *Journal of Ecology.* 23: 470-487.

———. 1938. "Life Forms of Pasture Plants in Relation to Treading." *Journal of Ecology.* 26: 452-454.

Bateson, P., et al., eds. 1989. *National Parks and Tourism.* New South Wales National Parks and Wildlife Service.

Bätzing, W. 1984. *Die Alpen: Naturbearbeitung und Umweltzerstörung: Eine ökologisch-geographische Untersuchung.* Frankfurt am Main: Sender Verlag.

Baud-Bovi, Manuel and Lawson, Fred. 1977. *Tourism and Recreation Development.* London: The Architectural Press, Ltd.

Bayfield, N. G. 1974. "Burial of Vegetation by Erosion Material near Ski Lifts on Cairngorm." *Biological Conservation.* 6: 246-251.

———. 1979. "Recovery of Four Montane Communities on Cairngorm, Scotland, from Disturbance by Trampling." *Biological Conservation.* 15, 3: 165-179.

Beaman, Jay, Heyman, Susan and Du Wors, Richard. 1991. "Price Elasticity of Demand: A Campground Example." *Journal of Travel Research.* Summer: 22-29.

Becheri, E. 1991. "Rimini and Co.—The End of a Legend? Dealing with Algae Effect." *Tourism Management.* September: 229- 235.

Becker, Christopher. 1969. "Die Anziehungskraft kleiner Inseln auf den Urlaubsverkehr." *Zeitschrift für Wirtshaftsgeographie.* 4: 121-124.

———. 1988. "Entwicklung und strukturelle Bedeutung neuerer Formen des Tourismus." *Moderner Tourismus*: 585-601.

Becker, R., Jubenville, A. and Burnett, G. 1984. "Fact and Judgment in the Search for a Social Carrying Capacity." *Leisure Sciences.* 6, 4: 475-486.

Beeton, James. 1989. "Tourism and Protected Landscapes." In Bateson, P., et al., eds. *National Parks and Tourism.* New South Wales National Parks and Wildlife Service. 33-49.

Bender, Barbara and Edmonds, Mark. 1992. "Stonehenge: Whose past? What past?" *Tourism Management.* 13, 4: 355-357.

Birnbaum, Jesse. 1991. "Just Too Beastly For Words." *Time.* June.

Blangy, Sylvie and Nielsen, Todd. 1993. "Ecotourism and Minimum Impact Policy." *Annals of Tourism Research.* 20: 357-360.

Boisvenue, M. 1990. "La deterioration des sites de camping: une realite sournoise." *Operational Geographer.* 8, 2: 34-35.

Bonner, Raymond. 1993. *At The Hand of Man.* New York: Knopf.

Boo, Elizabeth. 1990. *Ecotourism: Potentials and Pitfalls.* Washington: World Wildlife Fund.

————. 1991. "Ecotourism: A Tool for Conservation." In Kusler, Jon, ed. *Ecotourism and Resource Conservation: A Collection of Papers.* 2 vols. Madison: Omnipress. 517-519.

Boreyko, Volodymir and Lystopad, Oleh. 1994. "Waging War on Nature: Reflections on the Medobory Reserve." *Surviving Together.* Spring: 41-44.

Bormann, Herbert, Balmori, Diana and Geballe, Gordon. 1993. *Redesigning the American Lawn.* Yale: Yale University Press.

Bornet, B. 1979. *Tourism et environment: faut-il souhaiter uneconcentration on une deconcentration touristique?* Aix-en-Province: Centre de reserche touristique.

Bosselman, F. P. 1978. *In the Wake of the Tourist: Managing Special Places in Eight Countries.* Washington: The Conservation Foundation.

Bounds, J. H. 1978. "The Bahamas Tourism Industry: Past, Present and Future." *Revista Geografica.* 88: 167-219.

Bowles, J. M. and Maun, M. A. 1982. "A Study of the Effects of Trampling on the Vegetation of Lake Huron—Sand Dunes at Pinery Provincial Park." *Biological Conservation.* 24, 4: 273-283.

Brard, Jean-Pierre. 1993. "L'integration de L'environment dans les systemes de compatibilite nationale." *Ecodecision.* Juin: 70-71.

Brauer, Christiane. 1989. "Südinseln-Touristenziele mit ökologischen Problemen." In Euler, Claus, ed. *Tourismus und Ökologie: Ökozid* 5. Giessen: Focus Verlag: 149-158.

Britton, R. A. 1977. "Making Tourism more Supportive of Small State Development." *Annals of Tourism Research.* 4: 268- 278.

Britton, S. and Clarke, W., eds. 1987. *Ambiguous Alternative Tourism in Small Developing Countries.* Suva: University of South Pacific.

Brody, Jane. 1991. "Water-Based Animals are Becoming Extinct Faster than Others." *New York Times.* 23 April: C4.

———. 1992. "Doses of Pineal Gland Hormone Can Reset Body's Daily Clock." *New York Times.* 3 November.

Bromley, Daniel. 1991. *Environment and Economy: Property Rights and Public Policy.* Oxford: Basil Blackwell.

Brooke, E. 1992. "As Forests Fall, Environment Movement Rises in Brazil." *New York Times.* 2 June.

Brooke, James. 1988. "Niger Works to Save a Species and Bolster Tribe." *New York Times.* 9 May.

———. 1991a. "Venezuela Befriends Tribe, but What's Venezuela?" *New York Times.*

———. 1991b. "Brazilians Take Pains to Save Sea Turtles." *New York Times.* 17 December.

———. 1991c. "Brazil's Forest in the Balance." *New York Times.* 19 May.

Browne, M. W. 1992. "Folk Remedy Demand May Wipe Out Tigers." *New York Times.* 20 September.

Browne, R. and Wall, G. 1979. "Patterns of Use in the Algonquin Park Interior." In Wall, G., ed. *Recreational Land Use in Southern Ontario.* University of Waterloo Dept. of Geography Publication Series No. 14. Waterloo: University of Waterloo.

Brzezinski, Zbigniew. 1993a. *Out of Control: Global Turmoil on the Eve of the 21st Century.* New York: Charles Scribner & Sons.

———. 1993b. "Power and Morality." *World Monitor.* 28 March: 22-28.

Bryden, J. 1973. *Tourism and Development: A Case Study of the Commonwealth Caribbean.* New York: Cambridge University Press.

Buchwald, Rainer and Dilger, Robert. 1989. "Wissenschaftlicher Tourismus: Imperialismus im Forscherlook." In Euler, Claus, ed. *Tourismus und Ökologie: Ökozid* 5. Giessen: Focus Verlag: 149-158.

Budowski, G. 1976. "Tourism and Environmental Conservation: Conflict, Coexistence or Symbiosis." *Environmental Conservation.* 3: 27-31.

Bulatov, V. I. 1993. *200 yadernykh poligonov SSSR: Geografia radiatisonnykh katastrof i zagryaznenii.* Novosibirsk: CERIS.

Burch, W. 1981. "The Ecology of Metaphors—Spacing Regularities for

Humans and Other Primates in Urban and Wetland Habitats." *Leisure Sciences.* 4, 3: 213-230.

———. 1984. "Much To Do about Nothing—Some Reflections on the Wider and Wilder Implications of Social Carrying Capacity." *Leisure Sciences.* 6, 4: 487-496.

Burkart, A. and Medlik, S. 1975. *Tourism Management.* London.Bury, R. 1976. "Recreation Carrying Capacity— Hypothesis or Reality." *Parks and Recreation.* 11, 1: 22-25, 56-57.

Butler, Richard. 1980. "The Concept of Tourist Area Cycle of Evolution: Implications for Management of Resources." *Canadian Geographer.* 1: 5-12.

———. 1986. "The Impacts of Tourism: Divots, Depression and Dollars." *Tourism and Environment: Conflict or Harmony. Symposium Canadian Society of Environmental Biologists:* 75-83.

———. 1990. "Alternative Tourism: Pious Hope or Trojan Horse?" *Journal of Travel Research.* Winter: 40-45.

———. 1993. "Tourism An Evolutionary Perspective." In Nelson, et al., ed. *Tourism and Sustainable Development: Monitoring, Planning, Managing.* University of Waterloo: Department of Geography Publications Series No. 37: 27-43.

———. 1993. "Richard Butler Interviewed by Bill Bradwell." *Journal of Sustainable Tourism.* 1: 137-142.

Buzzelli, D. 1990. "Ethical Leadership: An Imperative for the '90s." *Globe 90 Conference.* Unpublished speech. Vancouver, B.C. 20 March.

Cabryn, L. 1974. "Wolf Population Fluctuations in Jasper National Park, Alberta." *Biological Conservation.* 6: 94-101.

Cairncross, F. 1992. *Costing the Earth.* Cambridge: Harvard University Press.

Canadian Environmental Advisory Council. 1991. *Protected Areas—Vision for Canada.* Ottawa: Minister of Supply and Services Canada.

Canadian Society of Environmental Biologists. 1986. *Tourism and Environment: Conflict or Harmony?* Symposium Canadian Society of Environmental Biologists, Edmonton, Alberta.

Canadian Wildlife Service. 1989. *The Benefits of Wildlife.* Ottawa: Environment Canada.

Candela, R. 1982. "Piste de ski et erosion authropique dans les Alpes du Sud." *Mediterranee.* 3-4: 51-55.

Canestrelli, E. and Costa, P. 1991. "Tourist Carrying Capacity: A Fuzzy Approach." *Annals of Tourism Research.* 18: 295- 311.

Cappock, J. 1982. "Tourism and Conservation." *Tourism Management.* December: 270-276.

Cazes, G. 1989. *Le tourisme international—mirage ou strategie d'avenir?* Paris: Hatier.

Ceballos-Lascurian, Hector. 1991. "Tourism, Ecotourism, and Protected Areas." In Kusler, Jon, ed. *Ecotourism and Resource Conservation: A Collection of Papers.* 2 vols. Madison: Omnipress: 24-30.

Chermayeff, P. 1992. "The Age of Aquariums." *World Monitor.* August: 54-57.

Chrisholm, B. J. 1994. "Cooperation in the Taiga: The Key to Saving the Amur Tiger." *Surviving Together.* 12, 1: 36-39.

Christensen, H. and Davis, N. 1984. "Vandalism: Law, Violations, and Intervention in Recreation Settings." *Trends.* 21, 1: 12-16.

Chubb, Michael and Ashton, Peter. 1969. "Parks and Recreation Standards Research: The Creation of Environmental Quality Controls for Recreation." Michigan State University: *Technical Report No. 5.*

Civili, F. 1987. "The Pollution of the Mediterranean Sea and its Repercussions on Tourism." *Tourismus und Umwelt.* Starnberg: Studienkreis fur Tourismus.

Clark, Roger and Stankey, George. 1979. *The Recreation Opportunity Spectrum: A Framework for Planning, Management, and Research.* U.S. Department of Agricutlure, Forest Service. General Technical Report: PNW-98.

Clawson, M. and Knetch, J. 1966. *Economics of Outdoor Recreation.* John Hopkins Press.

Cleverdon, R. and Edwards, A. 1982. *International Tourism to 1990.* EIV Special Series 4. Cambridge: Abt Books.

Cohen, E. 1974. "Who is a Tourist?" *Sociological Review.* 22, 4: 527-553.

———. 1978. "The Impact of Tourism on the Physical Environment." *Annals of Tourism Research.* 5, 2: 215-237.

Colchester, Marcus and Lohmann, Larry, eds. 1993. *The Struggle for*

Land and the Fate of the Forests. Penang: The World Rainforest Movement.

Cole, David N. 1987. "Effects of Three Seasons of Experimental Trampling on Five Mountain Forest Communities and a Grassland in Western Montana, U.S.A." *Biological Conservation.* 40: 219-244.

———. 1989. "Recreation Ecology: What We Know, What Geographers Can Contribute." *Professional Geographer.* 41, 2: 143-148.

Coltman, Michael M. 1989. *Introduction to Travel and Tourism: an International Approach.* New York: Van Nostrand.

Commoner, Barry. 1990. *Making Peace with the Planet.* New York: Pantheon Books.

"Conservation by Conflict." 1992. *Earthwatch.* 11, 3: 5.

Copeland, Emma. 1992. "The Role of Airlines in the Tourism and Environment Debate." *Tourism Management.* 13, 1: 112- 114.

Cooper, C. P. and Ozdil, I. 1992. "From Mass to 'Responsible' Tourism: the Turkish Experience." *Tourism Management.* 13, 4: 377-386.

Covington, Richard. 1993. "Drawn by their Rugged Grandeur, Are We Loving the Alps to Death?" *Smithsonian.* November: 46-58.

Crutzen, P. 1992. "Ultraviolet on the Increase." *Nature.* 356, 6365: 104-105.

Cullen, R. 1986. "Himalayan Mountaineering Expedition Garbage." *Environmental Conservation.* 13, 4: 293-297.

D'Amore, Luis J. 1992. "Promoting Sustainable Tourism—The Canadian Approach." *Tourism Management.* 13, 3: 258-262.

Davidson, R. 1989. *Tourism.* London: Pitman Publishing.

Dawood, R. 1988. *Stay Healthy Abroad.* New York: Penguin Books.

———. 1989. "Tourists' Health—Could the Travel Industry Do More?" *Tourism Management.* December: 285-287.

De Blij, H. and Muller, P. 1986. *Human Geography: Culture, Society, and Space.* New York: John Wiley & Sons.

Defert, Pierre and Pichot, Robert. 1988. "Le Tourisme, solution aux dettes du Tiors-monde." *Revue de Tourisme.* 2: 2-5.

Defeyt, Philippe. 1993. "Les Ecotaxes." *Ecodecision.* Juin : 16-17.

De Groot, R. S. 1983. "Tourism and Conservation in the Galapagos Islands." *Biological Conservation.* 26, 4: 291-300.

de Kadt, E., ed. 1979. *Tourism—Passport to Development?* Oxford: Oxford University Press.

Delaney, L. and McVeigh, G. 1991. "Imagery." *Prevention.* September: 117.

De Soto, Hernando. 1993. "The Missing Ingredient." *Economist.* 11 September.

Diamond, Jared M. 1986. "The Environmentalist Myth." *Nature.* 324, 6 November.

Dieke, P.V.C. 1991. "Policies for Tourism Development in Kenya." *Annals of Tourism Research.* 18: 269-294.

Dilsaver, Lary. 1992. "Conflict in Yosemite Valley." In Janell, Donald, ed. 1992. *Geographical Snapshots of North America.* New York: The Guilford Press.

Dold, Catherine. 1992a. "Hearing of Manatees may Prove to be Key to Protecting Species." *New York Times.* 25 August.

———. 1992b. "Study Casts Doubt on Belief in Self-Revival of Cleared Forests." *New York Times.* 1 September.

Donevan, William M. 1992. "The Pristine Myth: The Landscape of the Americas in 1492." *Annals of the AAG.* 82, 3: 369-385.

Donnelly, Peter. 1987. "Creating National Parks—'A Grand, Good Thing.'" *Tourism Management.* December: 349-351.

Dowling, Ross. 1993. "Tourism Planning, People and the Environment of Western Australia." *Journal of Travel Research.* Spring: 52-58.

Doxey, G.V. 1975. "A Causation Theory of Visitor—Resident Irritants: Methodology and Research Inferences." *Proceedings of the Travel Research Association.* Sixth Annual Conference, San Diego. 195-198.

——— 1976. "When Enough is Enough: The Natives are Restless in Old Niagara." *Heritage Canada.* 2: 26-27.

Driver, B. L., Nash, R., and Haas, C. 1987. "Wilderness Benefits: A State of Knowledge Review." In Proceedings: National Wilderness Research Conference: Issues. *State of Knowledge, Future Directions.* Compiled by Lucas, R. 23-26 July. Fort Collins. USDA Forest Service. Technical Report. INT-220: 294- 319.

Dunbar, Gary S. 1991. *Modern Geography: An Encyclopedic Survey.* New York: Garland Publishing.

Dunbar, M. J., ed. 1974. *Environmental Damage and Control.* Montreal: McGill University Press.

Durning, A. T. 1992. *How Much is Enough? The Consumer Society and the Future of the Earth.* New York: W. W. Norton & Co.

Eckholm, E. 1976. *Losing Ground: Environmental Stress and World Food Prospects.* New York: W. W. Norton & Co.

Edington, J. M. and Edington, M. A. 1986. *Ecology, Recreation and Tourism.* New York: Cambridge University Press.

Edwards, F., ed. 1988. *Environmentally Sound Tourism Development in the Caribbean.* Calgary: University of Calgary.

Edwards, J. 1987. "The UK Heritage Coasts: An Assessment of the Ecological Impacts of Tourism." *Annals of Tourism Research.* 14, 1: 71-87.

Edwards, Jonathan and Barks, Mario. 1990. "Environment, Tourism and Development." *Tourism Management.* September: 266- 267.

Egan, T. 1991a. "Outcry Over Hunt of Endangered Grizzly." *New York Times.* 22 September.

————. 1991b. "Anger Grows in West Over City-Slicker Neighbors." *New York Times.* 22 December.

————. 1992. "Strongest U.S. Environmental Law may become Endangered Species." New York Times. 26 May.

Ehret, C. and Scanlon, L. 1983. *Overcoming the Jet Lag.* Berkley Books.

Ehrlich, P. 1991. "Can We Respond to the Growing Environmental Threat to Civilization?" In Wolbarst, ed. *Environment in Peril.* Washington: Smithsonian Institute Press. 110-137.

Ekins, Paul. 1992. *A New World Order: Grassroots Movements to Global Change.* London: Routledge.

Ekins, Paul, Hillman, M. and Hutchison, R. 1992. *The Gaia Atlas of Green Economics.* New York: Anchor Books.

Eldredge, N. 1991. *The Miner's Canary: Unravelling the Mysteries of Extinction.* New York: Prentice Hall Press.

Elliott, J. 1987. "Government Management of Tourism—A Thai Case Study." *Tourism Management.* 8, 3: 223-233.

El Samra, Gamal. 1984. "Health and Tourism." *UNEP Industry and Environment.* 14, 11-12 (Jan.-Mar.): 7-11.

Elsasser, Hans, Frosch, Rainer and Diener, Roth. 1992. "La Saturation Touristique a L'example du Canton des Grisons." *Revue Geographique de L'Est.* 3: 201-215.

Emery, F. 1981. "Alternative Futures in Tourism." *Tourism Management.* 2, 1: 49-67.

Environment Canada. 1983. *The Importance of Wildlife to Canadians: Highlights of the 1991 Survey.* Ottawa: Environment Canada, Canadian Wildlife Service.

Erasmus, Udo. 1990. *Fats and Oils in Health and Nutrition.* Burnaby: Alive Books.

Erlanger, S. 1989. "Indonesia Takes Steps to Protect Rain Forests." *New York Times.* 26 September.

Euler, Claus, ed. 1989. *Tourismus und Ökologie: Ökozid 5.* Giessen: Focus Verlag.

Farrell, B. and Runyan, D. 1991. "Ecology and Tourism." *Annals of Tourism Research.* 18: 26-40.

Feshbach, Murray and Friendly, Alfred. 1992. *Ecocide in the USSR.* London: Basic Books.

Feurstein, G. 1976. *Strategies for Tourism Development in Mountain Regions.* Final Report. Vienna: Council of Europe, Committee on Cooperation in Municipal & Regional Matters.

Fitzgerald, M. 1991. "Saving Babar's Kingdom." *World Monitor.* May: 22-26.

Foin, T. C., et al. 1977. "Quantitative Studies of Visitor Impacts on Environments of Yosemite National Park, California, and their Implications for Park Management Policy." *Journal of Environmental Management.* 5, 1: 1-22.

Foster, D. 1985. *Travel and Tourism Management.* London: McMillan.

Foster, Harold. 1992. *Health, Disease and the Environment.* London: Belhaven.

Fridgen, J. 1984. "Environmental Psychology and Tourism." *Annals of Tourism Research.* 11: 19-39.

"From Tradition Spa to Modern Forms of Health Tourism." Congress Report. *Journal of Travel Research.* Winter 1990: 38-39.

Fondaciòn Neotropica. 1992. *Analisis de Capacidad de Carga Para Visitation en las Areas Silvestres de Costa Rica.* San Jose: Fondaciòn Neotropica, Centros de Estudios Ambientales y Politicas—CEAP.

Galbraith, J. K. 1967. *The New Industrial State.* Boston: Houghton Mifflin.

————. 1991. "The Economic Case for the Environment." In Wolbarst, A., ed. *Environment in Peril.* Washington Smithsonian

Institute: 26-37.

Gale, F. and Jacobs, J. 1987. *Tourists and the National Estate: Procedures to Protect Australia's Heritage.* Canberra: Australian Governmental Publishing Service.

Garcia, Asun. 1989. "Macht euch die Erde untertan: Das Bild vom Abendteuer—Trekking—und Elebnisreisen in aktuellen Prospekten." In Euler, Claus, ed. *Tourismus und Ökologie: Ökozid 5.* Giessen: Focus Verlag.

Gartner, W. 1987. "Environmental Impacts of Recreational Home Developments." *Annals of Tourism Research.* 14, 1: 38-57.

Gauthier, David. 1993. "Sustainable Development, Tourism, and Wildlife." In Nelson, J. G., Butler, R. and Wall, G., eds. *Tourism and Sustainable Development: Monitoring, Planning, Managing.* University of Waterloo: Department of Geography Publications. Series Number 37: 97-109.

Gayray, M. 1981. "Threats to the Terrestrial Resources of the Caribbean." *Ambio.* 10, 6: 307-311.

Gee, C. 1981. *Resort Development and Management.* East Lansing: Educational Institute of the American Hotel and Motel Association.

Getz, D. 1982. "A Rationale and Methodology for Assessing Capacity to Absorb Tourism." *Ontario Geography.* 19: 92- 102.

———. 1983. "Capacity to Absorb Tourism: Concepts and Implications for Strategic Planning." *Annals of Tourism Research.* 10: 239-263.

Giles, Kent; Fouhy, Ken; Staller, Paul and Zahodiakin, Phil. 1991. "Days of Reckoning." *Chemical Engineering.* February: 30- 31.

"Globe 90." 1990. *An Action Strategy for Sustainable Tourism Development.* Vancouver: Tourism Stream, Action Strategy Committee.

Godfrey, P. and Godfrey, M. 1980. "Ecological Effects of Off-Road Vehicles on Cape Cod." *Oceanus.* 24, 3: 56-67.

Goudie, A. 1990. *The Human Impact on the Natural Environment.* Oxford: Basil Blackwell.

Gore, Al. 1992. *Earth in the Balance: Ecology and the Human Spirit.* Boston: Houghton Mifflin.

Goulet, Dennis. 1977. *What Kind of Tourism? Or, Poison in a Luxury Package.* Montreal: McGill University.

Greenwood, D.J. 1972. "Tourism as an Agent of Change: A Spanish Basque Case." *Ethnology*. 11: 80-91.

Grenon, M. and Batise, M., eds. 1989. *Futures for the Mediterranean Basin: The Blue Plan*. Oxford: Oxford University Press.

Groetzbach, E. 1985. "The Bavarian Alps: Problems of Tourism, Agriculture and Conservation." In Singh, T. V., and Kaur, J., eds. *Integrated Mountain Development*. New Delhi: Himalayan Books.

Grossman, David. 1981. "Combating Pollution: The Record so Far. *Focus*. 22, 1: 5-15.

Grossman, G. and Krueger, A. 1991. Paper presented at a conference. Brown University. 18 October.

Guidelines For Understanding and Determining Optimum Recreation Carrying Capacity. 1977. Bethlehem: Urban Research and Development Corporation.

Gunn, Clare. 1987. "Environmental Design and Land Use." In Ritchie, J. and Goeldner, C., eds. *Travel, Tourism and Hospitality Research: A Handbook for Managers and Researchers*. New York: John Wiley & Sons.

————. 1988a. *Tourism Planning*. New York: Taylor & Francis.

————. 1988b. *Vacationscape: Designing Tourist Regions*. New York: Van Nostrand Reinhold Co.

Gutfeld, G., Rao, L. and Sangiorio, M. 1992. "Bronze Shots: Tan Injections Darken and Protect Skin." *Prevention*. June: 28-29.

Hall, D., ed. 1991. *Tourism and Economic Development in Eastern Europe and the Soviet Union*. London: Belheaven Press.

Hall, C. Michael 1992. "Tourism in Antarctica: Activities, Impacts, and Management." *Journal of Travel Research*. Spring: 2-9.

Hamele, H., ed. 1987. *Tourismus und Umwelt*. Starnberg: Studienkreis für Tourismus.

Hammitt, W. E. and Cole, D. *Wildland Recreation: Ecology anad Management*. New York: John Wiley.

Harrison, R., Clark, R. and Stankey, G. 1980. *Predicting Impact of Noise on Recreationists*. San Dimas: USDA, Forest Service, Equipment Development Center.

Hartshorn, R. 1962. *Perspective on the Nature of Geography*. Chicago: Rand McNally.

Hassan, Shankat. 1993. "Grassroots Dilemma: State Versus the Environment." *Ecodecision.* June: 24-26.

Hastings, Alan and Higgins, Kevin. 1994. "Persistence of Transients in Spatially Structured Ecological Models." *Science.* 263: 1133-1136.

Haulot, Arthur. 1978. "Tourism and Coastal Environment." *Tourism Review.* 1: 10-11.

Havel, Vaclav. 1992. "Rio and the New Millennium." New York Times. 3 June.

Hawkins, D. E., et al., eds. 1980. *Tourism Planning and Development Issues.* Washington: George Washington University, Dept. of Human Kinetics and Leisure Studies.

Health Information for International Travel. Published annually. U.S. Department of Health and Human Services, Public Health Service, Centers for Disease Control.

Health and Tourism. 1979. Geneve: IUOTO.

Hendee, J., Stankey, G. and Lucas, R. 1990. *Wilderness Management.* Golden: North American Press.

Hill, Theo L. and Lundgren, Jan. 1977. "The Impact of Tourism in the Caribbean, A Methodological Study." *Annals of Tourism Research.* 4, 5: 248-267.

Hilts, P. 1991. "US Aides Retreat on Wetland Rule." New York Times. 23 November.

Hodgson, A. 1987. *The Travel and Tourism Industry—Strategies for the Future.* Oxford: Pergamon Press.

Höfels, Thomas. 1991. "Tourism: Environmental Culprit and Victim. How to Secure Longterm Success of Travel Industry." *The Tourist Review.* 4: 13-17.

Holder, J. 1988. "Pattern and Impact of Tourism on the Environment of the Caribbean." *Tourism Management.* June: 119- 127.

Hoole, A. 1978. "Public Participation in Park Planning: The Riding Mountain Case." *Canadian Geographer.* 22, 1: 41-50.

Hudman, Lloyd E. 1991. "Tourism's Role and Response to Environmental Issues and Potential Future Effects." *The Tourist Review.* 4: 17-21.

Hughes, G. 1991. "Are the Costs of Cleaning Up Eastern Europe Exaggerated? Economic Reform and the Environment." *Oxford Review of Economic Policy.* 7, 3.

Hussey, A. 1989. "Tourism in a Balinese Village." *Geographical*

Review. 79: 311-325.

Ibrahim, Y. 1992. "Kuwait Struggles with Oil Damage." *New York Times.* 24 April.

IISD. 1992. *Trade and Sustainable Development.* Winnipeg: International Institute for Sustainable Development.

Ilina, L. and Mieczkowski, Z. 1992. "Developing Scientific Tourism in Russia." *Tourism Management.* 13, 3: 327-331.

"Impact of Tourism on the Environment of the Mediterranean Basin." 1985. Communication by the Secretary-General of WTO. *World Travel.* 184: 25-26.

Ingram, C. Denise and Durst, Patric B. 1989. "Nature-Oriented Tour Operators: Travel to Developing Countries." *Journal of Travel Research.* 3: 11-15.

Inskeep, E. 1987. "Environmental Planning for Tourism." *Annals of Tourism Research.* 14, 1: 118-135.

Isbister, J. 1991. *Promises not Kept: The Betrayal of Social Change in the Third World.* West Hartford: Kumarian Press.

Iverson, M., Hinckley, B. and Webb, R. 1981. "Physical Effects of Vehicular Disturbances on Arid Landscapes." *Science.* 212: 915- 917.

Ives, J. 1985. "The Mountain Malaise." In Singh and Kaur: "In Search of Holistic Tourism for the Himalaya." *Integrated Mountain Development.* New Delhi: Himalayan Books: 30- 69.

Ives, J. and Messerli, B. 1989. *The Himalayan Dilemma: Reconciling Development and Conservation.* New York: Routledge.

Jackson, Ivor. 1988. "Interpretation of Tourism and Environment through Resource Planning and Management." In Edwards, F., ed. *Environmentally Sound Tourism Development in the Caribbean.* Calgary. University of Calgary: 47-55.

Jacobs, M. 1991. *The Green Economy: Environment, Sustainable Development, and the Politics of the Future.* Vancouver: University of British Columbia Press.

Janell, David, ed. 1992. *Geographical Snapshots of North America.* New York. The Guilford Press.

Jamot, C. 1988. *Thermalisme et villes thermales en France.* Institut d'Etudes du Massif Central, Université de Clermort Ferrand.

Järviluoma, Jari. 1992. "Alternative Tourism and the Evolution of Tourist Areas." *Tourism Management.* March: 118-120.

Jarvinen, Julie and Schmid, William. 1971. *Snowmobile Use and Winter Mortality of Small Mammals.* Proceedings of the 1971 Snowmobile and Off-Road Vehicle Research Symposium, Technical Report No. 8. Recreational and Planning Unit, Michigan State University.

Jenking, C. L. and Henry, B. M. 1982. "Government Involvement in Tourism in Developing Countries." *Annals of Tourism Research.* 9: 499-521.

Jerome, J. 1977. "Skiing and the Environment." *EPA Journal.* 3: 11- 14.

Johannes R. 1973. "Pollution and Degradation of Coral Reef Communities." In Wood and Johannes, eds. *Tropical Marine Pollution.* Amsterdam: Elsevier Scientific Publishing: 13-51.

Johnson, Brian. 1986. "Conservation, Adventure Tourism and Development: Patterns for Emulation?" *Landscape Architectural Revue.* 7, 5: 10-14.

Jones, Arwel. 1992. "Is there A Real 'Alternative' Tourism?" *Tourism Management.* 13, 1: 102-103.

Jones, Clayton. 1990. "Japan Will Pay Malaysia to Save Tropical Forests." *Christian Science Monitor.* 30 November.

Jones, H. and Barbott, F. 1977. "A Multi-Channel Digital Noise Measuring Apparatus for the Measurement of Noise Propagation." *Internoise* 77. Proceedings: B148-154.

Jones, Roy and Selwood, John. 1991. "Fallout from Hallmark Event: Freemantle after the Departure of the America's Cup." *Royal Australian Institute of Park and Recreation.* Conference Proceedings. 2: 14/1-14/9.

Justice, B. 1988. "Think Yourself Healthy." *Prevention.* June: 100.

Kamm, H. 1986. "Sea Turtle's Breeding Ground is Overwhelmed by Tourism." *New York Times.* 2 September.

Kaplan, M. 1975. *Leisure: Theory and Policy.* New York: John Wiley & Sons.

Kariel, Herbert. 1990. "Factors Affecting Response to Noise in Outdoor Recreational Environments." *The Canadian Geographer.* 34, 2: 142-149.

Kaspar, C. 1990. "A New Lease on Life for Spa and Health Tourism." *Annals of Tourism Research.* 17: 288-289.

Kaye, Evelyn. 1991. *Eco-vacation: Enjoy Yourself and Save the Earth.* Blue Penguin Publications.

Keller, Bill. 1993. "Cheetah's Race with Fate: U.S. Couple to Rescue." *New York Times.* 17 May.

Keyfitz, Nathan. 1991. "Interdisciplinary Analysis in Four Fields." *Options.* June: 4-11.

———. 1993. "The Right Steps at the Right Time." *Ecodecision.* June: 31-37.

Klemm, Mary. 1992. "Sustainable Tourism Development: Languedoc-Roussillon Thirty Years On." *Tourism Management.* 13, 2: 169-180.

Klostermaier, Klaus K. 1991. "Possible Contributions of Asian Traditions to Contemporary Environmental Ethics." *Humanities Association of Canada.* Bulletin 18, 1: 35-49.

Kneubühl, U. 1987. "Die Entwicklungssteuerung in einem Tourismusort—untersucht am Beispiel Davos." Bern: Geographisches Institut der Universität Bern.

Knickerbrocker, Brad. 1993. "Activists Take Aim at Logging Roads, as Scientists Point to Rare-Species Decline." *Christian Science Monitor.* 17 September.

Kohnen, Karl-Heinz and Braun, Rudiger. 1989. "Cash Apes—Das Geschäft mit dem Gorilla-Tourismus." In Euler, Claus, ed. Tourismus und Ökologie: Ökozid 5. Giessen: Focus Verlag.

Kolberg, W. 1993. "Quick and Easy Optimal Approach Path for Non-Linear Natural Resource Models." *American Journal of Agricultural Economics.* 75: 685-695.

Komarov, Boris. 1980. *The Destruction of Nature in the Soviet Union.* White Plains: M. E. Sharpe.

Kostrowicki, Andrzej. 1970. "Zastosowanie metod geobotanicznych w ocenie przydatnosciterenu dla potrzeb rekreacji i wypoczynku." *Przeglad geograficzny.* 42, 4: 631-645.

Kostyal, K. M. 1992. "The Ecotourism Alternative." *National Geographic Traveller.* 9, 2: 32-35.

Kotov, Vladimir and Nikitina, Elena. 1993. "Russian Environmental Protection." *Environmental Protection.* 35, 10: 11-20.

Kreib, Yorn. 1989. "Vorreiter eines umweltverträglichen Tourismus?—Naturschützer/innen auf großer Fahrt!" In Euler, Claus, ed. *Tourismus und Ökologie: Ökozid 5.* Giessen: Focus Verlag.

Krippendorf, J. 1967. "Regionalplanung im Dienste des Fremdenverkehrs." *Plan.* 4.

———. 1975. *Die Landschaftfresser: Tourismus und Erholungslandschaft—Verderben oder Segen?* Stuggart: Hallwag Verlag.

———. 1982. "Towards New Tourism Policies—The Importance of Environmental and Sociocultural Factors." *Tourism Management.* 3, 3: 135-148.

———. 1986a. "Tourism in the System of Industrial Society." *Annals of Tourism Research.* 13: 517-532.

———. 1986b. *Alpsegen-Alptraum. Für eine Tourismus Entwicklung im Einklang mit Mensch und Natur.* Bern: Kümmerly & Frey.

———. 1987. *The Holiday Makers: Understanding the Impact of Leisure and Travel.* London: Heineman.

Kunstler, James H. 1993. *The Geography of Nowhere.* New York: Simon & Schuster.

Kusler, Jon, ed. 1991. *Ecotourism and Resource Conservation: A Collection of Papers.* 2 vols. Madison: Omnipress.

Laarman, Jan G. and Perdue, Richard R. 1989. "Tropical Science and Tourism: The Case of OTS in Costa Rica." *Tourism Management.* March: 29-38.

Landals, Archie D. 1986. "The Bloody Tourists are Ruining the Parks." *Canadian Society of Environmental Biologists:* 89- 99.

Leary, W. 1991. "First U.S. Refuge for Plants Sought in Florida." *New York Times.* 18 June.

Legro, Bruce. 1993. "Noise-Proof Your Health." *Prevention.* January: 51-125.

Legro, Bruce; London, C. and Sangiorgio, M. 1992. "Ozone Alert." *Prevention.* July: 65-124.

Lemire, M. 1992. "Evolution du concept de capacite de support recreatif et application aux activites de plein-air." *The Operational Geographer.* 10, 3: 6-10.

Lewis, D. 1992. "Soldiers on Eco-Patrol." *World Press Review.* November: 47.

Lichtenberger, E. 1979. "Die Sukzession von der Agrar-zur Freizeitgesellschaft in den Hochgebirgen Europas." *Innsbrucker Geographische Studien.* 5: 401-436.

Liddle, M. J. 1975. "A Selective Review of the Ecological Effects of Human Trampling on Natural Ecosystems." *Biological Conservation.* 7: 17-34.

Liddle, M. and Kay, A. 1987. "Resistance, Survival and Recovery of Trampled Corals on the Great Barrier Reef." *Biological Conservation.* 42: 1-18.

Liddle, M. J. and Scorgie, H.R.A. 1980. "The Effects of Recreation on Freshwater Plants and Animals: A Review." *Biological Conservation.* 17: 183-206.

Lime, D. W. and Stankey, G. H. 1971. "Carrying Capacity: Maintaining Outdoor Recreation Quality." *Recreation Symposium Proceedings.* Syracuse: U. S. Department of Agriculture, Forest Service: 174-184.

Lindberg, Kreg. 1991. *Policies For Maximizing Nature. Tourism's Ecological and Economic Benefits.* World Resources Institute.

Lindsay, John J. 1980. "Compatibility Planning for Different Types of Outdoor Recreation and Natural Resources." In Hawkins, D., et al., eds. *Tourism Planning and Development Issues.* Washington: George Washington University, Dept. of Human Kinetics and Leisure Studies: 139-147.

Liu, J. and Sheldon, P. 1987. "Resident Perception of the Environmental Impacts of Tourism." *Annals of Tourism Research.* 14: 17-37.

Lovelock, J. 1979. *Gaia: A New Look at Life on Earth.* New York: Oxford University Press.

Loventhal, David. 1990. "Awareness of Human Impacts: Changing Attitudes and Emphases." In Turner, B.L., et al., eds. *The Earth as Transformed by Human Action: Global and Regional Changes in the Biosphere over the Past 300 Years.* Canbridge: Cambridge University Press.

Lozato-Giotart, Jean-Pierre. 1992. "Geographical Rating in Tourism Development." *Tourism Management.* March: 141-144.

Lucas, R. C. 1974. *Forest Service Wilderness Research in the Rockies.* U.S. Department of Agriculture.

Ludwig, Donald, Hilborn, Ray and Walters, Carl. 1993. "Uncertainty, Resource Exploitation, and Conservation: Lessons from History." *Science.* 260, 2 April.

Lundgren, Jan. 1987. "Touring Tourist Research from Riviera to the Arctic Circle." *Operational Geographer.* 13: 49-54.

Lupandin, D. and Gayer, Ye. 1989. "Chernobyl on the Chukot Peninsula." *Moscow News.* 34: 5.

Lusigi, Walter. 1982. "New Approaches to Wildlife Conservation in

Kenya." *The Ecologist.* 12, 3: 101-106.

Lvovich, M. and White, G. 1990. "Use and Transformation of Terrestrial Water Systems." In Turner, B.L., et al., eds. *The Earth as Transformed by Human Action: Global and Regional Changes in the Biosphere over the Past 300 Years.* Cambridge: Cambridge University Press: 235-250.

Machliss, G. E. and Tichnell, D. L. 1985. The State of the World's Parks. Boulder: Westview Press.

Mader, H. 1984. "Animal Habitat Isolation by Roads and Agricultural Fields." *Biological Conservation.* 29: 81-96.

Mäder, U. 1987. *Vom Kolonialismus zum Tourismus—von der Freizeit zur Freiheit.* Zürich: Rotpunktverlag.

———. 1988. "Tourism and the Environment." *Annals of Tourism Research.* 15, 2: 274-277.

Manning, R. 1979. "Impacts of Recreation on Riparian Soils and Vegetation." *Water Resources Bulletin.* 15: 30-43.

Mansfield, Howard. 1991. "The New Zoo." *Design Aid.* Jan./Feb. 64-67.

Margolis, M. 1992. *The Last New World: The Conquest of the Amazon Frontier.* New York: W.W. Norton & Co.

Marinos, P. 1983. "Small Island Tourism—The Case of Zakynthos, Greece." *Tourism Management.* September: 212-215.

Marks, R. 1989. "Skin Cancer in Australia." *Skin Cancer Foundation Journal.* No. 8.

Marsh, J., ed. 1986. *Canadian Studies of Parks, Recreation and Tourism in Foreign Lands.* Peterborough: Dept. of Geography, Trent University.

———. 1986. "National Parks, Tourism and Development: Easter Island and the Galapagos Islands." In Marsh, J., ed. *Canadian Studies of Parks, Recreation and Tourism in Foreign Lands.* Peterborough: Dept. of Geography, Trent University: 215-240.

Mathieson, A. and Wall, G. 1982. *Tourism: Economic, Physical and Social Impacts.* New York: Longman.

Matthews, H. G. 1978. *International Tourism. A Political and Social Analysis.* Cambridge: Schenkman Publishing Co.

Maner, Richard. 1993. "Harm from Alaska Spill Goes On, Scientists Say." *New York Times.* 6 March.

May, V. 1991. "Tourism, Environment and Development." *Tourism Management.* 12, 2: 112-118.

Mayer, Jonathan D. 1989. "Clinically Applied Medical Geography: Its Role in Travel Medicine." *Professional Geographer.* 41, 4: 421-428.

Mazur, D. 1975. *A Method of Land Analysis and Classification for the Canadian Shield Portion of Manitoba.* Winnipeg: M. A. Thesis, Dept. of Geography, University of Manitoba.

McBoyle, G. and Wall G. 1992. "Great Lakes Skiing And Climate Change." In Gill A. and Hartmann R., *Mountain Resort Development. Burnaby: Centre for Tourism Policy and Research:* 82-92.

McCool, S. 1978. "Recreation use Limits: Issues for the Tourism Industry." *Journal of Travel Research.* Fall: 2-7.

McHarg, Jan L. 1971. *Design with Nature.* New York: Natural History Press.

McLaren, Digby J. 1993. "Population and the Utopian Myth." *Eco-decision.* June: 59-63.

McTaggart, W. D. 1980. "Tourism and Tradition in Bali." *World Development.* 8: 457-466.

Meade, M.; Florin, J.; and Gesler, W. 1988. *Medical Geography.* New York: The Grifford Press.

Meadows, Donella; Meadows, Denis and Randers, Jorgen. 1992. *Beyond The Limits. Confronting Global Collapse, Envisioning a Sustainable Future.* Post Mills: Chelsea Green Publishing Co. Meier, B. 1992. "Refuges Feel Strain as Wildlife and Commerce Collide." *New York Times.* 1 December.

———. 1994. "U.S. Tries to Hide Indian Ruins from Intruders." *New York Times.* 19 May.

Melé, Andre. 1993. *Polluting for Pleasure.* New York: W. W. Norton & Co.

Mercer, D. 1990. "Recreation and Wetlands: Impacts, Conflict and Policy Issues." In Williams, Margaret, ed. *Wetlands: A Threatened Landscape.* London. Blackwell: 267-295.

Merriam, L. and Smith, C. K. 1974. "Visitor Impact on Newly Developed Campsites in the Boundary Waters Canoe Area." *Journal of Forestry.* 72: 627-630.

Mestel, Rosie. 1993. "Only the Tamest Survive Tourists." *New Scientist.* 7 August.

Mieczkowski, Bogdan. 1978. *Transportation in Eastern Europe:*

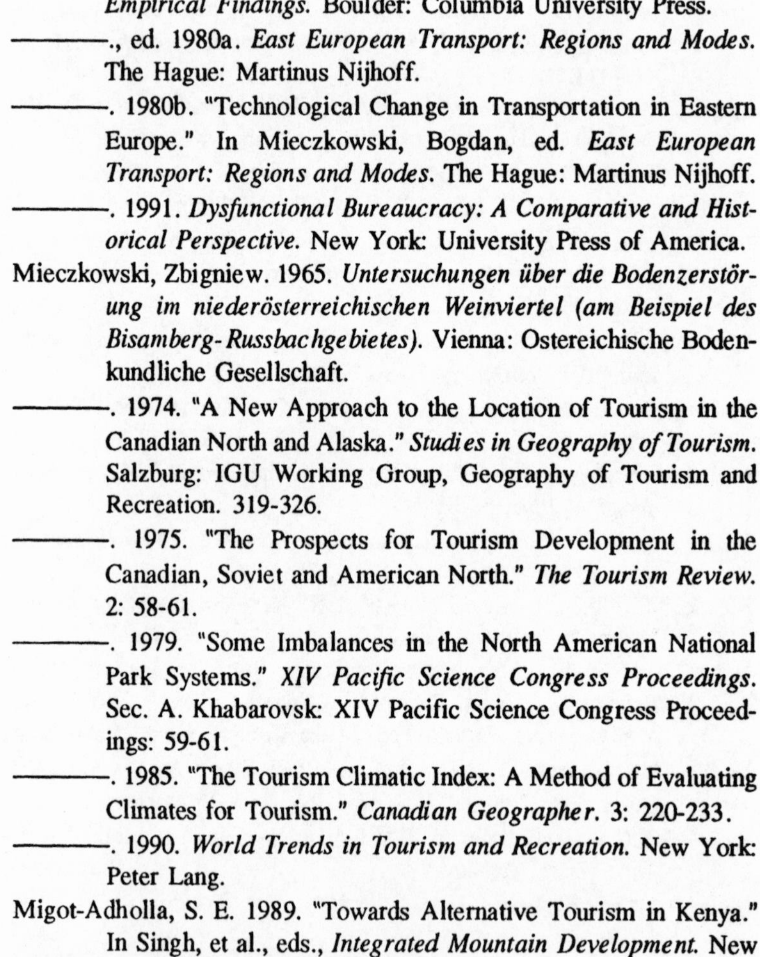

Empirical Findings. Boulder: Columbia University Press.

———., ed. 1980a. *East European Transport: Regions and Modes.* The Hague: Martinus Nijhoff.

———. 1980b. "Technological Change in Transportation in Eastern Europe." In Mieczkowski, Bogdan, ed. *East European Transport: Regions and Modes.* The Hague: Martinus Nijhoff.

———. 1991. *Dysfunctional Bureaucracy: A Comparative and Historical Perspective.* New York: University Press of America.

Mieczkowski, Zbigniew. 1965. *Untersuchungen über die Bodenzerstörung im niederösterreichischen Weinviertel (am Beispiel des Bisamberg-Russbachgebietes).* Vienna: Ostereichische Bodenkundliche Gesellschaft.

———. 1974. "A New Approach to the Location of Tourism in the Canadian North and Alaska." *Studies in Geography of Tourism.* Salzburg: IGU Working Group, Geography of Tourism and Recreation. 319-326.

———. 1975. "The Prospects for Tourism Development in the Canadian, Soviet and American North." *The Tourism Review.* 2: 58-61.

———. 1979. "Some Imbalances in the North American National Park Systems." *XIV Pacific Science Congress Proceedings.* Sec. A. Khabarovsk: XIV Pacific Science Congress Proceedings: 59-61.

———. 1985. "The Tourism Climatic Index: A Method of Evaluating Climates for Tourism." *Canadian Geographer.* 3: 220-233.

———. 1990. *World Trends in Tourism and Recreation.* New York: Peter Lang.

Migot-Adholla, S. E. 1989. "Towards Alternative Tourism in Kenya." In Singh, et al., eds., *Integrated Mountain Development.* New Delhi. Himalayan Books: 251-267.

Mill, R. C. and Morrison, A. M. 1985. *The Tourism System: An Introductory Text.* Englewood Cliffs: Prentice Hall Int.

Molotsky, Irvin. 1993. "New Rules for Air Tours." *New York Times.* 14 March.

Moore, C. 1992. "Bush's Nonsense on Jobs and the Environment." *New York Times.* 25-September.

Morris, A. and Dickinson, G. 1987. "Tourism development in Spain: Growth versus Conservation on the Costa Brava." *Geography.*

72, 1: 16-25.

Morrison, Karl and Wall, G. 1979. *Depreciative Behavior in Outdoor Recreational Settings: Annotated Bibliography*. Vance Bibliographies, Public Administration Series, Bibliography #P346.

Mosimann, T. 1985. "Geo-Ecological Impacts of Ski Piste Construction in the Swiss Alps." *Applied Geography*. 5, 1: 29-37.

Mrosovsky, N. and Salmon, P. 1987. "A Behavioral Method for Accelerating Re-entrainment of Rhythms to New Light-Dark Cycles." *Nature*. 330: 272-273.

Müller, H. 1985. *Touristische Vernetzungsmatrix: eine Methode fur eine umfassende Schaden-Nutzen-Analyse*. Bern: Forschungsinstitut für Fremdenverkehr Jahresbericht, Universität Bern.

Muller, Robert A. and Fielding, Bruce. 1992. "Storm Hazards along Louisiana Coastlines." *Geographical Snapshots of North America*. Donald G. Danielle, ed. New York: The Guildford Press: 172-175.

Mungall, C. and McLaren, D., eds. 1990. *Planet Under Stress: The Challenge of Global Change*. Toronto: Oxford University Press.

Murphy, Peter. 1983. "Tourism as a Community Industry: An Ecological Model of Tourism Development." Tourism Management. September: 180-193.

———. 1985. *Tourism: A Community Approach*. New York: Methusen.

———. 1986. "Conservation and Tourism: A Business Partnership." *Canadian Society of Environmental Biologists:* 117- 126.

———. 1988. "Community Driven Tourist Planning." *Tourism Management*. June: 96-118.

Murphy, Peter and Bayley, Robin. 1989. "Tourism and Disaster Planning." *The Geographical Review*. 79, 1: 36-46.

Myers, Norman. 1972. "National Parks In Savannah Africa." *Science*. 178, 4067: 1255-1263.

———. 1987. "The Extinction Spasm Impending: Synergism at Work." *Conservation Biology*. 1, 1: 14-21.

———. 1994. "The Sad Irony Behind Saving Africa's Elephants." *Christian Science Monitor*. 20 May.

Myers, Phyllis. 1976. *Zoning of Hawaii: An Analysis of the Passage and Implementation of Hawaii's Land Classification Law*.

Washington: The Conservation Foundation.

Nadeau, Roger. 1982. *Le Tourism, aspects theoretique et practiques au Quebec.* Montreal: Sodilis.

Naisbitt, John. 1984. *Megatrends.* New York: Warner Books Edition.

Nash, N. 1991. "Volcano Ash is Smothering Vast Area of Argentina." *New York Times.* 21 October.

National Tourism Policy Study: Ascertainment Phase. 1977. *Report on the Ascertained Needs of the State and Local Government and Private Sector of the Tourism and Travel Industry.* Washington: U.S. Govt. Print. Off., Congress, Senate, Committee on Commerce, Science, and Transportation.

Nelson, J. G.; Butler, R.; and Wall, G., eds. 1993. *Tourism and Sustainable Development: Monitoring, Planning, Managing.* University of Waterloo: Department of Geography Publications Series Number 37.

Neumann, P. W. and Merriam, H. G. 1979. "Ecological Effects of Snowmobiles." In Wall, G., ed. *Recreational Land Use in Southern Ontario.* University of Waterloo Dept. of Geography Publication Series No. 14. Waterloo, University of Waterloo: 263-272.

Newman, J. 1979. "Effects of Industrial Air Pollution on Wildlife." *Biological Conservation.* 21: 181-190.

Newson, Eric and Newson, Malcolm, eds. 1992. *Managing the Human Impact on the Natural Environment: Patterns and Processes.* London: Belhaven Press.

Newson, Malcolm. 1992a. "Environmental Economics: Resources and Commerce." In Newson, Eric and Newson, Malcolm, eds. *Managing the Human Impact on the Natural Environment: Patterns and Processes.* London: Belhaven Press.: 80-105.

———. 1992b. "Planning, Control or Management." In Newson, Eric and Newson, Malcolm, eds. *Managing the Human Impact on the Natural Environment: Patterns and Processes.* London: Belhaven Press. 258-275.

Nicolls, Leland L. 1982. "Project Turis—Coastal Tourism Development in Southern Brazil." *Tourism Management.* September: 196-199.

Nielsen, L. 1989. "International Standards for Acoustics and Noise Control." *Noise Control Engineering Journal.* 32, 2: 67-72.

Nordheimer, Jon. 1994. "Beach Project Pumps Sand and Money." *New York Times.* 12 March.

Norgaard, R. 1992. *Sustainablity and the Economics of Assuring Assets for Future Generations.* London: Pluto Press.

Noronha, R. 1976. "Paradise Reviewed: Tourism in Bali." In de Kadt, E., ed. *Tourism—Passport to Development?* Oxford: Oxford University Press: 177-204.

Noy-Meir, I. 1974. "Stability in Arid Ecosystems and Effects of Men on It." *Proceedings of the 12th International Congress of Ecology.*

Odum, H., et al. 1987. *Florida Systems and Environment.* Preliminary Draft.

OECD. 1980. *The Impact of Tourism on the Environment: General Report.* Paris: Organization for Economic Co-operation and Development.

Oglethorpe, M. 1982. "Recent Developments in Maltese Water Supply." *Geography.* 67: 62-64.

Otichillo, W. 1987. "The Causes of the Recent Heavy Elephant Mortality in the Tsavo Ecosystem, Kenya, 1975-80." *Biological Conservation.* 41: 279-289.

Oxley, D.; Fenton, M. and Carmody, G. 1974. "The Effects of Roads on Small Mammals." *Journal of Applied Ecology.* 11: 51-59.

Passell, Peter. 1991. "Washington Offers Mountain of Debt to SaveForests." *New York Times.* 22 January.

Pawson, I.; Stanford, D.; Adams, V.; and Nurbu, M. 1984. "Growth of Tourism in Nepal's Everest Region: Impact on the Physical Environment and Structure of Human Settlements." *Mountain Research and Development.* 4, 3: 237-246.

Pearce, Douglas. 1978. "Tourist Development: Two Processes." *Travel Research Journal.* 1978: 43-51.

———., ed. 1980. *Tourism in the South Pacific.* The Contribution of Research to Development and Planning. Proceedings of UNESCO Tourism Workshop, Rarotonga, June 10-13. Christchurch: Nat. Comm. For UNESCO, University of Canterbury.

———. 1980. "Tourism and the Environment: Frameworks for Research and Development." In Pearce, Douglas, ed. *Tourism in the South Pacific. The Contribution of Research to Develop-*

ment and Planning. Proceedings of UNESCO Tourism Workshop, Rarotonga, June 10-13. Christchurch: Nat. Comm. For UNESCO, University of Canterbury: 115-124.

Pearce, Douglas; Markandya, A.; and Barbier, E. 1989. *Blueprint for a Green Economy*. London: Earthscan Publications.

Pedevillano, C.; and Wright, R. G. 1987. "The Influence of Visitors onMountain Goat Activities in Glacier National Park, Montana." *Biological Conservation*. 39: 1-11.

Perlez, J. 1991a. "Whose Forest is it, the Peasants' or the Lemurs'?" *New York Times*. 7 September.

———. 1991b. "An African Park in Peril." *New York Times*. 19 May.

Peters, R. and Lovejoy, T. 1990. "Terrestrial Fauna." In Turner, B. L., et al., eds. *The Earth A Transformed by Human Action: Global and Regional Changes in the Biosphere over the Past 300 Years*. Cambridge: Cambridge Unviersity Press.

Peterson, Iver. 1992. "Linking Bits of Leftover Land to Put Parks Closer to Home." *New York Times*. 8 January.

Pigram, J. 1980. "Environmental Implications of Tourism Development." *Annals of Tourism Research*. 7, 4: 554-583.

———. 1983. *Outdoor Recreation Management*. New York: St. Martin's Press.

Place, Susan E. 1991. "Nature Tourism and Rural Development in Tortuguero." *Annals of Tourism Research*. 18: 186-201.

Plog, S. C. 1987. "Understanding Psychographics in Tourism Research." In Ritchie, J. and Goeldner, C., eds. *Travel, Tourism and Hospitality Research: A Handbook for Managers and Researchers*. New York: John Wiley & Sons: 203- 212.

Plüss, Christine. 1989. "Nach uns die Sintflut: Tourismus und Umwelt am Beispiel der Malediven." In Euler, Claus, ed. *Tourismus und Ökologie: Ökozid 5*. Giessen: Focus Verlag: 133-148.

Price, L. 1981. *Mountains and Man*. Berkley: University of California Press.

Priddle, G. and Wall, G. 1979. "Anti-Social Behavior in Ontario Provincial Parks." In Wall, G., ed. *Recreational Land Use in Southern Ontario*. University of Waterloo Dept. of Geography Publication Series No. 14. Waterloo: University of Waterloo: 281-296.

Prokhorov, B. 1979. *Medico-Geographical Information for the Devel-*

opment of New Regions of Siberia. Novosibirsk: Nauka.

Pyle, G. 1979. *Applied Medical Geography.* New York: Halsted Press.

Racey, G. D. and Euler, D. 1983. "An Index of Habitat Disturbance for Lakeshore Cottage Development." *Journal of Environmental Management.* 16: 173-179.

Rajotte, F. 1980. "Tourism in the Pacific." In Rajotte, F. and Coocombe, R., eds. *Pacific Tourism—As Islanders See It.* Suva: Institute of Pacific Studies, University of South Pacific. 1-14.

Rajotte, F. and Coocombe, R., eds. 1980. *Pacific Tourism—As Islanders See It.* Suva: Institute of Pacific Studies, University of SouthPacific.

Ranwell, D. 1972. *Ecology of Salt Marshes and Dunes.* London: Chapman & Hall.

Raykh, Ye. 1987. *Medico-Geographical Research of the Quality of Environment.* Moscow: Nauka.

Repetto, Robert, et al. 1989. *Wasting Assets: Natural Resources in the National Income Accounts.* Washington: World Resources Institute.

————., et al. 1991. *Accounts Overdue: Natural Resource Depreciation in Costa Rica.* Baltimore: World Resources Institute.

Repetto, Robert, Dower, Roger, Jenkins, Rubin and Geoghegan, Jacqueline. 1992. *Green Fees: How a Tax Shift can Work for the Environment and Economy.* Washington: World ResourcesInstitute.

Richling, A. 1971. "Pare Uwag na Temat Oceny Przydatnosci Terenu dla Potrzeb Rekreacji i Wypoczynku." *Przeglad Geograficzny.* XLIII, 3: 451-454.

Richter, L. K. 1985. "State-Sponsored Tourism: A Growth Field for Public Administration?" *Public Administration Review.* Nov.-Dec. 832-839.

Riding, A. 1991. "Pact Bans Oil Exploration in Arctic." *New York Times.* 5 October.

Ritchie, J. and Goeldner, Ch., eds. 1987. *Travel, Tourism and Hospitality Research: A Handbook for Managers and Researchers.* New York: John Wiley & Sons.

Ritter, Wigard. 1966. *Fremdenverkehr in Europa.* Leiden: A. W. Sijthoff.

————.1986. "Tourism in the Arabian Gulf Region—Present Situation, Chances and Restraints." *Geo Journal.* 13, 3: 237-244.

Romeril, Michael. 1985. "Tourism and Conservation in the Channel Islands." *Tourism Management.* March: 43-49.

————. 1989. "Tourism and the Environment—Accord or Discord?" *Tourism Management.* September: 204-208.

Ropelewski, C. 1992. "Predicting El Niño Events." *Nature.* 356, 9 April.

Rosencranz, A. and Scott, A. 1992. "Siberia's Threatened Forests." *Nature.* 355, 23 January.

Rosenthal, Elisabeth. 1993. "Flaws are Seen in the Diagnosis and Control of Lyme Disease." *New York Times.* 15 June.

Ross, John. 1994. "An Aquatic Invader is Running Amok in U.S. Waterways." *Smithsonian.* February: 41-51.

Rostenow, J. and Pulsipher, B. 1979. *Tourism: The Good, the Bad, and the Ugly.* Lincoln: Century Three Press.

Rother, L. 1991. "In Florida, Gators and Humans Vie for Same Turf." *New York Times.* 9 October.

————. 1992. "Treasure-Hunt Ban is Fought in the Keys." *New York Times.* 21 June.

Ruschmann, Doris. 1992. "Ecological Tourism in Brazil." *Tourism Management.* March: 125-128.

Ryan, Chris. 1991. *Recreational Tourism: A Social Science Perspective.* London: Routledge.

Saglio, C. 1976. "Tourism for Discovery: A Project in Lower Casamance, Senegal." In de Kadt, ed. *Tourism Passport to Development.* Oxford: Oxford University Press: 321-335.

Satchell, J. E. and Marren, P. R. 1976. *The Effects of Recreation on the Ecology of Natural Landscapes.* Strasbourg: Council of Europe.

Sauro, U. and Finlayson, B. 1992. "Saving Caves: Towards an International Protection System for Karst Environments." *27th International Geographical Congress, Technical Program Abstracts.* Washington: International Geographical Union: 558.

Sax, J. 1980. *Mountains Without Handrails: Reflections on the National Parks.* Ann Arbor: University of Michigan Press.

Scace, Robert. 1993. "An Ecotourism Perspective." In Nelson, J. G., Butler, R., and Wall, G., eds. *Tourism and Sustainable Development: Monitoring, Planning, Managing.* University of

Waterloo: Department of Geography Publications Series, No. 37: 59-82.

Schmidheiny, Stephen, et al., eds. 1992. *Changing Course: A Global Business Perspective on Development and Environment.* Cambridge: The MIT Press.

Schneider, K. 1992. "E.P.A. Head Allows Project on a Lake Michigan Marsh." *New York Times.* 9 May.

Schram, G. and Warford, J., eds. 1989. *Environmental Management and Economic Development.* Baltimore: John Hopkins University Press.

Schumacher, E. F. 1975. *Small is Beautiful: Economics as if People Mattered.* New York: Harper & Row.

Schwartz, David. 1994. "Over Hill, Over Dale, On A Bicycle For...Go." *Smithsonian.* June : 75-87.

Seabrook, Jeremy. 1991. *Promises and Illusions.* Montreal: Black Rose Books.

Sena, A. 1988. "Megatrends in International Tourism." *Journal of Travel Research.* Winter : 45.

Sessa, A. 1983. *Elements of Tourism Economics.* Rome: Catal.

Shabecoff, L. 1984. "Common Cause: Environmentalists and Industry." New York Times. 14 April.

Shackleford, Peter. 1984. "WTO—Thirty Years of Commitment." *World Travel.* 177: 27-31.

Shelby, B. and Heberlein, A. 1986. *Carrying Capacity in Recreational Settings.* Corvalis: Oregon State University Press.

Siebert, L. 1992. "Threats from Debris Avalanches." *Nature.* 356, 6371: 658-659.

Simmons, P. 1988. "Apres Ski Deluge." *New Scientists.* 14 January: 49-52.

Simons, Marlene. 1992a. "The Wetlands Home of Many Species is Threatened by Spain's Great Thirst." *New York Times.* 27 May.

———. 1992b. "Massive Ozone and Smog Defile South Atlantic Sky." *New York Times.* 12 October.

———. 1993. "Mining is Ravaging the Indian Ocean's Coral Reefs." *New York Times.* 8 August.

Singh, Tej Vir. 1989. *The Kulu Valley: Impact of Tourism Development in the Mountain Areas.* New Delhi: Himalayan Books.

Singh, Tej Vir and Kaur, Jagdish, eds. 1985. *Integrated Mountain*

Development. New Delhi: Himalayan Books.

———. 1985. "In Search of Holistic Tourism for the Himalaya." In Singh, Tej Vir and Kaur, Jagdish, eds. *Integrated Mountain Development.* New Delhi: Himalayan Books: 365-401.

Singh, T. V.; Teuns, H. Leo and Go; Frank M., eds. 1989. *Towards Appropriate Tourism: The Case of Developing Countries.* Frankfurt am Main: Peter Lang.

Singer, Peter. 1975. *Animal Liberation: A New Ethics for our Treatment of Animals.* New York: Avon.

Smart, J. E. 1981. *Recreational Development Handbook.* Washington: Urban Land Institute.

Smil, Vaclav. 1984. *The Bad Earth: Environmental Degradation in China.* Armonk: M. E. Sharpe.

Smith, Graham. 1993. *Impact Assessment and Sustainable Resource Management.* Burnt Mill: Longman.

Smith, M.J.T. 1991. "Aircraft Noise Measurement: The Case for Rationalization." *Noise and Vibration Worldwide.* 22, 5: 10- 14.

Smith, Russel. 1992. "Beach Resort Evolution: Implications for Planning." *Annals of Tourism Research.* 19: 304-322.

Smith, Valene and Eadington, William, ed. 1992. *Tourism Alternatives: Potentials and Problems.* Philadelphia, PA: University of Pennsylvania Press.

Snepenger, D. and Moore, P. 1989. "Profiling the Arctic Tourist." Annals of Tourism Research. 16: 566-570.

Sorensen, Jens; McCreary, Scott; and Hershman, Mark. 1984. *Institutional Arrangements for Management of Coastal Resources.* Renewable Resources Information Series Coastal Management Publication No. 1. Washington: National Park Service.

Southgate, D. and Disinger, J., eds. 1987. *Sustainable Resource Development in the Third World.* Boulder: Westview Press.

Staatsblad van het Koninkrijk der Nederlanden. Jaargang 1992. Besluit van 3 juni, No. 297 and 298.

Stadel, Ch. 1982. "The Alps: Mountains in Transformation." *Focus.* 32, 3: 1-16.

Stankey, George. 1981. "Integrating Wildlife Recreation Research into Decision Making: Pitfalls and Promises." *Recreation Research Review.* 9: 31-37.

———. 1982. "Recreational Carrying Capacity: Research Review." *Ontario Geography.* 5: 57-72.

———. 1989. "Tourism and National Parks: Peril and Potential." In Bateson, P., et al., eds. *National Parks and Tourism.* New South Wales National Parks and Wildlife Service: 11-17.

Stankey, George and Baden, John. 1977. *Rationing Wilderness Use: Methods, Problems, and Guidelines.* Ogden, Utah: USDA Forest and Range Experiment Station.

Stanley, D. 1989. *South Pacific Handbook.* Chico: Moon Publications.

Stansfield, Charles. 1969. "Recreational Land Use Patterns Within an American Seaside Resort." *Tourist Review.* 4: 128-136.

Stansfield, Charles and Ricket, John. 1970. "The Recreational Business District." *Journal of Leisure Research.* 2, 4: 213-225.

Stevens, William. 1994. "Pesticides may Leave Legacy of Hormonal Chaos." *New York Times.* 23 August.

Stevenson, Anthony. 1992. "The Geography of Conservation." In Newson, E. and Newson, M. eds. *Managing the Human Impact on the Natural Environment: Patterns and Processes.* London: Belhaven Press: 37-55.

Storbeck, D. 1988. *Moderner Tourismus—Tendenzen und Aussichten.* Trier: Materialien zur Fremdenverkehrsgeographie, Heft 17.

Stroud, H. B. 1983. "Environmental Problems Associated with Large Recreational Subdivisions." *Professional Geographer.* 35, 3: 303-313.

Tangi, M. 1977. "Tourism and the Environment." *Ambio.* 6, 6: 336-341.

Thefft, S. 1989. "Saving Wildlife—and Livelihoods." *Christian Science Monitor.* 2 March.

Teye, Victor B. 1992. "Land Transportation and Tourism in Bermuda." *Tourism Management.* 13, 4: 992-405.

Thresher, Philip. 1981. "The Present Value of an Amboseli Lion." *World Animal Review.* 40: 30-33.

Tobias, Dave. 1991. "Valuing Ecotourism in a Tropical Rain Forest Reserve." *Ambio.* 20, 2: 91-93.

Toffler, A. 1990. *Powershift: Knowledge, Wealth and Violence at the Edge of the 21st Century.* New York: Bantam Books.

Tudge, Colin. 1991. *The Last Animals in the Zoo. How Mass Extinction Can be Stopped.* London: Hutchinson Radius.

Turner, B. L., et al., eds. 1990. *The Earth as Transformed by Human Action: Global and Regional Changes in the Biosphere over the Past 300 Years.* Cambridge: Cambridge University Press.

Turner, K. and Jones, T., eds. 1991. *Wetlands: Market and Intervention Failures.* London: Earthscan Publications.

Turner, L. and Ash, J. 1975. *The Golden Hordes: International Tourism and the Pleasure Periphery.* London: Constable.

Tüting, Ludmila. 1989. "Trekking Tourismus in Nepal: Das 'Annapurra Conservation Area Project' als hoffnungsvoller Ansatz." In Euler, Claus, ed. *Tourismus und Ökolgie: Ökozid 5.* Giessen: Focus Verlag: 112-132.

U.S. National Park Service. 1988. *Air Quality in the National Parks.* Washington: U.S. National Park Service.

Vadrot, C. 1977. *La Mort de la Mediterranee.* Paris: Seuil.

Van der Zande, A. N. and Vos, P. 1984. "Impact of a Semi-Experimental Increase in Recreation Intensity on the Densities of Birds in Groves and Hedges on a Lakeshore in the Netherlands." *Biological Conservation.* 30, 3: 1-6.

Van Harsel, J. 1982. *Tourism: An Exploration.* National Publishers.

Van Linge, Joost. 1992. "How to Out-Zoo the Zoo." *Tourism Management.* March: 115-117.

Varley, R. 1978. *Tourism in Fiji: Some Economic and Social Problems.*Cardiff: University of Wales Press.

Vickerman, Sara. 1992. *Stimulating Tourism and Economic Growth by Featuring New Wildlife Recreation Opportunities.* Portland: Defenders of Wildlife.

Wagar, J. 1974. "Recreational Carrying Capacity Reconsidered." *Journal of Forestry.* 72, 3: 274-278.

Wagner, R. *Environment and Man.* 3rd ed. New York: W. W. Norton & Co.

Waldsterben und Luftverschmutzung. 1984. Bern: Eidgenop. Department des Innern.

Walker, J. 1990. "The Coastal Zone." In Turner, B. L., et. al. *The Earth as Transformed by Human Action: Global and Regional Changes in the Biosphere over the Past 300 Years.* Cambridge: Cambridge University Press: 271-294.

Wall, Geoffrey, ed. 1979. *Recreational Land Use in Southern Ontario.* University of Waterloo Dept. of Geography Publication Series. No 14. Waterloo: University of Waterloo.

———. ed. 1989. *Outdoor Recreation in Canada.* Toronto: John Wiley & Sons Canada.

———. 1983. "Cycles and Capacity: A Contradiction in Terms?" *Annals of Tourism Research.* 10: 268-270.

Wall, Geoffrey and Priddle, G. 1979. "Anti-Social Behaviour in OntarioProvincial Parks." In Wall, Geoffrey, ed., *Recreational Land Use in Southern Ontario.* University of Waterloo Dept. of Geography Publication Series. No 14. Waterloo: University of Waterloo.

Wall, Geoffrey and Wright, C. 1977. *The Environmental Impact of Outdoor Recreation.* University of Waterloo Dept. of Geography Publication Series No. 110. Waterloo: University of Waterloo.

Wallace, George N. 1993. "Wildlands and Ecotourism in Latin America." *Journal of Forestry.* 91, 2: 37-40.

Wallace, I. 1990. *The Global Economic Systems.* London: Unwin, Hyman.

Washburn, R. 1982. "Wilderness Recreational Carrying Capacity: Are Numbers Necessary?" *Journal of Forestry.* 80, 1: 726-728.

Weaver, David. 1991. "Alternative to Mass Tourism in Dominica." Annals of Tourism Research. 18: 414-432.

———. 1993. "Contention for Deliberate Alternative Tourism." *Annals of Tourism Research.* 19: 788-791.

Weaver, J. and Dale, D. 1978. "Trampling Effects of Hikers, Motorcycles and Horses in Meadows and Forests." *Journal of Applied Ecology.* 15, 2: 451-457.

Weeden, Robert. 1979. "Are there Non-Consumptive Uses of Wildlife?" *The Trapper.* August: 70-71.

Weiner, Eric. 1991. "Ecotourism: Can it Protect the Planet?" *New York Times.* 19 May.

Welch, R. V. 1984. "The Meaning of Development: Traditional View and more Recent Ideas." *New Zealand Journal of Geography.* 76: 2-4.

Wells, Michael. 1993. "Neglect of Biological Riches: The Economics of Nature Tourism in Nepal." *Biodiversity and Conservation.* 2: 4.

Wenger, K. 1984. *Forestry Handbook.* New York: John Wiley.

Western, David. 1976. "A New Approach to Amboseli." *Parks.* 1, 2: 1-4.

———. 1982. "Amboseli National Park: Human Values and the Conservation of a Savanna Ecosystem." *Proceedings, World*

Congress on National Parks and Protected Areas. Washington: Smithsonian Institution Press.

Westhof, V. 1962. "The Ecological Impact of Pedestrian, Equestrian and Vehicular Traffic on Vegetation." *Ecological Impact of Recreation and Tourism on Temperate Environments.* Morges: International Union for the Conservation of Nature and Natural Resources, Proceedings and Papers.

"What Price Posterity?" 1991. *Economist.* 23 March.

Wheatcroft, Stephen. 1991. "Airlines, Tourism and the Environment." *Tourism Management:* 119-126.

Wheeler, B. 1992. "Is Progressive Tourism Appropriate?" *Tourism Management.* March: 104-105.

———. 1993. "Sustaining the Ego." *Journal of Sustainable Tourism.* 1: 121-129.

Whelan, H. 1988. "Nature Tourism." *Environmental Conservation.* 15: 182.

Wilkinson, Paul F. 1989. "Strategies for Tourism in Island Microstates."*Annals of Tourism Research.* 16: 153-177.

Willard, Beatrice and Marr, John. 1971. "Recovery of Alpine Tundra under Protection after Damage by Human Activities in the Rocky Mountains of Colorado." *Biological Conservation.* 31: 181-190.

Williams, Margaret, ed. 1990. *Wetlands: A Threatened Landscape.* London: Blackwell.

———. 1994. "Making ECOnnections To Save the Sea of Okhotsk." Surviving Together. Spring: 39-44.

Williams, Mervin C. 1988. "Coastal Zone Management Strategies: The Caribbean Experience." In Edwards, F., ed., *Environmentally Sound Tourism Development in the Caribbean.* Calgary: University of Calgary.

Williams, Peter W. 1987. "Evaluating Environmental Impact and Physical Carrying Capacity in Tourism." In Ritchie, J. R. and Goeldner, Ch., eds. *Travel, Tourism and Hospitality Research: A Handbook for Managers and Researchers.* New York: John Wiley & Sons.

Williams, Vivian. 1977. "Infrastructural Development." *World Travel.* 133: 45-49.

Wilson, E. 1984. *Biofilia.* Cambridge: Harvard University Press.

Wilson, E. and Raven, P. 1992. *The Diversity of Life.* Cambridge: Harvard University Press.

Witt, Stephen and Gammon, Susan. 1991. "Sustainable Tourism Development in Wales." *The Tourist Review.* 4: 32-36.

Wolbarst, A., ed. 1991. *Environment in Peril.* Washington: Smithsonian Institution Press.

Woodland, D. and Hooper, J. 1977. "The Effect of Human Trampling on Coral Reefs." *Biological Conservation.* 11: 1- 4.

Woodley, Stephen. 1993. "Tourism and Sustainable Development in Parks and Protected Areas." In Nelson, J. G., Butler, R. and Wall, G., eds. *Tourism and Sustainable Development: Monitoring, Planning, Managing.* University of Waterloo: Department of Geography Publications Series, No. 37: 84-95.

World Commission on Environment and Development. 1987. *Our Common Future.* Oxford: Oxford University Press.

World Development Report. 1991. *The Challenge of Development.* New York: Oxford University Press.

World Health Organization. 1992. *World Health Organization Statistical Yearbook 1992.*

World Health Organization/United Nations Environmental Program. 1992. "Earth Global Monitoring System." *Urban Pollution in Megacities of the World.* Oxford: Blackwell.

World Tourism Organization. 1983. *Study on Tourism's Contribution to Protecting the Environment.* Madrid: WTO.

World Tourism Organization, United Nations Environmental Program. 1983. *Workshop on Environmental Aspects of Tourism.* Madrid: WTO.

————. 1992. *Guidelines: Development of National Parks and Protected Areas for Tourism.* Madrid: WTO.

World Tourism Organization. 1993. *Sustainable Tourism Development: Guide for Local Planners.* Madrid: WTO.

Wright, Pamela. 1993. "Ecotourism: Ethics or Eco-Sell?" *Journal of Tourism Research.* Winter : 3-9.

Yalden, D. 1992. "The Influence of Recreational Disturbance on Common Sandpipers Arctis Hypoleuncos Breeding by an Upland Reservoir in England." *Biological Conservation.* 61, 1: 41-50.

Yapp, Graham and Barrow, Graham. 1979. "Zonation and Carrying Capacity Estimates in Canadian National Park Planning."

Biological Conservation. 15: 192-206.

Young, A. M. 1986. "Eco-Enterprises: Eco-Tourism and Farming of Exotics in the Tropics." *Ambio.* 15: 361-363.

Young, G. 1973. *Tourism: Blessing or Blight?* Harmonds North: Penguin Books.

Zinnburg. 1978. *Kleine Fremdenverkehrslehre.*

Zurick, David. 1992. "Adventure Travel and Sustainable Tourism in the Peripheral Economy of Nepal." *Annals of AAG.* 82: 608- 628.

Selected Periodicals and Newspapers

Christian Science Monitor
Earthwatch
Economist
Ekonomicheskaya Gazeta
Environment
European
Financial Times
The Guardian
The Independent on Sunday
Land
La Presse
Newsweek
New York Times
The Ottawa Citizen
Poznaj Swiat
Prevention
Rossiyskaya Gazeta
Der Spiegel
Süddeutsche Zeitung
Sunday Times
Sustainable Development
Time
Tourism Intelligence
Tourism Management
Traditional Spa
Trends
Vostochno-Sibirskaya Gazeta
Waldsterben und Luftverschmutzung

Wellness Letter
Winnipeg Free Press
World Monitor
World Press Review

Index